An Ideal Theater includes founding visions for:

The Actors Studio · The Actor's Workshop · Alley Theatre
American Conservatory Theater · American Repertory Theater
Arena Stage · Barter Theatre · Bread and Puppet Theater
The Carolina Playmakers · The Chicago Little Theatre
Circle in the Square Theatre · The Civic Repertory Theatre
Cornerstone Theater Company · The Federal Theatre Project
Ford Foundation Program in Humanities and the Arts
The Free Southern Theater · The Group Theatre
The Hull-House Dramatic Association · KRIGWA Players
The Living Theatre · La MaMa Experimental Theatre Club
The Mark Taper Forum · The Mercury Theatre
Minnesota Theater Company (Guthrie Theater)
The National Theatre of the Deaf · The Negro Ensemble Company
The Negro Theatre Project, Federal Theatre Project
The Neighborhood Playhouse · New Dramatists
The New York Shakespeare Festival · The Open Theater
Oregon Shakespeare Festival · The Performance Group
The Provincetown Players · The Repertory Theater of Lincoln Center
The Ridiculous Theatrical Company · Roadside Theater
The San Francisco Mime Troupe · The Second City
Steppenwolf Theatre Company · El Teatro Campesino
Theater '47 · The Theatre Guild · The Theatre of the Living Arts
The Washington Square Players · The Wisconsin Idea Theater
Yale Repertory Theatre · The Yiddish Art Theatre

An Ideal Theater

An Ideal Theater

Founding Visions for a New American Art

EDITED AND INTRODUCED BY TODD LONDON

THEATRE COMMUNICATIONS GROUP
NEW YORK
2013

An Ideal Theater is published by Theatre Communications Group, Inc., 520 Eighth Avenue, 24th Floor, New York, NY 10018-4156.

The publication of *An Ideal Theater*, edited by Todd London, through TCG's Book Program, is made possible in part with public funds from the New York State Council on the Arts with the support of Governor Andrew Cuomo and the New York State Legislature.

TCG books are exclusively distributed to the book trade by Consortium Book Sales and Distribution.

LIBRARY OF CONGRESS CATALOGING-IN-PUBLICATION DATA
An ideal theater : founding visions for a new American art / edited by Todd London.
p. cm.
ISBN 978-1-55936-409-6
eISBN 978-1-55936-425-6
1. Theater—United States—History—20th century. I. London, Todd.
PN2266.I43   2013
792.0973—dc23   2013014536

Book design and composition by Lisa Govan
Cover design by Mark Melnick

First Edition, August 2013

For

Sandy Moffett, who gave me the books that, almost forty years later, led to this one

Naomi Thornton and David Wheeler, my first founders
(Theatre Company of Boston, 1963)

Peter Zeisler and Lindy Zesch, who showed me around

We've got our own theater. It's not in a very good neighborhood; it's been closed for years, and it's in pretty bad shape. But it's a theater, and it's ours. It's got a stage, and it's got seats, and that's all we care about. [. . .] We haven't got very much money, but we've got youth, and, I think, talent. They'll tell you the theater is dying. I don't believe it. Anything that can bring us together like this, and hold us to this one ideal in spite of everything, isn't going to die.

—*George S. Kaufman and Moss Hart,*
The Fabulous Invalid, *1938*

Idealism . . . may in itself be put down as the first ideal of the art theater.

—*Sheldon Cheney,* The Art Theater, *1917*

Table of Contents

Acknowledgments

This collection is, more than anything, a family tree of the American theater in which I work, as it took root and branched out in the twentieth century. My deepest gratitude goes to the founding artists themselves, those I've had the honor to know and those I've admired from afar or posthumously. Many of them speak from these pages, and many more don't. I am, though, indebted to all of them for helping me through the crisis of faith and inspiration that led me to this project.

Many colleagues served as guides along the way, directing me to specific founders or writings, as Robert Leonard pointed me toward Robert Gard and Gary Anderson toward W. E. B. Du Bois. My thanks go to them and to Ben Cameron and, later, Teresa Eyring, at Theatre Communications Group, for W. McNeil Lowry's published and unpublished papers, and to Joan Channick for introducing me to Nan Martin's journals. Lynn Thomson and bookseller Richard Stoddard were among those whose important hints allowed me to track down key material. Karen Hartman, Jenny Levison and Joshua Waletzky made it possible for me to sneak the Yiddish Art Theatre into the book at the last minute. Of course, Robert Brustein is one of the founders I refer to above, but I have to thank him here, too, for his intellectual example and for allowing me, over the years, to grill him about the field he helped create. Twenty years ago, Gary Clare hired me to write a five-part documentary for WNET in New York about the American theater. Gary died of AIDS in 1994, and the series was never filmed, but the research—and Gary's passion for the project—is a foundation of this anthology.

Terry Nemeth and Kathy Sova at TCG, too, have made this book possible through their patient support, as has Ted Thompson, by securing rights to these documents so I didn't have to. I'm afraid to recall the mess of prose and factual error this book made before Nicole Estvanik Taylor, my editor, got her hands on it. This is a work of amateur history, and she stood on the side of history and against amateurism, for which I can't thank her enough.

An Ideal Theater covers a short span of time, a mere hundred years, during which the American art theater has germinated, blossomed and spread. I've been fortunate to teach this material at the Yale School of Drama as I gathered it, thanks to Victoria Nolan, Joan Channick and Ed Martenson. I'm aware that my students at Yale and the New Dramatists interns who have assisted me will carry that century's legacy well into the next hundred years, planting and tending a transformed field of their own. This book was my collaboration with them, and I used them ruthlessly. My gratitude follows them wherever they may lead. Special thanks to Anne Erbe, Heide Janssen, Belina Mizrahi, Lindsey Turteltaub and Lauren Wainwright for uncovering buried treasures (only some of which appear here), and to Iris O'Brien Dodge, Roberta Pereira, Sergi Torres and Jen Wineman for supplementing my research with theirs. Will Arbery, Sam Lahne and Emily Zemba provided much needed administrative support during their semesters at New Dramatists. Aaron Kellner began the research on this book with me and Deborah Yarchun completed it. In fact, Deb is almost solely responsible for collating the crazy lot of materials that boiled down to the final manuscript; I never would have finished without her careful, devotedly obsessive, help.

I have dedicated this work to my teachers—Sandy Moffett for passing books to me freshman year at Grinnell College, Naomi Thornton and the late, great David Wheeler for their stories about the Theatre Company of Boston, which they founded, and Peter Zeisler and Lindy Zesch, who brought me to TCG in 1986 and toured me around the country, talking me through a national theater I knew embarrassingly little about. I thank them again here and further dedicate this collection to all my teachers (at least the good ones) and to theater teachers everywhere, who fight to keep interest in the invalid alive.

First, last and always, my love and life-gratitude goes to my wife, Karen Hartman, who is everywhere in this book, my heart, and all I do. I would have stopped work on this a dozen times, if it weren't for her. In fact, I never would have started it at all.

Tickets to a Revolution

> [My purpose] is to talk up a revolution. Where there are rum-
> blings already, I want to cheer them on. I intend to be incendi-
> ary and subversive, maybe even un-American. I shall probably
> hurt some people unintentionally; there are some I want to hurt.
> I may as well confess right now the full extent of my animus:
> there are times when, confronted with the despicable behavior
> of people in the American theater, I feel like the lunatic Lear on
> the heath, wanting to "kill, kill, kill, kill, kill, kill."
>
> *—Herbert Blau*

I wish I'd written that. It's the opening paragraph of Herbert Blau's 1964 manifesto *The Impossible Theater*. Herbert Blau, if you don't know, was, with Jules Irving, co-founder of the important Actor's Workshop in San Francisco and, briefly, co-director of the Repertory Theater of Lincoln Center.[1] Almost fifty years later, the "full extent of his animus" still shoots directly into your heart. You feel the roaring impatience of that original impulse, the crashing idealism that pulls someone into the theater in the first place.

I wish I'd written that but, since I didn't, I edited this book, an attempt to collect theatrical visions that similarly quicken the pulse and enlarge our sense of the possible (including—thank you, Mr. Blau—flying in the face of the impossible). Blau's is just one overheated voice from the fanatical chorus of American theater's artistic mothers and fathers—not, in most cases, when

---

1. Sadly, Blau died, at eighty-seven, as this book went to press.

they were running multimillion-dollar institutions, but when they were kids with an attitude and a world to change. I hope you'll find in these pages what I find in their pioneering visions: roaring impatience, crashing idealism, compelling fanaticism and the over-the-top belief—against all odds and reason—that theater matters and can help us change the world.

I will steal from Blau and say that the purpose of this book, like his, is to talk up a revolution, but not the coming revolution—rather, the one that happened over the course of the past century. I want to share with you some underlying ideals of that revolution, as I understand them, in order to reignite those ideals and the challenges they pose. Possibly the biggest challenge of all is the one that requires us to believe, with the fanatics, that we can make a new kind of American theater (i.e., a new kind of world); that the present doesn't hold the reins of the future; that what might be isn't dictated by what is. The revolution at the center of this anthology, then, is a revolution of idealism.

Every theater begins as an ideal. Every theater begins in dream form. And so this collection invites you to consort with dreamers of theaters. Their dream visions get articulated in many forms—manifestos, memoirs, letters, diaries, statements of purpose and desire. Some of these visions precede the theaters they imagine into being, and others invoke the lives of theaters in retrospect. They come to us in the words of theater pioneers as diverse as the Federal Theatre Project's Hallie Flanagan, the Guthrie Theater's eponym Tyrone, and Ellen Stewart, La MaMa of us all. You'll hear from the bohemians of Greenwich Village; builders of institutional theaters; and fearless activists, from the deeply rooted Bread and Puppet in Vermont to the Living Theatre, wanderers of the earth. There are singular geniuses here, like Orson Welles and Charles Ludlam, and collective geniuses, such as the seekers from the Open Theater and the young brainiacs of Second City. Once in a while, as with the Group Theatre's Harold Clurman, one beautiful dreamer can put into words values shared by many others.

In his autobiographical *All People Are Famous*, Clurman tells the story of meeting the French author André Gide. "Gide remarked, 'The problem in the theater is to find good plays,'" Clurman writes. "'The problem in the theater,' I rejoined, 'is to create a Theater.'" I have always taken Clurman to mean "theater" as both a single artistic entity and as a cultural enterprise. It's with the former that this book is concerned—the making of theaters, which, like the people who create them, have ambitions, spirit, mind, heart, psychology, history, society and intention, both conscious and unconscious.

Ordinarily, the history of theater gets told as a history of plays, performance styles and performers, artistic movements and epochs. In twentieth-century America, though, the history of theater is, as much as anything, a history of *theaters*. Not theater buildings—playhouses—but theaters, artistic ideas and ideals expressed through the gathering of creative company. All sorts of theaters in all sorts of places—cities and towns, universities, churches, settlement houses for immigrants, seaside shanties and the tent cities of migrant farmers—this rough proliferation mirrors the nation itself.

Theaters come and go. Some, including those with the most enduring, even mythical, influence, last only a handful of years (the original Provincetown Players, six; the Federal Theatre Project, four; the Group Theatre, ten). Some live on, long past their founders, even beyond the life span of their founding ideas. This is a history of theaters, then, but more precisely it is a collection of pioneering tales, an anthology of influence.

Fully envisioned or inchoate and impulsive, every theater begins in someone's mind and heart. And every theater defines the place of its nativity—rural North Dakota, civil rights–era Mississippi, New York's Lower East Side. Every American theater defines and is defined by a corner of America. By looking at the pioneering of American theaters, we look at America. What does it mean to make art in a democracy? What does it mean to make artistic community in a capitalistic economy? If all theater is local, how do you build a national theater? *Do* you? Conversely, when culture concentrates in magnetic, thriving cities, what does it take to decentralize, to encourage—even validate—artistic efforts across a broad land?

You may have figured it out: This is a book of questions. It begins with the simplest: What is a theater? How does it live in a place, a community, a culture? And more: How does a theater reflect and embody the genius of its founders? Of its artists? Of its geographical place? Of its community or audience? Of its historical moment? How does a theater continue when that moment passes? Does a theater have a life span?

While each of these (approximately) twentieth-century theaters is its founder's own unique answer to these questions, they share many underlying principles. And, so, the study of them offers a ticket to the revolutions these men and women aspired to stage.

Revolutionary Ideal #1: In the words of the Federal Theatre Project's Hallie Flanagan: "Democracy speaks in many voices . . ."

In more than a decade of research, my biggest epiphany was this: The theater as we know it—the noncommercial, non-Broadway theater—began as an immigrant theater. Its *first* impulse was to celebrate cultural distinctions while searching for a common tongue. Specifically, it began at Hull-House, a settlement house for new Americans in Chicago's urban ghetto near the end of the nineteenth century. The Hull-House Dramatic Association—or, as it came to be known, the Hull-House Players—made theater as part of making America. We cobble one world from the stories of many different worlds. Multiculturalism, or whatever you call it, didn't begin in the 1980s, though we sometimes behave as if it did. Hull-House reminds us that ethnic, racial and cultural diversity is, in fact, our theater's foundation. Diversity was, simply, our field's *originating premise*.

Revolutionary Ideal #2, from W. E. B. Du Bois: About us, by us, for us, near us.

When Renaissance man—sociologist, historian, novelist, playwright, editor, activist, NAACP founder—William Edward Burghardt (W. E. B.) Du Bois called for the formation of a Harlem-based "Negro Folk theater," about, by, for and near his African American community, he was articulating a new idea of theater that was also as old as theatrical expression itself. Theater is local. It can help a people shape its identity. If a theater is to be for a people, it must be *of* them. If it serves a community, it must be near that community. To be about "us," we must be its authors. Fargo, North Dakota, 1905. Chapel Hill, North Carolina, 1918. Delano, California, 1965. Central Appalachia, 1975. Who will tell our stories, if we don't?

Revolutionary Ideal #3: "The gifted amateur [has] possibilities which the professional may have lost." —Susan Glaspell

We all begin as amateurs. So it has been for our theater. It was customary in the nineteen-teens, during the first great boom of art theater in America, to recount that the word "amateur" comes from the French for "love," the love of what we do. The Chicago Little Theatre, the Neighborhood Playhouse, the Provincetown Players, the Washington Square Players were all passionately amateur in the beginning. Their beginning was, directly, ours. The great-grandfather theaters, founded before the regional boom of the late forties and after, all began as amateurs, too, though their intentions may have been otherwise: Oregon Shakespeare Festival, the Cleveland Play House, the Pasadena Playhouse.

"Life is worth play!" proclaimed the exultant George Cram Cook, known as "Jig," who with his wife Susan Glaspell rallied their bohemian friends to form the short-lived Provincetown Players. Provincetown became spiritual godmother to every experimental theater after. It began as a fervently amateur enterprise and, as such, forged a community whose spirit-bonds are elusive for professional companies. In the amateur theater we are connected, adventurers together—audience, writer, player, all one.

Revolutionary Ideal #4: "The individual can achieve his fullest stature only through the identification of his own good with the good of his group, a group which he himself must help to create." —Harold Clurman

Sometimes the genius of a theater lives in an individual; sometimes it lives in the group. If a theater's going to last, it had better live in both. There may be great examples internationally of theaters thriving under the visionary leadership of a single, prominent artist. In the U.S., however, it rarely works that way. Consider the nascent, soon-to-be mythic Steppenwolf ensemble, founded in a rolling fashion by a high school student named Gary Sinise and his friends and friends' friends. They incubated in the basement of a suburban church, and out popped a miracle of talent: founders Sinise, Jeff Perry and Terry Kinney; along with John Malkovich, Laurie Metcalf, Moira Harris, Alan Wilder, and joined in short order by Joan Allen and Glenne Headly. How does such a startling convergence happen? What set the stage for the abundance of talent known as the Wooster Group (which sprang from the Performance Group, represented here) or seen in the early acting companies of Arena Stage and the American Conservatory Theater? Unlike, for example, a great massive novel, where the marvel is how capacious Melville or Tolstoy or George Eliot can be, the theater excites through the wonder of confluent gifts, the alignment of powerful individuals "harnessed to the whole shebang," as John Steinbeck put it. Or, in Clurman's words, "We must help one another find our common ground; we must build our house on it, arrange it as a dwelling place for the whole family of decent humanity."

Revolutionary Ideal #5: "Theaters or institutions?"

Okay, that's not a revolutionary statement. This time the energy is in the question. The interrogative form holds the principle. What is the relationship between a theater and an institution? What does it mean to live in a theater culture whose great accomplishment to date is the building and maintenance of hundreds of what Arena Stage founder Zelda Fichandler calls "instrumentalities"? What does it say about our ingenuity that American theater administrators are so excellent and its artists so confused? What does it say about the contemporary American theater if we believe, to use the phrase Fichandler lifts from *Hamlet*, that the art is in some ways still "fusting in us unused"?

Revolutionary Ideal #6, from Julian Beck of the Living Theatre: "You must enter the theater through the world."

We need heroics. At least I do. They pump us up, encourage our little selves toward magnificence. They urge us to action. Almost every political theater in America offers such incitement—the Living Theatre, the San Francisco Mime Troupe, El Teatro Campesino and the Free Southern Theater. "If there is a single driving force which characterizes the New York Shakespeare Festival," that organization's founder Joseph Papp said, "it is its continual confrontation with the wall that separates vast numbers of people from the arts—[a wall] spawned by poverty, ignorance, historical conditions."

Both literally and figuratively, everyone who enters a theater—artist or audience—enters from and through the outside world, and to that world returns. Theater is no land apart. For theaters that take this contiguity to heart, theater practices must be, to steal another word from Julian Beck, "ameliorative." Activist theater (aka political theater) exists not simply to put on shows, but to make the world better.

One more revolutionary ideal, the seventh but also the first. This principle runs through the genesis stories of American theaters. It might be the most challenging to our world-wise, pragmatic, quantitative age. From Sheldon Cheney, who founded *Theatre Arts Magazine* in 1916:

Revolutionary Ideal #7: "Idealism . . . may itself be put down as the first ideal of the art theater."

An Ideal Theater is organized by the themes that constellate around these principles. Of course, theaters don't come into being by theme. They do, though, when looked at from a distance, side by side, carry some kinds of meaning, reasons for being, more strongly than others, sometimes by design, sometimes by existential implication. The Negro Ensemble Company, for instance, began with a call for a professional African American theater to speak to and cultivate "a sufficient audience of *other* Negroes." Identity and spirit are, in its case, inseparable. Cornerstone Theater Company, on the other hand, founded largely by young, white Harvard graduates, initially sought out socially and geographically different American communities in order to make theater within them, among people different from themselves.

Each company, even one sharing a genetic code with another, becomes its unique self. The Washington Square Players were determinedly amateurs, while the Theatre Guild, which rose out of the Players' ashes, is one of the most professionally accomplished companies in our history. The Federal Theatre Project set out to create a native theater and, to do so, laid out an unparalleled national vision; the Wisconsin Idea Theater, like the Carolina Playmakers, on a similar mission, dug deeply into local soil.

The life of a theater is revealed by what it does artistically and by how it does it. Artistic values, then, can also be reflected in organizational structures. "The Regional-Resident-Repertory-Theater Movement" was, according to Zelda Fichandler, one of its true mothers, an organizational revolution. This revolution, unlike the bohemian capital-*R* Revolutions envisioned in New York's Greenwich Village in the second decade of the twentieth century or Off-Off Broadway in the sixties, has created a relatively stable network of theaters-as-institutions. These institutions teach us ways to stay the course, while the art theaters and little theaters and collective/experimental/avant-garde theaters send up flares to illuminate the edges of—that word again—the possible.

I've also grouped companies that strive to create a political theater or a civically responsible one. The Living Theatre is an obvious example of the former, and Papp's New York Shakespeare Festival gave rise to the feistiest, most powerfully fought-for theater in the civic ring. This is one of the categories, however, in which my thematic scheme breaks down. Theaters fall out of almost every box I try to put them in. Is El Teatro Campesino, begun as part of the National Farm Workers Association strike in the mid-sixties, a theater of shared identity first or primarily a political theater? How can I leave Eva Le Gallienne's Civic Rep out of the section on civic theaters? Well, win some, lose some. The point is to make sense—generally, inevitably too sweepingly—of the reasons theaters come into being.

Finally, I've created a section on theaters that live as laboratories as well as theaters (though they may not even be theaters—e.g., the Actors Studio and New Dramatists, the playwrights' lab where I've worked since 1996). Yale Repertory Theatre is a theater and a school, and the Open Theater and La MaMa ETC are theaters but not schools. Nevertheless, the artist's growth, exploration and discovery run through each of these with great animating force, so I've pushed them into bed together.

Ultimately, this book delineates a family tree, a genealogy of inspiration, vision and influence. What I want is for whoever reads this to see these theaters in conversation with each other and with us. I want you to see their connections and their differences, their juts forward and back, their relations. Contrast and relief—rather than strict chronology—is, I believe, the best way to show them to you.

Despite its length, this anthology is in no way comprehensive. There are hundreds of worthy theaters (and visionaries) left out (including, maybe, some of your own favorites). I have personal favorites, too, that I've left out—Circle Repertory Company, the Theatre Company of Boston, Caffe Cino, the Chelsea Theater Center, Trinity Square Repertory Company, the American Place Theatre. Numerous theaters of enormous historical importance are missing from these pages—the Cleveland Play House, the Hedgerow Theatre Company, Goodman Theatre, the Pasadena Playhouse, East West Players, and many many more. The reason for this, beyond the constraints of space, is simple: The founders of these companies either didn't write enough down or their writing wasn't strong enough to hold up in book form. In other words, the quality of writing has been a guiding principle for this book almost as much as the uniqueness and impact of the vision itself. If the founders of these companies had captured their theaters in words the way Zelda Fichandler has done with Arena Stage, or if they'd had collaborator-spokesmen as brilliant as John Houseman or diligent as Lawrence Langner of the Washington Square Players and the Theatre Guild, I would never have neglected them.

Ultimately, bringing these visionaries together was a personal project, and, so, the curatorial choices were necessarily personal (as I note occasionally throughout). For me, this project has been a search for inspiration and influence. Why do certain theaters exert a hold on our imaginations over time? How can the voices from groups that lasted briefly and flamed out decades ago make my blood burn when the theater field I live in too often leaves me cold? Where is our sense of unique, passionate mission in a world of nearly identical mission statements, in which we leave the articulation of visions to fundraisers and vet them in marketing departments? I began this project at a moment of searching in my professional life, when I felt my own lack of inspiration, and looked around the country in hopes of feeling a jolt from my contemporaries. I found the jolt I was looking for in the past, the forefathers and mothers of our current theater.

In correspondence with San Francisco Mime Troupe founder R. G. Davis, I mentioned the personal nature of these selections. His response delighted me, as it seemed to reflect a lifetime steeped in Marx and Brecht and, in particular, the awareness that we are all social beings, forged in relationship, never in isolation:

> This can't be a "personal book"—you will be defining history, revising people's notions, your own take is not just yours—your publisher, your mother, your friends and your editor's assistants plus your own theatrical experiences and belief systems taught to you by ye old system and the bourgeois culture we grew up in. Zappo do di da . . . (Sing along with Ronald Reagan.) Now "personal"? I have personal thoughts too—all traceable to a number of other people or experiences.

Of course, Davis is right. This "personal" selection is a study in influence— from the teacher who handed me Pierre Biner's *The Living Theatre* and Robert Pasolli's *A Book on the Open Theater* in Grinnell, Iowa, in 1975, to the last Yale School of Drama student to describe to me a theater that changed her life. Our theater—even my own personal idea of it—as Davis points out, is a collection of intertwined people, places and things, where even the new is part of "ye old system and the bourgeois culture we grew up in." That's how it works in the theater, and maybe in everything else, too. Even in our isolation we are connected. Even when we are unaware of our history, it acts upon us.

Those of us who currently work in, or otherwise support, the American theater are stewards of the principles built into its foundation. We are stewards of these founders' fanaticism and idealism, their love of play, their devotion to making a world from all its stories. We carry their questions and, if lucky, their courage. If we live in a time of fear for the form of theater itself, and I think we do, we have them to reach to for comfort and inspiration.

This book is such a reach. It's one attempt to hear the voices from the past that call us to our future.

Todd London
New York
July 2013

All footnotes are those of the editor, unless otherwise indicated.

Chapter 1

What Is America? /
What Is an American Theater?

Democracy speaks in many voices . . .
—*Hallie Flanagan*

The Hull-House Dramatic Association (later, Hull-House Players)

FOUNDED 1897

Jane Addams

The American art theater begins as a search for American identity. It is forged in the melting pot. That our stages can be a place where the American Babel celebrates cultural distinctions while finding a common tongue is evident in the vision of the nation's first art theater, founded by reformer Jane Addams in a settlement house in the urban ghetto of Chicago near the end of the nineteenth century.

Credited by many as the first little theater in the U.S., the Hull-House Dramatic Association—or, as it came to be known, the Hull-House Players—was one of many artistic, cultural and educational activities of the Chicago-based settlement house from which its name comes. Hull-House proper was founded in 1889, and started offering classes and staging plays in the late 1890s, including some of the earliest American productions of work by Shaw, Ibsen, Gerhart Hauptmann and Lady Gregory, to audiences of immigrants from Ireland, Germany, Italy, Bohemia, Greece, Russia, Poland and Mexico, all clustered in the tenements surrounding the corner of Halsted and Polk, where the house stood.

At this crossroads, Hull-House was a contradiction of identification and assimilation, as the transplanted played out the stories of their national identities *and* began to steep in the American melting pot. Although the organization announced it would cease operations in January 2012, the first-ness of Hull-House reminds us that ethnic, racial and cultural diversity was an originating premise of our theater, not a late-twentieth-century concept applied after the fact.

"A house, easily accessible, ample in space, hospitable and tolerant in spirit, situated in the midst of the large foreign colonies which so easily isolate themselves in American cities . . ." This was how Jane Addams, Hull-House's founding, guiding angel pictured it. Inspired

SOURCE: *Twenty Years at Hull-House*, by Jane Addams, 1910.

by British social reformers and, especially, by the Toynbee Hall settlement in the London slums, Addams's utilitarian fervor—her belief in education, progressive reform, self-expression and democracy—led not only to the birth of this American art theater, but to other firsts as well—public baths, pools, gymnasiums and kitchens in Chicago; women's labor unions; local investigations of sanitation, tuberculosis, infant mortality and cocaine distribution. Though not widely remembered today, Addams was, by 1931—when she became the first American woman awarded the Nobel Peace Prize—one of the most famous women in the nation.

The following excerpt from her 1910 autobiography, *Twenty Years at Hull-House*, tackles the question of what makes an American theater. And she poses a bigger question, one that we're still grappling with more than a century later: What is America?

—TL

One of the conspicuous features of our neighborhood, as of all industrial quarters, is the persistency with which the entire population attends the theater. The very first day I saw Halsted Street, a long line of young men and boys stood outside the gallery entrance of the Bijou Theater, waiting for the Sunday matinee to begin at two o'clock, although it was only high noon. This waiting crowd might have been seen every Sunday afternoon during the twenty years which have elapsed since then. Our first Sunday evening in Hull-House, when a group of small boys sat on our piazza and told us "about things around here," their talk was all of the theater and of the astonishing things they had seen that afternoon.

But quite as it was difficult to discover the habits and purposes of this group of boys because they much preferred talking about the theater to contemplating their own lives, so it was all along the line; the young men told us their ambitions in the phrases of stage heroes, and the girls, so far as their romantic dreams could be shyly put into words, possessed no others but those soiled by long use in the melodrama. All of these young people looked upon an afternoon a week in the gallery of a Halsted Street theater as their one opportunity to see life. The sort of melodrama they see there has recently been described as "the ten commandments written in red fire." Certainly the villain always comes to a violent end, and the young and handsome hero is rewarded by marriage with a beautiful girl, usually the daughter of a millionaire, but after all that is not a portrayal of the morality of the ten commandments any more than of life itself.

Nevertheless the theater, such as it was, appeared to be the one agency which freed the boys and girls from that destructive isolation of those who drag themselves up to maturity by themselves, and it gave them a glimpse of that order and beauty into which even the poorest drama endeavors to restore the bewildering facts of life. The most prosaic young people bear testimony to this overmastering desire. A striking illustration of this came to us during our second year's residence on Halsted Street through an incident in the Italian colony, where the men have always boasted that they were able to guard their daughters from the dangers of city life, and until evil Italians entered the business of the "white slave traffic," their boast was well founded. The first Italian girl to go astray known to the residents of Hull-House was so fascinated by the stage that on her way home from work she always loitered outside a theater before the enticing posters. Three months after her elopement with an actor, her distracted mother received a picture of her dressed in the men's clothes in which she appeared in vaudeville. Her family mourned her as dead and her name was never mentioned among them nor in the entire colony. In further illustration of an overmastering desire to see life as portrayed on the stage are two young girls whose sober parents did not approve of the theater and would allow no money for such foolish purposes. In sheer desperation the sisters evolved a plot that one of them would feign a toothache, and while she was having her tooth pulled by a neighboring dentist the other would steal the gold crowns from his table, and with the money thus procured they could attend the vaudeville theater every night on their way home from work. Apparently the pain and wrongdoing did not weigh for a moment against the anticipated pleasure. The plan was carried out to the point of selling the gold crowns to a pawnbroker, when the disappointed girls were arrested.

All this effort to see the play took place in the years before the five-cent theaters had become a feature of every crowded city thoroughfare and before their popularity had induced the attendance of two and a quarter million people in the United States every twenty-four hours. The eagerness of the penniless children to get into these magic spaces is responsible for an entire crop of petty crimes made more easy because two children are admitted for one nickel at the last performance when the hour is late and the theater nearly deserted. The Hull-House residents were aghast at the early popularity of these mimic shows, and in the days before the inspection of films and the present regulations for the five-cent theaters, we established at Hull-House a moving picture show. Although its success justified its existence, it was so obviously but one in the midst of hundreds that it seemed much more advisable to turn our attention to the improvement of all of them or rather to assist as best we could the successful efforts in this direction by the Juvenile Protective Association.

Long before the Hull-House theater was built we had many plays, first in the drawing room and later in the gymnasium. The young people's clubs never tired of rehearsing and preparing for these dramatic occasions, and we also discovered that older people were almost equally ready and talented. We quickly learned that no celebration at Thanksgiving was so popular as a graphic portrayal on the stage of the Pilgrim Fathers, and we were often put to it to reduce to dramatic effects the great days of patriotism and religion.

At one of our early Christmas celebrations Longfellow's "Golden Legend" was given, the actors portraying it with the touch of the miracle play spirit which it reflects. I remember an old blind man, who took the part of a shepherd, said, at the end of the last performance, "Kind Heart," a name by which he always addressed me, "it seems to me that I have been waiting all my life to hear some of these things said. I am glad we had so many performances, for I think I can remember them to the end. It is getting hard for me to listen to reading, but the different voices and all made this very plain." Had he not perhaps made a legitimate demand upon the drama, that it shall express for us that which we have not been able to formulate for ourselves, that it shall warm us with a sense of companionship with the experiences of others? Does not every genuine drama present our relations to each other and to the world in which we find ourselves in such wise as may fortify us to the end of the journey?

The immigrants in the neighborhood of Hull-House have utilized our little stage in an endeavor to reproduce the past of their own nations through those immortal dramas which have escaped from the restraining bond of one country into the land of the universal. A large colony of Greeks near Hull-House, who often feel that their history and classic background are completely ignored by Americans, and that they are easily confused with the more ignorant immigrants from other parts of southeastern Europe, welcome an occasion to present Greek plays in the ancient text. With expert help in the difficulties of staging and rehearsing a classic play they reproduced the *Ajax* of Sophocles upon the Hull-House stage. It was a genuine triumph to the actors, who felt that they were "showing forth the glory of Greece" to "ignorant Americans." The scholar who came with a copy of Sophocles in hand and followed the play with real enjoyment did not in the least realize that the revelation of the love of Greek poets was mutual between the audience and the actors. The Greeks have quite recently assisted an enthusiast in producing *Electra*, while the Lithuanians, the Poles and other Russian subjects often use the Hull-House stage to present plays in their own tongue, which shall at one and the same time keep alive their sense of participation in the great Russian revolution and relieve their feelings in regard to it. There is something still more appealing in the yearning efforts the immigrants sometimes make to formulate their situation in America. I recall a play, written by an Italian playwright of our neighborhood, which depicted the insolent break between Americanized sons and old country parents so touchingly that it moved to tears all the older Italians in the audience. Did the tears of each express relief in finding that others had had the same experience as himself, and did the knowledge free each one from a sense of isolation and an injured belief that his children were the worst of all?

This effort to understand life through its dramatic portrayal, to see one's own participation intelligibly set forth, becomes difficult when one enters the field of social development, but even here it is not impossible if a Settlement group is constantly searching for new material.

A labor story appearing in the *Atlantic Monthly* was kindly dramatized for us by the author, who also superintended its presentation upon the Hull-House stage. The little drama presented the untutored effort of a trades-union man to secure for his side the beauty of self-sacrifice, "the glamour of martyrdom," which so often seems to belong solely to the nonunion forces. The presentation of the play was attended by an audience of trade-unionists and employers and those other people who are supposed to make public opinion. Together they felt the moral beauty of the man's conclusion that "it's the side that suffers most that will win out in this war—the saints is the only ones that has got the world under their feet—we've got to do the way they done if the unions is to stand," so completely that it seemed quite natural that he should forfeit his life upon the truth of this statement.

The dramatic arts have gradually been developed at Hull-House through amateur companies, one of which has held together for more than fifteen years.[1] The members were originally selected from the young people who had evinced talent in the plays the social clubs were always giving, but the association now adds to itself only as a vacancy occurs. Some of them have developed almost a professional ability, although contrary to all predictions and in spite of several offers, none of them have taken to a stage career. They present all sorts of plays from melodrama and comedy to those of Shaw, Ibsen and Galsworthy. The latter are surprisingly popular, perhaps because of their sincere attempt to expose the shams and pretenses of contemporary life and to penetrate into some of its perplexing social and domestic situations. Through such plays the stage may become a pioneer teacher of social righteousness.

I have come to believe, however, that the stage may do more than teach, that much of our current moral instruction will not endure the test of being cast into a lifelike mold, and when presented in dramatic form will reveal itself as platitudinous and effete. That which may have sounded like righteous teaching when it was remote and wordy will be challenged afresh when

1. The Hull-House Players, which, under the leadership of Laura Dainty Pelham, a professional actress, earned the distinction of becoming America's first art theater.

it is obliged to simulate life itself. This function of the stage, as a reconstructing and reorganizing agent of accepted, moral truths, came to me with overwhelming force as I listened to the Passion Play at Oberammergau one beautiful summer's day in 1900. The peasants who portrayed exactly the successive scenes of the wonderful Life, who used only the very words found in the accepted version of the Gospels, yet curiously modernized and reorientated the message. They made clear that the opposition to the young Teacher sprang from the merchants whose traffic in the temple He had disturbed and from the Pharisees who were dependent upon them for support. Their query was curiously familiar, as they demanded the antecedents of the Radical who dared to touch vested interests, who presumed to dictate the morality of trade, and who insulted the marts of honest merchants by calling them "a den of thieves." As the play developed, it became clear that this powerful opposition had friends in Church and State, that they controlled influences which ramified in all directions. They obviously believed in their statement of the case and their very wealth and position in the community gave their words such weight that finally all of their hearers were convinced that the young Agitator must be done away with in order that the highest interests of society might be conserved. These simple peasants made it clear that it was the money power which induced one of the Agitator's closest friends to betray him, and the villain of the piece, Judas himself, was only a man who was so dazzled by money, so under the domination of all it represented, that he was perpetually blind to the spiritual vision unrolling before him. As I sat through the long summer day, seeing the shadows on the beautiful mountain back of the open stage shift from one side to the other and finally grow long and pointed in the soft evening light, my mind was filled with perplexing questions. Did the dramatization of the life of Jesus set forth its meaning more clearly and conclusively than talking and preaching could possibly do as a shadowy following of the command "to do the will"? The peasant actors whom I had seen returning from Mass that morning had prayed only to portray the life as He had lived it and, behold, out of their simplicity and piety arose this modern version which even Harnack[2] was only then venturing to suggest to his advanced colleagues in Berlin. Yet the Oberammergau folk were very like thousands of immigrant men and women of Chicago, both in their experiences and in their familiarity with the hard facts of life, and throughout that day as my mind dwelt on my faraway neighbors, I was reproached with the sense of an ungarnered harvest.

Of course such a generally uplifted state comes only at rare moments, while the development of the little theater at Hull-House has not depended

2. Adolf von Harnack (1851–1930), a German theologian.

upon the moods of anyone, but upon the genuine enthusiasm and sustained effort of a group of residents, several of them artists who have ungrudgingly given their time to it year after year. This group has long fostered junior dramatic associations, through which it seems possible to give a training in manners and morals more directly than through any other medium. They have learned to determine very cleverly the ages at which various types of the drama are most congruous and expressive of the sentiments of the little troupes, from the fairy plays such as *Snow-White* and *Puss-in-Boots*, which appeal to the youngest children, to the heroic plays of *William Tell*, *King John*, and *Wat Tyler* for the older lads, and to the romances and comedies which set forth in stately fashion the elaborated life which so many young people admire. A group of Jewish boys gave a dramatic version of the story of Joseph and his brethren and again of Queen Esther. They had almost a sense of proprietorship in the fine old lines and were pleased to bring from home bits of Talmudic lore for the stage setting. The same club of boys at one time will buoyantly give a roaring comedy and five years later will solemnly demand a drama dealing with modern industrial conditions. The Hull-House theater is also rented from time to time to members of the Young People's Socialist League, who give plays both in Yiddish and English which reduce their propaganda to conversation. Through such humble experiments as the Hull-House stage, as well as through the more ambitious reforms which are attempted in various parts of the country, the theater may at last be restored to its rightful place in the community.

—JA

The Carolina Playmakers

FOUNDED 1918

Frederick H. Koch

We have cherished the locality, believing that if the locality were interpreted faithfully, it might show us the way to the universal. For if we can see the lives of those about us with understanding—with imagination—why may we not interpret that life in significant images for all? It was so with the Greeks before us, and with our own English forebears. It has been so in all lasting art. It should be so for us here in America.

—*Frederick H. Koch*

The question of what America is goes hand in hand with another question: Where is America? In our theater, this question of identity and geography was posed, initially, in universities, far from the historical—and commercial—center of New York's Broadway. In the early years of the twentieth century, a group of intrepid educators pioneered theater training in the U.S., fighting great resistance to establish the practices of theater—indeed, arts training at all—as a legitimate area of study. They initiated courses in acting, production, technical theater and playwriting, often as part of college extension programs, at such schools as Cornell (1912), Carnegie Institute of Technology (1912), Harvard (George Pierce Baker's influential "47 Workshop" launched in 1912) and the North Dakota Agricultural College (circa 1907).

One of these pioneers, Frederick H. Koch, affectionately known as Proff Koch, most fervently tied place and playwriting together, aimed at generating a distinctly American—local and universal— dramatic literature or, as he put it, "folk plays." Koch founded two companies out of this drive to create a new kind of theater from the heart of a young nation, the Dakota Playmakers in North Dakota (which began in 1910 as the Sock and Buskin Society) and its offspring, the Carolina Playmakers at the University of North Carolina–Chapel Hill in 1918–19. His vision included cultivating the native soil for drama and spreading the fruits of that labor through touring, a project he carried out with missionary zeal.

As an early observer, Sheldon Cheney, wrote in 1925, Koch "has been able to win over a whole state to a desire for drama in a few

SOURCE: "Drama in the South," an address delivered by Frederick H. Koch at the Playmakers Theatre in Chapel Hill, North Carolina, on April 5, 1940, for the Southern Regional Theatre Festival, commemorating the founding of the Carolina Playmakers.

short years, so that dozens of towns look forward to the coming of his troupe as one of the red-letter events of the year. He accomplished it by forgetting that the business of theater existed, digging up native actors, stimulating native playwrights to dramatize familiar materials, and then going out and offering his resultant productions wherever there were enough people living to make an audience." His long association with the Pulitzer Prize–winning playwright laureate of the South, Paul Green, and his early support of novelist Thomas Wolfe helped propel the indomitable Koch's cause. Koch became, as producer Norris Houghton put it, "the arch prophet of regional drama in this country."

In the following 1940 speech, Koch commemorates the founding of the Carolina Playmakers—which still exists, as PlayMakers Repertory Company—twenty-plus years earlier.

—TL

Today the Playmakers of Carolina welcome you to our home town of Chapel Hill, to our historic little theater building, the first state-owned theater in America to be dedicated to the making of its own native drama. We are thinking today of the simple beginnings of the Carolina Playmakers on the improvised stage in our village high school auditorium twenty-one years ago. And the little homespun plays that found an eager and lusty response. Before this, Barrett Clark[3] avers that North Carolina was regarded by Samuel French, leading publisher of plays in the United States and England, as a "dead" state so lacking in dramatic interest that the entire state had been stricken from their mailing list as not being worth the price of postage to carry their catalogs! The immediate success of the first little *Carolina Folk Plays* suggested to us here the hope for a possible oasis in the South, dubbed by H. L. Mencken, "the Sahara of the Bozart."

Dakota Folk Plays

And in thinking of our adventure in native playwriting in Chapel Hill, now coming of age, we remember too the twelve years of pioneer experiment at the frontier University of North Dakota before that time—when the Little Theater Movement was still to come. Maxwell Anderson, now a distinguished American playwright, was one of the founders of our first dramatic society there and out of the group of which he was a charter member came the Dakota

---

3. An editor, critic and historian, Clark encouraged many of our early experimental theaters—e.g., the Provincetown Players and the Washington Square Players—and was a strong proponent of folk drama and native playwriting.

Playmakers and the first *Prairie Folk Plays*. On receiving a playbill of the first original Dakota plays young Anderson wrote from California, where he was then engaged in teaching: "If there is anything that would bring me back to the old sod, it is a dramatic revival; and honestly, it seems to me that if the interest and enthusiasm keep up we may yet have one comparable to the recent flowering in Ireland. I would be willing to walk all the way back to the Dakota prairie to get in on that." And when later he went to New York the first play he wrote, you remember, was *White Desert*, a play of the vast winter plain of Dakota—its loneliness—a native play of the prairie. He had made a beginning.

The plays of Dakota were often crude, but they were honest. Simple folk plays, near to the good, strong, wind-swept soil—plays telling of long, bitter winters in the little sod shanty. But plays singing, too, of the prairie springtime; of unflected sunshine, of the wilderness gay with wild roses, of the fenceless fields welling over with lark song; plays of the travail and achievement of a pioneer people!

The Beginnings in Carolina

The only male member of the first playwriting course at Chapel Hill in the fall of 1918 was Thomas Wolfe, "Tom" to us, a lanky six-and-a-half-foot-tall mountain lad with burning eyes. The other twelve members of the class were co-eds. After the meeting of the class that first day he said, by way of apology, "Proff, I don't want you to think that this Ladies Aid Society represents Carolina. We have a lot of he-men seriously interested in writing here, but they are all disguised in army uniforms now. I tried to get into one myself but they didn't have one long enough for me."

His first play—and his first published work—*The Return of Buck Gavin*, a tragedy of a mountain outlaw, included in the second volume of *Carolina Folk Plays*, was one of the plays in our initial production that first season. We couldn't find anyone to play the part and I said to him, "I guess you'll have to play it yourself, Tom. You may not know it, but you really wrote that part for yourself!"

"But I can't act, Proff, I've never acted."

"You're a born actor," I assured him, "and you *are* Buck Gavin."

I shall never forget his first performance. With free mountain stride, his dark eyes blazing, he became the hunted outlaw of the Great Smokies. There was something uncanny in his acting of the part—something of the pent-up fury of his highland forebears.

In his foreword to *The Return of Buck Gavin*, Tom wrote for all beginners: "It is the fallacy of the young writer to picture the dramatic as unusual and remote . . . The dramatic is not unusual. It is happening daily in our lives."

Of his playwriting that first year he wrote: "I have written about people I have known and concerning whom I feel qualified to write. [The plays] have suggested a train of thought that intensely interests me, and is, I believe, of vital importance to me. My writing, I feel sure, has been made easier and better by their production.

"If they have affected my writing to this extent—if they have indirectly caused an analysis of my work, and a determination of my future course—are they not worthwhile, even though they be but the amateurish productions of a youngster?"

It is interesting to recall now the first efforts of the young writer. Like Anderson, he wrote what he knew. Those who have followed him through the years cannot fail to see in his first hastily written little plays the indications of his later achievement in *Look Homeward, Angel* and *Of Time and the River*.

The Carolina Folk Plays

As far as we have been able to determine, the first use of the term "folk play" in the American theater was the Carolina Playmakers' announcement: "*Carolina Folk Plays*," on the playbill of their initial production in Chapel Hill twenty-one years ago. The first play presented was *When Witches Ride*, about folk superstition in Northampton County, by Elizabeth Lay of Beaufort, North Carolina (now Mrs. Paul Green). Now the term is not unfamiliar in the expanding scene of our American theater. Witness Paul Green's *In Abraham's Bosom*, Lula Vollmer's *Sun-Up*, Dorothy and DuBose Heyward's *Porgy*, Jack Kirkland's dramatization of Erskine Caldwell's *Tobacco Road*, Lynn Riggs's *Green Grow the Lilacs*, Thornton Wilder's *Our Town* and Robert Sherwood's *Abe Lincoln in Illinois*.

From the first our particular interest in North Carolina has been the use of native materials and the making of fresh dramatic forms. We have found that if the writer observes the locality with which he is most familiar and interprets it faithfully, it may show him the way to the universal. If he can see the interestingness of the lives of those about him with understanding and imagination, with wonder, why may he not interpret that life in significant images for others—perhaps for all? It has been so in all lasting art.

Folk Drama Defined

The term "folk," as we use it, has nothing to do with the folk play of medieval times. But rather it is concerned with folk subject matter: with the legends, superstitions, customs, environmental differences and the vernacular of the common people. For the most part these plays are realistic and human; sometimes they are imaginative and poetic.

The chief concern of the folk dramatist is man's conflict with the forces of nature and his simple pleasure in being alive. The conflict may not be apparent on the surface in the immediate action on the stage. But the ultimate cause of all dramatic action we classify as "folk," whether it be physical or spiritual, may be found in man's desperate struggle for existence and in his enjoyment of the world of nature. The term "folk" with us applies to that form of drama which is earth-rooted in the life of our common humanity.

For many years our playwrights of the South—indeed of all America—were imitative, content with reproducing the outlived formulas of the old world. There was nothing really *native* about them. Whenever they did write of American life, the treatment was superficial and innocuous.

Trouping

From the first the Carolina Playmakers have been interested in the making of a native theater throughout the state and beyond their own borders. Traveling in their Show-Bus, with three sets of homemade scenery atop, portable lighting equipment, costumes and stage properties, they have played all over North Carolina, in crossroads villages in the mountains and in "neighborhoods" by the sea—in school auditoriums, old-time opera houses and outlived town halls.

The Playmakers' present trouping facilities offer a striking contrast to the first tour of the Dakota Playmakers over eight hundred miles of treeless plains, when it was necessary to spend several hours at a junction point sometimes, waiting for an "accommodation" train to take them to a little prairie town at the end of a branch line. Then the players drew lots to see who would peddle the handbills to advertise their arrival in town. Now the Playmakers ride in royal fashion over the hills and through the valleys of the Blue Ridge, blossoming with dogwood and flaming with the Judas trees of a Carolina spring; now announced in three-sheet posters in gay colors, and by high praise in the newspapers, their coming is like a triumphal entry.

The thirty-six tours of the Playmakers have not been confined to North Carolina. We have played in 121 different towns and cities—all the way from south Georgia to Boston, Massachusetts, and as far west as the National Folk Festivals at St. Louis and at Dallas, Texas, playing 322 performances to a total audience of more than three hundred thousand. In their thirty-six tours the Carolina Playmakers have played forty-five of the folk plays written and produced originally at Chapel Hill. They have played in the beautiful University Theatre at Yale, on three successive tours at Columbia University in New York City, and twice at the Fine Arts Theatre in Boston, where the troupe was greeted by Governor Frank Allen at the Massachusetts State House. On our first visit to Washington, D.C., we were cordially received at the White House by President Calvin Coolidge, who actually went so far as to say he thought our work was "very interesting."

Of the Playmakers' first appearance in New York the reviewer of *Theatre Magazine* wrote: "The rare characters and the homely qualities of these plays linger in one's memory long after some of the more sophisticated plays of Broadway have been forgotten. In fact, each time we witness a program of the *Carolina Folk Plays*, we feel for the moment that we, too, are just 'folks'—along with those other folks on the other side of the footlights, who transport us for a brief but happy period back to their hill country, with its rich traditions, legends and folklore."

The Carolina Play-Book

Besides publishing plays the Playmakers have issued twelve volumes of a unique little quarterly, the *Carolina Play-Book*, devoted to the making of a native theater. The *Play-Book* has the distinction of being included for two seasons in the International Exhibit of Periodicals at the Century of Progress Exposition in Chicago as one of only three American theater journals—the other two being *Theatre Arts* and *Stage*. A valuable supplement to the *Play-Book* is the *Carolina Stage*, an attractive publication in mimeographed form, designed to meet the practical needs of the members of the Carolina Dramatic Association.

Communal Drama of American History

Paul Green's *The Lost Colony*, you recall, was written and produced originally in the summer of 1937 to commemorate the 350th anniversary of the first English settlement in America. It has played for three seasons now on Roanoke Island to tens of thousands of people in an outdoor theater on the actual site of the landing of our first English colonists. Brooks Atkinson, in an article in the *New York Times* not long ago ("Ought We to Found a National Theater?"), is eternally right in saying that *The Lost Colony* has become a permanent part of the culture of the people on Roanoke Island. He goes on, "As long as they live, these people will have a grander notion of our heritage than they had before this reverent drama was written."

In November of the present year Mr. Green wrote a second drama for the American people's theater, *The Highland Call*, commemorating the bicentennial of Scotch settlement in the Cape Fear River valley of southeastern North Carolina, the stirring events of revolutionary times and the heroic leadership of bonny Flora MacDonald. Extending the idea of communal playmaking in *The Lost Colony*, *The Highland Call* was produced in Fayetteville by the Carolina Playmakers in collaboration with the citizens of that historic town. It evoked such enthusiasm there that plans have been completed for its annual production.

Now Mr. Green is at work on the third drama of his trilogy of early American history. It is to be given for the first time in old Williamsburg, Virginia, beginning early in June and closing before the opening of the summerlong run of *The Lost Colony* on Roanoke Island. Mr. Green holds that America was regarded by the underprivileged classes in the old world as a "land of opportunity," and that this was the compelling motive and promise which brought all classes to our shores and which America must fulfill to validate her beginnings.

Brooks Atkinson observes further in the above-mentioned article that we are just coming to realize that our country is rich in folklore and "should yield an abundant harvest of drama, and a national theater that will serve the entire country should develop regional plays and contribute to a deeper national understanding." I know of no better way toward an imaginative, a spiritual expression of our tradition of democracy.

Coming of Age

From the first we have thought of our Playmakers as a fellowship of young people working happily together toward a single ideal—the making of a communal, a people's theater in America. Walt Whitman happily expresses it, "An institution of the dear love of comrades." Important as the individual is in the theater, it is well for us to remind ourselves constantly that the dramatic is essentially a social art. Whatever the Playmakers have achieved is due primarily to their holding fast together to such an objective. Whatever we have done, we have done together.

We have come a long way in twenty-one years. Beginning traditionally in the Department of English as a one-man theater, we now have a separate Department of Dramatic Art with a full-time theater staff; and, in lieu of the traditional research thesis in English for the Master of Arts degree, a student may submit an original play.

A year ago the department entered the field of cinema and radio. Films from the Museum of Modern Art library are shown regularly in the Playmakers Theatre, and old favorites from the Playmakers' repertory (and new scripts, too) are now being broadcast from the university radio studio over a network of the Mutual Broadcasting System every Saturday afternoon at

3:30. The production this week is the first "Carolina Folk Play" of twenty-one years ago, *When Witches Ride*, by Elizabeth Lay.

Now we are wondering how long it will be before we take on television!

Those Who Come After

Time alone can tell what will be the effect, for good or bad, of our folk play-making. According to the editor of *Holland's*, "The Magazine of the South," the influence of the Carolina Playmakers "has spread indubitably into the associated fields of the novel, the short story and even nonfiction works. From the basic idea underlying their work and philosophy stem such writings as those of [Erskine] Caldwell, [DuBose] Heyward, [Caroline] Miller, [Roark] Bradford, [William] Faulkner, [T. S.] Stribling and other younger novelists. Not that many more influences have not impinged sharply and deeply on Southern writers and on Southern thought generally; but the Carolina Playmakers and their example have been a centralizing, crystallizing and vitalizing force unequaled in Southern literature to date."

From the first we have believed in the South, we have held that the South had something rich and strange to contribute to America, something of native honesty and of beauty. Dr. Albert Shaw, in writing of the beginnings in Dakota and in Carolina, interpreted our hope in an editorial article in the *American Review of Reviews* of September 1919: "When every community has its own native group of plays and producers, we shall have a national American Theater that will give a richly varied, authentic expression of American life. We shall be aware—which we are only dimly at present—of the actual pulse of the people by the expression in folk plays of their coordinated minds. It is this common vision, this collective striving that determines nationalism, and remains throughout the ages the one and only touchstone of the future."

In thinking of the next twenty-one years I go back to a conversation of my high school days with one of Walt Whitman's friends. On his last visit to the Singer of America he remembered Old Walt standing in the door of his little home in Camden and calling out in farewell, "Expecting the main things from those who come after."

—*FHK*

Barter Theatre

FOUNDED 1933

Robert Porterfield

Among the tales of American theater foundings, there may be none as vivacious as that of Barter Theatre in Abingdon, Virginia:

- Imagined in the depths of the Great Depression by a sometimes-employed actor;
- Established in a farming community of fewer than two thousand people;
- With a repertoire of plays given rights-free by luminary Broadway producers and playwrights;
- Performed by a company of New York actors, many of whom hitchhiked six-hundred-plus miles to southern Virginia, near the North Carolina and Tennessee borders;
- Tickets sold not for coin but for local livestock and produce, brought nightly to the box office.

That story is told here by founder Robert Porterfield, who in the summer of 1933 returned to his hometown and the farmland where he'd grown up to bring live theater to a skeptical, even hostile, population, some of whom saw actors as kin to the devil. At the heart of the story—of the vision—is the method of payment that gives the theater its name. "With vegetables you cannot sell, you can buy a good laugh," the theater boasted when it opened its doors, filling its seats with customers who paid in eggs, produce, jam and livestock—"hams for *Hamlet*." Porterfield died in 1971, leaving behind a continuously operating theater (it's still going) and this unfinished memoir.[4] Its voice captures something of Porterfield's charming persona—a gentleman farmer and theatrical raconteur with a well-oiled story to tell.

—TL

Patron Saint of the Impossible

The year was 1932, a year that anyone who lived through the Depression remembers. The closing days of the Hoover Administration, sullen, silent, hopeless. The year wages had been dropping steadily ever since the great crash

SOURCE: An unpublished memoir by Robert Porterfield.

4. I am indebted to my student at Yale School of Drama, Belina Mizrahi, who tracked down the Barter's devoted historian, Robert McKinney, and to Mr. McKinney himself, who shared the unpublished manuscript with Belina for a class presentation.

of 1929; the year unemployment was still climbing as more and more employers had to cut down their payrolls. National income that year dropped to less than half of what it had been only four years earlier; American business, they say, was running at a loss of more than five billion dollars a year; and twelve million unemployed Americans were out looking desperately for jobs.

It's hard to make today's generation understand what the appalling statistics in business failures and unemployment accounts meant in terms of human living. The spectacular legends of stockbrokers leaping from hotel windows to their deaths do not convey the daily struggle for all the rest for mere existence, a struggle that was sometimes tragic, more often simply grim. The American standard of living which had fattened on luxury dropped suddenly to the sharp edge of necessity. Banks were closing, savings were disappearing, and on every street corner in Manhattan people were selling apples for five cents apiece.

Men with PhDs turned hobo for lack of anything better to do, and traveled across country skipping from boxcar to boxcar. Farmers watched land they had labored all their lives to own disappear on the auctioneer's block as banks foreclosed their mortgages. Whole families—women, children and old people—were working at factories for as little as fifteen cents an hour. Hotheaded young men, their idealism deprived of all other outlet, took fire with the excitement of the new doctrine of Communism, and gathered in little cell groups to remake the world. Capitalism had failed, they declared, and they looked out at the idle factories, and the bread lines; it was time to bring in a new order.

I was just another hungry young actor in New York then, out of work like almost everybody else I knew, so what touched me most about the Depression was the way it had affected the theater. A friend of mine who is an orchestra leader said that the first thing people can do without in a depression is symphonies, but if that is true then the second thing they can do without is drama. They were certainly doing without drama nicely in 1932.

On the surface, the Broadway season kept up appearances. Even after four out of five of its playhouses had closed down indefinitely, those that were left made a respectable showing. In a stroke of touching bravado, the *Stage*, a highbrow theatrical magazine of the era, outlined a solid week of playgoing, including matinees, which a visitor to New York might enjoy. The selection it offered him was not, in fact, undistinguished. *Dinner at Eight*, *Dangerous Corner*, *The Late Christopher Bean* and *The Threepenny Opera* opened that year, though none of them lasted very long. That was the year Jerome Kern and Oscar Hammerstein's *Music in the Air* introduced "I've Told Every Little Star," and Cole Porter's *Gay Divorce* featured Fred Astaire and a song called "Night and Day."

There was little reflection inside the theater that a disaster had befallen outside. Squalor had not yet become the fashion of the stage—farce, romance and murder, laid in elegant surroundings and dressed in jewels and furs, befitted the fancy of the season. The imperishable stars—Alfred Lunt and Lynn Fontanne, Tallulah Bankhead, Judith Anderson, Osgood Perkins—all had vehicles designed to display their art and graces. Lillian Gish, I remember, was in a melodramatic dramatization of the famous Lizzie Borden murder case in *Nine Pine Street*, and Ina Claire delighted her fans in one of S. N. Behrman's most polished drawing room comedies, *Biography*. That was the year Burgess Meredith got discovered.

I was one of the people who realized that the Broadway scene was not so gay as it appeared by footlights. Being out of work, a more or less chronic condition among actors in good times or bad, was new to me. But most of the other actors I knew were out of work, too, not only the extras and bit players. For all the stars that I have named by their performances, I could name a larger number who were all about jostling me in the bread line. Even among the plays that opened to such promising notices, there was scant chance of a long run. A "hit" might be good for two or three months, and its houses might be half empty even at that. Hollywood was, if anything, bleaker; and television, the great bonanza of actors "between jobs," was not yet in existence. A good many of America's twelve million unemployed, it seemed to me, were actors out looking for work. As we watched closing notices posted on theater after theater, the chances of things getting any better seemed to be dwindling away altogether.

One night late in 1931 I came home to my small apartment on 58th Street to find the room stripped of everything including the bed sheets, every stitch of clothing, even the knives and forks I had borrowed from Horn & Hardart. They didn't amount to much, but to me they were everything. Dismayed, I went to a friend and I learned that Walter Hampden was casting for a cross-country tour of *Cyrano de Bergerac*. I went to see him the next day. He looked at me as though he might have heard of my loss. At any rate, he gave me a part and I went into rehearsal. I borrowed a blanket and a couple of sheets until we went on the road. Then I gave up my apartment.

After the tour started I realized that the theater outside of New York had been even harder hit than the theater in Manhattan. Rural areas might not have been suffering so acutely as some of the cities because there was still food to eat, but no one could afford to buy it. Prices on farm crops had never been lower. Cotton was bringing less than five cents, wheat less than fifty cents and corn only thirty-one cents a bushel. It shocked me to see panhandlers and beggars roaming the streets, in the midst of this wasted abundance, to see wagonloads of sharecroppers traveling westward, escaping the first of the dust bowl disasters of the Southwest. I watched from the train windows and saw ramshackle farms and idle factories. And while the bread lines in cities grew longer, the box office lines outside our ticket windows got shorter and shorter. People didn't have the money to spend on theater tickets, even to see a matinee idol like Walter Hampden in one of the greatest hits of his career. Banks were closing on all sides of us; one closed just in time to swallow up our weekly paychecks before they could be forwarded to another bank. Mine was, I must admit, quite small. I was playing a cadet of Gascony at the time, and doubling as the cardinal, and on the nights we played theaters too small to accommodate our horse, I helped Edward Everett Hale III[5] cart Roxane's carriage into the fourth act. (The horse usually remembered the cue better than we did.) For all this I was getting the minimum road salary, which was not large in 1931. But when it was lost, I was absolutely broke.

Through it all, Walter Hampden was wonderful. He was the last of the great actor-managers—a great and generous man. He was a great manager and an actor with a magnificent command of technique, but he was above all a gentleman. I never saw him lose his temper. The week the banks closed on our paychecks, he paid our expenses out of his own pocket. All this couldn't change one hard fact, though; we were closing the tour ahead of schedule because of poor business.

Some of us were sitting in the club car, heading across the prairies back to Broadway and another fruitless job hunt, when I first found expression for the wild idea that was beginning to form in my mind. The rich-looking fields and grazing cattle and crops piled outside of farm doors seemed to contradict the long lines of people on relief in the cities; nature had been bountiful that season. Save for the dust storms in western Kansas and eastern Colorado, there had been none of the great droughts or floods or pestilence that one usually associates with economic disaster. Prices on farm crops had never been lower. I think it was said that the price of wheat was lower than it had been since the days of Queen Elizabeth I. It was piling up and rotting away, nevertheless, because nobody had any money to buy it with.

To anyone who ever grew up on a farm, or to any boy who ever traded jackknives for marbles, the idea comes naturally to swap what you can't buy. It occurred to me that *we* had something to swap, too—culture, entertainment, spiritual nourishment for body nourishment. Why not? My fellow actors and I talked late into the night, taking fire with the novelty of the

---

5. American actor, later famous for his character roles in the movies of Fred Astaire and Ginger Rogers and, for those of us who grew up in the 1960s, for narrating the "Fractured Fairy Tales" on the *Rocky and Bullwinkle* cartoon show.

idea. The next morning I went to Walter Hampden—a job that took a deal of courage for a simple cadet. Following the tradition of the great actor-managers, he had always kept himself aloof. He always traveled with his wife, for he was a devoted family man. To his company he was an ever-courteous, ever-thoughtful manager, but hard to know. However, I gathered up my courage. "Mr. Hampden," I said, "people aren't buying tickets because they haven't got the money. Why don't we let them pay for their tickets in farm produce, things we could eat—vegetables, eggs, corn, turkey, ham . . ."

I got to that word *ham* and his face fell. It wasn't a very happy choice of words. He was an actor of the old school who had come to stardom through years of touring the English provinces. Perhaps he could still envision vegetables hurled across the footlights. Or perhaps he was just sensitive on the topic of pork, for the popular swashbuckling heroic style of acting had gained him and his contemporaries the reputation as "hams." At any rate he shook his head. With his unfailing courtesy, he told me that my idea, though novel, was completely impractical.

Walter Hampden was the first to tell me that my scheme wouldn't work, but he wasn't the last. I kept thinking about it and talking about it when we got back to New York the end of that season, and it seemed to me that my idea was the most positive, the most concrete solution anybody had to suggest for meeting the crisis of the theater.

Earlier in the Depression I had always been able to find some kind of job. I had done some modeling for art students. I had worked for the New York Athletic Club, collecting tips from time to time—a dime from John D. Rockefeller, one from Mayor [James J.] Walker, another from Lindbergh—and worked my way up from back elevator operator to front elevator operator to desk clerk to dining room supervisor to official host. That was a miserable year, I remember. I learned more about running a residence and about serving and preparing and handling of food than I expected to use in half a dozen lifetimes, and I had hated it.

Now I couldn't even find a job doing that. I juggled my budget to about three dollars a week, salvaged from what savings I had managed to accumulate. I lived on a box of graham crackers and a quart of milk a day, which I had figured out gave me the greatest amount of nourishment for my money, but all the while I couldn't help thinking about my father's farm, Twin Oaks in Glade Spring, Virginia, and the one he managed in Saltville.

The Depression had hit rural Virginia, of course; no one had escaped it. Banks had closed, never to reopen. You rarely saw cash for no one had money to buy the tobacco and corn and pork that were our mainstays. On a visit home I saw Haviland china hidden under attic floorboards lest it fall victim to the auctioneer's hammer, and heirloom sterling and silver tea sets offered for sale at the price of a song. The two private schools in nearby Abingdon had been forced to close as luxuries nobody could afford.

My own father, like so many rural Virginians, had become "land poor," buying up property through the wooded hills and cattle pasture of my native Washington County. Now, unable to meet the mortgages which the banks were calling in, he had to give up everything except the home place, abandoning his dream of leaving to each of his five sons a farm along with a good education. But the family, at least, was eating as well as they had ever eaten before. The only food we actually bought anyway was coffee and sugar, and after the Depression came we tapped our maple trees and used the syrup for sweetening. We had even made our own soap at home; I still have the recipe in my mother's old cookbooks.

I was luckier than a lot of people; I could go home to eat if I wanted to. But the last job I had in Glade Spring was painting outhouses. It gave me painter's colic, and I had left home determined to make my career in the theater, by damn. What did that leave—the bread line?

Because the gamble of life is part of an actor's daily existence, there were few theatrical people, if any, so shattered by the Depression that they took to leaping out of windows. Some of them fled to Hollywood and dreams of a Bolshevist Theater there.

Others—not an appreciable number of the whole—turned to the radicals and the lure of Marxism. Down at the Workers' Laboratory Theatre, close to Union Square, a handful of young playwrights got together to speak with the voice of revolution. Clifford Odets was among them, living, he said later, on ten cents a day while he was writing his first play. They wrote impassioned pieces of propaganda. The Communist Party, riding on the crest of such enthusiasms, organized the New Theatre League to propagate the workers' drama, and make its plays available to avant-garde little theaters everywhere without charge. It soon died out, however, for lack of suitable scripts—more politicians were attracted than playwrights and propaganda is not art. Most of us in the theater didn't care about bringing in a glowing new order for the ages; we just wanted to act.

Our chance to do so got smaller every day. But although eight out of ten shows were total flops in that 1932–33 season, although two-thirds of our playhouses had been shut since 1931, although thousands of us couldn't so much as get jobs operating elevators, there was a warm, poverty-based esprit de corps rarely found among so self-centered a group of people as actors. Among ourselves, we managed by and large to take care of our own. A Stage Relief Committee had been set up, composed of some of the outstanding theatrical personalities of the decade—Brock Pemberton, Arthur Hopkins, John Golden, Antoinette Perry, Austin Strong, Jane Cowl and a half-dozen others. A little canteen was set up in the Actors' Chapel, where actors could stand in line for bread and soup. There you were as likely to meet stars whose latest show had just folded as you were to find young understudies just out of the American Academy of Dramatic Arts. At the Little Church around the Corner, traditionally the actor's church under the pastorate of Dr. Randolph Ray, a theater guild had been set up to make sure that actors got their bite to eat. Everybody helped. Things were set up on a voluntary basis, not unlike at the Stage Door Canteen of the war years to come. We took turns cooking and serving.

I had never been lured by the hotheaded idealism of the young radicals. Too much of the downright country boy remained in me for that. But I found it awfully easy to get used to living off somebody's donation, particularly if you had the self-righteous feeling there wasn't anything you could be doing about it. I don't know what there was in me that kept me from staying in the bread line like so many others. Pride, to some extent, of course, but I think it also had something to do with the fact that the actor's philosophy had always been giving, not getting. And it also must have had something to do with the sense of responsibility I had been brought up to in Virginia.

For almost all of my boyhood that I can remember, I lived on a farm of twenty thousand odd acres. I grew up as a child thinking of it as the end of the world, because when the train got to Saltville it turned around and went back again. My father was manager of the entire farm, which extended for miles around and included all the village of Saltville, the Mathieson Alkali Company and thousands of cattle fattening on the good Virginia bluegrass. Whenever anyone was sick or in trouble they came to my mother—I guess there were literally hundreds of babies named "Miss Daisy" for her. When people needed clothes it was often our clothes they got. We grew up, my brothers and I as well as my mother and father, with a sense of responsibility for everyone who lived on those twenty thousand acres and, willingly or not, I couldn't shake off that same sense of responsibility for myself and my fellow actors who were walking up and down Broadway looking for jobs that didn't exist.

I suppose this is what kept me going in the months to come, as I waited in the offices of actors, producers and directors, of the Stage Relief Committee and the Dramatists Guild and Actors' Equity. My impossible dream seemed more urgent than ever and when everybody told me that the idea of a barter theater was insane, I kept at it harder than before. I even compounded my lunacy by saying that we should not only sell our tickets for butter and eggs; we should perform our plays in hinterland towns that never before had known professional theater.

All through the *Cyrano* tour, looking out the train windows, I had become aware that we were taking our drama not to the farmers and the small towns, but to the cities. Being small-town bred myself (I had never seen a professional play until I was in my freshman year in college), I kept wanting to ask, "Why don't we ever stop at the towns and the rural communities? Why shouldn't they have the niceties of life, too?" Ever since I fell in love with the theater, I have wanted to share it with other people. I didn't like to see the country people—my people—discriminated against. I didn't ask my question, of course; I knew only too well that the answer would be dry and economic. Who could afford to play *Cyrano* for a town with a population of 3,005?

I could, I decided. With the boldness of youth and madness, I marched into the Algonquin Hotel one afternoon and made an appeal to the Stage Relief Committee. They presented an awesome spectacle to a struggling young actor living on three dollars a week. I couldn't help thinking that any one of them could have given me a job had he been so minded. There was John Golden, producer, writer and musician, one of the wealthiest men in the theater. He could make you feel, when you walked into his presence, that all the world truly was a stage, and nervously you wondered what part he had chosen for you. A patronizing man, jealous of his success, he was one of the most conceited men I ever knew. He could also be, on occasion, one of the nicest.

Antoinette Perry[6] was there with Brock Pemberton.[7] A gracious blond lady who looked like a peach, she was a wonderful director and a first-rate organizer. And as for Brock, he had a disdainful look and a heart of gold. He had acquired for himself the reputation of being mean and crotchety; he needed it, he told me later, to protect himself from his own soft-heartedness.

Jane Cowl was there, the leading lady incarnate, and she looked every inch the queen of the American stage that she was. She was at that time at the height of her success in *Camille*. With her enormous black eyes and her regal carriage, she was one of the most beautiful women I have ever met.

Next to her was Rachel Crothers. Her first play, *Nora*, had been produced in 1904; since then she had turned out a succession of highly successful comedies and gained the reputation of a tireless worker. Actors were frightened of her perfectionism and energy, but there was not a humanitarian cause in the theater—the Actors' Fund, the Theatre Wing, the Stage Relief Committee and half a dozen others—which was not more successful because of her unflagging devotion and brisk efficiency.

If these were not enough to strike terror into the heart of someone who had last been playing a cadet and a horse on tour, there were also Arthur

---

6. Actress, director and co-founder of the American Theatre Wing. The Tony Awards are named for her.

7. Broadway producer and director who co-founded the Tony Awards.

Hopkins, aloof on his pinnacle of success as one of the top producers on Broadway; the playwright Austin Strong; and Frank Gilmore, president of Actors' Equity, the union to which all professional actors must belong.

I have always liked to talk—"run off at the mouth," my mother called it. I began by telling them something they all knew—namely, that there were a lot of hungry actors walking the streets of New York. There were two kinds of hungering, I told them, hungering in the body and hungering in the soul. I wanted to bring together the actor who was hungry in the stomach and the people I knew best, the people of the Virginia highlands, because I had a hunch they were hungry for the spiritual nourishment the theater could bring them. I thought they were hungry enough for it to pay in the vegetables and chickens and jam they couldn't sell.

I intended taking a company of actors to Abingdon, Virginia, I told them, a town of some three thousand population about twenty miles from Saltville, and I intended putting on any plays I could get royalty-free. Our patrons would pay for their tickets in edible produce, and when the performance was over the actors would go home and eat the box office. The economics were simple, but there would be a little cash involved in transporting the players 603 miles from Times Square and back. If I were to take some of the hungry actors out of their bread lines, I thought it was only fair of the Actors' Stage Relief Committee to provide me with enough money to transport them.

It seemed elementary enough, but those wealthy and successful ladies and gentlemen of the theater, city bred and sophisticated, looked at me as though I were proposing a voyage to the moon. A few of them asked questions. How did I expect to house a company of players in the Bible Belt of Virginia? Where did I expect to perform our plays? As a matter of fact, where *was* Abingdon, Virginia?

I told them proudly that Abingdon was the oldest incorporated town on the headwaters of the Mississippi River, and nestled in the southwest mountains of Virginia. I told them that among its many charms was a town hall erected in 1830, with a stage upon which Joseph Jefferson, [Helena] Modjeska, Fay Templeton, Edwin Booth and even his notorious brother John Wilkes Booth had performed long ago. It also had a school, I said, the Martha Washington Female Seminary for Women, which had closed during the Depression. I had already been to Abingdon and arranged to play on the stage of the old "Opry House" that was now the town hall, and for us to sleep in the dormitory of the seminary. Like the troubadours of medieval days who sang for their supper and a place by the fireside, like the company of players that had visited Hamlet in the far-off castle of Elsinore long ago, we would be "well-bestowed," sheltered and fed. Who knows, we might even take in a few pieces of silver. If we had any left over at the end of the summer, I vowed audaciously, throwing plausibility to the winds, we would turn it over to the Stage Relief Committee.

They went into a huddle in the corner while I waited. It seemed to me they took an awfully long time. At length they came and John Golden was their spokesman. The verdict was *no*. The Stage Relief Committee had no money to supply my actors with transportation to the highlands of Virginia.

So they thought it was impossible. All of them but one. I was walking wearily out the door when someone tapped me on the shoulder. "Young man," she said, "Don't let them discourage you. With your youth and your faith and your enthusiasm I'm sure you can carry it through. Go to it!" It was Jane Cowl—Saint Jane, as I call her now.

I had another friend on the Stage Relief Committee that afternoon, Mrs. Chappell.[8] She agreed that my idea was impossible, but she did something about it. She gave me a tiny lead statue, about an inch high, of Saint Rita, Patron Saint of the Impossible. "I want you to take this with you," she said. "And if you ever find somebody who is trying to do something more impossible than what you are trying to do, I want you to pass it on."

They are all dead now, those people to whom I appealed at the Stage Relief Committee that afternoon. Most of them lived to play some role in the history of the Barter Theatre. As a group, they turned me down flatly, but as individuals they had liked me, in spite of themselves. They seemed to think of me as a sort of lovable lunatic. Perhaps as a tribute to the influence Jane Cowl had among them, perhaps because the whole idea was all so impractical and unfeasible, and yet stirred their imaginations, they began offering help here and there.

Austin Strong took me to the Authors' League, and there helped me draw up in writing one of the most unusual arrangements in theatrical history. In exchange for the right to produce any play written by a member of the Authors' League (to which all playwrights for the Broadway stage then belonged) I agreed to pay in royalty one Virginia ham. It was a tongue-in-cheek agreement on their part, but not on mine. I had every intention of putting on those plays, and paying for them. I thought it was only right, in the sort of barter theater that I planned, to give the playwright as well as the actor a chance to eat the box office. A Virginia ham seemed a fair, convenient and poetic medium of exchange. Austin Strong did the rest of the Drama-

8. With the kind help of John Calhoun at the New York Public Library for the Performing Arts, I've identified this generous soul as Edna James Chappell, then wife of producer Delos Chappell (she divorced him in 1939). As Edna James, she was an actress; as Edna Chappell she co-adapted Alexandre Dumas, fils' *Camille* (with her husband and Robert Edmond Jones) for the actress Lillian Gish, within a year of Porterfield's encounter.

tists Guild one better. He offered to me his own popular success, *Three Wise Fools*, and he didn't ask me to count my hams before they got cured.

Antoinette Perry came next, with the offer of a beautiful silver satin cyclorama she wasn't using. Meanwhile she and Brock Pemberton began negotiating to get us some used scenery. And I started making a few calls on my own. One of the first people I went to see was John Golden. He had turned me down in committee, but I thought perhaps I could get his help as a private individual. I went around to his office and told him so, as simply and straightforwardly as possible. He had piercing eyes, and he looked at me for a long time. "Why are you doing this?" he finally asked.

I looked out onto the streets of Manhattan, crowded with job seekers and apple sellers. The International Apple Shippers Association had donated their surplus fruit to the jobless, who sold the apples at five cents apiece. In November of that year, six thousand apple sellers had taken a stand on the sidewalks of New York. It was better than going on the dole, I suppose, but I had been eating so many apples, when there wasn't anything else to eat, that I'd gotten acidosis and fumigated my apartment thinking it was "itch."

"I am an actor," I said. "I'd rather be doing this than selling apples."

"All right," said John Golden. "I'll help you." He gave me the rights to his current hit, *After Tomorrow*, royalty-free.

By the time the rest of the nation was going wild over Roosevelt's election, I was ready to accumulate actors. In the bread line at the Little Church around the Corner where I went to cook soup from time to time, and sample a little bread under the counter, I found plenty of them. To my amazement, however, I discovered that actors out at the elbows were just as skeptical of my project as the wealthy people on the Stage Relief Committee had been. To the actors who fed upon the vitality of Manhattan, little Abingdon, Virginia, had a remote and lonely sound.

There *were* summer theaters in existence in 1932, many of them longstanding ones, in such places as Skowhegan, Maine; Cape Cod, Massachusetts; and Westport, Connecticut. They were all within a fairly easy day's hitchhike from New York City. A playhouse south of the Mason-Dixon Line—more than three hundred miles south of it, in fact—was unheard of. And did I really intend to pay them in potatoes? How quaint!

However, a real actor would rather act than eat when he is hungry. Nell Harrison, a widely known character actress with a heart full of gaiety and an American flag sticking out of her hat, agreed to come and bring her daughter and son-in-law, Eleanor and Charles Powers, who had just closed in a show with Ethel Barrymore. I had known Mildred Quigley in the David Belasco production of *Mima*, and she promised to come as my leading lady. Beautiful Emily Woodruff (who was to marry Hume Cronyn a year later) and young

Bob Thomsen would both be graduating from the American Academy of Dramatic Arts in June, and they were avid for stage experience. Arthur Stenning had been with me on the *Cyrano* tour; he was a British character actor who had fought in the Boer War and mined for diamonds in South Africa, and he accepted my offer with alacrity—I suppose it appealed to his sense of adventure. Robert Hudson, white-haired, florid-faced and courtly, was playing with Tallulah Bankhead in *Forsaking All Others*, but knew he'd be out of work as soon as the show closed. Slowly I gathered together a company of twenty-two. They were not kids; they were mature men and women of the theater and most of them were older than I was. Some of them were better actors than others, but they were all professionals, and they all needed the work. A few days before I left, H. H. McCollum—elderly character man with a wonderful bass voice—came to me and said he had heard I was offering jobs to hungry actors. He wasn't much of an actor, I knew, but he was awfully hungry. I agreed to bring him along.

I was ready to go to Frank Gilmore, to see how the union felt about my plan for meeting the payroll. I don't think he took me seriously, but he was glad enough to see even a faint prospect of actors eating and working, and together we wrote up the following agreement. It seems, in retrospect, a little pretentious:

> We the undersigned members of the stock company which is to open a summer season at the Barter Theatre, Abingdon, Virginia, on June 10, 1933, severally acknowledge agreements heretofore entered into with Robert Porterfield, Manager, by which we are at the Barter Inn during the time we shall play, and also a share in the net profits of the Barter Theatre's operations—the share to be thus divided among the company to be at least one-third of such net profits, while the balance of such profits (not more than two-thirds of their total) shall be donated to the Stage Relief and Dramatists Guild funds.
>
> We also acknowledge that individual agreements, embodying a clear and definite understanding as to methods and expenses of our transportation (and including incidental costs en route) from New York to Abingdon, Virginia, and return, have been entered into by each of the undersigned respectively with the above Manager.

By and large, that "clear and definite" agreement about transportation expenses involved hitchhiking. If Frank Gilmore knew about it, and I suspect he did, he winked. I had actors now, and plays, and the blessings of our respective unions. I had an impressive list of patrons, headed by Jane Cowl and Walter Hampden. I had everything but an audience, and that was up to me.

My original visit to Abingdon had netted more than a promise of a theater and lodging for a company of actors. In an ice-cream parlor named Louie's, I had met Helen Fritch, a blue-eyed young woman who had taught at the Martha Washington Female Seminary. I managed to enlist Fritz, as she was called, in the cause of culture. She was with me when I drove down to Abingdon several months in advance, trying to talk up the idea of our theater and get the school dormitory in readiness for the summer.

We planned our southbound trip through Washington. On the morning of March 4, 1933, crowded in a throng of people that had braved mist and a cold wind to see their new president for themselves, we watched Franklin D. Roosevelt inaugurated for his first term of office. As I joined the roar of applause that greeted his ringing inaugural address—"We have nothing to fear but fear itself"—I felt an upsurge of hope. The morale of the country had taken a sudden upswing, and my own with it.

I was going to need it. We arrived in Abingdon the next day. The trustees of the Martha Washington Female Seminary for Women had given us their gracious, white columnar buildings, large enough to house two hundred with ease, and its surrounding estate, complete with lovely old trees, golf course, swimming pool and tennis courts. But their generous hospitality had its limitations. All the beds and bedding in the building had been removed to the sister institution, Emory & Henry College, eight miles away. So had the china and the cutlery. We were literally camping in a vast and empty hotel resort. My first act as a producer was to beg every unused bedstead in town. I wrote the actors to bring their own sheets and, if possible, hammers.

Early in June they began to arrive. Robert Hudson came first, getting in on the afternoon train from New York, suffering from his more or less annual bout of the D.T.s. We put him to bed in one of the downstairs bedrooms, and a small Negro boy was set to look after him. Most of the rest of the company hitchhiked. They made up what I'd call now a nice motley crew. Their appearance didn't do much to offset the general chilly atmosphere of indifference among townspeople; Abingdon looked askance at the style of manners and dress affected by actors in New York. Even I, from only twenty miles up the road, knew nobody in town I could call by his first name. I did know plenty of people, however, who looked upon the theatrical profession as the nether limbs of Satan. I knew plenty of people who weren't disposed to take very seriously a band of actors who work their hair in ducktails. I sat on a lot of front porches, I rocked and I visited, I talked culture to anybody I could get to listen. Most of them seemed bent on ignoring me.

I must admit that the good people on the Stage Relief Committee had reason for doubts when I talked of bringing theater to Abingdon, Virginia. Better reason, perhaps, than they realized. Now that I was actually here, I remembered we had entered a territory where the actor was scorned, not idolized. My own father, when I had announced my theatrical intentions to him at the age of ten, had thundered, in classical romantic tradition, "Not one of my boys is going into that wicked show business!" He had meant it, too. He belonged to the great bulk of solid citizens of town and country far from Broadway who thought of actors as second-rate citizens, rootless, without morality, sordid and lowly. All that he knew of the theater, after all, was cheap vaudeville and the few fifth-rate shows that came through town staffed by a bunch of hoodlums. Nobody had thought of bringing any other kind of drama anywhere near Saltville, Virginia. I hadn't met an actor until I was eighteen. Then, as now, most of the people who prayed for the salvation of the actor's lost soul were the people who had yet to go inside a theater. My father may not have actually been praying for the rescue of my soul (I think he had too much real humanity for that), but he was a long way from backing up any of my theatrical shenanigans.

Well, some of our ways *were* a jolt. We rehearsed on the lawn of our "Barter Inn," and there were plenty of people curious enough to watch. One day I was down in the kitchen doing a little supervising when Rufus, our hefty Negro chef, came rushing up to me out of breath. "Mr. Bob! Mr. Bob. You better come quick! There's a white man out in the yard tryin' to choke a white woman to death!" He was watching his first rehearsal.

At the theater, which continued to double as a town hall, we had plenty of other spectators. Next door to the dressing rooms were a couple of jail cells, in use from time to time, and the police headquarters. At the front of the house, where I was busy setting up a rudimentary box office, was the mayor's office. Upstairs were the town council chamber, the public library and a dentist's office.

We were too busy to spend much time worrying. Rehearsals had started, and the actors were deep in collecting props and memorizing lines. I set people to printing posters and scattering them abroad through Washington County. We had to get installed in the theater, build scenery out of practically nothing and try at least to make the inn habitable. It had a remarkable collection of antique plumbing, and every day precipitated a new crisis that sent us running for the crotchety old plumber that we kept in business.

The actors, those seasoned Broadway performers accustomed to commanding the stage, fell to work with a will. Proud professionals, they didn't complain when they found themselves assigned to build sets, focus spotlights made of tomato cans, usher, lay linoleum and peel potatoes. It beat being on relief in New York. I made Fritz business manager of our company, and sent a couple of the men out to an old barn which was falling down, where they hammered out enough nails, rusty hinges and incidental hardware for us to put together the scenery.

On the first Sunday morning that we were together in Abingdon, six days before our opening night, I issued a call to my twenty-two actors and led them en masse to the Sinking Spring Presbyterian Church on Main Street. I could feel the coldness around us as we filed into the church. Nobody in Abingdon had heard that Queen Victoria had knighted Sir Henry Irving for his services to the theater a generation past, and that actors had therefore become socially respectable. To the good people of the Sinking Spring Presbyterian Church, we were outlanders, and scandalous ones at that. I suppose there were many of them who would have joined with the Reverend Dan Graham, our local fire-and-brimstone prophet, in praying for the salvation of that "cesspool of iniquity" at Barter Inn. However, we took our places in the church, aware that every eye was on us. "Oh, Lord," someone whispered in my ear, "why didn't we stay up North where sin don't count?"

As it happened, there weren't enough hymnals for this sudden influx of visitors, and some of us were left without. But when we got up to sing "Rock of Ages," H. H. McCollum, the old character man reared back and put his whole heart and rich strong baritone into singing it—without a hymnbook. Every head turned to watch him but he didn't miss a word. Out of the corner of my eye, I could see icy stares melting into warm smiles of approval. The thaw had set in.

After, I went to Mr. McCollum and thanked him for the timely public relations his hymn-singing had given us. "Lord, Bob," he told me, "it's a good thing they picked 'Rock of Ages.' I had to learn it for a part I played a couple of years ago. I haven't been inside a church in twenty years."

Anyway, that turned the tide of public opinion in our direction, and there were people standing at the church doors after the sermon to invite us home to Sunday dinner—the first square meal some of us had had in a good long time.

We had set the schedule for the opening week. Saturday night we would open in Abingdon, Monday we would appear in Glade Spring, then we would move on to Damascus on Tuesday, Marion on Wednesday, Wytheville on Thursday, Saltville on Friday, and close the following Saturday in Bristol . . . playing in an overall radius of some fifty miles. Tickets were to go on sale for thirty-five cents or its equivalent in produce. Children could come in for a dime. I had chosen John Golden's *After Tomorrow* for the debut, and proudly we put our posters on display. Their line proclaimed: "With vegetables you cannot sell, you can buy a good laugh."

I had decided not to act in the opening show. I was going to greet people, sell them their tickets, show them their seats, and then dash back to pull the curtain. I found myself hoping there were going to be people to greet, for I realized on the morning of the day we opened that no one had as yet forked over his thiry-five cents or the equivalent in "vittles" across the mayor's desk that was now the box office. I suddenly felt the sharp burden of responsibility of the twenty-two people who had followed me in faith all the way from Manhattan. I knew I was right about the actors who were hungry in the stomach. I just hoped I was still right about the Virginia highlands people who were hungry in the soul. In my pocket I had exactly one dollar. I also had Saint Rita.

The Bartered Pig

I don't suppose at any other time we would have found a community like Abingdon so receptive to our venture. The Depression, in the midst of all the hardship and suffering it created, had nevertheless created the same esprit de corps of poverty in Abingdon that I had found in New York. When everybody was just about as poor as everybody else, there wasn't much sense of snobbery, and there weren't any Joneses to keep up with. There *was* a lot of the milk of human kindness flowing, and people who had suffered had a feeling of responsibility for their neighbors. I daresay in a more prosperous year we would have met with a lot more indifference and a good deal less appreciation. As it was, our jobless predicament, and the fact that we were trying a unique way to work ourselves out of it, caught at people's imaginations.

We were still improvising in the matter of furniture and eating utensils. The morning after the church service I decided to send the troupe out in teams to cover the town and get us some. A skillet here, a cup and saucer and a couple of forks there; we soon accumulated enough to do full justice to whatever we could take in at the box office. The Cumbow China Decorating Company donated a whole barrel full of cracked and chipped china, all varieties; Nell Harrison drank her coffee out of an antique mustache cup all summer long. More homes opened to us when we went out in pursuit of stage properties and "set dressings"—the mirrors, pictures, candlesticks and knickknacks we needed to adorn our meager scenery. The housewives opened their front doors and they began to discover that actors are people. I had picked my company then, as I have every year since, with the idea of choosing not only talent, but also ladies and gentlemen who would fit in with the community mores of a small Southern town, ladies and gentlemen I could introduce with pleasure in any company. It was one of the strongest assets I could have had in facing that opening night. We had begun to soften up the prejudices of the townspeople, and now the great question in all our minds was: would they come?

Along about eleven o'clock on the morning of June 13, they did start to come—farmers, teachers, shopkeepers, tourists. I've talked to many of them since, and I haven't been able to find anyone who remembers much about the play itself. Most of them don't even remember the title. What they do remember is that on that June day in the highlands of Virginia, in the teeth of improbability, magic began to happen. It began happening long before the old roll curtain of the Opry House, complete with its advertisements for snuff and patent medicines, went up on our makeshift setting. It started, I believe, when an old farmer plunked down two heads of cabbage on the mayor's desk and asked for a ticket. It went on to the moment I traded a season ticket for a very small calf, dashed back to pull the curtain, and hurried back again to the front of the house to put in chairs for an overflow of guests. It hovered over the head of my father, sitting in the forefront of the audience, giving him the first inkling that my playacting might possibly bring pride and not disgrace to the Porterfield family name. It went right on through the absorbed, well-mannered attention of our patrons, interrupted only once or twice by the cackle of chickens from the box office, and up to the triumphant curtain calls at the end. Living, breathing, *professional* theater had come to the Virginia highlands.

One of the best accounts of that memorable opening night, leavened with the exuberant enthusiasm of youth, came from Bob Thomsen, who wrote about it to his mother:

It's Sunday morning and most of the cast is seated around a long table writing letters about last night. It was really swell. I never in all my life had a better time. I guess this is as good a time as any to try to describe the theater—a large town hall. I learned last night that the last performance given there was over seven years ago. All I have written about Booth's stuff lying around is no exaggeration. It is. But the most exciting part of the place is the fact that the stage is right over the town jail. You can look through a hole in the stage and see the prisoners. I am awfully keen to know what they thought of my performance.

The dressing rooms are right next to their cells, which adds color to say the least. Another outstanding point is that the back stage looks right out on Mrs. Henry's cow pasture—and her animals are not very well trained. At the most dramatic moments in the play they will give forth—great resonant *moos*. I think their favorite actress is Agnes. They never fail to respond to her line, "I hate you, I hate you!"

Yesterday morning went pretty well. We ran through scenes till about twelve and then came back for lunch. After lunch we sat around here and went through our lines. People started appearing with "barter" about eleven o'clock and by the middle of that afternoon the box office was filled with the most amazing lot of stuff it has ever been my pleasure to see. The first ticket was bought with a very small baby pig, which has a squeal that can defeat any actor's voice. We put him outside as a barker. We got enough onions to keep us for a century, lettuce, corn, a chocolate cake and the biggest black rooster I ever saw. It was the strangest sight—stock and vegetables for a ticket. We got to the theater about seven to find the box office looking like the rear end of Lexington out front and people were actually turned away. Several carloads from North Carolina couldn't even obtain standing room. It was wonderful.

[. . .]

The stories of our box office larders have taken on an almost legendary quality by now; I can only add that they are almost all true. There was the old man, for instance, who came up to the box office with a solemn face one afternoon when I was on duty. "I ain't got no victuals to bring you," he announced.

"Well, what do you do?" I asked. We were glad enough to let people pay for their tickets in professional services; that was the way we got our hair cut and our teeth filled.

"I'm in the underground business." He said it kind of furtively, and I didn't quite know what to make of it.

"Underground"? I asked.

"Yep," said the old man. "I make coffins."

"Not this season, thank you, I don't believe we're going to need any." We had gotten into the knack, by then, of believing we might survive. But the old man stood there for a while longer. "I also whittle out walking sticks," he finally said. "If you let me in to see your show I'll bring you one, and if my old woman comes I'll bring you two."

It was a deal. He came and he brought his old woman, and they liked it so much that before long I had more walking sticks than I knew what to do with. I ended up giving them out among theatrical people in New York, and for a while they were almost as popular as our Virginia hams. He made them out of roots dug up from trees of sassafras and apple, and they were wonderfully light and strong.

Another lady came for every show and always brought a carton of cottage cheese. I never was too particular about the exact value of the rations people brought in; so when she said she had thirty-five cents worth of cottage cheese in that carton, I took her word for it. One day, though, she brought a bowl that was a little bigger than usual. "I'd like ten cents change, please," she said. I reached into the bowl and pulled out ten cents' worth of cottage cheese and handed it right back to her.

The story that has become my trademark is the story of the man with the cow. I've told it many times before but I'll tell it once again—people seem to expect it of me. He came up to the box office window about a half hour before curtain time and asked, using one of the hand-me-down Elizabethan terms so often found among Virginia mountaineers, "How much milk does it cost to get into your opry?" I did a little mental arithmetic, and I told him it would come to just about a gallon. He nodded gravely, and went back outside. I'd noticed a cow tied to a tree on the Martha Washington lawn, and I watched him take out a pail and milk this cow. Customers came and went, and just before the show started he was back at the ticket window. There was a woman standing over on the lawn leaning against the flank of the cow. "Isn't that your wife?" I asked him.

"Yep," he allowed.

"Don't you think she might like to come see the show, too?"

"Yeah, but by God she can milk her own ticket!" The first act was half over by the time she came in.

There were a few people, of course, who always paid in cash. With the admissions that they bought, we managed our only cash expenditures—gasoline, electricity and water. But ninety percent of the people who came to see us brought barter. They brought everything from rattlesnakes in a cage ("Them snakes is good eatin', ma'am," the old mountaineer told the terrified Fritz.) to Lady Baltimore cakes. As food piled up in our larders, the town's Negroes across the railroad tracks learned that they could come down to the kitchen after supper for leftover bread and ham and onions. In what had once been the library of the seminary, pint jars and crocks full of homemade preserves and blackberry jam piled up to be packed into barrels and sent to the Actors' Home in New Jersey.

Many people ask me how we set a valuation on the barter people brought in. We simply put a market price tag on it, based on the local Piggly Wiggly, and if a dozen eggs were bringing thirty-five cents, they were good for one admission. If I didn't know the exact value, I was apt to take the person's word for it, and it didn't take me long to find that our patrons were, by and large, scrupulously honest. And sometimes very literal.

Dad, who had not yet relented in his attitude toward the theatrical profession in general, was nevertheless attracted by the excitement our experiment had generated, and he could often be seen at the box office before an opening night helping us appraise the livestock market. One night a truck rolled up to the theater with fourteen people and a calf. He allowed that the calf was fair exchange for fourteen tickets, no more and no less. The farmer took his word. He deposited the calf at the stage door, took the rope off its neck, and led his family inside the theater, leaving Dad and me with the problem of corralling the calf and finding a new rope to tie it up. Curtain was five minutes late that night.

Occasionally I got an irate call from someone whose watermelon patch or apple tree had been robbed by a young patron of the arts. But people were really apt to err more often on the side of generosity. I have only one recollection of being downright cheated. We had been getting so much apple butter that we were all sick of it, but when two kids brought in several mason jars full of the gooey reddish brown of apple butter, I let them in. When we got it to the kitchen, it turned out to be red clay. I figured that if anyone wanted to come to the theater that much, he deserved to get in.

I cannot deny that we had our critics. Some of them, without coming near the theater at all, merely prayed for us. But we had others, including directly underneath the stage, the drunks in the town jail. The hole in the stage floor gave them better than average acoustics. Unfortunately, we could also hear *them*. One night, during a scene that happened to be noisy and rather dull, a drunk raised up his head and groaned in a voice that penetrated to the balcony, "Oh my God, why don't you shut up?"

For the most part, however, the theater-starved people of Washington County and our neighboring communities were delighted with whatever we brought them.

[. . .]

Our profit for the season added up to $4.35, two barrels of jelly and one sow pig. It seemed a little futile to take two-thirds of the $4.35 and divide it up among the twenty-two actors, so I just sent the lump sum along to the Stage Relief Committee. The leftover jelly went to the Actors' Home and I kept the sow pig.

It was, if you remember, the same little pig that had bought one of the first tickets and played the barker on our opening night. I sent her out to Twin Oaks instead of to the butcher's knife, for I said in the back of my mind as soon as I saw her, "This is where I get my royalties." She grew up on the farm, and became a husky sow, worthy of a season ticket for a family of five by any box office reckoning. The following spring she presented us with what the Associated Press called an octuple blessed event—eight squealing piglets.

Henry Wallace and the Agricultural Adjustment Act[9] were in the headlines that year. To bring up the price of farm crops, everybody was plowing things under for the good of the national economy. It didn't make much sense to me, but a sow that farrowed more than seven little pigs was just plain unpatriotic. Didn't she know she was wreaking havoc with the carefully planned shortage of produce?

By the time our sow pig produced her first litter, I had produced a summer-full of seven plays. I had an agreement in writing with the Authors' League that I could pay for them in hams instead of cash, and I thought the whole arrangement made a lot better sense for the national economy than the rule of plowing under. I raised hell with Henry Wallace, but the AAA ruled sternly: the eighth piglet must be plowed under. Sorrowfully we obeyed the law.

That was not the end of the story of the Barter sow. She was prolific. The next season she presented us with *another* family of eight, and this time, before our fight to salvage the eighth piglet could assume epic proportions, the Supreme Court stepped in. Eight piglets, even nine piglets were to be permitted to survive. Henry Wallace's program of plowing under had been plowed under itself.

What with the AAA and the Dramatists Guild, though, that sow pig and her descendants have made the Associated Press twenty-eight times. Within the next several years hams of her lineage were gracing the tables of Noël Coward, George Kaufman, Philip Barry, Robert Sherwood, Sidney Howard, Rachel Crothers, Howard Lindsay and Clare Booth Luce. George Jean Nathan was delighted with his—said it cut down on his income tax returns and saved him an agent's percentage. News of their succulence reached as far afield as the front page of the *London Times*, which ventured to comment with rare critical acumen that it was a royalty which overpaid most plays.

Two years later, one of these hams occasioned an emergency meeting of the venerable Theatre Guild in New York City. This dignified body happened to handle American rights to all George Bernard Shaw's plays. I sent them one of our finest Virginia hams in receipt for our right to *Candida*, and they were having trouble dividing the percentages. I didn't hear how the emergency meeting came out, but they must have sent him all or part of the ham, because I got a postcard from Ayot St Lawrence not long afterward. "Don't you know I am a vegetarian?" Shaw complained testily. "If you must pay in produce, send spinach." We compromised on a crate of Virginia apples.

---

9. Drafted in 1933 by Wallace, Roosevelt's Secretary of Agriculture, the Act paid farmers to cut crops by thirty percent and to halt production of milk and butter. The goal was to stop prices from the free fall caused by overproduction, and thus to help farmers from defaulting on their heavily mortgaged land.

The long line of stage celebrities and playwrights who began to receive our Virginia hams have sometimes been a little shy of taking one. Some of them may have taken it personally. Not Fred Allen. He took his with gusto, looked it over with a gleam of malice in his eye, and then asked cheerfully, "Anyone we know?" Hams of that old sow pig's lineage have gone on to pay off the royalties on practically all the plays we've ever done at the Barter Theatre. All in all, I expect she had done more for the cause of culture in Virginia than any foundation or individual.

—RP

The Federal Theatre Project

FOUNDED 1935

Hallie Flanagan

> In an age of terrific implications as to wealth and poverty, as to the function of government, as to peace and war, as to the relation of the artist to all these forces, the theater must grow up. The theater must become conscious of the implications of the changing social order, or the changing social order will ignore, and rightly, the implications of the theater.
>
> *—Hallie Flanagan*

In 1935—as America continued to slog its way up from the Great Depression—the U.S. government gave birth to a national theater program more extensive than any in the country's history. Conceived in detail by Hallie Flanagan, director of the experimental theater at Vassar College, the Federal Theatre Project blanketed the country, from big city to small town, factory to farm, radiating from regional and urban centers, connected to Washington, D.C., by an endless length of red tape. It worked on a model that mirrored the country itself, a "federation of theaters, subsidized nationally but administered locally." FTP offered something for everyone, including circuses and children's shows, new American plays and world classics, light-hearted musicals and up-to-the-minute docudramas—Living Newspapers—of the day's events.

SOURCE: *Arena: The Story of the Federal Theatre*, by Hallie Flanagan, 1940.

Begun as a relief project under President Franklin D. Roosevelt's Works Progress Administration (WPA), the Federal Theatre Project intended to get those theater workers who were part of the nation's more than twenty percent unemployed back to work at what they did best. It accomplished much more. In fact, as Flanagan writes, its outstanding achievement was "the discovery and development of a nationwide audience," as FTP reached more than twenty-five million people, a quarter of the nation's population, in four years, introducing many to live theater for the first time.

Often described as a "practical idealist," Flanagan envisioned not only her national project but, remarkably, the future of the American theater. She saw a future that is, in many ways, still working itself out—a panoramic American theater: cheap, accessible to all, simultaneously local and universal, technologically sophisticated and reflective of the realities of the day; a national, living theater as varied as the people of America. In her words: "The Federal Theatre is a pioneer theater because it is part of a tremendous rethinking, rebuilding and redreaming of America [. . .] not merely a decoration but a vital force in our democracy."

The Federal Theatre Project lived a mere four years. It was "killed" by an act of Congress in 1939, after a struggle to become what Harry Hopkins,[10] director of Roosevelt's Federal Emergency Relief Administration, called "a free, adult, uncensored theater." In these excerpts from Flanagan's 1940 history of FTP, *Arena*, an astonishing work that captures both the tortuous detail of the endeavor and its monumental vision, she describes the project in the throes of birth and death.

—*TL*

Danger: Men Not Working

In 1932, 1933, 1934, the people of the theater—directors, actors, designers, costumers, stagehands—turned to any sort of job that could be found, however temporary, however poorly paid. They were willing to dig ditches and they did dig ditches, but unskilled labor was also unemployed and could dig better ditches. A violinist, a circus clown, a sculptor, a stagehand—these people are trained in one profession and one profession only. Try as they would, they could find no recourse except charity. In New York and other

10. A nod to origins: Flanagan and Hopkins met in the small town of Grinnell, Iowa, where they grew up together and where they were students, a year apart, at Grinnell College. It was as a student at Grinnell in 1974 that I first learned the name of Hallie Flanagan, because the school's experimental theater was named for her. It was there, too, in the offices behind the Flanagan, that my teacher, Sandy Moffett, gave me my first inspirational books about American theater companies, the books that, thirty-five years later, led to this book.

cities friends formed various actors' organizations such as the Dinner Club, where those who could afford to buy a meal might buy another for an unemployed actor in return for entertainment offered as an attraction.

Thus the actor became one with thousands of fellow professionals in the fields of music, painting, writing. He was a small part of a portion of our population, the unemployed, developing in numbers at a terrifying rate.

Steps were taken to remedy the general unemployment condition and should it be asked what has this to do with theater, the answer is that this economic situation was the rock from which the first government theater of the United States was hewn.

The first Relief Act passed by Congress, March 31, 1933, in addition to providing relief for unemployed adults, set up the Civilian Conservation Corps, the immediate object of which was to find jobs for unemployed youths. Six weeks later Congress established the FERA (Federal Emergency Relief Administration) for the purpose of granting federal funds to states to assist in caring for the unemployed. On November 9, 1933, Congress established the CWA (Civil Works Administration) for the purpose of creating four million jobs for men and women desperately in need. In all of these agencies the emphasis was on immediacy. Under CWA in the administration of Harry Hopkins in nine weeks more than 4.2 million men were put to work, laying sewer pipe, building and improving roads, playgrounds, schools and athletic fields.

. . .

With the setting up of the Works Progress Administration[11] by Congress on April 8, 1935, a new approach to the problem of unemployment based on experiences of FERA and CWA was indicated in three departures from earlier methods:

1. Only *employables* were to be taken from the relief rolls of the states.
2. To these employables, work was to be offered within their own skills and trades.
3. Unemployables were to be returned to the care of the states.

Each state set up its own welfare organization to certify the needy for relief or for WPA jobs. These organizations were guided by two definitions: *employable* was to mean a healthy, unhandicapped person certified as to ability to work and as to need; *unemployable* to designate "those unable to work

11. The CWA was dismantled in February 1934; it closed officially in April, its unfinished work being carried over to the Work Division of FERA. [author's note]

and those who should not, for society's sake as well as their own, compete in the labor market: mothers who should be enabled to be homemakers, children who should be in school, and workers old enough to have earned retirement."[12] Around the differing methods used by the various emergency relief agencies in the forty-eight states to determine need and employability revolved much of the turmoil and argument over Federal Theatre; as of the entire WPA program.

This new emphasis of the Works Progress Administration on social, as well as on human, values meant that for the first time in the relief experiments in this country the preservation of the skill of the worker, and hence the preservation of his self-respect, became important. People in vast numbers had been put to work by the government before; now the problem was to sort them out, get them into their own line of work and insist that the work they turn out be of a standard compatible with payment by the government. The very name of the new organization, with its absence of any reference to the word *relief*, struck an emphasis on work growing progressively better.

Could the theater have a place in this new conception of work for the unemployed? Could a nationwide plan be devised for theater activities?

. . .

A plan began to take form in my mind, dictated not by an art theory or an academic idea, but by economic necessity. No one knew how many unemployed theater people there were or where they were. Actors' Equity said there were five thousand unemployed actors in New York City alone. Counting workers in allied theater skills, WPA estimated a probable twenty to thirty thousand. Where were they? Who were they? Numbers on cards in relief offices from one end of the country to the other. The primary task would be to set up volunteer boards of theater people in each state to audition the applicants. When a sufficient number of professionals was found in any state, we could start a company. This, however, was not enough; we must have a broad plan encompassing the whole country, outlining the general policy in plays, sketching the relationship of these companies to their various communities.

Because of the size of our country and because of the origins and aims of the project, the type of theater needed could not be modeled on a government-operated enterprise of any other country. Government subsidy of the theater brought the United States into the best historic theater tradition and into the best contemporary theater practice, but there the similarity ended. This was not France or Germany, where a galaxy of artists was to be

12. *Spending to Save*, by Harry L. Hopkins, W. W. Norton & Company, Inc., New York, 1936. [author's note]

chosen to play classical repertory. Nor was it Russia, where the leaders of the state told the theater directors what plays to do and what not to do. Neither was it Italy, where theater performances took the form of largesse distributed to the people. This was a distinctly American enterprise growing out of a people's need over a vast geographic area.

Knowledge of plays and techniques absorbed through years of theater study here and abroad would be useful, but in the central conception what was immediately needed was a knowledge of the United States. I was glad at this point that I knew my country, that I had been born in South Dakota, educated in Iowa and Massachusetts, that I had traveled in almost every state, lived in cities—Chicago, St. Louis, Detroit; in a small town, Grinnell; in a village, Sonora; and on a farm in Iowa. I studied the map, and the plan developed: five great regional theaters—New York, Los Angeles, Chicago, possibly Boston, possibly New Orleans, each one a production center for a professional company; each a retraining center for the actors who would undoubtedly be of varying ability and from various backgrounds; each a service, research and playwriting center for its own region. Eventually the plan should include a metropolitan theater built in each area, labor for such a building to be furnished by the WPA; and in these theaters, resident companies would do new plays and classical repertory and everything that commercial theaters cannot always afford to try; companies from each of these centers would tour the region, playing a circuit of smaller theaters; university or civic theaters in each of the regions would work with these government theaters in developing playwrights who would build up a body of dramatic literature, each for his own region.

[. . .] We laid a great deal of stress upon the development of local and regional theater expression, rather than on the New York conception of theater or of ideas emanating from Washington:

> If any important creative work is to be done in the theater in the West it will be an outgrowth of life in these regions. The plan here proposed is an effort to stimulate the development of genuinely creative theater in these regions.

And again, we stated the aim:

> To set up theaters which have possibilities of growing into social institutions in the communities in which they are located and thus to provide possible future employment for at least some of those who now present an immediate and acute problem to the government . . . and to lay the foundation for the development of a truly

creative theater in the United States with outstanding producing centers in each of those regions which have common interests as a result of geography, language origins, history, tradition, custom, occupations of the people.[13]

In short, the plan was based on that of the federal government itself: the general policy and program would be outlined in Washington, but the carrying out, with modifications dictated by local conditions, would rest with the states. It was not a national theater in the European sense of a group of artists chosen to represent the government. It was never referred to by me as a national theater, though critics increasingly spoke of it as such. It was rather a federation of theaters. That was the origin and meaning of its name.

[. . .] No more natural place for the announcement of a nationwide government theater could be imagined than the National Theatre Conference at the University of Iowa, where people from all over the United States met for the laying of the cornerstone of an institution which was to be not only a civic and university theater, but a regional center for the entire Midwest. After the ceremony we all went back to the hall of the Art Building where, after dinner, President [Eugene] Gilmore of the university introduced Elmer Rice, Paul Green and other speakers. Harry Hopkins spoke of the new kind of theater we hoped to create in America; he concluded with a fearless statement of policy: "I am asked whether a theater subsidized by the government can be kept free from censorship, and I say, yes, it is going to be kept free from censorship. What we want is a free, adult, uncensored theater."

I took this declaration seriously, as did my associates, and that is the kind of theater we spent the next four years trying to build.

.   .   .

On August 27, 1935, I took the oath of office, swearing to protect and defend the Constitution of the United States against all enemies foreign and domestic. The oath was administered in a theater, the old Auditorium in Washington, a vast hulk of a building which, symbolically enough, was under reconstruction to accommodate several thousand WPA, PWA,[14] and other government workers. In those August and September days the Auditorium was a madhouse of rushing people, whirring electric fans, riveting machines going full blast, workmen slinging lumber about and plasterers slapping on cement.

---

13. *A Plan for the Organization of Regional Theatres in the United States*, by E. C. Mabie (WPA Federal Theatre Records, Washington, D.C.). [author's note]

14. The Public Works Administration, under Secretary of the Interior Harold Ickes, was a massive national construction project aimed at work relief and the building of dams, bridges, hospitals and schools, part of the New Deal effort to revive the economy.

The airless hall was divided by gray partitions into a labyrinth of cubicles, and in one of these, under the glare from overhead electric lights, Lester Lang[15] and I, with a staff of three people, sorted the mail dumped daily on our desks, studied involved WPA procedure, and planned a program to put some ten thousand theater people back to work. In order to be ready when the allotment came through, we worked out with the aid of the statistical and legal divisions the plan which I had sent to Washington on August 17, the premises of which were as follows:[16]

1. That the reemployment of theater people now on relief rolls is the primary aim.
2. That this reemployment shall be in theater enterprises offering dramatic entertainment either free or at low cost.
3. That whenever possible regional theaters developing native plays and original methods of production shall be encouraged.
4. That the WPA will pay:

   a. *Labor costs* of unemployed people enrolled on the project at the wage stated by the local WPA administration.
   b. *Superintendence cost*, on an average of one person not on relief rolls to twenty who are, at a small wage.
   c. *A small percentage* (not to exceed ten percent) *of labor costs for production costs*, depending on the nature of the project.

5. That if the sponsoring organization is a public enterprise, or a nonprofit-making cooperative, or can be incorporated as such, any funds made by admissions may accrue to the project.

[. . .] In answer to the hundreds of letters asking for funds we sent out a questionnaire which, after stating what the government could do, listed the following points to be answered by any organization, group or individual interested in working with Federal Theatre:

1. How many theater people, *now on relief rolls*, does your plan propose to put to work?
2. At what date?

15. Flanagan's associate at Vassar College, and later administrative assistant at FTP.

16. *Theatre Project for Works Progress Administration*, by Hallie Flanagan. Enclosed in letter to Bruce McClure, on August 17, 1935 (WPA Federal Theatre Records, Washington, D.C.). [author's note]

3. Are directors available in your community? If so, state education and theater experience.
4. List any civic, state or local organizations actively interested in the support of your project.
5. State the entertainment and cultural value of your project.
6. State the practical working plan under which you will operate (i.e., repertory, stock, touring, etc.).
7. Give estimated superintendence cost and operating cost.

Most of the people who had written in so grandiosely or belligerently about what should be done, when faced with the necessity of getting practical ideas together, were never heard from again. [. . .]

Blasting: Work Suspended

The entire history of Federal Theatre points to one dynamic fact, profoundly significant for the future of the stage: that the theater, often regarded even by members of its own profession as dead or dying, still has tremendous power to stir up life and infuse it with fire. It is probable that during the last four years more discussion of the theater took place in the House and Senate and in congressional committees than in all the other years of our congressional history put together. Scenes from Federal Theatre plays were enacted on the floor of Congress; eloquent speeches were made for and against the theater as an art and as an institution; Shakespeare came into the discussion, and Marlowe and Aristotle. A senator who fought for Federal Theatre told me that months after that institution was ended, fights about its merits and demerits were still going on in congressional cloakrooms. No one fights over a dead art or a dead issue.

In June of 1939 forces of the theater world from New York to Hollywood united in a spectacular campaign to save an organization which four years earlier many of them had ignored or attacked. Some were actuated by growing admiration of the work of the project, some by a sense of fair play, some by a fervor of belief expressed by Orson Welles in his broadcast when he said, "Federal Theatre is the very life blood of the commercial stage." The variety of organizations and individuals coming out publicly for the continuance of Federal Theatre included every theatrical union, representing a combined membership of thousands; the Screen Actors Guild, the Screen Directors Guild, the Screen Writers Guild, speaking for the vast Hollywood industry; entire companies of plays on Broadway, dramatic critics from coast to coast; distinguished actors, producers, directors, designers from New York and Hollywood; college and community theaters from the

North, East, South and West; the Federation of Arts Unions representing painters, sculptors, musicians and artists of every field.

Further, no movement sponsored by the art world ever received wider and more varied civic and state backing than that given the pleas of the commercial stage to continue Federal Theatre; their requests were reinforced by similar ones from churches, Catholic and Protestant of many denominations; from schools, colleges and universities throughout America; from a great number of American Legion posts and other patriotic bodies; from every conceivable type of civic and philanthropic organization; from social, medical and welfare institutions; from business houses and industrial concerns; from many civic committees and mayors throughout the country.

How was it possible, with such overwhelming support and with a record of accomplishment so substantial, that Federal Theatre was nevertheless ended by Act of Congress on June 30, 1939?

It was not ended as an economy move, though this was the ostensible reason given: the entire arts program, of which Federal Theatre was one of five projects, used less than three-fourths of one percent of the total WPA appropriation; and that appropriation was not cut one cent by the end of Federal Theatre; the money was simply distributed among other WPA projects.

It was ended because Congress, in spite of protests from many of its own members, treated Federal Theatre not as a human issue or a cultural issue, but as a political issue.

It was ended because the powerful forces marshaled in its behalf came too late to combat other forces which apparently had been at work against Federal Theatre for a long time. Through two congressional committees these forces found a habitation and a name.

As an American who believes it the center and core of our democratic way of life that decisions rest not with any one man or group but with the people through their elected representatives, I can feel no resentment that Congress had, coequal and coexistent with its power to create a government-sponsored theater, the power to end it.

Congress, in the case of Federal Theatre, however, was misinformed by witnesses before two committees, by members of those committees, and by other congressmen: first, by witnesses before the House Committee to Investigate Un-American Activities (chairman Martin Dies) during the period from August to December 1938; later by witnesses before the subcommittee of the House Committee on Appropriations (chairman Clifton A. Woodrum), set up for investigation and study of the Works Progress Administration, in the spring of 1939; and finally by Congressman John Taber (Republican, New York) and Congressman Everett M. Dirksen (Republican, Illinois) on the floor of the House of Representatives; and by

Senator Robert Reynolds (Democrat, North Carolina) and Senator Rush D. Holt (Democrat, West Virginia) on the floor of the United States Senate.

In July 1938, when I first read a statement in a New York paper that Federal Theatre was dominated by communists and that you had to belong to the Workers' Alliance in order to get on the project I released an immediate and unequivocal denial. This was an infraction of the rule that only the WPA information division in Washington answered press stories and I was told by WPA officials that on no account was I to reply to these charges. It was the fashion at that time, in the WPA and out, to laugh at the Dies Committee; but it never seemed funny to me. As days went on and the papers gave more and more space to the testimony of a few unqualified witnesses, it seemed to me increasingly incredible that the congressional committee called no officials of the project and no theater experts from outside the project.

On August 5, 1938, when the WPA was still ignoring the whole matter and still refusing to allow me to issue statements to the press, I wrote to Representative Dies asking him to hear me and six regional directors who constituted the National Policy Board; I told him that regional and state offices were waiting to give cooperation to the Committee, but that as yet no use had been made of available information, while in the meantime a half-dozen witnesses, no one of whom was in any position to know the broad sweep of project operation or administration, were making statements which, as the Committee could easily ascertain, were biased, prejudiced and often completely false.

To this letter I received no answer.

The WPA still refused to take the continued attacks seriously. Many people believe that this was because that organization had already decided that Federal Theatre was a political liability and wanted to end it before 1940. I do not think, however, that the appeasement policy, in the air in Washington in the spring and summer of 1939, started as early as this. I incline rather to the belief that WPA was following government tradition that attacks on people in government service are not answered by anyone except heads of departments. Any agency like the WPA which depends for its continued existence upon periodic appropriations wants to keep out of the papers. It goes on the supposition that if you do not answer an attack, the attack will cease.

These attacks did not cease. Again I wrote Chairman Dies, saying that the jobs of thousands of people were being jeopardized and that I wished to put the record of their work before the Committee. Again no answer. In the meantime the allegations left their mark on the public mind and the project morale.

Emmet Lavery, who had charge of the final clearance of play contracts, in August wrote a vigorous letter to Chairman Dies saying that he was a

Catholic and that he had never authorized a communistic play for the project and that he demanded to be heard. The letter was not answered. On September 1, Congressman J. Parnell Thomas (Republican, New Jersey) declared in the *New York Herald Tribune* that "practically every play was clear unadulterated propaganda." Mr. Lavery immediately challenged Representative Thomas to debate the production record of the project on the radio, play by play. That challenge, like all others, went unanswered.

I have often been asked why we did not demand to attend the hearings of the Committee, insist that project officials or professional theater people be called, see that the project record of the witnesses be examined by the Committee; and above all why we did not bring libel suits against some of these congressmen, including Representative Dirksen, who called our productions "salacious tripe."

The answer is that citizens are not able to insist on the same measure of due process of law in Congress that they receive in the courts. A congressional committee may hold its hearings in public or private, as it sees fit, may or may not hear witnesses as it pleases, may cite for contempt witnesses who do not respond to its subpoena but on the other hand may not be compelled to hear people who demand to testify. At the bar of a trial court an accused person may demand through his lawyer that accusing witnesses be cross-examined, that evidence be relevant and legally probative; the accused has the advice of counsel and may summon expert witnesses for the appraisal of technical points. These are rights granted at the bar of our courts; but congressional committees operate as quasi-judicial bodies which are a law unto themselves; and a congressman is immune from libel suits for statements he makes while engaged in the conduct of his official duties.[17]

Thus it came about that during the year from June 1938, to its end on June 30, 1939, a project, in which ninety percent came from relief rolls, the vast majority of which showed membership in theatrical unions (American Federation of Labor affiliates), was accused of being made up largely of nonrelief amateurs; a project which had brought in cash to the government approximating two million dollars,[18] a record which so far as I know has never been equaled by any WPA project, was accused of being inefficient;

17. Article I, Section 6, United States Constitution, provides that "for any speech or debate in either House they (senators and representatives) shall not be questioned in any other place." The decision in the case of *Kilbourn v. Thompson*, 103 U.S. Reports, 168, indicates that the protection provided is not necessarily limited to statements made on the floor of either house. [author's note]

18. The figure given by the Division of Statistics of the WPA, through March 31, 1939, was $1,925,919. This did not include final figures on *The Swing Mikado*, *Run, Little Chillun* and other outstanding box office successes of the spring of 1939. [author's note]

and a project which from first to last had stood on American principles of freedom, justice and truth, was accused of being, through its plays, its audiences and its personnel, subversive, communistic and indecent.

. . .

On December 6, I was called to testify. It was indeed much later than the WPA thought. Could a few hours offset the months in which allegations had gone unanswered, and charges had been magnified by the press?

Before me stretched two long tables in the form of a huge T. At the foot was the witness chair, at the head the members of the Committee. At long tables on either side of the T were reporters, stenographers, cameramen. The room itself, a high-walled chamber with great chandeliers, was lined with exhibits of material from Federal Theatre and the Writers' Project; but all I could see for a moment were the faces of thousands of Federal Theatre people: clowns in the circus . . . telephone girls at the switchboards . . . actors in grubby rehearsal rooms . . . acrobats limbering up their routines . . . costume women busy making cheap stuff look expensive . . . musicians composing scores to bring out the best in our often oddly assembled orchestras . . . playwrights working on scripts with the skills of our actors in mind . . . carpenters, prop men, ushers. These were the people on trial that morning.

I was sworn in as a witness by Chairman Dies, a rangy Texan with a cowboy drawl and a big black cigar. I wanted to talk about Federal Theatre, but the Committee apparently did not. Who had appointed me? Harry Hopkins. Was that his own idea or did somebody put him up to it? I said I had no knowledge of any recommendations made in my behalf; I said that while the Committee had recently been investigating un-American activity, I had been engaged for four years in combating un-American inactivity. The distinction was lost on the Committee. I sketched the project's concern for the human values, the return of over two thousand of our people to jobs in private industry, but the Committee was not interested in any discussion of the project. Wasn't it true I taught at Vassar? Yes. Went to Russia? Yes. Wrote a book about it? Yes. Praised the Russian theater? In 1926 I had been appointed as a fellow of the Guggenheim Foundation to study the theater in twelve European countries over a period of fourteen months; Russia was one of the countries in which I carried on such observations. What was it I found so exciting in the Russian theater? It was at that time an interesting theater about which little was known. It was my job at that time to study it. That, I pointed out, was twelve years ago. It was part of the background of my profession—the American theater. The Committee was giving more time to the discussion of the Russian theater than Federal Theatre had in the four years of its existence.

[Congressman Joseph] Starnes was curious about my visits to Russia. Had I gone there in 1931 as well as in 1926? Yes, for three weeks. Was I a delegate to anything? No, I had gone, as had many American theater producers, to see the Russian theater festival. Did I meet at the festival there any of the people later employed in the Federal Theatre? Certainly not.

Hadn't I written plays in Russian and produced them in Russia? I had not (I remembered my struggles to learn to order a meal or buy galoshes in Russian).

Then back to the project. Had communistic propaganda been circulated on the project? Not to my knowledge. Were there orders on my part against such activity? Yes, stringent orders which appear in the brief. Mr. Starnes took a different tack: Did I consider the theater a weapon? I said the theater could be all things to all men. "Do you see this?" Congressman Starnes suddenly shouted, waving a yellow magazine aloft. "Ever see it before?" I said it seemed to be an old *Theatre Arts Monthly*. This described a meeting of workers' theaters in New York in 1931. Hadn't I been active in setting them up? No. I had never been connected in any way with workers' theaters. I wrote a report on such theaters for *Theatre Arts Monthly* under the title "A Theatre Is Born." This theater, however, was not born through me; I was simply a reporter.

How about these plays that had been criticized by witnesses before the Committee? Were they propaganda? For Communism? "To the best of my knowledge," I told the Committee, "we have never done a play which was propaganda for Communism; but we have done plays which were propaganda for democracy, for better housing . . ."

How many people had we played to so far? Twenty-five million people, a fifth of the population. Where did our audience come from? Was it true that we "couldn't get any audiences for anything except communist plays"? No. The list submitted would show our wide audience support. Back to the article, "A Theatre Is Born," and the phrase where I had described the enthusiasm of these theaters as having "a certain Marlowesque madness."

"You are quoting from this Marlowe," observed Mr. Starnes. "Is he a communist?"

The room rocked with laughter, but I did not laugh. Eight thousand people might lose their jobs because a Congressional Committee had so prejudged us that even the classics were "communistic." I said, "I was quoting from Christopher Marlowe."

"Tell us who Marlowe is, so we can get the proper references, because that is all we want to do."

"Put in the record that he was the greatest dramatist in the period of Shakespeare, immediately preceding Shakespeare."

Mr. Starnes subsided; Mr. Thomas of New Jersey took over.

How about this play, *The Revolt of the Beavers*? Didn't Brooks Atkinson of the *New York Times* disapprove of the play? Yes, he did. But Mr. Hearst's *New York American* thought it a "pleasing fantasy for children," and an audience survey by trained psychologists brought only favorable reactions from children such as "teaches us never to be selfish," "it is better to be good than bad," how the children would "want the whole world to be nine years old and happy."

Was it true that we had been rehearsing *Sing for Your Supper*, the musical in New York, for thirteen months? It was true and the delays were not of our choosing. We kept losing our best skits and our best actors to private industry. Was that, I asked, un-American? Mr. Mosier[19] brought us back to the question of propaganda. Had we ever produced any anti-fascist plays? Some people claimed that Shaw's *On the Rocks* was anti-fascist and others thought it was anti-communist; Shakespeare's *Coriolanus* caused the same discussion.

"We never do a play because it holds any political bias," I declared. "We do a play because we believe it is a good play, a strong play, properly handled, with native material."

Was it true that Earl Browder[20] appeared as a character in *Triple-A Plowed Under*? Yes. Did he expound his theory of Communism? He did not; he appeared as a shadow on a screen along with Al Smith,[21] Senator Hastings[22] and Thomas Jefferson. Had we ever produced plays that were anti-religious? On the contrary, we had produced more religious plays than any other theater organization in the history of the country. Was I in sympathy with communistic doctrines? I said:

"I am an American and I believe in American democracy. I believe the Works Progress Administration is one great bulwark of that democracy. I believe Federal Theatre, which is one small part of that large pattern, is honestly trying in every possible way to interpret the best interests of the people of this democracy. I am not in sympathy with any other form of government."

What percentage of the four thousand employees on the New York project were members of the Workers' Alliance, Mr. Thomas wanted to know. We had no way of knowing. Was it a very large percentage? No, we knew it could not be large because the vast majority belonged to the standard

19. Harold G. Mosier, congressional Democrat and member of the Dies Committee.

20. Political activist and general secretary of the Communist Party of the USA in the New Deal years.

21. Three-term New York governor and 1928 Democratic presidential candidate. Smith lost a second bid for his party's presidential candidacy to Franklin D. Roosevelt.

22. Two-term Republican senator from Delaware.

theatrical organizations like Actors' Equity and the various stage unions, and these unions did not permit their members to join the Workers' Alliance.

Chairman Dies asked if we were out to entertain our audiences or to instruct them. I said that the primary purpose of a play is to entertain but that it can also teach.

"Do you think the theater should be used for the purpose of conveying ideas along social and economic lines?"

"I think that is one justifiable reason for the existence of a theater."

"Do you think that the Federal Theatre should be used for the purpose of conveying ideas along social, economic or political lines?"

"I would hesitate on the political."

"Eliminate political, upon social and economic lines?"

"I think it is one logical, reasonable and, I might say, imperative thing for our theater to do."

Could I give the Committee one play, dealing with social questions, where "organized labor does not have the best of the other fellows"? Certainly. I mentioned *Spirochete*, the Living Newspaper on the history of syphilis, endorsed by the surgeon general of the United States Public Health Service. I mentioned the Living Newspapers being prepared on flood control (*Bonneville Dam*); the history of vaudeville (*Clown's Progress*); the history of California real estate (*Spanish Grant*). The chairman waved these examples aside. Didn't *Power* imply that public ownership of utilities is a good thing? Is it proper for a government theater to champion one side of a controversy? We do not choose plays by picking sides in a controversy.

On this matter of the writing of plays it was apparent that the Committee confused the Theatre [Project] and the Federal Writers' Project. Chairman Dies insisted that he had received admissions from Federal Theatre workers who were communists, communists who had placed their signatures openly in a book. I said this had not happened on our project.

"Well," declared the chairman triumphantly, "Mr. De Solo said he was a communist."

"But he is not on Federal Theatre Project."

"He is on the Writers' Project."

"Yes, but not our project."

Suddenly Mr. Starnes remarked that it was a quarter past one, the chairman announced an adjournment for an hour and said that Mr. Alsberg would be heard when they resumed.

"Just a minute, gentlemen," I interrupted. "Do I understand that this concludes my testimony?"

"We will see about it after lunch," the chairman promised.

"I would like to make a final statement, if I may."

"We will see about it after lunch," the chairman repeated and the gavel fell. We never saw about it after lunch.

As the hearing broke up I thought suddenly of how much it all looked like a badly staged courtroom scene; it wasn't imposing enough for a congressional hearing on which the future of several thousand human beings depended. For any case on which the life and reputation of a single human being depended, even that of an accused murderer, we had an American system which demanded a judge trained in law, a defense lawyer, a carefully chosen jury and, above all, the necessity of hearing all the evidence on both sides of the case.

Yet here was a Committee which for months had been actually trying a case against Federal Theatre, trying it behind closed doors, and giving one side only to the press. Out of a project employing thousands of people from coast to coast the Committee had chosen arbitrarily to hear ten witnesses, all from New York City, and had refused arbitrarily to hear literally hundreds of others, on and off the project, who had asked to testify.

Representative [John] Dempsey, who throughout the hearing had been just and courteous, came up and told me that he felt my testimony had been "completely satisfactory." Congressman Thomas was jovial.

"You don't look like a communist," he declared. "You look like a Republican!"

"If your Committee isn't convinced that neither I nor Federal Theatre Project is communistic I want to come back this afternoon," I told him.

"We don't want you back," he laughed. "You're a tough witness and we're all worn out."

Mrs. Woodward[23] and I weren't satisfied. We told the secretary of the Committee that I had not finished my testimony. He said, "In any case your brief will be printed." He accepted the brief for inclusion in the transcript. It was not included.

After the testimony, one thing stood out in my mind: the brief must be made public. Mr. Niles,[24] when approached on the point, said that my apprehension was groundless. "They'll have to include the brief. They can't suppress evidence. However, I'll tell you what to do. You send five hundred of those mimeographed briefs to my office and if the Committee does not print it I will then see that copies are distributed to every senator and to a number of members of the lower House." We sent the briefs to Mr. Niles's office. They were never distributed to members of Congress.

23. Mrs. Ellen S. Woodward, assistant administrator in charge of women's and professional projects of the WPA.

24. David K. Niles, assistant administrator for the Federal Theatre Project.

We made one more attempt to give the Committee a realistic view of the project. On December 19, I extended an invitation to each member of the Committee to come to New York for the opening production of *Pinocchio* at the Ritz Theatre on December 23, or for any of the holiday performances.

"You might be especially interested in this production," I wrote Congressman Dies, "not only because it represents one of our major efforts in the field of children's theater, but because it is a visualization of what we have been able to do in rehabilitating professional theater people and retraining them in new techniques. In *Pinocchio* we use fifty vaudeville people who were at one time headliners in their profession and who, through no fault of their own, suddenly found themselves without a market. Now they are artists in a new field and I feel certain you will find that this re-creation of theater personalities is no less exciting than the presentation of the play itself."

The Committee, however, proceeded to its final deliberations with its theatergoing record intact: officially it never saw a production of the project under examination.

The Dies Committee Report, filed with the House of Representatives January 3, 1939, may in the future be of as much interest to students of jurisprudence and government as of theater. A great amount of space was given over to condemnation of the Federal Writers' Project; but on the case of Federal Theatre, six months' of sensational charges tapered down to one short paragraph:

> We are convinced that a rather large number of the employees on the Federal Theatre Project are either members of the Communist Party or are sympathetic with the Communist Party. It is also clear that certain employees felt under compulsion to join the Workers' Alliance in order to retain their jobs.

It will be noted that the report did not say a word in criticism of three of the major points dwelt upon by witnesses and about which I had been questioned: type of plays; type of audience; type of leadership. Just what constituted "a rather large number," what amounted to "sympathy" or how many "certain employees" ever felt any "compulsion" was left to the imagination of the public.

[. . .]

For the last performance of *Pinocchio* at the Ritz Theatre, New York, Yasha Frank provided a new ending. *Pinocchio*, having conquered selfishness and greed, did not become a living boy. Instead he was turned back into a puppet. "So let the bells proclaim our grief," intoned the company at the finish, "that his small life was all too brief." The stagehands knocked down the sets in view of the audience and the company laid Pinocchio away in a pine box which bore the legend:

BORN DECEMBER 23, 1938;
KILLED BY ACT OF CONGRESS, JUNE 30, 1939.

Meantime at the Maxine Elliott, George Sklar's *Life and Death of an American* presented for the last time the life of Jerry Dorgan, "first kid of the twentiethth century, born at twelve seconds past midnight, born to grow with America, with the century." Production and direction by Morris Ankrum and Charles Freeman enlarged the implications of the story, as did Howard Bay's settings. Emerging out of space, a single screen set on a diagonal afforded for each scene its own psychological as well as physical background. Thus the gymnasium hung with bunting for the high school dance was not so much a place as an enchantment felt by the boy and girl as they danced together: by the same eloquent economy of means, emotional reverberations were suggested in the scenes of the boy's first job, his marching away to war; his return to joblessness, his despair, his growing realization that his destiny was a part of America's destiny. "What does one person count?" his wife asks bitterly. Jerry answers, "Everybody counts."

At the Adelphi, as the project ended, in *Sing for Your Supper* actors who knew what the words meant were singing:

Ain't it lucky, ain't it swell
I ran all the way home to tell
I'm so happy it's just like ringing a bell—
Papa's Got a Job!

The stage filled with neighbors, congratulating the family on the earth-shaking event, the hurdy-gurdy played, children danced in the street, the policeman unrolled the red velvet carpet and Papa came in, borne on the shoulders of shouting friends, to be met by the mayor, presented with the keys to the city, and photographed by enterprising newsreel men.

Sing for Your Supper reached its climax in "Ballad of Uncle Sam," which since that time, as "Ballad for Americans,"[25] has been performed under many circumstances: it was sung over a nationwide hook-up by Paul Robeson, and CBS was buried under an avalanche of letters saying, "This is the voice of America." It was sung by the Schola Cantorum in the Lewisohn Stadium

---

25. "Ballad for Americans," copyright © 1940, Robbins Music Corporation, New York. Used by permission. [author's note]

in New York to the music of the Philharmonic Symphony Orchestra, and thousands of people rose and cheered. It was chosen as the theme song of the Republican National Convention in Philadelphia in 1940—probably without knowledge of its Federal Theatre origin, or of the fact that Congressman Woodrum had said, "If there is a line or passage in [*Sing for Your Supper*] that contributes to cultural or educational benefit or uplift of America, I will eat the whole manuscript." Yet it was never sung under circumstances more momentous to human beings than on the last night of the Federal Theatre by the project that originated it. As the revue of Uncle Sam surveying his world reached its climax, the stage began to fill with:

> Engineer, Musician, Street-cleaner, Carpenter,
> Teacher, Farmer, Mechanic, Housewife,
> Stenographer, Factory-worker, Beauty Specialist,
> Bartender, Truck-driver, Seamstress, Miner, Ditch-digger—
> All the et ceteras
> And the and-so-forths
> That do the work.

Over the silent house the words of the questioner and the answers of the chorus took on urgency. Did they all believe in liberty in those days?

> Nobody who was anybody believed it
> Everybody who was anybody they doubted it . . .

But:

> Out of the cheating, out of the shouting . . .
> Out of the windbags, the patriotic spouting,
> Out of uncertainty and doubting . . .
> Out of the carpet-bag and the brass spittoon
> It will come again
> Our marching song will come again:
> *Adopted unanimously in Congress July 4, 1776:*
> We hold these truths to be self-evident
> That all men are created equal
> That they are endowed by their Creator
> With certain inalienable rights
> That among these are life,
> Liberty,
> And the pursuit of happiness.

Thus Federal Theatre ended as it had begun, with fearless presentation of problems touching American life. If this first government theater in our country had been less alive it might have lived longer. But I do not believe anyone who worked on it regrets that it stood from first to last against reaction, against prejudice, against racial, religious and political intolerance. It strove for a more dramatic statement and a better understanding of the great forces of our life today; it fought for a free theater as one of the many expressions of a civilized, informed and vigorous life.

[. . .]

The President of the United States in writing to me of his regret at the closing of Federal Theatre referred to it as a pioneering job. This it was, gusty, lusty, bad and good, sad and funny, superbly worth more wit, wisdom and imagination than we could give it. Its significance lies in its pointing to the future. The ten thousand anonymous men and women—the et ceteras and the and-so-forths who did the work, the nobodies who were everybody, the somebodies who believed it—their dreams and deeds were not the end. They were the beginning of a people's theater in a country whose greatest plays are still to come.

—*HF*

The Wisconsin Idea Theater

FOUNDED 1943

Robert E. Gard

> If you try, you can indeed alter the face and the heart of America.
> —*Robert E. Gard*

Robert Gard may not be the literal father of grassroots theater in America, but he is surely, among its pioneers, one of the best and most influential articulators of its hopes and practices.[26] Working the ground cultivated by forerunners in rural and community theater in

SOURCE: *Grassroots Theater: A Search for Regional Arts in America*, by Robert E. Gard, 1955.

26. Many thanks to Robert H. Leonard, founding artistic director of the Road Company (1972–98) and now a professor of theater arts at Virginia Tech, who first told me about Robert E. Gard. Of course, once I'd "discovered" him, I found his influence everywhere, including the next two offerings in this book, by Dudley Cocke and Cornerstone Theater Company.

America—including Alfred G. Arvold (North Dakota) and Frederick H. Koch (North Dakota and North Carolina), and his mentor at Cornell, Alexander M. Drummond—and building on foundations laid in Wisconsin by Thomas H. Dickinson's Wisconsin Players (founded in 1911), Gard laid out a vision for finding the art in the places and people of America, one playwright at a time.

After several years of collecting plays written in and about upstate New York as part of Drummond's New York State Play Project, Gard, a thirty-five-year-old playwright and educator, came to the University of Wisconsin in Madison as a professor. There, as part of an adult education "extension" program, he began planning the Wisconsin Idea Theater. In those unlikely surroundings he set out to grow a popular American art, deeply connected to the places, traditions, and themes of a region—a native theater grown on native soil out of the native talents of its people.

—TL

In retrospect, the lights and shadows of the nine years spent in the creation of the Wisconsin Idea Theater stand out clearly. The shadows were predominant in the early years. My convictions about native literature were sincere, strong. I saw a native literature emerging as in Alberta and New York from a feeling for places. But soon after I had started work in Wisconsin I understood that I could not work as I had in New York, for example, where the university theater itself furnished the center and the home base for my efforts with native playwrights.

There was no . . . sympathy for native playwriting in the university theater at Wisconsin. The Wisconsin theater staff was overburdened with teaching and with duties connected with play production and had little or no time for the discussion of regional drama problems. The attitude of the theater staff was a blow which left me confused. I fear that I wasted some of this early period in futile bitterness. I believe now, however, that failure to establish a center for my work in the university theater was actually the factor that saved my program. For I was thrown toward the backstage and became familiar with the Wisconsin Idea, with the extension men, the specialists, the crusaders.

I was reluctant at first. I was somewhat mistrustful of the Extension Division[27] at Wisconsin, especially when I learned the division was to be the actual administrative unit for my work. The whole format of my project, however, was unique, and the Extension Division seemed to me, shortly

---

27. Adult education division.

after my arrival in Madison, to offer a more promising base than the university theater, which offered nothing.

My entire program was to be conducted by three separate branches of the university: the College of Letters and Science, the College of Agriculture and the Extension Division. Financial support would be divided among the three branches, with Letters and Science and Agriculture providing one-half of my salary and the Extension Division providing the remaining half as well as office space, secretarial help and other facilities. Although the new program was to be a joint undertaking of these three university branches it was placed under the administrative jurisdiction of the Extension Division, and during its first year (1945–46), all budgetary matters not relating to salary were channeled through the division's Department of Debating and Public Discussion.

One hot afternoon in September, I walked into the catacombs of the building called Science Hall, where the Department of Debating and Public Discussion was temporarily housed. I presently found an office in which a fellow with a brush of kinky gray hair was working at a roll-top desk. The director of the Extension Division, a young administrator named Adolfson, had told me that this gray-haired fellow, who was the director of the Department of Debating, would give me an office and help me get started.

The man with the kinky gray hair was Leslie E. Brown. He had been an Iowa farm boy with a passionate hunger for education for himself, for everybody. He wanted the schoolhouses lighted at night for the men and women who had never had a chance to get any daytime education, or who wished to continue their education. He developed ultimately into one of the national leaders in adult education and became a dean of Cleveland College. I liked him instantly. He said warmly: "You're Gard! I'm certainly glad to see you."

I sat down and we spoke of inconsequential things. Then he said, "What are you going to do in Wisconsin?"

I thought for a moment. Looking back, I knew that in Kansas, Allen Crafton had opened a whole new world of theater for me; that in New York, [Alexander M.] Drummond had taught me how to apply feeling for places and ideas about theater to regional life. In Alberta I had tested and developed these ideas and, while I did not know exactly what I was going to do in Wisconsin, I thought that I could safely say that I wanted to try in many ways to stimulate and develop the creative forces in the people. I answered him the best I could then.

Brown and I became fast friends. In practical terms, I suppose that Brown's real role throughout our early association was to assist me in matters of university policy, to help to acquaint me with the state, and to orient me to previous activity in the drama field. But during the time he remained in Wisconsin he was a constant source of inspiration. He was overburdened, often tired, and sometimes sick, but he was never too tired or too sick to discuss my problems. Much of my knowledge of the early history of the Wisconsin Idea came out of my many conversations with Brown and out of his comprehension of what I hoped to accomplish. From Brown I learned that "adult education" was not at all alien in theory to my hopes and dreams about people's expressiveness, and from my association with Brown began my tolerance for the great backstage.

By late September 1945, with Brown's help, I was ready to summarize some of my impressions, suggestions and ideas relating to the possible development of a Wisconsin regional theater program. These were gathered together in an informal written proposal called "Notes for a General Wisconsin Drama Plan." In this paper, I observed that in the creative arts, especially, new work needed to be undertaken to relate the arts to people's lives. That the people themselves desired such a relation seemed to me to be indicated by the interest in local scene and tradition I had found in America. From such desire, I believed, a good popular art could grow. It seemed to me the undertaking I was proposing could add to the increasing awareness that our American picture was not a completed work in itself but a composite of developing regional pictures in every state and community in the nation.

My work in drama I hoped to relate as closely as possible to the Wisconsin scene. I hoped to make such work mirror the outstanding tradition and themes of the region and to develop the native talents of the state. I proposed a statewide playwriting project in an attempt to bring the regional themes to the fore, and I hoped to relate to the field of drama some of the general experiments in the other arts being conducted by the university. I had in mind particularly the statewide programs in painting and in music being conducted by the Extension Division.

The playwriting phase, I noted, would be conducted somewhat as the one Drummond and I had conceived for New York State. Lists would be compiled of persons interested in writing a Wisconsin play, of persons who might be able to provide regional materials for playwriting, and of persons who might be interested in producing Wisconsin plays. Criticism and instruction would be offered to interested writers through correspondence and simple manuals on play construction, and through conducting one- or two-day institutes in playwriting.

Fundamental to such a playwriting experiment would be a central try-out laboratory theater located somewhere on the university campus. I foresaw the formation of an annual Wisconsin Idea Theater Conference to bring together once a year all the dramatic activities in the state, including not only the actual drama producing groups of the state but also interested individuals from all aspects of community life. I felt that the failure of drama experiments was most often brought about through setting up the play and its production as something for the few or as something only superficially connected with the everyday life of the people. I hoped to make the Wisconsin work broad enough to include a large proportion of the population.

The "Notes for a General Wisconsin Drama Plan" went on to suggest that a magazine be established to serve as a medium for the expression of ideas and as a means of offering some needed instruction. This publication would serve as a clearinghouse for the statewide organization of groups and individuals. I also noted the need for research projects and hoped that I might find time for some research and writing myself. (I fondly remembered the modest success that I had had with playwriting in New York State and in Alberta, and I had pleasant recollections of my journeys in search of folklore, out of which grew my book *Johnny Chinook*.) I concluded that I considered the fundamental principles of the proposed drama plan to be a reflection of contemporary and past life and themes of the region. In this sense it was proposed as an educational service for developing the native talents of the region and for raising general dramatic standards. I hoped to make the drama a living factor in the people's lives. I noted, finally, that since I wanted to establish a living work in Wisconsin, the beginnings of such a work must be carefully planned with the roots of the work in the people.

A number of copies of "Notes for a General Wisconsin Drama Plan" were prepared and sent to over a dozen University of Wisconsin officials whose advice and counsel were considered of importance prior to the initiation of a drama program. Early in October 1945, a meeting of these individuals, the deans of the sponsoring colleges, members of the University Speech Department, rural sociology specialists and others was held for the purpose of discussing in detail all phases of the proposed plan.

Brown kept careful notes of this meeting. These notes indicate that practically everyone in attendance was in substantial agreement on the plan. It was pointed out by John Gaus (now professor of political science at Harvard University) that "the essence of the entire program rests on the attempt to create a favorable climate in which a worthwhile regional expression may grow." John Kolb[28] emphatically stressed the need for better and more complete drama training in rural areas, the need for breaking down the traditional barriers between rural and urban people and the desirability of keeping the emphasis broad in scope yet centralized at the university. Beyond points such as these I was encouraged to develop the entire program slowly

28. Professor John H. Kolb arrived at the University of Wisconsin in 1919 to chair the department of rural sociology.

and carefully and to feel free to make use of every facility within the province of the three sponsoring colleges.

By January 1946, I was deeply engrossed in gearing the new theater project to the machinery of the great backstage. A name for the project then became a major concern. Since I was still unfamiliar with much of the earlier theater tradition in Wisconsin, I took some time at this point to probe a bit into such background. I hoped that a name for my project would emerge.

I presume that my selection of the title "Wisconsin Idea Theater" for the new drama program was the result of this probing into backgrounds. I was greatly impressed by what I had read about Thomas Dickinson and the Wisconsin Dramatic Society. The society's purpose had encompassed a regional approach to drama very similar to my own. It was soon after I had learned the details of the Wisconsin Dramatic Society that the idea of calling the project the Wisconsin Idea Theater simply occurred to me as I was walking across the campus. I knew instantly that it was a far better name than Wisconsin Theater Program, Wisconsin State Theater Project or the dozen other inept titles I had been considering. "Wisconsin Idea Theater" seemed to indicate a number of points about the plan, including its statewide scope and its fundamental idea (already accepted by me as essential) of integrating the meaning of the Wisconsin Idea in education with the need for a broad penetration of the field of the cultural arts. So with the name decided, a version of the final draft was again sent to university officials, to newspapers and to other interested persons.

It was a brave name full of brave hope. My optimism was boundless, and I could only consider that the Wisconsin people would welcome the new Wisconsin Idea Theater with open arms. And indeed, the opening publicity guns brought forth a mass of comment both oral and written which fluttered down on Leslie Brown and me and lifted us to wild dreams of a truly overpowering cultural emphasis in the Badger State. "Maybe even beyond Wisconsin," Leslie muttered one afternoon as we inspected our pictures over a tremendous front-page story in an influential state newspaper. Looking at the headline, which intimated that a playwriting boom was about to strike the Middle West, I agreed with Brown that almost certainly our idea was on the way.

In fact, the lavish publicity became at times almost unbearable. Our statements that the spirit and tradition of the Wisconsin portion of the upper Middle West were to be investigated and turned to creative use were pounced upon by eager and inventive reporters who seemed willing to go to any length to plumb the comic news of my arrival in Wisconsin.

I was caught by reporters one afternoon in the rathskeller of the Wisconsin Union. A dozen coffee cups were quickly placed on the table in front of me and a quick-triggered news photographer caught my homely visage like a pale and doubtful sun above the small mountain of cups. A caption above the picture on the front page of the *Wisconsin State Journal* stated that "Cawfee helps a man think" and the story under the picture characterized me as a deceivingly tired-looking addition to the University of Wisconsin faculty who moved with a lope not far removed from the plowed fields and whose idea of real pleasure was to wander into the hinterland of wherever he happened to be and just "sit around talkin' and sittin' and drinkin' cawfee until he had absorbed the local folklore."

As a matter of fact, under different circumstances I might have found the reporter's idea of my mission in Wisconsin good fun, but in those days I did not do much sitting around and drinking coffee. I was after a big thing—a major cultural movement—and I wanted action. [. . .]

· · ·

My impressions of the state of Wisconsin are, of course, selective, emotional, intuitive and, in any real sense, nonhistorical. I can see no overall trait that characterizes Wisconsin people, and my impressions are like short pieces of music each with its own tempo and color. My search in Wisconsin (as always) has been for the flavor and variety of place, and what understanding I have of Wisconsin is based on these things. Yet a portrait of place was extremely important to the whole early development of the Wisconsin Idea Theater and to me personally as its director. It was essential to my personal happiness that I establish an attitude toward Wisconsin which might make it as appealing as Kansas, or New York, or Alberta had been. Perhaps I have been able to do so. At least, the flavor and variety of Wisconsin are inseparable from the work of the Wisconsin Idea Theater, for I believe that theater and its allied arts should reflect the personality of the area, refine its lights and shadows, and define its poetic and dramatic climaxes. [. . .]

· · ·

Emily Sprague Wurl is a Wisconsin writer who has been writing plays for a long while now without very much to show for her work. No one doubts her ability. She has won high praise for her verse and has published a very commendable volume of poetry. She was Zona Gale's protégé years ago when Emily was a young girl. Emily is interested in writing poetry and fiction, but her real interest is in playwriting. She has that intense, uncommon conviction present in a selected few writers that playwriting is her medium and that no other will do. She has been associated with playwriting schemes, plans, classes, whenever these things were in evidence. She wrote plays in the old Drama Guild days in Wisconsin when there were competitions for original plays in the state. Her work was always thought to be superior. She has been associated with the Wisconsin Idea Theater since its earliest promotion and has continuously worked for the success of the project and, she has hoped, for her own success. She has an unusual sensitivity to the sights and sounds of her Wisconsin, a sensitivity which has helped her create warm and intensely human stage characters. She is in middle years now and teaches kindergarten in Wauwatosa.

Realistically, Emily does not have much hope of attaining success as a Broadway playwright. What she has always thought might be within her grasp is a successful career as a playwright within her own state. She often looks at Wisconsin with a hopeful but rather suspicious eye, for she has received continuous rebuffs from the organized community theaters to which she has taken her plays. "We can't produce your plays, Emily," the directors tell her. "Your plays are good enough, all right. We concede that. But they're local products. Our audiences won't stand for that sort of thing. Our budget won't stand for it either. We're not in community theater so much for art, Emily. We're in it for entertainment, and our entertainment comes from doing Broadway stuff."

Emily sometimes attempts to reply: "But your community theater is the only living theater in town. You have a responsibility . . ."

"Sorry, Emily."

She has tried writing plays especially for the rural theater, too, but here she has encountered opposition of a slightly different kind. Her plays are poetic. They probe rather deeply into human motives. As a sincere artist she writes as she must and the musts within her do not appeal greatly to a country theater for which the rural comedy *Goose Money* is the prototype. Folks in rural areas want comedy, insist on it in fact, because they are unfamiliar with a fine, serious theater.

Emily knows now that rural folk for the most part expect to laugh when they attend the local plays and—well, there are parts in Emily's scripts which just cannot be laughed off, or laughed at. She hopes that the situation will change some day. "After the educators stop putting so much emphasis on the group and work more with the individual," she says, "maybe the situation will be different. Or when there is not so much attention paid to recreation in the countryside and more paid to art. That might help, too."

The Emily Wurls are extremely important to my grassroots theater, for in them I see the chief hope of its coming into being. They are the talented ones, the ones beyond the recreative arts. They are the ones whose expressiveness is a little beyond the levels of small community appreciation, the ones who are having a bad time of it spiritually because they cannot understand why they are not made a part of a vital native theater movement. It is hard to make them believe that they are a part of my grassroots theater when there are few productions of their plays. They find it extremely hard to understand when I tell them that the communities of the region must be prepared to accept their work. They cannot understand. They are ready, but they see little in their communities that is apt to change in favor of sincere, homegrown playwriting. Yet they never quite give up hope.

My search for grassroots theater is forever a search for the Emily Wurls, the hopeful ones, the sincere, sensitive ones. And my search is also for ways to develop the responses of the region—responses tuned to the idea that fine living theater can be created by playwrights who have no desire to take their plays far away from home.

—REG

Roadside Theater

FOUNDED 1975

Dudley Cocke

Appalshop, in the coal-mining country of central Appalachia, is a child of President Lyndon B. Johnson's "War on Poverty." Founded in 1969 in the Kentucky city of Whitesburg (population approximately 1,600), the only rural pilot program in that war, as led by the federal Office of Economic Opportunity, Appalshop began as a way of training local kids for jobs in film and TV. The federal money dried up after two years, but the cameras kept rolling, and in 1975 Roadside Theater joined Appalshop's programs, determined to use storytelling to reflect the community back to itself, to heal and inspire, to work with the people of the region to give public voice to their culture and concerns, and so direct their own future. Over the years, Roadside has excelled in using story to connect its community to others, across the country and around the world.

From the beginning, the prospect of success seemed unlikely. As Roadside's long-term managing director Donna Porterfield has written, "Born in the late 1940s, we were educated in substandard public schools where we were told that our parents did not speak or live correctly, and that if we were ever going to amount to anything in

SOURCE: Posting on Roadside Theater website, by Dudley Cocke, 2008.

this life, we would have to change everything about ourselves, leave the mountains and never look back. The national media, where we regularly saw shameful hillbilly stereotypes of ourselves, emphatically affirmed this message. [. . .] We opened *Life* magazine and saw ourselves, our friends and our neighbors, depicted as raggedy, shack-dwelling, forlorn-looking people."

This 2008 essay, by founding artistic director Dudley Cocke, is less a picture of a founding vision than the articulation of an evolving one—and the specific ideas and practices that grow to fulfill that vision. It's a vision that builds on those that have come before, notably the work of Robert Gard and Hallie Flanagan. Cocke's look at Roadside's democratic, participatory methods also provides an eloquent depiction of the ways class influences culture, a vital aspect of that theater's search for America.

—TL

———

Class and the Performing Arts

Alexander Hamilton, political rival of Virginia planter and slave owner Thomas Jefferson, proposed that the president and Senate be elected for life. Hamilton wrote: "All communities divide themselves into the few and the many. The first are the rich and wellborn, the other the mass of people. The voice of the people has been said to be the voice of God; and however generally this maxim has been quoted and believed, it is not true in fact. The people are turbulent and changing; they seldom judge or determine right."

The Founding Fathers rejected Hamilton's elite proposition in favor of Jefferson's declaration of equality. Thus began our nation's journey—still not completed—to align the Deed with the Creed.

Several months before the 2000 presidential election, a Florida reporter interviewed citizens about why the vote was important. She approached two retirees relaxing by the pool: "Why is the upcoming presidential election important to you?"

Without hesitation, the first responded, "The Supreme Court." The second added, "The economy." Then, almost in unison, they said, "The culture."

The reporter blinked and wondered, "What do you fellas mean?"

The first retiree looked squarely at her and answered, "Who controls the culture . . ." The second jumped in and finished the sentence, ". . . controls the story the nation tells itself."

The past quarter century has been unkind to the democratic impulse in the arts. A 2002 poll by the Urban Institute found that ninety-six percent of respondents said they were "greatly inspired and moved by art." However, only twenty-seven percent said that artists contribute "a lot" to the good of society. National surveys (including those by the League of American Theatres and Producers and the 1991–96 Wallace Foundation–sponsored AMS[29] survey) consistently report that audiences are eighty-plus percent white and originating from the top fifteen percent of the population, as measured by income and education levels. The widening income gap between rich and poor is threatening to create a permanent underclass. In a twenty-seven-year-long trend to apply market values to our social life since the presidency of Ronald Reagan, we have embedded our spiritual, emotional, intellectual and political life in the economy. And economic globalization has been the steroid of this trend. The exact opposite should be the case.

I will argue that culture—and its concentrated expression, art—has an important role to play in realizing our nation's democratic aspirations. But in the not-for-profit performing arts—and many other arts fields as well—progress toward leveling the playing field has stalled, leaving our many U.S. cultures without an equal chance to express themselves, to develop and cross-pollinate. The good news is that knowledge and new opportunities do exist to remove obstacles blocking arts' progress toward inclusion.

Art in a Democracy: Four Historical Vignettes

Ever since our forebears began putting on dramas, the U.S. theater has been a social forum where race and class, cultural power, and separatism versus integration have been debated.

In 1996–97, it was the playwright August Wilson going at it with Harvard theater director and critic Robert Brustein. In 1821, it was the African Grove, in Manhattan, where a growing community of free African Americans was mounting productions of Shakespeare, as well as original plays like *The Drama of King Shotoway*, which called for a slave rebellion. The African Grove's audience was racially mixed, although the theater's management found it necessary to segregate whites, as some did not know "how to behave themselves at entertainments designed for ladies and gentlemen of color."

It's January 16, 1936, Des Moines, Iowa. At the Shrine Temple Auditorium the curtain rises on the encore performance of the opera *The Bohemian Girl*. Regina Steele, twelve years old, steps from the wings and in a clear voice, which carries to the last person in the audience of four thousand, brings the story of the opera to the second act. The cast of 150 is from fifty of Iowa's hundred counties. They are farm girls and boys, farm men and women. Regina

29. AMS Planning and Research is the name of the firm that conducted this study for the Lila Wallace Foundation.

is wearing her blue 4-H uniform. "Who can measure the rewards of such an event?" wrote Marjorie Patten at the time. "Perhaps the greatest value lies in the rich experience of each person who took part in it, the growth through good training, the joy of having had a part in producing a lovely thing and the freeing of some craving for expression."[30] As one cast member put it, "We have no new linoleum on the kitchen floor, but we have sung in opera!"

In 1991, I invited Robert Gard, founder of the venerable populist Wisconsin Idea Theater, to a meeting of one hundred grassroots theater practitioners at Cornell University. It was to be his last public address. He described a vision he had when he was twenty-seven years old: "I felt the conviction then that I have maintained since: that the knowledge and love of place is a large part of the joy in people's lives. There must be plays that grow from all the countrysides of America, fabricated by the people themselves, born of toiling hands and free minds, born of music and love and reason. There must be many great voices singing out the lore and legend of America from a thousand hilltops, and there must be students to listen and to learn, and writers encouraged to use the materials."

After politically motivated investigations by the congressional Dies and Woodrum committees, at midnight on June 30, 1939, only four years after its inception, the WPA's Federal Theatre Project—the apotheosis of the theater's democratic impulse—was closed by Congress. The Project's director, Hallie Flanagan, put its aims succinctly: "National in scope, regional in emphasis and democratic in attitude." In its first two years it had presented forty-two thousand performances to more than twenty million people of all races, creeds and classes. According to meticulous audience surveys, sixty-five percent of those attending were seeing a live play for the first time.

Finding Answers: A Contemporary Case Study

Roadside Theater, which I direct, is a working-class ensemble based in the central Appalachian coalfields, where ninety-eight percent of the population is white. The theater has performed in thousands of communities in forty-three U.S. states and around Europe. The demographic profile of Roadside's audience is the inverse of the national norm: seventy-three percent have annual incomes under $50,000, according to a Wallace AMS survey, and thirty percent earn $20,000 or less. Seventy percent live in rural communities. One-third are people of color. How did this happen?

---

30. *The Arts Workshop of Rural America: A Study of the Rural Arts Program of the Agricultural Extension Service*, Columbia University Press, New York, 1937.

In 1990, as Roadside was preparing its strategy to diversify the audience for the professional American theater, many experts advised us we would fail. We found ourselves wrestling with tough questions. What is a public space? What is an affordable ticket? What are acceptable protocols (e.g., must a show start promptly? should children be admitted?)? What community organizations should be our partners?

We determined the key was finding presenters and local leaders who would join us in wrestling with such questions. Over six years, using a process of trial and error, Roadside developed a cultural development model that guaranteed audiences that looked like the whole community. In *Bowling Alone: The Collapse and Revival of American Community*, Robert Putnam describes our approach as "mustering diverse local folks to celebrate their traditions and restore community confidence through dramatization of local stories and music." The model's methodology rests on five pillars:

- Active participation;
- Partnerships and collaborations with an inclusive range of community organizations;
- Local leadership;
- Engagement over the course of several years;
- Flexibility to alternate between the roles of leader and follower.

Roadside's method can be represented as a circle that rests on these pillars, but the different points on the circle don't necessarily occur as discrete events. Here's how it works.

The first point of the circle is when we come into a community and perform from our repertoire of original plays. People see and evaluate what we do. We explain our history and process in workshops after the performances.

In the second phase of our residency, we prompt the creation of community music and story circles, so the participants can begin to hear their own voices. We pick a theme—maybe a local historic incident—and community members start listening to each other's stories and songs. They often hear new information about a common experience. The songs and stories, which are often recorded, become the ingredients for community celebrations at the end of the second phase. These often involve potluck suppers; people play music, sing, tell their stories. Through such big, structured celebrations, the community voice proclaims itself.

In the third phase, the community's own stories and songs become a natural resource for creating drama. Nascent and experienced local playwrights, producers, directors, actors and designers use this material to make plays. We fill in the gaps in inexperience. The fourth point comes after the drama is up and running. We suggest ways for the community to honor its artists and leaders, and we help establish a theater in the community. We then introduce our new colleagues to the national network of artists and communities that are engaged in similar explorations.

Roadside's model is labor-intensive. It requires that each Roadside artist become a producer (Paulo Freire's writing oriented us to this new role). Early on in each multiyear residency, the assigned Roadside producer sits down with community leaders to articulate common aspirations. The farming and ranching community of Choteau, Montana, completed the circle and established a theater company. Here is the agreement that guided our partnership:

- *The plays will be given their voice by the community.* The artists will be part of the culture from which the work is drawn. Their histories and feedback will inform the work. The audience will not be consumers of, but rather participants in, the performance.
- *The plays will witness a commitment to place.* They will be grounded in the local and specific, which, when rendered faithfully and creatively, can affect people anywhere.
- *The traditional and indigenous are integral to rural life.* They help us maintain continuity with the past, respond to the present and prepare for the future.
- *The project will strive to be inclusive in its producing practices.* We will partner with community organizations. Performances will be in places where the community feels welcome. Tickets will be affordable.
- *The project will recognize that management structures and business practices are value-laden.* We support broad participation, self-reliance and collective responsibility.
- *The project will be consciously linked to struggles for cultural, social, economic and political equity.* Advocating equity often meets resistance, and such resistance, when articulated, is an opportunity for positive change.

This kind of residency work is never smooth sailing. Even so, we were rewarded by the AMS survey results. After all, we had demonstrated that there were no insurmountable barriers to attendance—a good thing for the box office, for democracy and the art form. We expected that the arts field would be excited by our success, but there was no such reaction. Apparently, we had misunderstood something. Looking back, the warning signs were clear.

One warning sign confronted us in Alabama. We had arrived at the northern Alabama venue greeted by a crowd—"twice as many people as show up for our performances," exclaimed the presenter. The audience was a cross-section of the city. The working-class people had a great time because they understood our Appalachian working-class play better than many who were from the more formally educated class. But they didn't invite us back. After our third follow-up call, the presenter said, "We've not had such a big crowd before or since. But our board of directors just didn't like the way y'all talked." Alabamans didn't like the way Appalachians talked! Apparently, for some folks, the arts are like a country club—a chance to be with their own kind.

Another example of what the Brooklyn poet Marianne Moore described as "people not liking what they don't understand" occurred in Scottsdale, Arizona. We were performing at the charming, upscale Kerr Cultural Center. The event, sponsored by Arizona State University, was supposed to bring together a diverse audience: wealthy white patrons, folks from the Chicano community, and Native Americans from the Pima Reservation. The culture clash occurred around the performance protocols. Some Chicanos and Native Americans showed up an hour early. They were made to wait outside in the cold for thirty minutes until the doors officially opened. Others arrived ten to fifteen minutes after the 8 P.M. curtain and were not admitted. The kids from the local Boys & Girls Club (our special guests, performing their own stories) were made to sit on bleachers "to control their behavior." (It reminded me of Ngūgī wa Thiong'o's experience in post-colonial Kenya. It was not censorship of his words, Thiong'o had said, but censorship of the desired configuration of the performance space and of his audience's other cultural norms.)

Despite such attitudes, Roadside has become adept at removing barriers. A long-standing Roadside collaborator is Junebug Productions, an African American theater in New Orleans. One of our co-creations, *Junebug/Jack*, is about the relationships between black and white working-class Southerners. As we toured the U.S., naturally we wanted black and white working-class people to attend the play. The problem is that black and white working-class people do not go out together (or separately, for that matter) to the professional theater. Our solution was to ask the sponsors of *Junebug/Jack*, which is a musical, to pull together singers from different parts of their community—from the white Methodist church to the black AME Zion church to the integrated public high school. Out of support for their church, family and friends, as well as sheer curiosity, large numbers of people showed up for the performances who would not otherwise have attended. The disparate parts of each community came together to sing. Only then began the journey of understanding each other. [. . .]

Strategic Directions

The community itself is the answer to the problem of the class gap. Outside expertise can help. Here are some approaches that, in our experience, are demonstrated to work:

· The principles of community cultural development as articulated above;
· Diverse and equitable community partnerships which free the partners from the prejudices of their silos;
· Learning together through manageable cycles of action and assessment;
· Storytelling;
· Remembering that those with the problem are the basis for the solution.

These are some things that, we have concluded, do not work:

· Community outreach (what is required, instead, is community *in-reach*);
· Allowing the community to select which development principles to include in a project;
· Trying to make one community's cultural development project fit all communities;
· Allowing large power imbalances among community partners (too much power can be a deterrent to learning);
· Inhibiting the community from taking the lead.

[...]

Conclusion

A joke from the Depression: Two black men are standing in a government breadline. One turns to the other: "How you making it?" The other looks up the line: "White folks still in the lead."

For a sustainable future, society needs creativity and innovation from a healthy arts ecosystem. For twenty-seven years, we have failed to advance the fundamental principle of cultural equity, or, as my mentor Alan Lomax[31]

31. An eminent twentieth-century American folklorist and ethnomusicologist, Lomax collected music from the United States, the Caribbean, the British Isles and elsewhere. In his lifelong commitment to musical diversity, he amassed an astonishing archive of songs and world music, and pioneered a new way of listening across cultures.

insisted, "to tap for our common good the inherent genius of every cultural community." There are, however, indications that now might be a moment of opportunity:

- *Unprecedented numbers of young people are seeking opportunities for civic engagement*, often motivated by a search for meaning—religious, spiritual or humanist.
- *Colleges and universities are offering a steady supply of new community cultural development courses*, programs and engagement opportunities. (Syracuse University chancellor Nancy Cantor was recently honored by the Carnegie Corporation for her efforts on behalf of public scholarship. She is co-founder of Imagining America, a coalition of eighty colleges and universities devoted to creating knowledge in the arts, humanities and design to help communities and campuses transform into centers for civic engagement.)
- *A lot of the action is happening at the intersections of disciplines, of fields and of cultural boundaries.* Unlikely suspects, such as environmental activists and politicians, are finding themselves drawn to collaborations with artists.
- *A critical mass of analytic writing* has accrued, bringing attention to community cultural development theories and practices that have been gathering force over the last fifty years.
- *As ever, the folk arts remain vibrant and flying under the radar.* Their audience already looks like the whole community.
- *New concern about how the U.S. is negatively perceived by many in the world is awakening government leaders* to the need for restarting international arts exchange programs which demonstrate our nation's commitment to pluralism and cultural diversity abroad as well as at home.

As any Darwinian will tell us, when challenged by change, the fatal response is denial. At a time when the arts should be innovating broadly (not just in a narrow, avant-garde sense), we have become too uptight, too hesitant, too risk-averse. We must encourage citizen participation and bridge the inequalities that divide us. More than the law, politics or the economy, democratic participatory arts connect us to our fellow human beings in the most powerful ways.

—DC

Cornerstone Theater Company

FOUNDED 1986

Bill Rauch and Alison Carey, et al.

The stories are irresistible: a theater company of eleven, all in their early twenties, most of whom met as undergrads at Harvard, head into the heart of America in a fifteen-person van, their hearts full of idealism, their heads full of classics. In a little over a year they've spent three months or so in Virginia, North Dakota, Texas, Florida and Kansas. They've put on plays—adaptations of the classics with songs and dances added in, parts rewritten, characters and references contemporized, dialogue translated into the local tongue. American theater luminaries support them; the national press tracks them to the corners of the country. They mount a Wild West *Hamlet* in North Dakota; *Tartuffe* in Norcatur, Kansas, with a six-foot-nine farmer whose last appearance on stage was in the eighth-grade Christmas show; an interracial *Romeo and Juliet* in the almost totally segregated Port Gibson, Mississippi.

They work their asses off, trying to make truly American theater that matters with casts of dozens, blending their group of young professional actors with "real people." (Remember Tom Stoppard's line in *Rosencrantz and Guildenstern are Dead*? "We're *actors*—we're the opposite of people!") In the process, they seem to tap an old strain of American theater—grassroots, regional, national in scope—even though at the time they are more aware of their immediate avant-garde precursors (Peter Sellars, the Wooster Group) than of their natural ancestors (Robert Porterfield, Robert Gard, Hallie Flanagan, John O'Neal). They are founding a new kind of itinerant community-based theater, until they settle in Los Angeles five years after their journey begins.

Cornerstone is the youngest theater in this book, if you go by founding date, and, in the following newsletter—the founders' second, from October 1987—you can hear their original youth. Everything they have done is in this newsletter, everything they're doing, and everything they want to do (and will). It's the voice of vision in action.

In the words of journalist Robert Coe, whose 1989 article on Cornerstone's Port Gibson *Romeo* in *American Theatre* magazine captured their unique project as well as anything else written about them: "Urging a renewed faith in that infinite moment of connec-

SOURCE: Newsletter, October 1987, Act Two, Scene 1, by Cornerstone Theater Company, Bill Rauch and Alison Carey, co-founders, et al.

tion between the stage and the world, Cornerstone creates singular communities which ripple outward through a playwright's vision like pebbles tossed in a pond."

—TL

———

Dear Friend,

At 9:45 P.M. one week ago today we pulled into Norcatur, an agricultural community of 190 people in northwestern Kansas. At the city limit, we were greeted by a large, hand-painted sign that read "Welcome Cornerstone," a good omen of what lay ahead.

We now live in what used to be the Norcatur Rural High School, which was closed in 1970. Senior class pictures and sports trophies dating back to 1926 still decorate the locker-lined hallways. Our bedrooms are ten classrooms with wooden floors and blackboard walls. Our office is the former sewing room, our kitchen the former home ec room, and our bathrooms the locker rooms. Our theater is the gym/auditorium right smack in the middle of the building, a realization of a Cornerstone fantasy; we are rehearsing and performing a show in what is essentially our living room.

One hundred and seventy-five people came to eat pancakes and sausages and look at slides from our past shows at Monday night's "get acquainted with Cornerstone" supper. On Wednesday and Thursday, over eighty people came to audition and sign up to build, paint, sew, usher and do just about everything. Last night we performed our school assembly, *I Can't Pay the Rent*, to an all-ages audience of two hundred, and the text was used this morning in the sermon at Norcatur's only church. We are now in the middle of casting the play: *Tartoof, or An Impostor in Norcatur—and at Christmas!*, based on Molière's original.

But we're getting ahead of ourselves.

A few weeks ago, director Melissa Babb and the cast and crew of the newly founded Marfa Community Theater opened their first production. We congratulate them, and the news reminds us to take a few steps back in time to where our last newsletter left off: our residency in Marfa, Texas.

"Let's do a small show" was our 1987 New Year's resolution as we drove into Marfa (population 2,400) last January. After our first half-year of epic productions, we wanted to pull back focus on a smaller-cast, simpler project; we chose Noël Coward's nine-character comedy *Hay Fever*.

What we ended up with was *That Marfa Fever*. Transplanted from the English countryside to the mountains of West Texas, rewritten to include Spanish dialogue and folk songs, with an added chorus of five Canasta Tea Gals who commented on the action while doing arts and crafts, and with a guest appearance by Nina from Chekhov's *Seagull*, our "small?" show included Lynn Jeffries's set of eight magnificent hand-built tables with pop-up furniture, which spun around the Beta Hall (a World War II USO hall and our theater) and eventually landed together in a corner of the room to become a complete Memphis-style living room.

That Marfa Fever played for three weekends, a luxury in our tight schedule of residencies.

During the residency, we lived in remodeled World War II barracks, located a block from the sector headquarters of the U.S. Border Patrol and run by the delightful wine-and-cheese queen Willie Null. The complex, which once housed German prisoners-of-war, now houses the works of minimalist sculptor Donald Judd and a herd of highly cultured antelopes. Yes, this Mexican border town boasts a grasslands parade of avant-garde cement cubes. Many residents are skeptical, to say the least. The antelopes like to sharpen their horns on them.

In Marfa, we were able to continue the Cornerstone tradition of occasional days off, and filled them with exploration of the Texas countryside and beyond. Emergency-rescue-style rubber rafts took us down the Rio Grande, treacherous mountain roads took us to the Mexican city of Chihuahua, and wildly inappropriate footwear took us sliding down into the heart of New Mexico's Carlsbad Caverns.

Days off, however, were forbidden in the face of our schedule in Dinwiddie County, Virginia, our March through May residency site. Some of you may recognize Dinwiddie from our first newsletter; last summer we lived there for three weeks doing research for our original play, *The Pretty Much True Story of Dinwiddie County*.

Nine months and countless rewrites later, the product of that research and Cornerstone playwright Douglas Petrie's insightful imagination opened on Dinwiddie's tree-nestled, rain-soaked outdoor stage. Despite the torrents, the opening night audience voted unanimously during the first-act intermission that the show must go on; their enthusiasm was a great reward for the actors, who faced not only ankle-deep mud but the backstage remains of a copperhead snake who made the mistake of visiting our final dress rehearsal.

As the skies cleared for the rest of the run, several hundred county residents braved the new threat of killer mosquitoes to watch the play and vie for door prizes—including a fifty-pound bag of fertilizer—that had been collected from local businesses by local actor and copperhead-killer Johnny Bain.

Thirty-five Dinwiddie residents portrayed characters from eight periods of three hundred years of Dinwiddie's past, present and future, including a jailbreaking Revolutionary War counterfeiter, a murderous plantation owner and his unwilling slave accomplice, an injured Union soldier recuper-

ating in a Confederate home, a Depression-era schoolteacher and her vaga-
bond sweetheart, and two sisters playing in the woods on the eve of school
desegregation. Commenting on these interwoven tales, in their own pretty
much true fashions, were a first act chorus of white gentlemen pulled from
their real-life daily meeting place at the Dinwiddie Drug, a second act chorus of black churchgoing ladies, and a third act multiethnic Family of Man.
Back during the casting process we had been warned not to let our Family
suggest interracial marriage, but we never heard another word about it after
the whole cast gathered around the Family's huge dinner table to sing the
closing hymn.

But we're getting ahead of ourselves again . . .

In the fall of 1986, we had been asked by the Virginia Commission
for the Arts to develop a show for its new Arts on the Road program. (We
have recently been honored to learn this program was actually inspired by
Cornerstone's working methods.) During our Marfa residency, we started
work on our first commissioned show: a single, epic evening of theater—*The
Maske Family Musical*—based on a trilogy of plays by German playwright
Carl Sternheim. Rewritten, *Maske* follows the rise of an immigrant family
from rags to riches between 1918 and 1988. In Dinwiddie, we made *Maske*
performance-ready.

The Maske Family Musical is a Cornerstone touring show, and Cornerstone touring shows can only involve Cornerstone members. So, along
with teaching workshops and performing *Rent* in all twelve of Dinwiddie's
schools and working evenings and weekends on *The Pretty Much True Story*,
nine Cornerstone members—including managing director, development
director, technical director, playwright, and stage manager—took roles in
Maske. A kindly donated lakeside lodge housed our last-night staging and
musical rehearsals; meanwhile, in the storefront of our Dinwiddie home—an
abandoned Stuckey's at exit 12 on Interstate 85—Methodist minister Dick
Sisson helped us (almost) complete our sets. (The sets were finally completed by a paintbrush-wielding Brownie troop, who earned their drama
badges for the work.)

On the outdoor stage of a 4-H center ninety miles west of Washington, twelve blanket-bundled audience members saw the chill-April world
premiere of *The Maske Family Musical, Part 1: The Underpants*—with German Expressionist, two-and-a-half-dimensional furniture and a skewed-
perspective wall that eventually encased the actors in a wildly spinning box.
Part 2: The Businessman—set in a fifties-style, black-and-white honeymoon
suite fashioned from the skeleton of Part 1's wall—had a sweaty late-May
world premiere in a tiny nineteenth-century church in the mountains of
western Virginia. During intermission, stage manager Tim Banker enlisted

audience members to take their seats, literally; the church was so small that we couldn't make the necessary set change with the audience chairs in place.

Before we finished out the tour, however, we headed North to give some of our big-city friends a taste of Cornerstone. In the shadow of Wall Street's skyscrapers we unpacked lighting instruments, scenery and photographs and, thanks to the generosity of Kate Levin, Mark di Suvero and Enrico Martignoni, transformed a fourth-floor artists' loft into a theater and bar for two days. Generous, check-bearing audiences ate pâté imported from Boston caterers Eleanor and Janice Moore, watched sections of *Rent* and *Maske* and applauded Patti Perry, the mayor of Marmath, North Dakota, who had flown in to speak firsthand of Cornerstone in residence.

In Boston, we packed the Harvard Club with a similar fundraiser, and then took the show across the Charles; at the invitation of Cornerstone board member R. J. Cutler and as part of the American Repertory Theater's Monday night series, we twice performed *Maske* at Radcliffe's Agassiz Theater, and once performed *I Can't Pay the Rent* for adults as part of a twenty-fifth reunion week symposium.

We also had the once-in-a-lifetime experience of performing *Rent* in front of our own worst nightmare. Our biggest challenge in developing a school assembly was to make it both good theater and a good educational tool; thirteen thousand engrossed and enthusiastic students in Virginia and Texas made us proud of our solution. Three-hundred children of Harvard alumni taught us that we hadn't planned for every audience; we had encountered lively and vocal crowds before, but never the repeatedly shouted suggestion that we use our American Express Gold Card to "pay our rent."

As a relaxing end to our rushed urban tour, we held a fundraiser in Washington, D.C.'s National Theater under the watchful gaze of a portrait of Helen Hayes, and with the cooking and help of Nancy and Alyson Rauch. All in all, our big-city fundraising receptions gave us over fifteen thousand dollars to kick off our second year. Thank you, hard-working honorary chairpeople, for making them possible!

Then back to rural Virginia: two final weeks of our Arts on the Road tour, which would take us to June 30, 1987—exactly one year from our first day of operations, and exactly forty thousand miles on the big blue van.

Spending two days each in eight rural Virginia towns, we would perform *Rent* and *Maske* and hold workshops for both adults and children. Churches, schools, gymnasiums, libraries and the great outdoors became theaters-for-a-day, and we became expert at restaging our shows for spaces of any size and shape. With the guidance and brute strength of technical director Benajah Cobb, we managed to cut back our *Maske* load-out time from five hours to one hour and thirty-seven minutes. Although our houses were usually small, we closed out the tour in front of fifteen hundred people on a public green as part of the Wytheville Arts Festival. Several of the fifteen hundred approached us after the show with this (whispered) review: "You might hear that it was a little too sophisticated and, well, scandalous for other folks around here, but I just loved it." We never did hear from those other folks.

As we packed away the sets in our 1971 vintage milk delivery truck that constantly surprises us by running, we did so with plenty of regret. When we headed off to our year-end, three-week vacation, playwright Doug Petrie, stage manager Tim Banker and actor Amy Brenneman headed back to civilization for good. Even in Kansas, four months later, we still miss them badly.

Hundred-degree heats. Palm trees. Drug deals on the corner at three o'clock in the morning. Abandoned, gutted, pink-painted hotels standing like sand castles in the wind, mocking the glory of decades gone by. The place you have all come to know from crime thrillers and Friday-night television is where we started our second year.

Miami.

Cornerstone residencies are all learning experiences, but some are bigger learning experiences than others.

Miami.

Our Miami residency—where we developed a play addressing the issues surrounding the AIDS crisis—was far and away our hardest to date. We chose Miami because it had the third highest incidence of AIDS in the country and the highest incidence of pediatric AIDS, and yet has little citywide recognition of the problem. We were warned plenty that the residency would be emotionally grueling because of the play's subject and the people we intended to cast; people with AIDS or AIDS-related complex, their lovers, friends and families, health care workers, people who are HIV-positive, and anybody who had been touched by the crisis.

But our problems didn't come from that at all.

We should admit now that part of our problems stemmed from our own stupidity. We planned the residency just a few months in advance, driven by an immediate desire to do something about the crisis. What we forgot was the cities are different from small towns: theaters are booked a year in advance, the community identity that usually gives us our participants and audiences is infinitely diffused, and the logistical and financial problems of one little transient theater company are easily ignored. Finally, our Miami project was to benefit our host, the Health Crisis Network, the city's only AIDS counseling and referral center; we had talked them into being associated with the project to begin with, and their interest was never more than cursory.

Which is not to say we were ready to give up without a fight, at least not alone. Second-year reorganization gave us a new, stay-in-Boston-and-avoid-the-distraction-of-life-on-the-road development director, Stephen Gutwillig, to meet our second-year funding challenges. Gail Berrigan undertook the newly named job of company manager, whose in-residency responsibilities she had already been facing. Stage manager Susan Rosen filled our Miami roster, and we looked forward to the addition of actor Nela Wagman in Kansas.

A chance to use the Cameo Theater—a renovated 1920s movie house turned turquoise rock-and-roll palace—steered us to Miami Beach, so we settled into nine pulmanettes (whatever they are) at the nearby Collins Plaza Hotel in the heart of Miami Beach's red light district. A chance for the Cameo to book a hot heavy-metal band left us without a theater (and without our rental deposit, which we are *still* trying to get back with the help of a new board member, attorney Frederick Fogel); it was a full five weeks into residency before we found a filthy, gutted Las Vegas–style showplace in the fifties-splendrous Carillon Hotel. The hotel's ever-generous owner, Mr. Roger Falin, let us renovate and use the theater for free and even covered the cost of utilities.

We took the W. H. Auden and Christopher Isherwood 1935 black-comic original and created *The Dog Beneath the Skin: An Epidemic Epic*, featuring actor Christopher Moore as a crew-cut and confused young man who travels a plague-wrenched world. With the daily help of local cast member Arthur Curtis, we rewrote scenes to make them fit into our new issue-play, rushed them to the theater for rehearsal and comments from the cast, and took them home again for more rewrites. Never before has a Cornerstone cast contributed so much to a script and made it such a labor of love. Also never before have we rewritten a last scene nine times during production week, the last draft getting into the actors' hands only three and a half hours before opening.

The thirty-eight-by-seventeen-foot clear plastic curtain didn't go up on our Miami show; it was ripped down by actors, as were a couple of giant cardboard sea creatures and a post-execution, blood-splattered backdrop. Against a jungle-gym, cross-stage grid, twenty-six Miamians filled our cavernous theater with eighteen heady and haunting songs from musical director David Reiffel. Nightly standing ovations from distressingly small houses met the nine *Dog* performances, during which "dog in heat" took on new meaning for actor Peter Howard, who played the title character; his furry, polyester costume, complete with specially designed and donated prosthetic forelimbs, was so hot that a three-person crew—including visiting VCA regional coordinator Cynthia Schaal—was needed to pack him in ice and fill him with water and Gatorade during his offstage moments.

Coincidentally, four *Dog* actors portrayed members of the press. They had plenty of research material . . .

The credit for the Cornerstone press revolution goes to the *Wall Street Journal* reporter Meg Cox, who responded to a brief informational mailing with a phone call saying that she would be arriving in two weeks to cover our work in Marfa. She wrote a thorough, smart article, and it opened the floodgates.

Newsweek's piece appeared in late September, and industry bible *American Theatre* will have a page on us in the November issue. This week we have been busy juggling the shooting schedules of crews from *The Today Show* and *CBS Evening News*, and both stories will air after our Kansas production opens, probably in early December. *People* magazine has a reporter in Norcatur now, and will send back a photographer to fight out the perfect shot position with the *Entertainment Tonight* cameraman at the early December performances of *Tartoof*. CNN covered our work in Miami, as did *West 57th*, which is still facing the challenge of editing the twenty-five hours of tape it filmed down to a twelve-minute segment; the piece should air sometime this season.

Even more important to us, however, has been the support of local press, which gives us most of our auditioners and audience for community projects. Most thanks here to Peter Howard, who, after volunteering to write a weekly column for *Marfa Independent*, eventually became publicity director as well as actor.

Because substantial press coverage is new to us, we are still learning the ropes. Chris was astounded one morning to find a camera crew surreptitiously filming his early morning jog, and Gail was asked not to use a camera in her rehearsal portrayal of a *Dog* journalist for fear that *Newsweek*'s photo editors would think they had a picture of a competitor's real-life photographer.

And then there are the bigger, really real-life questions that all this press attention inspires. As we carefully word proposals to prospective residency hosts, does the value of theater for a community play second fiddle to the value of national press coverage? How many nearly identical interviews can we all give about the methods and goals of Cornerstone before our words begin to lose their meaning? Is there a point when we believe our own ever-enthusiastic talk and forget that Cornerstone needs constant reevaluation and improvement to do what it does as well as it can?

We'll keep you posted.

Still, as always, we are full of ideas and plans for the future. January will bring a new "Arts on the Road" tour; last year's pilot program, under the wise management of Patty Parks, was so successful that AOTR is now a part of the VCA's annual program. The spring of 1988 will find us on a Paiute Indian reservation in Nevada, for an experimentally long sixteen-week residency. After that, we are juggling work with the elderly in a trailer park, loggers in Washington State, and factory workers in Wisconsin. Next winter will probably find us in Alaska's eternal night, and beyond that . . . Will Cornerstone settle as a residential theater in years to come? And how many years? And what of this mysterious "alumni show" idea?

You'll hear all about it in our next newsletter, a short six months away. Until then, please keep in touch. We thrive on hearing from our friends.

—BR, AC, et al.

Cornerstone Wish List

A copier
A computer/word-processing system
A dot-matrix printer
An amplifier
A mixer
Speakers
A two-track tape deck
A four- or eight-track tape deck
Electric, good quality typewriters
An air compressor
An air hammer
An air stapler
An electric planer
A router
A spotlight
Other theatrical lighting instruments
A wet/dry shop-vac
An electric grinder wheel
A portable table saw
A photographic enlarger
An eight-foot A-frame ladder with eight-foot extension
A pickup truck
An overlock machine
Black duveteen
A free-of-charge auditor for our books

Chapter 2

About Us. By Us. For Us. Near Us.

A theater evolving not out of negative need, but positive potential; better equipped to employ existing talents and spur the development of future ones. A theater whose justification is not the gap it fills, but the achievement it aspires toward . . .

—*Douglas Turner Ward*

The Yiddish Art Theatre

FOUNDED 1918

Maurice Schwartz
(Translated from the Yiddish by Joshua Waletzky)

By the early days of the twentieth century, New York had become the largest center of Jewish population in world history. If this immigrant influx—an estimated half a million Jews came to New York between 1905 and 1908 alone—marked the advent of a new world, the theatrical traditions these Jews brought with them were strictly old world. That old world was the *shtetl*, the small towns and enclaves of eastern Germany and Tsarist Russia—Poland, Lithuania, the Ukraine, White Russia and beyond. If that word, *shtetl*, describes a locale, it also encapsulates a way of life and the people who lived it, the spirit and customs they carried with them. The earliest Yiddish theater started in the *shtetl* and, in a sense, stayed there. Its audiences were made up largely of uneducated, often illiterate workers, "greenhorns," who were scorned by Americanized, educated Jews who didn't want to be associated with their backward ways.

The theater these immigrants brought with them, beginning in the 1880s, was, at first, likewise scorned. It was broad, lowbrow entertainment of the worst kind. The plays were swollen with melodrama, the Yiddish a babel of dialects, the productions lacking in unity, and the characters stock—the idiotic mama's boy or *Schmendrik*; the hunchbacked, pop-eyed moocher, *Yonkel Schnorer*. It was *shund* (trash). According to the great Yiddish theater actor Jacob Adler (father of another great, Celia Adler, and of Celia's half-brother and sister, Stella and Luther Adler, both part of the Group Theatre), this *shund* theater went through its infancy in the vast changing lands of Russia, where it began in the mid-1800s. It was in

SOURCE: "Can New York Support a Better-Quality Yiddish Theatre?" by Maurice Schwartz, published in *Der Tag*, 2 March 1918: 3 (translated for this publication by Joshua Waletzky).

America, Adler tells us, that the Yiddish theater "grew to manhood and success."[1]

Before it matured, though, the Yiddish theater boomed. After a rocky start, professional Yiddish theater flourished across the nation. Between 1890 and 1940, there were more than two hundred Yiddish theaters or touring Yiddish theater troupes in the United States. As many as a dozen Yiddish theaters existed in New York City, mostly in what is now the East Village (then still part of the Lower East Side), along Second Avenue, a theater district to rival Broadway, sometimes referred to as the "Jewish Rialto."

The Yiddish theater grew, but it didn't really grow up until 1918 when Maurice Schwartz founded what would, three years later, be called the Yiddish Art Theatre. Also known as Mr. Second Avenue, Schwartz was, along with Jacob Adler, one of the prominent actor-managers in the Yiddish theater of the time. But it was Schwartz who created the bridge between the old styles and the newer literary ones coming out of Europe, who introduced Jewish audiences (and others) to the experimental staging associated with the Russian innovator Vsevolod Meyerhold and the naturalism pioneered by Théâtre Libre's André Antoine. Schwartz, most agree, put the "art" in the Yiddish art theater.

Schwartz ran the YAT for 32 years, from 1918 to 1950, though he continued its activities until his death in Israel in 1960. In an irony of history, his company opened at the Irving Place Theatre, which had been a German theater but, due to WWI-era anti-German sentiment, was shut down, its German repertoire banned. Schwartz and his business partner, Max Wilner, referred to in Schwartz's plucky manifesto below, made an immediate success, finding a voice and an audience with their first offering, Perez Hirshbein's *Farvorfen Vinkel* (*Forsaken Nook*). Lifson describes the play as a "*Romeo and Juliet* in a village setting" without the tragic ending, a peasant play that celebrates the ebullience of youth and a love for the earthy peasantry of the author's origins. The fervent reception, critical and popular, of this literary work marked the beginning of a true Yiddish art theater. (More irony: Schwartz had originally rejected the play but was backed into doing it by another leading actor of the time and sometimes-member of YAT, Jacob Ben-Ami. Schwartz, an enthusiastic egotist, took credit for the runaway success and even tried to convince Hirshbein to guarantee him rights to all his future plays; the playwright was unconvinced. "If a man borrows a pail to fetch water," Hirshbein allegedly said, "does it mean he has all future rights to the pail?")

---

1. Another scion of this extraordinary theater family, Tom Oppenheim, the late Stella's grandson and director of her acting studio, gave me his great-grandfather Jacob's memoir, *A Life on the Stage* (Applause Theatre Books, New York, 2001), cited here. I'm also drawing heavily on David S. Lifson's exhaustive *The Yiddish Theatre in America* (Thomas Yoseloff, New York, 1965).

In his theater's first season, Schwartz also premiered in Yiddish Shaw's *Mrs. Warren's Profession* and Ibsen's *Ghosts* and *A Doll's House* (which he called *Nora*). He built on the work begun by the passionate amateurs of the Folksbuehne, associated in its early days with the Neighborhood Playhouse. A man of great ego and gusto, with all the "pathos and sovereign air of a great trouper" (according to Heinz Politzer, writing in *Commentary* in 1949), Schwartz was relentless and indefatigable. You can hear it in the surety of his writing voice. He was a showman with a mission: not merely to bring theater to the Jewish masses—that was being done in great force—but to bring *art* theater to them—and to bring the American Jewish experience (and its deep roots) into the art.

—*TL*

Can New York Support a Better-Quality Yiddish Theater?

For the last few years there have been rumors going around town about plans to open a People's Theater;[2] there have even been some who have opened theaters and called them "people's theaters," and later, for various reasons, changed the name. Many of these poor souls who cry "people's theater" don't know what the term means. (It's a theater that belongs to the people; or it's a theater with cheap seats, where it's possible for plain folk to attend frequently.) In short, they are confused, poor things. But there are many who *do* know what character a people's theater ought to have and are ready to throw themselves, body and soul, into the noble task of creating a "People's Theater," where one would see plays of better quality than what is now available, and where the people—who in reality sustain the theater—would have a say in how this theater is run.

However, two things argue against the realization of this project. First, it requires a colossal capital investment; second, and much more importantly, "Who will lead?" It's an institution after all, so there must be directors and committees at the top. And here is where everything reaches a standstill. Because everyone wants to be the first, everyone wants to be the "Trotsky," and so it's going to take a rather long time until one will be able to open a true "people's theater," able to operate under normal conditions.

For over two years I've been carrying around a plan to assemble a troupe dedicated to playing good literary works, works that would be an honor to the Yiddish theater. I have spoken with several performers, who were enthused with the idea, among them also several writers, critics and

---

2. Yiddish word is *folks-teater*. [translator's note]

dramaturgs.[3] We've gotten together, had meetings, made plans to first try summer performances for cheap tickets, and so forth. But as soon as it got to the money question, to how we should divvy up the cash, to who should be the director, who the manager, who should set the tone, the flame of envy was ignited in each of us. And I'm not pointing any fingers: it is, after all, all for one and one for all: *our* enterprise, *our* possession, each one has the same right to it . . . And thus the plan fell through. Many thought us lunatics, daydreamers. Until, after two years of daydreaming, we were able to come up with the most beautiful theater, the best I could imagine. A small theater with a big, splendid stage, where we'll be able to mount beautiful good plays. And most important: the mood will be there.

It's a fact that in the Irving Place Theatre, the Germans produced wonderful plays, magnificently performed. Because the theater has an historical significance. The greatest artists have performed there. And therefore, when the news broke that I had taken over this theater for ten years (with an option for another eleven years), there were some who still considered me a lunatic, a daydreamer. Because the prevailing opinion is that such a theater cannot survive. The complaint is that the people screaming for good plays don't pay for tickets, they ask for comps; and that the current theater managers are not as guilty as they are made out to be. The large theaters currently have nuts of four to five thousand dollars a week. One flop and they're running a considerable deficit. And so everyone is looking for the hoped-for "hit" with "punch," that will have people weeping and laughing. And when the manager can enter the theater and see the house sitting and weeping like it was Yom Kippur in the synagogue, he strokes his belly and goes home to sleep peacefully, because he knows that on Saturday he'll be able to meet the payroll and make a profit. And aside from that, there is another big impediment to good plays of literary significance. The theaters are too large; better plays get lost in them. An actor's blink of the eye is too small for all two thousand in the audience to see. So you've got to, actually, make a wide-eyed stare. A quiet moan gets lost. And the public says—as does the critic swayed by the public—that the actor or actress has no temperament, no soul, no passion, and so on. And as you want to show that you have temperament, you start chewing up the scenery (a theater expression for screaming and shouting). In all English-language theaters where quality plays, even operettas, are pro-

3. Yiddish word is *dramaturg*, which Schwartz may have used in the sense of "playwright." But it is more likely, for two reasons, that he was using the word in its more contemporary sense of "dramaturg." First, he refers to writers in the same breath. Second, we know that he was familiar with German-language theater (see later reference to German theater in this article), and the term "dramaturg" was used in its contemporary sense in the German theater of the nineteenth century. [translator's note]

duced, they are mounted in a theater of a thousand or twelve hundred seats. The spectator then feels like he is at home, where he can easily see and hear everything, and get into it. And that enables the stage actor to give a better performance, because he feels that he's being paid attention to.

And that's why I want the large audience that is looking for a small theater, where the performers dedicate themselves wholeheartedly to art, where the management, the magnificent, comfortable theater, and all things taken together will work toward one goal: elevating Yiddish theater to a level at which the horrible "hits" with the fifteen "curtain calls" disappear. Let this audience know that they will now get the chance to have what they are looking for.

My partner, who has invested a large sum, has agreed to my condition: that the theater be massively different from others. Simply opening a theater is not so called for—business is not spectacular (with only two exceptions). In order to make the theater a financial success, it must first be a moral success. And on the following principles, I count on its being a double success:

1. The theater shall be a kind of sacred thing, where a festive and artistic mood shall always reign.
2. A company of young artists who will enjoy striving to bring Yiddish theater to a beautiful level.
3. Performing quality dramas, honest comedies, glittering farces and beautiful operettas. If, once in a while, a melodrama, then a melodrama with interest and plot logic.
4. Every play produced as it should be and where the author has a say. Sufficient rehearsal time, so that the actors have enough time to learn their roles. Also, each play will get a general rehearsal with costumes and scenery.
5. Establish a subscription system, so that everyone who wants to can have an assigned seat for this and that date. We will also set it up so that, aside from telephoning, one will be able to order tickets by mail at our expense. And aside from our critics from the press, we will also pay attention to the critiques of each audience member who wants to write to us.
6. The press and the theater shall go hand in hand. And if the press, the public and the theater unions give us the necessary support, I am certain that the Irving Place Theatre (the name will probably change) will be a point of pride for the Jews of New York.

—MS

KRIGWA Players

FOUNDED 1926

W. E. B. Du Bois

How does a theater serve a place? How does it serve a people? Does a theater reflect its community or help form it? What does it mean for a theater to share, with its audience, a cultural identity? These are just some of the questions that arise from the articulated ideals of theaters steeped in cultural, ethnic or racial struggle. And while the theaters that follow differ by degrees in aesthetic approach and political intent, while some are integrated theaters and some are not, they are all built around this sense of shared identity—among the players, between the company and the audience.

It's hardly a coincidence that one of the first visionaries to call for a theater for, by, about and near a particular race of people was the man who wrote, "The problem of the twentieth century is the problem of the color-line." William Edward Burghardt (W. E. B.) Du Bois was many things—sociologist, historian, novelist, editor, cultural critic, political activist, Pan Africanist, organizational founder (including of the NAACP—National Association for the Advancement of Colored People). He was also a playwright. His plays, such as the sweeping pageant *The Star of Ethiopia*, were designed to teach American blacks about their history and their connections to Africa and the Pan African world. He wrote to provoke thought among his people. He wrote protest drama to agitate in the white world, especially by revealing the Negro "as a human, feeling thing," connecting him to "almost every event in American history," and by stirring white liberals to join the fight for equal opportunity. "All Art is propaganda and ever must be, despite the wailing of the purists," he writes in the 1926 essay "Criteria of Negro Art." "I stand in utter shamelessness and say that whatever art I have for writing has been used always for propaganda for gaining the right of black folk to love and enjoy."

From his longtime perch as editor of the NAACP's magazine, *The Crisis*,[4] a job he writes defined "the span of my life from 1910 to 1934," he called for the formation of a "Negro Folk theater," modeled on the Abbey Theatre in Ireland, which would tell the story of the African American people to the African American people in one of their central communities: Harlem, New York City. The Crisis

---

SOURCE: This essay, by W. E. B. Du Bois, was first published in *The Crisis*, July 1926.

4. *The Crisis*, which originally carried the subheading, "A Record of the Darker Races," has been the official magazine of the NAACP for more than one hundred years. Du Bois helped found it and was its first editor, starting in 1910 and ending with his resignation in 1934.

Guild of Writers and Artists (KRIGWA) Players Little Negro Theater grew out of a series of playwriting contests Du Bois sponsored, a way of supporting the development of the kind of dramatic writing he espoused. KRIGWA ended almost as soon as it began—in part because of a dispute over prize money he withheld from playwright Eulalie Spence to reimburse production expenses. (Interesting anecdote: according to Errol G. Hill and James V. Hatch's *A History of African American Theatre*, Spence, an actress and director, as well as a writer, was later credited by New York Shakespeare Festival producer Joseph Papp for "scrubbing" his Brooklyn accent off his tongue.)

Although there has always been debate in the African American community over the best uses and approaches to drama, the importance of this call by Du Bois can't be underestimated. If art would be for a people, it must be *of* them. If it would serve a community, it must be near that community. If it would truly be "about us," those who form that "us" must be its authors. "Thus it is the bounden duty of black America to begin this great work of the creation of Beauty, of the preservation of Beauty, of the realization of Beauty . . ."

Du Bois died in Ghana on the eve of Martin Luther King's 1963 "I Have a Dream" speech on the Washington Mall. His death was reported, minutes before King's appearance, by Roy Wilkins, then head of the NAACP. In the "postlude" to his majestic biography of Du Bois, Pulitzer Prize–winning author David Levering Lewis notes:

> Legendary Dr. Du Bois (for few had ever dared a more familiar direct address) appeared to have timed his exit for maximum symbolic effect. [. . .] In a real sense, Du Bois was seen by hundreds of thousands of Americans, black and white, as the paramount custodian of the intellect that so many impoverished, deprived, intimidated and desperately striving African Americans had either never developed or found it imperative to conceal. His chosen weapons were grand ideas propelled by uncompromising language. Lesser mortals of the race—heads of civil rights organizations, presidents of colleges, noted ministers of the Gospel—conciliated, tergiversated and brought back from white bargaining tables half loaves for their people. Never Du Bois.
>
> *—TL*

A Little Negro Theater

Today, as the renaissance of art comes among American Negroes, the theater calls for new birth. But most people do not realize just where the novelty must come in. The Negro is already in the theater and has been there for a long time; but his place there is not yet thoroughly normal. His audience is mainly a white audience and the Negro actor has, for a long time, been asked to entertain this more or less alien group. The demands and ideals of the white group, and their conception of Negroes, have set the norm for the black actor. He has been a minstrel, comedian, singer and lay figure of all sorts. Only recently has he begun tentatively to emerge as an ordinary human being with everyday reactions. And here he is still handicapped and put forth with much hesitation, as in the case of *The Nigger*, *Lulu Belle* and *The Emperor Jones*.[5]

In all this development naturally then the best of the Negro actor and the most poignant Negro drama have not been called for. This could be evoked only by a Negro audience desiring to see its own life depicted by its own writers and actors.

For this reason, a new Negro theater is demanded and it is slowly coming. It needs, however, guiding lights. For instance, some excellent groups of colored amateurs are entertaining colored audiences in Cleveland, in Philadelphia and elsewhere. Almost invariably, however, they miss the real path. They play Shakespeare or Synge or reset a successful Broadway play with colored principals.

The movement which has begun this year in Harlem, New York City, lays down four fundamental principles. The plays of a real Negro theater must be: *One: About us.* That is, they must have plots which reveal Negro life as it is. *Two: By us.* That is, they must be written by Negro authors who understand from birth and continual association just what it means to be a Negro today. *Three: For us.* That is, the theater must cater primarily to Negro audiences and be supported and sustained by their entertainment and approval. *Four: Near us.* The theater must be in a Negro neighborhood near the mass of ordinary Negro people.

Only in this way can a real folk play movement of American Negroes be built up.

Our Playhouse

The KRIGWA Players Little Negro Theater is a free stage. It has been equipped by the joint effort of the Public Library and the Players. It will be further decorated by colored artists. Any one who has a play or any group which wishes to give a play is invited to use the playhouse, under certain easy conditions which the library and the Players will formulate. We hope by plays, lectures and informal social gatherings to make this room a place of wide inspiration for all dark people everywhere and for all their friends.

—*WEBD*

5. By Edward Sheldon, Charles MacArthur and Edward Sheldon, and Eugene O'Neill, respectively.

The Negro Theatre Project, Federal Theatre Project (aka, Negro Theatre Unit, Harlem Theatre Project)

FOUNDED 1935

John Houseman

The New York Negro Theatre Unit of the Federal Theatre Project was the largest of sixteen such units across the country—in Seattle, Los Angeles, Boston, Philadelphia and elsewhere—organized around East, West, South and Midwest regional centers. Housed at the Lafayette Theatre in Harlem, it was the first New York unit to open a show: Frank Wilson's *Walk Together Chillun!* on February 4,[6] 1936. It also proved one of the most vital and influential FTP troupes, producing an eclectic range of new works by African American playwrights, adaptations of classics, vaudevilles and musical reviews, and Living Newspapers. Orson Welles's production of what became known as the "Voodoo *Macbeth*," described below, may be the single most famous (not to mention fabulous) production of the Federal Theatre Project's short life.

John Houseman, a Romanian-born jack-of-all-theatrical trades, son of a Jewish-Alsatian father and a Welsh-Irish mother, had little producing experience when he was tapped to run the unit. Raised throughout Europe and educated—through high school—in Britain, he'd arrived in America in his early twenties, become a wildly successful businessman in the grain-export business, lost everything in the stock market crash of 1929, and kicked around for several years, translating and co-authoring plays, following his actress wife on the road, hanging out with New York artists and intellectuals and dabbling in directing and producing. He tells the story of his involvement with FTP's Negro Theatre below, part of his breathtaking autobiography, *Run-Through*.

Houseman reappears later in this book, again alongside Orson Welles (see chapter 4 on their Mercury Theatre), and remains fixed in the American cultural pantheon in numerous ways—as the producer of infamous theater productions of the thirties and major movies of mid-century and as, arguably, America's most prolific theater founder: as head of two units of the Federal Theatre Project, co-founder of the Mercury Theatre, the first artistic director of the American Shakespeare Festival Theatre in Stratford, Connecticut, the

SOURCE: *Run-Through: A Memoir*, by John Houseman, 1972.

6. I've also seen this date reported as February 2 and February 5.

head of a new drama division at the Juilliard School and the founder of the Acting Company there, as well as producer of the Los Angeles–based theater group that would ultimately become the Mark Taper Forum. For all this pioneering activity, he is most widely remembered as Professor Kingsfield in the film *The Paper Chase* and as the commercial voice of Smith Barney: "They make money the old-fashioned way; they *earn* it." What does it say that two of our nation's most outsized theater pioneers—Welles and Houseman—were known to successive generations mostly as TV pitchmen, the one selling wine and the other financial services?

—*TL*

———

By 1935, halfway through the energetic confusions of Roosevelt's first term, the outline of the New Deal had begun to appear. One significant symptom was the changeover from relief—from a national acceptance of "defeated, discouraged, hopeless men and women, cringing and fawning as they came to ask for public aid"—to the revolutionary idea of work relief. To twenty million Americans dependent on public charity (amid cries of socialism, communism and worse), work was to be supplied by the federal government within their own skills and trades. This mutation took place during the dog days, with only moderate attention on my part; it was not till September that the Works Progress Administration, newly formed under Harry Hopkins, received an allocation of five billion dollars of federal funds, to be spent at the rate of 420 million a month. Of this, a small fraction (less than one percent) was to be devoted to the arts—including the theater.

The Federal Theatre of the Works Progress Administration, which, within two years, was to be described by a leading critic as "the chief producer of works of art in the American theater" and which came to play such a vital part in so many of our lives, was not primarily a cultural activity. It was a relief measure conceived in a time of national misery and despair. The only artistic policy it ever had was the assumption that thousands of indigent theater people were eager to work and that millions of Americans would enjoy the results of this work if it could be offered at a price they could afford to pay. Within a year of its formation, the Federal Theatre had more than fifteen thousand men and women on its payroll at an average wage of approximately twenty dollars a week. During the four years of its existence its productions played to more than thirty million people in more than two hundred theaters as well as portable stages, school auditoriums and public parks the country over.

To guide and administer this, the most controversial of all his work projects, Harry Hopkins had chosen a national director who was not drawn from the commercial hierarchy of Broadway but from among the dreamers and experimenters—the eggheads of American theater. Hallie Flanagan, like Hopkins a graduate of Grinnell in the Middle West and head, since 1925, of Vassar's famed Experimental Theatre, was a wild little woman who believed and publicly stated her conviction that "the theater is more than a private enterprise; it is also a public interest which, properly fostered, might come to be a social and an educative force"; a fanatic, armed with millions of taxpayers' money, who, on assuming office, had heretically announced that "while our immediate aim is to put to work thousands of theater people, our more far-reaching purpose is to organize and support theatrical enterprises so excellent in quality and low in cost, and so vital to the communities involved, that they will be able to continue after federal support is withdrawn." To those who were fortunate enough to be a part of the Federal Theatre from the beginning, it was a unique and thrilling experience. Added to the satisfaction of accomplishing an urgent and essential social task in a time of national crisis, we enjoyed the excitement that is generated on those rare and blessed occasions when the theater is suddenly swept into the historical mainstream of its time.

My own connection with the project began quite suddenly one evening in Rosamond Gilder's apartment on Gramercy Park. As associate editor, with Edith Isaacs, of *Theatre Arts Monthly*, she had come to form part of the inner circle of Mrs. Flanagan's aides and advisers. She told me my name had come up in discussions over the formation of the New York WPA Negro Theatre. She asked if I would be interested; I told her I would. Two weeks later my friend Rose McClendon, the Negro actress, called and asked me to meet her in Hallie Flanagan's office. She was late as usual and I spent half an hour alone with Mrs. Flanagan—a small, forthright, enthusiastic lady with strong teeth, whose matted reddish hair lay like a wig on her skull and who seemed to take her vast responsibilities with amazing self-confidence and sangfroid. When Rose arrived, there was a general meeting with Philip Barber, Hallie's assistant, and Elmer Rice, newly appointed head of New York's Federal Theatre Project.[7] By the end of it I had been offered and had accepted the post of joint head of the Negro Theatre Project in association with Rose McClendon, with instructions to fill out papers and begin work the following morning. In the confusion of transferring three and a half million men and women to the federal payroll before Christmas, it was not noticed that I was not only an alien but also illegally residing in the United States under a false name. Or maybe nobody cared. My application went

7. Elmer Rice was the only successful theater man to throw in his lot, actively, with the Federal Theatre, from which he resigned five months later on the issue of censorship. [author's note]

through as urgent, nonrelief, executive personnel at a salary of fifty dollars a week. It was not until many months later that I understood the true circumstances of my nomination to a job which I took on eagerly, with only a confused awareness of its hazards and implications. I was not stupid enough to underestimate the difficulties that lay ahead, but for anyone who was as frightened of life as I was, there was an irresistible attraction and even a perverse sense of safety in my commitment to such a manifestly impossible task.

. . .

I had known Harlem in the mid-twenties as a late-night playground; I had found it again, eight years later, as the scene of my first and happiest theater experience. Both times, in different ways, I had been made sharply aware of the corrosive misery that filled its streets and houses. The so-called Harlem Riots of March 1935 shocked and frightened New Yorkers but surprised no one who knew conditions in that unhappy, restricted corner of Manhattan. It was the sudden boiling over of a long-fermenting mess of corruption, exploitation and official indifference. Harlem had a church on every other corner; it also had the highest crime rate in the city. Vice, gambling and bootlegging in its various forms were Tammany preserves of long standing; rents were double or more what they were in any equivalent white area of the city, with no leases given, no control or inspections enforced and an organized landlords' blacklist against protesting or "troublesome" tenants. Local businesses and stores (many of them survivals from the days when Harlem was a New York suburb) refused, almost without exception, to employ Negro help. Unemployment had long been endemic in Harlem; with the Depression, it became critical. Under the spur of despair, passive resignation turned into active resentment—stirrings of revolt in which the Left found fruitful ground for its expanding activity. The first Negro unemployed demonstrations had been met with police brutality; soon after, the Harlem edition of the *Daily Worker* began to call itself the *Liberator* and the Communist Party's vice presidential candidate in the two next national elections was a Negro. Yet the party's influence remained limited and superficial, for Harlem followed the typical minority pattern: united in misery, it remained fragmented in every other respect. Father Divine[8] was in his heyday. The churches, with their multiple denominations, continued to perform an important and soothing

---

8. The influential and charismatic African American founder of the International Peace Mission movement. Though he lived and led congregations elsewhere, Divine had relocated to Harlem by the 1930s, where his activities, and tens of thousands of followers, were centered. Claiming to be God and attracting both adherents and critics (some consider him an early American cult leader), he also made great strides toward economic independence and racial equality for his followers. [author's note]

function in the life of the community, though many of their preachers were considered old-fashioned, in some cases mercenary, and generally suspected of "Uncle Tom" attitudes. Roused by Mussolini's threat to Ethiopia, small groups gathered on street corners to listen to advocates of "Back to Africa" and to participate in various small Negro nationalist movements—echoes of Garvey and forerunners of Black Nationalists and Muslims. "Segregation" and "integration" were still academic words, in use among the intelligentsia, but devoid of any wide emotional affect.[9] Economic discrimination, on the other hand, was general and acutely felt; it was the main and immediate cause of the rage and fear that filled Harlem's littered and neglected streets during the worst of the Depression. "Don't buy where you can't work!" had become a battle cry long before the riots. Still, nothing was done. Rents and unemployment continued to rise; so did the anger in the streets. The riots were inevitable—a spontaneous explosion of hysterical despair rather than part of any organized campaign of protest. Now, six months later, the New Deal's continuing increase in federal relief and the promise of local works projects on a large scale had taken some of the fever out of the Harlem crisis without curing its underlying causes. Discrimination and rent gouging continued; so did the bitterness and the disunity.

The Negro Theatre Project of the Works Progress Administration was announced in mid-September and immediately became Harlem's leading topic of agitated dispute. It was known that between seven and eight hundred actors, technicians, service personnel and theater staff were about to be hired: this would make the project the city's largest employer of Negro workers in one unit, with activities that promised to be far more attractive than leaf raking, street cleaning, construction or office work. For years show business had occupied a special place in Negro city life as one of the few open roads to self-expression and fame; here was a chance to enter it—at government expense. No wonder that from the first day, and increasingly as rumors began to fly, the question was asked in curiosity, suspicion and anger: Now that Harlem was finally to have its own project—who was going to run it? And not only "who?" but "of what color?"

There were three theatrical factions in Harlem at this time. The first centered around the former Lafayette stock company, which had enjoyed a long and successful career before talking pictures in that same theater building in which the WPA was now about to house its project. Ex-members of the Lafayette Players and their friends felt that the government's effort to

---

9. The word "black" was taboo. "Negro" was in official and general use, though there was some ideological disagreement as to whether it should be spelled with a small or a capital *N*. [author's note]

revive Harlem theatrical life should be entrusted to veterans who had run their own show once before without a white man—and who needed one now?

They were opposed by a second, larger and more influential group. Among the intelligentsia—the teachers, social workers and race relations experts—there was a general feeling of condescension toward Negroes in show business, who were felt to be lacking in the experience, the education and the vision required to administer a major Negro project in a white man's world. This group recommended the appointment of a white man "of stature," flanked by Negro advisers, whom they were eager to supply. Between these two stood a third small but powerful group of successful Negro performers, respected union members whose talent had won them full acceptance in the white world. Many of these were now torn between a desire to lead their people into the theatrical promised land and a reluctance to be sucked back into the Harlem broil from which they had only recently emancipated themselves. They, too, for all their strong racial feeling, were generally of the opinion that without a white man at its head—with connections in government circles and some reputation on Broadway—the Negro unit would receive scant recognition or respect in Washington or New York.

There was one other element which, finally, came to exert a determining influence in the choice of a project head for the Negro Theatre. This was the Communist Party, which, having few acceptable candidates of its own, threw its support behind those Negro "names" who had shown a willingness to collaborate (for artistic or other reasons) with United Front organizations. One such name was that of my friend Rose McClendon. Rose was not well— ravaged already by the cancer that carried her off six months later. Besides, she was a performer, not an administrator or a director. When the job of heading the Negro Theatre Project was offered her by general consent, she demurred, then finally accepted on one condition: that a suitable white associate be found who would work with her, on a basis of complete equality, as her artistic and executive partner. Asked if she had any suggestions to make, she gave my name as that of someone she knew and trusted.

Our collaboration was never put to the test. In the early days of the project she made one or two formal appearances before she fell finally and hopelessly ill. My visits to her bedside after we got under way gave her a feeling of participation, but soon she was too ill even for that and resigned. By then the project was so far advanced that no one was willing to risk the delays and confusions that would have resulted from a change of leadership. Besides, by that time, things seemed to be going surprisingly well for the Negro Theatre of the WPA.

. . .

Our first month had been devoted to one single activity—getting people off relief and onto the project. This transfer took place in a temporary building on lower Madison Avenue, in a vast area of bare concrete floor with makeshift partitions amid hurriedly assembled secondhand desks and benches. Here, day after day, the hallways, elevators, stairways and improvised waiting rooms were jammed with hundreds of men and women, many with children, who arrived and stood around in herds, sent by their local relief agencies to be interviewed, processed and transferred to WPA jobs for which they were more or less qualified.

For admission to the Negro unit the rush was such that guards had to be summoned to control the flow of milling applicants, many of whom arrived downtown in a state of bewildered and angry hysteria. Besides the established relief cases, hundreds of new applicants had suddenly appeared, excited by rumors of jobs and opportunities in a work area where skills and credentials were almost impossible to verify. Anyone with an authentic relief status was hired, sight unseen; as the days passed and the rolls began to fill up, our task was to make sure that men and women with legitimate theatrical backgrounds got on the project even if their relief status (through pride or bureaucratic confusion) was not entirely satisfactory.

In making these vital and sometimes distressing decisions about people with whose background and circumstances I was totally unfamiliar, I had to rely on the advice of two Negro aides. One was Edward Perry, my stage manager from *Four Saints*;[10] the other, who became my counselor, protector, instructor, deputy and intimate friend, was Carlton Moss. One of the Negro "new generation," a graduate of Morgan College in Baltimore, he had directed a community project for the New York Public Library and worked as a drama counselor for the Civil Works Administration and a writer in radio. When he came to work for the WPA at the age of twenty-five, he was already a bitterly skeptical man. But behind his smiling pose of protective sarcasm lay a deep and sympathetic understanding of the inner workings of the Negro world. For ten months he was my Machiavelli—briefing me before every meeting, sitting by my side and whispering to me or slipping me scribbled notes along the table each time he saw me getting ready to make a fool of myself or to surrender some essential point of which I had failed to grasp the importance.

These meetings were held in various places—in vestries, boardrooms and the back rooms of shady bars. And each was entirely different. Around

10. Prior to his work for the Federal Theatre Project, Houseman had made a name for himself as director of his friend Virgil Thomson's opera, *Four Saints in Three Acts*, with a libretto by Gertrude Stein, followed by Ibsen's *The Lady from the Sea*, Maxwell Anderson's *Valley Forge* and Archibald MacLeish's *Panic*, which he produced.

the polished table of the Urban League, sober, conservative, well-spoken men and women were interested mostly in employment, culture and decorum and were concerned lest the Negro Theatre's offerings be too exclusively concerned with squalor, violence, bawdry or sex. Here I brought my English accent into play and marshaled my artistic record of *Four Saints*, Ibsen and *Valley Forge* for further reassurance.

The Party, on the other hand, represented by the perennial vice presidential candidate James Ford and his white advisers, wanted no "handkerchief-heading" on the project: they wanted plays of social protest and a voice in the assignment of executive jobs. I did my best to reassure them, citing my production of *Panic* as evidence of my liberal position.[11]

"We believe we will find on the relief rolls people with the energy, ability and talent to achieve any program set up," Mrs. Flanagan had declared. But for added safety, to ensure the artistic and professional standards of the Arts Projects, a special dispensation was granted by WPA which permitted each unit to hire up to ten percent of its creative and executive personnel from outside the relief lists, at relief wages of between twenty and thirty dollars a week.

[...]

[One] non-Negro member of the project was a plump, pink-cheeked, bouncing Jewish virgin named Augusta Weissberger. We desperately needed a secretary; she was moderately competent; there was no one else available and she was willing to work in Harlem. But most of my nonrelief appointments—black and white—were on the creative side. These included a number of the country's best Negro actors, whom pride and an obstinate sense of status had kept off the relief rolls. Their names appear with honor on the cast lists of that year's Lafayette productions. Negro writers included Countee Cullen and Zora Hurston, a young female novelist from Florida. Clarence Yates was our best-known dancer and choreographer; Perry Watkins, who designed our first show, was that rare thing—a Negro member of the scene designers' union. Among our musicians, we had the great Eubie Blake, Joe Jordan and Leonard de Paur, who, years later, founded and led one of the country's most distinguished male ensembles—the Infantry Chorus. Langston Hughes was a frequent visitor, but he already formed part of the Writers' Project and saw no reason to change.

The rest of our artistic staff came from among my own friends and associates. They included Manny Essman and Nat Karson, the designers;

11. Five years later, when Orson Welles and I produced Richard Wright's *Native Son*, there were two separate sets of protesting pickets in front of the theater on opening night—the Communist Party's and the Urban League's. [author's note]

Virgil Thomson, who had the title of musical supervisor; and Abe Feder as technical director and lighting expert, with his inseparable assistant, Teddy Thomas. They came, certainly not for the thirty dollars a week, nor primarily out of friendship for me, but because they saw in the project a wide-open field for those creative activities which they were denied within the narrow limits of the commercial theater; also, perhaps, out of a vague, undefined feeling that, as cooperating members of the Negro Theatre unit, they were helping to start something new and significant in the cultural life of their country.

Late in October 1935, about the time Mussolini was invading Ethiopia, the Negro Theatre Project, with its more than 750 men and women and its battered desks, chairs and filing cabinets, began its move from lower Madison Avenue to Harlem. Soon after that, while the Japanese were invading the Chinese mainland, we started to take down the rotting boards which had long covered the doors and windows of the old Lafayette Theatre on Seventh Avenue between 132nd and 133rd Streets. Built around the turn of the century when Harlem was a theatrical tributary of Broadway, the Lafayette was a sordid, icy cavern when we moved in—with peeling plaster, a thick accumulation of grime, burst bulbs, rotting carpets and broken seats in the hairy recesses of which lurked rats, lice and other horrors. Within a month the auditorium had been restored to some semblance of respectability and warmth. On stage, behind the lowered, flaking asbestos safety curtain, equally miraculous changes were being wrought by a stage crew that was the equal in zeal and skill to the best of Broadway. Consistently refused admission to the stagehands' union on grounds of color, these carpenters and electricians had been forced to make their living for years outside the nonexistent Negro theater. Now they were back in their chosen profession: the miles of new rope and cable that Feder had requisitioned, the scores of up-to-date electrical units hanging overhead and the six portable dimmer boards with their dozens of multicolored switches and levers were a source of excitement and pride that made theirs the most consistently enthusiastic department of the project.

Of our 750 workers, between four and five hundred were officially classified as actors, singers or dancers. Of these, approximately one-third had never acted, danced or been on a stage or a concert platform in their lives. Half of the rest had, at one time or another, danced in a chorus, sung with a group or appeared as extras in films. This left us with around 150 professional performers, including African drummers, veteran stock actors, Broadway stars and locally celebrated elocutionists like Venezuela Jones. To devise productions in which we could properly employ even a fraction of such variegated talents—this became my main challenge as the project got under way.

None of the tried and obvious ways would work. In the current temper of the Harlem community, the old "stock" pattern of performing recent Broadway hits with Negro casts was undesirable, if not downright offensive. Equally unsuitable, for different reasons, was the revival of such celebrated Negro successes as *The Emperor Jones, In Abraham's Bosom, All God's Chillun Got Wings* or even *Porgy*, which Harlem audiences had applauded downtown but would resent on the stage of their own community theater. This same inhibition seemed to apply to the revues and musicals that had long been the Negro performers' main source of theatrical fame and employment; under ideological censure from both Left and Right, they were regarded as "handkerchief-head" and so, for our purposes, anathema.

In the solution of this problem, Virgil Thomson, with whom I was sharing the first of the five Manhattan apartments we inhabited together over the next two and a half years, was of inestimable aid to me. He reminded me that our casting of *Four Saints* had been done on purely artistic and theatrical grounds. Our black singers had been chosen because their voices, diction and movements were perfectly suited to the execution of a work that had nothing Negro about it. Their performance had justified our choice and this encouraged me in the position I now took—that our only hope of functioning in a vital and constructive way lay in dividing the performing personnel of the Negro Theatre into two separate, though still interrelated, halves. One would be devoted to the performance of plays written, directed and performed by and for Negroes, in Negro locales and, preferably, on contemporary Negro subjects. The other would devote itself to the performance of classical works of which our actors would be the interpreters, without concession or reference to color. The choice as to which group they joined was to be made by the project members themselves, with the clear understanding that they could, if they chose, shift their allegiance from production to production. This would give diversity to our shows, increase our use of manpower and stimulate public interest in our activities. It would also arouse a feeling of emulation that would, I hoped, act as a sharp and constant spur to our morale.

For this fine scheme to work, there was one essential condition—that the quality of these "classical" productions be exceptionally high. It would be fatal to undertake the risky and difficult business of producing Shakespeare in Harlem until I had found a director of whose creative imagination and power I was completely confident. With this in mind I went down one evening to the basement apartment on West 14th Street into which Orson and Virginia Welles had just moved. Orson had spent a feckless summer in Wisconsin—his impresario having gone broke even before he opened. On his return to New York, in order to keep himself and Virginia alive, he had been forced into what soon became a meteoric career in radio, where his magnificent voice was put to such base uses that fall as the Shadow, the voice of chocolate pudding and the Great McCoy, besides his weekly imperson-ations on *The March of Time* of such diverse characters as Haile Selassie, Hindenburg, Sir Basil Zaharoff and the Emperor Hirohito.

I told him of my plans for the Negro Theatre and formally invited him to join us. I suggested that our dream of staging a whirling Elizabethan drama might now be realized under unusual but attractive conditions—with Uncle Sam as our angel. Orson said yes immediately, then called me at two in the morning to announce that Virginia had just had an inspiration: our first production would be *Macbeth*, laid in the island of Haiti in the early nineteenth century, with the witches as voodoo priestesses! Within a week he had constructed out of Plasticine, on a sheet of laundry board, a scale model of what later appeared on the stage of the Lafayette as the basic unit of *Macbeth*. At the same time he and Nat Karson, with Virginia as their leg-man, began to amass research on Directoire modes, Napoleonic uniforms and tropical vegetation.

As soon as it was known that we were considering doing *Macbeth*, it became a matter of general controversy in Harlem. The community was fas-cinated but wary: some thought this Shakespearean venture an unnecessary risk, others saw it in a white man's scheme deliberately hatched to degrade the Negro and bring the Theatre Project into disrepute. Our first auditions tended to confirm these misgivings. I had announced that we would hear anyone who wished to try out for the classical wing of the project. For the best part of a week, they followed each other onto the platform of a large rec-reation hall belonging to the Ancient Order of Monarch Elks: old and young, male and female, singers, dancers, semiliterates and intellectuals—some in deadly earnest, some giggling in self-conscious embarrassment; still oth-ers who came suspiciously, regarding the whole thing as an elaborate joke. By the end of the week more than three hundred had been auditioned and classified under mysterious symbols that signified rejects, dancers, soldiers, witches, walk-ons and principals. Within another week, with Edward Perry as associate supervisor, *Macbeth* was in rehearsal. Orson had asked me to stay away for the first few weeks. Overwhelmed by the problems of getting the theater open, I was only too glad to oblige.

For obvious reasons it was desirable to open the Lafayette with an "indig-enous" and, preferably, a realistic contemporary Negro work. And here, immediately, I had encountered our first predictable hazard—the absence of performable Negro scripts. Precedents were scarce: [George Sklar and Paul Peter's] *Stevedore*, notwithstanding its use of the Negro as victim and hero, was, essentially, a white play; Hall Johnson's *Run, Little Chillun*, for all its boundless energy, was less a play than a choral and declamatory tour de force. Of the many scripts submitted to us, two were possible, though far from good: *Turpentine* by Peter Morrell and Gus Smith—a powerful actor of the Left—was a stereotyped play of protest laid in a turpentine-workers' camp in South Carolina; Frank Wilson's *Walk Together Chillun!*, which he was eager to direct himself, was an awkward hodgepodge of theatrical clichés, complete with church scene, dance-hall sequence, comedy routines and a preachment that could offend absolutely no one. Wilson was one of America's best-known black actors, the creator of Porgy, a church member and a man whose confused and voluble sincerity had won him the patronizing approval of most organized sections of the community. I chose his play for tactical reasons, fully aware of its weaknesses but equally aware of its advantages for our opening show. My assignment, as head of the project, was not, primarily, the production of masterpieces. I had been instructed to find suitable theatrical activity for the hundreds of needy men and women on our payroll and to find it quickly. *Walk Together Chillun!* seemed to meet this requirement.

For all their many divisions, every member of the project seemed to agree on one thing: that the Negro Theatre must be the first New York unit to open its doors to the public. With this objective very much in mind, we put *Walk Together Chillun!* into rehearsal early in December, first in a church, then on the reconditioned stage of the Lafayette. And, in spite of our difficulties with the play (half the second act was removed in the fifth week of rehearsal) and the problems normally attendant upon the opening of a dark theater, it soon became evident, following the cancellation of the Living Newspaper's first show, *Ethiopia*, that we would, in fact, be the first major project to present a WPA Federal Theatre production in New York City.

Walk Together Chillun! opened with a suitable official flurry on the night of February 5, 1936. Its reception was cordial but not enthusiastic. Harlem was relieved that the project's opening show was neither a disaster nor an "Uncle Tom" piece and proud that the first Federal Theatre play in New York should be a Negro production. People who remembered the old Lafayette were impressed by the condition of the house, the size of the pit band led by Joe Jordan and the lavishness of the new technical setup—the lighting particularly. Downtown was generally uninterested. Brooks Atkinson's reaction in the *New York Times* was condescending but kind:

> After displaying patience enough to make Job envious, the New York Federal Theatre raised the curtain on its first legitimate production, *Walk Together Chillun!* According to Broadway standards, it is artless and sometimes unintelligible, but its actors attack their parts as vigorously as though a Broadway manager was footing the bill . . .

Setting his play in an unnamed city in the North, Mr. Wilson shows how an infusion of Negroes from Georgia makes trouble and precipitates a race riot which stirs up the whole town. When the Negroes are in trouble their sectional differences lose importance. When the whites are aroused, they draw no distinctions. *Walk Together Chillun!* concludes with an impassioned plea for racial solidarity.

. . . Although *Walk Together Chillun!* is a patchwork play by Broadway standards, there is obviously more to it than any white man is likely to understand. Mr. Wilson is talking to his comrades. He is not appealing for Times Square applause.

This, our opening production, ran for less than a month to moderate attendance. Our second—also from the "contemporary" wing of the project—was *The Conjure-Man Dies* by Rudolph Fisher, a well-known Harlem physician and novelist. It was less earnest than its predecessor and a lot more fun. Directed by Joseph Losey, it was a comedy-mystery in three acts with fourteen scenes, whose theme song was "I'll Be Glad When You're Dead, You Rascal You!" It opened on March 11 (three days before the first of the WPA's Living Newspapers, eight days before [T. S. Eliot's] *Murder in the Cathedral*) and it was a smash. Unlike Wilson's ingenuous preachment, this was big-city entertainment—fast-moving, topical, crammed with inside allusions and bitter minority jokes (e.g., the detective, [played by] Dooley Wilson, stands beside the police doctor in the morgue as he looks through his microscope at a suspicious blood smear. "It's not moving," says the doctor. "It must be colored blood," says Dooley[12] to roars of laughter). An earnest white man's perplexity was reflected in the *New York Times* review:

HARLEM MUMBO-JUMBO

To a paleface, fresh from Broadway, the new play seemed like a verbose and amateur charade, none too clearly written and soggily acted. But the Lafayette Theatre was bulging with family parties last night who roared at the obese comedian and howled over the West Indian accent of a smart Harlem landlady. This column doesn't know everything after all.

---

12. Five years later Dooley Wilson was starring with Ethel Waters and Katherine Dunham in Broadway's *Cabin in the Sky*; two years after that, as Sam in [the film] *Casablanca* with Ingrid Bergman and Humphrey Bogart, he was launching one of the year's biggest song hits, "As Time Goes By." [author's note]

From every practical point of view, even from that of those who disapproved of it, *The Conjure-Man Dies* was good programming, an asset to the project and a welcome escape from the many stresses and anxieties that continued to harass us. Its success allowed me to turn all my attention to our next opening—the first production of our classical wing, which was generally referred to, by this time, as the Voodoo *Macbeth*.

My functions on the project, so far, had been essentially administrative and diplomatic. Though I had personally supervised both our contemporary shows and, in the case of *Walk Together Chillun!*, actively intervened as a director when I thought it necessary, I had not identified myself creatively with either of them. The gauge of my success, so far, had been the efficacy and harmony with which the project was conducted, rather than the theatrical or artistic quality of its productions. Now, suddenly, with *Macbeth*, all this was changed. For besides its potential value to the project in opening up new fields for black performers, I could not help regarding this production as a direct, personal challenge and the first serious test of my theatrical collaboration with Orson Welles, on which I was setting such high hopes and on which I was preparing to risk not only my own future but that of the Negro project as well.

I had acceded to Orson's request that I stay away from early rehearsals of *Macbeth*. When I finally visited the Elks' Hall, what I heard and saw delighted but in no way astonished me. I had never seriously doubted the company's ability to speak Elizabethan blank verse when they encountered it under the right conditions and, though he had never staged a play except at school, I had complete faith in Welles's ability to direct them. We had chosen the cast together: Jack Carter, the creator of Crown in the original *Porgy*, was the Thane, with Edna Thomas as his murderous lady. For the Macduffs we had Maurice Ellis and Marie Young; J. Louis Johnson was the Porter, Canada Lee was Banquo and Eric Burroughs (a graduate of London's RADA) played Hecate, a composite figure of evil which Welles had assembled out of fragments of witches' lines and to whose sinister equipment he presently added a twelve-foot bullwhip. Our supernatural department was very strong at the Lafayette. In addition to the witches and sundry apparitions called for by the Bard, we had a troupe of African drummers commanded by Asadata Dafora Horton (later minister of culture of the Republic of Sierra Leone). Except for their leader, who had a flawless Oxford accent, they spoke little English: the star of the troupe, Abdul, an authentic witch doctor, seemed to know no language at all except magic. Their first act, after they had been cast in *Macbeth*, was to file a formal requisition for five live black goats. These were brought into the theater by night and sacrificed, hugger-mugger, according to approved tribal ritual, before being stretched into resonant drum skins.

This supernatural atmosphere added to the excitement that was beginning to form around our production of *Macbeth*. By the end of February it had become the most debated subject in Harlem—one on which the entire future of the Negro Theatre Project was felt to depend. Partly, this had to do with the nature of the show—the first full-scale, professional Negro Shakespearean production in theatrical history. Partly it was the effect of sheer mass. For *Macbeth* had grown steadily with the months until it had become an undertaking of such magnitude that the whole project was beginning to sag under its weight; backstage at the Lafayette, to make room for the huge slabs of scenery and acres of painted backdrops that continued to arrive from the shops, *The Conjure-Man Dies* was gradually being edged down toward the footlights, to the fury of its director and cast. And, in the basement, the glow of hundreds of Karson's gorgeous uniforms, stiff with gold braid, the sheen of satin ball gowns and the gnarled and hairy horror of the witches' hides could not fail to arouse the envious resentment of members of the project's contemporary wing, who were confined to the realistic drabness of street clothes and denim. Soon, ugly rumors began to fly: someone had been told downtown by an authoritative source that *Macbeth* would never open; so much of the project's money had been spent by me on my boyfriend's folly that all future productions of the Negro unit had been canceled. And a stale but dangerous whispering campaign was revived: that what was being so secretly prepared was, in reality, a vast burlesque intended to ridicule the Negro in the eyes of the white world. As a result, Orson was attacked one night, as he was leaving rehearsal, by four alcoholic zealots determined to prevent this insult to their race.

Partly, too, there was the agitation generated by the show itself. Since the first day of rehearsal, from behind the locked doors of the Elks' Hall, waves of excitement had been radiating in ever-widening circles through the Harlem streets. These were created in part by Orson, whose demonic energy was transmitted first to his leading actors, then to his exhausted and bewildered but enthusiastic company and finally, through them, to the whole puzzled community. When the *Macbeth* troupe came out of hiding and began to rehearse, often all through the night, on the stage of the Lafayette, this sense of anxious anticipation continued to grow—especially after drummers, dancers and sound effects had been added and could be heard, like distant thunder, seeping through the walls of the theater into Seventh Avenue and the surrounding streets.

Including his regular Midtown radio jobs, to which he commuted by taxi (sometimes two or three times a day), Orson was now working about twenty hours out of the twenty-four. When he was not drilling the company in mass scenes of battle, revelry or witchcraft, or rehearsing individually with the Macbeths and Macduffs, he was working with Virgil on music, Karson on costumes, Feder on lights or Asadata on voodoo.

It was during the preparation of *Macbeth* that Orson revealed his surprising capacity for collaboration. For all the mass of his own ego, he was able to apprehend other people's weakness and strength and to make creative use of them: he had a shrewd instinctive sense of when to bully or charm, when to be kind or savage—and he was seldom mistaken. With Feder, who was a garrulous masochist, Orson was abusive, sarcastic and loud. At light rehearsals he would set him impossible tasks, then howl at him, shamefully and continuously, before the exhausted company, who were so delighted to hear someone else (a white man, especially) catching hell, that they persevered with their own stage maneuvers long after their normal span of patience had run out. As a result Orson completed his light rehearsals, preserved the morale of his troupe and retained Feder's professional devotion—if not his love. With Virgil Thomson it was less easy. For here Orson was dealing with a temperament, intelligence and an attitude of a kind he had seldom encountered. Virgil was wary of the boy genius:

> You brought Orson to the flat where we were living on 59th Street. We argued late one night and as an older man I tried to beat him down because I felt he was full of bluff and because his verbalization of what he wanted to do in the theater was not entirely convincing. I argued hard and not always fairly against Orson and you told me later to stop it because he was a very, very good man in the theater. You were the one that believed in him . . .

Then as they began to work together, things got easier.

> Orson was nearly always likable. He was never hateful or brutal with me, though I was a little terrified of his firmness. He was extremely professional and he knew exactly what he wanted. He knew it so well and so thoroughly that I, as an older musician with a certain amount of pride, would not write him original music. I would not humiliate myself to write so precisely on his demand. On the other hand, I respected his demands dramatically. So, as your employee, I gave him sound effects and ready-made music—trumpet call, battle scenes and percussive scores where he wanted them—and, of course, the waltzes for the party scene.
>
> Orson and I never quarreled—as you and he did; but we never really agreed. We used to take each other out to elaborate dinners; and it was I who taught him to drink white wine, and not whiskey, at rehearsals . . .

Another quite different set of problems arose during our collaboration with Asadata Dafora Horton and his troupe of African drummers. With the exception of Abdul, the witch doctor, who several times during rehearsals fell into deep and agitated trances from which not even his fellow witches could rouse him, our Gold Coast contingent was thoroughly professional, adaptable and eager to please—except in the matter of spells. One day, after Orson, Virgil and I had been auditioning their voodoo numbers, we complained to Asadata that his chants did not sound evil enough. Virgil, as usual, got right down to the point.

"Are those really voodoo?"

"Oh, yes. Yes, indeed, sirs. That is absolutely real, authentic voodoo."

"They don't sound wicked enough."

"Sirs, I . . ."

"Sometimes for the theater you have to exaggerate."

"I am sorry, sirs. You can't be any more wicked than that!"

I stayed behind with Virgil and the drummers. As fellow musicians they argued for most of the afternoon. Finally Asadata admitted what those chants of his really were: they were strong spells intended to ward off the beriberi—not to induce it. He dared not give us the real thing, he explained. It might have worked.

Later, when we insisted, they did somewhat darken the tone of their incantations. For that reason I was unnerved when, one night, in the first witch scene, through the moaning and banging of drums, I quite distinctly heard, amid the incomprehensible sounds of Abdul's unknown tongue, the words "Meesta Welles" and "Meesta Houseman" several times repeated. I never told Orson, for he was ridiculously superstitious. Besides, he was haunted throughout rehearsals by the old English theatrical tradition that of all the plays in the canon, *Macbeth* is the most ill-fated and accident-prone. (It was, in fact, the only play I ever did with him in which he neither sprained nor broke a limb nor otherwise incapacitated himself before or after its opening.)

The *Macbeth* troupe, including understudies, stage managers, cripples, children and dependents, finally numbered 137. Orson led them with an authority that was extraordinary in a boy just out of his teens. He had the strength; but he also had the infinite and loving patience which, in my experience, distinguishes the great from the competent director. And he displayed a capacity for total concentration without which our whole perilous venture could never have been brought off. For this *Macbeth* troupe of ours was an amazing mishmash of amateurs and professionals, church members and radicals, sophisticates and wild ones, adherents of Father Divine and bushmen from Darkest Africa. It was one thing to handle them administratively and paternalistically as I did (firm but understanding, not always truthful but generally fair) and quite another to lead them creatively through unknown country during months of rehearsal in an atmosphere of gathering enervation and doubt. Orson kept them going by the sheer force of his personality. His energy was at all times greater than theirs; he was even more mercurial and less predictable than they were—driving and indolent, glum and gay, tender and violent, inflexibly severe and hopelessly indulgent. I once estimated that a quarter of his growing radio earnings during *Macbeth* went in loans and handouts to the company; another quarter was spent on the purchase of props and other necessities (including a severed head) held up by bureaucratic red tape; a third quarter went for meals and cabs; the rest was spent on the entertainment of Jack Carter.

Jack Carter was the most furious man I have ever known. Six-foot-four, elegant and malevolent in his bespoke shoes and his custom-made English suits, he had bright blue eyes and a skin so light that he could pass as white anywhere in the world, if he'd wanted to. He didn't. The son of one of the famed beauties from the original Floradora Sextet, born in a French chateau, unaware of his own Negro blood and brought up in the lap of European luxury, he had never heard of a race problem until he returned to America in his teens. What he then discovered made an outlaw of him; he became a pimp, a killer and finally an actor. As Crown in *Porgy* he scored a big personal success, which was soon threatened by bouts of misbehavior. His favorite diversion on tour was to register in a town's leading hotel, then invite his black friends, male and female, up to his room and fight till the blood flowed when they were denied admission. He had not worked much in recent years, but made a living somehow through his underworld connections in Harlem. His life was a nagging torment, not knowing whom he despised and hated most—his mother's people for submitting to humiliation or his father's for inflicting it.

When it became known that Jack had been cast for the part of Macbeth, in which he would be directed by a twenty-year-old white man, eyebrows were raised all over Harlem and people waited with mixed emotions for the outcome of their first encounter. If they hoped for mayhem, they were disappointed. From the moment at the first reading when Orson threw his arms around Jack, his eyes brimming with tears of gratitude and admiration, a close and passionate friendship had sprung up between these two giants who, together, measured close to thirteen feet. For four months they were seldom apart, driven by a need for each other's presence which caused Jack to appear at every *Macbeth* rehearsal, whether he had been called or not, and which sent them, when work was ended, at four or five in the morning, roaring together through the late-night spots and brothels of Harlem till it was time to rehearse again.

I never really knew how much of all this was director's strategy calculated to nurse a difficult leading man through opening night or how much it reflected a true and urgent affinity between these two troubled and dangerous men. (I used to wonder, sometimes, seeing Orson returning from these nocturnal forays, if they did not perhaps evoke some echo of those other long, wild nights which he had spent as a boy, with his father, in the red-light districts of the Mediterranean, Hong Kong and Singapore.) This curious intimacy proved of inestimable value to the project. In the state of anxiety and exhaustion which the company had reached by the beginning of April, Jack Carter's loyalty was a major factor in sustaining its morale. Not only was he above reproach in his own behavior, but he constituted himself Orson's champion with the company—scornful of its fatigue, quick to detect signs of revolt and to crush movements of disaffection.

This zeal sometimes got us into trouble. One night, not long before opening, around four in the morning, a minor mutiny broke out on stage. In sheer exhaustion, weighed down by the heavy uniforms in which they had been working for almost ten hours, the company exploded suddenly into open anger and refused to go on. First Eddy Perry, then I, then Orson—sweating and gray with fatigue—pleaded with them, explaining that, for technical reasons, certain stage movements must be fixed that night or not at all. They shook their heads and started to scatter. At that moment a tall figure, superb in full Napoleonic regalia, vaulted onto the parapet of Glamis Castle and began to harangue the rebellious troops. Jack was in a towering rage; he looked and sounded magnificent, full of the unrestrained fury which Orson had been trying to infuse into the last act of *Macbeth*. He told them he was tired too, for he had a bigger part than they did; they might have worked for nine hours but he had been rehearsing for thirteen—and, anyway, what was a little fatigue when the whole future of the Negro Theatre was at stake? Here was the chance they had never been given before; the opportunity for which they had never even dared to hope. If these men (Orson and I, Harry Hopkins and the President of the United States) were willing to risk their reputations on such a project—to work on it as Welles had done, night and day, month after month, on their behalf, when he could easily have been earning a fortune in radio, as they goddamn well knew—there was only one thing that they, as self-respecting Negro actors and human beings could do: follow him, unquestioningly, to the ends of the earth and stop screwing up his wonderful production with their fucking stupid complaints. If they were tired, let them rest after opening! Because if the opening was a bust and the production failed through their fault—they'd have the rest of their goddamn lives to rest in!

The company listened in silence. When he finished they began to pick up their props and to drift back into their positions; the mutiny was over;

they were ready to rehearse till dawn or longer. It was then that the demon that drove him made it necessary for Jack Carter to add one more sentence to his oration.

"So get back to work!" he yelled. "You no-acting sons of bitches!"

In the brawl that followed, some scenery was smashed and a court lady was slightly injured when she was pushed off the stage. And no more work was done that night.

Finally, not an hour too soon, the end of rehearsals drew near for Orson Welles and his *Macbeth* company. April 14 (which also happened to be the first day of the national baseball season) was announced as our opening date: it promised the Harlem community an emotional release such as they had not known since the riots of 1935. Little else was talked about above 125th Street. The news that Haile Selassie's troops were in headlong flight before Mussolini's mechanized army and air force made no stir at all in a week that was entirely monopolized by the activities of the Lafayette Theatre. Nor did the downtown press neglect us. A reporter named Bosley Crowther was sent north by the *New York Times* to report on this latest version of "the Bard's most slaughterous drama."

Midnight was the time. It seems that twenty-four hours makes too short a day for the WPA's Negro Theatre and, with its house pretty well filled up by workmen during the day and the performances of *The Conjure-Man Dies* during the evening, the only time left for the final rehearsals of *Macbeth* has been from midnight on till dawn. Sounds fantastic, but it's true . . .

This scout, upon arrival, discovered a good-sized crowd of Negroes milling around the back of the theater. These were the Shakespearian thespians waiting to begin rehearsal. Not to them, however, but to John Houseman and Orson Welles, supervisor and director, respectively, of the Negro *Macbeth*, it was that this scout went for information. Why, he wanted to know, had they mustered the audacity to take the Bard for a ride? What sort of Thane of Cawdor would find himself in Haiti? Whither would Malcolm and Donalbain flee—to Jamaica or possibly Nassau?

Both Mr. Houseman and Mr. Welles were pleased to talk, brightly and intelligently, about their unusual creation. But they were also quite serious about it. "We were very anxious to do one of Shakespeare's dramas in the Negro Theatre," said Orson Welles, "and *Macbeth* seemed, in all respects, the most adaptable. The stormy career of Christophe, who became 'the Negro King of Haiti' and ended by killing himself when his cruelty led to a revolt, forms a striking parallel to the history of Macbeth. The costumes and settings of the production are therefore in the period of Haiti's grimmest turbulence. Place names have been altered with particular care to retain the rhythm to Shakespeare's lines. Malcolm and Donalbain don't flee to England but to 'the Coast . . .'"

As to the company itself, they seemed as alert and enthusiastic as the day—or night—they started. The New Deal, not only in the theater, but in Shakespeare, was meat and drink for them. And any actor who will rehearse from midnight until dawn, the rosy-fingered, must be interested in something more than a paycheck. At least that's the way it looked to this scout.

Some of this excitement was spontaneous; some of it was induced and stimulated. Three days before opening, Harlem woke up to find "Macbeth" stenciled in luminous paint on every street corner from 125th to 140th—from Lexington to Broadway. The Tree of Hope, a gnarled relic that survived with difficulty on Seventh Avenue in front of the Lafayette Theatre and which was credited with magic properties of some sort, was festooned with garlands and bright-colored ribbons for luck. By April 10 every seat in the theater (except those reserved for U.S. Government officials and the press) had been sold, sometimes twice over, as ticket scalpers became active in Harlem's fancier bars. A free preview, given two days before opening, drew three thousand more would-be spectators than the theater could hold—necessitating the calling of a police emergency squad to disperse the crowd. From the downtown WPA press department came word that every first-string critic in town would attend. (One of them, tactfully, requested that he and his wife should be seated, if possible, "not next to Negroes.")

On opening night, just before dusk, the massed bands of the Monarch Lodge of the Benevolent and Protective Order of Elks, in uniforms of light blue, scarlet and gold, began to march in two detachments through the streets of Harlem behind two huge, crimson banners that read:

MACBETH
by
William Shakespeare

By six-thirty they had converged before the theater where they continued to play eighty-five strong, standing around the Tree of Hope, while ten thousand people milled around them and dozens of police, including two on horses, tried in vain to keep a way clear into the Lafayette. As reported in the *New York Times*: "All northbound automobile traffic was stopped for more than an hour, while from trucks in the street, floodlights flared a circle of light into the lobby and cameramen took photographs of the arrival of celebrities." Later, someone wrote of "the flash of jewels, silk hats and ermine," but I was too nervous to notice and too anxious to get the curtain up before eight o'clock.

It rose, finally, following the customary overture, on a jungle set "luxuriant, savage and ominous with shadows," where the trees met in a great overhead arch of twisted trunks that suggested a gigantic, living skeleton. Within five minutes, amid the thunder of drums and the orgiastic howls and squeals of our voodoo celebrants, we knew that victory was ours.

> The witches' scenes from *Macbeth* have always worried the life out of the polite, tragic stage; the grimaces of the hags and the garish make-believe of the flaming cauldron have bred more disenchantment than anything else that Shakespeare wrote. But ship the witches into the rank and fever-stricken jungle echoes, stuff a gleaming naked witch doctor into the cauldron, hold up Negro masks in the baleful light—and there you have a witches' scene that is logical and stunning and a triumph of the theater art.[13]

The next scene to stop the show was that of the Macbeths' royal reception immediately following the murder of Banquo: dozens of shimmering couples in their court finery swirling with wild abandon to the crashing rhythms of our Thomson-orchestrated nineteenth-century waltzes—then, suddenly, a wild, high, inhuman sound that froze them all in their tracks, followed by Macbeth's terrible cry as the spirit of Banquo, in the shape of a huge luminous death mask, suddenly appeared on the battlements to taunt him in the hour of his triumph.

For Birnam Wood, Central Park and half of Rockland County had been stripped of their burgeoning boughs, till the floor of the stage became a moving forest above which Macbeth, cornered at last on the highest platform of his castle, first shot down the "cream-faced loon" who brought him the news of Macduff's approach, then kicked him, for an eighteen-foot drop, into the courtyard below. It was here that the defiant hero vainly emptied his pistol into the body of the tall, dark, bearded man whose wife and children he had murdered and of whom he discovered, too late, as they closed for their final duel, that he had been "from the womb untimely ripped." A moment later, as Macbeth's head came sailing down from the battlements, a double cry rose

13. Brooks Atkinson in the *New York Times*, on April 15, 1936, under the headline "Macbeth or Harlem Boy Goes Wrong." [author's note]

from the stage—of jubilation from Macduff's army over the tyrant's death, and of triumph from the assembled members of the Negro Theatre Project's classical wing at the successful outcome of their long and agonizing ordeal.

> At the conclusion of the performance there were salvos of applause and countless curtain calls as bouquets of flowers were handed over the footlights to the leading players.

Here again, the clapping and cheering that filled the theater for fifteen minutes had a double meaning: it was the natural enthusiasm of a delighted audience; it was also Harlem's explosion of relief at the project's final vindication after months of anxiety and doubt.

The notices the next morning were a joy to read: "As an experiment in Afro-American showmanship, *Macbeth* merited the excitement that fairly rocked the Lafayette Theatre last night," concluded the *New York Times*. Others wrote of "an *Emperor Jones* gone beautifully mad," of "the dark, sensual rhythms, the giant tropic fronds" and of "a tragedy of black ambition in a green jungle shot with such lights from heaven and hell as no other stage has seen." Arthur Pollock of the *Brooklyn Daily Eagle* commented on the "childlike austerity" of the performance: "With all their gusto, they play Shakespeare as though they were apt children who have just discovered and adore the old man."

There were reservations, of course. Atkinson, after rhapsodizing over our "fury and phantom splendor," questioned our company's grasp of poetic tragedy: "They speak the lines conscientiously, but they have left the poetry out of them." There were others with preconceived notions of "poetic delivery" and "vocal passion," who complained of the very thing that Welles had gone to such pains to accomplish with his Negro cast: the elimination of the glib English Bensonian declamatory tradition of Shakespearean performance and a return to a simpler, more direct and rapid delivery of the dramatic verse.

Because the Negro *Macbeth*, before and after it opened, was a news event as well as a show, the most revealing reactions are to be found in reporters' rather than in critics' accounts. Martha Gellhorn, describing her visit to Harlem, saw at once that

> . . . these Negroes had taken Shakespeare to themselves and that *Macbeth* would remain in this audience's mind from now on; as a play about people living in a Haitian jungle, believing in voodoo, frightened and driven and opulent people, with shiny chocolate skins, who moved about the stage superbly, wearing costumes that belonged to them and suddenly belonged to the play. Macduff, in

the battle scenes, wore a pair of epaulets a foot wide made of heavy red cord, complemented by a pair of satin striped red and white breeches. Macbeth wore superb military costumes of canary yellow and emerald green and shining boots. Women came on and off the stage in salmon pink and purple. The impression was of a hot richness that I have almost never seen in the theater or anywhere else.

The lines were spoken without Negro accent, but in those beautiful voices made for singing; and the gestures were lavish, but not amateur or overdone. The audience sat and watched and listened as if this were a murder mystery by Edgar Wallace, only much more exciting.

Roi Ottley, a militant Negro journalist, was less concerned with these picturesque aspects than with the racial significance of the production:

> The Negro has become weary of carrying the White Man's blackface burden in the theater. In *Macbeth* he has been given the opportunity to discard the bandanna and burnt-cork casting to play a universal character . . .
>
> From the point of view of the Community, Harlem witnessed a production in which the Negro was not lampooned or made the brunt of laughter. We attended the *Macbeth* showing, happy in the thought we wouldn't again be reminded, with all its vicious implications, that we were niggers.

Like all WPA productions, *Macbeth* was judged by standards that were not purely theatrical. Percy Hammond, dean of New York drama critics, representing the city's leading Republican journal, the *Herald Tribune*, wrote what was not so much of a review as an attack on the New Deal:

> The Negro Theatre, an offshoot of the federal government and one of Uncle Sam's experimental philanthropies, gave us, last night, an exhibition of deluxe boondoggling.

He went on to ridicule the whole idea of a popular theater supported by government funds, citing the size of our cast, the brightness of our costumes and the loudness of our music as evidences of criminal extravagance and presumptuous folly. As an example of political polemic it was savage but eloquent; as a theatrical notice it was irrelevant and malignant. It did not surprise us, nor were we unduly disturbed. But there were some that were.

Early in the afternoon of April 15, the day of the *Macbeth* reviews, Orson and I were formally visited in my office by Asadata Dafora Horton and his corps of African drummers, including Abdul, the authentic witch doctor. They looked serious. Asadata was their spokesman. They were perplexed, he said, and desired guidance. He then produced a sheaf of clippings from which he detached the *Herald Tribune* review. He had read it to his men, he declared, and it was their opinion, and his, that the piece was an evil one. I agreed that it was.

"The work of an enemy?"

"The work of an enemy."

"He is a bad man?"

"A bad man."

Asadata nodded. His face was grim as he turned to his troupe, to Abdul in particular, and repeated what I had said. The men nodded, then silently withdrew. Excited by waves of praise and a line a block long at the box office, we quickly forgot both them and Percy Hammond. We stayed for that night's performance, which was better played and no less enthusiastically received than the first. We thanked the company, had a brief, violent personal row on the sidewalk over the *Times* notice in which my name had been coupled with Orson's as director, then went home to get some sleep.

It was reported to us by our disturbed house manager when we arrived at the theater around noon of the next day that the basement had been filled, during the night, with unusual drumming and with chants more weird and horrible than anything that had been heard upon the stage. Orson and I looked at each other for an instant, then quickly away again, for in the afternoon paper which we had picked up on our way uptown was a brief item announcing the sudden illness of the well-known critic Percy Hammond. He died some days later—of pneumonia, it was said.

Macbeth played for ten weeks at the Lafayette with never an empty seat, then downtown at the Adelphi on 54th Street (in competition with *Tobacco Road*, *Three Men on a Horse*, *Mulatto*, *Dead End*, *Bury the Dead*, *On Your Toes* and *New Faces of 1936*) for an additional run of two months. This move was celebrated with a six-column Hirschfeld cartoon on the front page of the *Times* Sunday drama section and brought great renown to the Negro Theatre Project, but it had one unfortunate consequence: we lost our Macbeth.

Between Jack Carter and Edna Thomas—that amazingly handsome royal couple—there flowed an old and strong emotion, protective and tender on Edna's part, filled with ambivalence on Jack's. Orson had worked to enrich their scenes with these almost incestuous overtones and to create the feeling of an alliance in crime between a middle-aged wife-mother and a passionate husband-son. Perhaps none of this came across the footlights;

if it did, it was smothered in the thunder of voodoo drums until it erupted suddenly one night on the stage of the Adelphi. For five months Jack, against all predictions, had been the mainstay of *Macbeth*. Now he began to crack. I have always believed that playing before white audiences may have had something to do with the drinking on which Jack started soon after we opened downtown; once that began, his feeling of guilt toward Orson and Edna (the two people on the project of whom he was really fond) did the rest. He knew that it upset Edna to see him drunk; he felt he was embarrassing her in their scenes together and hurting both their performances. One night as they were leaving the stage together, she started to cry. Jack went back to his dressing room for the long intermission, removed and carefully hung up his bright uniform, washed, got into his street clothes and his bespoke shoes and left the theater—and the project.

Illness and mortality being alarmingly high among Negro performers, we had carefully protected ourselves with understudies. Macbeth was doubly covered—by Maurice Ellis (Macduff) as Jack's probable successor in the role, and by our chief stage manager, Tommy Anderson (formerly of *Four Saints*), who knew every word of every part as an added cover in case of emergency. When he called the second act and found Jack's room empty, Anderson telephoned first to Orson, then to me, failed to find either of us, tore a uniform off the nearest soldier and went on as Macbeth. No announcement was made and the audience, that night, had the strange experience of seeing the first half of Shakespeare's tragedy performed by a very pale, six-foot-four hero in a glittering, bright yellow costume and the second by a dark, wiry, mustachioed, five-foot-seven Macbeth in the dark red uniform of one of Macduff's barefoot soldiers.

After running through the long, hot New York summer, *Macbeth* was sent on a triumphal national tour of WPA theaters—to Bridgeport, Hartford, Chicago, Indianapolis, Detroit, Cleveland and, surprisingly, Dallas. In Indianapolis Maurice Ellis, who was playing Macbeth, fell ill. Orson had been waiting for just this chance; he flew out and played the role in blackface for the rest of the week.

—JH

The Free Southern Theater

FOUNDED 1963

Doris Derby, Gilbert Moses and John O'Neal

How do you create theater in a cultural desert? How do you stimulate self-expression and reflective thought among a colonized people, whose access even to their own selves has been severely restricted? These were two of the questions facing Doris Derby, Gilbert Moses and John O'Neal when, along with Bill Hutchinson and, later, Richard Schechner, they founded the Free Southern Theater out of the Tougaloo College Drama Workshop in Jim Crow–era Tougaloo, Mississippi, in 1963. Two years later Schechner, a professor at Tulane University and editor of the pivotal *Tulane Drama Review*, convinced them to move the theater's center of operations to New Orleans.

Known as "a theater for those who have no theater," FST grew out of the civil rights struggle in the South in the early sixties and, in a sense, became that movement's cultural arm. Both O'Neal and Derby were field secretaries for the Student Nonviolent Coordinating Committee in Jackson, Mississippi, and taught English to nonliterate adults at Tougaloo as part of SNCC's adult literacy program. Moses, a student at Oberlin College, was in Mississippi writing for the *Mississippi Free Press*. Hutchinson taught English and theater at Tougaloo. Together they conceived a permanent company, the heart of whose operations would be a touring ensemble, bringing free theater to people who not only had no access to theater but, segregated from the dominant culture and dependent on it even for images of themselves, essentially had little opportunity to think critically about their own lives. FST would tour summers, covering as much as 4,500 miles over five states in the Deep South. As a free theater, reliant entirely on contributions, FST was forced to do most of its fundraising in the North, specifically New York. The theater's first five-dollar donation came from the poet Langston Hughes.

Free Southern was, arguably, one of America's bravest theaters, having to perform, at times, under armed guard, trying to raise political consciousness through art in parts of the South where gatherings of blacks were open to attack from the White Citizens' Council or the theoretically legitimate authorities. Starting as an integrated company it was, by its very existence, a provocation. FST artists hid in fields while Ku Klux Klan members, alerted by the local sheriff, hunted them. Their

SOURCE: As you'll see, these excerpts, like the book they come from (*The Free Southern Theater*, by The Free Southern Theater, 1969), proceed in scrapbook fashion, including official documents, narrative context and collected letters of the founders of FST and their friends and supporters.

company manager carried a gun. "In Bogalusa and Jonesboro, Louisiana, armed members of Deacons for Defense, a militant Negro organization, patrolled outside the hall, just in case," writes Julius Novick, in the aptly named 1968 book *Beyond Broadway: The Quest for Permanent Theatres*. FST was, indeed, well beyond Broadway.

At a distance of years, it's a reminder that even modern-day America has had theater companies that thrived in a system of apartheid, like the Market Theatre in Johannesburg, South Africa, or under governmental sanction and threat, like theaters of Eastern Europe in the seventies or the Belarus Free Theatre now. America has bred such courageous companies, and preeminent among them was the Free Southern Theater.

—TL

———

Doris Derby, John O'Neal and I [Gilbert Moses] met in the winter of 1963 in Jackson, Mississippi, where they were field directors for SNCC [the Student Nonviolent Coordinating Committee] and I was writing for the Mississippi *Free Press. All of us were black, all of us had been involved in theater before we came to Jackson. After we met, and first talked about the need for theater, we got to where we felt we could put down a good case for a Free Southern Theater.*

We decided that Doris, an artist, would concentrate on scenic design; John, who'd just finished his studies at Southern Illinois University, would handle the production and organization; and I would direct and train the actors. We also wanted to sponsor benefits in Jackson, and ask black stars and performers to appear. We wanted to open Jackson up, to bring people there who normally were outside of state control and police authority. We wanted freedom: for thought, and involvement and the celebration of our own culture.

A General Prospectus for the Establishment of a Free Southern Theater

We propose to establish a legitimate theater in the Deep South with its base in Jackson, Mississippi.

Our fundamental objective is to stimulate creative and reflective thought among Negroes in Mississippi and other Southern states by the establishment of a legitimate theater, thereby providing the opportunity for involvement in the theater and the associated art forms.

We theorize that within the Southern situation a theatrical form and style can be developed that is as unique to the Negro people as the origin of blues and jazz.

A combination of art and social awareness can evolve into plays written for a Negro audience, which relate to the problems within the Negro himself, and within the Negro community.

Through theater, we think to open a new area of protest. One that permits the development of playwrights and actors, one that permits the growth and self-knowledge of a Negro audience, one that supplements the present struggle for freedom.

Mississippi: The Caste System in a Cultural Desert

The above-listed objectives are set in accordance with the following observations:

1. *The development of patterns of reflective and creative thought has been restricted.*

   a. *Education*: The segregated Mississippi Public School system restricts the learning process rather than nourishes it. School textbooks are controlled, discussion of controversial topics is forbidden, teachers have no choice in school programming and are under constant supervision and pressure. It is apparent that competent teachers and honest education will not be the concern of a school system fundamentally built to keep Negroes out of white schools.

Since the majority of the schoolteachers are products of the same system, the students' legacy is inadequate training and an unclear understanding of the world in which they live.

   b. *Mass Media*: The newspapers in Mississippi are not a source of information concerning the activities of the community or of the state. The distortions of these newspapers are twofold: (1) What is not printed—any valid information about Mississippi's economics and politics, (2) what is printed—highly distorted and biased articles supporting the Mississippi "way of life." The two Negro weeklies—excluding the *Mississippi Free Press*—financed, and in one case controlled, by the same association which owns the white newspapers, fail to convey true information to the Negro community and are virtually useless and retrogressive in purpose.

      i. Television: Controlled and almost never admits controversial topics.
      ii. Radio: Jackson, Mississippi, has one Negro radio station which is dedicated to rock-and-roll.

Conclusion: The civil rights movement has greatly affected the vacuum in which the Mississippi Negro lives. Yet, it is still probable that the Negro is the last to be informed of a situation which directly concerns him. *He has been unable to develop naturally because he has found himself in a society which excludes him from its public consciousness, which is, by necessity, his own public consciousness.*

    c. *The Negro Community and Its Cultural Resources*: Although Jackson is the largest urban area in Mississippi, with a population of approximately two hundred thousand, its seventy-five thousand Negroes are without cultural resources other than one recreation center controlled by the state, one movie theater, two inadequate Ys each with one thousand members, quite a few juke joints, and about 175 churches. The municipal auditorium is closed to Negroes.

In general, the cultural institutions in Jackson are engaged in a tense struggle for which there exists no immediate solution. Working within a controlled situation, they attempt solutions to problems within the Negro community, but are unable to affect the external cause of the problems.

    Conclusion: *Mississippi's closed system effectively refuses the Negro knowledge of himself,* and has stunted the mental growth of the majority of Mississippi Negroes.

    2. *There exists a wealth of talent that has been denied the opportunity of development and expression.*
    3. *It is necessary that an education program coincide with and augment the program of the Freedom Movement.*
    4. *There will be opposition from the present power structure to the theater program.*

A Free Southern Theater

While it is true that the theater which we propose would by no means be a solution to the tremendous problems faced by the people who suffer the oppressive system in the South, we feel that the theater will add a necessary dimension to the current civil rights movement through its unique value as a means of education.

To Movement Friends in New York and Atlanta:

We have organized and are having weekly meetings of a theater workshop. Gilbert Moses is the dramatic director of the workshop; Bill Hutchinson, professor of speech and English at Tougaloo College, is the technical director; Doris Derby and myself are operating in the area of public relations and general flunkies. Doris will help coordinate the concert series.

At the present time we are meeting and working in the Tougaloo College Playhouse. The group is primarily composed of students from Tougaloo and Jackson State Colleges. We are hoping to involve more and more people as time goes by who are not the sole property of the academic community. Our attendance has averaged twenty-five people, all of whom are responding enthusiastically. Several show great promise.

If things go as hoped for, the group will be ready for public showing within two or three months and we will be able to operate a modest touring and summer stock company by summer. Several contingencies are involved, however. We're trying to feel out the faculty at Jackson State now to see to what extent they will be able to cooperate with the program.

Hopefully, we'll get the material for a repertory company from this workshop which will be a permanent part of our program from now on. As we get people committed to the theater some means must be found for their support, if we are not able to raise enough money to provide for their subsistence.

I am in the process of negotiating with the local representative of S. B. Fuller products, whereby we may have a franchise for the door-to-door sale of his products in a given area. In such a manner the group could work and pay for itself and still be in control of our own time.

At the present time we have accumulated a total of three scripts for consideration, aside from stuff that either Gil or myself have done; two from Langston Hughes, *Jericho-Jim Crow* and *Don't You Want to Be Free*; and one from Nancy Henderson, with whom Gil spent some time in New York: *Lo, the Angel*. None of these seem appropriate for the kind of thing we want to do. We therefore are in need of scripts. All kinds of stuff, especially material from Young Black Cats who heretofore have not had the opportunity to have their plays considered for production. Material from old "established cats" would, of course, be all right. We have been promised material from John Killens, James Baldwin, Ossie Davis and Ted Shine already. They should all be reminded of our needs in this regard.

So concludes this report kind of thing.

Yours for a Free Southern Theater,
John O'Neal

. . .

March 9, 1964

To Carol Feinman:

Carol, I hope to arrive in New York either the 12 or 13 of March, to stay for a week and a half.

Why I am coming:

3. To talk, discuss, make plans for, see about immediate fundraising.
4. To finalize acquisition of technical equipment.
5. To help gather sponsors.
6. Gather new scripts where I may
7. and because there is a free ride leaving out of here at six o'clock in the morning.
8. To breathe freely, for a while, for a change.
9. To take a look-see at publicity.
10. I am dying, utterly, uncontestably (well, *incontestablement*).

It will be a very difficult trip. I see a picture of myself prancing around New York, talking about the theater in Mississippi . . . I feel like a vaudeville barker. Exhorting spectators to pay their dues. Step right up and see the fire next time in Mississippi.

Like the rest of America is about to pay their way to see a bullfight, to see the lions clawing the Christians.

Did you see the SNCC advertisement (on the back of the *Progressive* for March)? "It takes more than courage . . . to face the combined forces of the resistant South." The reason that this line returns to mind is due to its sadistic implications. This frank and bleeding statement as if the federal government didn't exist . . . as if the South were another country, an underdeveloped country, South Africa, apartheid, the SNCC Mau Maus. More than that—it is a new approach to civil rights—casual; understated, sits you back on your reflective haunches, softens the emotional tone of the movement, the freedom struggle, almost puts it in its properly crude and harsh context: a calculated battle, bloody, the Jews and Hitler, the Italians and Ethiopia, early Americans and the Indians, flesh against flesh, a broken head, "Get on out of here, Nigger, I'm the justice here." Broken teeth, a prison cell, a shotgun in the back.

Step right up. Hear the clanker and strut of tanks, the fattening of army ranks, the strained cries of a black face whipped with chains, as we in Mississippi prepare for war.

Pay your dues and watch.

Gil

.   .   .

John Baby,

   . . . Baby I know you are going to make it and that the letter you wrote to me is just one expressing that temporary fright before you unleash de blood hounds of hell and scrounge all available asses in to the barn and explode with the theater. You can do it. You will do it. You must do it. Wail, mother—dear.

   Tell Gil to cancel them got-to be-damned plans about going back to school. We learn where it's at and if it ain't at Jackson, Mississippi, it ain't no-where. All of New York is buzzing. There will be money to carry on. And there will be talent galore, so much so that traffic cops will be needed to direct the Nothingham Northerners in and out of the place. You guys stumbled onto the most exciting idea of the Movement in a century. It would be a crime against nature if you strayed away from this promise just to go to school. Please baby . . . please.

   Sit down and put your heart and soul into an article telling the folks why the rocks are crying out for a theater of the people and by the people and for the people. Wail, baby! [. . .]

Love,
Len[14]

. . .

Gilbert Moses: *We wanted the theater to deal with black artists and the black audience. But its political aims reflected the political aims of the Movement at that time: integration. One of the first steps of rebelling against the Southern society, then, was to make an effort to integrate anything. A large part of the excitement generated by the idea for the theater was centered around the fact that it would be integration operating in the Deep South, and integration operating in the mainly unintegrated American theater. So two generic ideas were in conflict from the beginning: The development of a black style of theater (or whatever term we came up with to call what we were doing), and an "integrated" theater, based on preexisting structures. We sent a copy of our prospectus to Richard Schechner, who was then professor of drama at Tulane University in New Orleans. Richard's brother Bill had been a roommate of mine at Oberlin.*

February 19, 1964
Dear Miss Derby, Mr. Moses and Mr. O'Neal,

   I tried to phone you just before I left for New York, but was unable to reach you—so this letter is a substitute. I have your plans in my hand and have read them over, and I am very impressed. I even discussed them briefly

14. Len Holt, a SNCC lawyer.

with some friends in the New York theater. I think the idea of bringing live theater, either as a separate program, or as part of the rallies, to Mississippi towns can have a real and important effect on the whole civil rights movement there; the idea is: (1) dignity and pride, and (2) social action.

If you can get the people I can arrange to spend a good part of June in Jackson directing a play or two so that you can perform them in Jackson and around Mississippi—any play you choose; my body and talents, so much as I have, are yours. I can't spend the whole summer, I have a book to finish, and work here to do, but June is yours.

Richard Schechner

Gilbert Moses: *Richard came to Jackson that June, John and I put him up on a makeshift bed in the corner of our living room, and the three of us settled into a three-day marathon meeting that resulted in Richard's acceptance of our offer to become a third producing director and the making of a new prospectus by the three of us, this one designed to raise money.*

The Free Southern Theater Fundraising Brochure

For the first time, live, integrated theater is being established in the Deep South. The Free Southern Theater of Tougaloo College[15] this fall begins its initial season with a permanent ensemble company in Jackson, Mississippi. The company will tour rural Mississippi, Alabama, Georgia and neighboring states, performing for Negro and, when possible, integrated audiences. Later, other Free Southern Theaters will be established in other states.

The plays: dramas concerned with the political and moral dilemma of our time, by such authors as James Baldwin, Bertolt Brecht, Ossie Davis and Langston Hughes, as well as musicals, comedies, classical works and improvisations.

The stage: specially equipped halls, churches, barns, fields—wherever there is space and an audience.

The companies: participants from local communities and, with the cooperation of appropriate unions, professional actors, directors and technicians.

By themselves, protest and political action cannot sufficiently alter the present situation. In the South today, there is an educational and cultural void which must be filled. For this purpose the theater is uniquely equipped.

---

15. Tougaloo, an accredited interracial college outside the jurisdiction of the Mississippi State Legislature, provided support to the FST in many vital areas. Because of this support, the FST, in its pilot project, called itself the Free Southern Theater of Tougaloo.

The Free Southern Theater will act as a stimulus to the critical thought necessary for effective participation in a democratic society.

The Free Southern Theater can:

- Promote the growth and self-knowledge of a new Southern audience of Negroes and whites;
- Liberate creative talent that has been denied the opportunity of development and expression;
- Provide a forum in which the Negro playwright can deal honestly with his own experience, express himself in what may prove to be a new idiom, a new genre, a theatrical form and style as unique as blues, jazz and gospel;
- Emphasize the universality of the problems of the Negro people
- Strengthen communication among Southern Negroes;
- Add a cultural and educational dimension to the present Southern freedom movement;
- Assert that self-knowledge and creativity are the foundations of human dignity.

The Free Southern Theater will run from September through June, presenting five plays the first season. Because of low incomes and community structure in Mississippi, the performances will be free of charge.

The Free Southern Theater will be structurally and administratively independent, with a National Board of Sponsors and a Local Board of Patrons. The National Board will provide artistic consultation and fiscal guidance, encourage the participation of professionals and assist in fundraising efforts; the Local Board will be concerned with the needs of its particular theater, enlisting the support and participation of the community.

The Free Southern Theater depends entirely on private donations. Contributions are tax deductible.

· · ·

July 11, 1964
Dear Richard,

John and I realized that we had never tried to start a theater in Jackson. Anyway, we've been dying of inactivity, atrophic. Some of us (me) have substituted this theater for our own creativity!

So, to assuage this situation, and because it is just a good thing, we're beginning with *In White America* immediately.

We're using a few local actors and one professional, Susan Tabor. Jackie Washington, a young folk singer from Boston with one Vanguard recording to his credit, will play the guitar. I will direct. John O'Neal will act and produce. It will be a simple production and we'll take it to the Freedom Schools[16] and communities.

Gilbert

July 14, 1964
Dear Gil and John,

Your letter received. Work must commence. Because you have not run a theater before is no proof that you shouldn't/can't run one now. In fact you have to run it.

You say [in another letter] that the final decision on New Orleans will be determined by your tour. We have already made that "final decision." The money-raising proposals and my participation depend upon New Orleans. If that decision is to be changed—and I certainly hope it is not—you must let me know at once. I am not about to make a fool of myself and spend vital energies only to find out that the theater has vanished. I mean—to keep my personal commitments out of this for the moment—I don't want to solicit money in formal proposals which must be written out and speak to the president of Tulane University about a plan that is not agreed on. We decided on the New Orleans move, the money from Rockefeller and Ford is geared that way, etc. Quite frankly: just as you have invested your personal lives in this thing, I have invested mine. The contacts in the theater which I have are good for one time only. If the project succeeds these contacts will continue to be helpful. If the project fails for the *wrong reasons*—inefficiency, incompetence—there will be no further help coming from these people. We can't call on Mac Lowry, Kazan, etc., twice. If the theater fails for the right reasons—harassment, lack of community interest—that's a different matter. I see no reason for it to fail for the "right reasons." We can make it go. But we must work. *IN WHITE AMERICA* IS A GOOD IDEA IF COUPLED WITH THE LARGER PROJECT IF IT IS TRULY A "PILOT" OF THE FST. To make it part of the larger project it must end its tour in New Orleans and work must begin there on the facility.

Damn it, you had this great idea for a theater—don't let it throw you now, and don't go back to the time-wasting, one show now one show later, amateur idea. Get the grand idea to work. And then we'll all be able to work *in the theater* and to achieve the Movement goals we all want to achieve.

16. Founded as part of the civil rights movement and located primarily in the South, the Freedom Schools were free, alternative schools for African Americans, aimed, like FST, at fostering social, political and economic equality.

Keep in close touch, because lack of communications can be killing. It has already damaged our faith in each other. I have lost faith in you doing what you are in Mississippi to do—namely to lay the groundwork for *the continued and long-range success of the FST*. Your production of *In White America* can dovetail brilliantly into this if you capitalize on its opportunities. You have lost faith in my cooperating with you, believing, I am sure, that I have "taken over" the theater. That can only be true if you allow me to take it over.

If I lose faith in you or if you lose faith in me then there will be no theater. Neither "your" FST nor "my" FST—nothing; there will only be wrecked feelings, misspent money and frustration. And no one, least of all the people we want to get to, will benefit. These are axioms; they are not debatable.

What must be done now is to repair the gap in our communications, to get to New Orleans with your production, to arrange the facility, to contact the community, to pick our plays for the season, to pick the core of our actors. THEN WE CAN TRULY BEGIN THE THEATER WORK.

Atrophy will only atrophy you more. It is a continuous, contagious disease and must be treated. You're right when you say that work is the cure. But that work must fit into the larger project. And that larger project is a theater that will endure and grow for many years.

I expect to hear from you at once on these things.

Richard

July 19, 1964
Dear Richard,

Your questions and anxieties are well and correctly directed.

The main fault is the breakdown in communication—you are unable to know what we're doing—and we are unfamiliar with your activities.

What we are doing now is an extremely important step in the larger idea of the FST for us. It is the realization in part of the original ideas—TO PRESENT PLAYS THIS SUMMER FOR FREEDOM SCHOOLS AND COMMUNITIES. It will allow us to make contacts in the best manner for the future FST tour. Rather than presenting an idea to the people here who are already disillusioned, who distrust new ideas, who are ignorant of the goals of the FST, we have something real to give them, and a promise of an even better example later.

When we come to them in December we will neither be seeing the people nor the stages we must play in for the first time. During this tour we will also search for talent. Who knows what we'll find.

This production will be simple—with a few lights and one platform, hardly one which we will be able to present in N.O. Although we must make publicity contacts in N.O. in re this production, I suggest we confine performance to Mississippi. We also fear the lack of time. For after this production, all attention must be turned towards N.O. and setting up the year's program.

Only one actor is professional, Susan Tabor, Equity; the rest are college recruits from the Summer Project.[17] These students have their own source of income, so the only expense will be travel. I have already written to Erika [Munk, managing editor of *TDR*], and will go to N.O. July 22, 23, 24, to make initial facility contacts.

When you read our proposed touring schedule, you will understand that we are in the process of mobilizing an audience for the FST. The first performance here in Jackson will be to a selected audience only. Three very prominent local Negroes are sending out invitations (donations requested at the performance) and are heading a theater committee in Jackson.

For us, these are the priorities: (1) to mount *In White America*, (2) to familiarize our public with FST, (3) to select facilities in N.O., (4) to choose the plays which will be done (for only then will we be able to select our company—when we have some idea of who we will need), (5) to select the company.

When I say *In White America* is important to us, I mean that O'Neal and I have a commitment to Mississippi. This production not only fulfills this commitment to Mississippi, and to the people who are interested in and working for the FST in New York, but to ourselves, as initiators of this idea. We have been to a large part paralyzed by the FST's bigness, by its importance, by the fact that under any and all circumstances *it must not fail* . . .

Please, I am not afraid to play the fool. In a sense, to spin such a golden web in New York when nothing has been accomplished in the South is to play the fool. We are tired of our parts. You say people have all along asked, "What are they doing now?" and "What will they be doing this summer?" and you were dumbfounded—*WELL, NOW YOU HAVE SOMETHING PROUD TO POINT TO!* You may say, "There is a simple pilot project now in Mississippi—one which will take stock of our audiences—one which will set up contacts and playing places—one which will insure protection for our official theater, etc., etc.

Never did we consider the FST not a dangerous undertaking. In talking to everyone we have stated that everything will be done to lessen this danger. We are now going to court this danger and *WE NEED YOUR SUPPORT.*

A sense of timing is extremely important. Both John and I feel that the time for a production is *NOW.*

17. Another name for Freedom Summer, the campaign begun in June 1964 to register black voters in Mississippi, where they had for years been systematically excluded from the democratic process.

You reiterate that the FST is a great idea. You know that ideas have no dimension and that the people behind them must supply their depth. Then it follows that what must be backed is people. You are at the moment not only backing yourself but *me and John*. There are obvious deficiencies on our end—age, experience, indecisiveness, yet we are determined and committed to this theater.

Your concerns are correct. Continue writing. We feel at this point we are doing a great deal of hard and important work. Besides, we are about to play the most exciting theatrical circuit in America. We will send weekly reports.

Gilbert

—DD, GM, JO

El Teatro Campesino

FOUNDED 1965

Luis Miguel Valdez

As *Times Saturday Review* critic Irving Wardle put it, seeing El Teatro Campesino was "like being in at the birth of commedia dell'arte. I have never seen any company with the capacity to create theater out of thin air." El Teatro Campesino was begun not just to create theater but also to create culture—Chicano culture—even as it drew on and explored the cultural roots that already existed.

Its founding was as local, as time-bound as one can be—in the migrant workers' camps of Delano, California, in 1965, in the early days of the grape pickers' strike against the Di Giorgio company and other growers, who refused to recognize the National Farm Workers Association. Cesar Chavez, NFWA's founder, led the strike, and Luis Valdez, a twenty-five-year-old man, born and raised in the workers' shanties of Delano before becoming the first in his family to graduate from college—San Jose State—became the leader of the strike's cultural wing, El Teatro Campesino, the Farmworkers Theatre. Having joined the San Francisco Mime Troupe out of college, Valdez returned to Delano when the strike began, as if answering a call.

SOURCE: "The Flat Bed Truck Years 1965–1970," by Luis Miguel Valdez, was first published in *Ramparts* magazine, July 1966.

The stages were flatbed trucks parked in the middle of the fields. The performers were young artists, amateurs and the workers themselves. They "rehearsed on the run and performed on the picket line," as Valdez puts it. The short sketches, or *actos*, were part expression, part protest and part entertainment, the beginning of a still-kicking attempt to create a new American audience made up of Chicano migrant workers, Filipinos and Mexicans—some literate, some not, some bilingual, some speaking only Spanish. The stories were theirs, as were the struggles. This was theater of, by and for farm workers.

Over the years, the reach of El Teatro Campesino's groundbreaking work, and Valdez's energy, vision and commitment as a playwright, director and activist, has profoundly influenced the American theater, as well as the film and television industries. These are Valdez's earliest writings for the theater, handbills announcing their activities and describing their goals and the theatrical means of achieving them.

—TL

El Teatro Campesino is somewhere between Brecht and Cantinflas. It is a farm workers' theater, a bilingual propaganda theater, but it borrows from Mexican folk humor to such an extent that its "propaganda" is salted with a wariness for human caprice. Linked by a cultural umbilical cord to the National Farm Workers Association, the Teatro lives in Delano as part of a social movement. We perform for the grape strikers at our weekly meetings, seek to clarify strike aims, and go on tour throughout the state publicizing and raising funds for the Huelga.[18]

Our most important aim is to reach the farm workers. All the actors are farm workers, and our single topic is the Huelga. We must create our own material, but this is hardly a limitation. Neither is our concentration on the strike. The hardest thing at first was finding limits, some kind of dramatic form, within which to work. Working together, we developed what we call *actos*—ten- to fifteen-minute skits, sometimes with and sometimes without songs. We insist on calling them *actos* rather than *skits*, not only because we talk in Spanish most of the time, but because *skit* seems too light a word for the work we are trying to do.

Starting from scratch with a real-life incident, character or idea, everybody in the Teatro contributes to the development of an *acto*. Each is intended to make at least one specific point about the strike, but improvisations during each performance sharpen, alter or embellish the original idea.

18. Strike.

We use no scenery, no scripts and no curtain. We use costumes and props only casually—an old pair of pants, a wine bottle, a pair of dark glasses, a mask—but mostly we like to show we are still strikers underneath, armbands and all. This effect is very important to our aims. To simplify things, we hang signs around our necks, sometimes in black and white, sometimes in lively colors, indicating the characters portrayed.

Practicing our own brand of commedia dell'arte, we improvise within the framework of traditional characters associated with the strike. Instead of Arlecchinos, Pantalones and Brighellas, we have *Esquiroles* (scabs), *Contratistas* (contractors), *Patroncitos* (growers) and *Huelguistas* (strikers). We have experimented with these four types in dozens of combinations. Being free to act as they will, to infuse a character type with real thought and feeling, the farm workers of the Teatro have expressed the human complexity of the grape strike. This is where Brecht comes in. As propaganda, the Teatro is loyal to an a priori social end: i.e., the winning of the strike. We not only presume Our Cause is just; we know it.

Every member of the Teatro, however, knows it differently. We vary in age from eighteen to forty-four, with drastically different degrees of education, but we are all drawn into the Teatro by a common enthusiasm to express what we individually know and feel. The freedom to do so lifts our propaganda into Brecht-like theater: Our Just Cause is many-faceted, like human nature.

The Teatro appeals to its actors for the same reason it appeals to its audience. It explores the meaning of a social movement without asking its participants to read or write. It is a learning experience with no formal prerequisites. This is all-important because most farm workers have never had a chance to go to school and are alienated by classrooms, blackboards and the formal teacher-student approach.

By contrast, our Cantinflas-inspired burlesque is familiar to the farm workers. It is in the family; it is *raza*; it is part of the Mexican people. They know that the Teatro discusses the Huelga, but the actors are fellow farm workers and strikers, not teachers. If the Teatro has a point to make, it is just a step ahead of the audience, and the audience takes the step easily.

In a Mexican way, we have discovered what Brecht is all about. If you want unbourgeois theater, find unbourgeois people to do it. Your head could burst open at the simplicity of the act, not the thought, but that's the way it is in Delano. Real theater lies in the excited laughter (or silence) of recognition *in the audience*, not in all the paraphernalia on the stage. Minus actors, the entire Teatro can be packed into one trunk, and when the Teatro goes on tour, the spirit of the Delano grape strike goes with it.

Last March and April, the Teatro toured with the pilgrimage from Delano to Sacramento. Part of the purpose of the *peregrinación* was to "turn on" the farm workers of the San Joaquin Valley, to expose them to our growing Huelga movement. The Teatro performed nightly at all the rallies we held in more than twenty farm worker towns. The response of the audience to the Teatro in all of these towns was a small triumph, within the greater triumph of the NFWA march.

Perhaps the best key to the "theater" of the Teatro Campesino is a description of our most successful performance on the pilgrimage. It occurred in Freeport, a small town just nine miles southwest of Sacramento. We were to arrive at the Capitol in two days, and Governor Brown had just refused to meet with us on Easter Sunday. He had previously promised he would meet the pilgrimage somewhere on the road, but that was off too.

The Teatro Campesino decided to bring the governor to the rally that same night. We revamped an old skit we had on Governor Brown, also involving the "Di Gorgio Fruit Corp." and "Schunley." The "Schunley" character was dropped because Schenley Industries had recognized the NFWA as its workers' sole bargaining agent two days before. We replaced "Schunley" with another grower type, a "Mr. Zunavuvich," which—believe it or not—sounds incredibly like the name of a ranching family in Delano. To supplement Zunavuvich, and to hit at another Di Giorgio interest, we introduced a new character, "Bank Amerika."

When the time for the Teatro came, the "Di Gorgio" character—complete with sign, dark glasses and cigar—leaped onto the one-and-a-half-ton truck used as a stage for the nightly rallies, and was quickly booed and reviled by the farm worker audience of over three thousand. Threatening them with loss of their jobs, blackballing and deportation, Di Gorgio blustered and guffawed his way through all the booing, and announced that his old high school buddy, the governor, was coming to speak to them that same night, and in Spanish. At this point, a car with a siren and a loudspeaker drove up behind the audience, honking and moving toward the platform. An authoritative voice commanded the workers to move out of the way, and the outside rally was momentarily halted as "Governor Brown" was pulled out of his car by his cronies and pushed onto the stage. The "governor" protested all the way that he couldn't speak Spanish, but Di Gorgio, Zunavuvich and Bank Amerika convinced him to try:

"*No Huelga*," they exhorted, "just say *no Huelga!*"

"And no *boycoteo*," insisted Di Gorgio.

The "governor"—played by long, thin, dark Agustin Lira wearing a huge fake paunch—not only spoke Spanish, though brokenly at first, he spoke so ardently that he turned into a Mexican. This is the turning point of the *acto*. Di Gorgio and his friends were forced to drag the metamorphosed governor off the stage, as he shouted, "Huelga! Huelga!" all the way down, to the laughter and applause of the farm worker audience.

It has never been easy to measure the actual effect of the Teatro as serious social propaganda, but we do receive indirect reports occasionally. After one Bakersfield performance we were told that two scabs vowed never to come to Delano as strikebreakers again, and they cited the Teatro's satire as the reason for their change of heart. More encouraging than anything is that farm workers on the march, as Delano strikers have been doing every week now for five months, kept asking, "Is there going to be a Teatro tonight?"

The first striker to join the Teatro was twenty-one-year-old Agustin Lira. An irrepressible songwriter and guitar player, Augie was born in Torreon, Coahuila, Mexico. He has been a farm worker all his life, following the crops from Texas to California with his mother and seven brothers and sisters. He was packing grapes in the Fresno area when the strike started in Delano. He joined it in the second week. Proud and rebellious, he expresses a fierce loyalty to the *raza* through his gentle and sensitive songs.

Stage manager and mask-maker of the group is Errol Franklin, twenty-eight, a native of Cheyenne, Wyoming, who prefers to think of himself as a cowboy. He has traveled far and wide across the United States, and has worked as a horse breaker, fisherman, apple picker, tomato picker, short order cook, waiter and longshoreman. Some months ago, he came to Delano to pick scab grapes, but joined the strike when the roving picket line arrived at the vineyard where he was working. He is proud of his Indian blood and is a good man with a tall tale. About two feet taller than the rest of us, he usually plays a rancher or a cop in the *actos*, lifting or pushing people as the situation demands.

Felipe Cantu, forty-four, is a comic genius. A family man and farm worker of practically no formal education, he was born and raised in Nuevo León, Mexico. He now lives in Delano with his wife and seven children. Felipe made his talents apparent on the picket line, where lively dialogues between pickets on the road and scabs in the field inspired his Mexican wit. He claims to have been everything from a "policeman to a clown" in Mexico, and resembles a Mexican version of Ben Turpin. Still, he can be a deeply serious man, especially when the well-being of his family is concerned. He speaks no English, but his wild, extravagant Cantinflas-like comic style needs no words. His tour de force is the role of a drunken scab who is needled by another character, his conscience, who reads him Jack London's "Definition of a Strike-Breaker" in Spanish.

Gilbert Rubio, eighteen, another valued member of the troupe, is third in a family of thirteen, born and raised in Lubbock, Texas. His family moved to California two years ago because there was no work in their home state, where many farm workers are still receiving fifty cents an hour for their labor. Always eager to learn, Gilbert got his chance to act as the rotten, smelly grape in the "Tres Uvas" *acto*. He sings, too.

These men are only a few of the many farm workers who have participated in the Teatro. Unfortunately for the Teatro, the actors, encouraged to express themselves, often showed leadership potential and were put to work doing other things for the association. Some of our best natural talents have been sent to organize or boycott in Los Angeles, San Francisco and as far away as Texas.

The Teatro by its mere existence condemns the real loss of human talent, the deadening of the human spirit, the brutalization of mind and body caused by the callous, feudal exploitation that is farm labor today. Beyond that we can now afford to laugh as free men. The Teatro Campesino lives and grows in that laughter.

—LMV

The Negro Ensemble Company
FOUNDED 1967

Douglas Turner Ward

In the summer of 1966, Douglas Turner Ward, an African American playwright, actor and director, was asked to write an essay for the *New York Times* on the place of the black artist in the American theater. He answered with a manifesto: "American Theater: For Whites Only?" In it he called for the "development of a permanent Negro repertory company." His call was answered.

By the following spring, with an initial grant of $434,000 from the Ford Foundation to cover the theater's entire operations (the first of approximately $1.2 million in Ford money over three years), the Negro Ensemble Company had been formed with a resident ensemble of fifteen, a training program for the acting company, a workshop for the education of an apprentice company and a playwrights' unit, to cultivate African American artists. This combination of production company and training program would present plays

SOURCE: "For Whites Only?" by Douglas Turner Ward, was first published in the *New York Times*, on August 14, 1966.

relevant to the black experience, train personnel for all areas of the theater, and cultivate what Ward calls "a sufficient audience of *other* Negroes."

In a sense, the Ford money brought the NEC to instant life, but the theater already had artistic and educational foundations. Robert Hooks, an actor best known for his performance as Clay in LeRoi Jones/Amiri Baraka's *The Dutchman*, had torn down the walls of his Lower West Side Manhattan apartment to begin a Group Theatre Workshop to teach acting for free to neighborhood kids. Out of this workshop grew the partnership between Hooks, Ward and manager Gerald Krone that became the governing administration of NEC. This partnership also led to the production of Ward's double bill of one-act plays, *Happy Ending* and *Day of Absence*, which ran more than five hundred performances Off Broadway, developing a reputation for Ward and inspiring the *Times* invitation. Thus began the most influential black theater in our nation's history—home and launching pad to more than two hundred new plays and four thousand black artists, and the birthplace of some of the most important and lauded plays of the 1970s and 1980s.

—TL

———

For Whites Only?

During the last decade—coinciding with the explosion of Negro Civil Rights movements into public consciousness—a number of Negro playwrights have gained considerable notice. Louis Peterson, Lorraine Hansberry, Ossie Davis, James Baldwin, LeRoi Jones and others . . . collectors of awards and honors . . . a few catapulted into international fame and dramatic prominence . . . critical barometers and Geiger counters whipped out to gauge possible winds, trends and resulting fallout.

However, this flurry of attention has tended to misrepresent the real status of Negro playwrights. Despite an eminent handful, Negro dramatists remain sparse in number, productions sporadic at most, and scripts too few to indicate discernible trends. Moreover, even when deemed successful— the critical and financial rewards reaped by *A Raisin in the Sun* excepted, and on a smaller scale, LeRoi Jones's *Dutchman*—few productions have managed to recoup capitalization. No, the millennium has not been reached.

Many factors contribute to this situation but, surveying the total landscape of American theater, results could hardly be otherwise.

The legitimate theater, that fabulous invalid which, compared to its electronic bedpartner, is still dreamed of as the repository of high culture and artistic achievement in America, hardly qualifies when examined from a Negro viewpoint.

Tirelessly, predictably, almost repetitiously on cue, theater critics and other Jeremiahs deplore rampant commercialism, the monopoly of escapist musicals, frothy comedies and the inadequacy of experimental ventures. They also leave the impression that a little minor surgery would work wonders, that palliatives could restore health. But the patient is sicker than even the most pessimistic diagnosis suggests. No matter how severe their prognosis, pundits seldom question the basic structures or assumptions of the theater.

With rare exceptions—an occasional native play of quality, or intermittent foreign infusions—American legit theater, even at its most ambitious seriousness, is essentially a theater of the Bourgeois, by the Bourgeois, about the Bourgeois and for the Bourgeois. A pretentious theater elevating the narrow preoccupations of restricted class interests to inflated universal significance, tacitly assuming that its middle-class, affluent-oriented absorptions are central to the dominant human condition. A theater rarely embracing broader frames of reference or more inclusive concerns. A theater—even if it tried—incapable of engaging the attention of anyone not so fortunate as to possess a college diploma or five-figure salary.

More specifically, a theater in its lofty modern niche—Broadway, Off Broadway, Off-Off Broadway, Happenings-land, wherever—overwhelmingly riddled with works of in-group concerns, belles-lettres pomposity, instant despair, stultifying boredom, humorless humor, hasty-pudding hijinks and pseudo-absurdity.

A Theater of Diversion—a diversionary theater, whose main problem is not that it's too safe, but that it is surpassingly irrelevant.

Occasional productions of stature and significance must usually display a cachet of foreign authorship and reputation to justify presentation.

Maybe this is all as it should be: computer consensus—as yet—doesn't spawn meaningful plays; the most powerful country in the Western world doesn't necessarily usher in a golden age of drama.

It is not surprising that the Negro playwright and the power of his potential fit only peripherally into this spectrum. By his mere historical placement in American society, the Negro exists as a disturbing presence, an embarrassment to majority comfort, an actuality deflating pretenses, an implicit witness and cogent critic too immediate for attention.

Also, just as in real life, a black playwright—sight unseen, play unheard—is soothsayed as too bothersome a prod to the sleeping conscience of numerical superiors. The stage establishment, like Hollywood, consigns even the most innocuous Negro subject to an ogre-category of problem drama. Even sympathetic advisers constantly bug the dark craftsman to shun racial themes and aspire to that pantheon of Olympian universality which all white playwrights, ironically enough, can enter by merely getting themselves born. As one naive, well-meaning, but frighteningly boorish scribe put it— "No longer Negro playwright, just playwright." Whoever heard of batting an eyelash of lower-caste condescension when Sean O'Casey is mentioned as an Irish playwright?

That the Negro playwright is more or less excluded from legit boulevards is not a revelation for concern. More important is the fact that, even when produced within this environment, the very essence of his creative function is jeopardized. His plays stand to be witnessed and assessed by a majority least equipped to understand his intentions, woefully apathetic or anesthetized to his experience, often prone to distort his purpose. Spectators who, though afflicted with self-imposed ignorance, demand to be taught ABCs at the very moment when the writer is impatient to explore the algebra of his thematic equations. Observers, even when most sympathetic, whose attitudes have been repeatedly shaped by preconceptions and misconceptions, warped by superficial clichés and platitudes—liberal, conservative or radical though they may be. Catering to such insistence presages barren results. With imagination short-circuited, valuable time is wasted clueing in, exposition is demanded when action should be unfolding, the obvious must be over-illustrated, and fantasy literalized.

Finally, when the curtain descends, whether the writer has pampered illusions, lectured ignorance, comforted fears, shouted for attention or flagellated consciences, probability dictates his defeat and the victory of customers—triumphantly intact in their limitations. With tears dried, the shouting quieted or the aches of the cat-o'-nine-tails subsided, the writer has been neatly appropriated, usurped, his creativity subverted.

For those Negro playwrights eager to volunteer for this function, there's no advice to offer. They know the rules, they play the game and take their chances.

But for a Negro playwright committed to examining the contours, contexts and depths of his experiences from an unfettered, imaginative Negro angle of vision, the screaming need is for a sufficient audience of *other Negroes*, better informed through commonly shared experience to readily understand, debate, confirm or reject the truth or falsity of his creative explorations. Not necessarily an all-black audience to the exclusion of whites but, for the playwright, certainly his primary audience, the first persons of his address, potentially the most advanced, the most responsive or most critical. Only through their initial and continuous participation can his intent and purpose be best perceived by others.

The validity of this premise has been borne out previously in other productions and, most recently, during the current run of my own plays, *Happy Ending* and *Day of Absence*, two works of satirical content written from an unapologetic Negro viewpoint. Throughout the run, Negro attendance has averaged close to fifty percent—hundreds witnessing a professional play for the first time. Besides contributing immeasurably to the longevity of the run, the freshness of their response, immediacy of involvement and spontaneity of participation have significantly underscored the essence of the works themselves and provided crucial illuminations for others. With Negroes responding all around, white spectators, congenitally uneasy in the presence of Negro satire, at least can't fail to get the message.

Any future hope for the Negro playwright depends upon whether or not this minuscule, singular, all-too-infrequent experience can be extended, multiplied and made permanent. As long as the Negro playwright remains totally dependent on existing outlets, he stands to continue as a pauper begging sustenance, never knowing from day to day, year to year, whether a few scraps will be tossed his way. Even burgeoning, tax-supported, privately endowed repertory companies are beyond the reach of his ambition (imagine rushing to present *Day of Absence* or any other work which would require jobbing in fifteen Negro actors when your roster only allows for two or three at most—often tokens at that).

Eventually, an all-embracing, all-encompassing theater of Negro identity, organized as an adjunct of some Negro community, might ideally solve the Negro dramatists' dilemma, but such a development—to me—must arise as part of a massive effort to reconstruct the urban ghetto. Small-scale cultural islands in the midst of the ghettos, separate and apart from a committed program of social and economic revitalization of slums, are doomed to exotic isolation.

Meanwhile, potential talent ready for exercise cannot wait. Without engagement, it lies dormant, stillborn. Time passes, aging proceeds. The talent withers and eventually dies of non-use.

If any hope, outside of chance individual fortune, exists for Negro playwrights as a group—or, for that matter, Negro actors and other theater craftsmen—the most immediate, pressing, practical, absolutely minimally essential active first step is the development of a permanent Negro repertory company of at least Off Broadway size and dimension. Not in the future, but now.

A theater evolving not out of negative need, but positive potential; better equipped to employ existing talents and spur the development of future ones. A theater whose justification is not the gap it fills, but the achievement it aspires toward—no less high than any other comparable theater company of present or past world fame.

A theater concentrating primarily on themes of Negro life, but also resilient enough to incorporate and interpret the best of world drama—whatever the source. A theater of permanence, continuity and consistency, providing the necessary home base for the Negro artist to launch a campaign to win his ignored brothers and sisters as constant witnesses to his endeavors.

This is not a plea for either.

This is not a plea for either a segregated theater or a separatist one. Negroes constitute a numerical minority, but Negro experience from slavery to Civil Rights has always been of crucial importance to America's existence. There's no reason why whites could not participate in a theater dedicated to exploring and illuminating that experience if they found inspiration in the purpose.

Also, just as the intrusion of lower middle-class and working-class voices reinvigorated polite, effete English drama, so might the Negro, a most potential agent of vitality, infuse life into the moribund corpus of American theater.

—DTW

The National Theatre of the Deaf

FOUNDED 1967

Bernard Bragg

It's hard to think about the National Theatre of the Deaf without picturing it before you—the physical impression made by NTD's performers is indelible. Blending American Sign Language, visual vernacular, mime, dance, gymnastics and just plain theatrical storytelling, this company relies on the wildly expressive bodies and faces of its actors. NTD began in 1967, under the umbrella of the Eugene O'Neill Theater Center in Waterford, Connecticut, as a way of bringing the rich visual language of the deaf to audiences.

The idea of a theater that would employ deaf performers and improve the image of the deaf in the hearing world was not a new one. Government leaders such as Mary Switzer of Social and Rehabilitation Services and Edna Simon Levine, a psychologist for the deaf, were part of that dreaming, as was the actress Anne Bancroft, after

SOURCE: "The Premiere," by Bernard Bragg (portions as signed to Eugene Bergman), is from *Lessons in Laughter: The Autobiography of a Deaf Actor*, 1989.

she played Anne Sullivan in William Gibson's *The Miracle Worker*, the first Broadway show to include sign language. The idea found the right champion in the person of theater designer David Hays, who had been, the story goes, inspired by a student performance of *Our Town* he saw at Gallaudet University.

Hays was the founder of NTD, and for decades its driving force, but here the story of that theater's genesis is told by a different founding member and principal actor and adaptor, Bernard Bragg, a leading light of the company. Bragg was originally invited by Hays to perform on an NBC-TV special to introduce the nascent company to the nation. He was instrumental, in 1968, in the formation of the Little Theatre of the Deaf, the young people's theater wing of NTD. The company utilized both television and the stage to launch, and was known, initially, for its adaptations of such classics as *Volpone*, *Woyzeck*, *Gilgamesh*, *The Three Musketeers* and *Under Milk Wood*. In 1971, NTD presented its first original, devised work, *My Third Eye*. The company has been touring, nationally and internationally, since its founding, and is one of the longest continuing touring companies in the U.S., seen by deaf audiences and, overwhelmingly, hearing ones.

Bragg writes his autobiography, *Lessons in Laughter: The Autobiography of a Deaf Actor*, from which this excerpt is taken, in a combination of written text (the passages in italics, presumably) and American Sign Language, which has been freely translated by Bragg's collaborator Eugene Bergman.[19]

—TL

The Premiere

I sometimes wonder if all the credit should go to fate? What is fate? Are not we masters of our own destinies? Perhaps half and half. How did fate lead me to the day in June 1966 when I received a letter from the man named David Hays, a Broadway set and lighting designer, asking me to join him in establishing the National Theatre of the Deaf? That theater was a dream I had long been trying to realize . . .

That dream had first begun to approach reality six years previously, in 1961, when I had received a letter from Raymond Levy, a Broadway "angel" who offered to help establish such a theater. I answered his letter and in the same year,

---

19. Bergman's life is, like Bragg's, worthy of memoir. (He wrote one: *Survival Artist*.) A deaf writer and educator, as a boy Bergman survived the Holocaust through a combination of hiding and fleeing, and ultimately escaped Nazi-dominated Poland by pleading deafness to the question of whether he was Jewish. In America, Bergman, fluent in at least four languages, became the first deaf person ever to receive a PhD in English.

after giving a performance in New York, I met Dr. Edna Levine, a psychologist with entrée to theatrical circles. She had picked up Levy's idea, also entertained by Anne Bancroft, of a professional theater of the deaf, and became sufficiently enthusiastic about it to apply for a million-dollar government grant. The grant was turned down, but she did not give up trying . . .

. . .

In the summer of 1966, on the very day school closed, a letter from David Hays caught me unawares. As I reread the letter while walking across the school's central plaza, one phrase in its first paragraph stood out: "many fingers point at you."

Hays had recently become a vice president of the Eugene O'Neill Theater Center in Connecticut and was casting about for a novel idea and program. When he learned of Edna Levine's failed efforts to obtain a grant to start a deaf theater group, he thought it worthwhile to give it a try and asked her to give it up to him. He was going to push it forward single-mindedly with all the energy at his disposal. She agreed, on one condition: "Get Bernard Bragg!"

There was one person above all I wanted to share this letter with. That was Kathee, my fiancée of three years, a black-haired girl with lovely brown eyes. I had first met her at a party given by Taras Denis when she had been teaching at Fanwood. We were immediately attracted to each other, as if we had known each other for a long time. She was such a fluent signer that at first I had thought she was deaf, too. The truth was she was hearing but had grown up in a deaf environment and been immersed in deaf culture because her father had been superintendent of the Illinois School for the Deaf and he and his family had lived in a house on the campus.

[. . .] So of course, when I got Hays's letter I hurried to show it to her. I was practically jumping with joy. She read it, handed it back to me, and said, "Looks like you are getting what you were waiting for."

Hays's letter, heaven-sent as it was, arrived at a chaotic time for me. I was directing the play *Moments Preserved* by Eric Malzkuhn, a creative deaf playwright and actor who had written it especially for the National Association of the Deaf meeting in San Francisco. In 1943, Malzkuhn had been responsible for staging a Gallaudet production of *Arsenic and Old Lace* on Broadway. I was also rehearsing a solo mime show for Bimbo's, a nightclub in San Francisco, and taping a television program, *What's New*. Yet somehow I managed to suspend everything and free myself for a week in order to fly to Waterford, Connecticut, and meet Hays.

When I arrived at Groton Airport I was welcomed with open arms by Edna Levine, who theatrically presented me to Hays, a short, sharp-faced man with intense dark brown eyes. We shook hands and then, as Mrs. Hays said later, all hell broke loose. We spent extremely fruitful days together, swapping ideas and fleshing out the concept of the National Theatre of the Deaf, or NTD.

Yet all that time I kept thinking of Kathee. There had been something puzzling in the way she reacted to Hays's letter, but at the time I was too caught up in my good fortune to pursue it. I kept thinking about her on the plane back to San Francisco. I had a vague premonition of disaster, but shook it off, telling myself that she would be happy for me, and I was anxious to tell her about my exciting and creative discussions with Hays.

When I got home I found a note from her saying that she would not be able to see me for two weeks as she was tied up with her course work.

I kept busy in the meantime, teaching, acting and corresponding with Hays. After two weeks, Kathee came to my apartment. I asked her why she looked so serious and wondered if she was okay. She signed, "I know you'll be shocked by what I am going to say. I came . . . I think . . . that we would be better off being apart."

"What do you mean?" I asked, stunned.

"I know how much you love theater."

"But so do you."

But she said, "It's not the same thing. You belong to theater. I cannot fit in your life."

We kept talking in this vein for some time until finally she declared, "Let me be honest with you. There is someone else, a man I've been seeing for a long time, and I am going to marry him."

When I asked who he was, she explained that he served in the Coast Guard. He lived on the floor below her apartment, and they had become friends. She ended her explanation, signing, "I want you to know that I will always love you."

I was too stunned to respond. Finally, I brought myself to say, "But I always thought . . ." She interrupted me, "So did I, but from now on the NTD will be your life."

I argued, "There is room in my life for you."

She shook her head, "No. You'll understand years from now. I hope we can remain friends. I want always to be your friend."

Thus she stepped out of my life, though not out of my mind. To this day she remains my dear friend.

I plunged back into other things in my life. Hays and I continued our correspondence. We discussed the new grant proposal for the NTD and our ideas about what such a theater should be like and what kind of sign language should be adapted to it.

One week before Christmas I flew to New York. Hays took me to a huge dance studio and introduced me to Joe Layton, the Broadway director and choreographer who had staged *Gone with the Wind* in Tokyo and London and had directed, among other things, the film *Annie.*[20] His forte was musicals, as he graphically demonstrated to me. Layton immediately asked me to demonstrate to him what I could do. I reached into my repertoire of songs and poems and did Poe's "Annabel Lee," Shakespeare's "The Seven Ages of Man," "I Left My Heart in San Francisco," and other pieces, accompanied by the pianist who was conveniently there.

Layton kept asking for more. He straddled the chair with his elbows resting on its back, which reminded me of a similar favorite pose of Marceau in 1956. Finally, I did a passage from *Oklahoma!* and stopped.

Layton's reaction was disappointing. He turned both thumbs down. Through a sign language interpreter he commented, "That was not very exciting visually. You just stand in place and wave your hands."

"But," I protested, "what about the music? The piano accompaniment? My hands move to keep step with the music, 'eye music,' so to speak. Didn't you notice?"

He answered, "Don't take it to heart. I'm not criticizing that. What I meant was lack of movement on your part. You have legs. Use them."

"Oh, you want me to sign with my legs?" I asked, half-jokingly.

"No, I want you to move your legs around."

So he started to teach me how to move around while signing. He imparted to me the valuable lesson that I should move my legs in the same direction as my arms, even when pirouetting, and that I could make leaps like a ballet dancer when signing.

When the holidays were over I flew back to Berkeley. Shortly afterward Hays informed me that NBC Television was going to tape an hour-long show in sign language, *Experiment in TV.* He asked me to help pick deaf performers for it.

Hays chose Gene Lasko, who had previously worked with Arthur Penn on, among other hits, the film *Bonnie and Clyde*, to direct various segments of the NBC show, and Joe Layton to choreograph three numbers. Lasko flew to Berkeley to see me and for three days we worked together on the program, which was mainly to include selections from *Hamlet, Prince of Denmark* and scenes from the play *All the Way Home.*

The deaf actors and actresses I had helped pick at the time subsequently became the core of the NTD ensemble, and some of them went their own way to become famous elsewhere: Audree Norton appeared on the TV show

20. Bragg's chronology seems to be off here, as some of this work of Layton's came years later.

Mannix, Phyllis Frelich won a Tony Award for her performance in *Children of a Lesser God*, Julianna Fjeld won an Emmy Award as the producer of *Love Is Never Silent*, Ed Waterstreet starred in *Love Is Never Silent* and is now is a freelance director, Linda Bove has been a regular on *Sesame Street* for many years, and Gil Eastman won an Emmy Award for hosting the TV show *Deaf Mosaic*. In addition, there was Lou Fant, a hearing man and a superb signer, who has made a name for himself on stage and screen as a character actor.

My performance was to be taped in the barn of the O'Neill Theater Center. Two cameras were set up, one downstairs and one on the stair landing from which I was to sign the first half of my song—"Gesticulate" from *Kismet*. I practiced for almost two weeks with Joe Layton, who choreographed my sign/dance movements, and then the taping started.

I was the last to be taped and everybody was anxious to finish on schedule. That was when trouble started. I was standing on the stair landing with everybody watching me, including Joe Layton, who stood behind the camera. He shouted, "Lights! Music! Camera!" and counted to four on his fingers. That was the signal for me to begin, and I pranced, leaped and climbed onto the railing, signing with my free hand, "Sweet hand, swift hand, spinner of fable and fantasy, faithful friend of my art, would they rend us apart."

It so happened that a rope was tied to a railing post. The other end of the rope touched the ground. This gave Layton a last-minute idea. He shouted to me through an interpreter, "Slide down that rope!" and motioned to Gleason, a heavyset lighting man, to hold the other end of the rope downstairs and stretch it slantwise so it would be easier for me to slide down to the ground.

When I signed, "Up! Into the sky, and we did fly," I grabbed the rope and was about to slide downward on it, when I suddenly froze, looking at the rope and at Gleason, who held its other end almost vertically instead of diagonally.

Layton, Hays and some television crewmen rushed upstairs toward me, asking, "What happened?" "Why didn't you slide?" "Why don't you move?"

I was so embarrassed that I felt my face blush, but I stood my ground and protested that the cloth wrapped around the rope was not thick enough to protect my hands—the invaluable hands of a deaf person. Layton's face betrayed impatience. He started talking rapidly to Hays and others, so rapidly that I could not lip-read him. He probably was not intentionally rude but just forgot about my deafness. Then he turned to me, "All right. We'll wrap thicker cloth around the rope. Remember, we don't have much time."

Somebody brought a length of cloth, which was wrapped around the rope, and Layton hurried back to his post behind the camera. Once more he shouted, "Lights! Music! Camera!" and counted to four on his fingers.

I leaped onto the railing, grabbed the rope—and froze again. I just could not bring myself to slide down it.

There was a big blowup. Hays rushed toward me, shouting, "What happened? Why did you stop?" I told him lamely that I still did not think the rope covering was thick enough.

I had never seen him so furious before. He muttered something that I did not catch. I stepped down, feeling frustrated, but also feeling that I just could not trust my hands, my most precious possession, to that rope.

Hays shouted some expletive. "I'll show you how! I will do it myself!"

He leaped onto the railing, grabbed the rope, and slid down it. Everything seemed to be fine, but when he landed on the barn floor, his body suddenly jackknifed. A stunned crowd surrounded him. He groaned and held out his hands, palms up. There were large red welts on them and we could almost see smoke rising from them. I watched this scene from the second floor, casually looking the other way and flicking off an imaginary piece of lint from the sleeve of my black sweater.

Joe called for a five-minute break and instructed a crew member to get more canvas, which was rolled around the rope until it was twice as thick. Then he asked me, "Ready?"

I nodded. He called out once more, "Lights! Music! Camera!" and counted on four fingers. When he straightened out his fourth finger, I "belted out" my song with redoubled energy, leaped onto the railing, grabbed the rope, whose other end this time was held by four more crew members in a much more gently sloping position, and slid down it. The moment my feet reached the ground I pirouetted and, ending my song, spread my arms wide as if embracing the world and finger-spelled each letter of "Gesticulate" to the beat of the music, with my hands intact.

. . .

The NBC special triggered a brouhaha which was not made public but which to this day is still remembered by the deaf community. There is an organization in Washington, D.C., devoted to the promotion of oralism, the A. G. Bell Association. It is richly endowed with funds, for it had been bequeathed fabulous riches by its founder Alexander Graham Bell himself, a strong advocate of oralism who happened to invent the telephone while pursuing one of his ideas for improving the speech ability of the deaf.

The head of the A. G. Bell Association in 1967, Dr. Fellendorf, was so outraged when he heard that NBC was going to produce a program in sign language that he wrote a letter of protest to the producers, expressing his fears that sign language would pollute innocent deaf children and affect adversely their attitude toward learning speech. This threatened to be a battle royal, but fortunately we won it by not turning it into a battle. Instead we got the support of educators of the deaf all over the nation. As a result, NBC decided to ignore Fellendorf and put the show on the air for all the world to see.

Those were heady days. Not long afterward I received a wire from Hays— "We got it!"—meaning that our grant proposal for the NTD was approved by the United States Department of Health, Education and Welfare, owing largely to its sympathetic consideration by a key official, Mary Switzer. Thus, the NTD came into being. Its first play, Puccini's opera Gianni Schicchi, *had been adapted to the NTD style of acting-cum-signing in the absence of music, under the direction of Joe Layton. This one-act adaptation, along with several other pieces that together made up an evening's performance, made the NTD so successful that in the second year of its existence the company performed on Broadway to enthusiastic reviews, and the following year it went on a national tour with the same repertoire.*

—BB

Chapter 3

Amateurs or Professionals?

The inhabitants of the third [Bohemia] seldom know where they live; they are too busy making beautiful things, which they give to one another, for they have no money. They have, however, wealth and health, for the deeps which surround their shores are rich with treasure of many colors and the tides are strong and their tang savory. They are fisher-folk, those inhabitants, fishers of men and of their own hearts, and dredge jewels from uncharted seas.

—*Maurice Browne*

The Chicago Little Theatre

FOUNDED 1912

Maurice Browne

When the Chicago Little Theatre went bankrupt and folded, five years after its founding in 1912, an editorial in *Theatre Arts Magazine* pronounced it the end of "the most important chapter yet written in the history of the art theater movement in this country."

The theater started in a former storage room in the Fine Arts Building in Chicago, founded by a British poet and future West End producer, Maurice Browne, as a passionately amateur endeavor, in the original sense of the word—the amateur as one who works out of love or passion. Browne ran the theater with his wife, Ellen Van Volkenburg (Nellie Van), an actress with a spectacular gift of memorizing—or channeling—entire productions, or as Browne puts it, "the strange, the almost unbelievable faculty of going to a play once and, without having read it before or after, reproducing it verbatim to an audience."

Uncompromising and anti-realist in his choice of plays—CLT produced Euripides, Synge, Yeats, Ibsen, Schnitzler, Wilde, Strindberg and Shaw—Browne influenced a generation of theatermakers, many of whom—like George Cram Cook and Susan Glaspell, who would start up the Provincetown Players later in the decade—lived for a time in Chicago, an artistic boomtown in the early twentieth century. "No one has more consistently refused to compromise over what he believed to be the foundation principles of the art of the theater," wrote the art theater's early commentator, Sheldon Cheney, "and no one has been the center of more spirited controversies." After the theater's demise, Cheney amended his earlier statement: "To put it rawly, the Chicago Little Theatre was too artistic to succeed financially at that stage of American culture."

George Bernard Shaw saw his own work produced at the Chicago Little Theatre and came to know Browne during his many successful

SOURCE: *Too Late to Lament: An Autobiography*, by Maurice Browne, 1956.

later years in the London theater, notably as producer of *Journey's End* and *Wings Over Europe*, a play about the atom bomb staged seventeen years before Hiroshima. Shaw later wrote of Browne's commercial triumphs, "None of these things matter a tupenny damn. The work this man [did] years ago on a fourth-floor-back in Chicago—this is what matters."

—TL

————

Lou Wall Moore, a sculptress friend, had a studio, an old ramshackle one-storied frame-building, far out on the city's south side; she offered it for rehearsals. One by one, actresses—amateur actresses—gathered: Bess Goodrich, Elaine Hyman, Miriam Kiper; actors—amateur, let alone professional—were lacking. This pointed straight to *The Trojan Women*; if necessary *I* would double, triple, the three male parts. I had no experience as an actor—nor for that matter as a director.

Bess looked like a Greek goddess: clearly Helen of Troy; Elaine had a maternal air; clearly Andromache; Miriam read lyrical verse divinely: clearly the leader of the chorus. That left Hecuba, Cassandra and the remainder of the chorus. I insisted on Nellie Van playing Hecuba; Nellie Van was not unwilling. Lou Wall ached to play Cassandra: Lou Wall was considerably older than the rest of us and had a harelip; but we loved her dearly and she had lent us her studio: Lou Wall played Cassandra. Four more amateur actresses miraculously materialized; five including the leader was—obviously—the ideal number for the chorus. And suddenly God sent from nowhere two men—two actual male men—to play Menelaus and Talthybius; regarded retrospectively, God was perhaps not a very good casting director. Now there were left only the Greek army and the gods of the prologue. Clearly the gods were superfluous. The Greek army? A foolish question.

For nearly eleven months, nine hours a day, seven days a week, we rehearsed—except when Nellie Van and I took two days off to get married, or when she gave one of her imitations, or I a lecture, for neither of us had private means and it was necessary to eat sometimes. By the end of those months we knew most things about one another, many about the play, a few about our job. And in their course our casting director built up, soldier by soldier, the Greek army; it had two men.

Some strange and given instinct guided us toward finding that first group of players. We did not so much choose as were chosen, they and we jointly, by our aim: the re-creation of poetic drama. We never wavered in our loyalty to that aim, though often we made wide detours in our attempt to follow so untraveled a road. Instinctively too we knew that the road map lay concealed somewhere in the Greek chorus: a choreographic map based on the beat of verse; a map of perfectly synchronized mood, movement and speech; a "dance," with words.

The beat of verse is as metronomically exact as that of music; and the beat of English verse for generations has been based not on the number of syllables in a line but on the thought-stresses; so the speaker of Murray's verse as of Shakespeare's needs above all else to know exactly what the poet-dramatist means and thus, before speaking, to know exactly where the thought-stress lies. During those eleven months, slowly, toilsomely, those nine wretched slave-driven girls and I learned to apply these principles. I call them wretched; they were as thrilled and happy as I. Fellow students, realizing the immensity of our ignorance, we had only our objective to guide us. Week by week, month by month, we learned; and gradually the head, the arm, the torso, the leg, the foot, the hand, the little fingertip, began to move, of their own accord as it were and through "the modesty of nature," synchronously with the speech. Nor synchronously alone: with dramatic purpose also; we were learning to "suit the action to the word."

We had put *The Trojan Women* in rehearsal with little thought of where, or indeed whether, we would play it. Performance an ultimate possibility, no more. But now the play was almost ready. Performance became a paramount necessity, a theater an imperative need. We talked about it all the time: finally we talked it into being. One morning to our incredulous delight we read about our activities in the *Tribune*. Other papers followed its lead; in a week we found ourselves "news." Letters came offering encouragement, cooperation, advice. One was from the manager of the Fine Arts Building: would I care to call and see him? The building, on Michigan Avenue, had been repeatedly pointed out to me by enthusiastic Chicagoans as the only skyscraper in the world devoted solely to the arts; perfectly appointed and immaculately kept, it was the antithesis of Lou Wall's studio. I raced toward it.

I was received by a benevolent gentleman with flowing white hair and beard, Mr. Charles C. Curtiss. He radiated goodwill; I bathed luxuriously in its warm waves. His building, his own building, dedicated to the Muses and situated almost opposite the Art Institute itself, housed, he told me, not merely the city's most vital artistic activities but also the very place which, he was convinced, I urgently and precisely needed: the Fine Arts Theater, superbly located, superbly equipped and seating five hundred—the perfect number. It and I were destined for one another. I asked the rental. He tried, not quite successfully, to hide his well-mannered shame at my crass British ways. Over the portal, he said, magical words were inscribed, words which would strike home to my heart: "Art alone endures." As I entered the building I had noticed that they were preceded by two other words which he did not quote, words ominous to would-be theatrical producers: "All passes." Again I was crude enough to ask the rental. He was gracious to tell me that, in my particular case, he would ask the merely nominal figure of twenty-five thousand dollars a year.

At the moment Nellie Van and I were rolling in wealth; we had been given as a wedding present a check for five hundred dollars by a friend and well-wisher, Mrs. Chauncey Blair. But even so, I felt that I was not quite rich enough yet to undertake such a commitment. Mr. Curtiss waved my scruples aside. I was young, brilliantly gifted; I would earn vast sums; Chicago was talking about me. "To be perfectly frank," the mellifluous voice continued, "my building cannot afford to let you be housed elsewhere." I set forth with equal frankness my financial position; there was a moment of strained silence. Mr. Curtiss and I compromised with mutual satisfaction on an empty space hitherto used for storage, the fourth-floor-back. The rental was a mere trifle, three thousand dollars annually, and the space convertible, he assured me, for an infinitesimal outlay into an ideal small theater.

The next few months were a madness of stonemasons, decorators, plumbers, electricians. One moment Hecuba's heart was breaking:

I have seen the open hand of God,
And in it nothing, nothing, save the rod
Of mine affliction.

The next moment she was arranging the installation of a fire escape, demanded at the eleventh hour by the Chicago Fire Department. The night we opened, early in November 1912, the last workmen were moving out as the audience moved in. I was ten thousand dollars in debt.

The theater seated ninety-one, and seated them comfortably with good visibility from every seat. They—more often nine than ninety of them— rode four floors by elevator and walked down a long gloomy corridor. Suddenly they entered a shining world unlike any other of that time: simple, austere, yet filled full by what Ficke in an early poem had called

The light beyond the sunset and the music
With which the night is silent . . .

Two minutes earlier the Loop had thundered on our ears; here as in a thirteenth-century chapel was stillness.

[. . .]

On stage left of the tiny auditorium as one entered it from the foyer, a balustrade with pillars ran the length of the "house." Five feet back from it was a row of French windows. When these were closed, audience and players suffocated. When they were opened, pianos deafened us; a piano store adjoined on its other three sides the tiny courtyard which those windows faced. Through an opening in the balustrade's center two steps led down to a wide aisle crossing the auditorium. Beyond this aisle lay the tearoom, its walls hung with Chinese tapestries and wood carvings, another gift from Mrs. Chauncey Blair.

The lights in the auditorium were on dimmers: something wholly new in the theater of those days. Our programs were printed on non-rustling Japanese paper with cover designs by Raymond Jonson; today only three sets of those programs are known to exist. Kathleen Wheeler's bust of Nellie Van stood on the book table beside the entrance from the foyer; above it hung Jerome Blum's portrait of me; on the adjacent wall hung Shunyei's *Oiran*. The color scheme throughout was stone and beige, touched with olive; we had copied it from the Shunyei.

On the book table were books and pamphlets, then all but impossible to give away, let alone sell, now all but impossible to buy: first editions—there were then no others—of the "Georgian" poets, Abercrombie, Brooke, Drinkwater, Gibson, Hodgson, Monro, and of contemporary American poets, Arthur Ficke, Helen Hoyt, Vachel Lindsay, Carl Sandburg; sets of *New Numbers*; current issues of *Poetry*, *Drama*, *Theatre Arts*, the *Little Review*; Lindsay's *Rhymes Traded for Bread*, the original edition of which no copy is now known to exist; and the original edition, published by us at thirty-five cents, of Brooke's only play, *Lithuania*.

[. . .]

The stage measured fourteen feet across, twenty feet to the back wall and eight feet to the solid ceiling above it. Stage left, four-fifths of the way downstage, a structural pillar three feet square stood like Stonehenge; except for this and a tiny toilet there was almost clear wing space of nearly two feet. In the back wall, side by side with the main door into the theater, was the stage door. Both were of average size; no object could be brought into the theater which would not pass through one or the other. [. . .] Upstage right another structural column, this time twelve feet square and as impervious to human prayers as Hitler, thrust its immensity into the right wing. Downstage right was five feet of solid wall.

In the three-foot gap between these two vast and immutable masses stood the switchboard, a bank of eight dimmers, operating three-circuit strips. We had no money at first to buy floods or spotlights; for the former we used dishpans from the ten-cent store, for the latter tin funnels. Nor did we then have footlights, I superciliously postulating that the sun and moon illumine Earth from above; when we found that we could not see the players' faces I reexamined the postulate and discovered to my surprise that reflected light from the pavements on Michigan Avenue struck the faces of passersby. Yet these crude and improvised beginnings, in conjunction with Livingston Platt's experiments at the Boston Toy Theatre, were the first germ in that test tube from which proliferated the complex craft of modern American theatrical lighting, both front-of-house and backstage, alike in theaters and cinemas.

Beside the switchboard a short flight of steps led down into the right wing, a space perhaps twelve feet by six, which served also as "prop" room, storeroom, scene-dock, wardrobe, carpenter's shop, paint shop and all those other manifold and necessary spatial adjuncts to the acted play. Off it opened the two tiny and airless dressing rooms, for men and women respectively; the men's dressing room served also as passage from front-of-house to back-stage. Every sound backstage other than a whisper could be heard in front; if the toilet was flushed, the whole theater echoed with the noise of rushing waters. The stage left entrance would admit one person at a time; the stage right entrance would admit two, nearly. Within these material limitations, as binding and kindly as a coffin, we learned our job.

Meanwhile in the intervals of rehearsals, lectures, contractors, I was try-ing to raise funds for the theater. Some years later a wealthy Chicago friend told me a little tale. "Do you remember," he asked, "coming to see me when you were starting? You had letters of introduction from half the social elite of Chicago. I thought that you would probably ask me for a hundred thousand dollars; I hoped that I might get out for ten thousand. You inquired, shyly, whether I would be willing to take a life membership in the Little Theatre. 'How much does it cost?' I asked. Terribly embarrassed by your own bold-ness, you murmured tremblingly: 'One hundred dollars.' You cannot imag-ine the relief and alacrity with which I reached for my checkbook."

We were perhaps the first English-speaking public theater to base our activities on subscription membership; some years later a similar policy, more carefully thought out, was put into practice by the New York Theatre Guild with skill and success. Membership cost ten dollars a year, and enti-tled the member to buy seats at half price (their regular price was one dollar); in return we made eight productions yearly. Membership fees gave us our working capital. But the public got a notion into its head that the theater was open to members only and, save for a few fanatics as impoverished as ourselves, stayed rigorously away; even among our members the poor rather than the rich were our most dependable patrons. Yet when we played *Anatol* a Chicago paper commented enviously on the five magnificent sets of velvet curtains with which the five scenes from the play—all that we performed—were hung: the gift, presumably, of a wealthy sponsor. We had used one set of curtains throughout, made of flannelette, with differently colored lights thrown on it for each scene.

We had planned to give two performances weekly but soon increased the number to three; later we increased it to five and finally to seven, not "in consequence of public demand" but because the work was fun. God had shown signs of improvement as a casting director, so we had decided to postpone *The Trojan Women* for a couple of months and to open with two more recent plays, Gibson's *Womankind* and Yeats's *On Baile's Strand.* In the last an oath of allegiance is given to the High King of Ireland by his subsidiary kings. We arranged a ceremonial in which, across a metal cauldron of fire held by two girls, the kings extended the hilts of their swords to the High King on his throne. The fire effect was produced from powder sprinkled by the girls alternately on a night-light concealed in the cauldron.

It was the opening night performance. Every seat in the tiny place was filled. Among the audience sat that Chicago fire inspector who had insisted on the fire escape. The ceremony began. As I stood in the left wing waiting for my entrance, it seemed to me that flames were leaping from the cauldron higher than at rehearsal. After a minute a surreptitious look passed between the two girls. The flames leapt yet higher. Again the girls stole a look at each other. After a third look they knelt, slowly and together, and set the cauldron on the floor: then, unseen by the audience, gently rubbed their fingertips against their costumes. These actions had not been rehearsed. The flames continued to mount. No one on the stage flickered an eyelash; we knew even in those days that an audience seldom sees a mistake unless it be audibly or visibly corrected.

Against a central entrance Elaine was decoratively draped. A stage table near her held a flagon. I crept behind the scenes as close to her as I could and whispered: "Bring the flagon from the table as if it were set business." She did so, still decoratively. The moment she came off stage she thrust it into my hands; I hurriedly filled it from the toilet bowl and thrust it back into hers. She entered nonchalantly and, more decoratively than ever, poured water from the flagon on the leaping flames. Steam swept magnificently to the ceiling.

When the curtain fell there was loud applause. Many people came backstage to congratulate us. They included the fire inspector.

"That was a magnificent ceremony, Mr. Browne," he said; "I have never seen a more convincing fire effect on the stage. But—forgive me for asking—did you have a naked light in the cauldron?"

"Merely a night-light," I said, as casually as I could.

"Indeed? Remarkable. How in the world did you manage so vivid an illusion?"

"A little powder," I smirked: "the tricks of the trade."

We laughed. Then he looked solemn.

"But—I am sorry to press the question—the night-light was a naked light?"

Reluctantly I admitted it.

"What a pity," he murmured, more to himself than to me; then: "I hate to say this, for that effect was truly wonderful, but I have my duty. You must not use that night-light, or any naked light, on the stage again. Those are my official instructions to you. Forgive me."

I did. We shook hands warmly.

When everyone had gone we examined the cauldron. The inside had not been cleaned after rehearsals, and melted wax from rehearsal night-lights had caught fire. Where the cauldron had stood on the stage when the girls set it down, a hole had been burned through the floor-cloth; the boards beneath were scorched brown. We nailed down the charred edges of the floor-cloth and throughout the theater's remaining years left them and those bare brown boards just as they were, in reminder of the obvious moral—of many obvious morals.

.   .   .

Chicago in the second decade of this century was a mentally disturbing and therefore, to a young man, a mentally exciting place. Metropolis of an inland empire, its god was the dollar and municipal corruption his handiwork. "No decent man will touch politics" was a phrase heard daily and self-defensively from the lips of every "decent" man. Extremes of luxury and squalor contrasted even more violently than in the Dublin of my childhood or the London of my youth. On the east its huge inland sea bounded the city; when the wind blew from the west, where the stockyards lay, the smell of blood, seeping through shuttered window and bolted door, filled every room of every house. In summer pitch from the city's pavements bubbled underfoot. In winter the streets leading to Michigan Avenue had ropes waist-high 'round corner buildings, for foot passengers to pull themselves past the corner against the gale; blizzards swept the city, paralyzing traffic. And in that climate, amid Chicago's material and moral filth, mental life fought for existence like a sapling in a jungle.

At the Art Institute visiting exhibitions followed one another swiftly. Some were a challenge: the first cubist exhibition in America, Sam Hume's exhibition of theatrical design (also the first of its kind) and the Buckingham Collection of Japanese prints. The *Nude Descending a Staircase* enraptured the self-chosen few, infuriated the nameless many. Hume's exhibition revolutionized American stage design; but I question whether one percent of its fifteen thousand visitors had ever bought seats for any play staged by any of the three American designers whose work was shown: Hume himself, Robert Edmond Jones and Raymond Jonson. The superb Buckingham Collection was ignored by the public.

In Orchestra Hall, a cold and costly building, fashionable music was played to fashionable audiences by the Chicago Symphony Orchestra. As the Thomas Orchestra it had played for decades music which was not yet fashionable to a handful of music lovers in back streets. When our hearts were at their lowest Mrs. Thomas would encourage us with tales of her husband's heartbreaking and lifelong struggle against the city's indifference and ill report. He had died fighting: she hoped that we would; it was not the artist that mattered but his art.

Chicago's literary life was microscopic but, like all else in that sprawling metropolis, vivid and intense. Margaret Anderson, with her cold and cameo-like beauty of feature, sat beside me on a bench in the Fine Arts Building to discuss the founding of a periodical; she flattered us by naming it the *Little Review*. George Cram ("Jig") Cook and his successors, Floyd Dell, Lucian Carey and Llewellyn Jones, were patiently trying to teach Chicagoans their literary alphabet through the columns of the *Evening Post*; thousands bought the books which Cook ordered them to buy; a dozen may have read them. A little later Martyn Johnson was editing the *Dial*, a liberal review with notable contents and scant circulation. Just before our theater opened, Harriet Monroe, brilliantly aided by her second-in-command, Eunice Tietjens, had founded *Poetry*, a magazine of verse; during its first years lyrics as magical and unpretentious as the Elizabethan appeared in almost every issue; and, when Rupert Brooke sent me his 1914 sonnets, he asked me to hand them to "the divine Harriet," for "I want to get good gold for them from the Yanks, too."

Theater lovers in Chicago were driven further afield. Donald Robertson[1] had pioneered bravely; he looked at us with heavy eyes and shrugged his shoulders: "There's not a hope," he said. But in Hull-House [see Hull-House in chapter 1] we found cause for hope. Jane Addams's social settlement on the far west side of the city stood amid the slums surrounding the stockyards. An amateur dramatic organization had been formed there many years earlier; about 1906 Laura Dainty Pelham had reorganized it; and now the Hull-House Players gave plays of distinction with skill, sincerity and understanding. Mrs. Pelham, not I, was the true founder of the American Little Theatre Movement.

---

1. A Chicago theater pioneer, circa 1900, Robertson headed the Donald Robertson Company of Players, as well as the Chicago Woman's Club Players' Theatre Association (later the Chicago Civic Theatre Association).

Hitherto the city's writers, painters, sculptors, musicians, had had no common meeting place. Orchestra Hall and the Art Institute were singularly unsuited for intimate discussion, and even the divine Harriet's office had an editorial air; besides, it was hard to reach. But when you were downtown, the Little Theatre was next door. Almost overnight it became the center and focus of Chicago's eager mental life. Eunice Tietjens or Cloyd Head had a new poem, Mary Aldis a new play, which it was imperative to read immediately—or at least the moment rehearsal ended. Leo Sowerby would shyly put his red head through the foyer curtains; a new sonata was running in it. Jerome Blum wanted to see Jonson's designs for the next production. Stanisław Szukalski—that amazing boy who never fulfilled his early promise of Meunier-like genius—came to collect scratch paper which we gathered for him because he was too poor to buy drawing blocks. And young architects and city planners [. . .] used to burst in on a soliloquy by Hecuba with dreams in their eyes, to prophesy "the city beautiful." Chicago mocked their dreams, and today those dreamers are dead. But the Chicago River, which stank like the Liffey, now has vistas of loveliness comparable with Venice; and Lake Michigan, which used to lap the Illinois Central [Railroad]'s unsightly sores, has been filled in over many square miles with driveways, trees, lawns, parks, where community buildings dreamed long ago stand in silent witness to the dreamers.

[. . .]

Three countries are called Bohemia. One is—or was—a geographical entity; the second is of ill repute; the third has seacoasts. With the first this tale is not directly concerned. The inhabitants of the second form cliques and clubs, usually expensive and always exclusive, where they sleep with one another's mistresses to prove their open-mindedness; at each opening stands a masked sentry. I have often visited that country, traveling via Bloomsbury or Greenwich Village; once or twice I have lived there. The inhabitants of the third seldom know where they live; they are too busy making beautiful things, which they give to one another, for they have no money. They have, however, wealth and health, for the deeps which surround their shores are rich with treasure of many colors and the tides are strong and their tang savory. They are fisher-folk, those inhabitants, fishers of men and of their own hearts, and dredge jewels from uncharted seas. That country is often invaded but never conquered; an invisible land washed by an intangible ocean has no frontiers. There too I have lived, sometimes in England, sometimes abroad: once, for six years, in Chicago.

—MB

The Neighborhood Playhouse

FOUNDED 1914

Alice Lewisohn Crowley

In the creative flowering that was pre–World War I New York City, a passionate amateurism took hold in the theater, giving birth to three theater groups that would define that era and artistic idealism for decades to come: the Neighborhood Playhouse, the Washington Square Players and the Provincetown Players. The first of these, the Neighborhood Playhouse, was founded by sisters Alice and Irene Lewisohn in the Henry Street Settlement house in Lower Manhattan. Daughters of a wealthy, philanthropic New York family, who came to this Lower East Side community center as volunteers to direct the youth club, the Lewisohns began staging plays, screening movies and holding dance festivals. In 1915 they opened a beautiful, well-outfitted new theater space at 466 Grand Street and consolidated their theatrical project, which would a few years later start to incorporate more and more professionals.

Part art theater and part social experiment, the Playhouse was, in a unique sense, a world—as opposed to strictly Western—theater drawing on drama, dance, music and ritualistic traditions from around the globe. It was also a radically local theater, meant for its largely immigrant community. "By the variety of its program," the theater claims in its opening announcement, "the Playhouse aims to appeal to a public of diverse tastes, interest and ages, and in this way to share in the life of the neighborhood." Its amateur ethic was both communitarian and spiritual, and the sisters' work groped after the invisible threads that tie human beings together. Alice Lewisohn Crowley writes: "The Neighborhood player must first and foremost be a person whose interest and belief in theater, whose desire for expression, was not confined to a personal desire to play."

"Few other little theater groups have ever experimented so widely," writes critic Joseph Wood Krutch in the introduction to Crowley's "theater scrapbook," *The Neighborhood Playhouse*. "The actual texts chosen for performance were of every conceivable kind—ancient and modern, realistic and fanciful, poetic and tendentious. They included Shaw, James Joyce, Lenormand and Browning, but also Yeats, Dunsany and Percy MacKaye; also the ancient Hindu *Little Clay Cart* and the Chassidic *The Dybbuk*. [. . .] Obviously the intention was to explore as completely as possible everything which

SOURCE: *The Neighborhood Playhouse: Leaves from a Theatre Scrapbook*, by Alice Lewisohn Crowley, 1959.

might help recapture those elements of ritual, poetry and mysticism which had tended to disappear from the realistic and commercial modern stage." All this reach, all this eclecticism, was part of a quest or, as Crowley writes later in life, "We were searching for a root [. . .] a trail to blaze to that inner world of reality which is the source of drama." What a fitting epigraph Crowley chose for her book, from Goethe's *Faust*: "Formation, transformation, / The Eternal Mind's eternal re-creation."

—TL

The Playhouse had grown out of an intensive urge of the amateur to realize an image of theater which could not be found at that time along highways and byways of the professional stage. I used the word "amateur" in its original sense, as one who loves his craft unconditioned by any personal gain or self-exploitation. Therefore, as a term for an instinctive creative urge; as, for example, the craftsmanship of primitive peoples, or their rituals worked out with meticulous care; or as the origin of classic drama of Greece, from the Dionysian cults, or the Eleusinian Mysteries; or again, the folk festivals of Europe—to mention only a few examples of culture unfolding out of creative instinct. For primitive or original art mirrors the throbbing pulse of nature. An interesting piece of research might be done about the creative contribution of the amateur to art at a time when the amateur has fallen into disrepute, a situation which always confronts us when technique, in and of itself, is glorified, and the will to power has overridden the instinct of relatedness. Nothing could be a healthier symptom of our present time than the little bands of theater groups again emerging throughout the country and the renewed interest in theater and its craftsmanship as an avocation.

Yet the amateur approach carries its own burden of difficulties. As the work and standards for production increased at the Playhouse, we were faced with a double-edged problem: how to keep pace with these developing standards and yet meet the stern realities of the situation? During the first five years, so crowded with experiment, we had gone beyond the horizon of the original vision, although the productions, up to this point, had been scaled to the experience of the amateur. Excellent as the work of the amateur was, fresh and vigorous for certain characterizations, we were limited and hampered in the selection of plays that depended on maturity and finesse and the careful interweaving of motifs that comes of prolonged rehearsal. But how could a professional attitude toward work be reconciled with the need of our players and backstage workers to earn a living and meet the obligations of daily life? Rehearsals presented increasing complications, for Sunday was the only day we were assured of full attendance by our amateur dancers and players. As our demands increased, the elusive goal seemed farther and farther beyond reach.

Little by little, it became apparent that the strain of the dual effort to combine practical necessities with the life of the theater was too great. Were we being driven after all toward professionalism and the pay envelope, which could so easily undermine the natural, spontaneous experience? Yet, under the conditions confronting us, how was it possible to do otherwise? Had we reached an impasse? After weeks and months of the most searching thought and questioning, the decision was finally made in 1920. A small professional company, prepared to give full time, would be installed.

Sport has long been recognized for its value in developing individual leadership and group loyalty, but I question if there is any game that demands more sportsmanship or personal equilibrium than theater. This testing was now lying in wait for the student body in the announcement that a professional company would enable the Playhouse to present a continuous repertory. However carefully presented, this statement served as a bomb; for they saw, at first, only their beloved home invaded by an enemy, its informality threatened by a new regime, and they themselves exiled in a certain sense. Instinctively they realized the end of an epoch which required the greatest fortitude to accept.

Actually, the decision to incorporate a professional company did not materially change the organization. It indicated, rather, a daring experiment in uniting the lyric program, still to be manned by amateurs, with a mixed professional and student dramatic group, available for a more exacting repertory than we had heretofore been able to develop.

The stimulus of an ardent student body seemed to us as important as the equipment of a professional. If it could be made to work, just this combination might give the essential impetus needed for further growth. It was obvious that the roots of the Playhouse were embedded in the festivals, and that the student body, including the children, belonged root and branch to its development. The Playhouse had grown in the spirit of a family, with its quarrels, devotions, loyalties and conflicts, and that family spirit had to be maintained at all costs.

The transition from the amateur period to professionalism was not achieved without growing pains on the part of the student players and the sacrifice of optimistic expectations by the directors. This was to be expected; we were familiar enough with the limitations of the students, as well as our own inadequacies as directors. But we were totally unprepared for what the ensuing skirmish for a professional company was to reveal.

The rank and file of Broadway actors who applied, though they responded with enthusiasm to the idea, were trained to exploit obvious stage types rather than individuality of character. Their technique was based upon theatrical effect rather than upon relationship to the inner experience. This was a time when the star system dominated, and any other approach was not only foreign but as a rule unwelcome. To find professional players willing to search behind the obvious form and character of the part—in short, to enter into rapport with the orchestral values of a production—soon seemed like a quest for the Golden Fleece. The situation was exaggerated of course by our own lack of professional contacts and the difficulty of translating the values we held into the usual theater idiom.

We were also to observe the Broadway system at closer range. In those days, when David Belasco's[2] star rode high, the stage designer was still a pioneer, just beginning to blaze a trail on Broadway, where scenery had been produced *en gros* with meticulous regard to photographic exactness, and costumes were bought or hired from one of those remarkable caravanseries, the theatrical costumer. It was rare to find a play in which costume and setting were looked upon as a creative part of production.

A few schools of acting existed in New York where conventional technique could be acquired. But stock companies were the primary training for the beginner who, if gifted, had a chance to develop memory, observation, repertory, and alas above all, the banality of theatricalism. Except for Professor Baker's 47 Workshop at Harvard,[3] there was no center of training for all the related crafts of the theater.

This was the era of specialization and glorification of technique, spoils of the West, inherited from World War I. Collectivism was supplanting the old image of personal values; the human claims of the individual had little chance. Industry's attempt to reap the spoils of a universal market had resulted in mass production and mass control, and theater as an industry was naturally influenced by the collective standard.

It was out of the urge to realize a new dimension in theater, freed from this tarnish of conventionalism, that a triangle of insurgent theater groups had emerged almost simultaneously out of several corners of Manhattan. All manned by amateurs, and unknown to one another, they had begun their independent careers, not in a revolutionary attempt to upset the existing order, but merely to voice another image of theater. Confronting the

2. A great American theatrical impresario (actor, director, producer) who reigned from the mid-1890s until his death in 1931, Belasco introduced a fastidious naturalism to Broadway.

3. America's first professional playwriting program within a university. George P. Baker launched his workshop in 1912 at Harvard. His illustrious list of pupils included George Abbott, Philip Barry, S. N. Behrman, Hallie Flanagan, Sidney Howard, Eugene O'Neill, Edward Sheldon and Thomas Wolfe. Baker moved to Yale in 1925 and helped found the Yale School of Drama.

Goliath of Broadway, they were as unprotected as the boy David with his sling. But what a sense of freedom there was, unshackled by "what ought to be," unconscious of anything but the image that moved us. The Washington Square Players, with their intellectual outlook and interest in glittering innovations, were a bubbling fountain of enthusiasm for the word, as well as for translating it into terms of theater. The Provincetown Players, dedicated to authorship, were a source of inspiration to personalities such as Eugene O'Neill and Susan Glaspell, their outlook a kind of reformation in theater, suggestive of a Quaker meeting house—austere, purposeful in pursuing their essential values.

And there we were, the third corner of the triangle, in the lower depths of Grand Street, experimenting toward a synthesis of expression. The theater, we believed, was neither a place for the intellect alone, nor for the presentation of the shams and foibles of the day, nor just a laboratory in experimental drama. We were searching for a root, or, one might say, a trail to blaze to that inner world of reality which is the source of drama. We held the value and need of the lyric form, in and of itself, as a stimulus to imagination, as well as in guiding us to mythological values as, for example, through the early religious festivals and the noh or later the *Salut au Monde* and *The Dybbuk*. Our task seemed to lie in developing forms not of the traditional theater, which might be released with simplicity of means. Another characteristic form that had possibilities was the spontaneous burlesque, growing out of the Playhouse experience; this was later to develop into *The Grand Street Follies*. These were potentialities which belonged to the function of theater, a never-ending round, nor could one side be divorced from the other, isolated or developed alone.

Theater meant to us a kind of pilgrimage into various dimensions, strata or areas of life, and an attempt to capture something of the mood and atmosphere of each. We visualized it in the round, with all its many-sidedness and interests; and if our experiments were slow of growth, they were not unlike the baffling conflicts that life itself presents.

In acknowledging ourselves first and foremost amateurs, we had naturally to submit to the suspicions of the public and the patronizing tolerance of the professional world. On the other hand, we had gained a direct experience in technical factors of theater which could hardly have been acquired by specialized courses or university degrees, even had such providential direction existed at the time.

And now another epoch was approaching which required the intensity of nightly performances with a professional company yet without any deviation in direction. To continue to create, to sense the need of each day, to experiment with faulty material and methods, but always with the need to probe inner forces—that was our reality. However naive or ineffective the attempt, behind it there was the desire to reach deeper levels of experience. Heaven knows how often we were plunged into confusion, how often the battle raged between outer needs and inner values. And yet it was only at such times, when we persisted in following an impulse regardless of rational consideration, that we realized something of the thrill in creative effort.

—ALC

The Washington Square Players

FOUNDED 1914

Lawrence Langner

When the twentieth century was in its teens, Greenwich Village was the center of the New World. Everything, it seemed, was new: the New Woman, the New Art, the New Morality, Sexuality, Politics and Psychology. The theater, then defined almost exclusively by what lawyer-turned-playwright Elmer Reizenstein (later Elmer Rice) called "crude melodramas and mechanical farces," as well as mindless musical entertainments and star-driven adaptations of best-selling storybooks, was ripe for a similar rebirth. This is where the Washington Square Players came in, staking claim to a newly intelligent, literary theater, one that tackled the new ideas of the day with a brave new spirit.

"Their capital was exactly nothing," wrote the *Independent* critic Hannah White, "their stock in trade boundless enthusiasm, indefatigable energy and a wide variety of talents. [. . .] They are all young and they are all idealists. They have convictions and they have the courage to carry them out. Their convention is unconventional and their motto is DARE!"

The epicenter of this daring world could be found at 133 and 137 MacDougal Street, home to the Liberal Club and a bookstore run by the Boni brothers, who also served as publishers for the new literary boom. Here, in the center of the new Bohemia, gravitated writers such as Theodore Dreiser, Edna St. Vincent Millay, Floyd Dell, Susan Glaspell, George Cram Cook, the *Masses* editor Max Eastman and his

SOURCE: *The Magic Curtain: A Story of a Life in Two Fields*, by Lawrence Langner, 1951.

actress-wife ("the Duse of MacDougal Street") Ida Rauh, as well as radical activists, including Emma Goldman, journalist John Reed and women's rights crusader Margaret Sanger. Anarchism was in the air, Socialism was a possible good, women's suffrage was worth fighting for. Free love was both a topic for conversation and a practice for consideration.

In 1914 a group of these passionate amateurs, including patent lawyer Lawrence Langner and Broadway actress Helen Westley, began reading and staging plays for themselves at the Liberal Club. At the suggestion of Robert Edmond Jones, who would become one of America's leading scenic designers and who had just returned from Europe, where he studied and worked with director Max Reinhardt, the group then fashioned a makeshift stage in the Boni brothers' bookstore to present the work to the public. Producing almost exclusively one-act plays, the group was so successful that it leased the Bandbox Theatre on East 57th Street, where, according to historian Richard E. Kramer, it "bearded the Broadway lion in its own den."

World War I would spell the end for the profoundly influential Players, who would reemerge as the majestic Theatre Guild after the war. But before closing down, they had changed the American stage forever and planted the seed that would, over the next fifty years, grow into Off and Off-Off Broadway. The story of the Players' genesis is told here by Langner, one of the troupe's founders and a future director—and chronicler—of the Theatre Guild.[4]

—TL

———————

Despite World War I, during the winter of 1914 the interest of young people in the theater in New York was growing rapidly, stimulated by the imaginative productions of Granville Barker and by the tour of Diaghilev's Ballet Russe with Nijinsky in his most famous roles, with costumes and scenery by Leon Bakst and other European masters. This tour, sponsored by the late Otto Kahn (who told me he incurred a loss of over $250,000 in presenting this magnificent company to an America which was still too undeveloped culturally to appreciate it), had a profound influence on the young American theater, and undoubtedly also began that interest in the ballet which has since spread throughout the country. But the general public of those days was indifferent to new art forms in the theater, and the attitude of the great

4. I'm grateful to Roberta Pereira, a student at Yale School of Drama, who led me to Richard E. Kramer's fine history of WSP, "The Washington Square Players: Art for Art's Sake" (*Theatre History Studies* 25, June 2005, pp. 149–171). Another book, *1915, The Cultural Moment*, edited by Adele Heller and Lois Rudnick (Rutgers, The State University, New Brunswick, NJ, 1991) deepens this history, by capturing the reach of this era of cultural revolution.

mass of Americans toward the ballet can best be illustrated by the reaction of an engineer friend of mine from Dayton, Ohio, whom I took to the Century Theatre to see Nijinsky in a superb program which included *L'après-midi d'un faune.* "Gee, Lawrence," he said angrily, turning to me as Nijinsky leaped miraculously through the air, "how I'd like to take a sock at that guy! Why doesn't he *work* for a living?"

I mention this to show what we who pioneered in the theater had to meet and overcome in the philistine attitude of the American public toward the arts, an attitude which was generally prevalent except for a small handful of people in the larger cities who were looked up as cranks, eccentrics or "sissies" by their fellow rugged individualists.

One evening at the Liberal Club, Floyd Dell, the novelist, informed me that the club had decided to form a dramatic branch to produce plays, and that the governing body wanted me to be its secretary. He also told me that he had written a one-act play for the new venture, about a young Spanish grandee and his gypsy sweetheart, and that he would like me to play the part of this young man. He added (somewhat too hastily, I thought) that he had offered me this part on account of my black mustache and Spanish appearance. I accepted the proposal with suspicion, and agreed to attend a trial rehearsal at the apartment of Theodore Dreiser in Greenwich Village, where Kirah Markham, an attractive dark-eyed young woman who had recently arrived from Chicago, was to rehearse opposite me. As she was to play the part of the gypsy, I suspect that she, too, had been cast to type. While Dreiser sat and watched us with ponderous amusement, Floyd directed the play, and during the rehearsal he criticized my faltering efforts on the ground that my diction was too British, and I was introducing a disconcerting nationalistic complication into the play. "This," he said, "is the way I want these lines read"—whereupon he declaimed his precious words in harsh Midwestern accents which set my teeth on edge.

"If that's the way you want the part acted," said I, sarcastically, "hadn't you better play it yourself?"

"Perhaps I will," said Floyd. "I'll think it over."

The next morning he called me on the phone and said, "I have decided to accept your resignation and to play the part myself." *Well*, thought I, *if he wants to ruin his own play, that's his affair.* The performance was given at the Liberal Club some weeks later, and Floyd was greeted with rounds of applause as the curtain fell.

Seated near me at the performance was an attractive, dark-haired woman, also with a touch of gypsy in her, named Ida Rauh, who was married at the time to Max Eastman, then editor of the *Masses*. "Lawrence," said Ida, when the play was over, "I could certainly play gypsy better than Kirah Markham."

"Yes," I replied, "and I could certainly play the Spanish grandee better than Floyd Dell, with his Iowa accent. Besides," I added, "one of my ancestors was a viceroy of Navarre, so the part would have fitted me like a glove."

"I, too, have Spanish blood," said Ida, looking at me with some personal interest for the first time. "I used to be in the theater before I married Max, and now I'm determined to return to the theater and act!" When a woman of Ida Rauh's character and willpower is determined to act, she can move mountains—and she did.

A week later I met Albert Boni[5] walking dreamily along the south Washington Square. "I have been talking to Ida Rauh," he said, "and she thinks the dramatic branch of the Liberal Club is absurd."

"So do I," I replied. "We ought to start a theater of our own. Maurice Browne [see the Chicago Little Theatre, earlier in this chapter] has done it in Chicago," and I described the Chicago theater to him. Albert, who loved starting things just as much as I did, suggested that we spend an evening with Ida to talk over the possibility of opening our own theater.

I spent the next evening at Max Eastman's home on West 13th Street, where Albert, Ida and I planned to bring together different groups of our friends who were interested in the theater. Albert agreed to invite the theatrically inclined members of the Albertson farm group,[6] including Robert Edmond Jones and Samuel Eliot, to join the organization. I agreed to discuss the matter with Edward Goodman, Philip Moeller and Josephine A. Meyer, who belonged to the uptown New York group associated with the Socialist Press Club, and we also added the names of George Cram Cook and Susan Glaspell, along with their friend, Lucy Huffaker, and Helen Westley, Ralph Roeder, Daisy Thompson and Dudley Tucker of the Greenwich Village group were also included. Thus, in the formation of this new theater, which almost immediately took the name of the Washington Square Players, there were representatives of all the artistic groups with which I had come in contact during my four years of traveling around the country.

We decided that an old cellar on MacDougal Street, which smelled most appetizingly of old wine and later became the Provincetown Playhouse, was too small, and Florence Enright suggested that we take the little Bandbox Theatre on 57th Street, just off Third Avenue. With a capital of a few hun-

5. Owner, with his brother Charles, of the Washington Square Book Shop, Boni went on to have one of the most distinguished publishing careers in post–World War I America, first with his partner Horace Liveright and later with his brother again. Among the authors he championed were Thornton Wilder, Ford Madox Ford, Theodore Dreiser and Leon Trotsky.

6. A group of "more liberally inclined young men at Harvard" who often visited Chestnut Hill Farm near Haverhill, Massachusetts, as guests of the farm's owner, Hazel Albertson.

dred dollars, mostly contributed by Dudley Tucker and myself, and with a handful of subscribers, we embarked on our new theatrical venture.

As soon as word spread around among the younger generation that we were going to start a theater, many of the young writers in the Village began to turn out plays. As none of us had the experience or patience to get further along than one act, we limited our efforts in the beginning to one-act plays, which was wise, for we were not sufficiently experienced to write longer plays, and our actors were equally unable to sustain them. Philip Moeller had already written a play for the Socialist Press Club, and started on another. Susan Glaspell and George Cram Cook wrote a one-act play called *Suppressed Desires*, which was the last word in modernity since it satirized Freud. Edward Goodman wrote a playlet called *Eugenically Speaking*, while I put the finishing touches to *Licensed*. Other authors who sent in plays were Murdock Pemberton, John Reed and a sylphlike lassie from St. Louis named Zoe Akins. Because of his experience with the Socialist Press Club, Edward Goodman was selected to be our director, while Albert Boni and I were the business managers, which, in a practical sense, meant that he and I were dedicated to the difficult task of raising the money needed to launch the enterprise.

It was decided, in a burst of misplaced idealism, to operate the Washington Square Players on a strictly democratic basis, and this meant that everyone in the group, including the actors and the clerical force, right down to the office boy, had a vote on the selection and casting of plays, with results which were frequently fantastic. After weeks of arguing, democracy got the worst of it, and a committee was set up which limited the decisions to a group of five persons who were thick-skinned enough to disagree continuously without losing their respect for one another. Philip Moeller, Helen Westley and I succeeded in surviving this experience, and imported the committee system bodily into the Theatre Guild some years later under the title of "the Board of Managers."

When the would-be actors of the Liberal Club Dramatic Group learned that we intended to produce real plays on a real stage, they rallied to our banner, and before long we had enrolled more prospective thespians than we could possibly use. Among these was Helen Westley, then a tall, beautiful, dark-haired woman who spent a great deal of her time with Cuthbert Wright, our assistant in the bookshop, of whom she was said to be enamored, and with whom she quarreled incessantly. Helen spent most of her time browsing around secondhand bookstores, and her apartment was lined with thousands of secondhand books, which overflowed into the kitchen and even into the bathtub. The theater was quite up Helen's alley, for she had been a professional actress in her own right, and had also married a well-known actor, Jack Westley, from whom she was then separated. Thus, there came to be associated with us, and later with the Theatre Guild, this remarkable woman who was one of the most refreshing personalities in the theater, as well as one of its most talented character actresses. But what made Helen Westley invaluable to the Washington Square Players, and later to the Theatre Guild, was her simple, direct enthusiasm for the greatest plays, her incisive mind which cut through any meretricious work like a surgeon's scalpel, her disregard for appearances, her dislike of mediocrity and her unwillingness to sacrifice art for money, of which latter commodity she was not unduly scornful but never to the extent of letting it interfere with her integrity in selecting plays for the Players or for the Guild.

Helen placed all her earnings, which were considerable in her later years, in the savings banks, and carried her bankbooks at all times on her person. "Good heavens, Helen," said Edna Ferber one evening at my home, when Helen was sitting in a comfortable easy chair, wearing a bilious green batik dress, and low-heeled shoes. "What are those large lumps on your legs?"

"My saving bankbooks," said Helen, "I keep them in my stockings."

"But why?" asked Edna.

"They're worth about seventy thousand dollars," replied Helen. "I couldn't possibly leave them anywhere else."

During her membership on the Theatre Guild Board, when she was frustrated by a contrary vote, Helen would often remark, "I'll outlive all of you, and then I'll run the Guild alone, and produce only the greatest plays in the world!" Alas, she was the first of our group to pass away.

To set forth the purposes of the Players, Edward Goodman, Philip Moeller and I prepared the following manifesto:

THE WASHINGTON SQUARE PLAYERS
AIMS AND ORGANIZATION

The Washington Square Players, Inc.—an organization which takes its name from the district where it originated—is composed of individuals who believe in the future of the theater in America, and includes playwrights, actors and producers, working with a common end in view. The fact that the Drama League can recommend at the present time, as worthy of the attention of its members, only three plays running in New York City (of which two are by foreign authors, while two productions are by English and part-English companies) is an incisive comment upon the present condition of the American drama. The Washington Square Players believe that a higher standard can be reached only as the outcome of experiment and initiative. Just as the finished productions of Mr. Granville Barker—which are now delighting New York audiences at Wallack's Theatre—are the culmination of a growth of some years in the development of new methods of acting and production in English drama, so we believe that hard work and perseverance, coupled with ability and the absence of purely commercial considerations, may result in the birth and healthy growth of an artistic theater in this country. Your wholehearted support—a sympathetic appreciation of the possibilities of our experiment—will encourage us to greater efforts.

We have only one policy in regard to the plays which we will produce—they must have artistic merit. Preference will be given to American plays, but we shall also include in our repertory the works of well-known European authors which have been ignored by the commercial managers.

Though not organized for purposes of profit, we are not endowed. Money alone has never produced an artistic theater. We are going to defray the expenses of our productions by the sale of tickets and subscriptions. Believing in democracy in the theater, we have fixed the charge for admission at fifty cents. If we can secure sufficient support by the purchase of individual tickets, or subscriptions for ten tickets (two for each of our monthly performances) at the cost of five dollars, we shall be able to continue our work.

If you are in sympathy with our aims, we shall welcome you in our organization. You may be able to help us in a number of ways, whether you be playwright, actor, producer or capable of assisting us in some executive capacity.

Our ultimate success depends upon our ability to accomplish our purpose *and* your interest.

If this wording in the light of today sounds somewhat grandiose, it nevertheless indicated our serious purpose in bringing intelligence, an interest in social matters and a serious critique of life into the theater.

On the eventful night of February 19, 1915, the Washington Square Players gave their first performance at the Bandbox Theatre. The opening bill began with my one-act play *Licensed*, which showed a young girl whose fiancé had died a few minutes before her marriage was to take place. Her mother having called in the clergyman who was to perform the marriage, the girl confesses that she is about to have a child. The mother begs the clergyman to fill out the marriage certificate as though the marriage had taken place before her fiancé's death, to make the child legitimate. The play ends with a long propaganda speech by the unmarried bride on the subject of birth control, which, in retrospect, has had little effect in reducing the number of unwanted children in the United States. Ida Rauh, who played the part of the bride, suffered considerably as an actress from having once been told that she resembled Sarah Bernhardt, wore her hair in a manner to emphasize the resemblance, and dressed in a flowing white wedding dress which underlined her somewhat matronly form; and since she was already, at the time, the mother of an eight-year-old boy, she did not look quite as virginal as I wished her to.

However, the performance, to my surprise, was well received by the audience, made up, I may add, of our friends and relatives who could not, under such circumstances, be expected to respond very differently.

The next play was a naughty piece of impudence by Edward Goodman, *Eugenically Speaking*, in which Florence Enright and Karl Karsten played the leading roles, and the plot of which was amusingly described by George Jean Nathan in the *New York American* the next day as follows:

> A young girl, who has run across a magazine article by Shaw in which the latter expresses a characteristic idea or two on the subject of mating, is so impressed by Bernard's philosophy that she picks up a massive streetcar conductor and totes him to her home. Once there, she proposes that he marry her. The conductor informs her that he is sorry, but he already has a wife. The girl is downcast and cries out her woe upon the bosom of her flabbergasted father. Whereupon the conductor, in passing out, tells the girl that Shaw was all right as far as he went in the article, but why stop there? And, as the curtain comes down, the girl's face lights up with a relevant idea (the censor interferes with a more concrete exposition).

This was followed by Maeterlinck's poetic *Interior*, after which came a divertissement entitled *Another Interior*, in which the mise-en-scène represented the inside of a man's stomach, into which various foods, portrayed by the actors, passed through the esophagus. In this unforgettable episode, Helen Westley, attired in a flowing gray robe, played the part of an oyster, while Philip Moeller, who had been known in his college days as Columbia University's best toe dancer, appeared last on the scene in the role of an irresistible liqueur. His advent caused all the other food on the stage to sway with a sickly, bilious rhythm, and finally rush out of the stomach. This pantomime, strange as it may appear, did not send the audience reeling out of the theater for the same reason but, on the contrary, was heartily applauded.

Much to our surprise, the following morning the dramatic critics praised the performance highly. Here is what some of them said:

> . . . every indication of fully realizing their aim, which is to present unusual pieces in an unpretentious and yet effective way in the hope of adding impetus to the artistic movement in the New York theater, which of late has assumed proportions worthy of recognition. If the Players can keep up their present pace they will make the Bandbox an institution.
>
> —*New York Times*

> NEW COMPANY GIVES TWO-DOLLAR DRAMA FOR FIFTY CENTS. WASHINGTON SQUARE PLAYERS OPEN THEIR SEASON AND MAKE A BIG HIT.
>
> —*New York Herald*

> If the American stage is ever to extend its exhibitions beyond the "tired businessman" type of music show and the farces and melodramas which have been such moneymakers in the last couple of seasons, it will be by reason of the competition of such organizations as the Washington Square Players.
>
> —*New York Tribune*

> The appeal is distinctly to the "highbrow" of revolutionary tendencies. That it will ever win an audience outside of the spiritual frontiers of Greenwich Village is not probable.
>
> —*New York Evening Post*

Encouraged by the audiences which stormed the Bandbox Theatre when we were not playing Chekhov (we had disastrous results with the *Seagull*, because, like most amateurs, we played it in semi-darkness), we decided after our second season to move to the Comedy Theatre on West 38th Street, a deserted playhouse which was leased to us by the Shuberts on unusually reasonable terms. We rented an empty loft building across the street, with a large number of rooms for our offices. This building ultimately resulted in our financial downfall, for we all began to engage assistants and sub-assistants to fill these rooms, which gave us the appearance of great prosperity while contributing to our impoverishment.

It was my duty, as business manager, to arrange for a lease of the Comedy Theatre with the Shuberts. Having made so many insulting remarks in our publicity about "the commercial theater," I was apprehensive of the reception I would receive on being told that Mr. Lee Shubert wanted to see me to discuss our proposition. My fears were not allayed when, along with Eddie Goodman, I called at the Shubert offices and passed through a series of ominous coffin-shaped doors into the small inner sanctum. There we were met by Mr. Lee Shubert, a small, neatly attired, keen-looking man with piercing eyes, who at that time vaguely resembled a young Indian chieftain without the head feathers. He put us at our ease and discussed the matter with great intelligence and kindness, quickly making the necessary business arrangements. It did not take me long to realize that Mr. Shubert was enamored of the theater, and that he was ready to gamble with any newcomers whose talents he felt would be productive—a kindly trait which has continued right down to the present day.

This was also the period when the Provincetown Players, headed by George Cram Cook and Eugene O'Neill, came into being and cradled the early works of O'Neill and Glaspell. This latter theater was always a more personal expression of the authors behind it than was our group, with the result that it tended to develop its authors rather than its audiences—a worthy and important objective, difficult to achieve, and deserving of the greatest praise. It was frankly experimental as to plays, while the Washington Square Players were attempting to present productions which would be in healthy competition with the plays of Broadway. The Washington Square group fought the issue of the art theater versus the commercial theater; it sought to produce its plays at the Comedy Theatre in competition with commercial attractions; it sent a traveling company on tour, and it operated a small and unsuccessful school of acting. It finally developed most of the producing talent which was later to become the Theatre Guild.

Among the acting talents which the Washington Square Players introduced to the American theater may be mentioned Katharine Cornell, Roland Young, Rollo Peters, Jose Ruben, Frank Conroy, Marjorie Vonnegut, Remo Bufano (of marionette fame), Arthur Hohl and Glenn Hunter; among its scenic artists, Lee Simonson and Rollo Peters. Edward Goodman and Philip Moeller both deserve special mention. Goodman held the helm of the Players with great discretion and artistry, and in later years has put his theater talents into teaching acting at the American Academy of Dramatic Arts. Philip Moeller, as a result of his training with the Players, became one of America's most brilliant directors, and in the direction of comedies he was unsurpassed in this country.

While my title in the Players was business manager, I was a member of its board of directors, in which capacity I helped select the plays, cast them and supervise the productions. Here was born the system, later imported into the Theatre Guild, which enabled me and the others to learn every branch of the theater without having sole responsibility for what is, in essence, a cooperative effort. In the mornings and afternoons I put in a full day at patents, and my evenings and weekends were spent with the Players, or in writing plays for them. My work was stimulating, and was progressing well in both fields; and I managed the difficult task of starting two different careers with a maximum of enthusiasm.

In the short three years from 1915 to 1917, the Washington Square Players presented sixty-two one-act plays, many of which were outstanding. The list included *In the Zone* by O'Neill, *The Magical City* by Zoe Akins, *The Girl in the Coffin* by Theodore Dreiser, *Suppressed Desires* by George Cram Cook and Susan Glaspell, *Trifles* by Susan Glaspell, *The Neighbors* by Zona Gale and many other fine plays. I recommend any group of young people who are energetic and ambitious to try repeating that program in thirty-odd months, and then throwing in for good measure the production of six long plays, including Chekhov's *The Seagull*, Ibsen's *Ghosts*, Shaw's *Mrs. Warren's Profession*, Andreyev's *The Life of Man*, Maeterlinck's *Aglavaine and Selysette* and last and undoubtedly least, Langner's *The Family Exit*!

Walter Prichard Eaton, then a drama critic, summed up the achievements of the Washington Square Players as follows:

> It accustomed a public, small perhaps, to look with interest on experimental work, and to relish the unusual work done for the sheer joy of the doing. Finally, it left among the workers themselves a sense of incompletion, of a vision striven for but not attained, a realization of mistakes, but a belief nonetheless that the vision was a sound one, that in a spirit of cooperation and united purpose some day it was not unattainable.

With the entrance of the United States into World War I, I was unable to give any more time to the Players, and regretfully resigned. One by one our best actors joined the armed forces, but Edward Goodman held the fort, aided only by his wife Lucy Huffaker, until he too joined the army. So the Washington Square Players came to an untimely end, leaving behind a handful of trained amateurs who were ultimately to lift the bedraggled face of the theater, as well as a substantial debt to the stagestruck Lee Shubert, who had long been inured to "holding the bag" for impecunious impresarios who attempted to fill his chain of theaters. Thus, with a record of artistic achievement and financial disaster, ended my first experience in the American theater.

—*LL*

The Provincetown Players

FOUNDED 1915

Susan Glaspell

> But yield who will to their separation,
> My object in living is to unite
> My avocation and my vocation
> As my two eyes make one in sight.
> Only where love and need are one,
> And the work is play for mortal stakes,
> Is the deed ever really done
> For Heaven and the future's sakes.
>
> —*Robert Frost, "Two Tramps in Mud Time"*

It began in the fishing community of Provincetown, Massachusetts, and it began in the Bohemian hotbed of Greenwich Village. It began casually, almost by accident. It began out of rejection—plays that hadn't been accepted by the Washington Square Players, among whose members were George ("Jig") Cram Cook and Susan Glaspell— and out of the mythic discovery of the son of a famous actor, a playwright figuratively born in a trunk and living, in his late twenties, with a pile of unproduced plays kept literally in a trunk. It flared up and flamed out in a matter of years, and its heat has radiated throughout American theatrical liturgy for nearly a hundred years.

The Provincetown Players belonged to the playwright. It belonged to Eugene O'Neill, who would become the Great American Playwright, the *ur*–Great American Playwright—O'Neill, whose varied and experimental early work would come to map the possibilities for nearly everyone who followed. It belonged to Glaspell, the other—relatively unsung—great playwright to come out of the Players. It belonged to every playwright who served as the first and final authority over the production of his or her work. Even the playhouse the troupe settled in, a former bottling works at 139 MacDougal Street in the Village, carried the name, proposed by O'Neill, of the Playwrights' Theatre, to assert that authority. The Provincetown Players existed "to give American playwrights of sincere purpose a chance to work out their ideas in freedom."

Even more than the other inspired, amateur ventures of the moment—the Neighborhood Playhouse and the Washington Square Players—the Provincetown gang were radicals, free livers, free thinkers, experimentalists. Their radicalism was instigated most directly

SOURCE: *The Road to the Temple: A Biography of George Cram Cook*, by Susan Glaspell, 1927.

by Jig Cook, Glaspell's husband and the prophet of the founding years. Cook was the inspirer, the visionary, the man of ecstatic language and fanatical, if fickle, enthusiasm. "Life is worth play," Cook believed, a belief that would encourage our country's first two major playwrights (O'Neill and Glaspell) and the birth of an experimental art theater upon whose foundations so many of our later companies would stand.

—TL

The Old Wharf

Winters we went to New York. Our friends were living downtown in "the Village," so that is where we lived; it was cheaper, and arranged for people like us. Nice to have tea before your glowing coals in Milligan Place, and then go over to Polly's or Christine's for a good dinner with friends. Every once in a while, in the Sunday paper, I read of Greenwich Village. It is a wicked place, it seems, and worse than wicked, it is silly. Just what Greenwich Village is now, I do not know. Through the years I knew it, it was a neighborhood where people were working, where you knew just which street to take for good talk when you wanted it, or could bolt your door and work all day long. You had credit at the little store on the corner, and the coal man too would hang it up if the check hadn't come. I never knew simpler, kinder or more real people than I have known in Greenwich Village. I like in memory the flavor of those days when one could turn down Greenwich Avenue to the office of the *Masses*, argue with Max [Eastman] or Floyd [Dell] or Jack Reed; then after an encounter with some fanatic at the Liberal Club, or (better luck) tea with Henrietta Rodman, on to the Working Girls' Home (it's a saloon, not a charitable organization) or if the check had come, to the Brevoort. Jig[7] loved to sit in the cellar of the Brevoort. He had his own corner, and the waiters smiled when he came in.

We went to the theater, and for the most part we came away wishing we had gone somewhere else. Those were the days when Broadway flourished almost unchallenged. Plays, like magazine stories, were patterned. They might be pretty good within themselves; seldom did they open out to where it surprised or thrilled your spirit to follow. They didn't ask much of you, those plays. Having paid for your seat, the thing was all done for you, and your mind came out where it went in, only tireder. An audience, Jig said, had imagination. What was this "Broadway," which could make a thing as interesting as life into a thing as dull as a Broadway play?

7. George ("Jig") Cram Cook, Glaspell's husband and the founder of the Provincetown Players.

There was a meeting at the Liberal Club—Eddie Goodman, Phil Moeller, Ida Rauh, the Boni brothers, exciting talk about starting a theater.

Jig spoke the first word spoken by the Washington Square Players; amusing, in view of his feeling about the audience as collaborator, that he spoke it from the audience: "I've had enough of this!" he cried. And I said, "S-sh"; but he went into a violent outbreak about it being a quarter of nine, and the curtain not yet up. Whereupon Edward Goodman, hastening before that curtain, explained why it wasn't up, and told what the Washington Square Players were about.

Two nights before Jig opened the season at the Bandbox,[8] [in his words:] "We got off the car in the neighborhood of exuberant pushcarts with flaring torches, black-eyed women in shawls, old men with patriarchal beards, and violent juvenile squadrons of roller-skaters. At number 466 we located the Playhouse. It looked like the eighteenth century when it was new." He always loved the Neighborhood Playhouse, walls like old parchment, letting you know just how bad the gilt rococo of the ordinary theater is. That opening night, when we saw *Jephthah's Daughter*, we knew why the things we had been seeing uptown found no feeling in us. "Full of a strong inherited religious feeling beyond the command of any commercial manager, danced the Jewish youths and maidens of that neighborhood, their drama, much of it taken from the Hebrew ritual, full of feeling immeasurably old, the tribal religious feeling of the ancient Jews still a living thing to some of the Jews of Henry Street."

That night, before the glowing grate in Milligan Place, we talked of what the theater might be. It is one of the mysterious and beautiful things of the world, if you are true to the thing you feel, across gulfs of experience you find in another the thing he feels.

That winter, while I was in Davenport, Jig saw the *Lysistrata* of Aristophanes:

I sat there in the darkness of the second balcony with the tears streaming. Something in the play (its beauty, its coming from so far away in time, its revelation of man and woman as they were two thousand years ago—and are—something in its great "abstain from love" [as we are abstaining], "I suffer—I suffer with need of you") struck something tremulous in me and made me very sad. I think maybe you were disappointed in not having a letter Monday, and I felt your sadness. Of course that may be only a fancy—that we can feel each other's emotion at a distance.

8. The Washington Squre Players' theater on 57th Street in New York.

I told Grace Potter of this sadness I felt at *Lysistrata* and tried to explain it as due to feeling through the Greek play something which was in Greek life and is not in ours—something we are terribly in need of. One thing we're in need of is the freedom to deal with life in literature as frankly as Aristophanes. We need a public like his, which itself has the habit of thinking and talking frankly of life. We need the sympathy of such a public, the fundamental oneness with the public, which Aristophanes had. We are hurt by the feeling of a great mass of people hostile to the work we want to do. We can write about taboos. If we do it just right, it will go. But that is not swinging free, like Aristophanes, with all the elements of life.

I've been thinking how a people reflects itself in literature, regardless of what such-and-such writers want to write. It's interesting.

There was the great strike in the Paterson silk mills. John Reed brought the strikers over for a pageant at the big Madison Square Garden—"the first labor play," though not a written play, not even a designed pageant, but what he was able to do in suggesting them into showing some things from their experience. He put into it the energy of a great desire, and in their feeling of his oneness with them they forgot they were on a stage. That too was a night when we sat late and talked of what the theater might be.

Those were the early years of psychoanalysis in the Village. You could not go out to buy a bun without hearing of someone's complex. We thought it would be amusing in a play, so we had a good time writing *Suppressed Desires*. Before the grate in Milligan Place we tossed the lines back and forth at one another, and wondered if anyone else would ever have as much fun with it as we were having.

We wanted our play put on—as who doesn't?—but even the little theaters thought *Suppressed Desires* "too special." Now it has been given by every little theater and almost every Methodist church; golf clubs in Honolulu, colleges in Constantinople; in Paris and China and every rural route in America.

Well, if no one else was going to put on our play, we would put it on ourselves. Neith Boyce had a play—*Constancy*. We gave the two in her house one evening. Bobby Jones[9] was there and helped us with the sets. He liked doing it, because we had no lighting equipment, but just put a candle here and a lamp there.

---

9. Robert Edmond Jones was one of the most innovative and influential stage designers (sets, lights and costumes) our theater has known. He was also an early member of the Provincetown Players and became, with Eugene O'Neill and critic Kenneth Macgowan, part of its leadership triumvirate in the 1920s.

A few minutes before it was time to give our play, Jig and I took a walk up the shore. We held each other's cold hands and said, "Never mind, it will be over soon."

But when it was over we were sorry. People liked it, and we liked doing it.

Neighbors who had not been asked were hurt, so we gave the plays again. Margaret Steele had taken for a studio the old fish-house out at the end of the Mary Heaton Vorse wharf, across from our house. She let us have this, so more people could come. Jig became so interested he wrote another comedy, *Change Your Style*, having to do with Provincetown art schools, a jolly little play. Wilbur Steele had written *Contemporaries*, and those two we gave together. Thus ended the first season of the Provincetown Players, who closed without knowing they were the Provincetown Players.

It might have ended there—people giving plays in the summer, [but in] Jig's dream city [. . .] there was to be a theater, and "why not write our own plays and put them on ourselves, giving writer, actor, designer, a chance to work together without the commercial thing imposed from without? A whole community working together, developing unsuspected talents. The city ought to furnish the kind of audience that will cause new plays to be written." "The Will to Form the Beloved Community of Life-Givers"— that is written through the papers of his years.

The summer people had gone. Jig would go out on the old wharf and "step" the fish-house. Weren't there two feet more than he had thought? He would open the sliding door that was the back wall, through which fish, nets, oars, anchors, boats used to be dragged, and stand looking across the harbor to the Truro hills, hearing the waves lap the piles below him. He would walk back slowly, head a little bent, twisting his forelock.

"To write alone will not content me. The blood of backwoods statesmen is in my veins. I must act, organize, accomplish, embody my ideal in stubborn material things which must be shaped to it with energy, toil."

We were back early in the spring, after seeing more Broadway plays. Jack Reed came home from Mexico, where he saw a medieval miracle play which has survived in unbroken tradition among the natives of a certain village, as the poems of Homer existed for some centuries in the Ionian villages of Asia Minor.

Students of dreams tell us our dreams use the things of the moment as vehicle, pattern, symbol, for the deeply lying thing. In our activities, as in our dreams, the accidental is seized to be shaped by our deep necessities.

"One man cannot produce drama. True drama is born only of one feeling animating all the members of a clan—a spirit shared by all and expressed by the few for the all. If there is nothing to take the place of the common religious purpose and passion of the primitive group, out of which the Dionysian dance was born, no new vital drama can arise in any people."

He and Neith Boyce said it together. He came home and wrote it down as an affirmation of faith.

The people who came back that next summer had little chance of escaping. Purpose had grown in him; he was going to take whom he wanted and use them for the creation of his Beloved Community.

We hauled out the old boat, took oars and nets and anchors to various owners, bought lumber at the second wharf "up-along," and Jig, [Bror Olsson Julius] Nordfeldt, [Edward J. "Teddy"] Ballantine, Joe O'Brien,[10] others helping, converted the fish-house into the Wharf Theater, a place where ninety people could see a play, if they didn't mind sitting close together on wooden benches with no backs. The stage, ten feet by twelve, was in four sections, so we could have different levels, could run it through the big sliding door at the back, a variety of sets surprising in quarters so small.

We gave a first bill, then met at our house to read plays for a second. Two Irishmen, one old and one young, had arrived and taken a shack just up the street. "Terry," I said to the one not young, "haven't you a play to read to us?"

"No," said Terry Carlin, "I don't write, I just think, and sometimes talk. But Mr. O'Neill has got a whole trunk full of plays," he smiled.

That didn't sound too promising, but I said: "Well, tell Mr. O'Neill to come to our house at eight o'clock tonight, and bring some of his plays."

So Gene took *Bound East for Cardiff* from his trunk, and Freddie Burt read it to us, Gene staying out in the dining room while the reading went on.

He was not left alone in the dining room when the reading had finished.

Then we knew what we were for. We began in faith, and perhaps it is true when you do that "all these things shall be added unto you."

I may see it through memories too emotional, but it seems to me I have never sat before a more moving production than our *Bound East for Cardiff*, when Eugene O'Neill was produced for the first time on any stage. Jig was Yank. As he lay in his bunk dying, he talked of life as one who knew he must leave it.

The sea has been good to Eugene O'Neill. It was there for his opening. There was a fog, just as the script demanded, a fog bell in the harbor. The tide was in, and it washed under us and around, spraying through the holes in the floor, giving us the rhythm and the flavor of the sea while the big dying sailor talked to his friend Drisc of the life he had always wanted deep in the land, where you'd never see a ship or smell the sea.

It is not merely figurative language to say the old wharf shook with applause.

---

10. Friends of Cook and Glaspell's, who also acted and participated in the first season at Provincetown.

The people who had seen the plays, and the people who gave them, were adventurers together. The spectators were part of the Players, for how could it have been done without the feeling that came from them, without that sense of them there, waiting, ready to share, giving—finding the deep level where audience and writer and player are one. The last month of his life Jig wrote:

> I who am audience insofar as the author is one with me,
> And author insofar as the audience is one with me,
> More than any person's name and fame
> I will to hear
> The music of the identity of men.

People sometimes said, "Jig is not a businessman," when it seemed opportunities were passed by. But those opportunities were not things wanted from deep. He had a unique power to see just how the thing he wanted done could be done. He could finance for the spirit, and was seldom confused, or betrayed, by extending the financing beyond the span he saw ahead, not weighing his adventure down with schemes that would become things in themselves.

He wrote a letter to the people who had seen the plays, asking if they cared to become associate members of the Provincetown Players. The purpose was to give American playwrights of sincere purpose a chance to work out their ideas in freedom, to give all who worked with the plays their opportunity as artists. Were they interested in this? One dollar for the three remaining bills.

The response paid for seats and stage, and for sets. A production need not cost a lot of money, Jig would say. The most expensive set at the Wharf Theater cost thirteen dollars. There were sets at the Provincetown Playhouse which cost little more. He liked to remember *The Knight of the Burning Pestle* they gave at Leland Stanford [University], where a book could indicate one house and a bottle another. Sometimes the audience liked to make its own set.

"Now, Susan," he said to me, briskly, "I have announced a play of yours for the next bill."

"But I have no play!"

"Then you will have to sit down tomorrow and begin one."

I protested. I did not know how to write a play. I had never "studied it."

"Nonsense," said Jig. "You've got a stage, haven't you?"

So I went out on the wharf, sat alone on one of our wooden benches without a back, and looked a long time at that bare little stage. After a time the stage became a kitchen—a kitchen there all by itself. I saw just where the stove was, the table, and the steps going upstairs. Then the door at the back opened, and people all bundled up came in—two or three men, I wasn't sure which, but sure enough about the two women, who hung back, reluctant to enter that kitchen. When I was a newspaper reporter out in Iowa, I was sent downstate to do a murder trial, and I never forgot going into the kitchen of a woman locked up in town. I had meant to do it as a short story, but the stage took it for its own, so I hurried in from the wharf to write down what I had seen. Whenever I got stuck, I would run across the street to the old wharf, sit in that leaning little theater under which the sea sounded, until the play was ready to continue. Sometimes things written in my room would not form on the stage, and I must go home and cross them out. "What playwrights need is a stage," said Jig, "their own stage."

Ten days after the director said he had announced my play, there was a reading at Mary Heaton Vorse's. I was late to the meeting, home revising the play. But when I got there the crowd liked *Trifles*, and voted to put it in rehearsal the next day.

It was a great summer; we swam from the wharf as well as rehearsed there; we would lie on the beach and talk about plays—everyone writing, or acting, or producing. Life was all of a piece, work not separated from play.

I like to remember certain times late at night. The audience had gone home, the big door had been drawn shut; the last actor who wanted a drink had the last drop there was at our house, and Jig and I might stroll out on the wharf before going to bed. The sea had taken it all again—the wharf was the old wharf and the theater the fish-house that had been there while so many tides came and went. Fishermen, people from deep in the land who wanted to write plays about both sea and land that—why? At such times one wondered. It seemed now, on the wharf that jutted out from a sleeping town, as if we had not been at all; and before many more tides came in, it would indeed be as if we had not been at all. And yet, would it? Perhaps we wanted to write plays and put them on just because we knew, more intensely than the fishermen, that the tide comes, the tide goes. You cannot know that and leave things just as they were before.

One night I was lonely in the house, suspected where Jig was and went out to find him. The theater a dark bulk behind him, he was sitting at the end of the wharf, feet hanging over. "Thinking about the theater?" I asked after a little—things hadn't gone so well that night.

He shook ashes from his pipe. "No," he said. "I was thinking about raft boats on the Mississippi."

. . .

I was appalled the day Jig said, "When we go to New York for the winter, we will take our theater with us." That, I thought, was a very different thing. I was afraid for him. I knew how it had been through the summer. Many had been interested, and some of them had worked hard, but after all the others worked when they wanted to. "What is Jig going to do about this?" they would say when a real difficulty presented itself. There were people who would be animated when they were with him, and then next day—"But really, I haven't time for it, you know," and they would have to be captured anew, or let go, and someone else captured. He was the center; for the most part, he made the others want to do it, as well as persuaded them it could be done. I felt the energy must go into keeping that fire of enthusiasm, or belief, from which all drew. It was hard to see Jig hurt—he always seemed so surprised it should be like that. He had so much trust, valuing people by the finest moment they showed him—sometimes largely a radiation from his own glow. And I was afraid people would laugh at him, starting a theater in New York—new playwrights, amateur acting, somewhere in an old house or a stable. He himself never thought of this, too concentrated on the thing to be done.

I said I did not think we were ready to go to New York; I feared we couldn't make it go. "Jack Reed thinks we can make it go," he said.

Those two were the first to believe—adventurers both, men of faith. "Impractical."

One of Jig's notes: "The deep and original creative feeling that is found in some American men."

"Where will we get the money?" I asked.

"Our associate members will subscribe for the New York season. That will be our nucleus."

It was one of Jig's warmest satisfactions that members of our audience that summer of 1916 were members every year thereafter. There was our strength, he said; we did not need to take money that would threaten what we were; our audience was part of us.

We were going to call ourselves the Provincetown Players, but Gene proposed we be also the Playwrights' Theater.

Two hundred and forty-five dollars in his pocket, in the glow of vision, energetic with belief, Jig boarded the train to look for a place for the Provincetown Players in New York. He stood alone on the back platform, waving to me. "Don't worry!" he called, as the train was starting, then something I couldn't hear, and I went running after him. He cupped his mouth with his hands to call back: "Write—another—play!" [. . .]

Fire from Heaven

"Writers, critics, adventurers, painters, having in common a feeling that it would be better to be destroyed than not to create one's own beauty." Jig said this of the group from which the Provincetown Players came.

You have the police to reckon with in creating your own beauty in New York; you have small boys who kick tin cans down MacDougal Street while the curtain is up, people upstairs who put their garbage in front of the theater just as the audience is arriving, the phonograph next door.

A little disheartening, when finally he found a ground-floor at 139 Mac-Dougal Street, to learn that two hundred of the two hundred and forty-five dollars (capital from Provincetown) must be paid for putting in a steel girder, or the partition which would give the stage couldn't be torn out.

When I arrived in New York, having dutifully written *The People*, my first glimpse of Jig was standing amid shavings, lumber and bags of cement, explaining the Provincetown Players to a policeman and an impersonal-looking person from the building department. "Now here is Susan Glaspell," he said, as if I had entered for just this. "She is writing plays. And there is a young Irishman, O'Neill"—turning to the Irish policeman. We all went downstairs to have a drink and talk it over. Broadway. That wasn't what we wanted to do. In fact, we weren't doing this for money at all. "My salary is fifteen dollars a week," said Jig. The person from the building department looked a little less impersonal as Jig talked to him of plays out of American life, quite as if this were one of the man's warm interests. The Irish police-man remained a friend to the last, more than once telling us what to do when we would have blundered.

I have heard Jig explain the Provincetown Players to firemen, electri-cians, women tenement inspectors, garbage collectors, judges. Our Italian landlady, our real-estate agent, our banker, were drawn into the adventure. "We are doing it for fun," Jig said to a judge, when the question of our play-ing Sunday nights was up. "Oh, of course, profound fun. The fun of death, for instance—the profound amusement of imagined death, followed swiftly enough, Your Honor, by the real moment."

The judge gave him a swift keen look. The look held between them.

"But what shall the sergeant do," said the gentleman from the police, "if they play again Sunday night?"

"Oh, tell him to do something else," said His Honor, and subscribed to the Provincetown Players.

It didn't always come out so charmingly. Many nights Jig would sleep a couple of hours, then figure in his little book how to prevent a threatened disaster. We had no theater license; often we did not know whether we would play once more, or be closed that night.

Hard, too, to create one's own beauty without dressing rooms, without space for shifting scenery. Even knowing we did it, I am disposed to say what we did that first year couldn't be done. I can see Jig, say, an afternoon of dress rehearsal, coat off, sleeves up, perspiring as any other laborer perspires, lifting, pounding, working to help finish a set; wrestling with a stage manager who says a certain thing can't be done, checking up on props— himself going over to Sixth Avenue for some of them—yes, sweeping the theater, if the woman who should have done it failed to come. "You must have your lunch," I say. He shakes his head. I go out and get a bottle of milk, and he works through till performance time—works as if it were death which waits if the thing is not done.

He believed that the gifted amateur had possibilities which the professional may have lost. It was with an amateur group he worked in those early years; with no money, the only hold he had on them was through making them want to do it. It was his intensity that held the thing together. They would cut rehearsals, be late—things professionals would not dream of doing. He would reorganize a whole scene-shift, rehearse it himself, drive it through to save three minutes, only to have the gifted amateur actress hold the curtain while she finished her makeup. There are people who are not equal to the intensity of the theater; they are there to thwart your own intensity, and from their superior calm look with amazement upon your righteous fury. "I sweat blood for that three minutes, and she threw it away powdering her nose!"

And the thing it was all for? The beauty created? Judging that first year by itself alone, it was not worth the struggle of making it possible. Bad acting and producing, plays there seemed little reason for giving. Sometimes it would be almost impossible to cast a play. Why then did his faith hold?

Because beneath fatigue and disappointment he believed in the thing as a whole. In a theater for experiment you may do things which in themselves are not worth doing. Yet he would feel something in that play—a thing that was on its way to something else. Why not give this boy a chance to see it in action, see how he can improve it in rehearsal? Let him know that here is a stage for the better play he can write.

In those years there were no tickets for critics. If they wanted to come and pay for a seat, they were as welcome as anyone else. We were not doing it for them any more than for other members of the audience. "We knew the joy of the theater last year in MacDougal Street," he writes at the beginning of our second season, and that joy, strangely uncommon in our great play-giving, play-going world is, like beauty, its own excuse for being. There ought, moreover, to be one theater for American writers to play with—one where, if the spirit move them, they can give plays which are not likely to be produced elsewhere. We mean to go on giving artists of the theater a chance to work out their ideas in freedom.

We have no ambition to go uptown and become "a real theater." We have a theater because we want to do our own thing in our own way. We believe that hard work done in the play spirit has a freshness not found in the theater which has become a business.

There are rich backgrounds behind the people of this group. They were accustomed to deal imaginatively with life before they came together and began to focus their creative impulse upon their untrammeled little stage. There are more interesting things latent in their minds than they have yet written or acted. Their hope is greater than it was in the beginning.

We are still not afraid to fail in things worth trying. This season, too, shall be adventure. We will let this theater die before we let it become another voice of mediocrity. If any writers in this country are capable of bringing down fire from heaven to the stage, we are here, to receive and help.

A beautiful thing had happened. That "fire from heaven"—had it been withheld? The scenery might totter at times, the waits were long, the ventilation bad and the seats uncushioned, but that audience is already an historic one. For one after another they were seeing those dramas of the sea written by Eugene O'Neill. No one else was producing him then, and I leave you the story of the unfolding of his career, of his growth in power upon that tiny experimental stage, as justification of the idea of this man George Cram Cook.

Yet because of his integrity of idea, that conspicuous success never made him see as less important the work of those who had not yet succeeded, who might never, in the usual sense of the word, succeed. If certain things we did reached the larger public, then perhaps our intensity should more and more go into the work which also had meaning, but which might be harder to project. The things that others would do were not so particularly our individual job. To *cause* better American plays to be written—that is what he kept saying.

—*SG*

The Theatre Guild

FOUNDED 1918

Lawrence Langner

The Theatre Guild began, as Lawrence Langner explains below, with the idea that "the little theater should grow up." By growing up, the Guild cut a path for the modern art theater in the commercial mainstream and so established one of the most consistent and long-lived artistic production records ever. Rising out of the ashes of the willfully amateur Washington Square Players, the Guild became the principal producer of fine contemporary theater on Broadway. It premiered plays by numerous American and European greats, including George Bernard Shaw, Eugene O'Neill, Maxwell Anderson and Robert Sherwood, and helped sustain the careers of some of our finest actors, including the incomparable Lunts. Though not without its detractors—preeminently the Group Theatre, whose three founders all worked at the Guild before launching their own upstart company—the Guild may still represent the pinnacle of art and commerce coming together in the New York theater.

The company pioneered the subscription season—regularly maintaining up to thirty thousand subscribers—and challenged audiences with category-defying works like *Heartbreak House*, *The Adding Machine*, *Porgy and Bess* and *Idiot's Delight*; such whoppers as Ibsen's *Peer Gynt*, Shaw's *Back to Methuselah* and O'Neill's *Mourning Becomes Electra*; as well as the ground-breaking musical *Oklahoma!* The Guild also thrived despite, or maybe because of, its unique governing structure, in which a powerful, opinionated governing board made all decisions collectively. Its six directors—actress Helen Westley, executive director Theresa Helburn, designer Lee Simonson, director Philip Moeller, banker Maurice Wertheim and playwright/patent lawyer Langner—selected plays together, oversaw all rehearsals, ran the administration, and planned the expansion of a theater that at its height in 1930–31 had eighty-five thousand subscribers in thirteen cities across the United States, each of which was promised a six-play season.

Below Langner depicts how the big theater grew out of the little one, and how it ran. The story he tells comes from *The Theatre Guild: The First Ten Years*, published to mark the Guild's anniversary, co-written by the theater's directors and edited by critic and author Walter Prichard Eaton. Eaton sums up the aesthetic of this remarkable company: "The Guild plays are for the most part the antithesis of the

SOURCE: *The Theatre Guild: The First Ten Years*, by Lawrence Langner, 1929.

type of drama supposedly popular and able to succeed on tour; they are for the most part plays with a sharp intellectual appeal, or with some edge of wit or style or sophistication setting them off from the ruck." And he goes on to sum up the Guild's ethic as well, the guiding principle—with the "force of a revolution"—that the directors steered by:

> It is less a theater of ideas than of an idea. That idea is shared by these six men and women, and by each one is held with passionate loyalty. [. . .] And what is that idea? Ridiculously simple! Merely that the theater is bigger than any workers in it, and in its ideal condition will not be employed for either personal or commercial exploitation, but for the creation, as carefully and lovingly as lies within one's power, of the best drama of one's time, drama honestly reflecting the author's vision of life or sense of style and beauty.
>
> —TL

The Washington Square Players, in the year of 1914, produced a program of one-act plays in the little Bandbox Theatre, seating 299 persons; its direct lineal descendant, the Theatre Guild, in the year 1929, is providing ten of the large cities in the United States with a program of from five to six artistic plays of the kind not ordinarily produced in the commercial theater, acted by some of the best acting talent available in the country, and running for a season of from five to fifteen weeks outside New York, to a full season of thirty weeks in New York itself. I shall try to trace the steps of internal development which have made possible the growth of the Guild to an art theater conducted on an unusually extensive scale, and to explain some of the principles which I believe to be entirely new in the history of the theater, and which have been utilized by the Guild in its development as a group organization.

Other members of the Guild Board have explained their special provinces in the Guild, which have brought its artistic and organization activities to its present stage of development. I shall deal here with the particular work in which I have been largely engaged—the planning of the Guild's future development—which work, like all the other activities of the Guild Board, has always been in the nature of collaboration with the other five Guild directors.

The Theatre Guild began with an idea, which was in my mind as well as in the minds of a number of others, after the demise of the Washington Square Players. It was that the little theater should grow up. The Theatre Guild, both in its inception and in its subsequent development, has always embodied this idea, and it is in this respect that the Theatre Guild has differed from the dozens of other art theaters in this country and abroad, which have been satisfied to remain in the little theater stage.

The beginnings of the Washington Square Players were humble indeed, far more humble than the beginnings of the Theatre Guild; for when we started the Theatre Guild we had behind us the experiences of the Washington Square Players. Nevertheless, it was in the work of the Washington Square Players that the germs of many of the ideas now forming a basic part of the Guild policy were developed.

In addition to the experience which was gained in this group, the Players contributed at least two extremely valuable organization methods, and an extremely valuable artistic method, all of which were later to be of great importance to the Guild. It inaugurated the operation of a theater under the direction of a board of managers, which performed the general function of controlling the artistic and financial policies of the theater, the work of the board not only including the selection of the plays but also the selection of the theater, the actors, the director and the scenic artist to be employed in each production, so that the direction of the organization was centered entirely in the board, while the various executives designated by the board carried out the policies which were agreed upon. This system has been the basis of the Guild's directorate. The Washington Square Players also developed a method of play production, under the supervision of its board of managers, which, so far as I know, was not used by any theater before it, but was eminently successful both with the Washington Square Players and, with modifications, with the Theatre Guild. Special rehearsals of each play are given before the board of managers during successive stages of the period of rehearsal, and after the rehearsal is over and the actors leave the theater, the director and the board have a conference, at which the various notes made by the board members are submitted. Each point in the production is examined and argued until a conclusion is reached, the board having the final say in any dispute.

Another organization method which the Guild inherited from the Washington Square Players was that of securing a membership audience, the members of which subscribe in advance for a series of plays, their subscriptions furnishing the organization with some of the funds necessary to produce the plays. This subscription method, having been adopted and greatly improved upon, has resulted in the Guild's extensive definite supporting membership of over sixty thousand members throughout the country. The members, by paying for their seats in advance, provide a guarantee against too great a loss on each production, which makes a subsidy unnecessary. The number of members obtained by the Washington Square Players by means of its subscription list was, however, never quite large enough to keep the group out of debt, so that the subscription system did not realize the same success with the Players as with the Guild, and financial help in the way of private subsidy was often necessary in the earlier group.

When the war came to an end, I suggested to Philip Moeller and Helen Westley that we should immediately start to work to create a new art theater, and, backed by their enthusiasm, I wrote letters to a number of former members of the Washington Square Players, inviting them to attend a meeting at the home of Miss Josephine A. Meyer, who had been one of the prominent members of the Washington Square Players, and whose spirit had been a source of inspiration to us all. Miss Meyer was ill at the time, but it seemed fitting that our first meeting should be in her home, always a sanctuary of artistic faith and idealism.

Josephine Meyer was not to live long after this meeting, but I like to think that her spirit has always been with the Guild. In spite of her weakened condition, she bravely undertook the duties of one of the Guild's play readers.

The atmosphere of our first meeting, which I well remember, was one of the greatest enthusiasm. We not only discussed the forming of an art theater, we discussed very fully the kind of art theater which we wanted to form. It is a tribute to the spirit and intelligence which characterized the discussion at this meeting, when I say that the conclusions which were set in writing after the meeting have formed the Magna Charta of the Theatre Guild, and have never been departed from in principle. For the benefit of those who are interested in the conclusions which were reached at the end of this first meeting of the Guild, I quote the following, which I noted down in a letter written directly after the meeting:

1. That we would form a group to carry out the idea of an expert theater; that is, a theater which would be entirely different from the Little Theatre or Provincetown Players type of theater, but would be made up only of artists of the theater who are experts in their work.
2. That we would either lease or secure the building of a theater seating a considerable number of people, and certainly larger than the usual Little Theatre (between five hundred and six hundred seating capacity), in some place where the rents were sufficiently low not to make rentals a burden.
3. To govern absolutely by a committee which will delegate its executive and administrative powers to members thereof.

[...]

Whereas the earlier theater had proven to be a splendid training ground for the amateur, this new theater was to be an adult theater, attempting the highest expressions of the theatrical art, and using the finest talent available in the theater for its avowed purpose, which, like that of the Washington Square Players, was to produce plays of artistic merit not ordinarily produced by the commercial managers. The group invited a number of well-known players who were sympathetic toward the art theater movement to join the Guild, and with a company composed largely of players recruited from the ranks of the commercial theater, with a few amateurs to fill in where professionals were not available, the performances of the two long plays of the Guild's initial season were given. The Guild, thus launched in its program, has never departed from this policy. It has produced the masterpieces of many countries, and has always attempted to do this with the best acting talent it could procure in the American theater.

What is there in this policy which makes it a desirable policy for an art theater to pursue—or which justifies any recommendation of such policy to others? At first glance it seems clear that the work of the earlier Washington Square Players, in developing new talent, was of considerably greater importance than the work of the Guild in utilizing talent already in existence. Indeed, since it was the Players which developed, in the main, the young talents of the Theatre Guild Group, it is obvious that, without the earlier work of the Players, the Guild could not have existed at all, just as a promising athlete could not become a football player without first learning the game. The earlier Players group had served its purpose; it had acted as the incubator for several talents in the theater. These talents were not teaching talents; if they had been, the Players might still be in existence, turning amateur actors into professional actors, and so forth. They were producing talents, and when the step of using the best actors available in the theater, and the forming of a company of such actors was decided upon, the Guild pushed the whole cause of the art theater into the vanguard of American cultural life by showing that artistic plays, when well acted, were as interesting, and indeed *more* interesting, than the rubbish which had passed for theatrical fare just before and during the war. In other words, instead of making the artistic play bear the brunt of bad acting performances and bad productions, as had commonly been the case with so-called "high-brow" efforts, the Guild realized that great plays needed great performances, and set out to secure them. It lost to a certain extent the capacity for experiment with raw material in acting talent. Indeed, it lost the general capacity for experiment which marked the first phase of the group, but it gained a competence in performances and production which won an audience away from the "commercial" theater; an audience which we confidently hope will continue to support the Guild so long as it continues in the policy of producing great plays, greatly acted and sensitively produced.

[…]

One of the most interesting of the Guild's activities has been its organization of its audience. Beginning with the idea that there was an audience which was eager for good plays in New York, and discovering later on, against the contrary opinions expressed by many, that there were audiences equally eager outside New York, the Guild set about systematically to unite itself with its audience in such a way that the Guild now consists of those who produce the play and those who go to see the play. I think it can be safely said that the most important bond which exists between our audience and ourselves is the mutual interest in the production of plays of an unusual character presented with the greatest possible resources of the theater. We have often noticed that our greatest support has come when we have made some unusually daring experiment, and especially an experiment which involves considerable financial loss, with very little likelihood of recouping it. Our production of *Back to Methuselah* is a case in point. I remember when I first visited Bernard Shaw in London, and arranged for him that the Guild should produce his plays in America, that I asked him for contract in order that we might produce *Back to Methuselah*. "A contract is quite unnecessary," said Shaw. "It is quite unlikely that another lunatic will want to put on the play." Several years later, Eugene O'Neill handed me the manuscript of *Strange Interlude* while I was on a visit to Bermuda. He informed me that he had already promised the manuscript to another manager who would produce it in case a well-known actress was willing to appear in it. I waited with a great deal of trepidation upon the verdict of this other manager. Fortunately for the Guild, he refused it, and the Guild produced the play purely in the spirit of experiment, fully intending to risk a considerable financial loss in the event that the play proved a failure from the popular standpoint. Both *Back to Methuselah* and *Strange Interlude* proved to be artistic successes of the first water, and the financial losses on the former were more than made up by the earnings of the latter.

[…]

There is one great, crying need for the Guild Board itself. It is the need of always attempting the production of something a little more difficult than has been attempted before. The Guild Board receives its greatest stimulus when attempting tasks which are more difficult than those which it has already accomplished. After producing *Strange Interlude*, it seeks restlessly for another test of itself. So long as this spirit continues in our organization, I do not fear either stagnation or satiation.

—*LL*

Oregon Shakespeare Festival

FOUNDED 1935

Angus Bowmer

Oregon Shakespeare Festival was born as an amateur project in 1935 and, after a six-year intermission for World War II, reborn as a professional organization in 1947. Its first flowering began on the weekend of the Fourth of July with three performances of two plays—*Merchant of Venice* and *Twelfth Night*, played for five hundred people. Over the next five years, the season grew: eight performances for 1,800 people. In its renaissance year following the war, that number had grown again, to sixteen performances and an audience of five thousand. In 2011 OSF offered 787 performances of eleven plays to more than four hundred thousand theatergoers. Amateur or professional, it never lost touch with two driving forces: 1) it embodied the enthusiasm and energy of its founder, Angus L. Bowmer, a teacher at the local Southern Oregon Normal School; and 2) it belonged to the audience.

Here's what Bowmer's successor, Jerry Turner, wrote about him:

> In the Rogue Valley of southern Oregon I met a man with three loves: shakespeare, art and people; and none of them were capitalized in his mind. The people in Shakespeare's plays were just that: people. [. . .] His art consisted of introducing them to each other and, like a gracious host, making conversation until both audience and character felt at home together.

This hospitality—introducing the people of Shakespeare to the people of the northwestern United States—has marked the Festival and made it a tourist destination, with eighty-eight percent of its audience traveling more than 125 miles to see its shows.

Despite its boom growth, OSF never has seemed to lose sight of its humble origins or its American roots. Bowmer erected the Festival's first Elizabethan stage—consciously modeled after the drawings of Shakespeare's own theater, as opposed to the realistic proscenium stages popular for Shakespearean productions of the time—within the embrace of the foundations of one of the nation's early Chautauqua arenas, the domed roof of which had been removed as part of Ashland's first WPA project under President Franklin Delano Roosevelt's New Deal. The Chautauqua was a late-nineteenth-century education and culture movement that brought traveling

SOURCE: *As I Remember, Adam: An Autobiography of a Festival*, by Angus Bowmer, 1975.

programs—lectures, speeches, concerts, dramatic readings—to people throughout the nation. The spirit of these tented meetings, with
attendees often numbering in the thousands, infused the spirit of
the early Festival. You can hear this spirit in Bowmer's writing—the
welcoming pioneer, eager to share his enthusiasms with the rest of
the community. It was the same spirit that rallied the community,
allowing the theater to run on volunteer help—more than a dozen
local committees and clubs staffing the Festival—for decades.

When, in 1970, OSF opened a second space, named for Bowmer,
Governor Tom McCall spoke of the Festival's founding days, and of
the spirit of community participation that, with Bowmer's leadership,
made reality of a dream:

> The dream did not, even in the beginning, walk alone. There
> were loving hearts and talented hands and a legion of unnamed
> laborers who soon came into the story. That was a brave and
> daring band back in the thirties. They flourished with what
> some professors like to call "the valor of ignorance." They
> didn't know that a Shakespearean Festival in a what's-its-name
> town way out in a whatcha-ma-call-it state is ridiculous.
>
> —*TL*

The two and a half years between my return to Ashland and the rebirth of
the Festival seem in retrospect to have been a kind of limbo. My professional
life was not dull, but neither was it particularly exciting. I suppose my own
activities lacked direction. I was treading water. It is possible that I could
have spent the rest of my life in this contented cow existence had it not been
for a conversation with Bill Healey, the secretary of the Ashland Chamber
of Commerce. Bill asked me if I would be willing to start the Festival again.

Bill Healey was an unusual, active, perceptive and considerably more
progressive secretary than the Ashland Chamber had been used to. His policies and tactics were so aggressive, in fact, that he made enemies as well as
friends for the Chamber. However, I have always credited Bill for having
sparked the fortunate move to start the Festival again. What I did not know
until recently was that he was pushed! Well, prompted at least.

Robert Dodge had been a member of the Festival Board all during the
pre-war years since the forming of the Festival Association. Bob and his
wife, Rae, had invited Bill and Mary Healey to their summer cottage at Lake
of the Woods for a weekend. Bob came from a family which, for several generations, had been sired by successful and public-spirited businessmen. Bob
tells me that his grandfather was instrumental in the establishment of Ash-

land's beautiful Lithia Park. Bill had, therefore, reason to listen with interest to the history of the Festival and to the estimates of its potential impact on the community, as related that weekend by Bob, whose business acumen Bill had reason to appreciate.

Thus it came about that the energetic secretary of the Ashland Chamber of Commerce asked me if I would start the Festival again. My answer, I suspect, caught him by surprise. It came readily enough, for there had been a lot of time for me to think about the kind of theater I had dreamed of for Ashland. In the nine years since the start of the Festival I had learned some lessons concerning the nature of that inseparable married couple: the theater company and its audience. There were certain firm convictions about what a great community theater should and should not be that shaped my answer.

Perhaps this is a good place to set them down. The list that follows extends far beyond those precepts which shaped my answer to Bill Healey, and some of them may have been conceived ex post facto. In any case, here is the list: what might well be called "The Oregon Shakespearean Festival Manifesto."

First, what it should not be:

1. It should not be a plaything for a group of stagestruck youngsters.
2. It should not be an exclusive watering place for the socially ambitious.
3. It should not be a platform for the exploitation of any single political, social, aesthetic or religious thesis.
4. It should not be a theater in which the talents of any one theatrical artist are exploited to the detriment of either the audience's enjoyment or the playwright's intent.
5. It should not have the clinical aura of academia.
6. It should not be a museum.

Then what it should be:

1. It should be a people's theater—that is, it should belong to its audience.
2. It should be a theater operated by professional theater experts.
3. It should have a clear, thoroughly efficient internal organizational structure.
4. It should be a theater which presents its audience with a wide variety of theatrical experiences, including those provided by the world's great playwrights of all ages.
5. It should be exciting.

6. It should be unique without being quixotic.
7. It should be solvent.
8. Above all, it should be an instrument of communication, utilizing trained artists in a theatrical environment to entertain, and
at the same time to make clear to its audience, by means of visual
and auditory data, ideas and emotions concerning the interrela-
tionships of Man and Man, Man and his Environment and Man
and his Gods.

This list is far from exhaustive, but I think it presents the nub of the Oregon
Shakespearean Festival idea.

But back again to 1947, when Bill Healey asked me if I would start the
Festival again. With a few of the above criteria a bit more firmly in mind than
they had been before the war, I answered in the negative.

"No," I said, "but if the people of Ashland want to start it again, I am
available—for a price." When pushed for a figure, I said I would produce
the Festival for five hundred dollars a year. Later that day, I called him and
revised the figure to one thousand dollars a year.

This materialistic answer came not from a newly developed acquisitive-
ness, but from a firm conviction that the relationship of the Festival to the
community must be changed if it were to be successfully revived. Before the
war, there had been a goodly number of wonderful, public-spirited people
whose help had been essential to the success of the Festival. But I felt there
was a limit to an artistic organization which depended upon the help of the
community for its success. The reverse should be true. We theater people
should be essential to the success of the community's artistic project. I was
also of the opinion that the people of Ashland must want the Festival very
much indeed if it were to survive another try. The money yardstick was
a measure we could all understand. If they wanted it a thousand dollars'
worth, I thought it was worth a second attempt.[11]

—*AB*

11. According to Paul Nicholson, the Festival's long-term executive director, Bowmer "went
home after his meeting with Bill Healey and told his wife Gertrude, who was a curmudgeon of
the first order, that he'd been asked to start the Festival again and had been offered five hundred
dollars. Very excited about it, Gertrude said, 'Absolutely not! If they are willing to pay five
hundred dollars, they'll be willing to pay one thousand dollars.' And so that's why he went back
with the higher price!"

Chapter 4

The Genius of the Individual, the Genius of the Group

One man cannot produce drama. True drama is born only of one feeling animating all the members of a clan—a spirit shared by all and expressed by the few for the all.

—*George ("Jig") Cram Cook*

The Group Theatre

FOUNDED 1930

Harold Clurman

> I'm sick of this dervish dance they've got us doing on steel springs and a General Electric motor. When it stops—as it must—there will be dissolution and devastation; everything will become as frightfully blank as today everything is fiercely congested. [. . .] Perhaps to rush out of line is to invite disaster. If so, let it come. [. . .] We must help one another find our common ground; we must build our house on it, arrange it as a dwelling place for the whole family of decent humanity.
>
> *—Harold Clurman*[1]

If, as it's been said, Harold Clurman talked the Group Theatre into being, many others shared the job of giving it life. Lee Strasberg, the Group's first teacher and director, brought it fire, with his fierce, demanding zealotry, the austere paternalism of his drive for truth. Cheryl Crawford, part of the triumvirate, with Clurman and Strasberg, to found and run the Group, gave the company legs and, taking on the more thankless, practical tasks of "reading scripts, working on finance and calming tempers," helped it to walk. A contentious and striving ensemble of, in Crawford's words, "twenty-eight fanatics" offered their individual talents in service of the most unified, coherent communal vision of theater that had yet been seen on this nation's stage. Clifford Odets, a supporting actor with the company and its major playwriting discovery, taught the Group to sing.

The three directors were all part of the flourishing Theatre Guild when they decided to strike out on their own. Clurman had begun as a bit player and graduated to a play reader. Strasberg was an actor

SOURCE: *The Fervent Years*, by Harold Clurman, 1945.

1. I am indebted to Wendy Smith's exhilarating book *Real Life Drama: The Group Theatre and America, 1931–1940* (Knopf, New York, 1990) for a much more complete—and many-voiced—portrait of the Group than Clurman's or, indeed, anyone's.

with the company and Crawford, a stage manager and casting director. But the Guild, for all its success, was a product of America before the stock market crash of 1929. Its directors were not makers or initiators of art. "They didn't want to say anything through plays," in Clurman's assessment. Through a series of weekly, late-night talks, the shy Clurman countered the more aesthetically neutral, Guild approach. He found passionate voice, groping toward an aesthetics of community, unity of production, and connection—performer to material, theater to the world. His lengthy torrential monologues attracted hundreds, including many who returned, Friday after Friday, just before midnight, from November 1930 until the following May. In June 1931 the newly constituted band of players, spouses, children and others retreated to a vacation resort in Brookfield Center, Connecticut, to begin the experiment that would become the Group Theatre.

That theater would last—with fits and starts—almost a decade. It would be finally pulled apart by myriad forces, notably the lure of Hollywood and tensions between the actors and the company's directors. It would fall victim to its own successes and to conflicts among the very artists this experiment encouraged to shared power, shared voice. It would embody the struggle between individual ambition and collective good that lies so deeply in the American soul. But first it would create a kind of theater never before seen in this country and change the course of American acting forever, by nurturing the talents of most of the nation's leading acting teachers and theorists of the twentieth century—Strasberg, Stella Adler, Robert Lewis, Sanford Meisner. It would incubate world-class actors and directors, notably Clurman and Elia Kazan, and, in Odets, an important playwright as identified with his time as any in our history. It would provide moments of glorious theater lore—that communal summer in Connecticut, for example, or an audience, rising to its feet, shouting, "Strike! Strike!" at the closing moments of the premiere of Odets's *Waiting for Lefty*.

More, the Group Theatre would come to embody a powerful, persistent *idea*: individual talent delivered up in service to a common goal, the common good. This is the way Odets vivaciously expressed it in his first entry in the Group's daybook, its shared diary:

I am done! done with chasing my febrile self down the nights and days. From the ashes of the phoenix! The clamoring hatred of Life has been hushed to less than a whisper. On the pivotal point of a quarter century of living (sweet Jesus, twenty-five years old this month!) I have begun to eat the flesh and blood of *the group*. I partake of these consecrated wafers with a clean heart and brain; and I believe—as I have wanted to believe for almost ten years—in some person, idea, thing, outside myself. The insistent love of self has died with strangulation in the night [. . .] I who cried from my inverted wilderness for strong roots with which to fasten to the swarming sustaining earth have found them at last in The Group. I am passionate about this thing!!!

—*TL*

Getting Together

It was Cheryl Crawford who now urged me to prepare for the future by seeking actors who might be selected for our permanent company. I would talk to them, excite their enthusiasm, and generate the momentum that would transform what had been a somewhat vague program into a going concern. When our company had been chosen, when our aims had become concretized through association and discussion, she might be able to enlist the [Theatre] Guild and others as sponsors for the new theater.

The first people we called on were, of course, those with whom we had already worked: [Franchot] Tone, [Morris] Carnovsky, [Sanford] Meisner, and the others. Down at the Civic Repertory Theatre there was a promising character actor, J. Edward Bromberg, who might be interested. Mary Morris from the Macgowan-Jones-O'Neill[2] days should be summoned. Stella Adler would now be willing to listen to me, and there were those people from the Lab[3]—Ruth Nelson, Eunice Stoddard—we had cast in *Red Rust*, as well as a number of youngsters—Phoebe Brand, Dorothy Patten—in the current Guild productions. From Broadway, Margaret Barker, who was playing an agreeable role in *The Barretts of Wimpole Street*, should be considered. These and more we would call together. We would explain—that is, I would, for I did most of the talking at that time—that we proposed a new approach to the theater, that we wished to get acquainted with all those actors who might come to share our approach, that we wanted to lay the foundations of a new theater. As for practical matters, the manner of our functioning, we would take them up only after we had established a common ground of understanding through our meetings together. We had no plays, no money; the meetings were to be entirely "unofficial."

---

2. Kenneth Macgowan, Robert Edmond Jones and Eugene O'Neill were the triumvirate that ran the Provincetown Players in its post–George Cram Cook incarnation.

3. The American Laboratory Theatre, where both Richard Boleslavsky and Maria Ouspenskaya of Moscow Art Theatre fame taught.

The first meeting was held in my room at the Hotel Meurice on West 58th Street in November 1930. Since my room was too small, later meetings were held at Miss Crawford's apartment on West 47th Street, and when her apartment became too crowded, owing to the increasing number of people who showed up, we repaired to a large room at Steinway Hall which some friend of a friend provided without cost. These meetings, held every Friday night at half past eleven, continued from November till May 1931 with hardly an interruption from week to week.

A curious thing happened from the first. Instead of telling the prospective actors of our theater what advantages would accrue to them through an association with us: that we believed in a permanent company which would guarantee them continuity of work and, consequently, security of livelihood, that we believed in developing the actor—not merely in hiring him—thus ensuring greater versatility—instead of all this, which would have been eminently to the point, I chose an almost metaphysical line which led away from matters of the theater. Cheryl Crawford, for this reason, told me she thought my first talk had been "lousy." Gerald Sykes, a literary friend, who was present at the first talk, came from the meeting with the conviction that "such passion can't arise from concern with the theater alone."

An article in dialogue form I had written in 1929 had begun this way:

THE LAYMAN: If you will omit the evangelical tone, you may talk to me about the theater.

THE THEATER MAN: Fanaticism is not only inevitable with us; it is almost indispensable.

I had observed elements of fanaticism in Copeau, in Craig,[4] in Stanislavsky—indeed, in almost every first-rate man of the theater. But in me this fanaticism—which antagonized some of my listeners though it attracted others—was intimately bound up with the nature of my message, which extended beyond the limits of the theater or a desire to make good in it. I was well aware of the fact that there had been other permanent companies in the recent theater (the Neighborhood Playhouse and the Civic Repertory had them). As for training actors, at least two other organizations proposed to do this. In fact, every one of the reforms our theater might bring had been announced, at least, by a previous organization.

My approach emphasized the theater's reason for being. New technical methods, no matter how intriguing in themselves, had a very minor value

---

4. Clurman's referring to the innovative French theater director Jacques Copeau, founder of the Théâtre du Vieux-Colombier in Paris; and Gordon Craig, the modern theater's great designer/director/thinker and the British-born son of actress Dame Ellen Terry.

unless they were related to a content that was humanly valuable. To what human beings, one might ask, were theater ideas to be valuable? First, to the theater artists themselves—to actors, since they were the theater's crucial factor; actors were citizens of a community before they took on their dubious connection with "art." Second, theater ideas were to be important to an audience, of which the actors were a focus, for it is the audience (seen as a "community") that has given birth to its artists. The criterion of judgment for what is good or bad in the theater—be it in plays, acting or staging—does not derive from some abstract standard of artistic or literary excellence, but from a judgment of what is fitting—that is, humanly desirable—for a particular audience,

The unity of theatrical production, about which Craig has spoken at such length, was a unity that does not spring, as Craig presumed, out of an abstract sense of taste or craftsmanship, but out of a unity that is antecedent to the formation of the theater group as such. It is a unity of background, of feeling, of thought, of need, among a group of people that has formed itself consciously or unconsciously from the undifferentiated masses. In the Broadway theater, productions are cooked up haphazardly for money-making purposes in the hope that they will appeal to a large enough number of customers to make them pay. This produced positive results when the elements thrown together were based on the rather primitive appetites of a large number of people. Action melodrama, a leg show, a conventional musical, or a knockabout farce was generally more satisfactory from the standpoint of completeness or unity of style than were the more ambitious efforts of the highbrow theater; Jed Harris's production of *Broadway* or the Ziegfeld *Follies* were capital because all the elements that composed them matched each other and were well related to the audience that paid speculator's prices to see them. The same could not be said for many of the "fine things" I had seen done at the Guild and other of our "better organizations."

A technique of the theater had to be "founded on life values." The whole bent of our theater, I reiterated time and again, would be to combine a study of theater craft with a creative content which that craft was to express. To put it another way, our interest in the life of our times must lead us to the discovery of those methods that would most truly convey this life through the theater.

If man was to be the measure of all things in our theater, if life was the starting point, and an effect on life the aim of our effort, then one had to have a point of view in relation to it, one had to define an approach that might be common to all the members of the group.

It was this that added a dimension to the talks and to the whole atmosphere around the Group, that was to become its distinguishing mark, its strength; its impediment, and its wound. Certain it is that there was added to all the technical discussion of the actor, the director, the scene designer, the audience and the problems of casting and administration a new note, an attitude that lifted these subjects from the realm of narrow craft to that of a general concern with our lives and the life of our times.

[. . .]

Since we were theater people, the proper action for us was to establish a theater in which our philosophy of life might be translated into a philosophy of the theater. Here the individual actor would be strengthened so that he might better serve the uses of the play in which our common belief was to be expressed. There were to be no stars in our theater, not for the negative purpose of avoiding distinction, but because all distinction—and we would strive to attain the highest—was to be embodied in the production as a whole. The writer himself was to be no star either, for his play, the focus of our attention, was simply the instrument for capturing an idea that was always greater than that instrument itself. The playwright too could be worked with, the power of his play could be enhanced by the joint creativity of the theatrical group as a whole, which saw in the play a vehicle to convey a motif fundamental to the theater's main interest. The director was the leader of the theatrical group, unifying its various efforts, enunciating its basic aims, tied to it not as a master to his slave, but as a head to a body. In a sense, the group produced its own director, just as the director in turn helped form and guide the group.

It did not matter at first that each person who attended these meetings put his own special interpretation on them, lent them the color of his own dreams. There were some who were nonplussed by the generalities, others who were shocked by the arrogant boldness of my expression, still others thought me a theorist, which signifies in theater parlance a practical do-nothing. One lady flatly stated: "The man is crazy," for she had never seen anyone so carried away by the expression of ideas. The playwright Lynn Riggs was worried by my emphasis on the contribution of actor and director: he was afraid this boiled down to a contempt for the writer's work. Some of the people came once or twice never to return again. I rarely besought them to alter their course. One actor, a young man who had played secondary roles in two Guild productions, confessed to me, after perhaps ten meetings, that he was just beginning to understand what I was talking about. His name was Clifford Odets.

The Guild Board got wind of these meetings. The theatrical trade papers, *Billboard* and *Variety*, announced—tabloid-fashion—that "revolt" was brewing in the Guild's ranks. [Guild Board member Theresa] Helburn questioned me. I explained the nature of these meetings and told her that when we had definitely chosen our people, we planned to address the Guild

Board, as they might want to help in what we were doing. We would present our ideas to the Guild in a paper; and we would make suggestions as to what they might do for us.

Cheryl Crawford drew up a report, listing the actors and playwrights interested in us, giving also some of our thoughts regarding the financially modest basis on which we could be subsidized as a Guild "Studio." In addition to this, I submitted a general statement. The Guild never commented on it; in fact, I never knew whether it was actually read. It was not unsympathetic, however. When Cheryl Crawford asked the board to release a play they held an option on—Paul Green's *The House of Connelly*—they were prompt to do so. More than that, they allowed us to engage Franchot Tone and Morris Carnovsky, who were then under contract to them, and they added the gift of a thousand dollars toward our expenses in rehearsing the play that summer.

For that is what we decided to do: to go away to some country place with twenty-eight actors and rehearse two plays till they were ready for production in New York. We would pay no salaries, but we would provide meals, living quarters, laundry expense. The three directors—that is what Cheryl Crawford, Lee Strasberg and I now constituted ourselves—had chosen a company from among the people we had come in contact with during our winter meetings. A good many—indeed, a majority—remained with us for years, some to the very last days of our functioning.

[. . .]

Honeymoon

Some of us owned cars; others were borrowed. On the morning of June 8, 1931, twenty-eight actors, some wives, two children, the three directors and a few friends left from the front of the Guild Theatre on 52nd Street for Brookfield Center, Connecticut.

When we arrived and quarters had been assigned, I was amused to find that the first visible activity of the newly gathered company turned out to be a baseball game on the main lawn. It had been started by Franchot Tone, who, he explained to me later, thought it a good way to overcome the natural self-consciousness of the occasion. The average age in our company at this time was twenty-seven. I noticed that Stella Adler looked out from her window somewhat sadly, almost frightened. These people were strangers: they did not behave like actors. To her, the place was like a camp for overgrown high school kids.

There was little time, however, for introspection. After dinner, at about eight-thirty, we all met in the rehearsal hall. This was to be a kind of opening exercise in which the three directors were to give the assemblage an emotional send-off. No record was made of our speeches, but that the meeting had a certain atmosphere of high dedication I am sure. In fact, for a few moments Lee Strasberg was unable to speak at all. He began twice and faltered. A man of intense feeling and an even more intense effort to control his feelings, he was deeply conscious, he said, of the responsibility of our task—his task, since it was he who had been chosen to direct our first play.

The meeting was short, although a few actors tried to add some words of their own to the occasion. One of them, William Challee, had difficulty in articulating his ideas or even his words, but I believe he stammered something about the feeling of being among "brothers." It was about ten when the actors left the hall. No one thought of sleep. The conversation was rather hushed, and in no time a number of phonographs were hauled into the open to play music of an elevated character. These little manifestations of our new life were as mysterious to me as they would have been to any visitor who might have happened on the scene. I had started something, but once begun, this life would gather a momentum of its own from which I was to learn many things.

The next morning, we collected in the main living room to hear Cheryl Crawford read Paul Green's *The House of Connelly*. In presenting to our actors this play about the decadence of the Old South and the emergence of a new class from among the poor tenant farmers, my emphasis was on the basic struggle between any new and old order. The actors immediately made the obvious parallel between this play and Chekhov's *The Cherry Orchard*, just as many other very different plays were later to be discussed by the reviewers in terms of the same Chekhov—parallels and analogies that are academic, empty and useless. But at this time—and perhaps the only time in our history—concern over the play gave way to the actors' far greater absorption in it as a vehicle for the strengthening of their craft.

Lee Strasberg was the natural choice for the director of our first production. Cheryl Crawford had been a little shocked at first by my insistence on this, as her background was obviously much closer to the play than Strasberg's, but I was concerned with the formulation of a technique of acting and production, a specific training that might be shared by the entire company. For this, Strasberg, with his experience (Off Broadway) and his peculiar gifts as a teacher, was best adapted. It was from no pedagogic dogmatism, however, that I insisted on the establishment of a single unified method for the company. It was a question of artistic necessity. You couldn't actually say what we wished to say in the theater by simply having a troupe of actors give "good performances." Talent, contrary to the accepted doctrine of Broadway, is not enough. Talent is accident; craft, in the use of talent, is a matter of some consciousness, of training. Talent might be sufficient for the individual actor; it didn't lead to the solution of the problem of a whole production, which is the relating of a number of talents to a single meaning. "For the elements of a theatrical production to be shaped into a true artistic organism," I had written, "it is not sufficient for them merely to be 'good.' They must be homogeneous, they must belong together, they must form an organic body." That day in June 1931 Strasberg began to make of the twenty-eight actors an "artistic organism" with its own special character and aims.

[. . .]

From consideration of acting and plays we were plunged into a chaos of life questions, with the desire and hope of making possible some new order and integration. From an experiment in the theater we were in some way impelled to an experiment in living.

I must warn the reader not to imagine from the foregoing that we spent the summer wading in emotional mud puddles. In the early days of our formation Aaron Copland had asked me if, in dealing so intimately with our actors, I wasn't afraid of the well-known fruits of familiarity. I asked Strasberg what he thought of the question. Strasberg answered that we were making a group, not hiring a company, and that a certain closeness to the very pulse of the individuals composing the group was essential to real leadership in it. We respected the individual—without such respect there can be no true culture or progress in our time—but the individual needed help and an objective aim beyond himself to avoid an isolation that would end by confusing and diminishing him.

[. . .]

Our actors followed their directors because they felt their true selves were being considered and coped with—something that had rarely occurred in the theater before. But they by no means took everything on faith. One of my earliest memories with an actor of this company was of Morris Carnovsky asking me: "What is this hocus-pocus?" when he was first introduced to the procedure of our acting method.

About our rehearsal method, and the famous Stanislavsky or Moscow Art Theatre system from which it derived, a great mystery was made in those days, and much nonsense was written and spoken. The reason for this was that while we considered the system vital as a method of training, a way of organizing the study of parts, and above all as a means of achieving concrete results in the interpretation of plays, there was no way of demonstrating its value except to actors at rehearsals, rather than through lectures, commentaries or critical debate.

[. . .]

The aim of the system is to enable the actor to use himself more consciously as an instrument for the attainment of truth on the stage. If we had been satisfied that such truth was achieved in most productions, there would have been little purpose in troubling ourselves over the system, for it was not something taught novices, but rather a method employed in all our productions with experienced actors. We were not satisfied with most of even the best previous productions, which seemed to us to show more competent stagecraft than humanity or authenticity of feeling. With few exceptions, what we saw in most shows was "performance," fabrication, artifice. Theatrical experience was, for the greater part, the antithesis of human experience; it bespoke a familiarity with the clichés of stage deportment rather than experience with direct roots in life. It seemed to us that without such true experience plays in the theater were lacking in all creative justification. In short, the system was not an end in itself, but a means employed for the true interpretation of plays.

[. . .]

The first effect on the actors was that of a miracle. The system (incorrectly identified by some actors as the use of the exercises) represented for most of them the open-sesame of the actor's art. Here at last was a key to that elusive ingredient of the stage, true emotion. And Strasberg was a fanatic on the subject of true emotion. Everything was secondary to it. He sought it with the patience of an inquisitor, he was outraged by trick substitutes, and when he had succeeded in stimulating it, he husbanded it, fed it, and protected it. Here was something new to most of the actors, something basic, something almost holy. It was revelation in the theater; and Strasberg was its prophet.

[. . .]

. . .

Writing in our logbook toward the end of the summer, I pointed out that it surprised me how few of the people, in their enjoyment of the summer's activity, reflected on the difficulties ahead. We had come on the scene to improve the theater, to relieve some of its ills; perhaps, too, we hoped to make some contribution to American life generally. But our task was not an easy one. All of us wouldn't necessarily be made happy because we had set ourselves these high purposes. Our job was a hard one, I wrote then, and in the ensuing years I reiterated the warning. I spoke as if we were going into battle, and presaged casualties, but to the others, "battle" meant only alarums and excursions, fanfare and drumbeat.

The night before our last in Brookfield Center we gave a run-through of *Connelly* which a few visitors, among them Winifred Lenihan, then director of the Theatre Guild school, attended. There was, of course, no scenery, no costumes, not even a stage. Rarely has a company of players been so captured by its own mood of sincerity and dedication. More even than the play's lines or situations demanded, the actors poured forth a concentrated stream of fervor that was like the pent-up rivers of all their young life's experience and the aspirations awakened and released through the summer's efforts. The company was exalted by its own transformation.

Miss Lenihan's reaction was that, although there were fine scenes in the play, the whole thing was "too slow." Two or three of our company were affected by this comment, and they repeated the old saw: "too slow." But most of us knew that "too slow" was not the salient feature to be singled out. Robert Edmond Jones in a letter we received next morning spoke in quite different terms.

The last night at Brookfield Center I alone spoke. It was my salute to the future. First I dismissed the kind of evaluation of our work, whatever its source, that expressed itself in such gems of discernment as "too slow." (I did not know then that in later years almost the entire critical vocabulary of most reviewers in regard to stage direction was to relate to the matter of pace and timing. What was slow was bad, what was fast was good.) Second I expressed my own high estimate of Strasberg's accomplishment and of the company's progress. Third, and most important, I spoke of the resistance that we might encounter in New York, not so much through mischief as through indifference. This resistance would not embitter us, but would serve as a challenge. Our heat would melt the city's ice. I quoted "Beanie" (Margaret Barker), who had answered a manager's offer of a part by a refusal. The manager had asked: "How long do you think you'll be busy with your present engagement?" She had replied: "If our play is a success—twenty years. If not—twenty years."

—HC

The Mercury Theatre

FOUNDED 1937

John Houseman

> Why, man, he doth bestride the narrow world
> Like a Colossus, and we petty men
> Walk under his huge legs, and peep about
> To find ourselves dishonorable graves.
>
> *—Shakespeare,* Julius Caesar

"I am the Mercury Theatre," Orson Welles announced to his acting company at the outset of the theater's second—partial, final—season. And he was: the star, auteur director, writer-adaptor, head of publicity and cynosure of it. He was the show. Through Mercury productions of *Julius Caesar, The Shoemaker's Holiday, Heartbreak House* and *Danton's Death*, all eyes and—with Mercury Theatre on the Air's radio broadcast of *The War of the Worlds*—all ears were on him. Even before he turned twenty-four.

George Orson Welles was a student at the Todd Seminary for Boys in Wisconsin when he began to make his mark as a theatrical Prometheus. He traveled to Ireland on a small inheritance after his father's death (his mother had died when he was nine), and talked himself into featured roles at the young Gate Theatre, attracting a kind of critical renown that would—along with some fortuitous contacts, including a letter from Thornton Wilder to Alexander Woollcott, a leading light in New York cultural circles—land him leading roles in Katharine Cornell's touring productions of *Romeo and Juliet* and *Candida*. When John Houseman, later head of New York's Federal Theatre Project's Negro Theatre Unit, saw the nineteen-year-old Welles play Tybalt in Cornell's *Romeo* (he'd been demoted from his earlier turn as Mercutio), both of their lives changed forever.

Houseman hired Welles to direct the famous "Voodoo *Macbeth*," (see the Negro Theatre Project in chapter 2) and in its powerful wake the two men created Project 891, the Federal Theatre Project's classical wing in New York. They enjoyed immediate success with *Doctor Faustus* and notoriety with Marc Blitzstein's *The Cradle Will Rock*. *Cradle* defied a FTP shutdown and the regulations of several artists' unions by premiering impromptu in the audience of the Venice Theatre on Broadway and, in doing so, created theatrical history. The restless pair lit out to form a theater of their own. Less than two years later, they abandoned it.

SOURCE: *Run-Through: A Memoir,* by John Houseman, 1972.

Their legendary achievements were as fraught as their codependent relationship. Welles created tempests wherever he reigned; Houseman enabled him. They made each other possible—and miserable.[5]

Ultimately, the Mercury Theatre stands in stark contrast to the Group Theatre's communitarian ethos. Rather than forming around the collective responsibilities and united voices of the company, the Welles/Houseman theater was built around the singular talents, vision and genius of one man, who, in the words of *New York Times* critic Brooks Atkinson, one of the Mercury's most serious cheerleaders, "is a thorough egotist in the grand manner of the old-style tragedian." Welles, Atkinson writes,

> is an intuitive showman. His theatrical ideas are creative and inventive. And his theatrical imagination is so wide in its scope that he can give the theater enormous fluency and power. [. . .] Plays have to give way to his whims, and actors have to subordinate their art when he gets underway, for the Shadow [a part Welles famously played on the radio] is monarch of all he surveys. It is no secret that his willfulness and impulsiveness may also wreck the Mercury Theatre.
>
> —*TL*

————

To start a repertory theater in New York City today would take a million dollars, months of high-minded discussion, a major real-estate operation, city, state and federal involvement and the benevolent participation of two or more gigantic foundations. The Mercury Theatre was conceived one summer evening after supper; its birth was formally announced ten days later and it opened on Broadway within ten weeks in a playhouse bearing its own name with a program of four productions, a company of thirty-four and a capital of $10,500.

We had no difficulty formulating a program, for we had announced our favorite plays the previous winter on the Federal Theatre and our tastes had not changed. We came upon our name on the cover of a two-year-old magazine in the corner of an empty fireplace at Snedens Landing; we were registered and incorporated four days later in Albany as the Mercury Theatre, Inc., with me as president, Orson Welles as vice president, Augusta Weissberger as secretary and a paid-up capital of one hundred dollars. It was mid-August and if we wanted our theater for the 1937–38 season we had not a moment to lose.

Our first step, once we had a name, was to find a home. Neither Orson nor I could conceive of running a company without a theater and in the

5. While Houseman's *Run-Through*, the first volume of his two-part memoir from which this except comes, tells the story of their partnership with startling honesty, the whole tale comes to novelistic life in Simon Callow's majestic, ripping biography of Welles, also in two page-turning parts.

state of the real-estate market at the time we were confident of finding one. Our search led us downtown to Second Avenue, where we looked at huge, desolate playhouses left over from the boom days of the Yiddish theater. We looked at the Irving Place Theatre, once the home of New York's German repertory, now sunk to burlesque and foreign films; it remained a handsome, dignified house, but too large and expensive for us to run. We got excited for a few days over an abandoned medical amphitheater in the East Forties. Then one morning, George Zorn [Houseman's Federal Theatre Project stage manager, and the Mercury's general manager] called and suggested we meet him at the Comedy Theatre on 41st Street and Broadway. One look— and we knew we had found our home.

The Comedy, an intimate, rococo, two-balcony theater with 687 seats and a good stage, was for many years one of Manhattan's most elegant smaller playhouses. Producers from [Harley] Granville-Barker to Cecil B. DeMille and the Washington Square Players had occupied it, and among the stars it had sheltered were John Barrymore, Holbrook Blinn and Katharine Cornell in her first Broadway appearance. It had also been used for small musicals, which accounted for the narrow orchestra pit and a booth for follow spots high up in the rear of the second balcony.

[Designer/production manager] Jean Rosenthal was hastily summoned from the basement of the Maxine Elliott two blocks away. While we made our way by flashlight through cobwebs and scuttling rats, exploring the twilit, long-abandoned desolation of our new home, Zorn hurried off to make inquiries about its availability. He returned in half an hour with a confused report that the house was currently controlled by an Italian known as the "Commendatore" who ran a bar on Eighth Avenue and fronted for a gangster in Chicago. More important—it was available at the reasonable rental of $187.50 a week, on a three-year lease, so long as it was clearly understood that the owner would not spend one cent to restore or maintain it.

So now we were incorporated; we had a theater available and a program to announce. But we had not one cent of backing and not the faintest notion of where to look for it. Clearly the time had come for a manifesto.

I made an appointment with Brooks Atkinson of the *New York Times*, whose Olympian benediction was desirable, if not essential, for such a project.[6] We met in the *Times* commissary, where I outlined our plans for an

---

6. Though it did not hold the monopolistic position it does today, the *New York Times*, through its drama critic, exercised a dominant influence in the theater of the thirties and forties. Brooks Atkinson, who occupied that position for over thirty years, took his responsibilities seriously and did his best to support what he considered new and valuable theatrical activities on and Off Broadway. His judgments were often emotional but overall his influence was salutary and protective of what was best and most vital in the American theater. [author's note]

independent, low-priced repertory season on Broadway; he approved and offered to publish our declaration of principles in the Sunday drama section, where it appeared on the front page on August 30, 1937, under the headline: PLAN FOR A NEW THEATER.

At the height of our success, *Time*, describing our origin, wrote that "the Mercury was at first just an idea bounded north and south by hope, east and west by nerve." Actually our venture was less rash than it seemed. The WPA had given us an opportunity to feel our power and to try our wings. It had done more than that: through our achievements with the Negro Theatre and Project 891,[7] we had acquired not only a national reputation but also a more direct and varied experience than anyone in the country in this kind of theater, in this particular climate and for this particular audience. We founded the Mercury with the sublime confidence of our youth and our reckless temperaments—and with a substantial accumulation of theatrical knowledge and skill. This was reflected in our "manifesto," in which I tried to avoid the tone of vague, verbose grandeur generally associated with the announcements of embryo, indigent artistic groups. In my third and final draft, completed an hour before deadline, I tried to convey an impression of self-confidence and continuity based on our successful operations of the past two years.

> When it opens its doors early in November the Mercury Theatre will expect to play to the same audiences that during the past two seasons stood to see *Richard II*, *Doctor Faustus*, the two *Hamlet*s, *Murder in the Cathedral*, and the Negro *Macbeth*.
>
> It was surprising that they came in such numbers; but that was not the only surprising thing about this audience. It was fresh. It was eager. To anyone who saw it night after night as we did, it was apparent that this was not the Broadway crowd taking in the hit of the moment. Even less was it the special audience one has learned to associate with "classical revivals." (A million people do not make a special audience.) One had the feeling, every night, that here were people on a voyage of discovery in the theater.
>
> Who were they? There were the silk-hatted few who buy their tickets from speculators. There were the organized groups that the Left Wing has brought into the theater in recent years—but, still more important, there came regularly to these plays a large group of persons who walked into the theater as into a new, unfamiliar

---

7. The Federal Theatre Project's classical theater unit that Houseman ran with Welles prior to founding the Mercury.

place, people who had never been to the theater at all, or who, for one reason or another, had completely ignored it for many seasons.

By filling out the questionnaires which were placed in their programs, about forty thousand people made their theatrical confessions to us. The results were quite startling. Half these people did not go more than once a year to the theater. (Reasons—prices and the movies.) A large number professed themselves disappointed in the regular run of Broadway attractions; now the theater had again assumed importance for them with the appearance of such plays as *Murder in the Cathedral, Richard II, Faustus,* etc. There were specific requests, varying in number with the evening's audience for (a) plays of social content, (b) O'Neill, (c) Shaw. But the steady and overwhelming majority of these nightly requests were for "more classical plays," "classical plays excitingly produced," "great plays of the past presented in a modern way."

This is the audience the Mercury Theatre will try to satisfy.

With no money, no theater, no company and no organization of any sort, it was essential that our initial release be specific and credible.

We shall produce four or five plays each season. Most of these will be plays of the past—preferably those that seem to have an emotional or factual bearing on contemporary life. While a socially unconscious theater would be intolerable, there will be no substitution of social consciousness for drama . . . We prefer not to fix our program rigidly too far ahead. New plays, new ideas may turn up any day. But we do know that our first production will be Shakespeare's *Julius Caesar.* As in *Faustus,* by the use of apron lighting, sound devices, music, etc., we hope to give this production much of the speed and violence that it must have had on the Elizabethan stage. The Roman senators, when they murder the dictator, will not be clad (any more than were the Elizabethan actors) in traditional nineteenth-century stage togas.

Next, we hope, given George Bernard Shaw's consent, to present what we consider his most important play, *Heartbreak House.* Also William Gillette's *Too Much Johnson;* Webster's *Duchess of Malfi*—one of the great horror plays of all time—and Ben Jonson's farce *The Silent Woman.* We expect to run our first play between four and six weeks. After that, without clinging to the European system of repertory, with its disturbing, nightly change of bill, the Mercury Theatre expects to maintain a repertory of its current season's productions. However, at no time will more than two different plays be seen in one week.

We expect to occupy a theater of medium size on the edge of the Broadway district. With a top of two dollars, there will be four hundred good seats at fifty cents, seventy-five cents and one dollar available at every performance.

When Orson returned from his ten-day retreat in New Hampshire, he brought with him a completely reedited text of *Julius Caesar*, including music and light cues, and a suitcase full of notes, sketches and a Plasticine model of his production. We had four weeks in which to adapt them to the Mercury stage. At Jean Rosenthal's suggestion we engaged a young scenic designer, a fellow graduate from Yale. He was a dynamic pollywog of a man with a crew cut and a strong accent, named Samuel Leve—known also as "the Rabbi" because he taught "shul" each Sabbath at a Talmud Torah uptown. He absorbed Orson's ideas and sketches, spent a day marching around the stage with him while Jean and I watched sight lines from the balcony; then, under her technical direction, set about converting them into working drawings and blueprints.

Later, when they saw *Julius Caesar*, many people were under the impression that they were watching a play performed upon a bare stage, and praised the Mercury for its return to theatrical simplicity. In *Caesar* he called for a series of huge, subtly graded platforms that covered the entire stage floor. First came the main downstage playing area—fourteen feet deep including the apron—which rose in a gentle rake to meet a set of shallow steps running the full width of the stage. These led to an eight-foot plateau, the mid-stage playing area, then rose again through another set of steps to a final narrow crest, six and a half feet above stage level, before falling back down in a steep, fanning ramp that ended close to the rear wall of the theater. This gave the stage an appearance of enormous depth and a great variety of playing areas—from the intimacy of the downstage scenes acted within a few feet of the audience, to the dominating mid- and upstage positions on the first and second elevated plateaus. Steps and platforms were honeycombed with traps out of which powerful projectors were angled upward and forward to form a double light curtain (the "Nuremberg lights") through whose beams all actors making upstage entrances had to pass and were suddenly and dramatically illuminated before descending to the playing areas below. It was a brilliant concept, but when the first estimates for lumber, construction and additional lighting equipment were added up they came to twice what we had budgeted or could afford. Moved by my distress, Orson made two concessions: four thirty-foot flagpoles were sacrificed and, at Jeannie's suggestion, he agreed to do without padding on the platforms. As a result they made a hollow, drumming sound which disturbed us during rehearsal until we discovered that they added an ominous and highly dramatic element to our mob scenes.

There was also the small matter of paint. What could be simpler and more economical than a few platforms and bare brick walls daubed with standard barn-red? Precisely because they *were* bare, it meant that hundreds of gallons of paint must be sloshed and sprayed from ladders and scaffolds over an acreage of more than five thousand square feet, including dressing-room stairs, stage door, steam pipes and fire extinguishers. The first fifteen hundred feet were done at night by bootleg house painters. Then the union stepped in and ruled, not without justice, that the walls, having become scenery, must be painted by accredited scene painters. Jean prevailed on her friend Horace Armistead (later designer of the Menotti operas and head of the design department at Boston University) to paint the remaining thirty-five hundred feet. He completed them with an assistant over a period of ten days at the reasonable price of $220.

An even more ingenious solution was found to the problem of our platforms. Jean unearthed a builder who was willing to construct them outside the New York metropolitan area in an abandoned movie studio at Fort Lee, New Jersey, then used as a warehouse by Wee and Leventhal, Broadway's most active shoestring producers and scavengers, who were in the habit of carting away Broadway productions on the night of their closing and storing them against a rainy day. It was from such salvaged lumber and fragments of old sets that our *Julius Caesar* platforms were built at a cost of under three hundred dollars. They were solid enough but, as a result, no two sets of steps were exactly the same height or depth. When the Rabbi pointed this out to Orson, he replied that he preferred steps to be uneven. When Leve continued tremulously that one of these steps might be as high as twenty inches, Orson said, "That's fine! We can use it to sit on!"

Costumes, fortunately, presented no problem. Our production came to be known, later, as the "modern-dress *Caesar*" and we were commended for our shrewdness in avoiding the expense of period costumes and armor. The decision to use modern dress was not an economic one and it was not conceived as a stunt. It was an essential element in Orson's conception of *Julius Caesar* as a political melodrama with clear contemporary parallels. All over the Western world sophisticated democratic structures were breaking down. First in Italy, then in Germany, dictatorships had taken over; the issues of political violence and the moral duty of the individual in the face of tyranny had become urgent and inescapable. To emphasize the similarity between the last days of the Roman republic and the political climate of Europe in the mid-thirties, our Roman aristocrats wore military uniforms with black belts that suggested but did not exactly reproduce the current fashion of the Fascist ruling class; our crowd wore the dark, nondescript street clothes of the big-city proletariat.

Welles, in his final cut version, had eliminated all formal battle scenes and, with them, all need for armor and weaponry. The only arms seen on our stage were the daggers of the assassins and short, bayonet-length blades for the final suicides. This was our greatest single economic break. Uniforms were easily procured on a rental-purchase basis from the Brooks Costume Company. They were old army tunics and overcoats, dyed a uniform dark green. For the rest, the actors wore their own street clothes, supplemented by dark coats and hats picked up in secondhand clothing stores on Orchard Street and the Bowery—all except Orson, who, as the aristocratic Brutus, wore a double-breasted, custom-made black pin-stripe suit with a dark tie "not unlike that which young Bob La Follette[8] might have worn for an afternoon wedding in Madison, Wisconsin." [. . .]

In the second week of rehearsal Orson began blocking his crowd scenes. Two days later he demanded the stage—platforms and all. Jeannie said that even if they were ready it would cost a fortune in crew bills to bring them into the theater ahead of schedule. Orson didn't care. I did. We were virtually bankrupt already and this would be the final straw. Where were these platforms? Orson asked. Across the river. So for the next ten days the entire company (forty strong by this time) made its way each morning by West Side subway to 125th Street, crossed the Hudson on the Dyckman Street ferry, then took a Palisades Park bus to where our platforms stood among mounds of moldering lumber in Fort Lee, New Jersey. Here, without a trace of heat, the mob scenes of *Julius Caesar* were rehearsed day after day amid the whir of saws, the banging of hammers and the perils of an unfinished set. To his mildly protesting troupe Orson explained that all this was for their own protection: by the time the platforms reached the theater they would be so familiar with the steps, ramps, risers and sudden drops that they would feel totally secure.

They needed every bit of this security, as it turned out. For when they arrived at the theater for the first of their all-night sessions, they discovered that the platforms had been pierced by four large stage traps—gaping holes located in strategic positions, each wide enough for the passage of a human body and each supplied with a narrow, almost perpendicular set of wooden steps leading down to the basement below. These open traps provoked some

---

8. Robert M. La Follette was a renowned progressive politician (congressman, governor, U.S. senator and presidential candidate) from Wisconsin.

grumbling among the actors, who regarded them as added and unnecessary physical risks—especially when they learned that they were expected to negotiate them in pitch-blackness. When they spoke to Orson about them, he was amazed and indignant. Were they not actors? And were not traps among the oldest and most consecrated devices of the stage? They must stop being amateurish and craven; they must get used to the presence of these traps and learn to use them like professionals!

At our first dress rehearsal, when the lights dimmed up on the assassination scene, all the conspirators were present except one—the honorable Brutus. Orson had been seen starting up the ramp with the others but now he was nowhere to be found. A hurried search of his dressing room (to which he sometimes retired for a quick nip) and of the mezzanine (to which he occasionally climbed to survey his staging) failed to locate him. Rehearsal stopped and the perplexed company waited for his return.

He was found five minutes later, still unconscious in the dark at the foot of the stairs after falling cleanly through an open trap and dropping fifteen feet before striking the basement floor with his chin. He was shaken but uninjured except for a slight sprain of his ankle, which got twisted as he was being helped to his feet. The next morning two of our manholes were plugged up. The others remained open and the company gradually got used to them, as Welles had predicted they would.

Throughout the run of *Julius Caesar* the problem of entrances and exits remained a tricky one on that completely open stage. All the dressing rooms except Orson's were located stage left in a three-story cell block served by a narrow cement staircase set in the wall, from which stage left entrances had to be made. All other entrances meant going on down into the darkened basement and coming up on the other side or through one of the traps. After some initial confusion the company became quite expert at getting into position and timing their entrances while keeping out of sight of the audience. Unfortunately they were not the only ones to use the stage. Since our stage door opened directly onto the acting area and we had a permissive doorman, it was not unusual for people to wander in off the street during performances. On the second night of *Julius Caesar* one critic noted the presence of a New York City fireman in uniform in the background of the assassination scene. Orson himself, arriving late from Longchamps or Bleeck's, more than once made his entrance into the Forum directly from 41st Street. And one Wednesday afternoon, a conscientious delivery boy, carrying a pressed suit on a hanger, made his way across the crowded stage to Orson's dressing room, where he delivered one garment, collected another and departed the way he had come without disturbing the matinee audience or the funeral oration. Other regular visitors were the rats—the size of small dogs—with whom we still shared the theater and who found in Orson's Elizabethan stage traps a quick and convenient route from the basement to the street. Undeterred by the presence of forty actors, the glare of two hundred projectors and the thunder of Marc Blitzstein's martial music, they trotted about the stage—singly, in troupes, or pursued by impotent cats.

—*JH*

The Second City

FOUNDED 1959

Bernard Sahlins[9]

> The audience was shoehorned into seating at small tables that were navigated by waitresses serving drinks before and during the show. [. . .] On stage, the cast of six or seven players (the men always outnumbering the women) worked in a small, plain space, with a pianist on one side providing the music and sound effects. Lighting and scenic effects became slightly more elaborate over the years, but costuming consisted principally and simply of a scarf, coat or hat to suggest character, and a shifting around of bentwood chairs remained the chief means of changing scenes. Props were minimal and often imaginary. There were no cups or glasses. To take a drink, the actor just cupped his hand, put it to his mouth, and sucked on the thumb knuckle.

Thus longtime *Chicago Tribune* theater critic Richard Christiansen sets the literal stage for the Second City, Chicago's ever-present and tidally influential comedy troupe.

But the figurative stage for the theater was set years before its 1959 debut in a former Chinese laundry at 1842 North Wells Street in the Windy City. It began with the improvisational theater games of a Chicagoan named Viola Spolin. Spolin had taken a course in "play" from Northwestern University–based sociologist Neva Boyd at Boyd's Recreational Training School at Hull-House. Spolin's own games were born at Hull-House, too, beginning in the thirties, when she taught and supervised creative dramatics for children while working with adults under FDR's Works Progress Administration.

SOURCE: *Days and Nights at the Second City: A Memoir, with Notes on Staging Review Theatre,* by Bernard Sahlins, 2002.

9. Regrettably, Sahlins died as this book was going to press in June 2013.

Spolin's son, Paul Sills, a brilliant director whose volatility and inarticulateness are as legendary as his genius and idealistic quest for truth in performance, brought Spolin's work into the world. He helped give birth to the Playwrights Theatre Club with friends he'd met as a student at the University of Chicago, his first stab at blending Spolin's games-training and theater practice. Over the Playwrights Club's two-year and twenty-five-play life, Sills used the games to move away from psychological acting and to build a sense of ensemble among such actors as Edward Asner, Mike Nichols, Elaine May and the woman who would be his second wife, Barbara Harris.

The Playwrights Club begat the Compass Players, founded by Sills and another idealist, one with some money in his pocket, David Shepherd. Compass created improvised plays based on scenarios worked out in advance, thus becoming the nation's first improvisational theater. Though the Compass folded, as its star players—Shelley Berman, Nichols and May—"graduated" to a national audience in New York, its influence was profound, especially once the Second City rose from its ashes. With the birth of the Second City—the brainchild of Sills, actor Howard Alk and producer Bernard Sahlins, who tells the story here—the satirists took the snide name given to Chicago in 1952 by *New Yorker* writer A. J. Liebling and spat it right back.

This lunatic band, which melded idiosyncratic talents into groups "who somehow set each other on fire," as actor Alan Arkin puts it, became a Chicago staple (it's still thriving) and spread its web of influence wide, most notably into television and film via generations of casts for NBC's *Saturday Night Live*. Beginning with Spolin and Sills, the Second City became—and still is—an eccentric international family, a brood that playwright Jeffrey Sweet once pegged as a cross between the Waltons and the Corleones.[10] Writing in the *Los Angeles Herald Examiner* about a 1985 reunion of some of the early players, Jack Viertel captures the excitement of the best Sillsian improv: "You can practically feel their brain waves screaming helter-skelter toward one another, hoping for that mystical collision that will produce a miracle: a laugh that's true."

—TL

————

April 1959

Several of us, Chicagoans, mostly in our early thirties, many of us graduates of the University of Chicago, had worked together as actors, directors and producers in many theaters for many years. We had presented plays ranging

10. Sweet's smart *Something Wonderful Right Away* (Limelight, New York, 1988; Avon Books, New York, 1978) is an oral history of the Second City, and a delightful model of its kind.

from the classics to new works still in manuscript. In some good weeks we had earned the princely sum of seventy-five dollars—in some weeks.

Some years ago the Japanese director Tadashi Suzuki described to me the regimen imposed on his actors, which included sweeping the stage before each rehearsal as an act of artistic purification. "We too did that," I said. "We too swept the stage—in fact we cleaned the entire theater, not for artistic reasons but out of economic necessity since we couldn't afford a janitor." I never thought to make it a requirement for artistic achievement.

Now in 1959, we were tired of the start-up-in-hope-and-go-down-in-flames cycle. We were pushing thirty and beyond. We decided to start another kind of theater, we hoped a "popular theater." We weren't aiming to "sell out," just to bend a little. Besides, there was a vaguely egalitarian virtue in working with popular forms that suited our politics.

It wasn't an entirely new idea for us. We had tried something like it in bars and showrooms around town. We took as our model those experiences plus some vague ideas of European cabarets, and dim memories of the Living Newspaper and the *Pins and Needles* revue done during the Great Depression by the WPA Theatre. We were especially influenced by Brecht and by what we had read of German cabarets. Although we were a bit undecided as to the exact form, it was a point of honor not to compromise our skills and intellect.

May 1959

The corner of Wells Street and Lincoln Avenue, a stone's throw from bustling, downtown Chicago, was in one of those lonely areas that circled the busy center of industrial cities in the era before gentrification. There we found a couple of storefronts at an affordable rent, which we hoped eventually to turn into a cabaret theater. A mile and a half south of us lay the Loop with its great stores and office buildings. A short distance east was Lake Michigan and the city's Gold Coast, and a mile north sprawled the trendy Lincoln Park neighborhood. Earlier in the century the area had provided the warehouses and distribution centers where trucks unloaded produce and supplies for the rest of the city. Now it was quiet, even desolate—small shops in old buildings, some rooming houses, a few Edward Hopper bars.

When it came to local theater production, Chicago in 1959 was a barren scene. Except for the Goodman Theatre, the major theatrical activity was provided by touring shows originating in New York, supplemented by a few summer theaters in the suburbs. Attempts at resident theaters had been few and short-lived. Now we were to embark on yet another.

December 16, 1959, 7 p.m.

The usual Chicago winter cold. If we were lucky, we thought, there might be an audience of twenty or thirty for the opening night of our new theater, which we called the Second City. Hadn't we failed often enough to now?

Three of us devised and founded the Second City. Paul Sills, a matchless director with a longtime interest in improvisation, was a golden boy—attractive, articulate, gifted, charismatic. He was barely thirty and had directed dozens of plays from every period. Paul is several kinds of genius. As a director he has that rare faculty of inhabiting each moment as it is born on the stage. Any slight deviation from the truth, any flash of uneasiness that arises from a false note—which for most of us is a passing, forgettable twinge—is for Paul an excrescence to be furiously excised. The wonder of it all is the way he carries out this operation. Although normally highly articulate, when it comes to conveying information to an actor he rushes to the stage emitting strange, incomprehensible grunts and burbles, meanwhile reinforcing with violent and seemingly random body language the message he bears. Lo, by some miracle of communication, the actors understand precisely what he wants to convey, and the rehearsal goes on. No false moment is allowed, no shortcuts. The fact is that Paul, like Chekhov, hates "acting" and loves truth. Anything hammy or affected is anathema to him.

In his work and in his person, Paul radiates idealism. He is a theatrical pied piper, inviting his actors to embrace the purest, highest ideal of the art and of themselves as artists, then leading them in a crusade against the Philistines. That is why some high-priced stars gladly work with him for a pittance.

I learned to direct from watching Paul Sills. I was never able to match the total effectiveness of his incoherence, but I did learn to detect what I now call "the awful fiction." This is when a character in a play does not notice, or pretends not to notice, something that is happening on stage until long after that character should have noticed and the audience already has. For example, a husband comes home from work sporting an air of gloom that would do justice to Cassandra. His wife greets him at the door and asks how his day went, as if he had entered normally. A simple, "What's the matter?"— a question that every audience member is already asking—would propel the scene forward.

Howard Alk, our pipeline to the counterculture, couldn't act, play the guitar or sing, but he managed to do all those things convincingly. Howard was a great bear of a man with a highly developed sense of irony, a voracious appetite for high-level gossip, and a well-developed nose for trends and fakery. Howard stayed with us only a few months and then went off to do whatever his thing was; but his incisive knowledge of young, avant-garde thinking was invaluable at the start.

And myself, Bernard Sahlins, fascinated with the theater and now, having sold my share in a tape-recorder factory, retired though not rich, in my mid-thirties. We three had met at the University of Chicago four or five years earlier and had tried various theater projects which had succeeded critically and failed financially. Now we and many of our actor colleagues were at loose ends. But I was the only one among us who had not committed to the theater as vocation. I had only dabbled in it, often and intensely, but never totally. Now I was leaving the world of business (where I never felt comfortable) for the world of theater. It took me a decade to feel I belonged, to achieve a level of comfort with my new life.

December 16, 1959, 8:30 P.M.

As I say, we would have counted ourselves lucky had there been twenty people at the opening. But a half-hour before curtain time there were more than a hundred. Our capacity was 120. Over the years at least five hundred of that 120 have introduced themselves to me, claiming to have been there on opening night.

We three had not come together to build a theater. We had been burned enough times doing that. This was still the time of the Beat generation, and we started out to found a coffeehouse where we idlers, including the actors whom we had worked with for years, could loll around and put the world in its proper place. We pictured ourselves there, drinking coffee and listening to poetry with a few of our friends, sort of a San Francisco Beat scene in Chicago. It is hard to imagine now, but in Chicago then there was no "scene" for theater aspirants: few places to work, almost no way to earn a living.

We searched the Near North Side for a location and found two adjacent storefronts. One had housed a hat shop, the other a Chinese laundry. Both of these enterprises had foundered, and the stores were empty. In the case of the Chinese laundry, the exit must have been precipitous: for several weeks after we took occupancy, people would knock and mournfully enter brandishing their laundry tickets. We were unable to help since Wong Cleaners & Dyers had left no forwarding address.

The rent was cheap because, despite its nearness to downtown and to the Gold Coast, this was hardly a high-traffic area. (Since then that section of Wells Street has flourished, first as a honky-tonk collection of bars and night spots, now as a trendy avenue with five coffeehouses, four Italian restaurants, and the city's best cigar store within two blocks.) We hired a couple of itinerant carpenters and sat back to await the opening of our coffeehouse.

But after a little while we grew restless. Maybe we ought to stage some sort of show.

People like Studs Terkel, who had participated in the WPA Theatre in the 1930s, recalled doing a Living Newspaper, that is, reading from a current newspaper and commenting on, even dramatizing, the news. This inspired us to think again of a topical revue in a setting where the audience could drink and smoke—a cabaret in the European sense. Hadn't we played with the revue form in previous ventures at other people's bars? Why not a cabaret of our own, with music and songs and scenes and blackouts? After all, we were already building the coffeehouse. We already had plans for tables and chairs and drinking and smoking. All we needed was a small stage. Certainly we had plenty of out-of-work classical actor friends to choose from. Most of them were hovering about before we hammered our first nail.

"Why don't you get a job?" We all heard that, from our parents and some of our friends. Work and life were balanced differently in those days. Older people (in their forties) remembered the Great Depression: the fear and misery of being out of work, the desperation. Considerations like "quality of life" were luxuries, perhaps dangerous to dream of. Blake's "I sometimes try to be miserable so I can do more work" found ready assent from our parents. But by 1959 a long period of affluence led to a rejection of these fears. The young were ready to fly.

"The theater? That's no life," sniffed my mother. "You should stay in the tape-recorder business." True, I wasn't quite as fancy-free as the others in the project. After all, I was a school generation older. I admit to a kind of shock at the fact that many male and female students were cohabiting as a matter of course, and that sex and travel and life decisions, the way young people loved and lived in 1959, were more casual than I was used to. Life wasn't that free when I was a student. We had to work hard to get laid. By today's mores it was all rather tame, but not to me at the time.

In other ways too, though I did my best not to show it, I was a fish out of water. My role with theaters had always been that of patron or adviser or even cheerleader. I looked at actors and directors across a divide, fascinated, distant and a little bit awestruck. Although I had been involved with these very people for years, I had never committed to that life. Now I devoted my days and nights to it. Now what had been a game was suddenly serious. I had traded a secure livelihood for the uncertainties (and the pleasures) of art. I did see it that way. But for a long time I belonged to neither world. Was it a Faustian bargain? I pretended to be at ease, but I never stopped peering at myself in this new life.

Our first company included Barbara Harris, Severn Darden, Mina Kolb, Eugene Troobnik, Andrew Duncan, Roger Bowen and Howard Alk. A short time after we opened, Bowen and Alk left. Alan Arkin, who as a youngster had studied with Paul Sills's mother, Viola Spolin, and Paul Sand, who had studied in France with Marcel Marceau, replaced them.

The Dream Team: Our First Cast

Partly by chance, partly by selection, the first Second City cast—intelligent, well informed—displayed a range and variety of talents that meshed like the gears of a fine watch. In skill and attributes they so complemented each other that they served as casting prototypes for years. A polymath Severn Darden type was sought avidly, as was a witty, pretty Barbara Harris type, a deadpan Alan Arkin, an affable Andrew Duncan. Of course we never found clones, but we did wind up with great variety in small compass.

Andrew Duncan. There is a reason that successful talk-show hosts command such high salaries. The ability to speak to an audience about everyday things in one's own person seems easy but is difficult, and rare. In all my years at the Second City there have been only three or four actors who could master this feat. Andrew was the first and perhaps the best. This was especially important at the beginning, when the rule was to introduce most scenes in direct address to the audience. Solid, not flashy, instantly ready to play Mr. Average Man, Andrew was an invaluable cast member. To him belonged the parodies of those official voices that blare at us from our radios, our television screens, and the public part of our daily lives.

Eugene Troobnik. He of the mellifluous voice. He was close to embodying the stereotype of the classical actor but self-aware enough to parody the type brilliantly. Invaluable at playing senators, executives and generals, Eugene is best remembered in a parody of Superman, doffing his shirt to reveal the logo of "Businessman"—"able to leap loopholes at a single bound."

Severn Darden. Sui generis in 1959 and not duplicated since. The legendary Severn, scion of an old-line Southern family, was a stocky, tallish man with a vacuum-cleaner mind that I swear retained and could instantly call forth every obscure fact, philosophical tenet and literary work ever produced by man. And whether in his famous art lecture devoted to explaining a blank canvas ("Featuring two shades of white in which both shades are exactly the same . . .") or in his scene as Oedipus Rex ("It's not my fault"), Severn could juxtapose all this information to devastatingly comic effect.

In his personal life too, Severn was the stuff of legends. The most famous concerns the night when he, together with his date, managed to enter the great gothic Rockefeller Chapel on the campus of the University of Chicago. Alerted by the sound of unauthorized organ playing, the campus police, advancing down the aisles, were treated to the sight of Severn throwing himself across the altar and screaming, "Sanctuary! Sanctuary!"

Barbara Harris. Barbara, who went on to a distinguished career on Broadway and in film, was the innocent-looking ingenue with the unexpectedly rapier-like mind. She combined accurate analyses of middle-class ridiculousness with a stellar acting talent to skewer the would-be bohemian suburbanite or the self-styled intellectual. But what set audiences back on their heels were the moments in an otherwise richly comic scene when, through the magic of her acting talent, they glimpsed a serious and emotion-rich inner life.

Mina Kolb. Mina was, in the best sense of the word, a clown. Although she came from a rich background in commercial TV and was the one cast member without extensive experience in theater, she more than held her own with her deadpan comic insights into the minutiae of everyday life.

Alan Arkin. If one were to meet Alan in ordinary circumstances, the last guesses one would make about this serious, somewhat taciturn man would be that he is a superb actor and a talented musician-performer, singer and composer. (Alan [co-wrote a version of] the famous "Banana Boat Song" and a great number of comic masterpieces, including "I Like You Because You Don't Make Me Nervous.") Alan is intense and relaxed at the same time, with a deadly sense of humor. Like many great actors, he has a superb talent for mimicry. After a moment of study he can walk like anybody, talk like anybody and sing like anybody.

Howard Alk. Although not a professional actor, Howard, a co-founder of the Second City, had a firm grip on what the counterculture was thinking and saying. He served as a balance wheel to our tendency to be awed by the intellectual and was quick with the witty analysis of life's contradictions. It was he who defined a Freudian slip as "meaning to say one thing and saying a mother." Howard quickly tired of acting and was replaced by Alan Arkin.

Roger Bowen. He of the devastating wit (he conceived the Businessman sketch for Eugene Troobnik) also quickly tired of the eight-shows-a-week grind and was replaced by Paul Sand.

Paul Sand. Sweet Paul Sand. If mime were a popular art form, Paul would be a major star. He was physically eloquent, riveting when playing a fish in our underwater ballet, touching when responding to the instruction from a phonograph record entitled "Make-a-Friend."

Bill Matthieu. A piano was an indispensable part of the show as we conceived it, not only to accompany songs but to underscore and to play scenes in and out. We were fortunate in meeting with Bill Matthieu (later known as Allaudin), a great musician who could parody any style on the spot and was sensitive enough to know when not to play.

By September the theater was shaping up, though between moonlighting carpenters and the natural propensity of show people to start their day at suppertime, I was groggy for many weeks. My biological clock took a long time in adjusting. All my working life I had been hard at it by eight in the morning. Now things began to stir only in mid-afternoon.

I was constantly reminded of the story about Ferenc Molnár, the Hungarian playwright living in Vienna at the beginning of the twentieth century. Molnár rarely went to bed before five A.M. and accordingly woke in the afternoon. One day a friend prevailed on him to be a witness in a court case, which is how Molnár found himself driving in a carriage through the streets of Vienna at the unlikely, ungodly hour of eight A.M. He was amazed, had never seen anything like it. The bustling streets were filled with people and vehicles—going to work, making deliveries, rushing to appointments. Who were these people? Puzzled, Molnár turned to his friend. "Tell me," he asked, "are they all witnesses?"

Eventually I did adjust.

Naming Time

Naming the theater was a collective endeavor that took weeks. Each day we and the actors would gather and offer the gems we had thought of overnight. The short list occupied four single-spaced pages.

At about this time a series of articles about Chicago, entitled "The Second City," was appearing in the *New Yorker*. As the appellation implied, their author, a wonderful journalist named A. J. Liebling, did not think much of our metropolis on the lake. In fact he was relentlessly negative about its citizenry and its culture. I think it was Howard Alk who suggested we definitely carry the title of the articles as our banner. It was one of those "of course" moments.

Thus it was: Paul directing, Howard on stage and I taking care of the rest. Most of the people we worked with were University of Chicago graduates, and the audiences, in our heads (and indeed, the majority of the real audience for our first six months), were made up of university students and faculty. They shaped our reference levels, our characters, our causes and our humor.

We took the summer and fall of 1959 to ready our space, with our moonlighting tradesmen working away at the theater, with our cast playing theater games, and with Jimmy Masucci designing our space. A couple of engagements in our past theater life had taken us to St. Louis. There a handful of bar and club owners in a Victorian area of the city known as Gaslight Square had embarked upon a frenzy of Victorian restoration—gilded chandeliers and mirrored bars, antique storefronts and botanical prints. Here was an odd sidebar to the taste of the times. While we, together with the venturesome, liberal club owners in St. Louis and the new breed of entertainment entrepreneurs in Chicago, embraced "modernism" culturally, we were retro in our visual tastes. Political rebellion was in, but when it came to design, plush Victorian nostalgia was cool.

At the design center of the St. Louis renaissance was a most remarkable figure. With very little formal education and no background in interior design, but with an incredibly inventive talent, Jimmy Masucci, a tall, thin, shambling man, became the guiding design genius of Gaslight Square. Jimmy was not the most articulate of men, but his taste was unerring. In St. Louis he not only found the antiques, he created the most fetching environments out of the most unlikely elements. We hired Jimmy, and what did he do? He bought telephone booths, which then consisted of four wooden panels, each some seven feet high, the top halves of which were glass. He painted them black and paneled the walls with them. In the center of each, under the glass, he installed prints from a set he had cut from a book on Roman antiquities. The effect was stunning, especially when highlighted by the electrified gas lamps extending from the walls and some jerry-built red velvet banquettes, all well within our meager budget.

By mid-November 1959, Paul and the cast had worked out a group of disparate scenes, songs, short blackout pieces and parodies. Paul's mother, Viola Spolin, who taught theater on the West Coast, had over the years developed a series of theater games designed to teach acting and the development of material.[11] Paul started with her theater games and from these gradually developed a full-fledged revue. Later I found that we, all unknowing, were working in a tradition that started in 600 B.C. with the short comic scenes arising from the Greek harvest festivals. In any event, we produced an hour and a half's worth of unconnected scenes and songs that we ourselves were not quite sure how to organize.

It wasn't as though we were reinventing the wheel. At the University of Chicago and in several ventures we had experimented with short scenes developed through improvisation, and we were happy with the individual pieces that Paul and the actors and Bill Matthieu had developed. But we felt there was something missing. We tried imposing a unifying theme, a rudimentary plot, but nothing seemed satisfactory.

For a year Mike Nichols and Elaine May had been the darlings of the New York scene. They came from our group, and success had descended on

11. Her books on theater games have been an invaluable source for theaters and schools and have remained in print for many decades. [author's note]

their two-person show with the intensity and suddenness of a hurricane. We called Mike and asked him to come to Chicago to give us a critical appraisal— we would pay his fare, of course—and he did. He looked at what we had and suggested we stop trying for a connection. The joy of the work, he said, was watching a skilled ensemble playing a great many roles and displaying a range of talents for singing, miming, acting and nimble witticisms. That, he said, was all we needed. And if we needed time between scenes, it would be an asset for the actors cleverly to introduce the next scene either in character or in their own person.[12] Don't change the scenes, he advised, don't add any structures, don't impose a theme. Stay with what you're doing.

We cheered. "By gosh! The man is right! How sensitive, how persuasive—how easy!"

It was years later when I realized that artistically we had upset the normal pattern of theatrical evolution. The classical theater, in its brief flarings and long dyings, had ever looked to the popular theater for actors and stagecraft. We reversed the process. From the theater of Shakespeare, Brecht, Sophocles and O'Neill, we brought what we knew to the popular theater. We lived by the classical theater watchwords:

· Respect your audience by playing at the top of your intelligence.
· Assume they are at least as smart as you are, if not smarter.
· Respect every character you play, even the darkest villain.
· Play all characters from within and never be superior to them.
· Bring every bit of your talent to the stage.
· Tell the truth.

Between June and December we had lots of time to discuss the deep philosophical issues of how close the tables should be, what kinds of ashtrays we should have and what sort of coat-check system we should use. The committee on plumbing made its urinal recommendations, and a management decision was made not to compose a manual for our wait staff.

Fortunately I was too busy to second-guess my decision to embrace the life of the theater. Had I looked up for a moment and thought about our dwindling finances, I would have panicked.

Meanwhile, we bought 150 bentwood chairs at auction for a dollar apiece, cobbled together tables with black Formica tops on cast-iron bases, equipped a bar and a kitchen from a bankrupt restaurant, and covered the

---

12. The introductions became a popular part of the shows. We introduced almost every scene with carefully prepared, funny and illuminating texts. As the years went by, with the acclimation of the audience to the quick cuts and transitions of film and TV, the introductions became fewer, then nearly disappeared. [author's note]

whole place with carpeting left over from business conventions at a dollar a yard. We hung a few stage lights (purchased used) over the small platform that was our stage. There was an untouchable, active gas pipe running floor to ceiling, upstage left. (The gas pipe remained as long as we occupied the space.) Our only scenery consisted of six of the bentwood chairs. We were equally parsimonious with costumes, deciding that only the elements of costume were compatible with our vision. An army jacket was enough to suggest a general; a white coat, a doctor; a fedora, a gangster. We had plenty of spectacle frames without lenses, hats galore and some bad wigs. We dressed the men in brown corduroy suits from Brooks Brothers and the women in black dresses.

November 1959: Enter the Mafia

Winter came early. In late November, just before we opened, a tall man in a gray fedora appeared. He wanted to talk to the "boss." With the three of us assembled, he announced that he was there to "help" us by seeing to it that we would have no "trouble" from unruly patrons or "undesirable elements"—which he assured us we would have if we didn't choose to use his services. Furthermore he offered us two ways of paying for this arrangement. We could either give him a percentage of the business or pay him a weekly fee. He spoke softly. He mispronounced words. The delivery, the syntax and the implied threat came right out of a bad B-movie. For a moment we thought it was a hoax. Then we knew it wasn't. We didn't know whether to laugh or cower under a table. "Here," continued our benefactor, "is my phone number. Think it over." At the door he turned. "I'll be back next week if I don't hear from you." That was scary.

After a quick powwow we decided to fight. We called the police and our local alderman, who was reputed to have some influence in certain circles. A policeman showed up with a large book of photographs, and we were able to make an identification. We were not reassured when the policeman pursed his lips and said, "Hmm!" We heard nothing for two weeks. Then on a Sunday morning we were summoned to the theater. Our plate-glass front had been shattered by a bottle of the most foul-smelling liquid, which was spilled all over our lobby. It took us two days to get rid of the noxious smell. Three weeks later the same thing happened. After that I guess we were considered adequately punished. But for many weeks I was wary when walking down dark streets.

Stink bombs aside, in early December we had a theater, a show, a wait staff and a bartender. We set our admission price at $2.50, with no minimum for the drinks.

Excelsior and Other Outcries was the name of our first Second City show. It was the first of a long series of names that had nothing whatever to do with the contents of the revue. Some of my favorites over the years include *Unanimous Raves from All the Critics*; *Truth, Justice, or the American Way*; *Freud Slipped Here*; *Jean-Paul Sartre and Ringo*; *I Remember Dada, or Won't You Come Home, Saul Bellow?*; *Orwell That Ends Well*.

December 16, 1959, 11:30 P.M.

Our stage lights were controlled by five small dimmers—more like living room than theater equipment—and they were operated by whichever actor happened not to be in the opening or closing of a scene. On that first night, when the entire company was taking a bow, there was no one left to bring the lights up and down, a situation that none of us had thought of before, and that I realized in the nick of time. I ran backstage and twirled the dimmers through interminable curtain calls. There it was, the delightful sound of people who would not stop telling us they had been moved. We were a hit! We couldn't believe the response. We sat around afterward and drank beer. Over the next few days the four newspaper critics (there were four daily papers in Chicago in those days, now two) confirmed the audience reaction.

Once the papers were on the streets, the phones started ringing. All of us were enlisted in taking reservations. We were now successful artists. What did that mean? Quit our day jobs? Look forward to long-term employment? None of us would go that far. We "knew" from our past experiences that it wouldn't last, and all our friends agreed. We would repeat to one and all the immortal words attributed to a local Chicago impresario, "If they don't want to come, you can't stop them." For many months after that first performance we remained certain that our luck would run out and that no audience would appear the next night. Even if it was a brutally cold Tuesday in February, one empty seat convinced us it was the beginning of the end.

So we kept things lean. The three "owners" would check the waitresses out after the show and come in during the day to place orders and get things ready for our part-time bookkeeper. And even though we were selling out, we ran our first show just eight weeks. We figured that was how long it would take us to run out of fans.

But what was this show that was causing such a stir, and why was it so exciting? It was—and still is today—a revue in two acts, with the actors (generally six in number) playing a great many characters in a great many places, from the president in the White House to the cop on the corner to the housewife in the suburbs. The elements are simple: fifteen to twenty-five short comic scenes, blackouts, musical numbers and parodies, strung together with no thematic connection. The form was already old in the fifth century B.C., but it is a serviceable vessel into which one can load rich cargoes. Without a set, just a back wall with two doors, without costumes, with just words and our great actors, there is pure theater magic on that stage.

Contrary to some predictions, having a bare stage in no way diminished our effectiveness. Whether it is a revue scene or a play, the impact of a theater piece, its authenticity, comes primarily from acting and text. It is difficult on a television show or in a movie to portray a living room convincingly with one potted palm and an easy chair. In these, media-realistic settings are almost mandatory. But for the stage, the old adage that all one needs is "two boards and a passion" is on the mark. I value lighting, costume and set, but the stage work can succeed if any or all of these are at a functional minimum. It will fail if the acting or the text is deficient. Paul Sills was a stickler for truthful acting and concise text, and that tradition has remained.

The show itself ran somewhere around an hour and forty minutes, including a fifteen-minute intermission. Since we were trained in improvisation but skeptical about its viability as a continuous presentational form, we had decided that the revue we presented and marketed would be polished, honed and more or less "set." But for our own amusement as well as that of the public, after we took our bows for the regular show we took suggestions for scenes from the audience. Half an hour later we returned to do a set of improvisations based on those suggestions. In confirmation of their hit-or-miss character, admission to the improvisations was free.

It took us only a short time to realize that the improvisations had another, very important function. They were the incubator for originating and polishing new material for the next show. As Alan Arkin pointed out, they turned out to be "public rehearsal." Improvisations that were well received were either repeated or worked on in rehearsal and then replayed in the improvisation section. (We were always careful to introduce these as "scenes we are working on.") Thus from the opening night of a show we were already preparing a new show. When it was time for that new show to open, we would have a group of tested scenes ready to go.

Here I want to clear up a long-held misconception. Although we were, and still are, perceived as an improvising theater, we almost never—except for an occasional "game" within a show and in the free period after a show—used improvisation as a presentational form. For us it was a tool for developing material. Paul Sills and Viola Spolin had perfected the use of improvisation as a vehicle for "writing" scenes. It turned out to be a faster, more equitable method for developing a show, since the actors could use themselves to their maximum ability. In effect, each cast member was a writer.

Part of the attraction of our show was due to the state of the nation. Senator Joe McCarthy was dead, but the shades of his communist witch-hunt still darkened the landscape. The Cold War was in full swing, and while it was not quite a period of repression, there was a certain wariness in the air. Political jokes and topical subject matter were scarce, confined to such enclaves of rebellion as San Francisco. Television featured fluffy sitcoms like *Father Knows Best*.

Even at the time, to speak of the decade of the fifties was to evoke images of conformity, of going along, of tract homes and the quest for identity. A corrosive miasma of paranoia and red-baiting still hung in the atmosphere. Not for nothing do we look back on those days as shrill and materialistic—even frightening.

But Allen Ginsberg had read his poem "Howl" in October 1955, and the Second City was part of the expression of a growing anti-establishment sentiment. The sixties, the rebellious sixties, were dawning as a counter to the conformist fifties, and questions were being asked. As usual, literature led the way. Burroughs, Kerouac and Ginsberg; Bellow, Roth and Glass; Mailer, Eldridge Cleaver and Norman O. Brown. In comedy, the careers of Dick Gregory, Lenny Bruce and Mort Sahl were beginning to be noticed beyond the counterculture. To put Eisenhower and Nixon on stage, indeed to do anything topical, to smash icons, to discuss the events of the day from the points of view of well-acted characters, was deliciously new and terribly exciting for young audiences. We were often treated to the phenomenon of openmouthed young people, hanging about forever after each show, bedazzled by hearing their concerns expressed on stage.

One of the joys of the revue form is its immediacy. A straight play can take years between its conception and its appearance before the public. With a revue scene, an idea conceived in the morning can be seen on the stage that night. And one can capture the sometimes ephemeral visit of the zeitgeist, reflecting the preoccupations of the actors and the audiences at a given moment in time. The revue form is flexible and can stretch to receive even the most abstract of concepts.

A certain amount of oppression is good for comedy. The firmer the taboo, the more excitement when it's violated—like Eve's apple made more delicious by being forbidden. But unlike the Beats, unlike Bruce, we represented the respectable, the acceptable face of dissent. We were neither hostile nor in a rage. We did not separate ourselves from the mainstream. Our irony was gentled by the fact that we included ourselves among its targets. We soon stopped trying to save the world in favor of laughing at it. We did not preach the apocalypse. Our audiences laughed the laugh of recognition.

We were, of course, political liberals. And we took our easy shots at the Ku Klux Klan, at Nixon, at racism. But we also recognized that the proper target of a satirist is himself and the members of his own class, their shibboleths, beliefs and dogmas. The worthiest scenes exposed our own culpability in the face of such issues as racial prejudice and injustice. Another reason for our success was not artistic but financial. Mostly through sheer dumb luck we had stumbled on a form, and a formula, that made for economic advantages unusual in the theater. We had a lower cost base than even a storefront theater. With no set, with a couple hundred dollars' worth of costume elements, with a small cast, with one musician and a stage "crew" consisting of one combination light, sound and stage management person, we were lean. There were other savings. We rehearsed a new show with the same cast that played the old one. We earned extra revenue from serving drinks. We never advertised.

These factors enabled us to keep our prices down. In a business notorious for being transient, we survived and even flourished with a relatively small theater.

But the chief reasons for our survival, aside from our favorable business setup, were the intelligent actors, highly skilled at both writing and acting, guided by the genius of Paul Sills. Plus the fact that not one of us, including our savvy, loyal waitresses, wanted anything other than a good, uncompromising show. Because we had a bar and served at tables, people often characterized us as a nightclub. To them I would explain that we were a theater that served drinks, not a bar that put on a show.

That is the sum of it. We appeared at the right time with a great format, a viable financial venture, a great director and marvelous actors. Although we were and still are known as political satirists, the fact is that politics was but a fraction of the subjects we considered. We often disappointed those who held the idea that we should be more heavily engaged in social critiques. But irony was our métier. We applied it to the family, to courting, to work and the workplace. We parodied Mozart and Superman. We sang songs about nature. We were young people talking to young people.

—BS

The Ridiculous Theatrical Company

FOUNDED 1967

Charles Ludlam

"A brilliant, one man way of theater," wrote *New York Times* critic Mel Gussow after Charles Ludlam's AIDS-related death in 1987. "Ludlam is a genius of redemption," Richard Schechner wrote upon seeing Ludlam's *Bluebeard* nearly twenty years earlier, "whose total commitment to his face, his body, the *shape* of his words makes us understand again what a *star* is." Schechner goes on, "His company is also gifted, but they are infected too. And, I think, Charles Ludlam is their plague."

The Ridiculous was a theater created to be as large as its creator and capacious enough to house the outsized personalities with which he surrounded himself. It was a theater whose ambition was to be, in the dream of its founder, "the national comic theater company."

"Charles had the idea then that the whole world was a stage and everyone was an actor," wrote John D. Brockmeyer, one of eight actors who defected with the twenty-four-year-old Ludlam when he was fired from John Vaccaro's Play-House of the Ridiculous after only a year in the company. Jack Smith, the performance artist and filmmaker who would later (and briefly) join the new troupe, gave it its name, the Ridiculous Theatrical Company.

Already, with the act of naming, the looting had begun, and before long Ludlam and company were pilfering from everywhere: the bohemian street life of the sixties, silent film, vaudeville, commedia dell'arte, and just about every theatrical tradition that came before. They appropriated everything they could from anywhere they found it. "Ridiculous takes everything seriously," Ludlam told *Village Voice* writer Michael Smith in 1972. "It's ecological theater—we take the abandoned refuse, the used images, the shoes from abandoned shoe factories, the clichés, and we search for their true meaning. We are recycling culture." Moreover, as the Ridiculous reclaimed and revived "a thousand traditions that had fallen into corruption, banality and disrepute," (*Voice* critic Michael Feingold's words, from his eulogy of Ludlam) it flew in the face of its contemporaries in the avant-garde. In place of authenticity and nakedness, Ludlam's crew celebrated artifice and adornment; in place of naturalism, it served up "theatricalism."

SOURCE: Unpublished essays, circa 1980s, later published in *Ridiculous Theatre: Scourge of Human Folly*, by Charles Ludlam, 1992.

Ludlam was often seen as a Shakespeare or Molière for his times; indeed he saw himself that way. He surrounded himself with idiosyncratic and outsized performers, rugged, competitive individualists—Black-Eyed Susan, Lola Pashalinski, Bill Vehr and Ludlam's protégé and lover Everett Quinton, for example—and that's the way he liked it. Still, he continued to be both author and star of the show, literally and figuratively. That's why he built the theater, as a place that would be grand enough even for Charles Ludlam. As a character says in his play *Stage Blood*, "We may be small, but we're pretentious."

—TL

———

The Ridiculous Theatrical Company is an ensemble repertory theater working in the modernist tradition. Our productions are avant-garde in the sense that we are interested both in exploring uncharted territory and in perpetuating or reviving theatrical conventions and techniques which we feel have been unwisely abandoned by our peers. In the latter sense our work is also traditional, because we consider the history of the theater an invaluable resource, which in this age of stultifying conventionalism on the one hand and narrowly based minimalism on the other is being worn thin by the commercial establishment and ceremoniously discarded by its radical counterpart. We believe that tradition has in the past been inspired and, indeed, can only be reinspired through the artful expression and evocation of newly evolved thoughts and feelings within the fabric of original plays which draw liberally from the history of the theater in its vast entirety.

All ensemble has to share a unified artistic point of view, and that's hard. In a way, the viewpoint is forged by the members of an ensemble: the leader leads because he embodies that viewpoint. He doesn't force his will on the group; he reflects the group's collective will.

Working with an ensemble of actors is a luxury in today's theater that would have been regarded as a necessity to our forebears. In the great ages of the theater, the plays that have since come to be considered masterpieces were realized by companies of actors whom the playwright had in mind when he wrote the roles. The ensemble of actors is the instrument on which the dramatist plays. To keep this instrument in tune requires constant practice, an almost year-round playing schedule which includes rest: time for contemplation, evaluation and inspiration.

This continuity reflects the classical concept behind the company: actors who play in repertory, devoted to new plays created by an artistic director with a strong point of view. We are able to resist the fads and fallacies of the contemporary theater because we draw on older authorities.

And I've been lucky that the Ridiculous Theatrical Company has afforded me the opportunity to do everything the way you're not supposed to do it. I've had the chance to grow and to learn from my mistakes. By now I've made so many of them that I'd almost have to strain to think of a new mistake to make.

It's ruthless, but it's not evil. I've created a very nice—though not ideal—atmosphere to work in.

[. . .]

In 1967 it all came together for me. I found that I could shape the ongoing needs of my theater by writing plays for myself. That's really how it evolved. I can't remember before then, except that it was depressing.

I started out as an actor. I had this company thrust upon me when the original Theatre of the Ridiculous broke to pieces and the actors were all kicked out. They decided I should direct the company. It was very much like a commedia dell'arte troupe. We had no theater to play in, so it was really a troupe of actors taking matters into their own hands.

I had nothing to lose, so I threw my cards in the air and let them land where they would. I didn't really care what happened in those plays so long as I could put over my own scenes.

.   .   .

When I was in conventional theater—even when I was going to school—people thought my acting was too broad, too pasty. So I had to create a theater where I could exist. I had to create, for my own survival, a world where I could take advantage of my talents.

Naturalistic theater is a very recent innovation, a corrective device. It wasn't the end of anything. It was a fashion to do things naturally. You can't really perform an unnatural act, unless you claim supernatural powers.

The idea of being natural becomes a very oppressive concept. It's shallow. Gradually, through training with Stanislavsky teachers, I realized they wanted me to behave in a civilized manner in a room, not to do anything extraordinary. But everything I'm interested in is extraordinary.

In naturalism there is always the tendency to be less than you are, to be more specific and less. That was always a terrible danger. It certainly didn't work for me.

.   .   .

We began in 1967 with a freewheeling approach to the theater. We did everything in a defiant way—radically wrong, you might say. It was a new-found freedom.

We felt that epic theater had great expressive possibilities, and we used them without holding back. We threw out the idea of professionalism and cultivated something much more extreme than amateurism. Actors were chosen for their personalities, almost like "found objects"; the character fell somewhere between the intention of the script and the personality of the actor. The textures of meaning were amazingly rich. Everything contributed to the effect: the script; the performers; even the accidents which were always happening on stage.

These Off-Off-Broadway things were thrown together—casts were thrown together and busted apart. I wanted to create an ensemble. I found some like-minded people in the theater, in underground movies. Friends, people I met on the street—I'd *invite* them. I created—invented—my own stars. I was building something by discovering people and creating a continuity for them.

Most actors don't get continuity. They get a job here and a job there. Their only continuity is in acting classes.

To create a company that performed all year round was a big challenge. We had no money—nothing. We lived like paupers on the Lower East Side, starving, but keeping the company working, trying to find places where we could perform. That took all my energy. That's what I did all the time.

We used to pay thirty-five dollars per night to play twice a week in a movie house after midnight. A lot of the Off-Off-Broadway people were playing in alternative spaces, church basements and so on. I wanted to play in a theater, not in an art gallery or a loft, because we'd done that kind of thing. I had the idea that if you used a movie theater after midnight, when there were no more movies, you'd have a theater with regular seats and you could get a grander feeling of going to the theater being an event.

Three years is a long time. We did *Big Hotel*, *When Queens Collide*, *Whores of Babylon* and *Turds in Hell*, all without funding. They were rather lavish productions, which we did entirely with volunteers and donated materials.

For years we had just five or ten minutes to set up the stage, and then we had to rush on and do it. We didn't have any time to prepare. We never rehearsed in a theater. We rarely had any money to work with, to advertise, to do anything. It is not fair to judge plays I did with no money and without any advantages.

At that time, all the actors, everyone, was in it for the adventure. There's a big difference between the times it was like a floating crap game and when it became a real theater.

· · ·

The first turning point came when I wrote a four-hour epic called *Big Hotel*, where we made a collage out of quotations, scenes, poems, one-liners—you name it—and put them together in different ways every night to see how they could work. We knew what the plot was, but I don't know if the audience did.

That wasn't really important. What was important for us was to break down that rote quality that you get in most theater—the conventions, the blocking, the techniques used over and over to get points across. The creative process was *human*. We didn't focus on rote. It was about having ideas and developing something that was exciting.

I was very influenced then by the ideas of John Cage. I wanted to find ways of getting beyond my own personal taste and avoiding aesthetic decisions. I wanted to get rid of that "no," to say "yes" to everything.

I took the extra liberty of a great modernist, not caring whether any of it made sense or ever came to an ending. We tried anything that popped into anyone's head. It was very surrealistic. It was a wonderful play—you could do anything with it.

I had been gradually trying to bring the artistic policies closer to the physicalities of Artaud's theater, as well as the verbal values. Costumes became more and more environmental. The costumes alone created the whole scene-value. The fans were gigantic.

At Hofstra[13] they put on big epics, so I learned how to put one on. And my Catholic background influenced my theater: we burned incense during the plays; there were many ritualistic things.

Our art was to bring everything in, to include everything until we finally admitted that the world was our work. We used banal counterbalanced with sublime. We used literature as the servant of the theater. When the thing had to be said we said it.

Our goal was that the audience would become part of the theater, that the theater would expand to encompass the world. It was almost a religious idea.

A pure physical theater from Artaud, with a verbal sound score. It was the solution for fitting dramatic literature into Artaud's theater, since he condemned playwrights. The mise-en-scène comes into its own when the actors allow the theater to admit its physicality.

．　．　．

Pornography is the highest development of naturalism. It was the seriousness of pornography that we were never into. It is not in depicting the sexual act that one becomes a pornographer; it is in demanding to be taken

13. Where Ludlam attended college.

seriously. Depicting sexual things—nudity and all that—we were taking a satirical view, rather than trying to arouse the audience sexually. We weren't peddling our asses. We were celebrating physical love, or criticizing it, or commenting on it. We were never into that tedious seriousness that pornography always demands of its audience.

One night we had a fight with the audience. We started throwing fruit and vegetables at them. A dummy was thrown into the audience. They threw it back to us. It was war.

· · ·

In the course of this experimentation I was perhaps mistakenly credited—or credited fairly, I don't know—with getting rid of plot—out of the play, out of drama—and maybe I did. Stefan Brecht was writing about my work at the time, really studying it closely, keeping a journal of developments. One day he called and said, "I hear you're rehearsing. What are you rehearsing?" I said, "There used to be that number where Alexis Del Lago came on in drag and sang 'Lady in Red.' I realized that just after that the Miraculous Mandarin was with Blondine Blondell in a scene of espionage, and I thought I'd put them together and have little tables, and when Alexis Del Lago as Mata Hari came on and sang the song, it would be like he was doing it in a nightclub." Stefan shouted, "You're making it more of a play!" I said, "I want it to be more of a play." And he said, "Oh no! Don't do that!" I realized that I was being credited with being a figurehead, the creator of something others would do that I would not do, which was to throw out the baby with the bathwater, take it into formless, nonstructured drama.

A lot of this came from Jack Smith, who was a genius at doing things for no money. Jack Smith could take people and objects that everyone else considered worthless and transform them into the most exotic creations. Unfortunately, he was impossible to work with. He performed with us for a while in *Big Hotel*, but one day he got sore at Chris Scott and punched him in the eye, and then he quit.

· · ·

This was far from popular theater, but we didn't intend to present popular theater. We weren't chic enough, although we did have glamour and grandeur.

We developed a cult following, but we had to work for free. The audience was reportedly mostly gay, and that may have been true on certain nights. But the fact is the audience was small in those days. Since there were fewer people, the proportion of gay people may have been greater then.

I played three women's roles: Zabina, Queen of Mars in my play *Conquest of the Universe, or When Queens Collide*; Norma Desmond in my play

Big Hotel; and the Emerald Empress in Bill Vehr's *Whores of Babylon*. Yet my male roles outnumbered the female ones. My flaw as a female impersonator lay in this: I always played women who wished they were men.

I always feel like a lesbian in drag. I am never content.

When I play female roles, they become collages of different actresses. Bill wrote this line in *Whores of Babylon* in which his character said to mine, "How well I understand that struggle in you between the warrior artist and the woman"—this was a wonderful self-revelation—and my line, that he wrote, was, "The woman? Don't you know there are a thousand women in me and I'm tormented by each one in turn?"

Since then I have never done a play in which I did not cast someone in the role of the opposite sex. The drag is always supercharged with theatricality, and theatricality is the hallmark of the Ridiculous Theatrical Company.

· · ·

I knew a lot of drag queens who would go into Whelan's Drug Store on Sixth Avenue for free makeup back then. They would go in and do their whole face from the counter samples. I knew Candy Darling then, when she was a street person. She was always out there on the corner, on the avenue, everywhere. She had no apartment, no place to live.

Candy had emerged as a kind of underground celebrity. She was in my *Turds in Hell* briefly, maybe one or two nights. I was playing a priestess and she pulled my loincloth off. She exposed me and I was stark naked. It wasn't in the play.

The main thing about Candy and Jackie Curtis was that they took female impersonation into the street—off the stage and into their lives. They tried to *live* it, twenty-four hours a day.

The Dionysian principle: you're drawing on your own personality; you are committing an act of self-destruction, because you are obliterating your own identity to create another one. And so we have these periods in which we must revive ourselves. You give a performance and come off stage, and you've got to get into yourself and rest, reconstruct your own true personality, indulge it. Only then can you go back and play the role again.

But once you start playing the fantasy twenty-four hours a day, you may have obliterated your personality on a more or less permanent basis. A mask can be a protection to preserve what's inside, but in the case of Jackie and Candy—particularly of Candy—they were always being overly generous with others, giving so much they didn't leave anything for themselves.

At a very early stage in our company's development, I was watching Bill Vehr's *Whores of Babylon* from the lighting booth. We had a lot of real people in it—not just actors, but people who were different, strange. They were acting the play and I was watching it from up there in this godlike perspective, and I found it terribly touching. I was so moved by it: those poor mortals down there on this stage of life, as fools. The play was very heroic, very highfalutin—like a court masque, very elevated. I was very touched by this—*suddenly it was my cue*! I'd forgot. I leapt up and ran down, and I had to run up the stairs—suddenly I was on. I realized that I was one of those pitiful humans, one of those poor people I was so moved by.

I made stars of bizarre people. I used drag queens off the street as Fire Women in *When Queens Collide* if they had outré wardrobe. I interpolated an entire play around Crazy Arthur Kraft, *Turds in Hell*. It ran for ten months, and there were nights when it got up over four and a half hours.

We never made a dime out of it, either. All the receipts went for the theater rental and the weekly ad in the *Times*. Bill Vehr was working days then as a clerk in a bank near the theater. He'd rush the weekend box office receipts in on Monday morning to cover our weekend overdraft.

. . .

Eventually, I began to feel I was pouring everything into an abyss. I felt drained, and yet we went on and did *The Grand Tarot*, which was even more complex. It was sort of a medieval mystery play that took in the whole world. That play never did get put together—it's still in fragments. It was great, but not aesthetically satisfying. I have plans to redo it. It's something I grow with.

It was performed in pieces in many places. It was like an opera, like a Wagnerian *Ring*. The twenty-two cards of the Tarot deck were like twenty-two plays.

The idea that it could be a finished play would be folly. It would always be a part of a play. It would never be complete. In its total journey through its existence, all its performances would be one performance, because it's a continuum.

Some people completely work that way. I personally feel that the endless drama—the infinite drama—is the negation of drama, because it's not isolated in time and space.

Here I come to my deadlock; my refutation of *The Grand Tarot*. It's infinite plot. The Tarot cards represent all of reality. Infinite plot is a negation of plot.

That was the period when I began to see everything falling apart. That's when I decided to abandon the epic form and write a well-made play.

—*CL*

The Performance Group

FOUNDED 1967

Richard Schechner

While the Performance Group may be most famous for its space in New York City's SoHo, the Performing Garage, and for its theatrical offspring, the Wooster Group, TPG's impact was, from its 1967 founding, both immediate and lasting. More important still is the legacy of its founder, Richard Schechner. Arguably the most influential American theatrical editor and theorist of the past fifty years, Schechner was also at the leading edge of experimental production and directing from the mid-sixties through the seventies. As editor of the *Tulane Drama Review* at New Orleans's Tulane University and, beginning in 1967, at New York University (when the journal became the *Drama Review*) he seemed to be present at most of the key moments in the American experimental and regional theater. He founded, with two others, the New Orleans Group and became one of the producing directors of the Free Southern Theater. As the Ford Foundation rose up to fund and instigate the decentralization of our theater, Schechner published on every major trend and moment in that movement. He created the preeminent "environmental theater" (TPG) and, essentially, fathered the field of performance studies out of the department by that name, which he continues to lead—spiritually and ideologically, if not always officially—at NYU.

"Sometimes the people I work with suggest that I direct plays so I can write about them," Schechner reports in *Environmental Theater*, the 1973 book from which this excerpt is taken. "But if this book has value, it is because in it I do something that I cannot do in 'the work.'" This double capacity—and his brilliant, if nakedly self-centered, theoretical mind—allows him to dig up something none of the other founders in this collection unearth: the structures that underlie the work of an ensemble—psychodynamic, sociological, mythic and performative. He creates the group. He leads it. He dominates it. He dictates terms. He submits to its terms. He is changed by it.

At the time he wrote this unique analysis-in-process, he was fleshing out the "Six Axioms for Environmental Theater" he'd outlined in *TDR* and his first book, *Public Domain*. These include:

1. The theatrical event is a set of related transactions (i.e., "Among performers. Among members of the audience. Between performers and audience.").

SOURCE: *Environmental Theater*, by Richard Schechner, 1973.

2. All the space is used for performance; all the space is used for audience.
3. The theatrical events can take place either in a totally transformed space or in "found space."
4. Focus is flexible and variable.
5. All production elements speak in their own language.
6. The text need be neither the starting point nor the goal of a production. There may be no text at all.

Part theoretical experiment, part gestalt therapy group, part Grotowski-inspired psychophysical training, and part revolutionary showmanship, Schechner's Performance Group broke down every boundary it could, especially those between the people "watching" the show and the ones "performing" it.[14] And it was always Schechner's group. "Schechner always thought of himself as a guru," according to one Wooster Group member, the late Ron Vawter. I love the description of Schechner on the back of *Public Domain*, quoted from his *TDR* associate editor, and later colleague at NYU, Theodore Hoffman. Schechner is, according to Hoffman, "vulgar and abrasive, amazed and ecstatic. He is an apostle of change whose wisdom comes from commitment. He speaks [. . .] with a tactical fervor that puts the pontificators to shame."

—TL

I began the Group as a workshop after announcing to my classes at NYU and to some friends that I wanted to continue work I started while with the New Orleans Group (1965–67). Also during the first three weeks of November I was in Grotowski's NYU workshop, and I wanted to apply some of what I was learning. During October I coordinated the planning for a street theater piece, *Guerrilla Warfare*, which was staged simultaneously in many areas of Manhattan on October 28. Some of the people I met while planning *Guerrilla Warfare* wanted to continue working with me. The workshop met at first once a week. Soon, however, meetings were increased until by mid–December we were meeting three and then four times a week in the evenings.

I never directly selected who was to form the nucleus of TPG. I simply announced very strict standards of attendance for the workshop. A person had to be on time; if he missed more than one workshop, he would not be

14. For this writer, at age eighteen, the Performance Group undid everything I thought I knew about the theater, altering forever the way I saw the audience/performer encounter. I spent a month in the sumer of 1975 studying with the Group and watching it rehearse and perform. My mind was blown, and my life was, in numerous, enduring ways, changed.

let back in. The work itself was physically difficult, combining exercises I learned from Grotowski with NOG work, tumbling, and some encounter group techniques. Although I was not entirely conscious of it at the time, the fact that many of the people in the workshop were also in my classes reinforced my authority greatly. Also in no small way I encouraged my own elevation as a father-leader. I was about ten years older than most of the people. By mid-January there were about ten people left from an original twenty-five. We decided to form a group and do our own version of Euripides' *The Bacchae*. But "we" is a tricky word. A corporation was formed by me in which I held all the powers. I took out a personal loan from a commercial bank in order to have enough money to look for a permanent theater space. Luckily Patrick McDermott and William Shephard found the Garage, and I rented it.

Soon a very complicated situation had grown up. Even at this distance I am not able to untangle it. Legally, the Performance Group was a nonprofit, tax-exempt corporation, with me as its executive officer. Theatrically, TPG was a theater of amateurs, myself included, training ourselves. We were fortunate in finding a theater space ideally suited to the new style of work we were doing. Group-wise I became a guru, loved and hated by the people I worked with. The nature of some of the exercises—the gropes, the hours-long improvisations evoking both mythic and intimate material, encounter and confrontation work—corroborated my position. Also I had difficulty speaking to people personally, one to one, in simple conversation. I was most relaxed in a highly structured situation—such as teaching exercises, arranging the rules for a theater game, outlining the shape of an improvisation. When I was confronted, I remained silent, justifying my lack of reaction by saying to myself that the performer needed me as a screen on which to project his/her feelings. Often I would communicate to the whole Group by writing out my notes and distributing them. I discouraged any kind of discussion during workshops. In fact, we followed strict procedures of silence. Every feeling that came up was focused into the work, made part of the work. I saw little of Group members outside of the work. In fact, I was very uncomfortable when a few of them wanted to become my friends.

But this situation was not stable. The commercial success of *Dionysus in 69* put off the inevitable reckoning—after all, maybe I did have some "magic" (went the legend), because the play was a hit. But even as the Garage resounded to full houses, things within the Group were deteriorating. Rehearsals for *Makbeth* during the 1968–69 season went very slowly. Our own experience with a formal therapy group demystified my position in the Group. I began to have deep doubts about my leadership abilities and about the structure of the Group. At the time I didn't know what was going on, and I fought desperately to keep my powers. Later I read Slater's[15] excellent summary of the dynamic.

> . . . the initial view of him [the leader] is highly suffused with an exaggerated and idealized parental image. But this fantasy of the group leader's omniscience is obviously doomed to decay. In the first place, it is based in considerable part on the feelings of abject dependence which are aroused by the initial lack of structure in the situation. The feeling calls for the desire and also activates the worldview appropriate to the feeling when it was first experienced. Relative to the helpless child the parent is omnipotent, and whenever such helplessness is felt again, authority figures will tend to be viewed in the same way. But as the group members gain inner strength this perception will correspondingly wither.
>
> In the second place, transference reactions bloom most richly in the absence of stimuli, and it is easiest to attach an idealized parental image to the group leader when he is unknown . . . Insofar as he does nothing and says nothing, the fantasy of his omniscience can be maintained . . . His nonretaliatory detachment bolsters and colors this fantasy, enabling the members to see him as "invulnerable" and a "superman." But gradually he, too, reveals more and more, and when he speaks he becomes mortal and fallible again and seems quite unsatisfactory by contrast with the idealized paternal image against which he has been silhouetted. Hence the members fluctuate in their attitudes toward him, seeing him now as omniscient, now as incompetent, and circulating bizarre rumors which serve to support both views.
>
> In time, the group leader is stripped of his magical image altogether—his secrets fathomed; his bag of tricks up-ended—and appears in all his naked mortality, a mere human, although apparently clever and well-intentioned. A revolt occurring this late in the game carries no thrill and yields no sense of triumph. If it is not a god but only a mere human who has been conquered and eaten, then what has the group achieved, and what has it added to itself?

The revolt came very late in the game. All during the spring of 1969 I felt my authority slipping away, and I did not want to let it go. In rereading letters

---

15. Philip Slater's *Microcosm: Structural, Psychological and Religious Evolution in Groups*. Slater is a sociologist, actor and playwright, among other designations, whose 1966 book (John Wiley & Sons, New York) was influential on Schechner's work with the Performance Group, as well as on many other companies who were focused not only on the making of theater, but, additionally, on the dynamics of the group process.

written to me by a Group member I realize how stupid I was. The arguments for sharing power, gracefully abdicating my omnipotence, were clear and well taken. But something in me made me want to hold on with a desperation that I can only describe in retrospect as life-saving. Somewhere I felt that if I let go, I would go down.

Instead of letting go I tightened up. On July 27, 1969, I read and posted the following notice:

RS has the following powers:

1. To admit and dismiss members of the Group.
2. To determine what plays should be produced, the casting, and directing assignments.
3. To set workshop work and rehearsals both in terms of the nature of the work and their scheduling.
4. To supervise the planning of the environment and other artistic but nonperformance matters.
5. To set fines for failure to do work, or disruption of work.

This does not signal an end to open discussion. I wish people to feel free to express their opinions. But discussion will not occur during exploratory work where it is necessary to get into the work and not evaluate it too soon.

Performers have the following responsibilities:

1. To perform.
2. To be in workshops.
3. To run workshops where assigned by RS.
4. To direct plays or projects where assigned by RS.

Behind this incredible document was another, drawn by the TPG lawyer at my request and dated July 1, 1969:

This will confirm the understanding reached between you and the Board of Directors of the Wooster Group, Inc.,[16] whereby we have employed you as Executive Director and Artistic Director of the corporation and of the Performance Group . . .

16. Although at a distance of more than forty years, we think of the Wooster Group as the astonishing experimental ensemble led by director Elizabeth LeCompte, which evolved out of and splintered off from the Performance Group, here Schechner refers to the legal entity that owned the Performing Garage at 33 Wooster Street in New York's SoHo.

We confirm that, in this capacity, you are to have sole charge of all artistic matters and overall administrative control of all operations, including, without limitation, the right to hire and fire members of the Performance Group and other employees, to select the works to be presented, to fix hours and places of employment, determine use of the theater and to establish rules and procedures for the group members and employees, subject only to the powers granted to this Board by statute, our certificate of incorporation and bylaws.

We understand that in the past you have referred certain matters affecting the Performance Group and the theater to the members of the group to decide. To the extent that you wish to do so, this is to confirm your authority to continue this practice and to extend or restrict the areas or subject matter to be treated this way, but in case of any dispute between the members of the group and you, it is our intention, and we hereby agree, that your decision shall prevail.

In the notice of July 27 I gave as my reasons for "clarifying" TPG structure:

1. Confusion of legislation for participation. The two are far from identical.
2. Confusion of argument for collaboration. Ditto.
3. Necessary to put most of Group's energies into the immense and interesting problems of *Makbeth*, professional improvement, exploration of self.
4. Experience over the past year has shown:

   a. Not growing fast or largely enough as performers.
   b. Increasing number of enervating and mind-wasting disputes.
   c. Decreasing concentration on work.
   d. Preoccupation with "interpersonal communication" which in many instances does not communicate but rather develops a private (to individuals, to the Group) code.
   e. Group has not emerged either as functioning community or functioning theater.
   f. People who needed special work did not get it.
   g. People who had developed capabilities not sufficiently challenged.
   h. Increasing self-indulgence on the part of the Group as a whole. Individually people want to work. Together, the work is sometimes avoided.

5. Therefore I am returning to some old disciplines which I feel most strongly will help us become finer performers and more whole persons.

It is hard for me to assess now (November 1972) my feelings then (July 1969). I was scared, disappointed, threatened; I had no faith in the way the work was going. I did not enjoy *Dionysus in 69* because images I had in my head were not being played out in the theater. Every time a performer would make a suggestion either about the mise-en-scène or about Group structure I read it as an attack on me. My experience in the Sacharow group sessions[17] did not facilitate my dealings with the others. The groups gave us a frame of reference, but this frame was of anger, resentment and perpetuation of the parent–child relationship.

The capper was the work on *Makbeth*. I had no confidence that the Group could do the play. Some of the best performers I could no longer speak to, much less work with; two others were leaving the Group, one permanently and one on a "leave of absence." I was afraid of failure. What if the critics hated *Makbeth*; what if there were no audiences?

The critics hated *Makbeth*; there were no audiences. The Group was plunged into its deepest crisis. Exactly a year before the *Makbeth* crisis that exploded the Group, I wrote another note to the Group dated December 10, 1968:

On Rules and the Withering Away of the Director:

In all perfectible societies the perfect state is one in which there are neither rulers nor ruled, but rather a harmonious unity in which all live with all. Not in peace, for that would be tedium, but in overt agreement over goals and procedures; active differences coming only over means and only to determine the "better way." These differences are worked out through discussion and action, a new "chairman" emerging for each encounter. The whole society is one rooted in trust and flowering in productivity.

Such a society does not yet exist; probably has not yet existed.

Rules measure the distance between where we are and that perfect state that is the end goal of perfectible societies. Rules are a confession of inadequacy; an admission of imperfectibility. Where rules exist, something is wrong.

17. The Performance Group had spent seven months in weekly encounter groups led by theater director Lawrence (Larry) Sacharow and his colleagues. Within a year of these sessions, that early iteration of TPG's ensemble broke up, possibly as a partial result of Sacharow's work, but Schechner continued to use some of the therapy group's rituals and techniques in rehearsals.

I am a relativist. I do not believe I will live in a perfect state; I do not think I am living in the worst of all possible states. I do not believe either in artistic anarchy or artistic totalitarianism. Artistic totalitarianism is a situation in which a man's whimsy = law. It is a situation which has traditionally been dominated by tyrants, but one in which the "people" (of a small group) could also be dominant. By that I mean, if a person decided not to do the work and by that decision he interrupted the work of all the others, his act would be (for him valid) for the others totalitarian.

The rules we have are essentially of two kinds: (1) societal and (2) artistic. The first kind—be on time, attend—keep us in existence and prepare the time/space for our work. The second kind—surpass yourself, express yourself within the terms of the work—are the root of our art. Insofar as we believe in the second kind, the first kind of rule will wither away. No one would miss work he found absolutely necessary and productive.

However, the human psychophysical mechanism (from toe to soul) is extraordinarily complicated, deceptive and cunning. We too often ask someone to be "human" when human beings can be nothing else but human. No desire for perfectibility will eliminate the beautiful complications of the nonperfect human being. Rules are established as boundaries, touchstones, guideposts. Within the brackets of the rules

$$\text{Must Do} \left[\quad \textbf{FREE} \quad \right] \text{Must Not Do}$$

the performer and the director are free. Our rules are to us what the circular arena and the limit of three actors was to the Greeks. Sometimes our rules are viewed as tyrannical episodes—the "acting out" of RS. In some views they are that; RS is no more perfect or perfectible than any other person.

The only specialty he can claim is that he is more knowledgeable about the process we are embarked on; and that he recognizes the restraints of rules and their necessity; the fact that they free more than they inhibit.

The time may come in the Performance Group when disciplinary societal rules are not necessary and artistic rules are simply implicit in our work. That would mean that TPG was fairly close to being a model of the perfect society. I would welcome, though I do not expect, that time.

Until then I would like you to think of the proposition that the rule of law is a circumscription that draws the area of our creativity and freedom; and not be swayed by the all too simple belief that any limitation is tyrannical.

Endnote on infallibility:

I am very aware that I am most fallible; that as a human being I am not complete. Not "through" as the existentialists would say. I hope not to be "through" until I am dead. Completion is not a state but a process and by definition an impossible project for the human being—but one which must occupy all who wish to be wise.

The nature of our work is innovative and experimental. That means a high proportion of failure. To do our own work is to fail much of the time. Your failure will be not to be able to answer specifically the questions of situation and specificity; not to be able to express effectively the answers when you have found them; and more tasks as well that we will come to later. My failure will be in concepts relating to the mise-en-scène; in allowing myself to be "subjective" but not "personal" in dealing with each of you; and more that I will come to later.

I believe that we need presently, and for some time to come, rules. Perfection is not my game; process is. A word, I might say, that few of us understand though many of us choose to use it either as a cloak or a dagger.

But instead of moving in the direction vaguely outlined in the above, a movement toward communality and collective decision-making, we moved to crisis, confusion, disruption and explosion. As I tightened my authoritarian grip, the group members increased their pressures against me. It was a classic situation. It also interiorized and then projected the situation from *Makbeth*. In some way I was playing old Duncan, and I was doomed. As Slater points out, the patterning of group life on a mythic model is common:

We seem to be dealing here with something akin to the magical force or *mana* of many nonliterate peoples. This force resides in the idealized parental image, and is present in the group leader only so long as he is identified with that image . . . What the group wants most when it revolts is to believe in its own strength and dependability. It will be successful as a group insofar as the members are willing to depend on each other rather than on the leader, and this will occur when the group as a whole is perceived as strong and able.

Thus the attack on me, and my bitter defense and counterattack, was not pure, but dripping with old themes, some of which we had rehearsed for more than a year and were performing nightly. And the conflict left no one the richer because it finally was a kind of stalemate. I fired people; people fired me. We argued, fought, made public pronouncements. Box office receipts were seized, legal notices sent. When January was over, *Makbeth* closed, and the Group split irreparably. I cannot speak for the others, but I did not feel triumphant, just exhausted. It was like the crisis of a sickness, a horrible but necessary vomiting of hatred and personal failure. And, just maybe, the chance for another beginning.

Before discussing the new beginning I want to reflect a moment on TPG in terms of the thesis in this chapter: the contradictory need for communal and analytic experience. TPG began as a workshop, but I knew from the start that I wanted to direct a theater. I think everyone in the workshop wanted a theater. We shared a hope that this theater could be made on a different basis from the commercial theaters. We did not want the part-time, amateurish Off-Off-Broadway kind of theater in which people held second jobs and were unable to give enough time to training or rehearsal. We did not want a stepping-stone theater in which people stayed just long enough to get known. However, I reacted negatively to suggestions that we form a community. I identified community with self-indulgence, freak-outs, undisguised pursuit of pleasures, especially sexual pleasures, at the expense of discipline, productivity and what I called "professionalism." I was trained as a critic and editor; my NYU job was as a professor. Expectedly I leaned toward the classical end of the scale. For all the reputation about being "Dionysian," I *taught* about Dionysian patterns—I did not live those patterns. At the same time I felt an overwhelming excitement during some performances of *Dionysus* and during some workshops, something *more than* theater was happening. This "more than" was the making of personal bonds among TPG members; suggesting ways of communal experience to audiences: in other words, the shamanistic kind of performance. But even as I was fascinated by this, drawn to it, I could not give myself over to it. I was afraid of what would happen to me, to my reputation, to the work I wanted to do. I did not trust the Group, which means I did not trust the people I was working with. Finally, they did not trust me either. As I lost my magic hold over them—as I became less and less a father—I substituted raw authority: I became a boss.

Subsequently I discerned different models of group structure. TPG began with the *leader outside the group*.

The ego boundaries of people in the group are weak while the leader's boundaries are strong and fiercely defended. He is outside, above, beyond, more powerful; the sense of identity of individual group members depends on the leader's attention, praise or punishment, assistance and personal presence. He is the father to the group. There are frequent *emotional epidemics* in the group to which the leader is immune. Cliques, struggles, ganging up and dumping on a scapegoat characterize group life. The leader is envied and hated for his immunity, unassailability and invulnerability. In this kind of group, rebellion against the leader is inevitable; and if the rebellion is thwarted, members feel depressed. A group with the leader outside can be transformed into its opposite, *a group in the leader*. This did not happen to TPG, but it is the kind of structure the Manson family has.

The leader is a messiah, a god, a supermind, the one to whom all is revealed. The members' ego boundaries are completely dissolved; they live in and through the leader, whose fantasy life becomes the actual life of the group. In fact, the leader is the only *person* in the group. The others are absorbed into him, they are parts of him, extensions of his body. Without his "love" they are nothing. Members spend hours interpreting the leader's actions, telling stories about him, embroidering his legends, adoring him, and keeping their experience of him in a perpetual mysterious elation. Like Mel Lyman of Boston's Fort Hill Commune, or the Mother of the Aurobindo Ashram of Pondicherry, members may think of their leader as the Avatar, the literal incarnation of god. The leader does not communicate in only a direct, discursive manner but through parables, mysterious gestures and allegories of action. The leader *manifests* himself. Heinlein's *Stranger in a Strange Land* is about the cult of such a leader, as is the New Testament.

TPG moved not toward this extreme, but often unshakably stable, structure, but toward other, more moderate, models. First we became a group with the leader in the group as a special member.

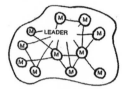

In this kind of group the leader has specific and well-known powers. He gives to the other members of the group but does not reveal as much to them as they do to each other and to him. There is still a large degree of mystification; the leader retains his function as a screen. He is not stripped of his parental role. This kind of group is unstable. The leader's unveiling of himself is deeply manipulative: it is a surface off which the others confront each other. The leader guides his behavior according to how he perceives the needs of the performers. The leader suffers delusions of omniscience: He *knows* what the others need. The others resent the fact that the leader's participation is somehow arranged, that he has jump on them. Let me be clear: it is not that the leader sits at home planning how he will behave at workshop; it is that he does not release his own feelings to the degree he expects others to do so. Thereby an irreversible imbalance is set up that gives the leader a manipulating upper hand.

TPG was this way from March 1970 until after my departure for Asia in October 1971. This very defensive and unstable group structure was my reaction to the terrors of the breakup of January 1970. It was from this stance that we made the first versions of *Commune*. But with Joan[18] and me gone the Group changed—if TPG were to survive, it had to change. I knew that when I went away: another subtle manipulation perhaps. But I didn't recognize the dimensions of the changes until after our return in April 1972. A few weeks after Joan and I got back the Group had a party. After supper people launched into me. They said things they had been feeling for two years; everyone wanted to make sure that I understood that things would not pick up in April where they left off in October. Person after person said angrily that they felt I had used them in making *Commune*; that they were not entirely conscious during rehearsals; that they didn't feel that the play meant what they wanted it to mean.

This second revolution was different from the explosion of 1969–70. During the first period of TPG I was secretive, autocratic and distant. Dur-

18. Joan MacIntosh, an ensemble member and, at the time, Schechner's wife.

ing the second period—the making of *Commune*—I was more like a broken-field runner, shifting my position in order to keep from being downed. In 1972 everyone wanted to keep working together—but in ways that were conscious and collaborative. We sought a form of structure that would be *conscious, stable and creative*: a difficult combination. As best I can perceive it, this kind of structure could take two shapes, with one leading to the other.

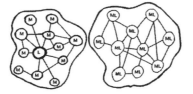

In A there is a single leader who leads with the consent and collaboration of the members. Many powers are shared and leadership diffuses. The leader interacts genuinely with members, taking the same risks they do. He serves at their pleasure and may be replaced if they wish. A is a democratic model. In B we have the mythical leaderless group—perhaps as rare as the unicorn. Every member is the leader depending upon circumstances. Decisions are collective, or a particular situation calls for someone who leads and gives up leadership when the situation changes. In both A and B, leadership is demystified, nonparental and flexible. The democratic and collective (or participatory) models allow for effective interaction among members. In the parental model the interaction is almost all in terms of rivalry either among siblings or between the members and the leader. In the messianic model there is total communion, merging and adoration but little nonfantasized interaction. And there is no power—literally no *mana* or *anima*—outside the leader and what he bestows.

In point of legal fact TPG adopted a new structure in May 1972. The corporation was restructured to include all members of the Group as members of the corporation; and no one who was not a Group member was included. The corporation members elect the board of directors who in turn elect the officers of the Group. Elizabeth LeCompte, Joan MacIntosh, Stephen Borst, Spalding Gray, Jerry Rojo and I all wanted to be on the board and were elected. Also elected to the board was Jeremy Nussbaum, the Group's lawyer. Borst and I were confirmed as co-executive directors of the Group. The "power document" of July 1, 1969, was redrafted to include both Borst and me; and we serve only at the pleasure of the board; and the board only at the pleasure of the members. This legal restructuring was one face of a more complicated and still developing restructuring. Presently the Group is not yet a collective. But leadership is spread around with several of us making decisions. Also the Group as a whole is not only consulted (as always) but *empowered* to make decisions. It is in the area of workshops and rehearsals—the daily artistic work—that a good deal still needs to be done. I don't know what needs to be done, but the process of collaboration, participation and collectivization is started, and not finished.

All kinds of groups can produce "good theater"—if by that one means performances that are moving and meaningful to audiences. But definitely different kinds of groups tend to produce different kinds of theater. The first kind of group is secretive in its actual distribution of power, and if it works, *the director seems to be absent,* as the skillful marionette manipulator stands above the performance he controls. The second kind of group produces hierophanies, extremely powerful but often mysterious and private images and acting out. This kind of messianic group blurs distinctions between out-of-the-theater reality and in-the-theater reality: the killings of Sharon Tate and her friends were, to members of the Manson family, a show, a performance, a real-life drama. The third kind of group shows the strong hand of the director. The fourth kind of group—especially the leaderless version—is the most flexible, capable of adapting its structure to meet different needs. Therefore the kind of performance such a group can make varies widely.

During the summer of 1972 a lot of the strictness of TPG work went out of style. For the first time we let people drop in on our rehearsals, which were open unless we needed to work alone. This was a full reversal of previous policy when all rehearsals were closed except formal "open rehearsals." Previously we let a few special people in to see our work—a professional courtesy. But we kept a "holy space, holy time" attitude. That attitude pretty well went down the drain. Students, faculty, visitors, dropped in to our UBC[19] rehearsals and stayed for a few minutes or a few hours. Some people came back again and again. Unless we got into very personal stuff we did all our work with people there. When we had to be alone, there was no hesitation in asking people to leave. Usually we kicked them out for a comparatively brief time—an hour or so—and then, after we worked through what was troubling the work, we invited our guests back in.

This loosening affected the work on *The Tooth of Crime* by making it inevitable that soliloquies and audience asides would enter into the production. Also, for the first time, the audience was truly part of the creative process at the very first stages of the work. There was one truly extraordinary workshop-rehearsal in which Timothy Shelton, playing Crow, was "given the room" by me. I told him that the rehearsal room and everyone in it were

---

19. TPG spent the summer of 1972 in residence at the University of British Columbia in Vancouver.

his. We were investigating what it takes to kill someone without using physical violence. Tim absorbed the power in the room, and some amazing interactions took place between him and audience who just dropped in to see a rehearsal. The exercise took more than two hours. During that time Tim and two spectators played several scenes that not only found their way into *Tooth* but affected the lives of those involved, including Tim and me. Lasting relationships were started, insights achieved. It was not psychodrama, but working through a theatrical problem at the level of personal encounter. Tim was able to turn the *whole room* into the place of his exercise. For a few hours in that small rehearsal room there was no distinction between the space of the performers and the space of spectators. Scenes took place wherever Tim/Crow initiated them. It took him nearly two hours to "kill" one person. The struggle between them was incredible—ranging across the whole room, dancing, singing, arguing, wrestling, talking, whispering, touching. In the midst of this other people came and went, as their afternoon schedule dictated. A few people stayed, left, and came back an hour later. (The other performers were not there, though a few dropped in toward the end. I think this helped Tim feel freer.) As we work on the play even now, Tim and I refer back to that afternoon as a deep well.

If our rehearsals are more open, our workshop work is not. We do our daily exercises alone with each other. And the "work on ourselves" is done privately. But there's a loosening of secrecy, and to the extent that secrecy is a mystification—a way of stimulating the curiosity of outsiders—it must be abolished.

All this is connected to the changes in basic group structure. As leadership is decentralized, the mysterious *mana* connected with the leader and infused in "the work" is redistributed and reduced. The mystery is not simply shared; it is eliminated. Reconstruction on the level of legalism has consequences on the level of art. The most illuminating consequence is that the two levels are shown to be inseparable.

—RS

Steppenwolf Theatre Company

FOUNDED 1974

Gary Sinise

> I got thinkin' how we was holy when we was one thing, an'
> mankin' was holy when it was one thing. An' it on'y got unholy
> when one mis'able little fella got the bit in his teeth an' run off
> his own way, kickin' an' draggin' an' fightin'. Fella like that bust
> the holiness. But when they're all workin' together . . . kind of
> harnessed to the whole shebang—that's right, that's holy.
>
> —*Jim Casy from* The Grapes of Wrath, *John Steinbeck*

Steppenwolf Theatre Company appeared, it seemed in the mid-seventies, out of nowhere. Its rowdy, still adolescent members came mostly from Illinois State University, in the unaptly named town of Normal, by way of Chicago's North Shore. But they hit that city's theater scene—and the national scene—like a Mack truck in the kitchen—a great, noisy, racing, smelly fluke.[20]

Steppenwolf—which has come to define a Chicago aesthetic for many people—admitted to no indigenous influences, except for rock-and-roll music, a couple of college teachers, some early movies by Martin Scorsese, Mike Nichols and John Cassavetes, and their moms in the suburbs. They were incubated and hatched in a church basement in Highland Park four years before they moved into a theater space at Hull-House downtown. "That's how we grew up together," says Jeff Perry, who founded the company with Gary Sinise, Terry Kinney and others, "totally dependent on each other for all society." He continues, "It was like adolescence, which we purposefully arrested for years."

Steppenwolf wasn't the first ensemble in Chicago by a long shot—they were preceded by the Second City, the gonzo-wild Organic Theater Company under Stuart Gordon, and David Mamet's St. Nicholas Theater Company (essentially Steppenwolf's contemporary). It was, though, the company that came to epitomize a certain Do-It-Yourself-With-Friends principle of theater foundings in that "big-shouldered" town, as well as a breed of rough-and-tumble naturalism. To outside eyes, Steppenwolf made Chicago into a city of ensembles.

Mark Twain described Chicago as "a city where they are always rubbing the lamp and fetching up the genie, and contriving and

SOURCE: "No Money, Just Each Other and the Theatre," by Gary Sinise, *North Shore*, August 1998.

20. As in the introduction to the Second City, earlier in this chapter, I have plagerized language here from my own article, "Chicago Impromptu," *American Theatre*, July/August 1990.

achieving new impossibilities." With Steppenwolf, nothing feels more impossible, more magic-lantern miraculous than the collection of talent it gave birth to: Sinise, Perry and Kinney, as well as John Malkovich, Laurie Metcalf, Joan Allen, Moira Harris, John Mahoney and Glenne Headly were all founding or early members, just the leading edge of so many of the monumental talents to come out of a suburban church basement.

Another of the many miracles conjured up by the Wolf gang has been the transformation of the company itself. Perhaps the first acting ensemble of national prominence to have survived its adolescence and come to institutional maturity, the original group found a way to build a theater that both kept its ensemble together and allowed it to grow and expand. It has navigated—with difficulty and grace—the pull of two media-rich coasts and the stardom of many of its members. While the Group Theatre, maybe its only equivalent in this anthology of visions, lasted a mere ten years—succumbing to, among other things, the lure of Hollywood—Steppenwolf is still going strong forty years after it arrived on the scene like a bat out of hell.[21]

—TL

———

We were kids starting a theater.

It was kind of like one of those old Mickey Rooney/Judy Garland movies: "Hey, kids! Let's put on a show!" That's really the way it was. It takes a few people to get something started and if those people are ambitious enough, insane enough, and have enough love for what they're doing, it can work. We happened to put a very talented group together. The ISU[22] people were all fine actors looking for what to do next. All of them, I think, decided that rather than go to New York or L.A. and play around looking for acting work, they wanted to join something that would give them the opportunity to control their own work. That's what Terry [Kinney], Jeff [Perry] and I wanted. I don't think anybody thought it would come this far.

In the fall of 1973, Jeff had gone off to college at ISU and I stayed in Highland Park to finish an extra semester of high school. Don't ask why. When I graduated in January of '74 I started Steppenwolf with some kids who were still in school. We did two shows in the Unitarian church on Half

---

21. In a perfect everybody-gets-into-the-act Steppenwolf ensemble moment, an email I sent to current artistic director Martha Lavey, asking for early writings from the company's founders, spurred responses—and searches for material—from at least five people at the theater, including Lavey and founder Jeff Perry. They sent me a packet that included this memoir from *North Shore*, a local publication. I also received this piece from a Steppenwolf-smitten student at Yale, Heide Janssen.

22. Illinois State University.

Day Road and one at the Indian Trail Elementary School, where I went to fourth and fifth grade. The second show at the church was *Rosencrantz and Guildenstern Are Dead* by Tom Stoppard. I called Jeff at ISU and he and Terry came up to do the show. The first time I met Terry was the night of our first rehearsal. I'll never forget picking the both of them up at the train station and driving straight to the church. It was June 1974.

That summer we solidified our plans for what we were going to do when Terry and Jeff got out of college. Then, in January 1976, we started having meetings at Illinois State in a tiny apartment that Terry shared with Laurie Metcalf. We already knew we were starting a theater company, but other people were trying to decide what to do after college. I would drive down to ISU on the weekends to meet with people that Jeff and Terry thought would be good to work with, and I remember going to watch [John] Malkovich in a rehearsal of *The Zoo Story*. He wanted to join, but I didn't know him. I also watched him in a rehearsal for *The Man Who Came to Dinner*, which Laurie and Al Wilder were in. I watched H. E. Bacchus and Laurie in a play by Lanford Wilson called *Home Free!* that Terry directed, and I also saw Moira [Harris] in *Cat on a Hot Tin Roof*. Wow!

The original nine members were Laurie Metcalf, Moira Harris, John Malkovich, Al Wilder, H. E. Bacchus, Nancy Evans and Jeff, Terry and me. Joan Allen joined us one year later.

At the same time we were looking for the actors on the weekends at ISU, I was also spending time during the week in Highland Park looking for a space for our home. I went to the head of the youth committee at the Highland Park Chamber of Commerce and asked him if he knew of any spaces we could get cheap. He took me over to the Immaculate Conception School on Deerfield Road. I remember going in with him and seeing the basement, which had been used as a kind of teen clubroom. They had it painted up, but it was basically just a big empty room that looked like it would be great for us. I went to the head of the school and he said it wasn't being used for the kids anymore and that we could have it for one dollar a year. They gave it to us as a tax write-off. It was pretty much a giveaway. I could be wrong, but I don't believe they ever charged us rent. How lucky was that?

I remember that McCormick Place had burned down, and somebody had a connection with somebody who had a connection and we got some seats that were spared in the fire donated to us. We put eighty-eight of them in three rows in this little space. Kevin Rigdon, our high school classmate who's our resident designer, designed the theater.

Jeff had one thousand dollars in his savings and we had five hundred or so left over from 1974. That's what got things going. Local business also was very helpful in donating certain things from time to time. After we got started, we formed a board with people from town and they were helpful with some fundraising and benefits.

People came up from ISU at the end of May or early June and we opened around July 21. We were still painting the walls an hour before the first audience came in. We were building night and day.

We did four one-act plays that first summer—*The Lesson*, *The Indian Wants the Bronx*, *Birdbath* and *The Lover*. I believe performances were Thursday, Friday, Saturday and Sunday, and I think we charged three dollars. And yeah, we actually got an audience. We did everything to get people in. We handed out flyers, walked in parades. Dororthy Andries gave us some good reviews in the *Highland Park News* that helped. Eventually Richard Christiansen came to see us, and then other Chicago critics followed.

Even so, we were struggling. None of us made any money. We didn't start paying ourselves until we moved into the city. I think the only one who got paid in Highland Park was our current director of audience development, Tim Evans, and this was because we were able to get a small grant from the State of Illinois to hire someone to help us with business. The rest of us supported ourselves as best we could. I worked on the loading dock at Neiman Marcus in Northbrook Court and as a groundskeeper at the Ravinia Festival. Moira was a receptionist in a lawyer's office. Laurie worked as a secretary. Malkovich worked at Chandler's Stationery in Evanston. Terry worked at J. Riggins, a clothing store in Northbrook Court. Jeff Perry made egg rolls at Northbrook Court. Wilder was a bus driver. I don't remember what Nancy did. She left after the first year.

We had our day jobs and then we'd go to the theater at night and work until the wee hours. We did everything ourselves—sell tickets, build the sets, clean the toilets. Everything. If we weren't in the play, we'd do something else. I ran the sound and lights or stage managed for some shows. We did everything we could to keep going. Sitting around with no money forces you into fending for yourselves and coming up with some clever alternatives. It was not about money and fame to us. It was about having our own thing. We could decide what we wanted to do. The sacrifice is, you don't make any money. That's the trade-off. The important thing to us was to be able to grow as actors and to have control over the work. We chose plays with as many good roles as we could find because, primarily, we were an acting company. We directed each other and with every play, we learned something new.

I think it was very important that our theater was so small in those days. We were into acting styles that were a bit filmic. Our focus was primarily on contemporary realism and naturalistic plays. There were only three rows of seats in our little theater, so we didn't have to talk very loud. The quieter you can be, the bigger the range. You can always be louder in theater, but can you be softer? If we started in a five-hundred-seat house we would have had to be bigger, but in our little basement, we could be intimate and small. In those days, Malkovich always whispered. You could barely hear him sometimes, but that was okay. We were doing it our way.

The thing about being trapped in a suburban basement isolated from theater life is that we were alone without any distractions, i.e., movies to audition for, other theaters to audition for. It was our private club to do whatever we wanted. We were a family and we became very uninhibited and comfortable with each other. We liked to entertain each other. We had a pretty good, infantile sense of humor among ourselves and we always could make each other laugh. I think that's one of the reasons we stayed together. We just enjoyed each other's talents. The more we worked together, the more supportive of each other and freer we got with our choices. It seemed like nothing was sacred, nothing was inappropriate. There were no restrictions in the basement. We've carried that with us for the past twenty-four years.

To us, theater was a medium that had no boundaries, and that's been our attitude toward theater wherever we go. During Malkovich's brief three-month stint as artistic director, we did Wallace Shawn's *Our Late Night* and it practically closed the theater. We didn't do it in Highland Park, though. I'm sure the Catholics would have evicted us. We rented the Hull-House in Chicago for that one.

Most of the plays we chose in those days were not "mainstream," but I can't think of anything we did that I'd consider inappropriate. Some other theaters might think that way, but we just did whatever we wanted to do and let the chips fall where they may.

Some performances, we had small audiences. There might be three or four people—a couple of friends and maybe one or two others. Some nights there were *no* people. We just canceled the show on those nights and turned it into a party. We called it Random Night and we would entertain each other with any stupid bit of behavior we could come up with. Terry would do mime. He'd be a Frenchman with a mime poodle doing dog tricks. Malkovich loved putting on that song "Blinded by the Light" and dancing and singing at the top of his lungs. Jeff and I did dueling Tartuffes, spouting Molière vocal inflections at each other. Moira would be a French singer who was tone deaf. She'd sing songs like "Fool on the Hill" really off-key with a terrible French accent. We'd sit and laugh at each other and entertain each other all night. We had more fun at the theater with each other than anyplace else. Then again, where else would we have gone?

We also made a Super Eight sound movie in the basement called *The Audition* about small-town people, auditioning for *Hamlet*. It was my directing debut and the others' film acting debut. I'm sure it's destined to be a classic.

In 1978, we decided to do *Rosencrantz and Guildenstern* again and it was kind of our first big "hit." As I remember, it was the first show we ever extended. We ran it through Christmas and did a New Year's show. So you see? We had our encouraging moments as well.

There also were times I didn't think we'd last another day. A lot of things threatened to dismantle us: personal stuff, fear, etc. We fought through it all and came out on top, but not without a struggle. Many times it looked like we might be finished, but we kept ourselves together and kept moving forward.

There was lots of immaturity there, struggling for power and everyone needing to have a voice. We'd be fighting or somebody would quit. They'd leave the company and we'd have to try to get them to come back. People would fight through the pettiness and find a way back to the group. We were always having meetings about something. One time, Terry Kinney quit the company, then he wanted back in. We had to have a big meeting to decide whether we should let him back in or not. He was upstairs pacing in the school building while we were in the basement having the meeting. At one point Moira, whose father was dying of cancer at the time, got very upset at the absurdity that we were even having a discussion about letting our good friend back into the company when there were far more severe things happening in our lives. It all got very emotional, and that brought it all into perspective. After that, the meeting was over. Needless to say, we let him back in.

In those early days, everybody voted on everything. We had to find our group voice. Yeah, we had our leaders, but we were always a collective. Without it, there was nothing for the leaders to fight for. After our move to Chicago the leaders were given more power to lead and make decisions for the group. Now it's different because, then, all we did was Steppenwolf. We had no money, just each other and the theater. The artistic director and a managing director pretty much make all the decisions now. It's been that way for years. The group rarely votes, if at all, anymore. That's due to the evolution of the company and people's own careers. People still remain members of Steppenwolf, but it's not their sole artistic effort the way it was in the basement.

As I look back at those early days in Highland Park, I am amazed at what we have accomplished. It doesn't happen very often that a group of young theater artists comes together and creates something that lasts this long. Somehow, the stars lined up and fate was on our side. When I look at all the things I've done in my own career, I think the most unique and special will always be the founding of Steppenwolf Theatre. It has been my school. My college. A grounding force in my artistic life. And it all came together in Highland Park.

—GS

Chapter 5

Theaters or Institutions?

Separately and then together, we forged these theaters, these instrumentalities, these constellations of activities, these collective outposts, these—God forgive me!—institutions in order to preserve and re-create, in new forms, the art of theater then fusting in us unused. We found a better way of doing things. Found? We forged a better way, we scratched it out, hacked it, ripped it, tore it, yanked it, clawed it out of the resisting, unyielding nose-thumbing environment.

—*Zelda Fichandler*

The Civic Repertory Theatre

FOUNDED 1926

Eva Le Gallienne

"America represents the world hope of the attainment of lofty ideals in dramatic arts," Eva Le Gallienne enthused to George Pierce Baker's students at Yale in 1925. "The myth of European supremacy in the arts is fast fading . . . Let us make the theater of America stand free and high up, with no world peers."

Le Gallienne, the British-born daughter of poet Richard Le Gallienne, is among the earliest and most invigorating of the American art theater's founding mothers. After considerable success on Broadway, notably in her star-making turn as Julie in Ferenc Molnár's *Liliom*, Le Gallienne set out to counter a commercial system that she compared to an "Indian totem pole, never growing in stature but gaining merely in the number of new grimaces carved on its surface."

At twenty-seven years of age, she founded the Civic Repertory Theatre, the nation's first sustained, professional, low-cost repertory company. It lasted for ten years, creating a new nonprofit model and setting a standard for ensemble performance and diverse programming. It was infused with Le Gallienne's own spirit—of serving a theatrical ideal, beyond the personality of star actors, beyond the tally sheets of producers. The company's guiding principle: "The theater should be an instrument for giving, not a machinery for getting."

Le Gallienne leased a theater building on New York's 14th Street for nine hundred dollars a week, forty weeks a year. With a glorious nineteenth-century past—Edwin Forrest, Edwin Booth and Mrs. Fiske played there—and an inglorious recent history, the building had gone to seed. The Salvation Army across the street may have appealed to Le Gallienne's sense of theater as the most generous venture. She, too, was out to save something.

"I could not see why America should not have a repertory theater subsidized by private capital in the same way that its opera companies

SOURCE: *With a Quiet Heart: An Autobiography*, by Eva Le Gallienne, 1953.

271

and symphony orchestras are," she wrote in this later memoir. "Why should the drama be the only neglected art? [. . .] Millions were spent on libraries, museums and music, but the theater was an outcast."

Le Gallienne produced thirty-seven plays, acting in most of them, including the first English-language staging of Chekhov in America (*The Three Sisters*, in the company's first season). The repertoire ranged over new plays, world classics, revivals of recent work and reconceived favorites like *Peter Pan* and *Alice in Wonderland*. A free school for select young actors influenced a generation of American artists. Ticket prices topped at a low $1.50, attracting Broadway regulars, students, workers, shopkeepers and audiences from nearby German, Russian and Eastern European immigrant communities. Despite Le Gallienne's creative programming and energetic fundraising, the theater folded in 1933, nearly one hundred thousand dollars in debt.

While the early assessment of William Lyons Phelps, distinguished professor of literature at Yale, may sound hyperbolic, he was not alone in holding it. "I regard the establishment of the Civic Repertory Theatre in New York by Eva Le Gallienne as one of the most significant events not only in the history of the American stage, but in the history of America, as the drama and civilization are inseparable." Le Gallienne's memoir, *With a Quiet Heart*, captures the audacious energy and passionate conviction of this pioneering lady of the theater.

—TL

———

Anyone strolling along 14th Street between Sixth and Seventh Avenues in the year of 1953 will search in vain for any trace of a theater there. But in 1866 a fashionable new playhouse, at the time hailed as the apotheosis of elegance, was opened on the uptown side of the street near the corner of Sixth Avenue—the French Theatre.

Through the years this playhouse suffered many vagaries of fortune. It knew triumphs and disasters—as all theaters do—but by the year 1926 it seemed irrevocably relegated to decay.

It stood, crumbling and shabby, flanked on one side by the hideous travesty of a medieval fortress known as the 14th Street Armory, and on the other by disreputable-looking buildings housing an anomalous collection of small private factories and stores, whose filthy windows rattled mournfully at the passage of the Sixth Avenue elevated trains.

The paint had peeled off the once-beautiful portico of the old theater; the plaster fell in dangerous showers from its dilapidated cornices; and a few tattered posters announced occasional performances of tenth-rate burlesque shows, and "foreign-language" presentations, mostly Italian.

But during the summer months of 1926 the building underwent a sudden change. The moth-eaten façade was encased in scaffolding on which painters worked feverishly. Windows were mended; sagging doors were reset on brand-new hinges; the filth of years was laboriously carted away in veritable mounds.

At last, over the marquee, electricians mounted one by one the large letters which proudly spelled the name CIVIC REPERTORY THEATRE, and, spanning the street, a blue and white banner erected by the 14th Street Association fluttered, bearing on the one side the words GOOD LUCK CIVIC REPERTORY and on the other WELCOME LE GALLIENNE.

On each pillar of the colonnade supporting the venerable portico neat frames appeared, bearing the titles of such plays as *Saturday Night* by Benavente, *The Three Sisters* by Chekhov, *The Mistress of the Inn* by Goldoni, *Twelfth Night* by Shakespeare, *The Cradle Song* by Martínez Sierra, *The Master Builder* and *John Gabriel Borkman* by Ibsen and *Inheritors* by Susan Glaspell. Passersby stopped in amazement to read these names, the like of which had not been seen on 14th Street for many a year.

On the evening of October 26, 1926, an unprecedented procession of cars and taxis drove up to the long-neglected doors, and a crowd of curious, somewhat skeptical first-nighters, bewildered at finding themselves so far from the familiar Broadway scene, surged into the brightly lighted lobby.

From the subway, elevated and Hudson tube exits streamed another crowd, making its way in eager expectation to the rush-seats in the gallery. Backstage high excitement reigned, for this night was the culmination of many months, indeed years, of thought and careful planning. It was the beginning of our attempt to realize a dream, a dream that we had been assured was impossible of realization, impractical, fantastic and foredoomed to immediate failure. We had taken up the challenge and now prepared to embark on our first battle.

What was this Civic Repertory Theatre, which, through the unique quality of its achievement, had already become a legend? What were its aims? What was its purpose?

The Civic was founded in an attempt to provide the people of New York with a popular-priced classical repertory theater similar to those that have existed as a matter of course for many years in every large city of Europe—not only in such great capitals as Paris, Berlin, Vienna and Moscow, but in such comparatively small towns as Brussels, Amsterdam, Prague, Budapest, Stockholm, Oslo and Copenhagen.

The first sixteen years of my life were spent in countries where such "libraries of living plays" were considered mandatory. These theaters were as important to the mental and spiritual well-being of the people as bread was to sustain their bodies. Their presence in no way precluded, or impinged upon, the lighter and more sensational forms of entertainment, which it is also the function of the stage to provide; but in European cities the theater was not limited, as it is in our country, to the best-seller of the moment.

It was this limitation of an art which I had been brought up to consider on a par with poetry, music and painting—and which can be, in its finer aspects, a synthesis of all of these—that shocked and startled me, as it does so many newcomers to our shores, on my first arrival in New York in 1915. There was plenty of cake in the showcases of Broadway, but the bread was missing.

I determined then and there that, once I had won my spurs and proved my worth, I would devote my energies and talents to filling this need in the American theater scene, and this determination never left me. In 1925 I felt ready to attempt the realization of my purpose. A series of consecutive successes, starting with Arthur Richman's *Not So Long Ago*, followed by *Liliom* and *The Swan*, had placed me in the front rank of the young actresses of that time, and enabled me to gain access to men and women of wealth and influence, some of whom, happily, saw the value of my scheme.

I started modestly with some special matinees of *The Master Builder* in the fall of 1925, and when these proved a success I added *John Gabriel Borkman* to my incipient repertoire. At first these plays were offered at the regular Broadway prices, but since popular prices were the crux of my whole plan, I cautiously presented the two plays on alternate mornings at a top price of $1.50. Even at the unlikely hour of ten-thirty A.M. the houses were packed, and hundreds of eager people had to be turned away.

After the Christmas holidays I took the two plays on a spring tour of the Eastern cities, charging as low a scale as the booking office would permit. The results were immensely encouraging, and during these months I worked out, down to the smallest detail, the schedule for a proposed season of repertory to open in the fall.

One morning, in Cincinnati, I called the company together and outlined my plan to them. I explained that the work would be hard and the salaries only moderate, but in spite of this they one and all decided to join me in my adventure.

The plan once clearly formulated and set down on paper, I flung myself wholeheartedly into the job of translating theory into practice. I was predatory and ruthless. No rich person was safe in my presence. My crusading zeal was such that few people had the strength to escape my attacks on their bank accounts. If I met with resistance I was quick to point out that since I, possessed of no fortune but my talents and industry, was willing to donate nine-tenths of my earning capacity to this work, it would seem niggardly of them, secure in their steady incomes, to begrudge me a tiny fraction of their wealth. This argument amused some and impressed others and usually clinched the matter; I seldom went away empty-handed. I never failed to make it clear that these sums were gifts, neither loans nor investments; there could be no hope of repayment of profit. The Civic was designed as a subsidized theater; only in this way, it seemed to me, could popular prices be combined with the necessary high standard of production, and the policy remain stable and safe from compromise.

There were three reasons why I chose the old theater on 14th Street. To my indignant surprise, the uptown theater managers refused to permit regular performances at the popular prices I had decided on—thirty-five cents to $1.50 top. They were afraid of lowering the prestige of their houses. I therefore had to find a place outside of their jurisdiction.

With few exceptions the stages uptown were too small to accommodate the repertory scheme, with its constant changes of scenery.

I felt, too, that since our theater in no way intended to compete with the regular run of Broadway attractions it might be best to remove ourselves completely from that particular arena. So it came about that the 14th Street Theatre was rescued from oblivion.

On that Monday night of October 26, when we opened our doors with Benavente's *La noche del sábado*—translated somewhat erroneously by John G. Underhill as *Saturday Night*—we had three other plays in readiness: Chekhov's *The Three Sisters* and the two Ibsen plays already produced the previous season.

The notices on Tuesday morning tried to be kind—the critics seemed to feel a respect for the venture, mingled with surprise and amusement at its sheer audacity—but they were far from being good. We were able to brush them off lightly, however, for we had many other strings to our bow and, thanks to my Robin Hood tactics with various wealthy patrons, we were assured of a full season, no matter how meager the box office receipts might prove to be. On Tuesday, our second night, we opened *The Three Sisters*, the first professional performance in this country of a Chekhov play in English, and over this Mr. Woollcott[1] flung his famous hat in the air, and there was general jubilation among his colleagues. By the end of our second week *The Master Builder* and *John Gabriel Borkman* had joined the repertory, and these four plays rotated on the Civic program while rehearsals were in full swing for Goldoni's *Mistress of the Inn*, which opened the Monday of our fifth week. This was the first Goldoni play ever to be presented professionally in English on the New York stage. Five weeks later Shakespeare's

---

1. Alexander Woollcott was the scabrous—some would say savage—critic and commentator for the *New Yorker* and a member of the famous Algonquin Round Table. Of course, he was immortalized in the character of Sheridan Whiteside in *The Man Who Came to Dinner* by fellow Algonquin wit George S. Kaufman and Moss Hart.

Twelfth Night took its place beside the other productions. In early February *The Cradle Song* was added to the lists and proved a veritable smash hit, and finally Susan Glaspell's *Inheritors* was produced, giving us an active repertory of eight plays. I remember that the last week of our first season we gave ourselves the luxury of playing a different play at each performance. I had not announced "repertory" for nothing!

We closed the end of May, and I retired to the country to plan our second year of work, making occasional sorties to the yachts and palaces of Long Island to strengthen our finances, for, as I had expected, the deficit that first year was very high.

I was amazed at the praise and honors that began to shower upon me, and decidedly embarrassed by all the eulogies about my "great sacrifice" and "unselfish devotion" to the theater. I felt lucky to be doing what I wanted; I could see nothing unselfish about that! Honorary degrees were conferred on me, gold medals and, best of all, the *Pictorial Review* Award for "the most outstanding accomplishment by an American woman"—a prize valuable from several angles, since it carried with it the handsome sum of five thousand dollars, with which I was able to refurbish the carpets and chairs in the orchestra and put cushions on the bare benches of the gallery rush-seats.

Each year we added four or five productions to our growing library, and by the end of the fifth season we had some thirty plays actively rotating in repertory. Besides the staples that should form the backbone of such a repertory—plays by such giants as Shakespeare, Molière, Goldoni, Chekhov and Ibsen—we had introduced Giraudoux to New York theatergoers (a fact often forgotten) through his *Siegfried*, and several other modern playwrights such as Jean-Jacques Bernard, Claude Anet, [Gustave] Wied and [Max] Mohr. We had won a Pulitzer Prize with Glaspell's *Alison's House*. We had inaugurated a free school, known as the Apprentice Group, whose graduates included such well-known actors as Burgess Meredith, John Garfield, J. Edward Bromberg, Richard Waring, Arnold Moss, Howard da Silva and many others. Our acting company had been strengthened by the presence of such artists as Alla Nazimova, Jacob Ben-Ami, Paul Leyssac and Josephine Hutchinson, and the Civic Repertory, from being a mad quixotic experiment, had assumed an air of permanence.

Many of our productions—notably *The Cradle Song*, *The Cherry Orchard*, *Peter Pan*, *Camille* and *Romeo and Juliet*—had been smash hits in the full Broadway sense of the words, and I had much difficulty in resisting tempting offers to cash in on these successes by moving them uptown and presenting them at the regular commercial scale. It seemed to me that such a step would be not only shortsighted but a betrayal of the basic purpose for which the Civic had been created. Since our aim was to establish a permanent repertory theater, I felt it would be decidedly foolish to throw away our trump cards. The full houses that these plays drew each time they were performed enabled us to keep alive our other productions, which, though all of them worthwhile, had a more limited box office appeal. I wanted to keep faith with the public that had shown faith in me, and by strictly adhering to its firmly stated policy the Civic won the loyalty of its many followers and the respect of critics and newspapermen in general. I was proud of the reputation we had acquired of always living up uncompromisingly to the plans that we announced, and when we rang down the fifth year on a performance of *Camille* the extraordinary demonstration that followed the final curtain was proof enough of the public's genuine appreciation of the consistent integrity of the management.

All those who were present on that memorable evening will, I'm sure, remember it as vividly as I do. It is only in the living theater that such a communion between audience and players can exist. From all over the house people shouted to us, "Come back! Be sure to come back! Don't go away!" Those in the gallery and the back of the orchestra fought their way down the aisles to get a closer view of us. The entire Civic personnel—office staff, stagehands and actors—stood on the stage with tears in their eyes as the curtain rose and fell to the seemingly endless applause; and when I came out to take a final call alone I suddenly found myself ankle-deep in flowers, thrown singly and in small bouquets from every part of the auditorium.

It was one A.M. by the time the crowd dispersed. People found their way backstage through the pass-door, and I stood on the threshold of my dressing room, shaking hands with these unknown friends as they filed slowly past. As I started upstairs to my apartment on the top floor of the building, exhausted by the emotions of the evening, the porter told me that there was still an immense crowd at the stage door, which refused to go away without a final glimpse of me, so I hurriedly threw a cloak over my Camille nightgown and went into the street to wave farewell. Again came the shouts—"Come back! Be sure to come back!" I was tempted then and there to abandon our year of respite and continue the work without interruption; yet I felt this much-needed break would bring us back armed with fresh ideas, a clearer perspective and renewed energy to serve. Little did I realize what this "much-needed break" held in store for me.

A few weeks later, when I found myself painfully struggling through my unexpected ordeal,[2] the memory of this demonstration of friendship on the

---

2. On June 12, 1931, after her season had ended, Le Gallienne was severely burned when she struck a match to light the propane heater in the cellar of her country home in Weston, Connecticut. She had burns all over her body, but worst of all were her hands, which had instinctively flown up to cover her face in the blast. The third-degree burns ravaged the bones of her fingers. Even after a number of reconstructive operations, she never regained full use of her hands, though she found ways to conceal the damage on stage.

part of the public was a potent factor in my fight for recovery. I felt that, like the legendary salamander, I must somehow emerge from the fire unscathed and keep the promise to "come back" to which I had pledged myself that evening.

—EL

Theatre '47

FOUNDED 1947

Margo Jones

> Let us stir up the practical realization of a potential, of a dream, of an ideal.
>
> *—Margo Jones*

Margo Jones imagined the American regional theater into being. She planted its seeds and worked the soil. She laid out the vision for a nation of theaters—regional, resident, repertory—and she articulated the principles of that theater—permanence, professionalism and a "violent" dedication to new plays and playwrights. She was the first of the three great mothers of the "movement" of decentralization (the other two, the Alley Theatre's Nina Vance and Zelda Fichandler of Arena Stage, followed in her footsteps). She pioneered the use of arena staging as a way of creating intimacy with an audience and making the founding and running of theaters affordable. She voiced the siren call of this new theater, as her biographer Helen Sheehy[3] puts it: "National theater . . . every large city . . . decentralization . . . nonprofit, resident company . . . new plays and classics—we have to have it . . . we must have it." And, thanks in large part to her, we now have it. But, tragically, she didn't live to see it.

"In her modest 198-seat theater," Sheehy writes,

SOURCE: *Theatre-in-the-Round*, by Margo Jones, 1951.

3. We are fortunate to have a biographer of Sheehy's compassion and intelligence devoted to the women—Jones and Eva Le Gallienne, specifically—who pioneered our nation's theater. Although much has been written of Jones and her impact on the regional theater, I've cribbed most of the above from Sheehy, because, frankly, her portrait is the most complete and compelling.

Margo had united two major forces in twentieth-century theater—the aspirations of the art-theater movement launched in
the beginning of the century by the Provincetown Players and
continued in the 1930s by the Group Theatre, and the move
toward decentralization of the theater that had reached its
height in the 1920s with the community-theater movement
and then in the 1930s with Hallie Flanagan's Federal Theatre
Project. To this synthesis she added her own unique contributions. [. . .] Margo's theater, the prototype for a national
theater, was incorporated as a nonprofit institution—the first
modern nonprofit, professional resident theater.

A woman of legendary energy and a can-do, will-do, won't-take-no
determination, Jones had worked in recreational theater, led her
own Houston-based community theater, directed on Broadway. She
brought to the founding of Theatre '47, whose name was updated
with each new year, a fanatic's love of plays. Indeed, the most striking photographic images of her show a woman with an ever-present
drink beside her, sitting on a couch or floor, surrounded by scripts.
This is how, essentially, she died as well, in 1955 at the age of forty-
three. Her kidneys compromised from hard drinking, Jones fell asleep
(or possibly passed out) on her recently cleaned carpet, surrounded
as ever by plays to be read. Despite the best efforts of doctors in the
days that followed, the combination of drink and toxic fumes from
the cleaning fluid, in a Texas-hot apartment with the air-condition-
ing off, ended her life.

Jones earned her mythic descriptions from many of the leading
mid-century playwrights whose work she nurtured. Jerome Lawrence
(co-writer of *Inherit the Wind*, which she premiered) called her "a
patron saint of playwrights." Thornton Wilder dubbed her a "fighter,
builder, explorer and mixer of truth and magic." Her dear friend and
collaborator Tennessee Williams, who described her as a "combination of Joan of Arc and Gene Autry—and nitroglycerine," gave her
the nickname that stuck: the "Texas Tornado."

Margo Jones's 1951 book *Theatre-In-The-Round* reads like a manifesto for theater lovers everywhere, the breathless exhortations of a
preacher for a new religion, with little time and endless work to do.
Her call has been picked up by many who followed. The work is still
being done.

—TL

Then and Now

The dream of all serious theater people in the United States in the middle of our twentieth century is the establishment of a national theater, in which playwrights, actors, directors, designers, technicians and business managers can find an expression for their art and craft as well as earn a livelihood, and which will provide audiences with beautiful plays. If this dream has not yet become a reality, it is mainly because of the economic problems involved, but a solution is imperative lest all the wonderful ideals remain in a misty realm. Dreaming is a great human experience, but unless you can make your dreams come true, you cannot be of much help in creating a great theater in America. Dreams and ideals must be combined with practical thought and action, and I firmly believe that this can be done in the theater. If you add achievement to idealism, you prove that it is not only spiritually compensating to be idealistic, but it is also smart and profitable.

We must create the theater of tomorrow today. We cannot postpone our dreams and ideals any longer. Our potential audiences all over America are waiting for the theater we have been promising them. They are eager and ready to see good plays well produced, and we must not disappoint them. Let us stir up the practical realization of a potential, of a dream, of an ideal!

What our country needs today, theatrically speaking, is a resident professional theater in every city with a population of over one hundred thousand. According to the 1940 census figures, there are over one hundred such cities in the United States. I believe it would be easier to start in the larger centers, although I am certain that once all these cities acquired resident professional theaters, smaller communities would want them, too; and possibly within some ten years the 107 cities whose populations run from fifty to one hundred thousand would also have their own theaters.

I have heard that there is the fantastic number of five hundred thousand groups which produce plays in this country. If this figure is even remotely accurate, it is both amazing and sufficient; but it does not tell us anything about the quality of their productions. I believe that the best way to assure quality is to give birth to a movement which will establish permanent resident professional theaters throughout the country.

I realize that this is not a new dream, but today it does not have to be merely a dream because there is a way to do it. One of the problems that has confronted promoters and directors who have sought to establish professional theaters previously has been the building situation. Theater construction in the United States is at a standstill, except for a few universities that have acquired handsome theaters in recent years. Former legitimate houses have either become moving-picture theaters or have been condemned or torn down. To build new theaters in desirable locations is a tremendously expensive, if not completely prohibitive, proposition if the investment has to be repaid, because the profits simply are not large enough.

The answer which I have found in Dallas and which many theater people are finding today lies in theater-in-the-round presentations. This form is also known as central staging, arena staging, circus theater and penthouse style. It means very simply that you dispense with the proscenium stage and place your actors in a lighted area, surrounding them on all four sides by the spectators.

Since this method has been rediscovered and since we know that it works, there is an urgency about starting theaters in every town in the United States as soon as possible and doing it in the best way. I want to show not only that it can be done, but that it must be done right or it is not worth doing. A new medium can be a challenge and a source of great theatrical excitement, provided it is not cheapened or exploited to do the same old things in the same old ways. It is the duty of everyone who works in the theater or intends to work in it, and who loves it to keep it alive, to bring more audiences into it and to improve it every minute, every month, every year.

Numerous groups have discovered that they can solve their housing problems by using theater-in-the-round. The vast majority of these have been nonprofessional; several, however, are of professional caliber. Here is a proven way for the immediate establishment of resident professional theaters. The only way we can have a true theatrical renaissance in America is to have resident professional theaters in all our large cities. I say these theaters must be resident because they should give the community as well as the staff an assurance of continuity, and they must be professional because, if we insist on the highest standards of production, the actors and staff must spend eight hours a day in the theater. If we want young people of talent and intelligence to go into this field and give the best they have, we must offer them the compensation of dignity and security.

Every town in America wants theater! It is the duty and business of a capable theater person to go into the communities of this country and create fine theaters. It takes time and courage and patience. Anyone who undertakes such an assignment must want to do it and want to do it terribly. If no substitute will be good enough, if no compromise is effected, if standards are not lowered, the objective will be accomplished. It is a matter of hard work, positive thinking, endurance and, above all, great faith. Theatre '50 in Dallas is not a phenomenon.[4] It can be done everywhere. If cities are ready for enlarged industry, for modern hotels, for fine shops, they are also ready for good theater.

---

4. As mentioned in the above introduction, Jones's theater changed its name with each passing year, an idea she got from a company in Prague. Theatre '50, therefore, is Theatre '47 four years in.

My seeming insistence on theater-in-the-round as a method is not fanatical. As I will point out later, I believe that ideally we should have flexible theaters, and I have as much love and admiration for the proscenium stage as for the open-air theater or theater-in-the-round. It would be absurd to say "we have found a practical way to create theaters, so away with all other types." Not at all. I think we should have all sorts of theater structures, and all new architectural developments should be followed and studied and utilized whenever the opportunity presents itself. But we have an urgent job ahead of us in the theater, and a way to do it without further delay is theater-in-the-round.

There is no doubt that a change has been occurring in the state of our theater. The diminishing number of Broadway playhouses is terrifying at first glance, but rather than a sign of death I interpret it as a sign of change. A theater is not decaying if, within five short years, it presents to the public two great playwriting talents like Tennessee Williams and Arthur Miller—to mention only the most outstanding—and new actors, directors, designers and musicians. Perhaps because of the severe financial demands on a Broadway production, the standards are very high. A certain unevenness is inevitable in any theater, but basically I believe Broadway is at a height of development in its standards of play selection and production. Too little has been said in favor of the Broadway scene. At the moment it still stands as the center of our theater, contains its best plays, the best actors and the best stage sets and lighting to be found in America. And it is also an experimental theater in the sense that it will risk its all on new plays and unknown playwrights. For this alone Broadway deserves the respect and admiration of every theater person in the country.

This theatrical center of ours, nevertheless, is frighteningly small. There are only twenty-eight legitimate playhouses in the Broadway area today, and rumors are persistent about one which is to be torn down and another which is to be taken over by a television studio. Whatever the reasons may be—and the real-estate situation in the New York theater is extremely difficult—it means that the center of our activities is narrowing down. It does not mean that the American theater is dying, for even in New York there are areas besides Broadway where the theater can flourish, and we have hundreds of cities where potential audiences are starved for good theater.

The fact that last season there were only sixty productions on Broadway, while twenty-five years ago there were over two hundred, is an unmistakable sign of change, as is the decreasing number of plays that go out on the road. In the late twenties, some hysterical notes were sounded because only seventy road companies were entertaining the nation, but in the 1949–50 season there were only thirty-two! Nor is the outlook good for the 1950–51 season.

[. . .]

Decentralization is good, but there is something else we need if we are to have a great theater in America, and that is a sound theater attitude. It is high time all of us who work in the theater—whether it is Broadway, resident professional, community, college or high school—adopted an attitude with the finest possible standards.

All types of theater are really *one*, because if theater is to be exciting its aim is always *one*: to present good plays in the best possible manner. What is most important in maintaining a sound theater attitude is the reason for choosing and producing a play; this reason should be that it is a fine play, you are excited by it and you can give it a good production. When a college director, for instance, chooses to do *The Taming of the Shrew* for this reason, he has a sound theater attitude. An automatic byproduct will be the training his students will receive from acting in this play, working on the production and observing it. Thus, as a result of his sound theater attitude, the director will also perform his duty as an educator.

A sound theater attitude implies a great want to do a play. If a director does not have a suitable cast for that particular script, sometimes his great desire to see the play on the stage, his enthusiasm and the quality of the play itself can pull the actors up.

True excitement in the theater stems from hard work. Anyone who decides to produce a play or to participate in its production must take his job seriously; working toward a goal of excellence will enable him to enjoy his work to the fullest extent and give him the enthusiasm which is essential in the theater.

There is one more element in having a sound theater attitude which I want to emphasize: the attitude toward the new playwright. The decision to do a new script is mutually beneficent for the theater and the dramatist; the writer is fortunate to have his play produced and the group to have found a worthy play to do. The author must be paid a royalty, and his script must be given the benefit of the finest production the theater is capable of offering.

I believe it is imperative in creating new resident professional companies to take a violent stand about the choice of plays. Personally I believe in the production of classics and new scripts, with emphasis on new scripts.

Our theater can never be stronger than the quality of its plays. We must, therefore, have a great number of good plays. The classics have proved their value throughout the history of the theater, and I believe we should draw on them as great literature and great theater. But if we produce only classics, we are in no way reflecting our own age. Our theaters must not only be professional, they must be contemporary as well. The most excellent seasons in New York are those which bring forth exciting new playwriting talent.

Too many people are saying, "I'll do a new play if I can find a good one." Certainly you must find a good one, but this attitude is not good enough.

The plays can be found if you look hard enough. And if you take the violent stand I have spoken about, you will feel obligated to search and search and search until the scripts are discovered. I have a belief that there is great writing in America today and that much of it has not yet been unearthed.

Great theaters have always had their playwrights. Shakespeare, Lope de Vega, Molière, Ibsen—all these were men around whom theatrical companies were functioning. The Moscow Art Theatre had Chekhov; the Abbey Theatre had Yeats, Synge and O'Casey; the Provincetown had O'Neill; the Group had Odets. We must have our new playwrights, and we will not have them unless we give them many outlets to see their plays produced. This is the best way in which they can learn to write better plays.

The production of classics is healthy, but it is not a step in the flowering we want to see in the American theater. We need progress, and the seed of progress in the theater lies in the new plays.

On Broadway it is not considered unusual or idealistic to do a new play. Why do theaters in other cities feel that it is? Enough of them have been very successful with the few original plays they have produced, yet they continue their policy of imitation. The Broadway producer has at least one quality which theatrical leaders elsewhere would do well to emulate—he has the courage to do new scripts.

A sound theater attitude in reading a new script is very simple indeed. It means you pick it up and read it. If your experience and taste and discretion tell you that it is a good play, that you like it, then it *is* a good play until such a time as presented to an audience which rejects it. This can happen, of course, if the play has no meaning for the audience; but if it had a meaning for the producer or director when he read it, he should have been able to impart this meaning to the audience. The failure of a play before the public is as often the fault of the production as of the script. The producer must, however, be prepared for a complete rejection or for a mixed reaction. After all, do all people like the same type of houses, clothes, furniture, paintings? Then, why must they all like the same play? Five New York producers discussing a play will disagree violently on its merits, but one of them believes in it, puts it on and may have a success on his hands.

Looking for a play is a great adventure. I know of no greater satisfaction than to pick up a script and find that it is good, that it has never been done before and that the opportunity is yours to present it before an audience. I consider myself exceptionally lucky because once I have found the script, I have the means to produce it. I feel the same thing should be happening to many people all over this great nation. [. . .]

· · ·

As 1943 was drawing to a close, I decided that my way in the theater pointed to the formation of a permanent resident professional theater with a repertory system, producing new plays and classics with an accent on the new script. How could it be done? I knew I had to find a place for it, and I knew it had to be a beautiful theater which would give actors and other theater people a place to work and audiences a place where they would be entertained and enlightened.

I wrote out a plan reasonably soon thereafter and started thinking in terms of a city where my theater could be established. Somehow all the roads pointed to Dallas. It is practically in the middle of the country; it is in a new, fresh, rich, pioneering part of the nation; it is a city already rich in theater tradition; it had always been a good road town; there were many sincere theater lovers there who were anxious to help; I had gone to school near Dallas and had worked there; it was my home territory; Dallas at that moment was without a theater of any kind and wanted one very badly. It was a logical choice for me.

I had spoken about my plan to John Rosenfield, drama editor and critic of the *Dallas Morning News*, and to a few other people in Dallas, and in one of our conversations Mr. Rosenfield said, "Why not here?" I was glad because I wanted it to be there. In the early spring of 1944, when the choice was made, Mr. Rosenfield was instrumental in having me meet people in Dallas who were interested in the project; from then on out the theater was being planned for a specific city.

Now I needed time to look into the problems of finance and organization, availability of scripts and personnel and existing theater buildings. With this in mind, I applied for a Rockefeller Foundation fellowship, outlining my program of travel and time to be spent in Dallas as follows:

1. Getting as complete a picture as possible of the present American theatrical scene—from the point of view of the knowledge being of practical value in starting a professional theater in Dallas. I should like to visit as many theaters as possible—professional and nonprofessional. I should like to talk to as many theater people as possible. I should like to watch the best designers, lighting men, directors and all technicians at work. I should like at the end of the year to have at my fingertips as much new knowledge and inspiration as it is possible to get in a year.

   I would especially like to meet and talk to the young playwrights. I want to collect new scripts and read at least three plays a day during the year of work. I would like to be able to read all the books on the theater that I have not yet had a chance to read. I want to talk to the authors of many theater books I have read.

I especially want to talk to some of the great and idealistic theater people whose works have so long influenced me—Robert Edmond Jones, Eugene O'Neill and many others.

2. I want to spend a long enough time in Dallas to begin to know the city. I want to know its people, its schools, libraries, museums, churches, clubs, etc. I want to use a definite number of months in Dallas to raise the funds. After this is done . . .

3. I want to talk to all the young creative theater people in the country I can meet and from them select a staff and company of twenty for the creation of a resident professional theater in Dallas.

4. I want at the end of the year to:

   a. Have a theater building ready to open.
   b. Have a staff of twenty workers ready to go to work.
   c. Have funds enough to provide these workers with security for the next ten years. (I can dream, can't I?)
   d. Have new scripts, new ideas and new dreams enough to keep us all busy for one hundred years.
   e. Have all the knowledge and wisdom I can possibly acquire in the year's time that will enable me to put this plan over in the way that it deserves.

Needless to say, I was expecting to accomplish too much within a year, but with slight variations, I did work toward the goals I had set for myself. The plan itself consisted of five points: finance and organization, personnel, plays and playwrights, theater plant and the philosophy of such a theater. [. . .]

This is a plan for the creation of a permanent, professional, repertory, native theater in Dallas, Texas: a permanent repertory theater with a permanent staff of the best young artists in America; a theater that will be a true playwright's theater; a theater that will give the young playwrights of America (or any country, for that matter) a chance to be seen; a theater that will provide the classics and the best new scripts with a chance for good production; a theater that will enable Dallasites to say twenty years from now, "My children have lived in a town where they could see the best plays of the world presented in a beautiful and fine way"; where they can say, "We have had a part in creating theater and working in it"; a theater to go beyond the dreams of the past (and they have been wonderful); a theater to mean even more to America than the Moscow Art meant to Russia, the Abbey to Ireland or the Old Vic

to England; a theater that will carry on, but adapt to our country
and time, the ideals of the Stanislavskys, the Copeaus, the Craigs;
a theater of our time.

Looking back on these words, I am certain that what I had in mind included
the creation of similar theaters throughout the country, for I do not believe
that in a country as large as ours one center could or should provide the
whole nation with theatrical entertainment. It would be against the principle
of decentralization, which holds true whether the center is located in New
York or in Oregon.

The officers of the Rockefeller Foundation were very sympathetic toward
my plan, and I obtained the fellowship in the summer of 1944. Since I had
been directing at the summer session of the Pasadena Playhouse, I started my
travels in the California area. Before I had a chance to cover much other
territory, I was interrupted by a call from New York to co-direct Tennessee
Williams's first Broadway production, *The Glass Menagerie*. It seemed to be
the wisest procedure to discontinue the fellowship and go to New York, for it
meant an opportunity to practice what I had been preaching— the gaining of
experience in all fields of the theater. And I realized that I needed the added
training of the Broadway stage. Another strong consideration was the fact
that I believed in Williams and loved the play. *The Glass Menagerie* opened
in Chicago on December 26, 1944. The rest is history. It was wonderful and
fortunate for me to have had my first Broadway experience with a great playwright and some of the finest theater artists in America.

After *The Glass Menagerie* was launched, I returned to Dallas in order
to start organizing the theater. I was accompanied by Joanna Albus, who
became my associate and worked indefatigably on the project, remaining
with it through our first season.

Almost immediately after our arrival, Mr. and Mrs. Eugene McDermott gave the theater the sum of ten thousand dollars as an organizational
fund. A board of directors consisting of forty-eight citizens, with an executive committee of eleven, was formed at once; it was a good cross-section of
the city and large enough to be representative. The following day the theater
was incorporated under the laws of the State of Texas as a nonprofit professional repertory theater, and an office was set up under the title of "Dallas
Theatre, Incorporated."

A financial campaign was in order, but before raising money for a theater, it is imperative to have a building. I canvassed the city and got well
acquainted with the real-estate situation. Our best chance seemed to be the
Old Globe Theatre, which had been erected as a temporary building on the
Fair Park Grounds during the Texas Centennial for the use of Shakespear-

ean players. Although the land of the Fair Park Grounds is under the control of the city park department, the State Fair Association supervises all buildings and activities. We obtained permission from the association with the approval of the park department to use the theater, and proceeded to have it approved by the city building inspector and the fire department. The location was excellent, for the Fair Park Grounds were quite a center of activity— symphony, light opera, football, aquarium and museum.

While the financial campaign to raise $75,000 for our theater was officially starting, Jo Mielziner flew to Dallas to look over the Globe in order to plan the structural changes I needed to convert it into a flexible playhouse. Mr. Mielziner felt that it was unwise to put any money into such a temporary structure. He realized the circumstances, however, and took all the necessary measurements and blueprints and left for New York, but not before advising me to try once more to find a better building. I went back into the problem of the theaters we had investigated previously, but there were no possibilities outside of the Globe.

Soon after Mr. Mielziner's departure we received a letter from the building inspector listing a number of things that would have to be done to the building before it could be occupied. I sent a copy of these requirements to Mr. Mielziner, asking him if it would be possible to meet these conditions for a reasonable amount of money. He replied that it would be possible, but the cost would be considerably higher than we had originally estimated. Still, we had to have a playhouse, and we threw all our energies into the fundraising activities.

And then, in the middle of this campaign, I was called into conference with the city building inspector and the fire department. The Globe building, I was informed, had been categorized as "No. 5 Type," which, according to the law, is out of question for a theater building. This was a most discouraging piece of news because having our building condemned placed our whole financial campaign in a rather ridiculous light. But I had a comforting thought: the people on the board of directors and on the financial committee were behind me and continued to have faith in the project.

Our search for a theater started again, although it seemed there was no place left to look. The war was drawing to a close, and the housing situation was terrible. To build a new theater would have been inadvisable, even if we could have raised the money for it.

[. . .]

"When there is no theater available," I asked myself, "and yet you must start a theater, what do you do?" I had found the answer once before, when I wanted to produce plays in the summer in Houston. Why not the same answer now? It took a great deal of determination, for this was not the kind of theater I had been talking about. But had I been talking about a building or about an idea? And couldn't the idea be applied just as well in theater-in-the-round? It could. When one runs out of solutions, the unusual solution will save the day. The board of directors liked my suggestion, and we set out to look for a different type of building. The problem was easier, but not nearly as easy as it seems in retrospect.

We found a beautiful and charming building made of stucco and glass brick, a modern structure, air-conditioned, lovely to look at, well-equipped and adaptable to theater-in-the-round. It was also located on the Fair Park Grounds and had been leased by the Gulf Oil Corporation. We were allowed to occupy it free of any charge but the payment of utilities. After the Gulf Oil lease expired, we obtained it from the State Fair Association for a nominal fee. In the spring of 1947 all papers were signed with the approval of the State Fair Association and the city park department. Within twelve hours I flew to New York to get started . . .

The building had to be put in shape but plans had been made before we had the final approval, so we were ready to go to work on the building of platforms, installation of seats (which were loaned to us at first), carpeting and lighting equipment. We discovered that, to avoid impairing sight lines or comfort and to allow enough space for an adequate playing area, our maximum seating capacity had to be limited to 198. Our technical director, Joseph Londin (who had been engaged previously), had already conferred in New York with Jo Mielziner and with Edward Kook, of the Century Lighting Company; our setup had been blueprinted and was ready to be installed.

I planned a first season of ten weeks. I chose a short season because it seems extremely advisable to have, before you start, enough financing to insure the completion of a season.

During two years, my associates (Joanna Albus and June Moll) and I had been reading plays continuously. None of the other problems which confronted us ever stopped us from that one pleasurable duty. I knew what plays we wanted to do and proceeded to choose four new scripts and one classic for the first season. All I had to do in New York in this regard was to confer with agents and sign contracts.

But my first task in New York was to find a first-class business manager. I cannot overemphasize the importance of this job in a professional theater setup. He must know the art and craft of managing a professional theater; he must have experience, ability, a hard-boiled business sense. To have the respect of the town, the theater must be run in as businesslike a fashion as a department store. I was very fortunate to find just the kind of person I was looking for in Manning Gurian.

I hired a company of eight actors, a number which at this time seemed more feasible than the twenty I had called for in my original plan. The business manager bought the actors their railroad tickets, and they arrived in Dallas three weeks prior to the opening.

In three weeks' time in New York I optioned four plays, hired a business manager and a company, while tickets and publicity and technical equipment were being prepared in Dallas. I would like to add that I could not have done this without the cooperation of unions, agents and other theater people in New York; they can be wonderful friends when the occasion arises and make one proud and happy to be a part of the American theater.

Theatre '47, as it was now called, opened in June 1947 with William Inge's *Farther Off from Heaven*. With staggered rehearsals, we had three plays in preparation at the time we opened. Our repertory system, which has varied since then, meant that each of the five plays was repeated after a new opening, and the last two weeks of the season were devoted to a repertory festival. The purpose of the festival was to enable visitors from other cities and people in Dallas who had not seen some of the plays to view our work.

The season started slowly at first, but built continuously, catching momentum with the third production. As a whole, it was a fantastically successful first season. But the task is not accomplished once the theater has opened. Productions have to be good; the standard has to be maintained and constantly raised. This means reading more plays, searching for good actors and technical improvements and working hard on public relations. It means that work is required morning, noon and night—and then some.

The name of our organization, suggested by a theater in Prague, is changed every year on New Year's Eve in order to remain contemporary at all times. The audience that night is asked to attend the performance a little later than usual to join the actors, after the play, in greeting the new year and the new name of the theater.

—MJ

Alley Theatre

FOUNDED 1947

Nina Vance

> Mrs. Vance had $2.17 in her pocketbook. In those halcyon days
> penny postcards cost a penny. The lady bought 217 postcards.
> She and several others addressed them and sent them out.
>   The postcards were postmarked October 3, 1947, at 11:00
> A.M. They read, "It's a beginning. Do you want a new theater
> for Houston? Meeting 3617 Main. Bring a friend. Tuesday,
> October 7, 8:00 P.M. —Nina Vance." [5]

Some theaters begin as part of a sweeping vision, as Margo Jones's
Theatre '47 did. Others begin in the deviling details: Where can we
meet? Where will we hang a sign? Who has chairs? What follows is
the story of a pioneering theater built from just such details, listed
out in wry specificity by the theater's leader, midway through the
nascent company's first season. The first detail—elaborated above—
has become mythic. Nina Vance, chosen director of the soon-to-be
Alley Theatre, turns copper into gold by using a couple bucks worth
of penny postcards to rally more than a hundred people to her venture. (In some versions, the $2.17 came from as many as four people,
pooling their change.)

From that nickel-and-dime beginning Houston's Alley Theatre
grew into what it is now: the regional theater movement's oldest professional company (there are some older troupes, but they
remained amateur longer) and, arguably, one of the most important.
It's no coincidence that the collecting of money and the gathering
of people are intertwined in this origin story. Money and people,
along with space, are the basic ingredients of any upstart institutional theater, another reason Vance's non-manifesto manifest feels
a bit like Everystory. Pocket change plus a hundred curious friends

SOURCE: "Alley Theatre: First Legitimate Playhouse on Main Street, Houston, Texas (we
hope)," by Nina Vance, 1947–48.
    As this manuscript was undergoing a final edit, Yale School of Drama student Lauren
Wainwright was able to do what I had been unable to do for the previous seven years: find
something written by the important Nina Vance that was suitable for publication, alongside the
words of the many fine leader/writers in this book. It was an eleventh-hour save (I'd already
written the introductory apology for leaving such an important figure in the regional theater
movement out of this collection), and I'm deeply grateful to her and to Pat Bozeman, who is the
Emily Scott Evans Professor in Special Collections and Archives at the University of Houston,
for leading Lauren to this.

5. Alley Theatre's twentieth anniversary book, *Thresholds: The Story of Nina Vance's Alley
Theatre* (Wall and Company, Houston, 1968).

plus a rented dance studio on Main Street equals a four-play first season and the start of something where there was nothing. Add a name—"Alley" was chosen over Vance's objection; she thought it sounded too bohemian—and a director who won't take no. This is Nina Vance's most basic math.

When the pioneering of theaters gets written about, its chroniclers often evoke the tenacity of its leaders. Vance, along with Margo Jones, who'd directed her in over a dozen productions and was a guide to her, is a prime example. The Alley's early design director, Paul Owen, summed her up this way: "What are little girls made of? Nina Vance *is* made of sugar and spice and everything . . . PLUS! It's that 'plus' that has separated her from the other little girls and has provided her with the stamina she sorely needed."[6] Maybe it was this "plus" that made it possible for Vance to claim, as she did to critic Julius Novick in 1966, "I clawed this theater out of the ground."[7]

Vance led the Alley through numerous phases and several spaces from 1947 until her death in 1980. Although she was originally invited to form the group with Robert and Vivien Altfeld, she quickly—and lastingly—became the dominant force. (The Altfelds found the first two spaces, Vivien's rented dance studio and an old fan factory, before resigning in 1954 when the company went professional.) Here, in a time capsule-like report from the company's early months, Vance lists out the Alley's early assets, and documents her own background as a pioneer from a pioneering family. She describes it all, including the theater's genesis, in the no-nonsense, just-the-facts fragments of a woman of action, too busy with building her theater to write complete sentences, a woman able to grow a major cultural institution out of a pocketful of change.

—TL

———

Physical Aspects

1. The studio room which is Alley Theatre and which is used in the daytime as a dancing studio is twenty feet by fifty feet with a post at one end. Architects say if the post were removed the building would collapse.
2. Built some beaver board screens, seven feet by ten feet, in order to make a backstage area.

6. Ibid.

7. *Beyond Broadway: The Quest for Permanent Theatres*, by Julius Novick, Hill & Wang, New York, 1968.

3. The playing area used is thirteen by seventeen feet.

4. Eighty-five folding chairs are rented for each performance, for the audience, although we have used ninety-two on crowded nights.

5. Chairs are placed on fourteen wooden platforms, four, six and twelve inches high by five feet wide by thirty-three feet long.

6. Part of the lumber was donated and part came by tearing up the director's sundeck.

7. Three fellows borrowed tools from the director's neighborhood with which they built platforms and hauled them to the Alley.

8. Theater now owns sixteen spotlights.

9. Original capital of theater was $2.17 for postcards, a donated typewriter, five hundred sheets of donated stationery, eight metal strips used to build bird's eye lights as additions to nine spotlights bought on credit at ninety dollars before the first show opened. Also, two rheostats were donated.

10. Before the first show could open, wiring installations at $150.00 cost was necessary.

11. We now own four ceiling fans, donated, and a large fan is being purchased for two hundred dollars for use during the fourth show, *Caroline*. Installation of this fan involves volunteer labor.

12. There is a tree growing in one corner of the room.

13. We have one toilet for actors and audience.

14. Two hundred and seventy-seven workers are on file. Fifteen hundred names on the mailing list. They are people who signed cards at performances, asking to receive notice of coming productions.

15. Sound is piped from playing area to dressing room by small inter-office communications system. This enables actors to hear the show in progress.

16. Director has Hollywood chair with name on back. It is the only chair the Alley owns and it was a gift.

17. Customers are accustomed to cigarette butts, junk and two large cement lions in the Alley.

18. We had no sign up until the second show. We made a rush trip to a geology office which is in the same building (3617 Main). They owned a front window as a part of their office, and we persuaded them to let us put placards in the window for the first show. After this, they refused because they were afraid to have their offices connected in any way with the supposed bohemianism of the group. Finally got a sign, three feet by three feet, which was put at the entrance to the Alley.

Nina Vance, Director

Only child, great-great-great-granddaughter of pioneer Green DeWitt, who settled DeWitt county, where I was born. Graduated from Yoakum High School with honors in 1931, salutatorian of the class. Graduated from Texas Christian University at Fort Worth in 1935, cum laude. Also made college beauty page—imagine! Member of Texas Poetry Society, Scholarship Society of South. Postgraduate work in radio at University of Southern California. Extra in movies. Attended Columbia University in New York for courses in stagecraft. Professional training at American Academy of Dramatic Arts, New York. While in New York, noticed everybody there had a makeup kit and a violin. Field seemed overcrowded. Returned to Texas.

Wanted to direct theater after graduation from TCU. Had no idea how to get a job. Papa got daughter a job teaching dramatics in Yoakum High School. Had a room with a small stage, etc. It was the best equipment I have ever worked with. Far superior to the Alley. Job was during the Depression and paid ninety dollars a month. Had said I would not teach in anybody's school for less than a hundred dollars a month. Produced twenty-eight shows in one year, mostly one-acts. (This set something of a high school record.) Cute gal comes to city.

Taught dramatics at Jefferson Davis and San Jacinto high schools in Houston. Played fourteen shows for Margo Jones. Saw theater-in-the-round for the first time. Married Milton Vance in 1941, a lawyer for the Houston National Bank. Agreed to work at Jewish Community Center for twenty-four dollars a month salary. Next season we had no facilities. I quit. Offered five hundred dollars a show. Did four more and quit. In mid–August of 1947, Bob Altfeld came by my house. He had worked with the Players Guild, the name under which I had produced three plays while with the Jewish Community Center. He said Vivien Altfeld was renting a dance studio at 3617 Main Street. Why not do one show and see what happened? If Schleuter, the owner, could be persuaded to let us work in the building at night, we could use the studio. No money. Some (?)[8] chance of Roussel backing.[9] Discussed the possibility of ten people giving fifty dollars each. As figured, the show budget would be five hundred dollars without director's salary or rent. [. . .] Nina said no. That would mean that ten people would want to run the theater. Told Bob to discuss proposal of a few circle shows and get reaction from theater friends. All were enthusiastic. [. . .] Went to post office. Had $2.17. Bought 217 post cards. Addressed one hundred and fifty or so from a personal file I had always kept of people interested in the theater.

8. Here Vance has added the word "No" in pen.

9. Presumably Roussel was a potential donor in Houston.

The first meeting was held late in October of 1947. Rented fifty chairs for thirty-five dollars. One hundred people came. Names for the group were submitted by the people at the meeting and they ranged from Genius Inc. to Circle Theatre. Alley Theatre was the big choice because of the long brick corridor leading from Main Street back to the studio. Director did not sleep that night after the name was chosen. It smacked of bohemianism. The name caught on, however, so decided to trade on bohemian quality. Announced eight possible shows. Did only one of those announced, *A Sound of Hunting*. Set up ten-cent voting fee for anyone who wanted to vote on policies of the theater. Announced yearly staff of workers, appointed by director. No officers. No board of directors, just workers. Group voted patron memberships would cost twenty-five dollars minimum. Just nineteen people contributed amounts ranging from fifty to seventy dollars before first show opened. No formal drive for patrons. No lists to be called. Workers talked to friends. Patrons got no tickets, nothing except knowledge that they were helping to launch an exciting theater venture. Twenty-seven patrons obtained before first show was ever produced. Patron money is never touched unless necessary and then is replaced from show take. For all we knew when we started this thing it might fold after one show for lack of audience. We wanted to refund patrons money if we failed to carry through on the first season.

After the production of author Harry Brown's *A Sound of Hunting* forty letters were mailed asking for patron contributions. Six additional checks arrived, including ones from Miss Ima Hogg and Hobby, neither of whom have ever attended a show. After the second show, Jeffrey Dell's *Payment Deferred*, which ran February 3 through February 14, 1948 (a twelve-night run to catch weekend trade), director went to New York. Paid her own way. Saw agents. Looked for new scripts. Brought back thirteen originals. Director reads thirty to forty plays a month. Has complete works of George Jean Nathan in library. Specializes in Broadway flops. Plays critically successful but not commercially so. Examples: *A Sound of Hunting*, which has been compared to the English classic *Journey's End*, rated the highest of critical praise during its run of thirty-eight performances. Probably failed in New York because it was brought in at the wrong time. [Lillian Hellman's] *Another Part of the Forest*, which ran for five months, again was highly praised by critics but was unpopular with New Yorkers. Could have been due to the viciousness of the play's theme. *Caroline* [by Somerset Maugham], Alley's fourth show, will open May 11 for an indefinite run. Think this is the first time this has been tried in Houston. Almost positive of it. It was produced in England in 1912 (?). Was brought to this country under the title *The Unattainable*. Folded at the end of three months. *Damask Cheek* [co-authored by John Van Druten and Lloyd Morris], directed successfully for Players Guild in 1946, was thin script but had charm. Folded in New York after a short run. Probably due to wrong casting. Believe Flora Robson too old for title role. Director thinks good comedy is the hardest type to find. Is ear-minded and always has a script read aloud by a few competent actors before choosing. Regards a play as a score of music. Each speech has a rhythm, each scene, each act and the whole show. Cannot often hear the rhythm of a sequence but must go home and study before I can explain to actors logically the reason for the pace I ask for in certain scenes.

Famous quotations of director to cast: "If you can't be good actors you can at least be loud and fast." "Producing a show is like having a baby." "I will not have my name attached to a sloppy production." "The Alley has succeeded because we love each other."

Director's duties include speeches to various civic clubs. Examples: College Women's Club, Girl Scouts, Lions. Drama classes, salesmanship, classes at University of Houston.

Director to be paid if anything left at the end of the first season's proceeds.

Are Workers Serious

1. No drinking fountain.
2. Director and worker hauled eleven men's army uniforms wrapped in a dirty tarpaulin out of theater down Main Street and into washing machine to save money.
3. In circus fashion the theater is moved out from the playing area to the backstage area every night after a performance. Moving includes a piano, rugs, furniture, ninety chairs, fourteen platforms, a seven-foot piece of plywood which is attached to the ceiling by means of screws and which covers mirrors on one wall. This must be put up and taken down every night because of dancing classes next day.
4. Entrances to playing area are made from the front door and an office door, also an aisle leading through the playing area. No crossover from backstage to office entrance was possible until a section of wall was torn out. Now actors practically bend double and crawl through a small opening to get to office entrance. This was done by several women actors wearing beautiful period evening gowns in Alley Theatre's third show, *Another Part of the Forest*.
5. Dressing room upstairs is one large room directly above playing area. It has two small mirrors, one small closet and is not sound-proof. Actors must sit during the show, no talk, no moving about. Creaky stairs leading from dressing room to backstage area, and actors must time their entrances five minutes early so that they can silently descend staircase into dimly lit backstage area.

6. Director insists on quick study. Actors must drop book on fourth night of the act being rehearsed. Acts are rehearsed on a schedule which involves an act a week and a week to polish.

7. No star complexes. One of the leads from first show carried platforms on second, wrote publicity on third. Glamour girl in second show selected and hauled all furniture from her bay home in a small truck for the next show. Character woman so ill she fainted after first act during one performance. She was taken care of backstage, pulled herself together and finished the show. Few jealousies over parts in theater where crew triples or quadruples number of actors used. Crew for a show involves stage manager (same for every production) twenty-year-old Geoffrey Raymer, a University of Houston student. Light installation, two to four men. Light operation, two workers. Prop collection, two or three workers. Prop management, two or three workers. Costumes one to ten workers. Door men, ten. Ushers, twenty. Box office, fifty. Music, two. Construction four to twenty. Script person, one. Program advertising three to thirty. Coffee, eight. Program design and execution, one to four. Stage hands, three to fifteen. Makeup, one. Publicity one or two people. Art work and posters, one to five. Secretarial, five to ten people.

8. No janitor. Everybody sweeps.

9. One small stove during freezing weather. Director huddled with an army blanket around her. Fearing that the audiences would not endure the cold brought purchase of stove for $139.00.

10. Coffee in five-gallon urns is made in penthouse upstairs and carried down five flights of stairs and given to audience free.

11. Rehearsal four weeks, every night, including Sunday afternoon and night.

12. Box office chairman sets up a mimeographed schedule and places in workers' hands. They sign up for all shows per year. Substitute names and phone numbers given at bottom of sheet. Worker calls substitute if unavailable for work. Workers' sheet is given to every person who comes to meetings or tryouts before he gets to sit down on the floor. No chairs are rented for meetings.

13. Casting is done at open tryouts.

14. Play readings once a month. Eighty to one hundred people attend. New script or classic is read aloud. Example: *Liliom* and *Lady Windermere's Fan*. Gives director a chance to hear new talent. Cokes and popcorn served for refreshment.

Director's Problems

1. Casting to type. Very small amount of makeup possible. Pancake generally.
2. Keeping workers happy. So few parts to distribute. The four shows this season have used thirty-nine actors. Only eleven women. Occupations range from housewife, dancing teacher, students, secretaries, advertising agency employee. Men's jobs include radio announcing, antique dealer, lawyer, speech teacher, manufacturer of springs and furniture, oil and barge business. Age range of workers and actors is twenty to forty years. One percent of group are over or under that level.
3. Finding scripts. Prefers those that have not been done by movies recently. Relies on old scripts, though constantly reading new ones. The white hope of the American theater is reputedly tryouts by nonprofessional groups of new scripts. This is fine for the development of new playwrights, a serious need in the American theater, but often is hard on audiences. The director's aim, since the theater is not subsidized, is a professional look with nonprofessional talent. Plays of good quality which the public buys as entertainment; and culture, only if disguised. Alley is not an experimental theater, although we are interested for the future in doing new scripts of worth, and most certainly look forward next season to the production of at least one classic, possibly *Ghosts* because of small cast and the impact of emotional plays is most successful at close range. (This is somewhat unusual, as Penthouse Theatre in Washington, one of the best circle theaters, has concentrated for some years on comedies.) Believe most circle theaters throughout the country use few heavy scripts. Actors at Alley range from ex-professional talent to beginners. This necessitates a strong play. With the fact that after-working-hours rehearsals are necessary, the use of a strong script is clear.
4. Feel variety in choice of scripts less important than strength of scripts which will use best talent available to me. While circle theater was chosen because less expense to begin and operate than stage productions, believe it to be a valid medium and probably would do no other type productions at Alley even if large financing were possible. Intimacy between actor and audience is advantage. It is playing which is close to movie technique. (Love scenes effective because of lack of necessity for projection to the back row.) Music dubbed in at Alley productions as in a

movie, without the use of actor tuning in radio or some other mechanical device. Bob Blase, local radio announcer and disc jockey for station KXYZ, is in charge of music, which he selects and records on a wire recorder to make music fit dialogue.

—NV

Arena Stage

FOUNDED 1950

Zelda Fichandler

Zelda Fichandler is, to my way of thinking, the great founding rabbi of the regional theater. She has, from nearly the beginning of Arena Stage in 1950, restlessly questioned the very field that she, as much as anyone, created. Although Fichandler never set out to become a writer, as John Houseman did, or to live by writing, as Harold Clurman and Robert Brustein partly did, she ranks among them as one of the most eloquent articulators in the twentieth-century American theater. Her essays and speeches capture both the play of her own dazzling, Talmudic mind, and the aspirations and contradictions of the capital-*T* Theater she pioneered. Even the title of the following essay from a 1970 issue of *Theatre 3* is posed as a question, one that rings through the years: "Theaters or Institutions?"

If Fichandler poses her challenge as an either/or, her writing, and her theater, prove her a genius of inclusion, of "this *and* that," as she puts it. If she had world enough and time, it appears, Fichandler's theater (and *T*heater) would have everything and everyone in it—classics and new plays, plays of esoteric intellectuality and of wide appeal, auteur direction and ensemble acting, socially activist art based in local and underserved communities (e.g., Arena's groundbreaking Living Stage under Robert Alexander) and popular musical comedies. Racial inclusion was a theme of her forty-plus-year tenure as artistic director of Arena as well. She worked tirelessly to integrate her acting company, nurture designers of color, and serve the multiracial District of Columbia—where, just three years before Arena's founding, the National Theatre had closed to keep from acceding

SOURCE: "Theatres or Institutions?" by Zelda Fichandler, in *Theatre 3*, 1969–70.

to Actors' Equity demands that it open its auditorium doors to the District's blacks. (The stage was allowed to be integrated; the audience was not.)

This blend of heart, mind, conviction and drive must have been evident to Edward Mangum, Fichandler's teacher in the graduate drama department of George Washington University. Mangum led the amateur Mount Vernon Players, introduced Fichandler to the "theater-in-the-round" aesthetic, having seen Margo Jones's theater in Texas, and joined her, aided by her economist husband Thomas Fichandler, in founding Arena Stage. Mangum relocated to Hawaii after Arena's second full season, at which point Alan Schneider, a Catholic University professor, joined Arena as production director, beginning one of the most distinguished directing careers in the American and international theater and the first such career to begin in the regional not-for-profits.

Even the shape of the stage at Arena became a source of inclusion and democracy. "With no seat more than seven rows from the actors," an early flyer boasted, "that makes every seat a best seat." This configuration gave name to the company in more ways than one. When city regulations demanded that Arena have a fire curtain—an impossibility for a round playing area—Arena became a "public hall," as Schneider tells it in his autobiographical *Entrances*, not a theater. Hence, Arena "Stage."

—TL

———

I have been asked to write about the future of what is called the regional or resident theater movement in this country and this is my third attempt. I am wishing they had given the assignment to someone else, for, you see, I have been with this "movement" for twenty years, was part of its beginning and will be part of its future, if it has a future; and my psychic energy remains equal to the task. I know too much about it really to know anything. Someone doing one of those personality stories on me (a painful business, that) called our son at home the other week and asked him what I was like, how he would describe me. I heard him say: "It's an impossible question, I refuse to answer, how can you know anyone you've lived with for eighteen years?!?" Intimacy is so much easier between strangers.

They should have gotten Julius Novick, who did the resident theater circuit a couple of times, and came out with a book filled with such perception and insight that I am quite smitten with envy. Or Martin Gottfried, who manages to describe us unequivocably, prescribe for us without need of consultation, and tinker with our morality, our aesthetics, our public visage and private heart with the authority of a high priest. And there are others I could list who might have been called upon, all so highly qualified, with diagnoses and opinions positively oozing from their pens and tongues. But if I follow out this train of thought, I will never get to my own, and that is what I am trying to do. Besides, I would end up in a battle fought on someone else's terrain with weapons that they have chosen. And something in me rebels at the thought.

Karl Marx reminded us that you can't tell from the taste of the bread how the miller lived. So I suppose the reason that I am writing rather than someone else is that I am the miller, or one of the millers, and not one of the masticators, and can, therefore, possibly, describe some of the felt meanings and not only the surface contours. And because I find the writings of Herr Critics and Travelers largely one-dimensional, like picture postcards of well-known buildings. And because, not knowing, perhaps I know better than anyone else who knows.

One more personal note by way of introducing a subject far too vast for this space ("a subject for a short story," a character of Chekhov says ironically, and there is a sadness in the words and a sense that the subject would not fit even into a very very large book and would need a lifetime of experience to plumb). One more personal note: The signs are not right. If one looks around with even a slight degree of open-mindedness, one can come quite quickly to the conclusion that the signs are not right and, indeed, the portents are dark for the survival of this wee beastie wearing the hat bizarrely labeled (from what attic did it come?) the Regional-Resident-Repertory-Theater of America. The signs are not right and I am not a good reader of signs, so maybe I can be of some help.

I learned to read by the see-say method, not phonetically. The flash cards flicked and we tried rapidly and intuitively to latch on to a meaning. Pick, pack, pluck, poke, park, puke. At the beginning it was a random process indeed. It got better with the help of context: obviously Daddy packed his bags, he didn't pluck them. But areas of fuzziness always remained. I remember once when I was five or six going with my father to his laboratory at the Bureau of Standards and waiting outside and wanting to pick the dandelions growing on the grass. But the signs said No Picking so I didn't pick. Years later, in retrospect, I realized that the sign had probably said No Parking, not No Picking. This was a key experience for me, however trivial on the surface. From it I learned that one's behavior is conditioned far more by what one thinks one sees than by what one sees in fact. "Reading the signs" is, to a degree that is worth taking into account, a subjective matter. Reality is very private.

Out of all the "signs" to be read in the world, one chooses those that "signify" according to personal vision and need. We carry a camera and choose our shots, enlarging precisely those we choose, excluding areas of reality outside our lens range and selecting sight. The sign that said No Parking had no meaning at all for me, even if I had read it right (later I think I did learn to do this) since I had no car to park. The sign that I read as No Picking had enormous meaning for me for it signified that I must leave my dandelions in the earth and wait impatiently for my father without them.

I want to say what signs I now see. Negative signs, most of them. And how I think we might angle them so that they may read better in the long run. Some remarks, too, that will catch up in the history of this movement (Genesis before Exodus?) and then place it within a framework, or pincer, which I think of as "Theaters or Institutions?". . . A subject for a short story.

The Regional-Resident-Repertory-Theater Movement was, to corn [sic] a phrase, an idea whose time had come. Its impulse was highly American, in that it represented a better way of doing things. This doesn't mean to imply that the revolution was not also aesthetic; but first of all it was, in my opinion, in its first birth cry, organizational. I again say that I do not mean to depreciate the artistic work that is done (nor, on the other hand, do I mean to overpraise it), or to underrate the hazards o'erleaped, or to minimize the courage, talent and initiative of any of us, because I think that we moved mountains. Or maybe even made them and then moved them. And surely, and at any rate, organization is creation. But I think we should all get it clear for ourselves that we started differently and therefore *are* different from the European models to which we so frequently turn for standards and precedents in the absence of any others. A lack of clarity about this has the tendency to get us off course, to keep us from seeing fresh paths, and to make us chastise ourselves for not being what we are not and cannot be.

This organizational revolution began around 1950 (a few years earlier for Margo Jones and Nina Vance, and still earlier for K. Elmo Lowe and Bob Porterfield,[10] and with a great leap of second-generation energy in the sixties which increased the number of theaters from about a half-dozen to about three dozen or more) when some of us looked about and saw that something was amiss. What was essentially a collective and cumulative art form was represented in the United States by the hit-or-miss, make-a-pudding, smash-a-pudding system of Broadway production. What required by its nature continuity and groupness, not to mention a certain quietude of spirit and the fifth freedom—the freedom to fail—was taking place in an atmosphere of hysteria, crisis, fragmentation, one-shotness and mammon-mindedness within the ten blocks of Broadway. The most that could be said for Broadway was that there was singular excellence even though the excel-

---

10. Jones, founder of Theatre '47 in Dallas; Vance, of Alley Theatre in Houston; and Porterfield, of the Barter Theater in Virginia, can all be found in their own chapters in this volume. Lowe, not a literal founder, acted with, directed for, and helped run the Cleveland Play House from 1921–69.

lence was always singular. On the other hand, the literature of the stage was being lost. Classics and revivals of still-living older plays simply had no market. New plays were done, yes, but it was the case of good deeds for dubious motives. And important plays like *The Crucible* never did find their audience in New York. Audiences themselves had ceased to exist. Even in New York high ticket prices kept away all but the well-to-do.

It even had to be proved that there *was* someplace outside of New York. We had to convince theater workers themselves that people lived and breathed out here; one actress in 1955 wanted strong assurances that she could get fresh tomatoes as far from New York as Washington, D.C. Outside of New York there simply *was* no audience for any kind of theater except for touring companies with stars. So we looked around and saw a mess, saw that the art of the theater was dying and thought of a way to keep it alive.

I say "we." There was a "we," though we didn't know each other. It was I, and him, and her out there someplace until around 1957 when Mac Lowry, the Ford Foundation's Mac Lowry, found us all and stuck some adrenaline into us by the very act of finding us and seeing us and taking notice, not to mention the grants to save our skins that came later, and introduced us to each other, saying, "Look, did you know there was someone else besides you working on this thing?" I met Jules Irving for the first time, and Joe Papp, and John Reich, and Herbert Blau[11] and a lot of my other co-workers through W. McNeil Lowry.

Separately and then together, we forged these theaters, these instrumentalities, these constellations of activities, these collective outposts, these—God forgive me!—institutions in order to preserve and re-create, in new forms, the art of theater then fusting in us unused. We found a better way of doing things. Found? We forged a better way, we scratched it out, hacked it, ripped it, tore it, yanked it, clawed it out of the resisting, unyielding nose-thumbing environment. We taught ourselves how to direct, produce, administer, raise money, entice an audience, work with acting companies, work without acting companies, make grant applications, raise budgets, raise standards, build buildings, teach and involve a community, change the taste of a community, fail and rise again like the phoenix or, in some cases fail and not rise again, play a season of plays, then another season and another, search out new playwrights, learn about the crafts of the theater almost without teachers. We taught ourselves how to survive. That we found a better way is our essential *apologia pro vita sua*.

11. Irving and Blau, both represented elsewhere in this collection, were founders of the Actor's Workshop in San Francisco. Papp, of course, gave birth to the New York Shakespeare Festival, also in these pages. Reich was largely responsible for Goodman Theatre of Chicago's evolution to professionalism during his tenure there (1957–72).

We must not forget that while this is so, the opposite is also true. Among us there has been no Antoine[12] rushing into his makeshift theater with his mother's dining room furniture and real meat from the butcher down the street, discovering the breathtaking reality of an actor daring to turn his back on the audience. No Stanislavsky and Danchenko[13] putting together out of an amateur theater and some acting classes, and out of the work of a genius playwright whose plays demanded a different vision, an entirely new system of behavioral acting based on the physiology of the human body and connected to allied biological and psychological research of the day. And where is our Molière? Inventing plays to act in for himself and his troupe, elevating and freezing into art his own interior experiences, building a dramatic tradition on the shoulders of the improvisational commedia form, mocking himself, mocking his age, mocking his fellow man and still catering to and pleasing both? Yeats and Lady Gregory and O'Casey and the Abbey, making a theater of protest after their own style, making a literature to help make a nation: We have not yet made one of those. Bertolt Brecht, where are you? To teach the masses so that they might remake the world . . . The masses stayed away and the intellectuals sat in their seats but in that institution the aesthetic was the cause and the cause was the aesthetic. Who is our Bertolt Brecht, theoretician, transformer of form, social architect, director-dramaturg-dramatist–institutional head all in one mind and body?

We are not even like the European models we most resemble. We are not like the provincial (if only the word vibrated with ideas of nature, or geography, and not with a kind of squarish isolation, a distance from the pulse!) repertory companies throughout England and Germany, companies which also find their life in the preservation and dissemination of theatrical expression. We are not like them. We are usually better. We have longer rehearsal periods, rely less on imported "names"; our contributing arts of scenery, costume and lighting are more advanced, our actors are far better paid—American company actors earn more on the average than Broadway actors—and are often of the highest level in the land. An English director will say of an actor he doesn't like, "Oh, he's so rep-py," meaning that he's a stock actor, where American directors use the term repertory actor to connote an actor of versatility and range, staying power and commitment, a gifted artist-citizen.

12. Fichandler is referring to André Antoine, founder of the short-lived but influential Théâtre Libre in Paris (1887–94), whose passion for authenticity and realism on the stage led to scenes of just this sort—and the breakthroughs that went with them.

13. Vladimir Nemirovich-Danchenko was Stanislavsky's partner in the founding of the world-changing Moscow Art Theatre, where he served as producer and dramaturg and championed the work of many modern dramatists, including Anton Chekhov, alluded to here, as well as Henrik Ibsen and Maxim Gorky, among others.

And there is no real way of likening us to other culture carriers such as the British National or the Royal Shakespeare Company or the present Moscow Art Theatre since we are all of us broke and have small companies instead of very big ones. We spend half of our life at fundraising dinners and defending play choices to citizen boards of directors (not here at Arena Stage, but that is only an accidental stroke of history) since with the impulse that we should have theaters in our land came also the impulse that the community should be part of them, should put up some of the money, should even have a voice in them and—now hear this!—should even, even commission theaters into being and hire artistic directors to run them—of which there seem to be precious few anywhere about. And if they do come as artistic directors, they soon leave out of enormous fatigue bordering on the Sisyphean, or out of wrath at nonprofessionals meddling in decisions that are hard enough to make all alone, or out of a general feeling of "who needs it, what I really want to do is direct, not run an inefficient branch of IBM."

The impulse, then, was to remedy a grievous fault and reverse a direful trend—the contraction and imminent death of the art of the theater. This goal has been, to a large degree, accomplished. Not secured, but accomplished. And in the process of the accomplishment, which has taken place roughly over the past twenty years—in itself a mammoth undertaking—we have also managed, if not entirely to shift then surely at least to cause to lean, the fulcrum of aesthetic excellence away from New York and toward these whaddya-call-'em theaters. Outside of the musicals, in which New York is unbeatable, and outside of specific and singular Broadway and Off-Broadway productions, these whaddya-call-'em theaters (and some of them *are* in New York since New York *is* a "region" within that definition of the word, whoever assigned us to it, and New York *does* have residents—you won't get any reverse snobbism from me!) have achieved the highest consistent (repeat, *consistent*) standards in the contributing arts of the theater—architecture, stage lighting, scenic design, playwriting, acting and directing. And insofar as playwrights and actors and directors are concerned they have done more to provide a laboratory and proving ground for their skills than any other theatrical mode, or modus, in our history. The American theater has begun to have a tradition: a past, a present, a future, a somewhat coherent way to look at itself and to proceed.

Theaters or institutions? In my mind now these two words exist in a state of uneasy tension, a kind of dialectic opposition, where once they seemed to me to be one and the same word. It seemed to me until quite recently that when a theater finally stopped being on the way to what it was to become and actually became it, then it would be an institution. Resonances that were very seductive to me hovered around the word: an end to the scramble, time for inwardness, time for creative rest and re-creation, a way of work evolved through continuity of association and a common vocabulary, the possibility of sharing power or even passing it on, an administrative environment for creative work that would release it, let it go outward without the random stuttering and bucking brought on by disorder; tension where it belongs, within the process itself, but purring in the machine; all good things. But it hasn't turned out this way, a seduction is what it really was, a leading-from-the-self. I wonder why?

Perhaps I do precisely what I warn that we must not do. I cling to European institutional models—the subsidized, well-staffed, anything-that-money-can-buy theater. I strain to give flesh to runaway dreams. Between the idea and the reality falls the shadow and I look at the shadow I cast and it has a surprising shape. I do not recognize it. It isn't what I had in mind. When you and I talk, six people are having a conversation: the person I am, the person you think I am and the person I think I am. And then there are the three of you. You say that we are institutional theaters (there was an article in the last issue of this publication which began by defining the three kinds of theater in this country: commercial, experimental and institutional) but I want to know what that means to you? To me? What *is* an institutional theater precisely? What is it when you look at it? What is it when I dream about it?

My thoughts continue apace. I travel around a bit and am on various committees and panels (as few as possible, but some) and I find work that is good—spirited, personal, inventive, vivacious, specific—and a lot of work that is simply there: repetitive, unoriginal, stylistically barren, coming from no particular individual vision, institutionalized. And I find myself too often restless, bored and boring in the presence of my opposite numbers, the conversation turning and then turning back with a dreary passion upon the life-and-death within subscription statistics, the cloak and dagger relationships with boards or heads of edifice complexes, the Name-of-the-Game-Is-Grants, the gold rush for new scripts that bring prestige—as important as money to irritated egos, and the general problem of how to get from this day to the next, this week to the next, this month to the next without dying, the general problem of how to endure, how to function as part sitting-duck, part magician, and still invent.

What is that look I see on the faces of my friends? It is a look that varies, of course, with the day and mood and personality, but it is a certain look that bears dissection. Secrecy? Hidden thoughts that best be concealed? Like dress designers before late-summer showings (what is it to be this year, two inches above the knee or two below?). Confusion? Where do I turn next? What is my list of priorities? What comes first, the chicken or the nest egg?

Loneliness? Nobody knows the trouble I've seen, nobody knows my sorrow. And I'd better not tell because to tell would be to admit self-doubt and weakness and all the secrets of one's heart and to reveal these is to be nakedly vulnerable in the presence of one's successful, smiling peers.

What price salvation now? What price institutions now? If this be living theater give us death. Joe Papp. Does anyone ever think how much time and spark-plug energy Joe Papp gives to the endless job of fundraising?—to the point where his bones ache with Joe's fatigue and his temper snaps with Joe's frustration and his stomach grows sad with Joe's own sadness. And for what? For money. What's Hecuba to him or he to Hecuba that he should weep for her? What would you do if you had the motive and the cue for passion that he has? On how many levels can a man be creative at one and the same time and still hang on to his humanity?

I was very rude to a close, close friend recently. He called me to say that the chairman of his board would be in Washington the next day and could she come to talk with us about the festivities one arranges to prop up the opening of a new theater building. I was deep in conference with a playwright trying to wrest the logic from inside the script—I was on the battlefront, I thought, and I didn't want to be bothered with peeling potatoes in the rear. But ten years earlier I, too, had opened a theater, I had been preoccupied with the same peelings, and I should not have been rude. Yet, I was justified.

"Style is world outlook," wrote a leading Russian director, [Yury] Zavadsky. And here we are at the heart of the artichoke. Style is world outlook. What is on our stages is who we are and the way we look at ourselves, each other, and at our world. The psychic engine (it is a biologic law, not a metaphor) requires inputs, returns, in order to generate new impulses. The artist requires that he hear his own voice, at best a highly intricate process because to hear it he must often turn away inside and pretend he's not listening so that the voice makes *itself* heard and does not sound because it is being poked at. Next to impossible within the cacophony of these institutions of ours. So the directors, the conductors of the collective creativity, supposedly the fount for the energy and spirit of the Thing, getting and spending lay waste their powers. Dust fills their brains and months and when it does not it is because they use up half their gut to keep it from pouring in.

So what road are we on and where's the next toll bridge? Over there, the Swedish National Theatre, the TNP,[14] the Royal Shakespeare Company, the Berliner Ensemble. Or if you want to take the other route, there are the loose, or looser, creative units such as Joe Chaikin's Open Theater, which

14. Théâtre National Populaire, a Parisian company that moved to Villeurbanne, France, in the early 1970s, where it became part of Roger Planchon's Théâtre de la Cité.

plays only briefly in New York, trying to stay clear of the settling down, or Judith and Julian Beck's Living Theatre, hounded to Europe, split into three units each trying to find its own way, the Becks coming back, trying to hang institution-free, trying to hammer out an aesthetic, a personal style-as-world-outlook artwork with which to penetrate the social barbwire, trying to do it with only as much institutional baggage as is necessary to get from one discovery to another. And Ellen Stewart. Café La MaMa. The seedbed of tumbling, heterogeneous creative projects. Until recently Ellen Stewart kept her dress-designing job to keep up her theater. Ringing her bell, passing the hat, juggling projects, she presided over the birth of new playwrights, new actors, new thoughts. Now she has a building and the responsibility of that (the power of that, and the responsibility) and of a continuum of productions.

What happens when the money comes in a little? When you get enough from the Ford Foundation or the National Endowment to move ten squares and buy the Atlantic City Boardwalk? Is it migraine headache time? What time is it when you are suddenly endowed with all the blessings of institutionalization? (Mind you, the blessings aren't something that are forced on you. They're something you ask for without quite knowing what you're getting.) Time for the Table of Organization? Time for specialization of labor? Time to begin to consider the internal distribution of wealth now that you've got some? the promotion, marketing and distribution of the product? ways to increase efficiency, ways to rationalize use of time and manpower, ways to diversify so as to appeal to a broader base, ways to close the gap between income and spending? It's headache time and surprise! surprise! time. One has become a private enterprise in a capitalistic society. The "not for profit" in your papers really says No Parking. Shades of Adam Smith and the Ford Motor Company of America—and Pan, where hast thou fled?

Next question: Can a group hang with it without a context of formal structure? Can an individual remain pure in a corrupt world, ask the parable plays of Brecht. How long can you stay angry? Mother Courage puts it to the soldier. A week? A month? A year? How many years? What's important is not your anger, she says, it's easy to be angry, what's important is how long it can last, this anger of yours, before you capitulate to things-as-they-are. How long can a theater stay poor? Long enough to carry out its aesthetic intention? Anything short of that is not long enough. How long is long enough? It took Joe Chaikin several years to evolve his two ritual dramas, *The Serpent* and *Terminal*, and they were "worth" every minute of the time. Does he have enough poor-time left (poor—not in the sense that Grotowski meant poor, which is really rich, rich in the quintessential meaning of the art, poor only in the trappings—but poor in the sense of hungry, insufficient, lacking in stuff with which to make the artifact: time, cloth, concentration), does

Chaikin have enough poor-time left in him to follow his work to the end of where it is leading him? Must institutionalization eventually follow, follow inevitably, must it then follow as day the night . . . ?

Last question: If money corrupts, does absolute money corrupt absolutely? I think not. We have all grown up in this pure society and know that the love of money is the root of all evil. And we have been taught by our well-bred mothers not to talk in public about how much things cost (I suppose for fear the gods will get angry and jealous and take all the stuff away!). But I, for one, do not fear the corrupting power of money and I do not feel alone in my courage. I agree with Tolstoy that art needs comfort, even abundance, and I know that the devils of the artist are within him and have their own well-stocked armory and need no help from the outside. On the contrary, I believe in the sublime benevolence of absolute money. Not unlimited money. Absolute money. No more is needed than the amount which will absolutely bring into existence the vision that is being born. It would, of course, be silly and would not meet the test of reason to give Jerzy Grotowski, evolving his work with six actors, able to accommodate only a maximum of one hundred hungry souls a performance, grounding his aesthetic in a poverty of physical means, the absolutely same amount of money as one would give to the National Theatre of Great Britain.

Stark Young wrote: "Behind every work of art is a living idea . . . a content that will achieve a form that will be inseparable from it. A perfect example in any art arrives not through standards but when the essential or informing idea has been completely expressed in terms of this art, and comes into existence entirely through the medium of it. This is perfection, though we may speak of a perfection large or small."

All we absolutely need is enough money to conduct the search for the form of our idea, each in his own way, and in the hope that there's a fighting chance of achieving it.

If that is not somehow done for us, then we must stop being teased with the concept of institutions, taunted with it, for it is a dance macabre that is being danced and can end only in despair and death.

There is so much indifference. The APA folded and nothing skipped a beat. A short column in the *New York Times*, one in *Variety*, the APA had folded and Ellis Rabb, who created it in the late fifties and steered it into being one of our leading theater companies, was moving into the acting company of the American Conservatory Theater in San Francisco (which is retrenching for this coming season, giving up its second smaller theater. There are troubled sounds from the Theatre of the Living Arts in Philadelphia, and the resident theater in Atlanta is going or gone, and the Loretto-Hilton Theatre in St. Louis is now no more, and the Seattle Repertory Theatre has been shook up, and Joe Papp had to shorten his summer season in the Park, and there are tremors reported throughout the land as I write). Whatever the reasons for the disbanding of the Association of Producing Artists—the money just gave out, or a bad season topped a series of other problems and down it went, or internal conflicts ripped open the structure—whatever it was, it all slid away so softly, so silently, we hardly knew it had left.

We all need more money than we are getting and we must get it in a different way. Arena Stage has just received a terminal grant from the Ford Foundation which, partially matched by a grant from the National Endowment for the Arts will just about cover our deficit for the last season and for this one and the next. We have also received other grants from these and from other foundations, among them a three-year grant for the training at minimal salaries of young craftsmen under a production intern scheme, a three-year grant to increase the salaries of a ten-person nucleus of an acting company. This was very early on, around 1958 or '59—to entice actors from the magnetic field of New York. And finally, we received a year-by-year grant which keeps at a minimum level of life our Living Stage, an improvisational troupe that performs action skits on the suggestion and with the participation of young people at various points throughout Washington's inner city.

I mention these in particular to make the point that while it may be better to have loved and lost than never to have loved at all, these grants had such a seminal meaning for our organization that when they were withdrawn or, more accurately, not renewed, the trauma was so intense that one wondered whether it would have been better not to have had them than to have had and lost them.

Not knowing from one year to the next whether there will be a spring, or only summer, winter and fall, one simply does not know how to organize one's closet. I suggest an end to this tithing tease. I suggest a recognition that subsidy is here to stay or we cannot possibly. And, further, I suggest an extension of the arc of thought on the part of the policy-makers from three to, say, seven (a lucky number that, with all kinds of mystic overtones) years, so that there may still be part of the grant left by the time we have learned to use it wisely and so that the benefits can endure for at least as long as it takes our skins completely to replace themselves. The seven fat years of the regional theater—yes, seven seems a goodly number.

A commitment of responsibility, then, and I think, the organization by someone who agrees and will take the initiative of a mixed bag of expectations: so much from this foundation, so much from that, so much from the federal government, so much from other sources such as state arts councils where such sources exist. I am not very strong on community giving, except perhaps when it represents only a small percentage of the total. I think we could well do without the hand that rocks the cradle, for the hand that rocks the cradle will also want to raise it in a vote and mix into the pie with it. For while a theater is a public art and belongs to its public, it is an art before it is public and so it belongs first to itself and its first service must be self-service. A theater is part of its society. But it is a part which must remain apart since it is also chastiser, rebel, lightning rod, redeemer, irritant, codifier and horse-laugher. Separateness is the first law of relationship. Nowhere is the paradox more profound and nowhere must it be more urgently insisted upon. The first law of the theater is success; without success there can be no theater. At one and the same time, success can be arrived at only obliquely, as a by-product of a personal point of view strongly expressed. Success in the theater cannot be voted on or voted in. The proof of the pudding will be in the eating.

There has been a kind of folksiness in the RRRT Movement, engendered chiefly by the principle of matching money: so much from the foundation, so much from the community. Historically, the motivation was sound—if these cities wanted their theaters, let's see tangible evidence of the desire and wherewithal. But the hope on the part of the foundations that the communities would continue to run with the ball after they had left the seedbed and withdrawn turns out to have been a false one. We have lived long enough to see how the grass grew. What we are seeing now is that, as the deficits grow larger and larger, the folks get tireder and tireder, for they discovered that the need for money has no bottom. As the folks get tireder and tireder they also get fuller and fuller of opinions about what is going wrong and why. In the world at large, two wrongs don't make a right. In the theater two rights don't even make a right! It has to be *one* right, for the tougher the artistic decision, the fewer the number of heads who can make it. So, then, let the money be given at a distance, once removed, and let it be awarded by a jury of one's peers. Let the audience be only the judge.

Money from a mixed bag of donors, yes, I think we would like that. And we must learn to protect for ourselves a share of commercial earnings from works which we have evolved. If we are of use to Broadway and the film industry, if our better way is now producing fruit, let us reap some of the benefits in a direct financial way. Let us have a share of earnings in the marketplace to feed back into our work. This seems an overstatement of the obvious. But our critic Martin Gottfried trembles over the loss of innocence that may result in a liaison with the sources of money (winding up a recent article with what must be the statement of the month!: "There's no sense in being naive about purity . . . But there's no sense in being cynical about purity either."). And it took Howard Sackler, author of *The Great White Hope*, to tell me how it really is, or ought to be. It was this play, nursed at

Arena Stage, that became the big baby boy that won the Pulitzer Prize, a sale to the movies for something like a million dollars, and wrenched the axis of dominance for the production of important new works toward the regional theater. When we asked Mr. Sackler for a small financial pat on the back, he consulted his morality for a while and decided that since we had posed to him as a high priestess of the arts, and were now reversing roles, we had disqualified ourselves from his responsibility. Let it be known that I am no high priestess of the arts. I am dedicated, fanatic even and, after a good night's sleep and with a production on the boards that I like, I may even exude a certain charisma. But I am of the world, not above it. I require and now have learned to demand a worldly portion of what we help to bring about. I speak for my brothers and sisters in this matter I am sure.

There are other signs that money will not right, but which cannot be righted without money since money is the exchange commodity of our life.

We have not found out how to evolve acting companies for our theaters. No, we have found out how to evolve them but not how to hold them together. Arena Stage has had three acting companies over its twenty-year history: one—and its best—in the first phase from 1950–55, which broke up when we closed our tiny 247-seat playhouse to seek one large enough to pay the bills (we were still self-supporting in those days), one in the Old Vat, our second phase, which drifted off [one] actor-at-a-time to Broadway or television or to other new companies then coming into being around 1960–65, and one which was split up by the transfer of *The Great White Hope* to Broadway in 1968. We have not abandoned the notion of company, although some of our fellow theaters have. But we have had to broaden our definition of what constitutes a company and enlarge our vision of how to create one.

Again, we have had to teach ourselves to be independent of European models. American companies, operating at a distance from the film and television centers where most of the money can be made, and not able to afford companies on a yearly payroll, must be conceived more fluidly. Company membership must be defined more by artistic point of view and shared experiences, and less by uninterrupted geographical residency—although, of course, there is no reason why a company nucleus cannot be held together in one place over a considerable period of time. Further, companies are not companies simply because the actors share the same working hours and dressing rooms. This is a parochial concept. It explains why our critics complain, and justifiably, that many of our theaters have yet to evolve an identifiable style and remain hard to distinguish one from the other.

A company is brought into being chiefly through the force and power of an artistic leader. A company develops as the aesthetic ideas of the leader are given body and substance by the individual talents collected around him. Brecht's actors were not Stanislavsky's actors were not Meyerhold's actors were not Grotowski's actors. Actors are not interchangeable ciphers and companies are not stamp collections. Companies also require leading actors in order to emerge and present themselves as individualistic units, although in this country, with its egalitarian ethic, we seem to feel ashamed to say so. The Moscow Art needed Olga Knipper and [Ivan] Moskvin; the Berliner needs Ekkehard Schall; the Group Theatre needed Luther Adler, Lee J. Cobb and Morris Carnovsky; the National Theatre of Great Britain, Maggie Smith and Robert Stephens. Not "stars," but leading actors to carry the weight, fill up the space, connect the audience to the play with their special strings, and give the timbre of uniqueness to the goings-on. Plays are written about exceptional people within exceptional circumstances and even ordinary people in ordinary circumstances are given incandescence by the magnifying and transforming art of the stage. We need large voices, both vocal and human, to head our companies.

When the artistic leaders of our theaters can be freed for the task of artistic leadership and when the theaters come to be seen by actors as a first choice for a way to live their lives, then we shall see if we can produce leading companies or not.

Along with ways to free artistic leadership to do its job, means must be found to train people to head up theatrical institutions. This is one lesson that we can afford to learn from Europe: the know-how, if not the temperament and talent, for artistic leadership can indeed be taught and learned. Some sort of planned discipleship had better happen soon in this country. Until we experience a successful transfer of one of our more personally created theaters from one pair of hands to another, the term institution is not only tedious but euphemistic. The closest we have come is with the recent assignment of Michael Langham to the post of artistic head of the Tyrone Guthrie Theater in Minneapolis, Peter Zeisler—the last one of the triumvirate who began it in the early sixties—having decided to leave. But this represents an idiosyncratic solution and not one that we can count on repeating. Michael Langham and his association with the Tyrone Guthrie tradition of theater began long before Minneapolis. Furthermore, not all of our theaters will want to perpetuate an English or Canadian style, but will want to develop in more personal and individual ways.

A transfusion of funds and a reassurance that artistic leadership can follow his or her shining star, and need not be tub-thumpers and board-pleasers, would serve to attract director-producers rather than administrator-business managers to the helm. This latter course has turned out badly in a number of instances. I most strongly recommend the joint participation of a funding agency and some of our artistic directors in planning love-match apprenticeships to their positions. The way things stand now, our theaters are destined to become the mules of theatrical history, incapable of reproduction.

Was it Napoleon who said that it is easier to conquer a city than to occupy it? It is also easier to fall in love than to stay there and to launch a revolution than to batten it down. Around 1965 we began to experience the seven-year itch, even those theaters who were two years old, time being a very subjective matter. This syndrome persists though I think that I personally have wrenched myself into the recovery phase. The malaise is a malaise of doubt: in the audience, in oneself to create and lead a meaningful artistic entity, in the "relevance" of our repertory, in the validity of theater itself within a technocratic society. For some of us it felt (or feels) that a whole artistic life had been misdirected and that, somehow, we were part of a great betrayal, with no one to blame but ourselves.

The younger people are going to the movies—at least seventy percent of the revenue now comes from those between sixteen and twenty-nine. "See me, feel me, touch me, heal me," sings Tommy in the rock-media opera at Fillmore East. And the lyrics of Paul Kantner exclaim that "we can be together." To a lot of young people of Woodstock, the Vietnam Moratorium and the marches on Washington these nervy "now" sentiments seem to have more to say than we do. Had we outlived our day even before we had served up lunch?

There is an article in *Theatre 1* by Harlan Kleiman (he was the manager of the Long Wharf Theatre in New Haven and has since left it) which says: "As we move into a more cybernated, electronically oriented era, the spoken word as a dynamic means of advancing theme or plot in the entertainment media diminishes in importance . . . it is not a matter of economics; theater as we know it is too static and nonsensual. It belongs to their [the young's] parents' generation." And the brilliant young critic, John Lahr, in an article in *Evergreen Review* a year or so ago, wrote (I think I recall the gist accurately) that Shakespeare was passé, came from an age whose manners and morals found no equivalent in today's society, his images and syntax were archaic, and that the best that remained were his large metaphors of power, fear, conjuration, psychic dislocation. This was by way of reviewing Richard Schechner's rendering of *Makbeth* which he liked very much—the audience as members of the feast where Banquo's ghost appeared, the witches hanging by their knees, downward, from branches of trees, etc.

Tyrone Guthrie's prediction, dating from the same edgy period of mid-sixties onward, was also dire. In his book *A New Theatre* he noted out of his own experience with the theater in Minneapolis which bears his name, that after the honeymoon period is over—the initial years of operation—the audience diminishes, as do the box office receipts, and consequently the very core of the theater, its repertory, is affected. "*Three Men on a Horse*," says Guthrie, "is immediately substituted for *Oedipus Rex* in an effort to broaden the appeal. Still the audience continues to dwindle to the point where the resident theater, which five years ago was hailed as the great salvation of the American theater, is now viewed as an additional fiscal burden on communities already overloaded with 'worthy causes.'" One cynic even went so far as to say, when asked to explain the regional theater: "If a play was produced on Broadway ten years ago and made an extraordinary profit, was then done in summer stock all over the country nine years ago and was again a box office success, it will now be done in the nonprofit theaters at a sizable loss." And we, ourselves, noted in a speech in August 1967 that while "the regional movement is such a big thing they ought to make a musical out of it," much of its size could be attributed to too much air whipped into the cream, that its overt communality was only the underside of a covert conformity and that the whole "Movement" in its shadowboxing relationship with its audience, its fickle and fleeing audience, an audience, whom we both loved and hated, could best be expressed by the jingle:

As I was walking up the stair
I met a man who wasn't there.
He wasn't there again today.
I wish, I wish he'd stay away.

Something sidetracked us from having to deal head-on with the signs represented by these criticisms and self-castigations of the mid-to-late sixties. That was the quite accidental success of *The Great White Hope* (for success is always an accident, it is only failure that can be counted upon) and the subsequent succès d'estime of *Indians*, both of which originated at Arena, both of which had roots deep within contemporary life. And the attention given to the Mark Taper Forum production of [*In the matter of*] *J. Robert Oppenheimer*, in Los Angeles and in its New York incarnation, and to *Murderous Angels*, and to other plays of other theaters which subsequently moved or tried to move in one form or another from their homes to Mecca. My good and respected friend Gordon Davidson has been so reassured that the new play's the thing that his conscience is entirely caught and he's now devoting an entire season to new works, and perhaps the future of his theater, though I don't know this latter for a fact.

It is not hard to fathom that new orientation. What more important move is there than to open our arms, to open our theaters to new voices now being raised, to say new things in new forms to new people who are living in a world that has never been lived in before. Shades of Margaret Mead: A

kind of world community exists that has not existed before within archeo-
logical time. "It is not only that parents are no longer guides, but that there
are no guides." The search for and the production of new works has its origin
in Good Deeds.

But is that the voice of the Tempter I hear? I am not sure. It is nothing if
not funny that the write-up of *The Great White Hope* in *Newsweek* magazine,
after singing the praises of James Earl Jones and Howard Sackler, then nodded in our direction. We had achieved a national reputation, Arena and I,
overnight with this production (a night of Biblical proportions, having lasted
some twenty summers and twenty winters!) and had demonstrated beyond
contradiction our right to be. Who can say for sure that it is not the voice of
the Tempter that we hear? The competition to do the premiere production
of a new play has become part of inter-theater politics since *TGWH*. There is
one theater director who was totally exercised over not having presented the
American premiere of a new script that he loved. But after it was premiered
in another theater he would not do it in his, even though it still would have
been new for his particular audience. What kind of love is that, that "bends
with the remover to remove"? Is it not, indeed, a love subject to temptation?

This does not mean that good deeds cannot be done out of questionable
or mixed motives. I call no names and look down no nose. But it does raise in
my mind a most interesting formulation, a hypothesis as it were, with which
to wind up this reading-of-the-signs. One can beg a question, but one cannot steal it away. The question remains. Broadway was onto it a long time
before we suffered our first little inkling. A new play with a good press and a
good word-of-mouth (in our particular situation we can even do without the
good press) means lines at the box office and a feather in our caps, as *Variety*
put it for us with *Indians* (a bad pun?). But what about the rest of it? Should
we nag ourselves to death with self-doubts on the subject of relevancy? Are
we out of sync with the rhythms and sounds of our time? Are our audiences
really gone? Is *Macbeth* done for? Without *The Great White Hope* what kind
of a hope are we? Are we worth the money it will take to keep us alive? What
do the signs tell us?

I don't know in an empirical way the answers to any of these questions.
I am in the position of most people who have to make decisions and follow
a course of action. We don't know enough to satisfy our intellect, we have
to use whatever facts we can get hold of and piece them out with our emotions, our inclinations, our prejudices. I feel more optimistic than I did three
Augusts ago. I am glad that I heeded Emerson, who exhorted one to work on
without despair, but if we despair, then to work on anyway.

Frantz Fanon was onto something when he wrote that language was
"the god gone astray in the flesh." There are two meanings here. One, that

language is the highest evolutionary achievement of the human animal, a gift toward the gods. And second, that language is a function of the body, of the flesh, not, in the medieval sense, of the "soul" or "spirit world." Man is the animal who expresses himself with his body, this expression sometimes emerging as speech. No gifted actor or director will find anything new in the book *Body Language* that is now the talking-piece of dinner parties.

Ask any good actor. The theater is a place of physical actions and physical adjustments that when they reach their height, their straining point, their necessity, burst into speech. Just as song is speech unable to contain itself. Or it is a place of physical actions and adjustments which are themselves a form of speech, a language of the body, either denying or demonstrating what is being "said." I don't know what kind of theater Harlan Kleiman was referring to as "static and nonsensual" except to theater that is dull and without style. When theater is alive, the words are an extension of gesture, both psychic and physical: or the gesture *is* the word: or the gesture and the word, together, are life made concrete. The experience is as mobile and sensual as life itself. That the theater's movement and sensuality are different from the film's is, of course, true, but that is not what Kleiman or others who agree with him are saying. It may even be true that the medium of the film is more readily accessible to the psychology and habits of today's young people, challenging as it does the one-at-a-timeness of events in the theater, freed by the camera as it is from the dimensions of time and space, exploding as it can the synapse between thought and the body, the connection for logic that theater requires.

On the other hand, at the cinema one is not immediately witness to the event. One is not present in the flesh or, more accurately, the flesh of the event is not present. So that the sensual experience is once removed, is it not? And why cannot we have both, the theater *and* the film. Our thirteen-year-old son saw *Alice's Restaurant* and a dress rehearsal of *The Cherry Orchard* last season, one right after the other on the same evening. I asked him for his feelings. "The movie is bigger and moves faster," he said. "But I wasn't there in the same room with the people when it was happening. I liked them both. Why can't we have both?"

There are more good films than good theater productions. There is too much theater, especially there is too much bad theater, theater with no roots in human soil. It is very easy for theater to be bad and very hard for it to be good. I believe that bad theater has done much to send kids to the movies, where at least the images and the transitions between images are outsized and rapid and exciting—and you can eat your popcorn and go to the bathroom and get a drink of water when you want to. Bad theater and, of course, habit. Young people are not in the habit of going to the theater because it is "good for them" and you have to go to the theater for the same reason you read a book or fall in love.

And this goes not only for the young people but for the young people's parents, who also find bad theater boring and lifeless and not worth leaving their television sets for. Imagination is the nose of the public: by this, at any time, they may be quietly led. I think it was Edgar Allan Poe who said this. But it is I who second it. It is I who, out of my experience with bad seasons and good seasons, changes in administrations, deep affronts from disappearing subscribers, horrendous problems with matters of urban decay, the increasing crime rate in the central city, the high cost of money, fury at critics who don't know bad work when they see it, much less good, the endless invention and reinvention required to keep the people coming and to replace the ones who leave, it is I—faced now with more per capita competition than any other city in the United States—the emotion rising up in me to counter the doubts and question marks—I who agree with him, who second him. Right on, Mr. Poe! Imagination is the nose of the public: by this, at any time, it may be quietly led.

Edgar Allan Poe aside, I disagree with everyone else. I disagree with John Lahr, with Dr. Guthrie and with the other critic who said we do the plays at a loss that Broadway and stock did at a profit. First of all, I think there is a place for *Three Men on a Horse* alongside *Oedipus Rex* in the repertory of an American theater for reasons of its theatrical exuberance, the deliciousness of its design and its sly, askew glance at the American way of killing the goose that lays the golden egg by not knowing when enough's enough. In its funny and unpretentious fashion, it deals with the precarious nature of the creative process itself—watch the poem too much, clutch too much, and it dies: so the poem is only a greeting-card verse, the meat is still in the stew! I may even produce it again some time. For a repertory is a place for finding things and *Three Men on a Horse* should be found, discovered, come upon by succeeding generations who have never before found it and to whom, therefore, it is new and—here's that word—relevant.

I once asked our older son (the boys are my zippers in the generation gap) what the word "relevant" meant to him. He answered me simply. A subject or, in this instance, an artwork, since that was where I was probing, was relevant if it tied in to what was currently of concern or importance to him. Or it was relevant if it was simply beautiful in its own right. Or it could be relevant on both counts. Of course, there is a beauty that is large or small, and we would be on sounder ground with *Oedipus*. But I feel on sound ground with *Three Men on a Horse* and it is good ground from which to make my point.

I think one must guard against uppishness. Plays like *Room Service* and *You Can't Take It with You* and *Three Men on a Horse* are not "trashy comedies" as our same Gottfried article calls them, nor do we produce them in an attempt "to alchemize dated commercial theater into American folk art." Nor is there any feeling of "scorning the audience" or "concealing the camp" when they are produced. The fact that the plays were once commercial successes does not automatically cancel them out as "folk art." Reasoning in reverse one could arrive at the point that because these comedies were popular successes they were "folk art" ahead of their time. I hold to neither view very strongly, but I prefer the second to the first. I do not have the same aversion to commercialism as do many of my friends. My aversion is to art that has everything but creative energy, everything but life.

At any rate, I produced *Three Men on a Horse* and *You Can't Take It with You* (and over a hundred other plays from the past, including Molière, Giraudoux, Shaw, Shakespeare, Pirandello, Brecht and O'Neill to an average of ninety percent of capacity over the years) for the life that is in them, and, particularly, for the life that, like a tuning fork, sets off and responds to vibrations that are in the air today. I produce them for the continuum of life that they provide and for the sight they permit into the astounding ebb and flow of experience, its repetition and circularity, though each time with a difference in the specifics of circumstance, choice and resolution. It's to laugh at and to cry over, to puzzle out, to give up on, to take sides with, to be put off by, to delight with recognition at. It's a face in the present looking at a face in the past and seeing something of itself. Doing old plays provides a bridge between past and present.

A work of art is always relevant. A work of personal genius has perpetual life. Human nature does not change so rapidly. Thornton Wilder, in that wise and gentle voice, wrote in his latest novel [*The Eighth Day*]: "Human nature is like the ocean, unchanging, unchangeable. Today's calm, tomorrow's tempest—but it's the same ocean. Man is as he is, as he was, as he always will be."

Why does John Lahr have troubles with *Macbeth* without the "k"? Could it be because he has seen productions without specific human reality or without an interpretation of the environment of the play that would make it come to life? Douglas Turner Ward and Robert Hooks of the Negro Ensemble Company once told me that they felt the "classics" held nothing for young black kids, and really nothing for the black population at large. But I wish John Lahr, Doug Ward and Bobby Hooks had been at Arena Stage to watch as I watched inner-city black high school kids watch Macbeth, propelled by the hunger of ambition, thrown out of control by it to the seducing of dark forces, to the blood of murder and the hallucination of deeds-gone-awry and, finally, to his own destruction. And they knew faster than anyone in the play could find it out that Lady Macbeth was up to no good, what burned in her heart, and why she went mad. And then there was the bonus of all that language that *Mission Impossible* (is it still on TV?) just never gave them and not so hard for them to penetrate as we might pre-judge, since the words rested on emotions and the emotions rode out high on physical action. Tomorrow and tomorrow and tomorrow and tomorrow and tomorrow. And life's a walking shadow. And life's a brief candle. And we're too far steeped in blood ever to turn back. And we're just poor players who strut and fret our little hour upon the stage and then are heard no more. All well within their lives to understand. And within ours. Within our life and times as social beings. And within us, deep within us, as human beings with such a brief and bloody history.

So let us not impale ourselves on doubt. Plays by new writers, of course. But the theatrical past will die, the past itself will die, will fall into shadow, unless we prevent it. There must be a tension between the old and the new. And the answer to the question: "Without *The Great White Hope* what kind of hope are we?" has got to be, "The only hope we've got." And the answer to the question: "Are we worth the money it will take to keep us alive?" is, "Yes, I think, on balance, we are. But from whence cometh our help?"

—ZF

Minnesota Theater Company (Guthrie Theater)
FOUNDED 1963

Tyrone Guthrie

Most founders of U.S. theater undertook their pioneering efforts when they were still unknowns. By the time sixty-three-year-old Tyrone Guthrie co-founded and became artistic director of the Minnesota Theater Company, he had already been knighted and published his autobiography. He was, according to no less a master than Harold Clurman, "one of the world's most gifted stage directors." Most theaters emerge gradually, in fits and starts, through trial and error. The Minnesota Theater Company (which soon took Guthrie's name) arrived full-blown. It became, in critic Richard Gilman's words, "the first permanent classical repertory company outside New York." Its founding was (Clurman again) "a signal date in American cultural history [. . .] the most ambitious civic theater project in this country

SOURCE: *A New Theatre*, by Tyrone Guthrie, 1964.

outside of New York." It began with two million dollars in capital—raised locally—a 1,400-seat venue, a company of forty-two actors, and a staff that grew in a mere five years to 155.

Though Guthrie was the name and the creative power behind the company's birth and early success, he wasn't alone. He was ably abetted by two men he knew from his work in New York: Oliver Rea (pronounced "Ray"), who had, with the legendary Robert Whitehead, produced *Medea* with Judith Anderson and Carson McCullers's *The Member of the Wedding*, among other Broadway shows; and Peter Zeisler, a Broadway stage manager (*Candide*, *The Sound of Music*), who would later spend more than twenty years at the helm of Theatre Communications Group. The three men shared a disdain for the New York commercial theater, and a desire to get away from it.

The story of their pioneering effort is, in Guthrie's hands, a great tell. It's the story of three wise men selling high culture to America, ready or not. It's the only story of its kind (with the exception of the fly-by-the-seat-of-their-pants tale of John Houseman and Orson Welles's Mercury Theatre) in which a great theater is born whole. It's also the story of how a highly organized, deeply devoted theater community got developed before a single play by the new company hit the stage. (The triumvirate organized volunteer efforts that sold 22,000 subscriptions before the theater had even opened.) More, it's the story of a search for something unusual and pure—what Guthrie calls "a creative audience."

The Guthrie redefined the "movement." Before its arrival, resident theaters grew from "acorns," in Joseph Wesley Zeigler's taxonomy (see *Regional Theatre*[15]), or began as "saplings." The Guthrie burst into bloom with everything in place—roots, solid trunk, broad branches. It was, as Zeigler writes, the first American theatrical "'oak tree,' planted fully grown."

—*TL*

———

A month or two after our meeting in Ireland we were all back in New York. We were agreed as to the general conception of our theater; a classical program, of which about one play in four should be an American play of potential classic status; this to be offered to any city which felt deprived of live theater and would take us under its wing.

15. Zeigler's enduring 1973 book, *Regional Theatre: The Revolutionary Stage* (University of Minnesota, Minneapolis, 1973), while personal and partisan (Zeigler worked at several nonprofit theaters in Washington, D.C., San Francisco and New York State before heading up Theatre Communications Group in the sixties), is still the best history of what Zelda Fichandler dubbed the "whaddaya-call-'em" theaters. Zeigler should not be confused with TCG's long-time executive director and Guthrie co-founder Peter Zeisler.

Did such a city, or cities, exist? We knew that most of the cities of America had virtually no live theater. Maybe they preferred to have none. How should we find out?

We decided to consult Brooks Atkinson, who was then the critic of the *New York Times*. We all knew him slightly, admired immensely his absolute integrity as a critic, and his disinterested enthusiasm for the theater. This enthusiasm, you might think, would be dampened by many years as a critic. At first, yes; for the first year or so, maybe the first five years, you might be able to go to a play four of five nights a week and still retain some freshness, some of the eagerness with which you embarked on the job. Atkinson had been at it for four times five years and still—in a hard-boiled, not at all naive, way—was stagestruck.

On one of those matchless, golden New York days of late September we lunched in Dinty Moore's. Atkinson, with his intelligent, quizzical hedge-hog's face, listened as we expounded our plan and the reasons which underlay its conception.

He didn't say much; but allowed us to see that he thought our hearts were in the right place, even if there were something wrong with our heads. He said he would mention the plan on the drama page of the *New York Times*. Something might come of it; you never know. He would also send us a list of plays which, in his opinion, had been somewhat overlooked and might be worth considering.

A shrewd, sensible, helpful list of plays arrived next morning. A day or two later a paragraph appeared in the *Times*, briefly summarizing the plan, mentioning our various qualifications to operate it and wondering whether there might be any takers.

It would be nice to be able to tell how the United States Mail was totally inundated by the avalanche; how a specially recruited force of secretaries waded waist-deep in a sea of paper; how each letter, more emotional than the last, implored us to found our theater in the writer's hometown. But strict truth compels us to face the fact that the grand total of applications for our services was seven. But quality compensated for quantity. They were sensible and realistic.

[. . .]

We still inclined toward the Twin Cities. Of all our suitors they were the farthest removed from Broadway. It is true that the population, both of the cities themselves and of the surrounding area, was a good deal smaller than that of Milwaukee or Detroit. But the population, we thought, was large enough to support a theater, and small enough to enable us to be a big frog.

We put considerable stock in the strong ties which seemed possible between ourselves and the university. It is already a vast institution, and envisages over the next ten years a colossal expansion. By 1970 an enrollment is expected of over forty-two thousand students.

It is, I guess, arguable whether such wholesaling provides the best educational results. There are many arguments for and against. What cannot be argued is that the alliance with, and goodwill of, such a behemoth is an absolute necessity for all other cultural endeavors in the region.

We had been impressed and touched by the generous and unselfish attitude of Frank Whiting and his staff. We did not at this stage see precisely how we and they could be useful to one another; but we felt confident that we could, and that here—in the bridging of just one gap between a professional and an academic theater—something of permanent value might be begun.

Finally, we put considerable stock in the goodwill and assistance of John Cowles Jr., and others whom we had met in Minneapolis and St. Paul.

Meantime the weeks were passing, the deadline was approaching, but out of Minnesota there came no sign. Let us "cut," as in a movie, from Rea and Zeisler in New York, scanning with dwindling hopes the horizon for smoke signals from the Northwest, to Cowles and his associates in Minnesota.

As the year 1959 was ending, a so-called Steering Committee had been formed to guide the incipient project. This committee consisted of John Cowles Jr., of the *Minneapolis Star and Tribune*; Otto Silha and Philip Von Blon, also on the staff of the newspaper; Louis Zelle, president of the Jefferson Bus Company; Frank Whiting, director of the University Theatre; Roger Kennedy, vice president of the Northwestern National Bank of St. Paul; Pierce Butler III, a lawyer from St. Paul; Justin Smith of the T. B. Walker Foundation; and Harvard Arnason, then curator of the Walker Art Center, later transferred to the Guggenheim Museum in New York.

These represented a responsible and influential section of society in the Twin Cities. Some, not all of them, were wealthy, but none of them needed this project for his own advancement, either socially or financially. Demonstrably they were giving their services for the benefit of the community.

They are a youngish group, most of them well under fifty, some under forty. I suppose that it would be right to assume that they are not exactly the community's top brass, who would be men in their sixties and seventies; but they are, perhaps, a generation of Heirs Apparent.

But absolutely these men do not form a compact little group of rich and powerful people. It is a highly diverse group, in background, wealth, religion, race and attitude. Only by being so, I think, were these men able to catch the public imagination and to plant the project firmly in the locality.

It is still too early to know whether, in fact, our theater is firmly rooted. But if it is, and if eventually it brings forth good fruit, it will be to this first, dedicated and extremely diverse group that thanks are due.

They met weekly, and first began to investigate the possibilities of remodeling existing theaters in the Twin Cities. Rather soon they decided that this idea was unlikely to be fruitful. They then started to work on plans for building a new theater on the campus of the University of Minnesota. But this hare didn't run far either. For some reason, the business community did not seem enthusiastic about giving money for a project on the campus.

Early in the spring of 1960 John Cowles Jr. made a proposal to the annual meeting of the board of the T. B. Walker Foundation. The Foundation had been considering building an auditorium to hold some of the activities which, in addition to the Art Gallery, it sponsors—concerts, lectures, performances by dance groups, chamber opera.

Cowles's proposal was that the board should donate land behind the Walker Art Center and, in addition, make some contribution to the theater project which he and his associates were sponsoring. In return the foundation should share the use of the building.

The site is central; yet it is quiet. It faces a green lawn and a formal flower garden, handsomely maintained by the city of Minneapolis.

The Walker Foundation agreed to give this beautiful and suitable site and, in addition, pledged a tiny cash contribution of four hundred thousand dollars.

In May 1960, no more than a week before the agreed Day of Decision, a wire was received by Rea and Zeisler, who had, more or less, written off Minnesota and were wondering whether to send a corsage, candy and a sapphire ring to Milwaukee or to Detroit. Would they meet the Minneapolis steering committee for luncheon in New York?

The private plane of the *Minneapolis Star and Tribune* brought the steering committee to the luncheon. Over the salmon mayonnaise many questions were batted back and forth about both the practical details of the project and its philosophical implications.

Over coffee, Cowles, as spokesman for the Steering Committee, said that they liked the project, would do their utmost to implement it, had the promise of what they considered a suitable site, to say nothing of four hundred thousand dollars. He believed that they could raise another nine hundred thousand, making a total of one million and three hundred thousand dollars.

Rea and Zeisler, the artistic, dreamy things, heads in the clouds, said, "If it takes more, do you think you can raise more?"

Cowles, the ice-cold, iron Man of Affairs, said, "Yes."

There was no promise. No documents were signed. No hyperbolical expressions were uttered of enthusiasm or confidence. But then I do not think anyone could describe John Cowles Jr. as a hyperbolical type. Enthusiasm was implicit in their having come to New York. Confidence was mutual.

Sweating heavily, trembling at the knees, our two Parises proffered the golden apple to Aphrodite, quite effectively disguised as a Steering Committee from the Upper Midwest.

I have suggested the reasons why we wanted the Twin Cities to support us. But reasons, I seem to have found out, are nearly always invented after a decision to defend, even excuse it. Inclinations, hunches have far more to do with crucial decisions than has reason.

We offered our rather runty little apple mostly because we wanted to work in the Twin Cities. Why? The weather? The people? The river? We have discussed it often and we simply do not know.

At this stage all we could say was: "If you want us, we're available. We will put our various skills, experiences at your service. We will create for you a professional theater, which you will own. We shall be no more than paid hands. If we are unsatisfactory, you can, but not till after three years, get rid of us. You, however, must undertake the formidable task of raising the dough."

During that summer (1960) the Steering Committee was formally constituted on a nonprofit basis as the Tyrone Guthrie Theater Foundation. Louis Gelfand was appointed as administrator, an office was loaned by the Walker Foundation in the Jade and Pottery Gallery. Never was a budding theatrical enterprise more elegantly, more splendidly housed.

Professor Ralph Rapson was now engaged to prepare plans for the building. Trained at the Massachusetts Institute of Technology, he had been for some years professor of architecture at the University of Minnesota and had, in addition to academic distinction, a very varied and considerable practical record.

Now the task of fundraising was begun in earnest. Four hundred thousand dollars had been pledged. The target was estimated at thirteen hundred thousand. Nine hundred thousand therefore remained to be found.

A finance committee was formed under the chairmanship of Louis Zelle. Its members undertook the arduous chore of personally soliciting contributions both from firms and from well-off individuals. In addition, scores of speeches were made to groups.

I do not know how all the others managed. I found it very hard work indeed. For no more than ten days that summer Oliver Rea and I joined the evangelical campaign. Kind hostesses would invite us and a group of their friends to lunch. Over the coffee we would Make Our Pitch. In the evening, masculine organizations—clubs, church groups, business associations—would give us dinner. Over the coffee we would Make Our Pitch. In between we would visit schools, talk on the radio, make winsome, but progressively more jaded, appearances on TV. After only ten days, neither of us ever wished to look a martini in the face again and had difficulty not making compulsive recruiting speeches to one another in the men's room or as we sped by taxi from one engagement to the next.

In October the architect's plans were submitted for bids from contractors. The very lowest bid exceeded the committee's expectation by several hundred thousand dollars. This was charming. The committee had no option but to instruct the architect to revise his plans. But even considerable revision did not relieve the necessity of raising the target for the fund drive. The finance committee, panting already and lolling its collective tongue, was informed that a further seven hundred thousand dollars would be required.

The Walker Foundation proffered a further hundred thousand over and above its already generous contribution. The rest was dredged up somehow, although not without difficulty, and thanks to the energy and splendid pertinacity of the committee and to the generosity of the community the necessary sum eventually was reached. Contributions came from nearly three thousand sources, from corporations, foundations, professional men, businessmen, from clubs and schools, even from things called Women. The largest contribution was from the T. B. Walker Foundation, the smallest from a Sunday-school class in Mankato, a small Minnesota town some eighty miles southwest of Minneapolis. The class raised six dollars and thirty-seven cents.

Meantime, talking of Women, Gelfand had recruited a group of thirty or forty lady-volunteers who, during this period, typed correspondence, worked a duplicating machine, stuffed and stamped envelopes, telephoned, filed and generally acted as unpaid but indispensable office workers.

In June 1962 it was suggested to one of these ladies, Mrs. Robert Wohlrabe, that she undertake to expand this group and organize it on a more official basis. She agreed, and under her presidency about two hundred women formed themselves into a society called the Stagehands. In addition to arranging a roster of office work, the Stagehands spent many hours in the preparation of a mailing list for the first ticket campaign.

By the end of 1962 the society expanded to a total of twelve hundred women, in preparation for a drive to sell season tickets. Members were recruited from towns all over Minnesota, and were organized into areas, each with its own chairman and officers.

On January 20, 1963, a meeting was held in the still uncompleted theater. In a temperature seventeen degrees below zero, more than seven hundred women assembled and sat themselves down on the cold concrete, listened to a rousing blast on the Horn of Roland delivered by Robert Preston, looked at Rita Gam and received, from their own officers, their final eve-of-battle instructions. They then went into action. Armed with literature and a disc upon which had been recorded not only Preston's Horn of Roland speech, but others by Hume Cronyn, Douglas Campbell and various persons about to be connected with the project, they launched themselves upon their various communities.

The ladies did not actually sell tickets. They sold the idea, glowed to friends and neighbors about the project, answered questions, urged people to order tickets and told them how to do so. It is computed that in the following eight weeks more than eight hundred coffee parties were held. One couple gave a dinner party for eight other couples and raffled a season ticket. Then they urged the other eight couples to go and do likewise. More than forty different dinner parties can be traced to that particular effort.

A Speaker's Bureau was organized, evangelists—thirty to forty men and women—were briefed and more than two hundred speeches were made to clubs, church groups and so on.

The campaign closed on March 25, 1963. Almost twenty-two thousand people had bought season tickets, giving them admission to each of the four productions. That is to say eighty-eight thousand seats had been sold for a total of rather more than $270,000—a very substantial result indeed.

Throughout the year a nucleus of two hundred Stagehands continued to work for the theater as office help, assisting the actors to find housing and doing all sorts of useful but inconspicuous bits and pieces.

At the end of 1963 the organization was again expanded to something like twelve hundred, in preparation for the second season's ticket campaign.

All this has been of immense assistance to the business side of the enterprise. But I think it has more significance than that. These women gave a great deal of their time and energy, and sustained their effort over a considerable period. This would not have happened if they had just been stagestruck. Quite evidently they had the Cause not only at heart but in mind. They wanted the community to have a theater of some quality and they were determined that it should not fail for lack of public support.

In fact, we have been able to offer them very little reward—no money, no glamour, really nothing but the feeling that the whole venture is in some part their own creation.

The Stagehands are perhaps the most conspicuous, but by no means the only instance of the solid support which the community has offered to this project. One of the members of the theater staff, Minnesota born and raised and therefore far better placed than I to know about all this, has written as follows:

> I feel very strongly that one of the primary reasons we were successful at the box office in the very first year of operation was because of the number of people in the Midwest in high schools, colleges,

community theaters and stock companies who had been working very hard for years to interest people in the living theater. All of these people had "prepared" an audience for us.

And then Don Stoltz has been working for years with his Equity Company at the Old Log Theater, refusing to give up, and continually trying to interest new people in theater. I am sure that through his efforts over the past nineteen years he has given us several thousand people who would not otherwise have been ready to accept and welcome what we offer.

I am convinced that this is true. I would estimate that less than half of those who saw our *Hamlet* had ever seen a professional production of a Shakespeare play; and less than a quarter of those who saw *The Three Sisters* had ever seen a professional production of Chekhov. Nevertheless it was apparent that they were prepared.

And as to Mr. Stoltz, where he might have been jealous and bitter that newcomers were established in a handsome playhouse considerably larger than his own and that our project was able to attract more public attention and more funds than his, he was generous and helpful. And where he might have feared that our arrival would damage his business, he was confident that we should assist one another. I am happy to say that his confidence has, so far, been entirely justified. Last season, when we were both in operation and both therefore competing for the same trade, his theater did better business than in any previous summer of its history.

[. . .]

It is our hope that gradually, as audience and management become mutually better acquainted, the audience will begin to create the sort of theater which it wants, which will be an expression of itself.

Only thus can the intention of this project be fully realized. It is much more than merely building a theater and creating a series of productions. The ultimate aim is to attract a creative audience.

The three greatest periods in the history of the theater—the Athenian stage of Aeschylus, Sophocles and Euripides; the Elizabethan stage in England which produced Marlowe, Shakespeare, Ben Jonson and half a dozen lesser but significant poets; the French stage of Racine, Corneille and Molière—all these could not have happened if the writers, actors and craftsmen had not been fortunate enough to live in an age and place where a highly intelligent, lively and demanding audience had helped to create a theater which was far more than a commercial business and far more than a frivolous pastime. Neither the artists and craftsmen nor the audience can do this alone. It is a shared process of creation, a fruitful union.

In sum, our project is to set up conditions where such a union may eventually be possible. No one can predict exactly how this new kind of theater will develop. We must all keep open, but not therefore empty minds. It is all too easy for those who work in a theater to be disproportionately puffed up by success and cast down by failure; and, as a result, to pursue too eagerly a popularity which is ephemeral and often achieved at the cost of eventual reputation. It is all too easy for the audience of a theater to take an irresponsible view of its share in the creation of standards; to assume that "support" is enough, without regard to the quality of the support.

That attitude belongs to an era when the theater was organized as a business and where the public had no more responsibility than a purchaser of merchandise. Those days are ending. If a particular public wants to have a serious theater it must undertake the responsibility not merely of a customer but of a patron. That involves the exercise of Taste.

The development of taste is not just a matter of sensibility. Taste is formed by experience. That is why at Minneapolis we are starting with a classical program: to enable an audience to form its taste by contact with what the best minds of several generations have agreed to regard as important expressions of the human spirit.

Later on, when both the management and the audience know better what we can and ought to attempt, and also what we can and ought to afford, then we may take the risk of producing, and possibly commissioning, new work.

The greatest works of art have, almost without exception, been created to please intelligent and sophisticated patrons. The greatest works of drama have, almost without exception, been written with a particular theater or particular public and a particular group of actors in mind.

When, and if, our theater can offer the right kind of conditions to a writer, or a group of writers, then we may begin to expect interesting and contemporary results. Meantime we believe that we can slowly begin to create such conditions.

Our policy may seem to many people more conservative than they would like. We must risk their disapproval; we must creep before we can walk. If our progress seems too deliberate, let me ask you to recall the result of the celebrated sporting event when the Hare raced the Tortoise.

—TG

Ford Foundation Program in Humanities and the Arts

FOUNDED 1963

W. McNeil Lowry

"Does anyone think for a minute that the resident theater could have developed without foundation support?" Guthrie Theater co-founder Peter Zeisler demanded of the *New York Times* in a 1969 letter. "Let resident theaters rely on their local communities entirely for all funding (direct and indirect) for ninety days and see what happens to growth and development—let alone existence," he suggested by way of an answer.

Zeisler could have substituted the name "Mac" for "foundation" in his question, because W. McNeil Lowry ("Mac" to those fortunate enough to receive his support) was as responsible for the existence—and survival—of America's resident theaters as any of the founders in this book. In his years at the Ford Foundation, initially as a program officer in Humanities and the Arts and later as a vice president still in charge of giving to both those areas, elevated to a major division at Ford, Lowry was at first the only—and then, with the entry of the Rockefeller Foundation into theater funding and the formation of the National Endowment for the Arts, the most significant—supporter of the regional/resident theater movement. "Without him, there would have been no regional theater movement," argues field documenter Joseph Zeigler.

From his perch at Ford, Lowry, who'd been a college teacher and journalist/editor, gave small grants to theaters in the late fifties, including important money for their leaders to travel and see performances elsewhere. Initially, he also gave grants to directors and playwrights for work with specific theaters. He gathered chosen heads of professional, university and community theaters, convenings which led to the formation in 1961 of Theatre Communications Group. Ford brought TCG to life with a four-year grant of $244,000 in 1961 and a second, five-year grant of $795,000 in 1964. In 1962, Ford turned from grants targeted for individuals in favor of those that would, according to Henry T. Heald, then president of the foundation, "help professional groups reach and maintain new levels of artistic achievement and financial stability."

SOURCE: This lecture was delivered at Brandeis University under the auspices of the Poses Institute of Fine Arts, on December 10, 1962, by W. McNeil Lowry, Director of the Program in Humanities and the Arts, the Ford Foundation. I'm grateful to Ben Cameron, former TCG executive director, for bringing it to my attention.

Lowry was more than Johnny Appleseed; through Ford he was bankrolling a gang of Appleseeds, sustaining theaters, funding their founding, and putting money into buildings to house them. Between 1956 and 1964, Lowry doled out nearly ten million dollars to seventeen theaters in New York and across the country; from 1962 to 1971, the number of theaters remained the same (as did, mostly, the list of grantees), but the figure rose to above sixteen million. Through Lowry, the nonprofit theater discovered what critic Martin Gottfried labeled "American Subsidy." In Lowry, the theater—indeed, all the performing arts—was blessed with, in New York City Ballet founder Lincoln Kirstein's words, "the single most influential patron [. . .] that the American democratic system has produced."

—TL

The Arts and Philanthropy

My subject is the arts and philanthropy, by which I hope we mean not only large organized trusts dedicated to the advancement of human welfare, such as the Ford Foundation, but also all acts of patronage beneficently performed by individuals, corporations or associations at either the local, state or national level. As you will observe, I have attempted to organize my discussion of philanthropy around the *motives* which prompt it into the arts rather than according to its *sources*. But before coming to this analysis, I think it is important to sketch in general terms the present situation of the creative and performing arts in the United States.

Analysis of the current American artistic scene reveals many paradoxical elements. On the scale of history and in comparison with some of the older countries, the arts in the United States are underdeveloped. With conspicuous exceptions, most professional artists lead precarious lives both psychologically and economically. The majority are concentrated geographically in two sections of the country. Their scarcity in the Southeastern, Plains and Mountain States leaves these areas generally underdeveloped except within academic halls and in a few museum collections from the past. Compared to other elements in the nation's life, the arts are also neglected financially. Institutions in the performing arts, from the largest to the smallest, regularly meet financial crises threatening their survival. The same influences of rising costs affect fine arts institutions differently; all but the most heavily endowed curtail their activities and their staffs while managing to keep their doors open. Tax support is slow to develop, and on the federal level, despite much agitation, appears unlikely to materialize in this decade.

Yet there are many conflicting elements in the picture. From the period when the arts reflected largely a social interest there remain a significant number of institutions operating with large budgets—the largest of all spending up to seven million dollars a year. These institutions are among the most aggressive in pushing for federal, state, foundation, corporate and private support. But the arts are no longer merely "social." The arts as an ethic or an aesthetic have taken on a new doctrinal urgency in many diverse segments of the society, and the argument is advanced by the most as well as the least affluent of artistic groups. Among other claims, the arts are said to be:

1. Important to the image of the American society abroad.
2. A means of communication and consequently of understanding between this country and others.
3. An expression of national purpose.
4. An important influence in the liberal education of the individual.
5. An important key to an American's understanding of himself, his times and his destiny.
6. A purposeful occupation for youth.
7. In their institutional form, vital to the social, moral and educational resources of an American community.
8. Therefore good for business, especially in new centers of population in the Southwest, West and other regions.
9. Components for strengthening moral and spiritual bastions in a people whose national security is threatened.
10. An offset to the materialism of a new and (generally) affluent society.

This is not the place to debate the validity of each of these claims. But they reflect a steadily growing interest in the arts in almost every part of the United States, even though that interest ranges all the way from concrete action to mere lip service. The first translation of this growing interest has come in buildings (or plans for buildings) as symbols of our cultural life. Another has been in the form of arts festivals, workshops, seminars and conferences at every level—local, state, regional. A third is in the new fashion of clustering the arts together to reach some supposed nth factor in creativity. A fourth is the rapid enlargement of academic training programs in the arts. Most recently, and only in a few communities, has come the attempt to give stability to proved artistic groups or institutions which were formed out of individual drive and energy but have not enjoyed financial patronage. And there are many other examples.

The causes for this growing interest in the arts, wherever known, are various (it is clear that some of them are as yet unknown). The most basic are the most subject to generalization. Three factors have roughly coincided in time: the closing of the American land frontier, the emergence of the United States as a world power and the numerical importance of the college-trained population. When the land frontier closed, not every able or compulsive citizen could find an outlet for his energy in the new frontiers of finance, economic development and industrial management. Even many who could do so had energies left over for other identifications in their communities. The complexities of America's new position in a threatened world order drove many minds inward, and at a time when a new affluence brought (though not universally) increased leisure. Meanwhile the universities, though doing a generally inadequate job in training young people as artists, had done an important job in training audiences for the arts. The whole style of theater known as "Off Broadway" is supported for better or worse by an audience that has been educated in colleges and universities; abstract expressionism is kept alive, critically and otherwise, by allied interests.

Each of these general factors has its corollary, or more than one: In the late thirties and forties, when the domestic soil was particularly fertile, there was an influx into the United States of some of Europe's most creative artists. Also, U.S. involvement in World War II and the presence of millions of young Americans in Europe undoubtedly stimulated the audience for opera and ballet; the surprising interest in the latter in almost every region of the country is strictly a postwar phenomenon. Probably related to all three general factors is a vague desire to escape both the materialism of the American past and the stresses of new international tensions. Many adults presumably look back upon their college experience and wonder if they paid enough attention to their cultural heritage or learned how to interpret it in their own lives. If a painting after all means more than an object for economic speculation, what does it mean?

[. . .]

Compared to other elements in the nation's life, in short, the arts have been neglected financially. There are variations in degree when one looks at each art separately. Music and the visual arts have had a large share of what has been available; theater and the dance scarcely any. Fortunately the importance of outside support of the arts has not been strictly equivalent with the amounts involved; often the effect of a single action has been crucial in the career of an artist or of an institution important to his development.

As I said at the outset, I think a more meaningful way by which to assess the role of philanthropy in the arts is through an analysis of the motives provoking the philanthropic act itself. I am sure each observer of the artistic scene might find a varying number of motives and label them differently.

From my own experience in the field in every part of the country over the past six years, I have selected five categories about which to group the argument. I am not completely satisfied with my own labels; but for want of better ones I shall speak of the status motive, the social motive, the educational motive, the economic motive and the professional motive.

The motive of status might almost be called the temple complex. In dozens of communities around the country, there are plans, drawings or actual skeletons of so-called cultural centers. Somehow in our country public, business and other lay leaders appear to believe that art begins with real estate, as if art is engendered by the four walls, if they be imposing enough. At the risk of appearing ungrateful for all the artistic activities breaking out in American communities, I believe we must guard against a failing which is characteristically American—the tendency to mistake the symbol for the thing, the intent for the doing, the name for the act. Is this just another example of our materialism, even as we become more active in the nonmaterial realms of the arts? I do not know, but it appears we are to have the audience before we are to know who will perform before it. The rash of cultural centers is one sign of the status motive. The rash of arts festivals is another. Exposure to the arts is a good; no one could be against it, particularly in a democratic society. But surely the artistic status of a community or region cannot be measured merely in terms of the facilities it can offer to imported artists and artistic creations. As a motive for philanthropy, the status motive is at the least imperfect, and if it prevailed over other motives, it would be quite simply disastrous. None of us can afford to be complacent about this phenomenon in our society. It is being fanned by every wind that blows, particularly those from the banks of the Potomac, and it will not ultimately make for the public happiness.

The social motive for artistic patronage is merely an older variant of the status motive. It persists from a time when few of us could afford status but those who could were willing to pay for it. It surrounds the openings of operatic and symphonic seasons, particularly the former, but it is not altogether missing from the openings of museum exhibitions and other ceremonial occasions of the artistic season. The director of one of our large opera companies told me that he could open his season with a thirty-minute concert from the orchestra in the pit, raise and lower the curtain, and get by without singers on the stage, so intent would be the first nighters on the dinner parties they had just attended and their studies of the ladies' dresses in the hall. Perhaps he exaggerated, but I can vouch for the fact that the description of the dresses worn at one of his opening performances occupied five complete pages, barring advertisements, in the local press.

It is of course true that certain of the performing arts make their artistic statement with the greatest impact when we approach them with at least a trace of solemnity or grandeur, in short, a sense of occasion. Like the status motive, the social motive for supporting the arts is by no means completely unworthy. Some of our greatest institutions in the arts (let us face the fact) were established because of this motive. But like the motive of status, the social motive is bad when it is dominant. When it takes control of an artistic institution or company, art evaporates. The whole enterprise becomes something that is not about art, but about society, about power, because what society is ultimately about *is* power.

The educational motive for philanthropic activity in the arts is more difficult to characterize. It operates in two ways. In the first, artistic enterprises are accepted as important to the community because they are somehow supposed to be "good for the schoolchildren." The stock example is the businessman who supports a symphony orchestra provided he is not expected himself to appear at Symphony Hall. He likes the idea that the schoolchildren possess an advantage he does not want to exercise himself. For some time orchestras and museums have partially supported themselves on the backs of schoolchildren; theater and opera companies are now making more strenuous efforts to do the same. The donor's motive is single, the beneficiary's triple: the beneficiary hopes not only to extend his sources of support and help to educate young people in the arts but also to train his adult audiences of the future. All three objectives are laudable. Whenever they distort the artistic enterprise, it is because art, when used for nonartistic ends, always risks distortion.

The second way in which the educational motive operates is through the use of an educational institution as a philanthropic base for the arts. I am not referring to the subject which on another occasion I treated extensively, the subject of the university and professional training in the arts.[16] I am now speaking of the role universities, particularly the state institutions, have often assumed, to serve a community or a region as an artistic entrepreneur. Some of our state universities have even conceived their role in the tradition of the German *Stadt*, which in turn took its own role from that of the German princeling. Particularly in areas where professional institutions in the arts were scarce, such universities have provided music, theater, opera, painting and sculpture both on the campus and in other communities within the state. Meantime, on their own campuses they have, like many other universities and colleges, provided through faculty appointments an economic base for writers, composers, painters and sculptors, even concert performers. This trend shows the adaptability of democratic institutions, and it gives no sign of abatement. Since the universities, particularly those with tax support,

16. Proceedings of the Association of Graduate Schools, New Orleans, on October 24, 1961. [author's note]

have a much easier time raising funds than do professional institutions in the arts, we confront here an important new development in artistic patronage. Recognizing it, even welcoming it, we should nevertheless not lose sight of its hazards. We are living in an age of a general speeding-up of communication throughout every fabric of our society. But some of us worry lest every vehicle of communication, including even our educational system, may tend, if we are not vigilant, toward a steady popularization and amateurization of those intangibles we call the arts.

A fourth philanthropic motive, and the newest, is the economic. The arts are now not only good for people but good for business. This development is an offshoot of the educational motive for artistic patronage. The mobility of our economy, spurred by science, industry and the need for national security, is intruding upon settled and somewhat provincial communities new concepts about their proper community resources. We must have not only good schools but other—and more specialized—cultural resources. A few months ago an important industrial corporation in a Southwestern metropolis lost out in competition with another city for the talents of a trained biochemist. Later investigation disclosed that the biochemist had taken a position in the second city because of its supposed greater cultural resources for himself and his family. In the Southwestern metropolis that had come out second best, a new vigor was felt in the cultural renaissance. Backed by the local press, the businessmen undertook an inventory of the city's cultural resources. The arts, which had been thought of as good for the schoolchildren or of interest to the ladies, were now good for business, too. Given the nature of our democratic and laissez-faire economic society, this evolution within it is undoubtedly a necessary step in the development of our cultural resources. But it antedates (by how long a period we can only guess) any realization that it is the highly talented and professionally trained artist on whom all depends; it lacks as yet, in short, discrimination as to what the arts are really about.

In the identification of motives for artistic patronage I have chosen as the argument for my discussion, the fifth and last is the professional, a feeble name, I am afraid, for the motive I desire to convey. Basically it means accepting the artist and the arts on their own terms. This does not appear to be a very unorthodox requirement when we consider how easily (in the main) philanthropy accepts, say, scientists or educators on their own terms. But individual patrons, corporations, public officials and, until recently, foundations have too frequently chosen to concern themselves with the educational or social uses of the arts, if they have indeed devoted their resources to the arts at all. Some of us have long hoped that the sources of money in the United States, private or public, individual or corporate, would find a greater share for the professional arts. A greater share for the arts is actually becoming visible, though by no means as yet proportionate to the importance of the arts in any society. But a paradoxical development is also emerging. We are beginning to see an enlargement in the funds available to the arts without too much prospect of channeling the new resources into the places where they are the most imperatively needed, places which traditionally have been subsidized by the artist himself through his Spartan determination. And in many quarters, public-spirited persons of goodwill are performing good works in the exposure of the public to art without too much thought as to what is being exposed or the results to be anticipated.

At its most basic level, art is not about money or facilities or social acceptance; it is about the surge of artistic drive and moral determination. It is about the individual professional artist or artistic director. And philanthropy, in the arts at least, is professionally motivated only when it accepts the artist and the arts on their own terms, and learns from the artist himself *at least* to recognize the atmosphere in which the artistic process is carried out.

What is that atmosphere? None of us can describe it to the complete satisfaction of anyone else, but as I have said on another occasion, it derives importantly from:

> the drive of fanaticism or whatever of the person who has made his choice, and will often have to eschew anything else—money, the elite identification of a university degree, even health—to develop the latent talent he hopes he has. It comes also from the pride of doing for oneself, of making ends meet, of giving society what it will pay for even if what it pays is inadequate to sustain a normal life, of working in the midst of a fraternity that will show the same fanaticisms and abnegations. It comes from the endless time, time, time spent on doing one thing, only one thing, and then, starting all over again. It comes, finally, from the acceptance of such distortion as a way of life—a way of life, you will note, that is in some ways completely antithetical to the ideal objective of a liberal and humane education. Some of the most professional, the most talented and the most mature artists I have met lack either the time or the capacity to sort out a decent personal life from the endless hours of their artistic concentration. Only a rare heredity or early environment and not, I am afraid, a very good education, has given some of these artists a humanity that separates them from the talented bums in their midst.[17]

17. Proceedings of the Association of Graduate Schools, New Orleans, on October 24, 1961. [author's note]

It is no accident that so many talented artists (you will have guessed by now that I use this word to apply to creators or performers in all artistic fields) who are thirty-five years of age or older speak of "the Depression psychology." Strictly speaking, however, this is a timeless phenomenon in the artist and not peculiar to an era when the entire social community is in severe economic straits. Many persons believe that the artist became socially motivated in the Depression era because the government itself accepted him as just as rightfully unemployed as a bricklayer or a mechanic. I am not, of course, merely repeating the romantic picture of the artist as a starveling or saying, with Matisse, that hunger will bring out the artist's creativity if he has any. The Spartan fanaticism of the driving, talented force is not purely a factor of the annual income of the artist or artistic director in whom the force is lodged. It is certainly not saintly, nor is sainthood the goal. It is neither moral nor immoral. It does mean, however, that the artist has chosen what he must do without the promise of security, not merely financial, but even emotional or social. If the concentration is great enough to develop the existing talent, it is great to the point of distortion. And distortion, as I said earlier, may itself have to become the way of life.

If any of this be true, then what the artist is about is not what society or education or business or physical magnificence is about. And if philanthropy—public or private, individual or organized—is to relate to the arts in any realistic and therefore meaningful way, it can learn how to do so only from the artists and artistic directors themselves. It is they who must, in short, become the chief participants in the whole philanthropic process.

It has been my privilege for five and one-half years to help carry out this sort of exploration for the Ford Foundation. Whether it is theater, music, painting, ballet or opera with which we are concerned, we attempt to talk to many artists and artistic directors in the field and to gain a realistic insight into the problems with which the art is confronted. Through our extensive fieldwork in every part of the country, through conferences and panels we call in New York, through interviews with individual men and women in our offices, we *listen*. Anything we know about the arts we do not read from books nor attempt to view from our own vantage point on Madison Avenue. We are catalysts rather than reformers, participants rather than backers, communicants rather than critics. And when we announce a specific program for individual artists, both the nominating and the selecting processes are in the hands of the artists and artistic directors themselves.

I wish I had time to tell you about the results of this activity, now beginning its sixth year, and the way it is reflected in so many parts of the country. That is not my subject tonight. Even though the Ford Foundation Program in Humanities and the Arts is expanding, I can tell you that all the sums the Ford Foundation may expend in the arts will not enable us to attack even the most urgent problems we have identified with the help of the artists themselves. I say this lest you think I am not the appropriate person to speak of the artist in his Spartan aspects. Our investments in the arts are not so much subsidies as they are levers. We are content not to change history if we can help to shorten it, even infinitesimally, in the career of the artist and his most rudimentary institutions. There are ways, I feel sure, to weaken artistic drive through subsidy, but if this happens one is either subsidizing the wrong thing or mistaking for an artist a person who has only a talent for visibility. And we are not very much moved by those who tell us that the public will not respect the artist until he commands an imposing financial position. Most of those who support this argument talk better about art than they either practice it or recognize it.

As the scale of the Ford Foundation's activities increases, important actions we shall take will appear to serve all five philanthropic motives I have defined—status, social, educational, economic and professional—as did, for example, the six million dollars in grants to strengthen the resident theater concept announced in October. Every important philanthropic action has both an organic and a nuclear relationship to its society, and it is always an action taken in concert. But only the professional motive can justify what we do, our acceptance of the artist and the arts on their own terms. This is the key to channeling new interests and new financial resources in the arts into effective development for the future. Other motives are important, but they are finally irrelevant.

—WML

The Repertory Theater of Lincoln Center

FOUNDED 1965

Jules Irving

The Repertory Theater of Lincoln Center began as a theater in search of a vision. It would die several times without finding one. Surely, RTLC holds some record for institutional floundering: it took the company twenty years, until its rebirth as Lincoln Center Theater in 1985 under artistic director Gregory Mosher and executive director Bernard Gersten, to establish itself as a stable part of the New York theater.

The Repertory Theater of Lincoln Center began as an urban renewal project, a "slum-clearance project," as critic Julius Novick put it,[18] a way for New York City colossus Robert Moses to transform Manhattan's Upper West Side from the tenement setting of *West Side Story* to a rich cultural mecca worthy of a Rockefeller (John D. the third was Lincoln Center's driving fundraising force and first president). The other tenants of the mecca-to-be, the Metropolitan Opera and the New York Philharmonic, were thriving concerns. A theater company had to be built, literally and figuratively, from the ground up. Instead, it was built from the top down, meant to be an American national theater, in the words of critic Martin Gottfried, "from the moment it opened its doors." Lincoln Center, Gottfried sniped, "looks like a graveyard and it is there that American Subsidy seems determined to bury art."[19]

While, over the first two years of its operation, many critics agreed with Gottfried's funereal appraisal, Lincoln Center at first appeared more likely to bury its artistic leaders. The first two casualties, whom at first glance must have appeared invulnerable, were Broadway greats Elia Kazan (director of *Death of a Salesman*, *A Streetcar Named Desire* and more) and the producer Robert Whitehead.

SOURCE: "Diary of a Madman, or How to Build a Classical Theater on Five Dollars a Day," by Jules Irving, was originally published in the *New York Times*, on July 16, 1972.

18. Novick's *Beyond Broadway*, published in 1968, offers something other contemporary histories of the regional and nonprofit boom lack: a critic's viewings of numerous productions at each of the theaters he encounters. It's not always possible to know whether or not to agree with Novick's assessments, but by covering the actual work on stage, he adds dimension to the portraits of theaters drawn by contemporaries like Joseph Zeigler (*Regional Theatre*), Martin Gottfried (*A Theater Divided*) and Gerald M. Berkowitz (*New Broadways*, Applause Books, New York, 1997).

19. Martin Gottfried's *A Theater Divided: The Postwar American Stage* (Hill & Wang, New York, 1968) is so opinionated and contentious that I find it almost unreadable today, at least as history. It does, though, offer some of the sick pleasure of vitriolic attack, especially in his skewering of subsidy in American theater.

What follows, then, is not a "founding vision" like the rest of the entries in this book, but a re-founder's vision under siege. As such, it offers one of the best, most sharply satirical, insider views I've read about running—and being run by—an institutional theater. It's also an account of a meeting of two worlds—the burgeoning regional, nonprofit, art theater world (embodied by Herbert Blau and Jules Irving—founders of the groundbreaking Actor's Workshop in San Francisco) and the world of New York, commercial, Broadway-centric, high-rolling, high stakes and real-estate obsessed. It was into this world that Blau and Irving came, two "cantankerously imaginative" men from the new theater movement. It was this world that greeted them, according to Theodore Hoffman,[20] with a resounding, "Who the hell is Herbert Blau?" It was this world that would, within a few years, chew them both up and spit them out.

At the time of this *New York Times* article, Blau had already resigned from Lincoln Center, heading off to a long and influential life in academia, which lasted until his death in spring 2013. Irving stood alone, a temporary survivor, describing the battle as it raged.

—*TL*

———

Diary of a Madman, or How to Build a Classical Theater on Five Dollars a Day

I have a recurrent dream. It used to be a nightmare, but now it's like an old friend: I've grown accustomed to it. There I am standing in front of the Vivian Beaumont Theater in Lincoln Center. Crossing the empty reflecting pool on the plaza, marching steadily through the glare of the afternoon sunlight, a host of pickets approaches.

A group of American actors is protesting my hiring that fine English actor Anthony Quayle to perform in a German play about the Italian Galileo. Ed Bullins appears, accusing me of running a plantation. From behind the Henry Moore sculpture, members of the Oriental Actors Guild eye me warily. Clearing the plaza fountain with a communal whoop, a group of Hopi Indians gathers for attack.

'Midst the chaos, a patroness is carried from the lobby, having tripped on the torn red carpet. My house manager approaches to tell me that the water from the empty pool hasn't disappeared—it's simply flooded the dressing room level of the Beaumont. A reporter emerges from nowhere, asking me what it's really like to be at the helm of the largest permanent theater company in the nation. I say, "You mean the one with the $9.5-million building

20. "Who the Hell Is Herbert Blau?" *Show*, April 1965.

and no permanent operating subsidy?" Simultaneously, my business manager appears, whispering that we can't possibly meet next week's payroll.

The dream, rich in detail and entertainment value, has endless variations. I always hold my ground, cheerfully order my wagons in a circle and, dauntlessly, wait for the dawn and the daily papers. In their pages and those of my meticulously kept diary, I find that it is all very real indeed.

You see, the theater breeds a unique kind of madness. And I'm sure that all resident theater directors have their own versions of my recurrent dream. Why? Probably because none of us has to hunt very far to feed our fantasies. Except for some isolated Walter Mittys, I expect the staffs of General Motors and AT&T—from president to clerk—keep their reality and fantasy lives pretty well separated. In the theater, they, more frequently than not, function as one. Resident theater directors seem to thrive on adversity. Every day is a glorious extension of the Mad Hatter's tea party.

The Repertory Theater of Lincoln Center differs from the resident company in Center City, Idaho, only because our party is slightly madder, our problems more expensive, the noise a little louder in the glare of the proverbial New York spotlight, and the stakes are higher.

In case you have your doubts, let me give you some light summer reading and a few random selections from that well-thumbed diary:

June 10, 1971: I fly to Stockholm to talk with Ingmar Bergman about his making his U.S. directing debut on the Beaumont stage next year. A remarkably shy, private and charming man who confesses to being terrified of New York. We have a freewheeling talk about the theater into the wee hours. He insists that we drive to the outskirts of Stockholm to a two-hundred-year-old wood-and-copper theater built by Gustav III next to the royal palace. This, it turns out, is where Bergman's love affair with the world of the theater began. What a rare treat to roam the quiet palace grounds with this gifted man, both of us dreaming out loud.

Bergman, like myself, feels that without careful planning, order and organization, there can be no great art. He likes the idea of working with my company enormously, yet is adamant about rehearsing only four hours daily over a ten-week period. This would be wonderful as a regular routine in New York, but impossible with our soaring union demands. The prospect of exposing my company to the rigors of the Bergman mind is so exciting that I must find a way to make it possible.

September 15, 1971: Last season's hit, [Friedrich Dürrenmatt's] *Play Strindberg*, is still selling out in its pre-season revival in the Forum, but ill winds are blowing in the direction of this jewel of an experimental theater beneath the Beaumont main stage. I simply cannot accept the plans in the offing that may relocate and destroy it in favor of three movie houses and a film museum. Surely, we can collectively find another, less destructive way to cut down our building costs and still have a museum of cinema without tearing apart this perfect little theater.

September 19, 1971: Ed Bullins brings his play *The Duplex* to me. We have lunch and discuss its production prospects here. I consider his talents huge and important, but *The Duplex* needs a large cast, a complex production, and a great deal of rewriting and restructuring. Can we possibly afford to do it?

September 28, 1971: I am directing the season's opener, [Friedrich Schiller's] *Mary Stuart*, myself and have been desperately fighting for time to do my Elizabethan homework to create a rehearsal atmosphere for the company as vibrant and richly textured as the period itself. [Translator] Stephen Spender's version of the confrontation between the two heady queens has not been done here and we haven't mounted a historical drama in quite a while. We begin rehearsals today. I wonder if the Mary-Elizabeth story will have any interest for a present-day audience.

September 29, 1971: Plumbing breaks down in rehearsal area on West End Avenue. May have to find another condemned building for rehearsals. This one is to be ripped down soon. We pray for a mild winter and consider rehearsing on the grass in Central Park.

October 2, 1971: Beverly Sills, who once sang Yum-Yum to my Nanki-Poo in *The Mikado* when we were both fourteen, calls to chide me about doing *Mary Stuart* before she opens in *Maria Stuarda* at the City Opera. We laugh about it, and I tell her that David Merrick had called also to reproach me for opening before his *Vivat! Vivat Regina!*

October 7, 1971: I leave rehearsal and spend the day at City Hall for the definitive City Council Finance Committee Meeting to decide the ultimate fate of the Beaumont building and the Forum. A gratifying turnout—playwrights, theater owners, directors, designers, critics, journalists and bankers—along with city officialdom.

Probably what I acknowledged in my speech to the gathering of the strangest collection of bedfellows in theater history encourages me to point out that the events of this day will surely be a bellringer, a test, for the quality of life not only in this city but in the country. The cancer eating into the very fiber of urban life had struck the Beaumont, and none of us could sit silently and let it happen without a very large and special fight. A theater with such a rigorous amount of creative energy can't be strangled by a real-estate maneuver, no matter how much power or money is at stake.

The groundswell of support gives me impetus to ask what has happened to our civic pride? Have we lost it with the skyscrapers and smoke, the bulldozers and the dust? Do we want more construction and more destruction?

Do we want a senseless and wasteful rape of the most beautiful building and little theater in New York? A wise man said that America was a land of promising first acts. Isn't it about time we progressed to the second?

Traveling back uptown, I am happy and relieved. The tide is changing. Many selfless people have worked terribly hard to defeat the proposal to turn the Forum into a cinematheque and the Beaumont into a construction site. An enormous strain has been lifted from all and we face the more typical daily problems with greater vigor. Back to that other famous feud, between Elizabeth I and Mary, Queen of Scots.

October 11, 1971: Thanks to the Rockefeller Foundation, a grant comes through, at long last, to have the workshop series, planned since 1965, for the Forum. We have called it "Explorations in the Forum" and have given Jack Gelber the first slot to stage two new plays by Merle Molofsky. We've run out of rehearsal space entirely, though. Should I call Urban Redevelopment and find yet another condemned building?

November 2, 1971: "Explorations" is inaugurated on Election Day. At least one hundred prospective patrons are turned away. A good start. There is interest in new work.

November 7, 1971: Last week, Nancy Marchand courageously shaved her head. In her red wig, she looks strikingly like the famous portraits of Elizabeth I. Today, she and Salome Jens arrive at the Raffles Club for a Repertory 500 fundraising fete resplendent in sixteenth-century costume. After being told how wonderful it was of her to leave rehearsal to mix and mingle with patrons, Queen Elizabeth was overheard saying with gusto and yet great regality: "You bet your ass it is."

November 9, 1971: We place *Voices from the Third World* into rehearsal, a montage of stage literature from minority writers created by a group of us for touring to New York City and State public schools. To date we've reached over seven hundred thousand students in their own auditoriums and over two hundred thousand who have come to performances at the Beaumont and the Forum through student rush lines, which we proudly initiated in New York, through special subscription rates and prearranged groups.

November 11, 1971: Mary Stuart opens and delights the critics and our audiences. (As it turns out, we seem to have started something. The Mary-Elizabeth plot becomes the vogue of the 1971–72 season.)

November 30, 1971: Rehearsals for new Peter Handke play. The time seems ripe to explore the devious and brilliant mind of the reigning enfant terrible of contemporary German letters. We are intrigued by his *The Ride Across Lake Constance* and have found the right director to control the idiom in Carl Weber, a former associate of Brecht's at the Berliner Ensemble. I am confident that Handke is in safe hands.

January 4, 1972: Deadlock in negotiations in process since September for new contract with stagehands' union. The holidays have passed by practically unnoticed because of the constant meetings. A state mediator is brought in and today's session lasts until three A.M.

January 6, 1972: Edward Bond's *Narrow Road to the Deep North* opens. Ironically Walter Kerr carps on the extravagance of the costumes with no awareness that our ingenious designer has once again pulled off a Beaumont production on a shoestring. The costumes Kerr writes of cost $21.98 apiece. The play, by England's hottest young playwright, has been highly touted by an eager press and public, yet it meets with disappointment. Rule number one of repertory: You can't win them all, even though you always try. The body of work is, after all, more important than the individual production.

January 8, 1972: Meanwhile, back at the Forum, I am in less safe hands. Following the first preview of *The Ride Across Lake Constance*, I am literally mobbed in the lobby by a group of patrons—some angry, some exhilarated, yet none unmoved by the work. The discussion is still erupting an hour later and an interesting pattern is set for the run, with the actors and director having impromptu discussions with the audience after each performance. I recall the uproar that greeted Beckett's first works.

February 3, 1972: Have decided to go ahead with the Ed Bullins play and begin rehearsals for a Forum production with an all-black cast, director, composer and costume designer plus four musicians. The atmosphere is decidedly vital and upbeat, but I know the play needs hard work from the author as well as this collection of talented people. Where the hell is Bullins?

February 14, 1972: Cable from Bergman confirms his get-acquainted trip to New York and the Beaumont for early April.

February 16, 1972: Spent an extraordinary afternoon at the Human Rights Commission answering charges by the Oriental Actors Guild about the casting of *Narrow Road* and, also, our production of *The Good Woman of Setzuan* from the year before. Bond has emphatically stated that his play was written for the Western actors and Brecht's parable has about as much to do with Setzuan as *Abie's Irish Rose* has to do with gardening in Ireland.

Shocked by the charge of racial discrimination during the hearing, I am forced to point out that at the moment we have an all-black production in rehearsal, a fully integrated touring company and a *Twelfth Night* with black actors in several key roles. The most militant of the Oriental representatives cries out for me to "stop the liberal hogwash. It's quite clear that in order to be a part of the Repertory Theater, you have to be white or black."

I am reminded of our Great Indian Uprising when we mounted Sam Shepard's *Operation Sidewinder*. We had hired several Indian actors to advise and participate in a theatrical version of a Hopi ritual and were careful to perform the sacred rite with accuracy. In spite of this, a militant Hopi Indian appeared angrily backstage after the first preview, protesting our use of authentic cornmeal and a Kachina doll in the sacred ritual. Hours of discussion ensued, a committee of Hopis was brought in, and we did modify the rite on stage and get the crisis under control.

February 17, 1972: I go to a scheduled hearing at City Center to speak out about the Special Citizens' Report on the State of the New York Theater released last week. An ambitious group of private citizens led by Eugene Black Jr. had worked long and hard on this study. Among other items, the report asked for much-needed city support for the Repertory Theater. I am highly gratified by this well-publicized acknowledgment of our need for permanent funding, whether it will come to fruition or not.

The turnout is spectacular and everyone has a say. I quoted the statistics that I'd learned from Bergman about his National Theatre in Stockholm, which employs a paid staff of 450 over a fifty-two-week period, eighty-four of whom are actors with eight weeks' paid vacation. The annual government subsidy is three million dollars and the top ticket is three dollars. No statement was needed to illustrate the stark contrast to the American theater. Two youngsters from local public schools arrived at the end of the day to tell the people left how much they treasured their introduction to live drama through performances they had seen at the Beaumont.

February 23, 1972: Usual publicity photographs call for *The Duplex*. Bullins appears for the first time. He poses for a photograph and leaves shortly thereafter, saying he will try to attend a rehearsal later that day. Later, Bullins was heard from, if indirectly. The *New York Times* calls to inform us that Bullins has asked that his play be withdrawn because we have turned it into a "coon show." Previews are scheduled to begin Friday. What's going on here?

February 23, 1972: Search continues for the right small cast, original single-set play to end the Forum season. Commercial producers are surprised when they find out that the labor costs of running this tiny theater are comparable to those of a Broadway house. And *The Duplex*, with a larger budget than usual, is becoming a bigger and different kind of crisis than we had bargained for.

February 24, 1972: I head down for the Dramatists Guild and ask that Bullins meet with me and the play's director. He refuses and sends his lawyer. In an age when everyone is asking for a dialogue, there's absolutely no communication between us whatsoever. Here we are making theatrical history again: never before has a playwright demanded that his play be withdrawn without attending rehearsals. Today we are called a "racist institution" in one of his many press releases.

March 3, 1972: Ushers' union negotiations begin. Where's the money going to come from for increased wage requests? I have nothing left to hock.

March 15, 1972: Announce David Wiltse's *Suggs* as the final play of the Forum season. Why *Suggs?* Perhaps because the lead character strikes a recognizable and sympathetic chord in me: adrift on a Kafkaesque Manhattan landscape, young hopeful Suggs learns in several short, swift, scenic lessons the bittersweet facts of life in New York.

March 16, 1972: A phone call from New York Theatre Strategy, a loosely structured, instantly organized group of playwrights. Their purpose is to "protect" Bullins from "the corrupting influence of the Repertory Theater." I extend an invitation to every member to see *The Duplex.* We arrange a meeting to discuss the "issues."

March 18, 1972: New York Theatre Strategy, led by Bullins, replete with gracefully worded placards ("Close This Play" and "Jules Irving Assassinates Playwrights") demonstrates in the Beaumont main lobby, where *Twelfth Night* is on intermission break. Many members of the audience wonder why Shakespeare needs this belated defense. I talk with the group and, in the interest of fairness, allow Bullins and company to enter the Forum. They harangue the well-integrated audience, which angers quickly and demands that the performance continue. The actors make a noble attempt to play the play, but Bullins refuses to leave the stage. One of the playwrights excitedly says to me, "Jules, this is what the real theater of now is all about." As I try to explain the events to a bewildered audience, which has paid to see a play and not a street fight, I am thinking that if this is what theater is all about, bring back vaudeville. One of the infuriated *Duplex* cast members, a marvelous character actress, has a refreshing fall from professionalism and walks on stage during the proceedings with a picket sign, too. Hers declares that "Ed Bullins Hates Black Women." A crazy, crazy week.

March 28, 1972: Ingmar Bergman cables that he is most distressed but cannot come to New York at this time and apologizes for the inconvenience to me. I pick myself up, hoping that he will change his mind, remembering fondly our good talks in his home city and understanding only too well how frightening this city can be for such a sensitive man.

April 1, 1972: The Duplex closes. Its run has been successful, the play has been called an exceptional work, but I am troubled by the knowledge that if the author had been on tap to work with the director and the company, *The Duplex* would have received the refining it sorely needed. So often in the theater the difference between good and great depends upon the proper work atmosphere. This way, no one truly gains.

April 27, 1972: Have felt for some time that the impact of Arthur Miller's *The Crucible* had been limited in its original production by being too close to the days of the McCarthy era. Tonight we opened the play on the main stage and my instinct is borne out: the play is hailed as Miller's best and the critics note that the powerful drama has acquired a much deeper universal meaning since its initial exposure in 1954.

May 4, 1972: Suggs opens to fine notices, too. Sadly, due to lack of funds, not interest, Forum engagements must be very short and often, by the time the good word travels to prospective ticket buyers, the show is about to close. In any event, patrons are practically climbing on stage for curtain calls upstairs and downstairs as our seventh season winds to a close. I am pleased when Robert Foxworth (who heads *The Crucible* company) and William Atherton as Suggs are notified that they have received this year's Theatre World Awards and that the Outer Critics Circle is citing Atherton and Lee Lawson for their work in *Suggs*.

. . .

After such a tumultuous season, it seems unthinkable that I have had to lay off the bulk of my small, devoted staff for the important summer months. These are the months full of hopes and preparation for the coming seasons. Our *Play Strindberg* has just opened in Phoenix, Arizona, and the major local reviewer has written that "you never see better acting on any stage than what Lincoln Center's Repertory Theater serves up." Good notices are satisfying, but you can't pay bills with press clippings. I wish there were some positive way to illustrate once and for all that companies differ from the buildings that house them. That even though we look like the Manse on the Hill, we are forced to operate like the town orphanage, without even the regular appropriation from the local welfare commission.

Europeans, like Bergman, are utterly amazed when they learn the conditions under which we have to produce. They're even more baffled when they see that we have the largest resident theater subscription audience in the nation and the highest rate of renewal, plus the biggest and most active student audience. Anyone who feels that film has supplanted the theater in our young people's lives should attend one of these student symposiums.

Although we've said it countless times, I feel it needs constant repetition because we are appreciably in the same financial position we were in seven years ago: we are *not* a municipal or state or federal institution. What we are is a privately funded, nonprofit permanent theater company— which will remain "permanent" only as long as we can eke out the barest sustaining funds through the help of the New York State Council on the Arts, other foundations, corporations, private donors and—if we can wait long enough—the National Endowment for the Arts. At one hundred percent capacity, we cannot possibly make it on box office receipts alone. And, although we are not a "public" institution, our long-term commitment is to responsible public service.

With a nod to Mr. Kerr, it's flattering to know that our staff can mount productions which tend to look as if they broke the bank at Monte Carlo when the production budget for our entire season is less than the cost of one Broadway musical which may open and close in an evening.

In spite of all this, the Repertory Theater has come of age. It has become an invaluable cultural asset to our town and our nation. We are virtually splitting the seams of the Beaumont with production activity. In the seven years since I assumed directorship of the Repertory Theater, we have had three board presidents, the *New York Times* has had four daily drama critics, a major New York repertory company has been allowed to fold[21] along with others across the nation, and the war in Southeast Asia keeps rolling along, sucking up funds that should be enriching rather than destroying life. The Repertory Theater of Lincoln Center has produced in this fleeting period twenty-two revivals and twenty-nine premieres. And it continues to be a battle of wit, wits and brinksmanship to make the weekly payroll.

If I've learned anything during these continuing years in Wonderland, it's that there's always room for one more at the Mad Hatter's tea party. What does it take to create and run New York's major classical theater on five dollars a day? A little madness, coupled with nerves of steel, a bullet-proof directing shirt, that PhD in brinksmanship and a steady and shining dream. What other way of life gives man the entire canvas of history and literature from which to gain his spiritual and emotional sustenance? And what other life but one in the theater gives us the opportunity to do our dreaming out loud? This vision is what we have to strive hardest to hang on to amidst the adversity.

A close associate of mine used to say that the streets of New York were lined with money that would one day roll into the anxious hands of my company. Well, we're heading into our eighth season and our hands are still outstretched and too often empty. But our hearts and minds are still relishing the prospect of a new season. There's enough richness in the annals of drama to fill the stages of the Beaumont for years to come, and enough creative talent to give pause to our frenetic urban lives for a millennium. The stage—those live moments on it which we call drama—touches that inexplicable part of all of us where spirit and intellect collide.

God willing (not to mention the fundraising efforts of our board of directors and the National Endowment) we'll see you in the fall—or in a dream before.

—*JI*

---

21. The APA (Association of Producing Artists), headed by artistic director Ellis Rabb, closed its doors in 1970, after a five-year merger with New York's Phoenix Theatre, a result of mounting debt and an increasingly rocky relationship between Rabb and the leadership of the Phoenix..

The Mark Taper Forum

FOUNDED 1967

Gordon Davidson

The problems encountered by the Repertory Theater of Lincoln Center, creating a theater from the moneyed top down, should have been lying in wait for the Mark Taper Forum in Los Angeles. Begun in a lavish, multi-arts complex, established by the wealthy (apparently for the wealthy) in a public space in the constructed "Center" of the downtown-less city, set up as a small second fiddle (742 seats) to the domineering Ahmanson Theatre (almost 2,100 seats), a commercial West Coast outpost of Broadway—the Taper appeared to be an accident waiting to happen. It was not. While Lincoln Center died many deaths, only to be born again under new leadership half a dozen times, the Taper found its leader from the beginning, and stuck with him for decades. Moreover, it bucked all odds by throwing its institutional weight behind the support and production of new plays, and so blazed a trail for many other large theaters to follow.

One of the secrets of the Taper's success was the homegrown, tested quality of the theater, even before it opened. In the late fifties, the Theatre Group opened at UCLA under the direction of John Houseman (previously head of the Negro Theatre Unit/Harlem Theatre Project and, with Orson Welles, the Mercury Theatre; see chapter 2), producing quality work on a low budget. Gordon Davidson, a stage manager Houseman had worked with at the American Shakespeare Festival in Stratford, Connecticut, came to the Theatre Group to assist Houseman on a remarkably successful production of *King Lear*, starring Morris Carnovsky. When Houseman left, Davidson took over the theater and then fielded the invitation to join the Center Theatre Group at L.A.'s impressive Dorothy Chandler Pavilion.

Once there, Davidson somehow managed to chart a course between the Scylla of wealthy patrons on one side and the Charybdis of operating a publicly owned building on the other. (The first play the Taper performed, John Whiting's erotically charged *The Devils*, brought the Los Angeles County Board of Supervisors down on its head, in what became a battle over censorship that threatened the nascent company's existence.) More surprisingly, Davidson's dedication to new plays, through the production (often under his direction) of such provocative contemporary work as Heinar Kipphardt's *In the Matter of J. Robert Oppenheimer* and Father Daniel Berrigan's

SOURCE: "Reflections on Beginnings," by Gordon Davidson, was originally published in *Theatre 1*, 1968.

The Trial of the Catonsville Nine, and the success of a Monday night series called "New Theatre for Now" led by director Edward Parone, brought the theater both national attention and local standing. The Taper was the only rival to the Guthrie Theater of Minneapolis's instant institutional might. But the L.A. theater staked out an opposite position: instead of the Guthrie's classicism, the Taper gambled with the currency of the contemporary. In place of a company of actors, the Taper cast Hollywood players, eager for stage time in a world of TV and film. In lieu of stories from the past, the Taper opted for the explosive events of now. Both theaters, like Lincoln Center, the third leg of full-blown institutionalism in the American nonprofit theater, discovered early on the tensions between the expectations of the marble façade and the uncertainties and urgencies of the art.

In the words of Joseph Wesley Zeigler, "[These theaters] had been willed into being by community leaders rather than being forged by individual artists; while this meant that they were more readily supported financially, it also meant that for them an individual identity was more elusive. They were official, formal, institutional—and much less personal."

—TL

Reflections on Beginnings

The façade is marble, the structure institutional and the colonnades and fountains pristinely impersonal. The furnishings are rather plush. And the ticket prices, while not too high, are certainly not geared for low-income audiences. From the moment one sets foot on the granite steps of the Los Angeles Music Center, the impressively regal setting for the three theaters shouts out to the theatergoer that he is moving in the world of the Establishment—that he has joined forces with and embraces it with every step he takes toward the glass doors of this small circular building. But the Mark Taper Forum has its very foundations in a special and exciting physical environment; its intimate open stage embraced on three sides by an audience of no more than 750. And once inside this remarkably warm theater, the hardy theatergoer must be prepared to open his senses to an interaction between the event on the stage and his idea of community as part of an audience. A dialogue is demanded between audience and actor, whether it be through the utilization of film and television projection or the simple platform for communication of a playwright's ideas, unencumbered by gadgets and machinery. Ideas and passions are being explored and exposed and this inevitably rocks the security of the Establishment foundation upon which this theater rests.

This small theater's larger environment is that of a handsome cultural center with all its attractive advantages and its inevitable institutional inhibitions. The fact that three playhouses (additionally a 2,100-seat proscenium theater and a 3,200-seat concert hall and opera house) exist in one setting—that audiences can assemble to hear and witness programs of opera, symphony, dance and drama—promotes significant focus of attention in the battle for the individual's leisure time and entertainment dollar.

Buildings by themselves can provide no answer to an artistic director's problems and challenges: often they create more obstacles than they solve, for in many instances the containing cart has come before the creative horse. The theater building represents a path by which a journey can begin. It is only a tool; not the creative end itself.

It is my belief, however, that physical structures (environment) help shape the personality, in this case, of the theater, and have a great influence on both participants—actor and audience. The Globe Theatre did not inspire Shakespeare—but the Elizabethan audience attending a performance of *Hamlet* or *Twelfth Night* was at one with both the material and the form of presentation. The religious experience of the Greeks assembling in the Theater of Dionysus to watch the sun actually rise at the moment it was required in *Agamemnon* is one of the earliest examples of society, theater and artist being of one mind. Perhaps such unity is no longer possible in our fragmented, Mod world. Perhaps the closest we can come to this sense of being at one with our lives and the reflection of our lives through art is a "be-in" or a "freak-out." I have hopes to the contrary.

Creating an audience is the first ingredient toward such a new and vital theater life, and this already has been handsomely met in Los Angeles. There is indeed an audience hungry for good, provocative entertainment (our subscription audience numbers close to thirty thousand) and with this capability of filling this new theater, half the battle has been at least joined, if not won.

The key factor in this audience, however, is not its size but its sense of continuity (thirty to fifty productions over eight years with the Theater Group at UCLA) which has helped create—or re-create—theatergoers as differentiated from playgoers or "star"-gazers. This known profile permits Center Theatre Group, now part of the Los Angeles Music Center, to build upon a common theatergoing experience as it strikes off in new experimental directions.

One of the dangers of a subscription audience—especially as it exists in a cultural center—is the danger of middle-class homogeneity. We have taken steps to encourage students, culturally disadvantaged minority groups, city and county employees and so forth to attend previews and regular performances at special prices. The seven preview performances for each production are now sold out.

Our sense of continuity can be furthered by the development of an acting ensemble. By the end of our third year, I hope to have worked with enough talented and interested actors who will, all conditions being favorable, form the nucleus of such a company. The key to this ensemble will be the development of the most exciting young actors we can find. We've already begun this through the use of journeymen actors, a training program tied in with the universities in the community, and special projects utilizing a company concept, such as our new playwrights program. I will always want to make it possible for the serious mature actor to work at the Mark Taper Forum, but long-range commitments are difficult to obtain. The seduction of the actor by movie and television offers and the livelihood that is peculiar to Hollywood is heartbreaking. It will be a long time before actors, agents and movie producers regard the theater not as diversion but as a necessary creative partner in the growth of artists. The enthusiasm and the sense of dedication of most of the actors who worked for us in the last two seasons give one the courage to move ahead.

I feel we've only begun to explore the possibilities of the Mark Taper Forum from the point of view of the use of the theater, the aesthetics of a thrust stage and the kind of acting, writing and directing that can happen in that theater. The programming of the first two seasons had to do with just such an exploration. The first season of four plays thematically explored "man's quest for values." Through affirmation and denial our audience shared an experience with John Whiting's *The Devils* and Dürrenmatt's *The Marriage of Mr. Mississippi* and two world premieres, *The Sorrows of Frederick* by Romulus Linney and *Who's Happy Now?* by Oliver Hailey. In this second season we are exploring the "faces of truth" through the farce of Molière's *The Miser*, the factual presentation of ideas and issues in the American premiere of *In the Matter of J. Robert Oppenheimer* by Heinar Kipphardt and the poet's fantasy of Tennessee Williams's *Camino Real*.

I think we've begun to find actors who can create both a sense of intimate reality as well as considerable style, but we haven't integrated this concept enough in our work. One goal is to try to solve the problem of continued growth and exploration in a play and in actors once a production opens to public performance, and then to extend that growth from play to play. While we're exploring these areas our audiences are being asked to open themselves up to a new kind of adventure which, while not always totally satisfying, encourages the joy of discovery.

Additionally, the reality, pressures and responsibilities of living and working in a publicly owned facility (Los Angeles County) are enormous. Political sensitivity to the righteous wrath of taxpayer pressure is immediate and disconcerting, but freedom of artistic expression is essential to any creative endeavor and ultimately the answer to our theater's work lies in the community's realization that we cannot be all things to all people. What we can and hope to be is a projection of and reflection of the special society in which we function.

I firmly believe that the thrust and force of our operation in the Mark Taper Forum is in the area of new work—not just because it happens to excite and stimulate our senses, but because I have a tremendous sense of obligation to the writing talent in this country to provide them with a responsible and high professional atmosphere in which they can create. It's a large responsibility but inescapable. We have not even begun to scratch the surface, in our community or in the nation. Not every play, especially not every good play we get, can be produced, but in some manner—informal reading, staged reading, modest productions—more plays must and will get done in the mornings, afternoons or evenings throughout the year. Our "New Theatre for Now" program of Monday night performances has met with both critical acclaim and sellout performances and, in a little over one year of operation, Center Theatre Group has presented the work of twenty-six playwrights.

I have always believed theater to be a total art form wherein every element must be in place and all of it related somehow to life. Once created, this type of total theater must then find its own special identity, its own statement and sense of timeliness. The Forum provides a unique and challenging opportunity to create just such a theater. Its very name—Forum—suggests a sharing of ideas, a spirited dialogue existing between audience and artist. Out of this, both the artist and the audience can experience provocative thought, perception and—ultimately—the excitement of mutual expression.

—*GD*

The Theatre of the Living Arts

FOUNDED 1967

André Gregory

> The past six months have not been happy ones for the regional theater. Resignations, firings and administrative turmoil have shaken theaters in Philadelphia, Pittsburgh, New Haven, Providence and Baltimore; Herbert Blau has left Lincoln Center. The artistic excellence and excitement we hoped for in the regional theater have generally not materialized; the ensemble companies we dreamed of have not come into being; the financial security of steady patronage has not developed; subscription audiences have proven to be mixed blessings. André Gregory, the founder and recently fired artistic director of the Theatre of the Living Arts in Philadelphia, writes of his experience. I expect his words will be the beginning of a long and difficult public colloquy.
>
> —*Richard Schechner, editor,* TDR: The Drama Review, 1967

Richard Schechner's cautionary report—or, should I say, collective eulogy—appeared in the summer of 1967, as an introduction to André Gregory's account of his departure from the Theatre of the Living Arts. TLA had begun in 1964 as the pet project of two local women with community and amateur producing experience, Jean Goldman and Celia Silverman, who hoped to bring Off Broadway to the City of Brotherly Love. Their organization, the Philadelphia Council for the Performing Arts, rallied volunteers and raised money to renovate an out-of-business movie house that would open, they hoped, with a production of Brecht's *Galileo*, directed by Elia Kazan or Harold Clurman. When neither of those legends was available, the nascent theater company engaged Gregory, a man who came as close to an enfant terrible as the early regional theater would know.[22]

Gregory had graduated from Harvard, trained with the Actors Studio, spent a year observing Brecht's Berliner Ensemble under the direction of Brecht's widow, Helene Weigel, and gone out to Seattle

---

Source: Untitled essay by André Gregory, originally published in *Tulane Drama Review*, Summer 1967.

22. Numerous sources, including contemporary newspaper articles, corroborate the story of TLA's founding as I tell it above. In a 2004 interview, however, Gregory recounted the story of TLA's founding differently. According to Gregory, he'd set out to found his own theater. Following the advice of Alan Schneider, the early regional theater's leading director, he identified Philadelphia as an interesting city with no theater. "I got a letter of introduction to an interior designer in Philadelphia and asked if he could help me create it. [. . .] Over two years I talked at, I think, 432 dinners, luncheons, breakfasts, cocktail parties. Out of that, literally one-to-one, I got ten thousand subscribers and I started my theater."

as Stuart Vaughan's associate artistic director at the fledgling Seattle Repertory Theatre. Time at the Rep ended badly and swiftly for both men—Gregory first—as board prerogatives did battle with artistic imperatives. Armed with Antonin Artaud's *The Theatre and Its Double*, revolutionary zeal and, as he would tell me forty years later, no small amount of anger and arrogance, Gregory took on the nouveau riche of Philadelphia. He chose and staged, in the new theater built on the edge of a black ghetto, a pair of the most provocative and intentionally shocking seasons found anywhere outside of New York City in the early days of the regional theater movement.

By all accounts Gregory was also one of the great directing talents of his generation, an assessment borne out by his future—leading New York City's experimental Manhattan Project and mounting landmark productions of *Uncle Vanya* and the works of Wallace Shawn. (His influence on film has been significant as well, notably through his and Shawn's groundbreaking indie, *My Dinner with André*.) "In Gregory the board of the Theatre of the Living Arts had chosen one of the few potentially major talents to be involved in the creation of a sapling theater," Joseph Zeigler wrote five years after Gregory's firing. (Resignation? Reports conflict.) "His talent was too large and too vaulting to be absorbed and served by a theater just born and not ready to support his ambitions."

Clearly Gregory was pushing toward some kind of excitement or provocation he didn't see around him. As he told a *Tulane Drama Review* conference in the mid-sixties: "I'm scared that the regional theater, by the time it is mature, will have bored the shit out of millions of people all over the country."[23]

—TL

––––––––

There's a sick, sad joke going around the country: regional theater directors are pouring into New York looking for a little security on Broadway. I'm writing this in Los Angeles, three thousand miles from my theater; and I'm feeling sorry for myself. I feel sorry for myself because after starting the Theatre of the Living Arts in a Philadelphia slum which the burghers assured me no self-respecting Philadelphian (white, not black) would enter, after working in that theater for three years, after seeing our subscription audience climb to eight thousand, after putting six thousand dollars of my own salary back into productions (for what I considered artistic necessities),

23. A much mellower Gregory wants today's readers to know that he'd write about these events quite differently now. He says, "Given the state of the New York theater these days, I'm not sure I'd feel the same way today. But, as I've not seen any recent regional theater (as I almost never go to the theater), I'm not in any position to comment."

after keeping a basic company together for three years, after presenting fifteen productions of which thirteen were box office successes and seven artistic successes, after the theater gained national recognition and a large grant from the National Endowment—after all that, my board of directors put the gun to my head and fired.

And I'm furious. Howard Taubman, with the best intentions I'm sure, wrote that perhaps it would have been better for me to wait before producing plays like Rochelle Owens's *Beclch* (a new American play which raised a furor in Philadelphia). Wait until the board was ready, until the community was ready.

Well, listen, Mr. Taubman, and listen, boards across the country: the theater is about life and the waters outside the theater are troubled. We're dropping bombs on children in Vietnam. But Philadelphia isn't ready for a play with the theme of violence. Is Philadelphia ready for the violence in its own streets? Should we wait for violence to subside, if it will, and do nothing meanwhile? Wait to do the new plays until the writers have become so discouraged from not having their plays done that they are no longer playwrights? If we wait until communities are "ready," the regional theater will disintegrate; it is already so badly compromised that most theaters have lost their integrity and their contact with the world around them.

The real causes of my dismissal were artistic policy, money and communication problems, in that order. The board and I were both working to create a theater in Philadelphia. The difficulty was that we were trying to create two different kinds of theater.

Two years ago I directed *Endgame*. It was one of our finest productions. When it was revived at Yale this year it was a tremendous success both at the box office and critically. But when it first played in Philadelphia the critics disliked it and the Main Line hated it; sixty percent of our subscription audience walked out each night. Last year I directed [Jean Anouilh's] *Poor Bitos*. In one scene a naked breast was exposed. The board president was nervous, but sanctioned the scene; the police came every night. The audience loved the production and the police loved the breast. This year, after consulting with the board president, who disliked the play but liked my production ideas, I optioned *Beclch*, our first new full-length American play. And the shit hit the fan.

The play is a violent, sexual, political piece set in Africa. The Main Line conservatives were up in arms. Some moved to have the production stopped. I was attacked at a board meeting for wanting "to make the theater into a theater of sex and violence," as one who wanted to "fill the theater with homosexuals, drug addicts and college students." The conservatives said that I wasn't doing plays which represented the tastes of the community. I pointed out, perhaps undiplomatically, that there wasn't a Negro on the board (in a city with six hundred thousand Negroes), that the Main Line couldn't possibly represent the community. They went out and got a Negro for the board.

The furor over *Beclch* grew. Contractually the board had the right to veto any play but could not veto one new American play of my choice each season. However, since there was such a furor, I decided to hold a meeting with the board to discuss *Beclch*. I spoke for two hours and thought the meeting was a success. I was wrong. I hadn't read the signals correctly.

On the opening night of *Beclch* two leading members of the board were appalled. Several days later a board member with a large, local foundation in his pocket resigned. (A year ago, one of the most influential board members, revolted by Saul Bellow's *The Last Analysis*, walked out of the show and reneged on a twenty-thousand-dollar pledge. This year he resigned from the board because of *Beclch*.) A Play Reading Committee was reactivated by the board for next season.

The local reviews for *Beclch* were bad and the box office was dead. But then reviews from New Jersey, New Haven, Wilmington and New York began to turn the tide. The audience began to build. In the fifth week of the run, *Beclch* did nearly as well as *Room Service*, our most popular play. The capper was the *Time* review, a rave. Ten days after receiving this good-housekeeping seal of approval, I was fired.

What does all this mean? Artistic directors and boards of directors have to get along. An artistic director has to be diplomatic. It was no accident that *Beclch* was squeezed in between *Room Service* and *The Time of Your Life*. At the same time, artistic directors must have the right to touch the nerve of their communities, to deal with social and political issues, to go all the way with production styles. Boards of directors have to be reorganized. They can no longer be Main Liners only; the poor, the intellectuals, the politicians, the artists, the students should also be on the boards. Repertories should be developed that stretch tastes, that span many interests in the community.

Ideally, Philadelphia should have five permanent theaters, each one with a specific point of view relating to a specific audience supported by a board which strongly underwrites that point of view. But this is clearly impossible today. Therefore, there must be a lot of give-and-take. *The Time of Your Life* for one part of the audience; *Beclch* for another. Too often our regional theaters are dominated by the taste of the board and this taste, though it represents money and a certain social milieu, is in no way representative of the *entire* community. Most of the community stays away from the theater simply because it does not like what is done there.

A permanent, professional theater is the only place where good artistic work is possible. And no permanent theater is without its troubles. But all of us—artists, boards, foundations—must stop jumping blindly at the bait. We must reexamine the structure and goals of the regional theater. We must wonder whether subscription audiences maintain or strangle a theater. What does each of us want and what is the best way for each to get it? There must be great patience and great logic if the regional theater is to survive. And if it does not survive, and there are no more permanent theaters, there will be no theater at all.

> CLOV: Do you believe in the life to come?
> HAMM: Mine was always that.[24]

—*AG*

---

24. *Endgame*, by Samuel Beckett.

Chapter 6

Toward a Political Theater

You must enter the theater through the world.

—*Julian Beck*

The Living Theatre

FOUNDED 1947

Judith Malina

> The trouble with most revolutionary thought is the lack of an alternative to the existing situation. Action is limited to dissent, and soon one feels the circular hopelessness of simply wishing against. Missing is the imagination to dream—to enter that area where dismay has not canceled out the alternatives. [. . .] The Becks demonstrate in their work and their activism that there are almost no boundaries, that no one need stay within the limitations which seem to be fixed. They represent a repudiation of the captive way of life.[1]
>
> —*Joseph Chaikin*

"In anger we began," writes Julian Beck of the Living Theatre in one of the meditations below. "All the sane theater of that time was beneath the dignity of childbearing women and vigorous men." But if the history of the Living Theatre shows anything, it shows a theater founded in love—love of theater, love of peace, the love of a woman and man for each other and for something like the transformative dream of our ideal humanity.

Was there ever a more passionate American theater, a more extreme experiment than the Living Theatre? And yet here it is, sixty years later, not only "the mother of them all," as theater scholar Margaret Croyden dubbed it, but the longest lived of the experimental and political theaters to which it gave birth. "However simplistic their ideas and however muddled their thinking," wrote Martin Gottfried in 1967, "they have delved more deeply into the idea of pure theater than anybody working in their own country. [. . .] They are basically and irrevocably American and they know it. [. . .] They belong in

SOURCE: Judith Malina's diaries, 1951, later published as *The Diaries of Judith Malina: 1947–1957*, by Judith Malina, 1984.

1. *Breakout! In Search of New Theatrical Environments*, by James Schevill, the Swallow Press, Inc., Chicago, 1973.

America. It is terribly like our country to reject its most original (and so most valuable) artists."

For most, the lasting images of *Le Living*, as it was christened by the French during its years of exile from the U.S. (1964–68), come from the sixties: A ragtag, revolutionary commune wanders Europe after its leaders, Beck and his wife, Judith Malina, are released from prison, where they've been locked up (Beck for six months, Malina for three) after nonpayment of taxes on their loft theater. They stage massive experimental spectacles—*Frankenstein*, *Paradise Now!* They call for the overthrow of the "Capitalist-Bureaucratic-Military-Authoritarian Police Complex" in theatricalized street protests. They are hippies, anarcho-pacifists, political-psychotherapeutic shock troops, dividing their audiences into fierce camps of despisers and defenders. They seek the overthrow of capitalism, the eradication of the state and abolition of money. They live, as Croyden points out, by Artaud's credo, "Between life and theater there will be no distinct division, but instead a continuity."[2]

These powerful images have obscured the very different beginnings of the Living Theatre: a young couple in the late forties, drunk on love for the theater (Malina more so than Beck, who was also passionate about his painting), dissatisfied with most of what they saw during years of obsessive theatergoing, drawn to the European and American avant-garde in painting, poetry, dance and music: "Joyce and Pound, Breton, [García] Lorca, Proust, Patchen, Goodman, Cummings, Stein, Rilke, Cocteau, *und so weiter*," as Beck writes. They had already embraced pacifism and, theoretically, anarchism, but they couldn't imagine what the future would hold for them. For the time, they were devoted to words, to poetry, to finding a theater that could catch up with the experiments in other arts, the painting of Pollock and de Kooning, the music and dance of their young friends John Cage and Merce Cunningham.

What follows are several entries from various periods in Beck and Malina's early writings—Malina's diaries in the late forties and early fifties, and Beck's meditations from successive years at the start of the sixties. They had met in 1943 when he was eighteen and she seventeen, and they'd gotten married in 1948. Both were New York Jews, Malina the daughter of a rabbi and Beck from a family of teachers. Their poetic dreams are evident in these confessional entries, as is the increased radicalism of their shared vision.

—TL

---

2. This is certainly the Living Theatre that I was introduced to when, in 1975, my first college theater professor, Sandy Moffett at Grinnell College, handed me a copy of Pierre Biner's *The Living Theatre* (Horizon Press, New York, 1972) and, thereby, blew my mind. It was this book, along with a few others, including Robert Pasolli's *A Book on the Open Theater* (Bobbs-Merrill Company, New Yok, 1970), that began my love of reading about theater companies and, thirty-five years later, led to this collection.

September 9, 1951

We work to capacity on the theater.

Death or glory.

Now we move ahead. On the Living Theatre letterhead, all the news is clearly printed in gray ink.

Dr. Faustus lights the lights in darkness and luminosity. The task, like the text: too clear and yet too obscure.

[. . .]

September 17, 1951

Work. Each day now a workday.

[. . .] In the subway, Julian and I sit across from a thin, ascetic man dressed like a worker, clothes neat, but soiled, as from a hard day's work.

And monstrous, hideous feet. I fantasize the taking of a vow, perhaps twenty-five years ago, not to wash his feet or remove the shoes that he was then wearing. The filth-coated feet are grown thick with sores, swollen, and hoof-like. The decaying shoes have merged with the skin which emits a gruesome, sickly odor. We did not leave the train. We felt bound not to.

[. . .]

September 25, 1951

A night at John Cage's.

His home is a bare white room, only the black piano gleaming amid the ceiling-high plants that breathe a chlorophyll cleanliness into the air. On the floor, there is matting, a large marble slab as table, ashtrays, candles and long strips of foam rubber against two walls for seating.

Both Merce [Cunningham] and John have an unassuming way of living more in present time than we. Merce's renowned grace extends even to his speech.

Above all, an affectionate attachment to their creative powers, neither careless nor fanatic.

When art becomes pleasure it will find its function.

Outside John's windows, the East River and a fantasy of changing lights, glowing and flowing.

It's effortless—like Cage when he smiles and his eyes narrow to nothing and laughter crinkles his plain features to a look that the beholder wants to emulate.

His is explaining his newest work to a music writer named [Nicolas] Slonimsky and the writer's fifteen-year-old daughter, Electra. The new piece is based on chance and on a Chinese "book of chance" which explains the exactness and mystery of the random. Can mystery be explained or only discussed?

Each note is determined by the flip of a coin—pitch, duration and intensity are tossed for. The notation represents a spatial relationship to duration. That is, time and the millimeters of music paper have equivalent value.

Interesting and intricate. It would be boring if there were no faith in mystery. Slonimsky asks, "What if you have bad luck?"

"There is no such thing as bad luck," says John.

John plays a small piece. "Valentine of the Seasons." This is the first time I have heard the famed fixed piano: melody in rich unexpected tones, celestial in quality. I am tremendously impressed with Cage's work. And with his whole esprit.

There is a Goshen in this Egyptian darkness in which we live, and coming close to it, we are filled with premonitions of promise.

Years back, walking in a daze of tears for some forgotten sorrow after a pointless revel in Val and Julian's room, I thought over and over in a tragic strain, "No, this is not it," as though detoured on some odyssey. Now I have a distant view, as of a place not yet visited with which I am already familiar by picture postcard.

Merce talks about their use of our theater for concerts and dance recitals.

John proposes a concert for a piano piece by Satie called "Vexations." The piece consists of 840 successive renditions of a minute-long composition. There are 840 minutes in fourteen hours.

If John had the theater all day, from ten in the morning through ten-thirty at night, the hour critics must leave . . .

We enjoy talking about the ramifications of this idea.

A round ticket like a clock is printed. Audiences come and go all day long. The piece is played over and over. Admission is not charged but the entrance time is punched and the minutes counted at the exit. And the longer one stays the less one pays. That is: one pays according to how much one can tolerate, not for the space one takes up. For ten minutes, $14.40; for twenty minutes, $7.20; for half an hour, $3.60; down to five cents for twelve hours.

And a printed timetable of performing artists, for John can get all sorts of artists to play, from painters to renowned pianists. It might read:

A.M.

9:18–9:23	John Cage
9:23–9:28	William Masselos
9:28–9:33	Richard Lippold
9:33–9:38	Richard Stryker
9:38–9:43	David Tudor

and in this way use dozens of people.

The score is mimeographed on 840 sheets of paper, each discarded after playing.

During the concert, talk, selling books, sandwiches, seat-hopping, etc. *Musique d'ameublement*, or furniture music.

We also talk of a David Tudor concert.

Merce is reading *Beyond the Mountains*, and would like to do the choreography, but his schedule is difficult.

John says he'd like to do a score for us.

John and Merce advise us not to use newspaper advertisements, but to concentrate on mailing lists. And to use sandwich men on stilts, or men with drums.

They make us more alive.

On the river the lights move.

September 28, 1951

Julian and I return like pilgrims to the Chinese Theater under the Manhattan Bridge only to be told, "Disbanded forever. Nevermore in New York."

We solace ourselves with the ballet, but the dancers' gestures seem absurd; even Youskevitch and Alonso too forced.

Cocteau's *Le jeune homme et la mort*, about the goddess, the desirable woman who crushes and kills her lover—what Graves calls the "eternal" theme.

October 1, 1951

At Merce Cunningham's home we pick up his mailing list.

Sudie Bond, whom we met at Bonnie Bird's when [Lou Harrison's *Marriage at the*] *Eiffel Tower* was performed, wants to work with us. She has an extraordinary face.

Yesterday, Gershon Legman read his pneumatic translation of *Ubu Roi* to us.

October 3, 1951

In synagogue, I think during the silences which I no longer fill with prayer.

It is necessary to be detached, stoic, distant. The problem is how to be detached, and still do what is necessary. To act with detachment, when detachment contradicts "to act." Karma yoga says: "Action without fruits."

October 5, 1951

The Cherry Lane is charged with unnameable energies. I walk through webs of tensions and networks of danger.

Memory and desire catch me across the entrance to Commerce Street, permeated with the recollections of many loves.

October 8, 1951

Sometimes I'm frightened by the amount of work involved. No one can know how much we do in one hour, or how Julian and I plan our minutes.

Mother's illness has gone on too long for her to bear it uncomplainingly. She can't walk easily and grows sad at her disability. She'll come to live with us after Yom Kippur.

October 10, 1951

Many problems. We shall have to raise six months' rent for the theater. And pay for license fees, violations, water.

Financial woes. Julian on edge.

Kenneth Rexroth sends several letters objecting to our doing all four plays of [his] *Beyond the Mountains* in a single evening.

8/X/51

Dear People—

I think you are very mistaken in attempting the four plays at once. Such an idea never occurred to me. I think the audience would be worn out halfway through—as well as the actors. The more I think of it the less inclined I am to consent to such a program. There is no use in throwing away the effectiveness of the plays . . . The dances, though not lengthy, do take up enough time to, for instance, fill up an evening with *Hermaios* and *Berenike*. The tempo should be leisurely—even slow—to get across the frozen, hypnotized effect of the people in *Beyond the Mountains*. The whole point is that, during the actual moments of the birth of Christ, they are living through the action of the *Oresteia* like sleepwalkers . . .

[The music] must be kept extremely simple—diatonic—"white"—like Satie's *Gymnopédie*—and with a minimum of "effects." It is very difficult to get a composer to understand just how stark and hieratic it must be . . .

I got an impressive letter from your musician. If he writes music as well as he writes about it, he should certainly do . . .

Once again—put out of your minds the scheme of doing the plays all at once, straight through. I really know quite a bit about the theater and I assure you you will just be throwing them away. Ask anyone with practical experience—radio—burlesque—musical comedy, or vaudeville—or the movies—NOT some highbrows—and you will get the same answer . . .

Faithfully,
Kenneth Rexroth

He has no idea of how ambitious we are. Now we have to convince him of the plausibility of doing the full program.

Cage, Cunningham and Johnny Myers[3] are against our doing *Beyond the Mountains*. They abhor the intensity of its emotions.

Isn't it a sign of an overdeveloped culture, to search for a more and more bloodless stylization as in the cool noh, or the unnatural attitudes of late Hellenistic sculpture?

John McGrew[4] said that a symptom of a decadent period is always a futile attempt at pastoralism.

October 18, 1951

Casting. Every ten minutes a new face. Yet an extraordinary personality would not be lost among them.

Rexroth writes, in answer to Julian's letter saying that Goethe, too, wrote some long plays:

X/15/1951

Dear Judith and Julian—

Goethe was wrong. Go ahead *BTM en gros* if you want—but I think you're ill advised. As to commercial vs. highbrow theater, there is more theatrical sense in one old carnival or burlesque man—or in somebody like Jolson or W. C. Fields—than in all the O'Neills and Tollers laid end to end. You cut the plays as you see fit. This can only be done in rehearsal anyway. That is where you can tell if the lines will cross the footlights—beauty or dramatic profundity is worthless if the actor can't manage it or the audience can't follow it. I doubt if masks are actually desirable. Actors always mismanage them and actresses naturally hate them. They do permit dancers to stand in—also they are hard to hear through. As for the dancers—no [Mary] Wigman, [Martha] Graham or Pearl Primus, please! What I envisage is an extremely slow but dynamic movement—even more normal than a regular pas de deux and very hieratic—especially in the *Phaedra* and *Iphigenia*. There are books of Hindu and Buddhist mudras and of Tibetan Buddhas and Bodhisattvas in all the regular mudras which would give the dancer a hint of what I mean. And of course the two basic positions are those of the Buddhas and their Shaktis in Tibetan sculpture and painting—one of which represents sexual intercourse sitting, the other standing. You can see these things in any book on Tibetan Art. BUT—the end product should *not* look

---

3. John Bernard Myers, art dealer and writer, known for promoting other New York artists and poets.

4. American painter and musician best known for his animation work under Chuck Jones at Warner Brothers.

oriental. The Huns' dance at the end of the book is a typical Chinese military dance of the kind given in the plays based on the three kingdoms. If you ask at the local Chinese movie they can tell you when they are going to give such a movie. They're common enough.

Faithfully,
Kenneth Rexroth

October 20, 1951

Four designers.

Each of them has made a peculiar contribution. Each saw us on the basis of the letter we sent.

Donald Oenslager in his office in the tower of the Times Building is a portrait of security, framed behind his large desk by an enormous screen like a backdrop. He reminisces about the Provincetown [Players] and Robert Edmond Jones and "the days when we were all dedicated."

The dedication has been lost in the old rarified air of our age of despair.

He scrutinizes Julian's designs and approves of them. He warns us about actors.

Do I delude myself that Oenslager seems envious of us? Not that he isn't proud and grandiose, but he seems to be struggling with a fond memory that threatens his complacency. For he has everything except what we have: a project to be committed to.

He says he will be on the advisory committee, that he would like to do real work for us.

"We were all dedicated then."

As if to say: "It is your turn now."

. . .

Horace Armistead, in his workmanlike studio on University Place, conveys friendliness without smiling often. He's a craftsman interested in construction and the details of execution. We weren't aware when we went to him that he's production manager for the Metropolitan Opera.

On an easel, a soft-hued oil painting for Anthony Tudor's *Lilac Garden*.

How do these people have the time for it? And the time to see us? He manages all the Metropolitan's productions and designs independently, and yet shows none of the wear we show. The energy seems to flow effortlessly from those who have some measure of success.

Does the success bring about the calmness, or does the calm bring about the success?

Armistead, too, will be a sponsor of the theater. He gives us the addresses of various theatrical suppliers.

. . .

Aline Bernstein. In a large, ill-furnished apartment on Park Avenue, the beautiful elderly lady lies in a small sunny bedroom. She is able to smile through her many troubles. In one hand a hearing aid stretched toward us, and the other went frequently to her face to shield the eye which is temporarily sightless from a hemorrhage.

Her backlog of remembrances: the Civic Repertory where she designed for Eva Le Gallienne; the Neighborhood Playhouse and the events there of which Thomas Wolfe wrote so innocently when he loved this lady.

She praises Julian's work.

She is sad, she says, to be "indisposed and out of things," but chats about the book she is writing and the sets she's designing and the rehearsals she's been attending. Next to her bed is a Dictaphone (to which she said "excuse me" when we entered). This work she considers "not working."

Framed above her bed are her famous designs for *The Little Clay Cart* and, in a rack, designs for a book of costumes which she complains no one will publish.

What is most striking is the energy and the strength of this woman, ill and handicapped and yet so capable.

She agrees to be a sponsor. She gives us warnings and advice:

"Beware of light on the stage; it dims the actors, makes the text fade out into silhouette.

"I always underdesign. I make elaborate notes. I describe the whole room, all the details, but I always underdesign."

Aline Bernstein says that she knows no one who works as hard on a play as she does.

. . .

Frederick Kiesler is a small man whose expansive spirit towers like some fire-bearing Prometheus. His is a German rudeness-kindness. He ushers us in and growls, "Well, what is going on here? What is this all about?"

Immediately his eyes have discerned everything about us. All our secrets are revealed, filed, evaluated.

He calls in an assistant, a beautiful Chinese girl who obviously adores her teacher. And he deserves to be adored. There is something of Piscator[5] in what he says, and in his self-esteem.

---

5. Erwin Piscator, a German director and proponent, with Bertolt Brecht, of the Epic Theatre, had been Malina's teacher at the New School in New York, drawing connections between politics and theater that would mark her work for decades.

He speaks often of the beauty of women.

Listens with many interruptions to our story.

"This is very fine, but I have only this to tell you: You work very hard. You work forty-eight hours a day. Very good. Very fine. But if you are not geniuses, this does not mean a gott-damned thing. You have to be a *génie*. In this is everything. If you are geniuses, I guarantee you that you make a success. And if you are not, all this work is nothing for."

We were forced to choose the alternative of being geniuses—the tactic of a great teacher.

He leans heavily upon the mise-en-scène; considers the key to production what Johnny Myers calls obligation to the text.

Kiesler gives us ample space to boast, which is a great pleasure. He allows himself that prerogative also.

He recommends a play called *The Nineteenth Hole of Europe* by Cyril Connolly,[6] a science-fiction fantasy set in a marsh fog that covers postwar Europe. With a eureka expression, he describes the scene: "The audience is given mimeographed pages of pictures of buildings—Westminster Abbey, the Cologne cathedral, all the landmark buildings of Europe—and the audience has, each of them, a candle and they can turn to whichever page they please, and this could be everywhere.

"On the stage, the actors sit on stools like my draftsmen, in very harsh light without costumes.

"How inspiring for the actors to look out and see all those candles in the audience."

It sounds like one of those ideas Piscator brought up in theater research classes, delivered with vigor and the pleasure of invention.

He places our success into the hands of chance, the chance that we have the *génie*. He understands us better than the other designers.

Kiesler knows how much depends on "the muse. She is a hard lady to please."

To the lady hard to please, then.

Kiesler is a sponsor of the Living Theatre.

On the wall, a painting in grays, browns, black and dull lavender of a large chrysanthemum. Kiesler proposes a riddle:

"If you know who is the painter of that you will be a success."

Julian recognizes the Mondrian.

Let us hope it is prophetic.

---

6. Malina may have this wrong; this play was probably written by Vivian Connell.

October 21, 1951

Casting. Faustus proves a problematical man to cast.

[...]

We do, we will, we must.

October 22, 1951

Dr. Faustus casting. Marguerite Ida and Helena Annabel: searching for someone who can convey Gertrude Stein's womanly view of this male legend: a Gretchen who does not redeem Faust, but dies in her own innocence.

Work on the directing book. Much freedom within the text. No stage directions in Stein.

Various printers: Trubow's little broken-down press for our tickets and stationery. And a fancy printer, who does work for Kenneth Patchen and other touchy jobs, for our announcements.

In search of a choreographer for *Beyond the Mountains* we call Tei Ko, the Japanese woman who danced the noh dances at the Poet's Theater. Her little boy is named after Prince Genji, spelled variantly so as to mean Way of Peace; he was born at the signing of the peace between Japan and the United States.

Way of Peace was dressed as a most unpacific cowboy: toting two cap-guns, which he exploded incessantly, causing his mother much distress.

Tei Ko is surely the right person to choreograph *Beyond the Mountains*.

October 21, 1951

We have seen at least 350 actors. Not a moment's quiet. We eat in their presence.

Still no Doctor Faustus. No Marguerite Ida.

October 25, 1951

How a landscape can blacken, all light eclipse, all sun hopes vanish. How swiftly what was a garden is wilderness.

The pressures of the theater sustain me; my obligations steady me.

October 27, 1951

The play is cast: We find Donald Marye, who has just that look of soft Faustian wisdom that can allure Marguerite, and a cynical depth that is beyond his own comprehension.

Kathe Snyder, a poetic girl from the Workshop, is Marguerite.

Ace King for Mephisto—how fitting that the spirit of evil is played by a playing card, as if to say, "It's all a game."

Remy Charlip, back from Black Mountain, will play, will dance, will choreograph the Viper's role. No one else could bring it so much.

October 30, 1951

Luncheon with Eric Bentley. The hard critic intimidates me more than the accomplished artist.

Bentley seems not to be forming opinions, but we know that he is constantly judging.

One would think him less brilliant than he is, as he looks away in apparent disinterest, and then an astute observation reminds one that he is acutely present.

Later he warms and recommends several plays. Wishes to direct a play for the Living Theatre if he likes the early work.

Rehearsals: I feel this play under me. I can take its pulse act by act, scene by scene. I can move it, hasten it, slow it. I may do a good job on it.

The cast believes in the play and the work of the theater. Donald Marye's an extraordinary actor.

Equity makes things difficult for us. Three of our actors are union members. Equity will try to force these people to leave the cast.

We had a long disagreeable talk with Willard Swire, who is in charge of Off Broadway at the Equity office. Equity shows total ignorance of the possibility of a theater not based on the financial standards of Broadway. Their demands—and even more so the demands of the "craft unions" —are impossible to meet.

Equity dictates that we must hire five actors who are union members, or no union members at all.

We don't know what to do; the actors want to appeal to Equity Council. The hardest days are now.

Hiatus valde deflendus

Two lost journals: written during the period November 1 to December 21, 1951.

During this time, the Living Theatre opened at the Cherry Lane Theater with *Doctor Faustus Lights the Lights* on December 2 and began rehearsals for its second production, *Beyond the Mountains*. Despite the satisfaction which the work gave me, it was an unhappy and alienated period.

It is "lost time" since I think of the journal as time held captive.

All I have left to record the opening of our theater is a letter from William Carlos Williams:

December 15, 1951

My dears Julian Beck and Judith Malina:

I'm walking in a dream, the aftermath of what I saw and heard at your Cherry Lane Theatre last evening—in all that snow. I'd be in there tonight if I didn't have a firm grip on myself—if I were younger nothing could hold me back. I belong there tonight but I dare not let myself go. And tonight is the last night of your play of Gertrude Stein's *Doctor Faustus Lights the Lights*. To me it was a wonderful, a truly wonderful experience to have witnessed it.

I want to tell you everything at once: about the excellently chosen cast, the evenness of their performance, the way they kept the interest up among them as well as the integrity of their individual performances (I was thrilled!), but there was something else that overshadowed all that. It concerned the stage itself, the overall conception of the play as something elevated, as pure entertainment, as something so well sustained, so far above the level of commercial theater that I tremble to think it might fade and disappear. I swear it lives in a different air from the ordinary Broadway show, it is as fresh as a day in the country, the first really serious, really cleanly written, produced and acted play that I have seen, well, in a long time.

I say I feel as if it was something that someone were going to snatch it away from before my eyes [sic]—that is one reason I am so driven to go again tonight. I can't believe it possible that that cast, in those parts, just as they were acted, is going to be dispersed. I don't trust my contemporaries. Such a beautiful thing. Such a truly entrancing experience! It's going to be let die without anyone having adequately celebrated it. I want you to know that as long as I live I'll never forget it.

I realize that I'm speaking in hyperboles, I'm doing it of a set purpose. If I did not use that figure I could not show you how far above the usual conception of the stage you have set your mark and how I appreciate it. It's an almost impossible shot. But you've succeeded in communicating to me what you all together, as a company, have set yourselves and I want you to know and never to forget that you have succeeded. You HAVE succeeded and it is important, I do not want you to forget, any of you, that you did communicate to me the elevated achievement you had in mind when you first conceived such a theater as you placed before your audience last night.

I don't know whether you'll succeed in the fiercely competitive field which the theater in New York represents. There is a sordidness which corrupts playwright, producer and actor alike which somehow, and sad to relate, brings in the coin while it strangles the entire range of what is offered. We all know this vulgarity, we all detest it. The only protest we make is to stay away from the performances—but there are plenty that go and so the appearance of success is achieved. I want to tell you that everywhere people are conscious of this state of affairs, that they long for something more satisfying to their sensibilities than these fifth-rate appeals to their emotions and intelligence represent.

You are young and, apparently, incorruptible. You know that there is a whole range of plays (not just Ibsen repertoire) waiting to be created for a public, actually to be created. And if you can maintain yourself by the skin of your teeth, writers will write more plays for you, poetic plays, excellent plays, the plays that an enlightened audience calls or will call for. I can't tell you how important it is for the theater that you want to CREATE new plays. It is the most thrilling thing that can be done on the stage today.

I wish I could give you a million to start at once on your plans to build a theater housed in the walls of a brownstone. I can't do it. But to begin with you've got the thing, the practical energy to have made a beginning at the Cherry Lane. May all success be yours.

Sincerely yours,
William Carlos Williams

—*JM*

The Living Theatre

FOUNDED 1947

Julian Beck

Meditation. 1961. New York City.

I am a man not interested in theater. The entertainments that demean our being. The dissemination of lies. Fun is destructive while joy creates. Eric Gutkind.

Life is being dreamed. An old mirage while we live in the desert. My whole life is a dream. Strindberg. We are dreaming one another. We go in and out of existence each moment. Have will and am willed. Each day I know less and less. This is my glory.

The theater of our time pretends to know too much. Most of what we think we comprehend is false. We don't have enough facts, the vision is too

Source: Julian Beck's meditations, 1961–63; later published as *The Life of the Theatre*, by Julian Beck, 1972.

limited, we are not free to see. Nor think. When the actor is free like any man, he can create, yet we go to the theater and bear to watch actors fettered by the madness of the bourgeoisie whose madness is its laws which are its life, a life of money which is also a law and drives men mad. Freedom now in its infancy and may die still a babe, and civilization, like the universe, rapidly expanding, and civilization but a child, and may die still a child. 1961 is not the pinnacle. Nor even dates we can't imagine. We go on forever tho death exists. Suicide exists too; choose life. If I want to preserve the world it's my own life I immortalize. As long as men live so do we all.

Narrow vision. Men vary. Huts and turrets. Rice and telephones. And no man differs more from another than from himself at some other time. Pascal.

The theater is a dream. It, like a dream, an image of the world. The world interests me. "M. Dalí," said his companion, "is interested in everything." "Why is your work so concerned with poverty?" And, leaning over the table Dalí asked Allen Ginsberg, "Is not gold the measure of genius?" Genius yes, concentrated creators among us, they keep the world in constant creation, but the people keep the world fed.

My conscience reels under the impact of the Jewish sky and that banner of the rabbonim on which it is proclaimed that the world is in the process of creation and that it is man's sacred duty to assist God in this process.

Buber speaks of "nearness to God" as "the difference between true existence and mere conscious being."

To all sides of a thing at one time. Levels. Simultaneity.

The great preoccupying discovery of the twentieth century. Unification impossible without it. Divided men never find the golden answer. My unique life.

One life. Woe is me. Choice. Shall I go to the Gaspé. Shall I be a salesman or a buyer. Shall I till the earth, feed the poor, add the accounts for merchants and friends, shall I tear up the world and make dust of the plumage, turn the rocks and rills to decomposing blood, infanticide, germicide, shall I pasteurize milk, or paint farting dolls, sleep with men, sleep with women, disturb, tranquilize, bestialize, love, sacrifice, write, torment, augment, embrace, water or decay. Shall I grow old or grow wise.

I do not choose to work in the theater but in the world. The Living Theatre has become my life the living theater. We devour each other. I can't tell one from the other. Judith and I merge in it. Others with us. There are actors who hang on like Jeffers's lice on the eagle. There are actors who are my eyes and technicians who are our wings. The nest we build may crawl with maggots. The eggs breed carnivores. My theater. I hold up the mirror till my arms ache. It falls on the heads of the spectators, leaving them bleeding and marred. Or it does nothing. I hold up a mirror which is only a crumbling ikon of shit, and I am buried under it. A mound of dung upon the stage where no man ought to look. A unique life of nothing.

How can I tell. All I can do is worry, never tell.

On the stage there is life. An actor who brings back from his adventures a moment of communicable penetration is a hero, the light of our lives.

I go to the theater instead of to the synagogue. Not to worship but to discover the way to salvation. I might find the experience of my life. I will soar, actually levitate like Horatio in Paul Goodman's *The Dead of Spring*. He taught me.

Worship doesn't look like salvation.

By observing what is beautiful we can learn what is meant to be. Judith.

Derived from the spell of God, spelled with God aimed at God fulfilled by men set out for glory. The ancients played in sunlight, we in electric light, light is the clothing of glory, though darkness has its day.

Passion. Agony. Despair. Work. The work, the hammers, the persistence, the brooms, the nails unite me with men, else I'd be but poetry and flight. I'd be no good alone. The theater is an exercise in pure community. No one man can do it, made by many, for many. But life on the kibbutz is tough. Everyone complains. I most of all. There is no help for it, but it is as perfect as the weather, always beautiful, like a calendar, always terrible, the day always dies, the sun disappears, the wind is wild and west.

I work out my life in the theater. With Judith, the angel of my life, without whom there would be no Living Theatre ever.

Je ne trouve pas, je cherche.

Meditation. 1962. New York City.

Someday we will have to account for our premature death. Artaud.

You must enter the theater through the world.

It is the holy mission that redeems the theater.

Everything exists, nothing has value. Without value there are errors, sins, losses.

In the secret quarters, in the underground, in Greenwich Village, Saint Germain, among the campus students planning sit-ins and freedom rides, in the hidden quarters of Africa, wherever change is initiated, in the music of changes, in the march to the sea, in the picket lines in front of embassies, the worth of the world is proclaimed. In the invisible lofts where the anarchists and pacifists defy money and the structure of society, where the lies are being examined and reversed, lies which are the allies of death, in these places is the poetry which is the language of God.

In madness which is the force that delivers us to the rim of the sphere in which we're encased, the sphere in which we die, the sphere that floats in the unreckoned universe which we are denied until we let the vision of the madness-force, Ginsberg, assist us to pass thru the wall of the sphere, puncture, into the creation of which we have only heard archetypal rumors. When the madness-force has done its work and we have learned to breathe.

Our way of life is not to be defended, the way of premature death, death from government, death from weapons, death from oppression, death from class, death from the draft, death from poverty, death from racist stomp, death from law, death from police, death from fallout, poison in the air, death from education, the terrible icebox death, death from well-being, death from possessions, death from falsehood, the pain in my stomach, the cancer in my back; the plagues that wrack the bodies more and more ill-made for living, the loss of being.

The falsehood of ideals. Death from Broadway. Ideal clothing, ideal speech. Death from compromise, certain death from luxury and lack of it. Aspects of the stage that are not the world but vanity. This is the vanity stage against which we have pitted our being, not yet knowing what tools to use, nor how to use them; unsafe, witless, a barefoot army of stragglers.

I do not like the Broadway theater because it does not know how to say hello. The tone of voice is false, the mannerisms are false, the sex is false, ideal, the Hollywood world of perfection, the clean image, the well-pressed clothes; the well-scrubbed anus, odorless, inhuman, of the Hollywood actor, the Broadway star. And the terrible false dirt of Broadway, the lower depths in which the dirt is imitated, inaccurate.

The acting at the Living Theatre has been despised for many years, particularly by other actors. Judith and I have worked to build a company without the mannerisms, the voices, the good speech, the protective coloring of the actors who imitate the world of the White House and who enact the trifles and suffering of the bourgeoisie. The world of conscious experience is not enough.

The actors at the Living Theatre are awkward, untutored, unconsciously defiant of the conventions which portray the people who live in democracies, who are rational, good, well balanced, and who speak museum verse. The actors at the Living Theatre want to be concerned with life and death.

The acting at the Living Theatre is only a hesitant gesture, an implication of further development, as if arms might become wings, legs fins, bodies something undreamed of. Something else. The Broadway theater seeks what it would like to see. What is surpasses all illusion. "Accuracies." William Carlos Williams.

You enter the theater through the world, world that is holy, world that is imperfect, you enter the theater through awareness of the indestructible ugliness. Life ugliness. You embrace that ugliness and forget what is beautiful. The way of transcendence. The Acropolis, all that striving, all that striving for the perfection myth, will dissolve in the mass of being which is goodness.

Can't care about anything else.

Ameliorative theater. In which it is possible to discover someone sitting on the toilet without embarrassment.

Rejection of all those who proclaim thru the convention of their playwriting the conventions of civilization, the ways to premature death. All or nothing.

The Living Theatre is at best an imitation, feeble, longing, corrupt, power-principled, dictatorial, arrogant, uncommunal, it yearns for the day when it will wither away. In this is its only opposition to Broadway, demon of the upper world, demon of the money changers, who seek to improve the value of the dollar, who accept a world of premature death. They are Errico Malatesta's "man in chains" (people so accustomed to walking in bonds that they cannot believe it would be easier without them).

All niceness must then be exploded.

Le Rappel à l'ordre. All the pseudo organization must be scattered. And when the wind or Greenwich Village has done its work, after the breaking up of illusion, the broken pieces may penetrate, puncture the outer universe where death is no longer the answer and the conclusion.

Every time the curtain rises on a Broadway play I strike my forehead with the palm of my hand, one hundred thousand dollars for what? Harold Rosenberg.

A setting that is "order," whose "order" denies the order of things as they are, whose most advanced design at best reflects a piquant balance, sentimental color. Sentiment, which is the substitution of false feeling for real (when nothing else can be felt).

Excellent form is a lie.

Too much perfection on Broadway. They make a graven image, all, all of them vanity; and their delectable things shall not profit; and they are their own witness; they see not, nor know; that they may be ashamed. The smith that maketh an axe and worketh it in the coals, and worketh it with the strength of his arms, yea he is hungry and his strength faileth. He that heweth down cedars; yea he maketh a god and worshippeth it, he maketh a graven image, and boweth down thereto. They have not known nor understood, they cannot see. He feedeth on ashes, a deceived heart hath turned his aside that he cannot deliver his soul, not say: Is there not a lie in my right hand? Isaiah.

"Ameliorative theater. To make something useful." Judith.

To make something useful. Nothing else is interesting. Nothing else is interesting to the audience, the great audience. To serve the audience, to instruct, to excite sensation, to initiate experience, to awaken awareness, to make the heart pound, the blood course, the tears flow, the voice shout, to circle round the altar, the muscles move in laughter, the body feel, to be released from death's ways, deterioration in comfort. To provide the useful event that can help us. Help.

I indulge in this polemic because it is the only thing worth saying. The journey to love is not romantic. Out of my negation will come the way to endless positive creation. Help.

Meditation II. 1963. New York City.

what is happening is happening in our theater because
it accepts the patterns of procedure of a homicidal society
and makes them seem admirable
it also makes much of trivia
in a life of tribulation
makes the intolerable seem tolerable
makes life seem entertaining and amusing and gives easy answers
and when i ask why do the spectators permit this to happen
i sadly see that it is indeed
because this life we are leading is becoming unbearable
and the deceit on the stages
is a comfort
tho no one believes it
but people prefer to pretend that it's true because then things are
    maybe not so bad
and thus the theater of our time is a place of fraudulence and mis-
    representation
what is happening there is deception for the middle class and aris-
    tocracy who want to be deceived
if you want to see the truth you have to be mad mad enough to
    confront a horror

Experiences, autobiography: If you want to know me come and live with me.

First plans for a theater—twenty, twenty-one years old. Disinterested in the theater of that time, portraiture of sub-human people, and patriotic too, patriotism as a fool's pastime except for that passion for the land and its people which is a lover's passion. Why the mere image of the theater of our time is enough to precipitate a revolution.

In anger we began. All the sane theater of that time was beneath the dignity of childbearing women and vigorous men. Anything happening worthy of the spectator was a kind of insane thing, gestures scooped from the actor's entrails, unconscious like the reflex motions of grasshoppers, the appendages twitching as pins slip thru the thorax, hands of the drowning, things like anonymous messages received during sleep.

We watched for things driven thru the fuse of the imagination gone wild, escaping. Those were the things the only things that beaconed from the abode where the immortals are.

Take the cue. Go into the madhouse and find out the truth: in the imbalance of the order of things, in the perversity of real love, in the bursting cysts of the mind. No more deception. If you want to see what's what, you have to be mad, able to confront the horror.

We went to the theater all the time, Judith and I. Everything was interesting and infuriating. Two three four times a week. So that by 1946 Judith knew that she didn't want to work in that theater. I, hung up on painting at that time, took six months to come in on it, and we said we'd make a theater that would do something else. Now, fifteen years later, we know we haven't. We also believed that there was some kind of sociological lag in the development of the theater. That is, we were reading Joyce and Pound, Breton, Lorca, Proust, Patchen, Goodman, Cummings, Stein, Rilke, Cocteau, *und so weiter*. 1944: the painting of Pollock and de Kooning was implying a life which the theater didn't know existed, a level of consciousness and unconsciousness that rarely found itself onto the stage. Judith studied with [Erwin] Piscator who knew that radical politics and social action were the Way. We talked about anarchism, Marxism, Greek myths and meters, dreams and Freud, youthful talks, and walked in the woods along the Palisades, and went to the sea a lot, beach beauty. Perhaps our most profound understanding: that the 1940s were not the pinnacle of human achievement, and yet that in the 1940s was, dispersed, all the glory the world would ever contain. The problem of finding, assorting, reassembling matter, feeling, and being. A theater for that.

You are what you eat and what you won't eat anymore.

I ate an entire handkerchief bit by bit at the age of six at a Metropolitan Opera performance of *Hansel and Gretel*. It is an opera much concerned with eating, candy houses, hungry children, breadcrumbs, fattening of Hansel and Gretel, cannibal witch who eats children. My father thought I was eating because I was nervous, which was true, but I was also eating along with Hansel to identify with him, the tasteless awful handkerchief—and then I didn't have to eat it anymore, all the children were free, out of the oven, uneaten, alive, and still to grow up. Everything I have ever done in the theater has been an attempt to free the yearning for freedom from the witch's prison cage, which the *Hansel and Gretel* experience gave me. The event convinced me of three needs in the theater for total experience: physical participation by the spectator participant, narrative and transcendence-which-is-revolution.

Narrative is important in the theater because if the theater is to be the world it cannot neglect what happens, the passing from one moment to the next. Specialized experience like sponges of blue ink tossed onto green glass can fascinate eyes, but the person who throws the sponge is always more interesting than the splashing ink. The problem is to make a theater in which this is clear. Your hand lifting the familiar coffee cup to your lips is more than a vermillion streak in the evening sky: whatever you do beats any scenery, this must be made clear. If we are to survive the landscape.

When we went to Robert Edmond Jones in 1947 to tell him about our theater he got very excited and asked us to come back again.

We did, I brought him my stage designs and we talked about plays we were planning to do. We talked a lot, he looked very sad and we asked him why. At first, he said, I thought you had the answer, that you were really about to create the new theater, but I see that you are only asking the questions. How much money do you have? Six thousand dollars, I said. That's too bad, he said, I wish you had no money, no money at all, perhaps then you would create the new theater, make your theater out of string and sofa cushions, make it in studios and living rooms. Forget the big theaters, he said, and the paid admissions, nothing is happening there, nothing can happen there that is not stultifying, nothing will ever come out of it. Here, if you want, take this room, he said, offering us his studio, if you want to begin here you can have it.

It was not until four years later, unable to locate a theater in which to work that we decided to do some plays in our own living room and not charge a cent nor spend a cent. It worked, he was right. But we still had not thoroughly understood. Therefore we have had theaters which advertise commercially and charge admission and pay taxes, as if those things made something happen, *la gloire* perhaps. Into the trap. Recognizing that we are in it we are at last beginning to discuss strategies for getting out.

> there is something awry when the paintings of picasso and the
>   music of schoenberg
> are emblazoned on the coats of arms of the power elite
> rockefeller collects de kooning
> on wall street they read allen ginsberg
> jacqueline kennedy adores manet
> they are taking everything away

Malraux and Frost sold their birthrights by serving the state with the excuse of trying to popularize national art. The state does not wish to bring art to the people; it seeks diamonds in its crown. Now what is really happening when the Élysée Palace names a lobster after Claudel is that art is being stolen, de-balled, and served up as chocolate. Spain now lures tourists with pictures of its great artists, Picasso, but not *Guernica*, not *Dream and Lie of Franco*; Lorca, but not the body of his work nor his body. Cocteau has said that the revolutionary artist is first ignored, then scorned, and when these things do not work they try to suppress you by loading you down with honors.

> theoretically you should not be able to like de kooning and build
>   bomb shelters (as rockefeller does)
> you cannot approve yevtushenko and stockpile bombs (as khrus-
>   chev does)
> art must either oppose the state or destroy its own life force
> when the state heaps honors on art it is a way of saying this
>   art is safe for the ruling class
> beware of approval and official support

> dorothy day at the catholic worker has spent thirty years living
>   in voluntary poverty and feeding and clothing and housing
>   the poor
> and when the fund for the republic a division of the ford foundation
>   offered her $10,000 i believe i may be wrong the sum may even
>   have been larger but not smaller
> the catholic worker refused it
> because they would not take blood money
> that is they would not take money that had been extorted from people
>   thru the devices of interest and investment and war production
>   and the cruelty of factory labor
> and use that money to feed the poor because by accepting that money
>   they would be assuaging the guilt of the system that is killing
>   us off and is producing the misery the catholic workers
>   are trying to ease
> in our hard society in these hard times it is hard for people to
>   understand this
> i have even known people to express rage as if dorothy day (and not
>   the vicious nature of money) had robbed the poor of bread
>   because
>   the catholic worker refused to accept blood money
> this is because people are always thinking about the expedient

and do not know that you really cannot accomplish good thru bad
that is also why people think that a theater which gives them
    something to think about, the intellectual theater popular today,
is a good thing
but a theater which accepts support from a society which is adamantly
    opposed to
change
is the theater of the finks
it is a mechanism for making a bad thing shrewder and stronger
the patient is dying and we are putting bandaids on the wounds
the people will tolerate much until they can tolerate too much
    no longer
in the theater we are beginning to approach that stage
the stage on which too much is no longer tolerable
and something else must happen

—JB

The Actor's Workshop

FOUNDED 1952

Herbert Blau

> I don't want to be doing *Mary, Mary* when the bomb drops.
> —Jules Irving

In 1961 Nan Martin, a New York–based actress and board member of the newly formed Theatre Communications Group, took what *Theatre Arts* magazine called "a physically harrowing journey" around the U.S. with a tape recorder, visiting university, community and professional theaters. Discouraged by much of what she saw—especially the arrogance and compromises of academic theater—she concluded that, outside of Broadway (and, I assume, the theaters like the New York Shakespeare Festival and Arena Stage, at which she regularly starred), "there is a terrible missing element."[7] Simply stated, this missing element was the "lack of commitment to a dream," "a leap

---

Source: *The Impossible Theater: A Manifesto*, by Herbert Blau, 1964.

7. "A Two-Way River: The Journal of an Actress," by Nan Martin, *Theatre Arts*, August 1962.

far beyond logic." She appears, however, to have found that missing dream at the Actor's Workshop in San Francisco, and in the two men who ran it, Herbert Blau and Jules Irving.

"You cannot equate business success with the artistic value of a production," Martin wrote, positioning the Actor's Workshop uniquely on the side of the artistic. The near-total dedication to "creative experimentation" and artistic success—even if it flies in the face of "audience taste"—"makes it difficult for a great many people to understand what the Actor's Workshop is trying to do. The goals of the Actor's Workshop will never be as financially supportable as the goals of Washington's Arena Theatre [sic] and the Alley Theatre in Houston. But they don't set out to be and they cannot be."

The Actor's Workshop of San Francisco may have been the institutional theater's great counterexample, a major force of decentralization so determined to go its own artistic way that its lack of concern with its own community and audience bordered on disdain. Despite setting out, as Herbert Blau recounts below, with no political ax to grind, it became the regional theater most strongly identified with the advanced thinking of the postwar era. It assumed, and became, an ideological force that no mainstream theater had embodied since the Group Theatre. Moreover, its lack of attention to institutionalization meant that, despite its track record of regional theater firsts— the first to experiment with nightly rotating rep with a company of as many as one hundred actors, the first Off-Broadway contract outside of New York, U.S. premieres of the work of Beckett, Pinter, Brecht and Genet—the theater folded soon after its founders left. (They were lured away after fourteen seasons to run New York City's Repertory Theater of Lincoln Center; see chapter 5.) It was a world (or, maybe, Western world) theater, more than an American one.

Even the radical intellectual bent of its leaders made the Workshop distinct. They were steeped in textual analysis and contemporary thought. They shared a stubborn, even arrogant, artistic ambition. "Both men made the same and united choices," Joseph Zeigler writes, "to be experimental, to embrace blatantly unpopular ideas, to stretch beyond their immediate obvious capabilities, and to speak out against rigidities of form and formality. Through these choices, they preserved the freedom to be themselves, but at the same time they forfeited the acceptance and stability that a more socially reasonable approach could have assured. Their choices were conscious, deliberate and belligerently uncompromising."

"Blau and Irving aren't unique theater specimens spawned on the slimy banks of San Francisco Bay," wrote Theodore Hoffman, an author, editor and teacher influential in the founding of the regional theater movement and its network, Theatre Communications Group. "They're just the most cantankerously imaginative representatives of a theater movement that is taking hold beyond the moldy shores of the Hudson."

Blau, especially, was, in Joseph Zeigler's words and many people's estimation, "one of the few real intellectual geniuses in all of the movement." His brilliant, dense, passionate *The Impossible Theater*, from which the following excerpt is lifted, is a uniquely heady document in the history of U.S. theatrical memoirs. Its roiling prose seems to sweep up every idea in its path. By doing so it evokes the generational, historical, political and psychological context of its era as vibrantly as any theater book I've found.[8]

—*TL*

In a curious mixture of sincerity and misrepresentation, a biography of the Workshop, prepared a few years ago for publicity purposes, reads as follows: "Begun in 1952 without stars, fanfare, real estate or capital, the Actor's Workshop is an act of imagination by two professors at San Francisco State College, Jules Irving and Herbert Blau, native New Yorkers who are convinced that the destiny of the American theater lies as far Off Broadway as possible, in permanent companies dedicated to ensemble playing."

As an account of developed values, the passage has merit; as an index of what we believed when the Workshop began, it does no more than identify a couple of important symptoms of our origin: that the founders were earning their livings as college teachers and that we had left New York. But, though Irving had been on Broadway from childhood and though he might have continued a career there, his departure, mainly to escape the rat race, was no real sign of artistic rebellion; mine less, for I never saw a Broadway play until my eighteenth year to heaven. When I finally made it, without a critical principle to my name, I even enjoyed *The Moon Is Blue*.

So let us beware of education.

I left New York with a degree in chemical engineering, and though I had aspirations as a playwright, they were mainly informed by a quick reading in my senior year of the Bennett Cerf anthology of modern American plays, the bloodless distinction of which must have given me courage, though I thought they were great then because they were collected. The theater was a postgraduate indulgence I could afford on the GI Bill. Privately I had every intention of returning to bubblecap towers and the Second Law of Thermo-

8. After he left Lincoln Center, Blau became a significant force in academia, first at the newly formed California Institute of the Arts, then at Oberlin College, where his KRAKEN theater company included students Bill Irwin and Julie Taymor, and at the universities of Wisconsin and Washington. While his writings have become increasingly theoretical, he published *As If*, the first brilliant volume of his autobiography in 2011. He died in 2013.

dynamics, which I understood only when I began thinking seriously about dramatic form.

There was a lot of naivete lurking behind that "act of imagination." True, by the end of 1951, Irving and I were working for advanced degrees and had been teaching for more than a year—he in theater, I in English—on the college level. However, we had developed no general aesthetic separately or between us, nor had we stayed up all night holding revolutionary conversations on the place of the theater in American culture. Social views? Aside from some study in business administration, Irving had spent most of his time in the theater, whether in college or on Broadway or overseas, in the Special Services cast of *Brother Rat*. It was not promising. He is voluble, with a bright, bantering mind, and the sort of political nature that doesn't suffer needlessly from playing the game because he never took it to be anything else; but he is not political. As for me, despite my technological background, I had a small history of social action, a superb collection of *PM* [9] saved through high school, and had been something of a Wallace progressive when I was editor of the daily at NYU—though my editorials usually consisted, like *PM*'s, of liberal slantings of news and opinion pilfered from the *New York Times*. Thus fortified, I could be very contentious.

[. . .]

It was only as I began teaching that I understood some of the lessons from those histories of dramatic art . . . and that I began to look upon the drama itself as a means of livelihood, in every sense. Personally, I was living a double standard in those days. There was a schizoid split between the principles I had acquired in my study of literature and those I thought possible to exercise in the theater. Because I wasn't that ardent about the theater, I wasn't that grieved by the cleavage. Not only did I not expect deeper resonances of experience or revelations of formal beauty in the theater, but like Harold Clurman prior to his founding of the Group Theatre, I suspected either that "there is something inferior in the theater per se or there is something wrong about the practical theater of today that escapes me." And unlike Clurman, I wasn't sure I couldn't live without the theater, for I constantly wondered why I bothered with it at all, since I often found myself bored when I saw plays, grew annoyed (because I knew they were right) when my friends in the Creative Writing Program disparaged the best of American plays, and fretted to be back in my study.

Among my teachers had been Yvor Winters, the poet and critic, who thought the drama an inferior form to begin with, the theater too silly to be

9. *Picture Magazine*, a leftist daily newspaper published for most of the forties in New York City and bankrolled by Chicago millionaire Marshall Field III.

corrupt. It was Winters, a much-embattled absolutist, who taught me that the most abstract ideas were worth fighting about and that poetry was a matter of life and death. (The world is dominated, he feels, by those who "judge definition the most fierce of crimes.") We fought about the theater, but I was upholding a cause in which I didn't really believe—though I couldn't deny the attraction of the stage and all its gregarious surroundings, to which I was drawn as I condemned them. I certainly preferred the English lyric to the American play, as I still do, but you couldn't perform a lyric—or could you? Maybe you can't. But it was a while before we began to consider questions like that at the Actor's Workshop.

Shortly before we talked about a studio of our own, Irving described, with the bated energy that is the other side of a canny poker player, the theater he and a teacher of ours were planning for a town near San Francisco. It seemed to me the best of all possible theaters under the circumstances, a very admirable prospect. Despite my misgivings, the theater as an institution was still too novel and glamorous to keep me from asking too much of it. (A lot of my ambivalences might be explained by the fact that I had just married an actress.) No repertoire was discussed, but I'm sure the intention was to offer the usual slate of comedies and musicals, a serious drama for relief, with a classic thrown in. And I wouldn't have been prompted then to offer any objections. Literally, they intended a *stock* company. That plan, however, needed twenty thousand dollars or so, and I recall saying in what must have seemed a moment of invincible ignorance (if not envy for my being left out) that we could start a theater for next to nothing.

I'm certain I didn't know what I meant.

Though I have since come to suspect myself of submarine proclivities, a certain affection for the abyss, I do know that when we started the Workshop in 1952, it was with no dissidence in mind and our hearts in a relatively conventional place. Somebody had called 1951 the year of World War II.5, but we weren't making any social protest; and though there was plenty of *Angst* aghast in me, I kept it pretty well concealed, like Dostoyevsky's Underground Man. For I would hardly have thought then that it was the theater's function to do something with "that cold, abominable half despair . . . that acutely recognized and yet partly doubtful hopelessness of one's position . . . that hell of unsatisfied desires turned inward, . . . that fever of oscillations, of resolutions determined forever and repented of again a minute later" which is the perverse dignity of the buried life, too outraged to really take shelter. And if I had at the outset pressed the claims of the buried life, the people in our group would have despaired over me.

The Human Condition had almost nothing to do with the founding of the Actor's Workshop, except by default. In a nation spending billions on guided missiles, able to create an entire city almost overnight to release energy for the annihilation of another city in an instant, whose affluence was such that it could in wartime supply two armies on two fronts in less than two years with so much surplus that it was almost forced into dropping holocaust unimagined by man so it could get on with the Reconversion; in a nation which could in a few years think seriously of digging a Randy "big hole" underground so that a seven-hundred-thousand-ton blast could be set off in secret, and which was at the moment financing a limited war in a remote land for reasons that almost nobody understood, Irving and I each plunked down about eighteen dollars a month and rented a loft behind a judo academy and went about our ingenuous business. We asked no existential questions; we were recouping no cultural losses, toppling no icons, breaking no classifications, rewriting no history, assuaging no ontological guilt, shattering no systems—as the Underground Man says scornfully—"constructed by lovers of mankind for the benefit of mankind." There was a little Sartrean nausea when we discovered rat shit in the garbage beneath the stairs, but we swept it all away, garbage, shit and all, in the common interest. There was something inviolably American in all that, which has never left us.

Though I could not remember from my study of physical chemistry part of the proof for $E=mc^2$, we believed that twice two does make four, and if we had any doubts they were mainly speculative. We were not committed to the Absurd. There was no spite, no sickness, no Messianic rage, no Quest for Identity, no demonic style. There was no style at all, and though I was teaching a course in literary form, very few ideas about it so far as the theater was concerned. If revolution is an affair of logical lunatics, we were at the time very practical young men of the theater—the lunacy was yet to come. And, in varying degrees and with some agitation in the cellarage, with *Angst* over the *Angst*, all the rest.

But for those in our company who like their lunacy pure, like a fifty-megaton bomb, it was never sufficiently deranged.

. . .

Unlike the Group Theatre of the thirties, then, we were not prompted by social idealism, nor did we consider ourselves "a training ground for citizenship." We had no "common cause with the worker," or—for that matter—identification with any class. No more than the young man of *Awake and Sing!* did we want life printed on dollar bills—but we had a few more than he did, and we'd lived through a period in which the desire for social justice had gone through all the lettered agencies of reform and turned into a proliferating bureaucracy, stimulated by our marvelous capacity to organize for war. If we thought about it, we knew that not all the great social issues had been solved by the New Deal, but the rhythm of picketing had dissipated, and the litany of Moral Realism encouraged us to live with our sins—until, perhaps, the omnipresent issue of Segregation raised its ugly head in Little Rock.

If there was no clear social motivation to our work, neither did we have any collective sympathy with the Dispossessed; that is, with the Alienated, the Disaffiliated, the Angry, the Beat (who were gone, gone, gone in San Francisco about the same time we started making the scene); with all those who had made the problem of Identity, the strategic defense of Self against the minions and dehumanization, the primary issue of their lives; who were as much disgusted by the debilities of the Welfare State, here or in England, as they were by the terrors of the Bomb; who considered Medicare a non sequitur in a world that was diseased in soul. And some of whom—while pondering the twentieth century's history of torture, murder, brainwashing, saturation bombing, fireballs, fallout and the threat of "spasm response"— could respond to that generation of Europeans who had made despair a way of life. For them, the political game is a *shuck*, the social order is bunk, the social contract a fraud, drawn up to kill us off. If one insisted on working in the theater (another shuck) rather than taking to the hills, it was one's duty to fight outrage with outrage.

While we were still in our loft, we were, on a practical level, sealed off from these sentiments. When we chose, however, to become a real theater and were faced with extinction every day, the general peril and our own became fused, and we wondered whether there wasn't, indeed, a conspiracy against us. As we began to realize what we were up against, economically and culturally, and as we improvised our way through a most eclectic repertoire, what we learned was that the questions we weren't asking had to be asked. Since we weren't, like the Group, inspired by the social urgency of the period, we had to ask ourselves by what else we could be inspired.

This aspect of our growth was defined several years later by a trivial altercation during our rehearsals of *Mother Courage*, a play which brought us all face-to-face with the implacable countenance of the Cold War. I was going rather hard at an actor who had been puzzled by some direction. It had something to do with the idea of Alienation, which I began to badger him with all over again, extending the immediate issue into the social context. Whereupon he said to me: "Cut it out, you're not Brecht." "That's all right," I answered, "when we started I wasn't even Herbert Blau."

I might have saved a little face, but the perennial nagging question remains: *Am* I Herbert Blau? And though the game of "Who am I?" can be a drag, I am not sure I am suitably identified yet by all the credit and courtesy cards that have my number. What isn't down on paper is up in the air. And fallout is only the worst of it.

As we gathered for our first session, the security measures of warfare had turned into the peacetime "torment of secrecy." Ten days after President Truman ordered work on the H-bomb and Albert Einstein had warned of total annihilation, Senator McCarthy waved a list before the Women's Republican Club in Wheeling, West Virginia: "I hold here in my hand . . . ," he said, and incriminated 205 unnamed people in the State Department, with General Marshall explicitly mentioned for good measure. Obfuscation had reached its political apotheosis, and took its toll on the theater. It was at the end of 1951—the atmosphere having grown so paralyzing in New York—that Brooks Atkinson remarked we were emulating the totalitarian countries by yielding our cultural life "to the Yahoos and hoodlums." He spoke of "something elusive and intangible" draining the vitality out of the theater; it seemed to him that people were playing it safe and that the "ignorant heresy-hunting and the bigoted character assassination" were succeeding. But it was a strange period. For as Atkinson was writing this passage about the American theater, we were confronted with the irony of Brecht and Felsenstein[10] developing two of the greatest theaters in the world in one of its most repressive sectors, East Berlin.

What were the prospects in San Francisco?

Land's end. A sort of populated Darien; the landlocked harbor overlooked by Mount Diablo; eight hundred thousand people—small enough to be embraceable, yet metropolitan, too; with the highest incidence of alcoholism and suicide in America; a gilded boom town grown urban on a fissure, suburbs sprawling over nine counties of the Bay Region; three million people in the vicinity, two great universities nearby, and a trolley college of high caliber; a great park of eclectic fauna; a Chinese ghetto which feels affluent and no conspicuous slums; sick comics in the bistros and a Bohemian Club of unregenerate squares; its Barbary Coast infested with interior decorators and Alcatraz still dominating the views; withal, a city reposeful and august, the old Pacific Union club on Nob Hill, home of the railroad kings, lording it over the new arrivals: the students, the dockworkers, the doctors of the Kaiser Plan, the Hadassah ladies, the vagrants from the valleys, the junior executives of the new Playboy set, the Beats from Tangiers and North Platte, all the questing intellectuals, and those who simply want to retire in a city whose weather is so equable you may complain of missing the seasons but feel imposed upon anywhere else; a turreted, towered, scalloped, hilly city, Mediterranean in western baroque, the old buildings being erased by freeways and the troughs filled in by redevelopment; below its splendid bridges, a city with a nervous graciousness, upholding a worldwide reputation for a

10. Walter Felsenstein, founder and director of the Komische Oper in East Berlin from 1947 to 1975.

culture it doesn't quite have, though what it has is, by the standards of other American cities, impressive—a city that is a myth, with the golden opportunity to live up to it.

If we were living at mid-century, as Eric Goldman put it, in "the nagging realm of maybe," San Francisco seemed to me the perfect geographic setting. There was a kind of weird Keatsian "negative capability" in that prosperous postwar town, with full employment expected, medical conquests in the offing, rocket engines nearing perfection, and Space looming before us, while across the bay they were developing an anti-proton. A friend of mine, a distinguished scientist who works at the university on cosmic rays, was called in to run some tests to certify the isolation of the new particle. His wife, who has acted with our company, tells the story of waiting for him to return, which he did several hours later. "Well? Well?" she said. "Well what?" he said. "I couldn't see the goddamn thing."

It was a city of prospects and ambiguities, the left-wing longshoremen and a monopolistic union; a resort for homosexuals; a place for fashionable women, and psychiatrists, everywhere; three hours behind New York, yet three thousand miles nearer the Orient with its rising revolutionary sun— and when the Workshop started, a queer sort of "shooting peace" in Korea, not a "cease fire" but a "seldom fire"; while GIs hung their laundry on tanks and were getting up pheasant shoots.

. . .

Negotiations in Panmunjom had been going on about five months when we began rehearsals of our first play in our studio. Now and then the question would arise: Are we or are we not at war? And what for? The U.N., hedging, called the battle in Korea a "police action" and the North Korean attack became a "bandit raid." There was not yet much talk about brainwashing, but a new generation of Americans was getting an education in the rigor mortis of power. Just before the turn of the year, Hanson Baldwin wrote in the *New York Times* of the coalition of Russians, Chinese and North Koreans, that they were either "(1) primitive men who have not yet outgrown the swaddling clothes of savagery; or (2) men whose god is power unhampered by restraint, who regard murder and cruelty as necessary techniques for the achievement of absolutism." A Chilean diplomat told the U.N. that "cannibalism" is Soviet dogma. If this were so (and most of us were prepared to believe anything to the extent we believed nothing), then all the more appalling was the apathy and capitulation of American prisoners of war, especially in comparison to the behavior of other troops who served in Korea for the U.N.

Never before in our history had such widespread and flagrant national betrayal taken place:

> The Dhow, the Gizee, and Rhee
> What do they want from me?[11]

In the most idiotic days of World War II, it was still possible for an infantry soldier to climb Monte Cassino and feel he was doing his part to save history from the barbarians. But Korea—with its bleak, unreal terrain—seemed an unlikely place to make the world safe for democracy. Description of the landscape and the strange objectless maneuvers read like the setting and action of a Beckett drama. And, indeed, the GI who fired his rifle into the air because he hadn't the slightest inkling as to why he was fighting to save rice paddies fertilized with human dung later became an ardent spectator at our productions of Beckett and Genet.

[...]

Meanwhile, in those first days of the Workshop, we were not even members of the Radical Middle.

As we sat around our coal stove in the loft we had rented, I recalled the opening of E. A. Robinson's poem about the Wandering Jew: "I saw by looking in his eyes that he remembered everything." And I thought it wasn't so much that we had nothing to say as that we had to find a way of saying it that wouldn't sound hollow, for we also thought we had heard it all. Yet we had a lot to learn, and there was a lot we didn't remember.

For the time being, though Irving and I talked impressively, it was mainly—as they said in committee—procedural; we would pick a play with good parts for all the actors and rehearse it until it was "ready." We said very little about the world outside, or what sort of play. Like our politicians, our group was cautious, politic and already committed to being uncommitted, or at least cagey about revealing commitments. It was an affable bunch, well educated, and though there was no palpable fear of each other, still it was in the rhythm of the time to bide it. All of the men had been in the service, we all had jobs, most of us had families. What would we, if we wanted to protest, protest about? —except the Bomb, and you don't protest your nightmares, at first.

[...]

Pragmatically speaking, then: if, when we formed our Workshop in 1952, it was without "stars, fanfare, real estate and capital," it wasn't because we had principles against them, but because they simply weren't available to us. Since then we have had stars (and prefer to do without them); we have had a modicum of fanfare (which we try to exploit, even while we distrust the

---

11. A ditty sung by American GIs in Korea, sarcastically expressing their lack of clarity about the fight they were engaged in.

way it rushes us beyond ourselves); and we are always seeking real estate and capital, like any other growing enterprise in the Cold War.

And, though we have closed down on them, we are still improvising our principles.

. . .

Since Irving did all the directing in those days, when I was away from rehearsal my wife would answer questions about me by referring to my "other work," which always sounded somehow abstract and sinister. It was. And while persisting in my own netherworld, that awful center of infernal spirits, I saw the terrors of the present through the despair of the ages. I remember trying at the time to write a poem about the cobalt bomb, which invariably turned facetious the more I saw it as the apocalyptic extension of Original Sin, which meant nothing to me as dogma but everything as metaphor. It wasn't that I was intellectually wrong, only the enormity of it all was such that when you did think about it you could only laugh or rage, or pick at your liver in silence.

My literary study was rife with outraged melancholy. Behind in my reading, I had quickly grown intimate with Yorick's skull and all the old chimeras of the atomized soul. My eyebeams had twisted over the devotional skepticism of John Donne, with all his haunting paradoxes, like "a bracelet of bright hair about the bone." And my mind had been collecting images of estrangement, not only from the fury of the patriarch Oedipus at Colonus (I was less than twenty-five at the time) and the monomaniac Ahab plunging his Pequod into the blind Atlantic, but from the probings of Freud, the unmaskings of Marx, the chthonic inquiries of Jung, the "gay science" of Nietzsche, the demonic principle that was our legacy from the deification of Milton's Satan, the whole Romantic Agony, and all the accumulated disinheritance represented in phrases and titles like these: *The Waste Land*, *The Hollow Men*, *The Beast in the Jungle*, *The Drunken Boat*, *The Circus Animals' Desertion*, *Zero at the Bone*, *The Iceman Cometh*, *The Dance of Death*, *The Lost Generation*, *The Lonely Crowd*, *The Age of Anxiety*, *Escape from Freedom*, *The Miscellaneous Man*, *The Stranger*, *The Outsider*, *No Exit*, *The Secret Life of Walter Mitty*, *The Dangling Man*, *The Victim*, *The Trial*, *The Burrow*, *The Idiot*, *The Sound and the Fury*—who couldn't make his own list? signifying nothing, and I do mean Nothingness, to the last syllable of recorded doomsaying.

Clurman was familiar with the imagery and had read a lot of these books when they were first published, but he was able in the thirties to put Eliot aside as bloodless or Kafka as irrelevant. In the trial of the Republic under the New Deal, redress was possible. Even at the chastened end of *The Fervent Years*, he could still invoke the optimistic side of Whitman: "I think it is to collect a tenfold impetus that any halt is made." Myself, I was just picking up on the dark side of Whitman, the suppressed passages of *Leaves of Grass* that resembled the bar sinister of the heroes of the Underground (it seemed ironic but right, for instance, that America's poet laureate should be a homosexual), and I was reading with rather morbid relish Dr. Josiah Trent's report (in *Surgery, Gynecology, and Obstetrics*) that Whitman at his death was "a veritable pathological museum." There was the beginning of a Litany of Fallout in the revised diagnosis, a recitative for shelter programs: "Pulmonary tuberculosis, far advanced, right; atelectasis of left lung; tuberculosis empyema, left; bronchopleural fistula, left; disseminated abdominal tuberculosis; tuberculosis abscesses of sternum, fifth rib and left foot; cyst of left adrenal gland; chronic cholecystitis and cholelithiasis; cerebral atrophy; cerebral arteriosclerosis; benign prostatic hypertrophy; pulmonary emphysema; cloudy swelling of kidneys; history of hypertension." In a period studying coronaries, the hypertension may have seemed the worst of it; but it was also very Jacobean, and I thought of it when we came to Beckett's Hamm.

As I acquired my apocalyptic vision, however, encouraged by the best that had been thought and said, I refrained from introducing it wholesale into the Workshop, which was meant to be a healthy coming together of sorts, mainly of relatively experienced actors who were tired of playing in little theaters or with college groups, there being no alternative in San Francisco. It was clear to me that every major artist of the twentieth century would see the Bomb as the superemblem of a lot of diseased energy and internal chaos in society at large, but I didn't make an issue of it at first for fear I would be incoherent if not irrelevant. Whether they could articulate it or not, some of the others may have been feeling things similarly; but it was symptomatic of the period that when suicide walked abroad, it wore a normal face. Perhaps out of vanity I felt like the astrophysicist Sir Arthur Eddington on "the theory of the exploding universe," which, he admitted, "is in some respects so preposterous that we naturally hesitate to commit ourselves to it. It contains elements apparently so incredible that I feel almost an indignation that anyone should believe it—except myself."

So it was a while before the worm gnawed at the body politic of our rehearsals.

[. . .]

Many of us had no politics. If the American theater of the thirties, infected by politics, seems naive in retrospect, the one thing we can say is that there has been no extension of range since then by keeping our political noses clean. And surely less excitement. *Waiting for Lefty* we can see (they could see it then) was no great play, but when Odets read it to the Group, Luther Adler said, "The Group has produced the finest revolutionary playwright in America." The first performance is a great moment in our theatrical lore. And Clurman summed up the spontaneous roar of, "Strike! Strike!" by saying "It was something more than a tribute to the play's effectiveness, more even than a testimony of the audience's hunger for constructive social action. It was the birth cry of the thirties. Our youth had found its voice."

Which it subsequently lost with the fall of Madrid in 1939: "Concurrently with this event," wrote Clurman, "came an almost unrecognizable change in the spiritual scene of American life. A certain flatness, a falling off of inspirational force, a kind of treadmill progression subtly characterized the environment from this time till the outbreak of war in September."

Saroyan's *My Heart's in the Highlands* seemed to reconcile the old passion for "a sound, affirmative nature" with "the need for unity, good behavior and humorous condonement of our sins." But Clurman grew impatient even with *Time of Your Life*, for all its sentimental affection for human failing, because of the Arab's refrain: "No foundation; all the way down the line." The refrain hardly had the foundation or the force it would have in the dramas of Beckett and Ionesco or the revivals of the early Brecht; but Clurman was still looking in Odets's *Clash by Night*, with its "noxious atmosphere," that seems so genial today, for some sound "portents of a clearer future." He found something in the young couple of the play, but even they "represented a kind of ideologic afterthought rather than the creative center of the play, which, no doubt about it, was pessimistic."

The pessimism grew through World War II, which was being fought as *The Fervent Years* was being written. The war's lampskin exposure of the limits of perfectibility put a damper on "the inevitability of the struggle against evil" which made Clurman, early in the Group's career, impatient with the violent ending of *The House of Connelly*. It was about this time that Odets was becoming silent in Hollywood, and soon after other members of the Group were either assimilated or blacklisted; or blacklisted, then assimilated. John Garfield, who played the boy who didn't want life printed on dollar bills, was to die in an aura of congressional investigations, which were blamed for it; and to a generation soon to adjust to the daily possibility of extinction, youth seemed passé. The elder statesman of the Group, Morris Carnovsky, put the case—taking refuge in Shakespeare and questions of technique: "If I was a little bit sanguine about the importance of theater as a social force, why—so I learned my lesson. Not too long after that came the McCarthy business, and some very depressing stuff happening in this country . . ." [. . .]

· · ·

In those first days in the loft, when we referred to the Group or any other famous theater, we were very careful of grandiose aspirations. A couple of the somewhat older hands among us then had seen a lot of zeal come to nought in the enthusiasm of the thirties and the WPA projects in San Francisco. The Federal Theatre played some of its last performances below the Bay Bridge at Treasure Island. Other groups had come and gone, municipal theaters could never get off the ground, repertory companies had failed from presuming too much too soon; and the little theaters our people had known had no interest in revolution. Besides, we wouldn't have known what to do with a forum if we had had one then. (Several years later a Beat joint in North Beach would have a Blabbermouth night for those who wanted to sound off: it was not so much a forum as an escape valve, which ranged from potted anarchy to nonobjective howls. But it was lively; if you really didn't have anything to say in public, at least you could flip—and when it became a fine art, taking off on everything and changing nothing, you had something approaching Lenny Bruce—or Beckett's Lucky.)

Following the formula Tocqueville had discerned, our actors were not drawn together by *ideas* either about life or art, but by mutual *interest* in an opportunity to work with better people than they had been working with. The older among them were mainly looking and seeing, skeptical of the outcome; and when Irving or I did in a slip from caution mention the Abbey or the Moscow Art Theatre, I could feel an inward scoffing. Perhaps we were too sensitive. We were both in our twenties; aside from some plays produced in the university, I was almost totally inexperienced in the practical theater, and the actors knew it. Even my wife, who had been trained in New York and gathered her ideas about theater there, laughed when I first began to insist we *could* make a theater in San Francisco.

The lack of adhesive ideas, however, was an impediment. Though Clurman started out with less concern about politics than I had, he was swept up—as were his actors—in the fusion of the new aesthetic of the twenties with the radical politics of the thirties. With the Great Crash came the dire necessity of social protest. Moral salvation and political salvation became one. Talking like an Odets character, Clurman told his friend Aaron Copland in the summer of 1929: "I'm sick of this dervish dance they've got us doing on steel springs and a General Electric motor." They wept together for the trouble ahead. It was inspiring. Meetings were held, techniques were discussed, fanaticism aroused, actors organized, and Clurman (who had moved in the ambiance of the Provincetown) sought with Strasberg "a unity of background, of feeling, of thought, of need, among a group of people that has formed itself consciously or unconsciously from the undifferentiated masses."

But that was a period in which the word *masses* meant something honorific and urgent, and Clurman could even in the most disillusioned days of the Group, even as late as *The Fervent Years*, use the word *togetherness* to express an ideal. To us—for everybody but the squarest squares—it had become a pretext for parody. We were practitioners and victims of that bare sufferance of language that arose out of its abuse and exhaustion by sociology, psychology and the mass media, as well as the sloganizing of the thirties—the sort of thing satirized by George Orwell in his essay "Politics and the English Language." If the Group "clamored for greater occasions, for closer embrace, for a more rooted togetherness," and if Waldo Frank was the oracle of a new America, instructed by Mexican nationalization and the Soviet experiment, we lamented the loss of unity, sought (while distrusting the phrase) peace of mind, and feared that "separateness" was the natural condition of social man. And David Riesman documented our fear, giving us an up-to-date version of that revolt of the masses which others had predicted would lead to estrangement, malaise and suicidal loneliness. (In a society where the heroes of Odets's early plays are now clipping coupons, it may lead—as Herbert Gold has shown in *The Age of Happy Problems*—to death in Miami Beach.)

Riesman is a representative thinker of the Cold War epoch. Turning issues about as on a spit in the barbecue of some suburban yard, he is the sociologist of the *via media*, of the age of nonpartisanship. He is free of the old liberal platitudes, but he has his own rough sociological beasts, autonomously directed. The early edition of *The Lonely Crowd* explored the shadows of affluence while trying to confirm the general good health of things. But as the computers got to work on the relative salvation of mankind by first and second strikes, his view darkened and he saw the Cold War not as a Manichean struggle but as "the failure of a way of life." The ambivalence was characteristic of those intellectuals who did not renounce America altogether as an armed madhouse, and go off to Tunis, Kyoto or Big Sur to await apocalypse.

The distrust or critique of language had become, in either case, our chief mode of inquiry. The tradition descended from diverse sources—say, from Hamlet (who knew a hawk from a handsaw, but was scornful of words, words, words) through Flaubert's *Dictionary of Accepted Ideas*, through Wittgenstein's *Tractatus*, to Ionesco's *Jack, or The Submission*: "O words, what crimes are committed in thy name." It is reflected in the addiction of some literary people, atoning for the crimes, to the stoic or ecstatic dumbfoundedness of nonobjective painting, to the *sesshins* of Zen, and the final end of jazz—to swing or be stoned, man, depending on which end of the horn you're on. At its glorious extreme, the old adage flows out of the Symbolist cornucopia: Silence is golden. In the drama, there was a growing interest in mime.

The objective: *not* to speak out, but to avoid saying what you knew couldn't hold up in the general decay of language, value and civilization itself. If every poem renews the language, the words working among themselves, every newspaper corrupts it, the words working for the power elite. Though there were plenty of poets, there was incomparably more newsprint; and while some of the poets were trying to reactivate the language by making a mess of it, some of the others—trained in the academic tradition of the New Criticism, careful of excess, full of tensions, paradoxes, icons, architectonics and the seven types of ambiguity—were growing weary of it all.

Having developed a sense of Evil along with their cabalistic techniques, they were beginning to feel duped by their own wiliness. Not yet able to accept the raging infancy which distorted Blake's Innocence, they pondered lost passion. (Or, like Richard Wilbur defending *Ceremony*, tried to be Augustan in a time of fallout.) When psychiatrists now speak of moral blandness as the characteristic neurotic symptom of the period, the poets, who had been the first to diagnose it, begin to wonder about themselves. Was this the end of inquiry? Of all that critical technique? To be tranquilized, too? If I may cite Tocqueville again, he described with uncanny prophecy that general malaise of the fifties by which they felt trapped:

> If society is tranquil, it is not because it is conscious of its strength and its well-being, but because it fears its weakness and its infirmities; a single effort may cost it its life. Everybody feels the evil, but no one has courage or energy enough to seek the cure. The desires, repinings, the sorrows, and the joys of the present time lead to nothing visible or permanent, like the passions of old men, which terminate in impotence.

Only in the last couple of years, with the Negro revolution, has the power of mass action become inspiring again. But even so, the spirit of gradualism rules over a possessed minority, the action oscillating between passive resistance and threats of violence.

In art, the breakthrough, like the cure, is easier proclaimed than accomplished. And among the poets who aren't claiming millenniums too soon, the malaise—born in the twenties to a dying fall and nurtured through the crippling ambiguities of the Cold War—remains. Robert Lowell, the most exciting poet of my generation, writes at the conclusion of a poem recently published:

> Young, my eyes began to fail.
> Nothing! No oil
> for the eye, nothing to pour
> on those waters or flames.
> I am tired. Everyone's tired of my turmoil.

Not only do we suspect the falsity of our public truths, but we are experts in the detection of our private phoniness. The best informed of our artists suffer from excess of knowing, in inverse proportion to the public density. W. D. Snodgrass, in an essay appended to *Heart's Needle*, writes on this autobiographical poem:

> I am left, then, with a very old-fashioned measure of a poem's worth—the depth of its sincerity. And it seems to me that the poets of our generation—those of us who have gone so far in criticism and analysis that we cannot ever turn back and be innocent again, who have such extensive resources for disguising ourselves from ourselves—that our only hope as artists is to continually ask ourselves, "Am I writing what I really think?"

I am defining a tone. A rhythm of mind. Few of our actors had read much poetry or even heard of the New Criticism. (And it was some time before we came to Ionesco's *Jack*.) But the poets were only more outspoken: the actors breathed the same psychic atmosphere. With them it took the obverse form of diffidence with ideas, fear of complexity, or a suspicion of ambiguities that leads to further ambiguities by default of intelligence. I am not going to make this an occasion for an assault on the limitations of actors as a species, for they are finally the most self-denying, the most generous, and the most vulnerable of artists, for all their legendary narcissism. We must love them for that, without losing sight of their special liability to the chronic indecision I have been describing. Actors or not, burning the books is no solution, even when you haven't read the books. And all the parables, from the Gospels to Faust, tell us you don't return to innocence simply by renouncing knowledge—even when you really possess it.

The depth of sincerity in Snodgrass's poem is convincing precisely in proportion to his acceptance of the sad fact that he "cannot ever turn back and be innocent again . . ." Though there were not many real opinions in that period, each man was still insisting on his sincere right to his own. To claim sincerity, however, is no verification of opinion, or even of sincerity. What we were able to bring to those early sessions at the Workshop was an analytical attitude toward the texts which was surprising and engrossing for the actors, but at some limiting point—when analysis darted from the text to them or their deranged world—became intimidating. Especially when it was accompanied by moral fervor. Claiming sincerity, some of them evaded both the issues and themselves by invoking the old smokescreen that an actor shouldn't think too much. Perhaps so. Which usually prevents some of them from thinking at all, reducing the feelings about which it was possible to have opinions.

Irving and I had neither the authority of a Strasberg at close range nor his psychiatric instincts. Nor was this particular group of actors either so zealous in self-inquiry or so submissive as I sometimes feel they become at the Actors Studio, where the emphasis on inner life—a salutary thing, a necessity—is such that you will find young people from Oregon and New Mexico being utterly true to themselves in the unregenerate rhythm of the stripped id, with its New York accent—which is somehow the sign of truth and virility; though the White Negro is now taking the stage away (witness *The Connection*[12]) from the inferiority complex of White Protestant America. Both of us from New York, with a feeling for the dynamics of that city, we were dealing in temperate San Francisco with that same sense of inferiority. Only it felt no reverent obligation to defer to us and, as Irving would say, "put a cap on the emotions" when we behaved with the gratuitous energy of a Kazan or did pry like Strasberg.

Still, almost all actors in America, even the least experienced and the most threatened, know they must base their work on personal inquiry. Their training may actually be quite artificial, but internal technique is in the atmosphere of their profession and they speak its language even if they don't have much of it—as young people who have never read them inherit a natural disposition for Marx and Freud. As Marx and Freud can be frightening in their depths, so Stanislavsky can be intimidating behind the mechanism of his theory. And while our actors might invoke him on units and beats, the objective division of the play's action into actable components, they were uncomfortable with his depth psychology and his moral fervor, forgetting he had written a chapter on ethics in the theater. In that chapter he said: "Do not come into the theater with mud on your feet." Who could avoid it? We were all doubtful cases. It would seem that Stanislavsky was not so demanding after all. Consciously, however, our group was quite content not to bring the mud into rehearsals; the trouble was that we left somewhat more of ourselves outside than, I think, Stanislavsky intended.

Moreover, our sort of discretion kept us from seeing (as they also fail to see at the Actors Studio, perhaps from too much mud) that there was behind Stanislavsky's technique the task of finding that vague, true path of which the Master had spoken so often. "In other words, one must train one's self, *one must think and develop morally and give one's mind no rest*." (Italics mine.) True, there is in the technique itself the same necessity for preparation that one needs, say, for psychoanalysis; free association and the recording of dreams require a practiced discipline. But with Stanislavsky, as with Freud, it was a moral discipline; they both liberated the id, but revered reason. [. . .]

12. Jack Gelber's 1959 play, made famous by the Living Theatre, a portrait of drug addiction among jazz musicians.

The experience of the Group Theatre—with Stella Adler's recharting of Stanislavsky's technique, as well as the rabid know-it-allness of the thirties—stood curiously between Stanislavsky and some of our actors. If some of our generation worried about thinking too much, they had had warning from the Group, whose "directors had once practiced the art of self-criticism on their own productions and had analyzed each of the actors' performances for educational purposes. The actors were apt pupils; they didn't necessarily become better actors; they became shrewd critics. With this new instrument of criticism they made deft incisions into each other's work, into that of the playwrights (who came to loathe them for it) and all other actors outside. After a time almost everyone in the Group worried over everyone else's performance. At times there was an invisible silent slaughter going on among the Group actors."[13] So they gave their minds no rest; and though there were more awesome reasons, it was part of our folklore, too, that the Group failed because it talked itself to death.

"People don't seem to talk to one another enough," Clurman said in one of the informal meetings that preceded the founding of the Group. "We are separate. Our contacts are hasty, utilitarian contacts or escapist. We must get to know ourselves by getting to know one another." And they did. Togetherness banished separateness. The summer retreat, the critiques, the disputation were endemic to the Group in the swing of the period. And even Franchot Tone, who would shout, "I am an American!" on the Fourth of July, when nobody else would shoot off firecrackers, was affected by the rhythm. The members of the Group did get to know each other, almost too well; and some of them, like Strasberg, haven't stopped talking yet. I do not say this in malice. The Group's talk and rapport gave America its first ensemble acting company of any distinction. When Franchot Tone complained that the Group actors at their summer camp acted only when they didn't talk, Strasberg answered, "Yes, we talk a lot because we are not simply rehearsing a play; we are laying the foundation of a theater. Our theater is more than just a matter of getting one or two plays produced."

It is one of the principles I have already enunciated for my own theater, and it is indebted to the Group.

By contrast, we did not get to know each other at first; we got to know the texts, which intermediated. There were those who wanted to go out and have coffee together, but in those days one had the feeling that the old liberal ideal of "communication" was a dodge; that one went out to have coffee because he didn't really believe in what he was doing; and that one talked over coffee, as we did when we did, about almost everything but what counted in

---

13. Blau cites no source for this quote, and I can't find one.

our lives, to the diminishment of our art. Thus, when we did begin critiques in our studio, the resistance—subdued, mute or self-protective—was fierce; and when I did begin to talk up and elaborate ideas behind the plays, some complained to Irving that they were being lectured at. Now I am a good lecturer, but if I was lecturing, it was hard to be at my best; and though in time the company became more receptive, even zealous, about seminars and critiques, the atmosphere was so seeded with distrust that we are still atoning for it. As I wrote to the company as late as 1959, rehearsing some old desires for more experiment: "In the process we must begin to talk again— there *hasn't* been enough talk among us—of collective style, of method, of plays and what they mean. Not that talk will make method, but neither will silence; and for all the satire at its expense, there is method in method. I must admit my own fault here, for . . . I somewhat adjusted my own directorial procedures to a certain impatience on the part of some of our people with discussion; this encourages the premature."

The formation of the Group was the fruition of an artistic and ideological ferment. There was a swirl of ideas and human urgency, of reformist conviction and technical desire, of acting method and social action. By contrast, though most of the nine people who were in our first play were college graduates and some of them, with Irving and myself, were college teachers, I had the impression we were proceeding in an intellectual and artistic vacuum. True, the place was jumping around us with those happenings that were named the San Francisco Renaissance—the new jazz, the poetry readings, the austerely slapdash followers of Still and Smith[14] at the Art Institute, the Beats, the *City Lights* magazine and the bookshop named after it. But, if we were soon identified with them, we were never strictly part of that scene.

Irving and I were relatively new to the city, and though there were some painters and poets among my friends, again I was leading a double life. When, in 1957, I testified at the "Howl" trial[15] as a "literary expert" for the defense, I had never met Ginsberg or Ferlinghetti (who was actually prosecuted), or for that matter some of the other experts, Kenneth Rexroth, Mark Schorer and Vincent McHugh. Those I did know—the novelists Walter Van Tilburg Clark and Arthur Foff and the critic Mark Linenthal—were colleagues in the Creative Writing Program at San Francisco State College. In the thirties, Clark had coached basketball and acted in a little theater, but while he reminisced amusingly about that, he was more or less reclusive; Foff, my closest friend at the time, wouldn't have cared for the theater at all if I weren't in it, and kept his

14. Clyfford Still and Hassel Smith were among the leaders of the San Francisco School of Abstract Expressionism.

15. The trial in which Lawrence Ferlinghetti of City Lights Books was prosecuted for distributing obscene literature for selling Allen Ginsberg's "Howl."

distance so effectively he is now in Damascus; and Linenthal, with whom I had gone to graduate school, talked far more with me about modern poetry, which I preferred teaching, than about the theater. None of them was involved in the Workshop's organizing phase or in a definition of its principles. It expressed nothing important for them or for any other artist.

In time, the Workshop became a locus of artistic interest in the city. Rexroth became a critical admirer, and other poets and novelists (e.g., James Schevill and Mark Harris) had been attracted to write for us. One of Ginsberg's friends, the painter Robert La Vigne, became our resident designer. But at our origin, we moved in the ambience of things, not with them. And actually, unlike those artists who helped inform the Group, those who came to work with us or circulated in our ambience were very different, if not hostile, in their points of view. As for my own view, I should say that while I could testify against the harassment of "Howl," I could not really testify *for* it. Fortunately it was the strategy of the defense to have each of the experts cover some aspect of the poem's technique or traditions; under the instructions of the salty trial lawyer Jake Ehrlich, we were going to murder the district attorney with erudition. (When Al Bendich, the young ACLU lawyer who had boned up on all the obscenity cases in the history of literature, tried to suggest a strategy to some of the academic people who had met for a briefing, Erlich interrupted: "Turn it off, Al, these professors are all red-blooded Americans. If the D.A. gets smart, they'll let him have it"—smashing fist into palm—"right in the fucking face.") While Rexroth, who thought it a better poem than I did, placed it in the tradition of apocalyptic literature, I gave witness to its affinity with Dada, "the art of furious negation"—the intensity of that negation, said I, keeping it from total despair: "It is a vision that by the salvation of despair, by the salvation of what appears to be [sic!] perversity, by the salvation of what would appear to be obscene, by the salvation of what would appear to be illicit, is ultimately a kind of redemption of the illicit, the obscene, the disillusioned and the despairing . . ." The rhetoric of my testimony came out of the darker musings of my study, that dialogue with the depths, that was coming up more and more in the plays we were doing by the time of the trial.

In 1952, however, there was no such dialogue in public. I did hint at it in the rather silky noncommitment of the program notes to our first play, Philip Barry's *Hotel Universe*; but these were written after the play was rehearsed. The play was chosen because it had substantial roles for all the actors, and because it could be done in modern dress around the unused brick fireplace across from the stove. Yet, though there were no more urgent specifications and the choice almost an accident, I can't help feeling it was also an appropriate choice, given our collective state of mind—for the play reflected our own spiritual drift and a certain soft tolerance about intellectual fuzziness like our own. As the notes said: "Barry's bewildered and badgered characters are representatives of the Lost Generation made famous by F. Scott Fitzgerald and Ernest Hemingway. It was Barry's own generation . . . The innocence of essential understanding of this period was a product of disillusionment, reeling standards and the incertitude of life in an atomized universe."

We find these characters—elegant, effete and exiled—in what used to be a small hotel, now an estate, on a terrace angled "like a wedge into space." The universe is Einstein's, the atmosphere is fantastic, the psychology is basic Freud, the action a kind of psychotherapy, with a muted Jesuitical stink. The notes, as they went on, might have been describing a prototypical play of the fifties, Eliot's *The Cocktail Party*, "no chorus and no ghosts," as Eliot said, but concealed origins and an air of chic mystery. With Hell, Purgatory and the Beatitudes designed into the living room, we learn to make the best of a bad job: "Barry, with his Catholic heritage, could not permit his creatures merely to wander laxly through the universe, decadent and unredeemed. The moral listlessness of the opening scenes is transfigured in a ritual of rebirth that is a curious and not altogether tenable mixture of the orthodox communion and the psychiatrist's couch."

The play was written in 1930. While there was an optimistic tinge to the miraculous, "The ambiguity of this catharsis, together with the haut monde, sophisticated weariness of his characters, offended the socially conscious critics of the proletarian thirties. The play was rejected and suffered a general neglect that its qualities of style, genuine wit, and refined earnest groping with the problems of man's fate did not entirely deserve . . . However much we may regret the ultimate obscurity of Barry's thought," I concluded, "we cannot but admire his dramatic sensibility, precocity and his desire to find peace—for the lost souls of his age and, no doubt, for himself." Indeed, the malaise of the opening scene has an unusual grace for an American play; and the inexplicable guilt of the characters for a young boy they had seen commit suicide has been a memorable image. Again out of apparent expediency—but why this?—we revived the play some years later when we were pressed for a production at a theater we had temporarily rented. And still later, traveling in Europe and fighting a lover's quarrel with the existential position, I remembered that scene in composing a play of my own.

Performed in the loft, the "production" was meant to be an exercise. It played after a couple of months of rehearsal to an invited audience of fifty, for one night, and that's all. Before it began, I made a short talk to the guests explaining our moderate aim: to provide the circumstances in which actors could practice their art. The guests were enthusiastic. We asked them to sign a mailing list. Urged to do the play again, we refused and went on to another project.

Irving and I watched the "bewildered and badgered characters" of *Hotel Universe* in front of our "fire exit," a dirt-encrusted window, with egress against a low wall and a blank alley. Before we left the loft, over a year later, we had formed a "partnership" and were totally liable. Even Lloyd's of London refused to insure us.

—HB

The New York Shakespeare Festival

FOUNDED 1954

Joseph Papp

> I am trying to build our theater on the bedrock of municipal and civic responsibility—not on the quicksands of show business economics. I am interested in a popular theater—not a theater of the few.
>
> *—Joseph Papp*

Even among the Olympian founders in this collection, Joseph Papp stands out as a colossus. The legendary story of his New York Shakespeare Festival—later to include the Public Theater—is a story of many stories:

- How a little-known television stage manager and young theater producer of unshakable principle faced down the House Un-American Activities Committee;
- How this same man, blacklisted, fought in court to keep his job at CBS—and won;
- How—to offer Shakespeare at no cost to the people of New York City—he bested Robert Moses, one of the giants of twentieth-century New York politics (Papp's biographer Helen Epstein calls Moses "one of the most powerful non-elected public officials in the United States");
- How he built a free theater for all in Central Park;

SOURCE: "The Price of This Ticket Is Responsibility," by Joseph Papp, was originally published in the *New York Herald Tribune*, on March 16, 1958; letter to Robert Moses, by Joseph Papp, was originally published in the *New York Times*, on May 4, 1959; "Sponsor of Free Shakespeare Says It Would Help More Than Hinder," by Joseph Papp, was originally published in the *New York Times*, on July 24, 1960; *Free for All: Joe Papp, The Public, and the Greatest Theater Story Ever Told*, by Kenneth Turan and Joseph Papp, with the assistance of Gail Merrifield Papp, 2009.

- How he took on Broadway and, then, to a great extent, took it over;
- How he never stopped fighting back against the theater's most influential critics and the *New York Times*;
- How he unilaterally established color-blind, multiracial casting;
- How he championed the most controversial of the new American playwrights and how he fell out with them;
- How he made a mainstream home for an eclectic array of work by writers of color—Ntozake Shange's *for colored girls who have considered suicide/when the rainbow is enuf*, Charles Gordone's *No Place To Be Somebody* (the first play by an African American to win the Pulitzer), Miguel Piñero's *Short Eyes* and the work of Papp's eventual successor at the Public Theater, George C. Wolfe;
- How he created an incubator for unlikely musicals—*Hair, A Chorus Line, Runaways*—and made Broadway history in the process;
- How a poor boy from Brooklyn, Joseph Papirofsky, whose parents spoke Yiddish, fell in love with Shakespeare at the public library and then set about to make a theater in the image of that library;
- How that poor boy became arguably the most influential American producer in history, built what former *Times* critic Frank Rich called "the most influential theater organization in the United States," produced more than 450 plays, including the entire canon of Shakespeare (minus one), did "more, perhaps, than any other single individual to widen the base of the American theater audience" (according to Julius Novick), and still managed to cast himself in the role of the little guy.

These are stories of battle and conflict—conflicts often of Papp's choosing. "There was an internal force within Papp," explains his first biographer, Stuart W. Little, "an impulse buried in the dynamics of managing and leading a complex arts institution such as the Shakespeare Festival, that impelled him whenever in crisis not to retrench but to expose his theater to more risk and move forward. Out of the history of the New York Shakespeare Festival one could write the Papp Principle: escalation or extinction, keep moving or die. With each crisis, each time he felt himself besieged, he had raised his sights."[16]

16. The natively dramatic Papp is the subject of two compelling biographies, one written twenty years into his theater's life and one published three years after his death. Stuart W. Little's *Enter Joseph Papp: In Search of a New American Theater* (Coward, McCann & Geoghegan, Inc., New York, 1974) catches the man and the theater in media res, while Helen Epstein's fine *Joe Papp: An American Life* (Little, Brown and Company, Boston, 1994) provides a complete and intimate portrait of the entire life and career.

Even as Papp became a Goliath in the American theater, his story—as well as his animus and ambition—was that of a David, the little guy, the street fighter, the immigrant and outsider. He fought for democracy and, therefore, for access—to the stage (for actors and writers) and to the audience. "If there is a single driving force which characterizes the New York Shakespeare Festival," Papp said, "it is its continual confrontation with the wall that separates vast numbers of people from the arts—[a wall] spawned by poverty, ignorance, historical conditions." Or, in the succinct words of historian Mary C. Henderson: Papp's manifesto is "one simple, direct and unwavering statement: 'everybody needs theater.'"

Papp, ever engaged in building a future, resisted looking back, as Kenneth Turan, the co-author with Papp of the oral history *Free for All*, makes clear. As a result, we had no diaries or autobiographical sources from him until his widow, Gail Merrifield Papp, made it possible for Turan to publish that book in 2009 though Papp himself had, after reading an early draft, shut the door on the project. What we do have from Papp (in addition to the remarkable testimonies in *Free for All*, some reprinted here), are a fighter's selection of letters—to the *Times*, to government officials, to critics—that lay out the rationale and vision for a theater that truly earned its nickname: "the Public."

—*TL*

———————

"The Price of This Ticket Is Responsibility"

By Joseph Papp
New York Herald Tribune, March 16, 1958

Mr. Papp is the producer of the New York Shakespeare Festival, which offers its productions free of admission charge. The following article is a reply to a suggestion, advanced recently by New York Herald Tribune *drama critic Walter Kerr in a Sunday article, that Mr. Papp charge admission to his shows.*

Thank you very much (Mr. Kerr) for your very thoughtful article, in which you offer some formidable arguments for a change in our policy of free admissions. As always, I sincerely appreciate your concern for our survival.

If by charging admission, I was convinced we would have a "minimum stability" to guarantee our program on the basis of our approach to the theater and to audiences, I would do it. I would have done it long ago. It would certainly be a less painful method of operation for me, personally.

The Threepenny Opera [Off Broadway] charges a $4.85 top in a house of under three hundred. The Circle in the Square has a $4.50 top in a smaller theater—197 seats. Our home at the Heckscher Theatre has a 650-seat capacity; it is in every sense a legitimate house.

OUT OF AUDIENCE REACH

If we were to charge admission and were able to obtain concessions from the entertainment unions, our top price would have to be $5.50. In the park, with a two thousand capacity, tickets would have to go for $3.50. These prices would immediately defeat the primary purpose of our existence—to reach large, new audiences for the classics.

Up to this point we have been very lucky. We have had a string of consecutive critical successes. On a paying basis, it would take just one or two "failures" to wipe us out—one or two rainy nights in the park to wash us out. Off Broadway and Broadway economics do not give us the right to fail from time to time and still stay alive. If we are to strive for stability we must develop a structure that gives us this right. It would be an act of irresponsibility on my part to subject the organization to the chaotic gambling of show business.

What may seem an idealistic approach to the theater is in reality the most practical for what we are trying to build. Broadway and Off Broadway live in a world of romance; the quick buck, the overnight success, the one big break, here today and gone tomorrow—hardly a solid base for operations.

A POPULAR THEATER

I am trying to build our theater on the bedrock of municipal and civic responsibility—not on the quicksands of show business economics. I am interested in a popular theater—not a theater for the few. I am interested in establishing a classical repertory company with a guaranteed annual wage for performers. This is impossible under the present conditions on or Off Broadway.

We are not ready to adopt the point of view that human nature being what it is, people must be made to pay for something to appreciate it. A theater will create its own respect on the stage. How many plays have we seen for which we have paid lots of money and disliked, much less appreciated? In fact, it was worse when you paid for it.

The only practical means of insuring the permanence of our theater is to tie it in with civic responsibility. The public library, an institution for enlightenment and entertainment, is a case in point. No charge is made for books. If people had to pay, most of the books would gather dust on the shelves. I know that if I had had to pay for books at the Williamsburg (Brooklyn) Public Library, it is doubtful that I would have read the plays of Shakespeare.

AN INSTITUTION

The important thing about the library is that it is free and available to people if they want to use it. I do not know how much they appreciate it, but nobody suggests charging for books as a method of obtaining appreciation nor as a way of getting stability. The library is an institution for the people and it stands. This is how I want our theater to stand, supported by two pillars— the city and private donors. This is the only economic base that can insure permanence for our kind of theater.

I see the Shakespeare Festival in the category of public recreation and public education, not show business. A business must stay out of the red to exist. Recreation and education do not (and should not) have to live this way. There are free museums and free public concerts. There is, in fact, an excellent marionette troupe subsidized by the Department of Parks. There is no charge for admission, and they do not have to pay their own way.

Our school system pays our money every day which "is spent immediately and is gone forever" and "no other conceivable income is envisioned." Financial crises appear regularly. Nobody suggests that the schools be offered half-free. Insufficient funds was never a basis for attacking the principle of free and universal education. A theater, like education, has the function of disseminating ideas and values. Nobody expects any more from the money going into education than that it helps to put something useful into the head of some boy or girl.

THEATER FOR EVERYBODY

By establishing our theater as an essential part of the cultural life of the people, we insure stability. In democracy, public and private enterprise exist side by side. I believe that in a city the size of New York and in a city where most of the people have yet to see a live professional production, it is of the utmost importance to have a public theater—a theater for everybody—yes, everybody: for those who can afford it and those who cannot.

We accept the responsibility that goes with asking for support to turn out plays of worth on the highest artistic level. I believe in bringing the youth to the theater through the schools, churches and community organizations. I believe in the theater as a vital cultural force necessary to help in the spiritual guidance of our people.

I hardly think that the foundations and individuals who have made substantial contributions feel that their money went down into a bottomless pit. They contributed this money in the first place because they supported the concept of free theater for new audiences. Most of them would not have given a cent on any other basis. The city would not have given us facilities, labor or equipment if we had functioned in any other way. And I am certain that our audiences—who have made voluntary contributions time and again—feel certain that their money was used for a very good purpose.

ONE MILLION DOLLARS NEEDED

We are now engaged in a campaign to raise one million dollars to insure operations for the next five years. Far from offering philanthropists, municipal authorities and the general public an "eternal siphon," an "open drain," an "invalid," we are inviting them to invest in a highly responsible and promising undertaking.

From its inception, the free Shakespeare Festival has striven for permanence. We have crises, but we manage to stay alive and grow. I believe we have never been stronger than we are right now. Though we do not have enough funds to keep our curtain up right now, we have enough potential to keep it up for ten years. I am far from ready to throw in my towel over the city's reluctance to come to our aid. Conditions change and so do attitudes. I have every reason to believe that support from the city will come and if I were a gambling man I would lay odds that it will.

I am also confident that foundations and philanthropists will continue to invest in the concept of a public theater. I am absolutely certain that the people of the city, our audience, will guarantee our existence for now and forever.

. . .

May 4, 1959

Commissioner Robert Moses
Department of Parks
Arsenal
64th Street and Fifth Avenue
Central Park
New York 21, NY

Dear Commissioner Moses:

In your letter of May 1st you state that the New York Shakespeare Festival will be granted permission to operate in Central Park if (a) the mayor will provide twenty thousand dollars for improvements and (b) that instead of your previous demand for a two-dollar and one-dollar admission charge, you now insist on a revised scale of one dollar, and fifty cents for seats.

These demands take no cognizance of our previously stated reasons for rejecting an admission charge to our performance to cover the city's costs in maintaining the grounds. If our position is still obscure, may I repeat that for the past three years our plays have been presented free to the public with your approval and support. Funds to cover the costs of mounting and operating the productions have been raised from private sources. To abandon our policy of free admissions would result in disenfranchising the very people we are anxious to serve. Furthermore, increased costs of operating a box office would create new and insurmountable financial problems.

That you still hold to the proposition that the Shakespeare audience must be singled out to pay for the privilege of using public facilities which are free to baseball players, zoo-goers and concert audiences is regrettable and we have no other course than to reject this discriminatory and anti-popular concept.

While we acknowledge your authority to regulate our operation in the park, we feel that it does not extend to the internal workings of the Festival. Since we are dedicated to the principle of free admissions, it is hardly within your purview to insist that we alter the basic purpose of our organization.

As for the twenty thousand dollars you are asking the mayor to provide for improvements in the area, I can only say that we would welcome the addition of better facilities. However, we cannot be a party to any scheme which places the burden of the costs of such facilities on the backs of our taxpaying audiences. Why these "improvements" have suddenly loomed as a critical issue, I am at a loss to understand. We have operated successfully for the past three years within the conditions without a crisis. To present this newly manufactured obstacle as a reason for keeping the Festival out of Central Park can hardly be sustained.

If there exists any real concern for "improvements" may I suggest (as I have done for two years) that the pathways leading to the theater side from the West Side on 81st Street and the East Side entrance on 79th Street be properly illuminated.

You say in your letter that I have not contributed anything to a calm atmosphere, and that I "have been busily circulating round robin letters which bear no relation to the problem . . ." Perhaps in politics you have learned that by standing the truth on its head you can get enough people to believe a lie. I seem to recall that you were responsible for circulating a letter questioning (amongst other things) my political background, and my probity in handling Festival funds. You offered this letter as a reply to critics of your arbitrary ruling. You disseminated this letter without a signature. This is hardly a contribution to a calm atmosphere.

The letter represented your second position for denying the Festival the use of Central Park. Your first was soil erosion.

Saturday, a newspaper reported that you didn't care about the grass at all, but that it was the muggers, the degenerates and pickpockets that concerned you. In position number three, you called the operation "a disorderly type of performance." May I bring to your attention the remarks of a prominent critic who described the Central Park audiences this way: "the long patient line of people hoping to get into an amphitheater that seats 2,300 is a humbling sight for anyone who believes in the theater. The alert attention of the people who do succeed in getting in chastens anyone familiar with sophisticated audiences."

Perhaps, if you had attended one of the performances, you would have been prepared with reliable information concerning the nature of the Shakespeare audiences in Central Park.

Every civic-minded organization has hailed the Festival in the park as a buffer against lawlessness. They have expressed the opinion that Shakespeare in the Park has had a civilizing effect rather than a disorderly one. One letter writer said, "Thank you for making the park safe again." To keep Shakespeare out of the park because certain elements "might prey on the audiences" is to say that we discontinue all gatherings of people in the park and leave it as a haven for crime. It is my conviction that the more activity in the parks, the less lawlessness.

I think everyone is growing tired of the distortions, outright fabrications and anonymous allegations put out by your office. No new excuse you can conjure will stop us from pressing for the right to continue the free presentations of Shakespeare in Central Park.

Very truly yours,
Joseph Papp

. . .

"Sponsor of Free Shakespeare Says It Would Help More Than Hinder"
By Joseph Papp, founder and producer of the New York Shakespeare Festival
New York Times, July 24, 1960

GOVERNMENT AID

Asking for government subsidy of the theater was represented by Brooks Atkinson in a recent Sunday column as an invitation to control. By this token, commercial theater, the very antithesis of government-supported theater, should be a veritable bastion of freedom, a powerhouse of provocative and unorthodox ideas.

Yet were a government committee to select our theater of private investment as a target for censorship, it would have slim pickings indeed. Unless it were to consider deleting a subversive bump from *Gypsy* or curbing the radical enthusiasm of the magnificent dancers in *West Side Story*.

Why, with all the apparent freedom of privately financed theater, are there so few plays that stretch the boundaries of freedom?

Though the commercial producer has absolute freedom of choice in the selection of plays, he instinctively turns to the one with the greatest potential gross. Is this not a significant encroachment on the freedom of the theater?

If we believe that the theater, to be worthy of its heritage, should stand in the vanguard of thought, should be an area for challenging ideas in both content and for a place for deep and stimulating experiences, then we must also feel unsatisfied with what we have.

The invisible villain of the piece is anarchy. We have a theater without scheme or purpose, without a consistent artistic leadership; a theater based on whim, subject to economic laws thoroughly at odds with creative objectives, a theater with pick-up teams of talent plucked from the overflowing pool of unemployment.

WASTING TALENT

This chaos, inspired by the freedom of commercial investment, restricts and in turn inhibits the real freedom necessary to a vital theater, the freedom that comes from the planned utilization of our now wasting talent resources—the freedom for our actors, writers and directors to develop artistically and consistently in permanent repertory companies.

When we ask the government to support the theater, we do so because we realize that the arts cannot operate on the profits principle. We also recognize that they are an essential part of our lives and necessary for our survival. These ingredients have motivated the government's entry into education, science and the postal service. The fact that these functions of society are too important to be left in private hands is the substance of my argument.

Since it is the area of ideas that concerns us most, let us take a look at education and the government. Schools are the crucibles of our thinking. Yet we accept without reservation the necessity for government-subsidized education. Now certainly this inherently means control. Though the danger is always great that some governmental committee or ambitious politician will try to invade the realm of education, it is no argument for the abolition of public education.

Therefore, how can we reasonably deny the theater the help we accept for our subsidized educational system in the fear of interference? The fear is real—but the conclusions unrealistic. In a democracy there is no alternative but to constantly defend the sensitive areas of thought and expression against incursions. There is only one way to guarantee freedom in the schools, the theater and elsewhere—to defend it—eternal vigilance being the price of freedom.

THE FOUNDATIONS

Mr. Atkinson suggests in his article that "private subsidy as opposed to government subsidy" is, when it is given, a guarantee of freedom. He cited foundation assistance as a case in point.

For the New York Shakespeare Festival, foundations have proven to be its main source of operating income. Without it the Festival would be hard put to survive. Therefore, to critically examine the role of foundations in their relationship to the theater is not to deny their necessity at a time when the only real alternative, government subsidy, is not in the offing.

In the long run, foundations are no answer to the problems of the theater and no guarantee of its freedom. To support this latter contention we make take the example of the Rockefeller Foundation, which rejected an appeal from the New York Shakespeare Festival on the grounds that free admission destroyed incentive.

The Ford Foundation likewise turned down a request. Here it was subtly hinted and cautiously intimated that free Shakespeare smacked too much of socialism. Whatever their justifications, it appears that these giant foundations, responsible for the largest grants in the field of the arts, would not necessarily guarantee freedom of the theater.

Furthermore, decisions concerning grants are made in private. The public has no knowledge of them, nor can it expect to have. There is comparatively little public pressure that can be brought to bear on these private organizations. On the other hand, were the government involved, one would, at least, have recourse to the system of checks and balances, to the principle that the government is responsible to the people. Under these circumstances it would be possible to cry havoc and petition our government for redress of grievances. Admitting that interference is undesirable, but having the choice of private or government interference in the theater, it would seem that the latter is preferable.

CONTINUITY NEEDED

Aside from the issue of control, the unpredictable and temporary nature of foundation giving leaves unresolved the key problem of the theater—guaranteed continuity; and it must be guaranteed to make any sense. Foundations gear their support to the understandable philosophy of a boost to help the recipient over a hurdle. Grants are not given in perpetuity. Their purposes are varied and subjective to change. Nor can they be expected to limit their commitments year after year to a single project.

The theater, like education, needs the security and comfort, if you will, of inclusion in a governmental budget. It may be cut. But it is there to be defended and fought for. Any discussion of freedom of the theater without considering its permanency is largely academic.

By making the theater a responsibility of government, it makes it also a responsibility of the people. Restricting the theater to private subsidy cuts it off from the mainstream of American life and perpetuates the growing separation of the theater from its vast potential audience.

Only with government aid can we have ticket prices within the reach of everybody, a greater number and variety of plays and a guarantee of continued existence for the theater. Private subsidy narrows the scope of the theater. Government involvement broadens its role into the larger area of education and contributes to the development of a greater, more intelligent and more responsible audience.

. . .

Free for All[17]

Joseph Papp: There were gates at the very top of the amphitheater, and though it was still light, there were hundreds of people outside waiting for the first performance. When the gates were opened, people rushed in pell-mell. Old people, young people, Jewish people, Hispanic people, a few black people—it was really the Lower East Side spilling into the theater, packing every seat. Word of mouth brought them. We had been rehearsing there for a month or more, and the whole neighborhood knew about us.

There were these huge projects right there, some of the earliest low-cost housing developments, built by the ILGWU[18] and the Amalgamated Clothing Workers after terrible, terrible tenements had been torn down. A lot of elderly Jewish people came from those, and during the course of the play you'd hear all these comments similar to what used to go on in the Yiddish theater. They'd yell to Caesar, "Watch out, he's killing you!" and, "Oh, it's a shame!" They would comment on it because they felt this was actually happening. You'd watch people, and they were really enjoying it.

When the play started, frankly, I was scared to death. I didn't have the faintest notion what to expect. Obviously, most of the people out there had never seen live actors before. They might stone us to death for all I knew.

Then came the great speech at the very beginning of the first act, where the tribune Marullus says, "You blocks, you stones, you worse than senseless things!" It's a very strong speech, kind of a crowd-pleaser, and toward

---

17. The excerpt starting here is from *Free for All*, by Kenneth Turan and Joseph Papp, with the assistance of Gail Merrifield Papp, 2009.

18. International Ladies' Garment Workers' Union.

the end of it, people started to cheer. It was really loud and it sounded like cheering anyplace—it could have been a baseball game, the kind you'd hear when someone gets a hit in the clutch. By the last lines, when Marullus says, "Fall upon your knees, pray to the gods to intermit the plague that needs must light on this ingratitude," I could tell that here was an audience that really identified. I never felt so relieved in my life.

Earlier that day, I had been walking down Grand Street. There was a Sherman cigar [store] there, and I really loved that tobacco smell. It was just before the opening, the sun was just about ready to go down and I said, "I'll take that cigar." It was a Corona and it cost me thirty cents, which at the time made it a great luxury. But that night, it seemed the right thing to do. And, boy, was that a great cigar.

Putting on plays at the amphitheater was more expensive than at the church: *Julius Caesar* fully costumed cost almost eight hundred dollars. And that was with me doing the trumpet calls by cupping my hands together and making an appropriate noise off stage. I was having to use my own money, as I much as I had left over from what I needed to live on, which wasn't much.

So I was always trying to raise a little money here and there. I'd try and get ten dollars from somebody, fifteen dollars from somebody else. We had enough money to do *Caesar*, but I wanted to put on *The Taming of the Shrew* as well. Henry Hewes, a critic for the *Saturday Review* who'd liked the first play, connected me with a philanthropic group called ANTA, the American National Theatre and Academy.

I was always working, so I came to the ANTA meeting, which took place on Fifth Avenue, in dirty work clothes. They should have asked me to wipe my feet before I walked in there. Everyone was sitting around this table drinking coffee and I was told, "Look, you're ahead now, you've established yourself, why don't you sit back a little bit, give yourself a chance to reorganize and do something in a better style."

"No," I said. "I don't want to wait. Like one swallow, doing one play does not a spring make. We have to do two plays. We're geared to do it and we're going to do it. I want money, and I want it now, to put this play on." I pounded my fist on the table a lot. I said, "I've done the work, now you provide the money, it's your responsibility," and I ended up with five hundred dollars, the amount I needed to proceed.

[. . .]

Joseph Papp: My aim was to get Brooks Atkinson down. He was all-powerful at the time. I didn't want a second-stringer to come down; I wanted the most distinguished critic in New York to come down. Had we not done it, I don't know if I'd be here today talking about this thing.

I went up to the *Times* and said, "I'd like to speak to Brooks Atkinson."

"He's not in now."

"Well, I'll wait."

"He's not going to be here."

"Well, I'll wait."

Every five minutes, someone came out, looked at me, and reported, "The guy's still out there." I refused to leave. I sat there for hours, and finally in walked Brooks Atkinson, followed by a man I later learned was Robert Whitehead, the producer. I stopped him and said, "Mr. Atkinson, can I see you for a moment?"

He was an extremely distinguished-looking man, but very friendly. He said he wanted to converse with Mr. Whitehead first. After about fifteen or twenty minutes, he called me in. And everybody else in the department was looking out from the other doors, saying, "He's in there now! How the hell did he get in?"

"Look," I said, "I'm trying to start this theater. We're working very hard to do this well. You have to come see it. I need you there to see it." I told him exactly what my goals were and he said, "All right. Will you pick me up at the Harvard Club at seven-thirty?" And I said, "I'll be there."

The night in question came and the only vehicle I had was this big, old, dirty two-ton truck I'd been driving around—a very serviceable vehicle for carrying lots of heavy stuff but hardly appropriate for the Harvard Club. I went in wearing my work clothes—I didn't have any other clothes—and asked for Mr. Atkinson. He came out to the truck wearing this elegant suit and I said, "Okay, here we go," and started to drive this damn thing.

We were driving on the downtown side of the FDR Drive and the amphitheater was on the uptown side, and I always used to take a shortcut. I said, "Just hold on for a minute, Mr. Atkinson," and I jumped the divider to great screeching of tires all around. By the time we got to the amphitheater, Atkinson was breathing hard.

After the show, he was very nice, but he didn't say a word to me. I didn't know how the hell he felt. I drove him back, and this time I didn't have to jump the divider.

I was backstage the next day and I got a call from this sweet woman, Clara Rotter, who was Atkinson's personal secretary. "Don't tell anyone about it," she said, "but Brooks has written a wonderful piece; it's going to be his first Sunday column of the season."

And it was a wonderful piece, and that was the document I was able to use to really raise funds on a larger level. It was the most important thing you could have. It came from the most distinguished critic and it gave me a certain entrée into some of these places.

I'd studied foundations like you'd study the palm of your hand if you were a palmist. I went through books on them. I'd say, "Which people can help us to do this?" I became an expert on foundations. The first place I took Atkinson's column was the Doris Duke Foundation and they gave me ten thousand dollars. That was a *lotta* thousands of dollars, and it broke the ice. I still had no office, I was still working out of my home, but I was already planning for next season.

What I was trying to do was create a theater. That's an enormous under-taking. It's like creating a living thing that will express my ideas and my feelings, that will give me a place to go day in and day out, that will enable me to say that I have a career, I have a profession. I was profession-less and career-less, and I always felt a need, not in any crazy way but in the simplest way, to have some identification.

There were people who'd say to you, "What do you do?" And I never knew what to say. At one point I'd say, "I'm an actor," but I didn't feel like I was an actor. I said, "I'm a director," for a while, but I didn't have enough experience to prove that. It was at this point, because I'd done it and I'd achieved something in the process, that I began to feel like I was a producer. I don't want to use the word "destiny," maybe it's more of a Buddhist idea, but there was something that said that that was the way I should go.

[. . .]

Joseph Papp: I always felt that we should travel. After all, Shakespeare did both: he had his own theater, and he also toured from time to time. True, he went to avoid the plague, but that notion was always there. I wanted to bring Shakespeare to the people, that was the whole idea. I had to reach the thousands of people who lived and died in their neighborhoods.

To do this we raised money from foundations—the New York Founda-tion, the Old Dominion Foundation, and others—a total of thirty-five thou-sand dollars. The Astor Foundation had never given money to anything like this before, but the woman in charge, who was from Queens herself, said to me, "I'd be curious to see how the people in Queens react to Shakespeare." That's what got her interested.

In order to tour, we planned a wooden folding stage, to be mounted on the bed of a forty-five-foot platform trailer truck. I'd gotten estimates, and we were talking like twenty thousand dollars, thirty thousand dollars. But I knew this guy in Brooklyn who had a kind of body shop and he was going to give me a bargain. "I have some old trucks back here," he said. "I can fix one up for you for three thousand or four thousand dollars." I went crazy about trucks for a while. I kept watching the way he was putting this thing together; I could hardly wait.

Even when the truck was finished, the tires on it had been worn down quite a bit and the whole thing was never totally steady. It was a very rough, barely put-together piece of work; the hinges couldn't really support the weight that well. The truck looked like it had come out of Eastern Europe. When it would go around a corner it would list to one side to an extraordinary degree; you'd think it would never recover. You talk about two planks and passion, that was it, and even the planks were kind of worn through. We looked awfully strange going through the city streets, but for the money we couldn't go wrong.

I guess everything was hard at the beginning, but the most difficult thing was getting through the bureaucracy at the Department of Parks. I mean, who was I? Rules and regulations were all over the place. You couldn't do this, you couldn't do that, you couldn't do this.

Finally, I managed to reach Stanley Lowell, a deputy mayor, and a tour was approved. We began at the Belvedere Tower area of Central Park in Manhattan and then went on to War Memorial Park in Brooklyn, Kings Park in Queens, Clove Lakes Park in Staten Island and Williamsbridge Oval Park—later changed to the Hunter College campus—in the Bronx.

[. . .]

HUAC AND ROBERT MOSES

> I am not now a member of the Communist Party . . . I just think it is wrong to deny anybody employment because of their political beliefs.
>
> *—Joseph Papp,*
> *Testimony before the House Un-American Activities Committee,*
> *June 19, 1958*

> As to Papp, he was and is an irresponsible Commie who doesn't keep his word or obey the rules and—again, anticlimax—he has no dough to pay the actors or run the show decently and therefore surreptitiously passes the hat like a damned mendicant.
>
> *—Parks Commissioner Robert Moses,*
> *Letter to Howard Lindsay,*
> *August 10, 1959*

Joseph Papp: The House Un-American Activities Committee hearings had already begun when I began to be pursued by two FBI men. They would meet me as I was leaving work at CBS, say, "We're from the FBI," and start to walk down the street with me. I kept walking.

"We'd like to talk to you about some of the people that you knew in California." They were more nervous than I was—they were shaking, actually.

"I have nothing to say to you."

"Well, it would be to your advantage—"

"Listen, I have nothing to say to you. If you want to do something official, do it officially. Otherwise, I have nothing to say to you."

So they'd leave and I'd go in the subway. A couple of weeks later, there they were again, starting what became a routine of trying to break me down. Meeting me in front of CBS was part of that—making me wonder whether I'd lose my job, whether they had already informed CBS that I was going to be called to testify:

"I think you'd better cooperate, if you know what's good for you," they said the last time they met me.

"Are you threatening me?"

"I'm just telling you what you should pay attention to."

A few days before I was called, there was an offer to go to Washington to appear at a closed hearing and not be subjected to an open proceeding. I turned it down, even though I knew it meant I would be subpoenaed. I was not going to engage in naming names. I saw people that I knew starting to repudiate everything they ever stood for. They found all kinds of rationales, excuses for naming people, for holding on to their goddamn jobs. And I found that disgusting. I was very disappointed in that kind of behavior.

Some of the most radical people would say, "I was young and I really didn't believe in it. I didn't know any better." I was young, too, but I always knew better. I was very clear why I was doing certain things. I have deep-rooted convictions which I've had all my life. I'm not saying it's good or bad, but it happens to be me. It comes out of my background, and I would never deny that one bit. On the contrary, I'm very proud of it, I think it's made me capable of doing what I'm doing now, doing a service to the community, to people.

I was gritting my teeth, waiting to get a subpoena. The worst that could happen to me, if I was held in contempt, would be to spend a year in jail. And, psychologically, I was prepared for that. The terrible thing was that people were afraid to talk to you. Everybody looked at you as though you were something to be avoided. You became persona non grata.

I thought that as a result, whether I went to jail or was just publicly disgraced, the Shakespeare Festival would be destroyed. I felt that none of the big organizations would give us any money—they'd be afraid and all that business. The Festival was getting someplace. As far as I was concerned, it was my life, and I felt that this would end it.

Peggy Bennion Papp:[19] That was a terrible time. It was so frightening because we didn't know how we were going to live. Everybody was worried about it, everybody. People who had not been as left-wing as he were blacklisted. The

19. Papp's first wife.

FBI used to come to our door all the time and try to get Joe to inform. When he went to work, a lot of people wouldn't speak to him, or they'd come over and say, "Take my name out of your address book and never speak to me again. I don't know you." He nearly blacked out one night from the anxiety. But he always lived on the edge of crises, there was always brinksmanship, he would always take an enormous chance that was far beyond his present capacity, and somehow or other, he'd gear himself up to that leap.

It was his belief that supported him and saw him through. When he went to testify, I said to him, "Oh, Joe, I am so scared." And he said, "Peggy, I can't be scared for myself. I'm too worried about what this means for the whole country and whole world, the terrible meaning it has for a lot of other people." Oh, those were the kinds of statements he made that I admired.

Merle Debuskey:[20] When Joe got a subpoena he called me. And I picked up the phone and called a marvelous man whose name was Ephraim London and who was very big in civil liberties.

"Eph," I said to him, "there's no money in this."

And he just very simply said, "Is he a decent fellow?"

"He is an especially decent, loving, significant guy."

"Well, fine, tell him to call me and come in."

Obviously, Joe was not going to be a cooperative witness. He understood what it was all about, and he wasn't going to demean himself for any momentary relief of the burden of being a decent, honorable person. And we evolved a whole program of how to parry the thrust of this guy being some kind of menace.

We compiled an enormous amount of material that by now had been printed about the Shakespeare Festival, including the cover story of a publication called *Amerika*, in which the State Department used him as the foremost example to demonstrate to Russia what America is and what it can do. By the end of it, a couple of committee guys walked up to Joe and congratulated him.

Joseph Papp: I was not aggressive before the committee; the circumstances were very intimidating. You can't understand, unless you were part of it, how grim those times were. You saw no future after testifying; you didn't see any light at the end of the tunnel. You didn't even see the tunnel, for that matter. Even if you took what might be seen as a heroic position, it was hardly something that you ran around bragging about. You just knew that your situation was terrible.

On the other hand, on the day I testified I felt very high, very emotional. It's a romantic notion, but for some reason when you get up there, you think

20. Press agent for the Shakespeare Festival.

that these people who are questioning you will understand your patriotism. You look for some sort of comprehension, but, of course, it isn't there. These people were simply insistent on getting what they wanted for their purposes.

But still I tried. I presented them with a copy of *Amerika*, a magazine published by the State Department and sent to Russia, where our work was depicted as representative of free democratic culture. It was just a piece of showmanship, but it was important to say that what I was doing was important. The guy was trying to find out if we were saying something subversive with Shakespeare. It was dumb.

My position was that I'd answer any question about myself, but I wasn't going to answer any questions about anybody else. Ephraim London suggested to his clients in that position that they take the Fifth Amendment.

"It's up to you," he said, "but once you begin to answer things, they'll force you to answer everything, and you're going to have to start mentioning names."

"No, no, no," I said. "I won't do anything like that." Even though most of the people I knew in California had already been called before the committee, I wasn't going to use that as an excuse to name them. That would have been succumbing to them, and I was determined not to do that.

That particular position was purely a position of pride. To me, being a stool pigeon, informing on somebody else, was the lowest form of life. I knew that people who are put under pressure to save their necks will historically name other people. But, first of all, nobody was torturing me. It was just a matter of prison, possibly. But, I figured, that's not the worst thing in the world. At least they pay for your room and board.

I testified in the morning, and then I left to do a news show at CBS that same evening. I was on the subway and I saw all around me the afternoon newspapers—the *Journal American* and the *World-Telegram*—with my picture on them. There I was, and all these people were reading these big huge headlines about me, the "I've Got a Secret" Man, refusing to name names.

I walked into the studio, and the stagehands, my best friends, wanted to know what my position was. "I took the Fifth Amendment," I said, "because if I went further, I would have to tell them everything about other people, and I could not do that." They were all very good about it, except one embittered guy who said, "Oh, you communist," and walked away. Another guy, a lighting designer I'd spent hours helping, came over to me. He was shaking.

"You didn't mention m-m-my name, did you?" he said.

"Why the fuck should I mention your name?" I said. "You're nothing."

I was about to start my show when I got a call saying that Don Darcey, the head of the stage manager's department, wanted to see me. I did the show first, and then I went up to his office, where Don looked awfully uncomfortable.

"Joe," he said, "I'm going to have to lay you off."

"What do you mean? Why?"

"Well," he said, his eyes shifting a little bit, "you know we're a little overstaffed."

"Come on, Don. What are you handing me here?"

He looked at me and said very quietly, "There was a meeting about your testimony. William Paley was very upset."

"So what?"

"We've got too many people here. We're trying to cut back."

"Come on."

"That's what it is. I have to do it."

"I don't accept that."

"What do you mean?"

"I'm telling you, I find this totally unacceptable. I'm a member of the Radio and Television Directors Guild, and I'm going to take this up with the union."

[. . .]

Now you wouldn't exactly call the Radio and Television Directors Guild a fighting union. I tried for weeks to get them to have a board meeting to discuss the issue, but they were very reluctant to get into it. Meanwhile, I was out of a job, I had no income, and I had a child and family to support.

One of the directors I'd worked with at CBS, Robert Mulligan, got a job on Broadway directing *Comes a Day*, starring Judith Anderson and George C. Scott, and he hired me as stage manager. One night, I was so distracted by all the things that were bothering me that while Judith Anderson was on stage alone giving a speech, I said, "Okay, hit the curtain." And, oh god, it was the wrong cue, she was only halfway through the speech. She sounded like she was struggling, strangling, but the guy kept bringing down this curtain. Boy, was she furious.

Finally, I got the board of directors to meet, and after going through a very complicated polling of the membership, they agreed to challenge the firing. That led to arbitration, and in November of 1958, CBS was ordered to reinstate me with $1,500 back pay. CBS had contended that my dismissal had nothing to do with my pleading the Fifth Amendment but had come about because I had concealed my association with the California Labor School. But the arbitrator ruled that CBS knew of that association for years, and since it had never confronted me about it, "it does not follow that six and a half years later it might rely on these omissions to justify a dismissal."

That was a major victory, I was feeling great, but when I came to CBS, I found they were assigning me to minimum tasks, saying people had not asked for me when I knew they had. I could tell they were starting to jerk me around, and I began to think, "Why am I hanging around this damn organization?" So I quit and devoted myself full time to the Shakespeare Festival.

Still, winning was most gratifying, and not just because I felt I'd made a point. It restored a faith I had in this democratic system, confirmed my feeling that you could still get satisfaction in this country. From the very beginning, I've always believed in the justice of the United States, when we're at our best.

Merle Debuskey: Joe became the first blacklisted person to be fired and rehired, and even though most people today hardly remember it, that was very significant. His case was a kind of cause célèbre in the world of television and theater. I mean, the blacklist was a pretty heavy hitter. It had knocked a lot of big boys out of the box, buried them, and here was Joe, not a major figure, coming out triumphant.

The Festival was not yet a truly significant element in the consciousness of New York, but it was ascending, and as Joe became someone of more substance, became more notable, that became part of the atmosphere which allowed this thing to grow.

Stanley Lowell:[21] First of all, you have to know Robert Moses. Robert Moses was a fixture in government. He had about four or five different government jobs, including parks commissioner and being the guy who ran the planning commission.

When Robert Wagner was elected mayor, about a dozen leaders of civic organizations came to visit him. They didn't think he should reappoint Moses to all the jobs he held, but when the mayor suggested each organization pass a resolution stating that this is what they wanted, they all said, "Oh, we can't do that. We might get in trouble ourselves if we propose to do that to Bob Moses."

When they left, Wagner said to me, "Very interesting. They don't have to run for office, but they do want me to do this. They want to tell me in secrecy and they're not prepared to support me publicly." That demonstrated just how powerful Robert Moses was.

Joseph Papp: Before the mess started, I rarely even thought of Robert Moses in relation to the parks. I dealt on a borough level, and he seemed outside the whole thing. If I thought of him at all, it was as a powerful, dictatorial person who smashed a lot of things, whose excuse for tearing up the city to put up

21. Deputy mayor under Robert F. Wagner, Lowell convinced Wagner to meet with Papp and give his blessing to Shakespeare in the Park. Lowell later served on the Public Theater's board.

new highways and housing projects was: "If you want to make an omelet, you have to break some eggs."

Robert Moses, though, was also a very cultured man, an expert in O'Casey, and we understood that he was, in his own way, kind of fond of us. In fact, in October of 1957, he wrote a piece in the *Herald Tribune* saying he was "tremendously interested" in our company. "They have been a conspicuous and widely heralded success," he wrote, "but they haven't got enough money to reopen next year, so we are setting about to raise funds to support them." And as of late January of 1959 he wrote me a letter saying, "We will be very happy to cooperate with you as we have in the past."

Robert Moses, Letter to Joseph Papp, March 18, 1959:

I have your letter of March 11 in which you ask that we permit you this summer to operate your New York Shakespeare Festival in Central Park, as you have in the past, on a free admission basis.

I regret that we cannot do this. First, there is no control in the area you have been using and a considerable park acreage is being damaged by your operation. We must have fencing for control if your operation is to continue.

Second, there are no sanitary or dressing facilities for your actors and others employed in your productions and no electric current is available for lighting. We were forced to run a portable generator at the site during your operating season. Adequate sanitary and dressing facilities must be supplied if you are to continue in Central Park.

Third, the area used by your audience needs seats and paving. We cannot permit your audiences to continue to use lawn areas in Central Park as theater seating areas. We can't maintain grass, and serious erosion problems will soon face us unless the area is paved.

The cost of the work the city must do if your Shakespeare in Central Park is to continue is between $100,000 and $150,000. If your performances are worthwhile, people will pay a reasonable charge to see them.

The concession agreement we have offered you will, if you have even moderate success, return about $10,000 annually to the city which will help to amortize the cost of necessary improvements and pay in part at least the cost of city help assigned to control and service your operation.

Unless therefore you are prepared to agree to charge admission and to enter into a regular concession agreement with the Department of Parks, we cannot give you a permit to operate in the City Park system in 1959.

Joseph Papp: That letter was a shock to me. I thought I had the support of this man, and then this came out of the blue. It was a complete turnaround, like getting hit in the kishkes.

Now, I had believed in free seats for a long time. Ever since my days watching the Goldman Band,[22] my basic philosophy was making theatrical entertainment accessible to the audience regardless of their ability to pay.

A year earlier, in response to a column by Walter Kerr suggesting I charge admission, I wrote back outlining my aims: "The only practical means of insuring the permanence of our theater is to tie it in with civic responsibility. The public library, an institution for enlightenment and entertainment, is a case in point . . . I know that if I had had to pay for books at the Williamsburg (Brooklyn) Public Library, it is doubtful that I would have read the plays of Shakespeare."

At that time in my life, I lived or died by that principle—it wasn't subject to some kind of interpretation. But people didn't accept it at face value; they were always asking me, "Why are you really doing this?" I'd get so mad at that. I felt something cynical in it.

I wasn't stupid. I could tell that the people who gave money responded to the fact that it was free, and not having to get involved with the unions was also a factor. But over and above that, my "art," if you want to put it in quotes, was this idea, this feeling of accessibility. It was my life.

But then came this letter from Robert Moses. I didn't know how to deal with it. I never felt intimidated; I just felt kind of helpless. He was the big shot and a powerful man, so powerful that I felt I couldn't win. I didn't feel like David versus Goliath—David had the Lord on his side—I just felt like I was the smaller figure in this battle with not the kind of power to really combat it efficiently.

For that reason, I initially didn't want an outside battle. In fact, I wrote him one letter saying I had "no interest whatsoever in provoking a public outcry." Moses wore so many hats, he was the head of so many things, he'd survived so many battles, I didn't know how I could beat him.

Moses's first assistant, officially the Parks Department's executive officer, was a man named Stuart Constable. He was a blustery person with a kind of British army officer's mustache. I would have cast him as the Constable in *The Pirates of Penzance*. I didn't like him at all. I could see he was anti-Semitic, anti-communist, anti-everything; he was one of those red-faced fanatical people, and he became the prime advocate of getting us out.

Then I heard that an unsigned letter was being circulated about me, making allegations that I was a communist and so forth. It seemed to come from a disappointed actor who had some kind of personal gripe. But the fact that Moses was doing something underhanded ended up working against

22. Formed in 1918 under Edwin Franco Goldman, the Goldman Band played free public concerts throughout New York City for ninety-three years.

him. A man so powerful, why did he have to do that? It was unbecoming to someone of such authority.

There was a lot of reaction; people felt it was underhanded and despicable. Even Mayor Wagner criticized him about it, and the *New York Post* ran an editorial headlined THE PARK AND THE GUTTER, saying, "No man with any claim to decency" would use such a letter. It was dismaying, but I wasn't as outraged as other people. My whole concern was: How does that affect our case? Were we going to get that theater back or not? That was what was on my mind.

[. . .]

EDITORIAL

New York Post, May 6, 1959

My name is Robert Moses, I'm Commissioner of Parks;
On the subject of free Shakespeare I have a few remarks:
If the people of this city want this theater on my grass,
They'll have to pay two bucks a head to get a Moses pass.
Now it is clearly logical that those who disagree
Are probably subversive or at least a threat to me.
That's why I took it on myself to McCarthyize Joe Papp;
Who questions my sagacity gets purged right off the map.

Merle Dubuskey: It became a media event. This though Joe was not very well connected, either with people with lots of money or people who were in powerful positions in the city, or even influential in his own profession.

But when we reached the point where the annual to-do in the park was apparently not going to happen, it was as if all of a sudden spring had happened without spring training. Things seemed to be out of joint. Somebody was attacking this thing that had no reason to be attacked. How could you object to this because it was free and suggest that admission be charged? One round after another was covered by the media—even the conservative press was up in arms about it—and Moses was getting very frustrated and playing into our hands.

Every time something happened, when an elementary Catholic school in deepest, darkest Brooklyn put their pennies and nickels together to help support this thing, we used it, we fully exploited it in the media. It became Little Joe Papp and Big Robert Moses, and all the Shakespeare Festival had on its side was its absolutely untarnished purity of purpose and with that it fenced off all kinds of weaponry. I think in its own way that tortured the shit out of Moses. He was a colossus in this state, and deservedly so, not even

Mayor Wagner would take issue with him, and all of a sudden, he was being confronted by this little ragamuffin.

Joseph Papp: I began to challenge this, I got into a fighting mode, and I'm good at that when I get started. I could not accept that this was the be-all and end-all, that this was going to be the end of the Shakespeare Festival. Even though we had no money and were in a lousy financial position, I said, "I'm going to save this thing from going under."

I accused Moses of discriminating against us while not charging baseball players, zoo-goers and concert audiences. I talked about the mothers who forced him to change his mind a couple of years earlier about turning a Central Park play area into a parking lot and said he hadn't been the same since he was hit in the head by a baby carriage. It was never a clever thing, though. I didn't think, "Well, god, if we win this, this will be terrific." I just wanted to survive.

Thousands of people had already seen the plays in the parks, so there was a lot of consciousness about us. When Moses said he was trying to save the grass, a lot of people came to the fore and began to send him big packs of grass seed. I didn't initiate anything like that, it was simply done. The public really began to move, and the newspapers sort of picked up on it. Not much else was happening in the world, and I began to get front-page attention.

All during this time, not only didn't I ever meet with Moses face-to-face, I never even talked to him on the phone. I tried to make contact from time to time, but he was not reachable. We always communicated by mail. Imagine, the boss of all these programs, all the things he had to do, and the thing that was getting him more than anything else was me.

At one point, I finally got Stuart Constable to consent to a meeting. He must have believed those things about communists carrying bombs, because he had four cops waiting outside his door. He made some accusations. I got up and said, "Now, listen . . ."And he said, "Police!" He claimed later I was going to hit him, but I would never do a thing like that. And they led me out of the damn place and threw me out. I said to myself, "What the hell is happening here?"

I was a little disappointed in Mayor Wagner. I thought he personally had more power than he used, but, on the other hand, this guy Moses was there year after year, while mayors disappeared.

There was a meeting between the two of them held, ironically, at the Players, which is a club for actors that was established by Edwin Booth. You'd think that something coming out of those surroundings would be favorable to a theater, but the mayor came out and said, "I'm sorry. I have to give up either my commissioner or Papp, and it has to be Papp." I didn't see that coming. I didn't see anything coming. Whatever happened happened, and then I would react to it.

The only initiative I really took was trying to get this into the courts. I went to John Wharton, a partner in this big law firm, and I said, "I can't let this go by. Can you represent us?"

"We do so much pro bono work," he said. "I really can't get involved anymore. Anyway, if we got involved, there are going to be some communist charges. We'd have to open that whole thing up."

"Open it up," I said.

"Well, if you don't mind, then."

"No, I don't mind. Open it up. Anything."

So he reluctantly said he'd help us. He assigned a young litigating attorney, Sam Silverman, a shrewd, smart lawyer with a great deal of integrity, to help us. He was no schlepp, and I admired him a lot.

Samuel J. Silverman: I felt I had a respectable case and that we might have a fair chance of winning. There's a doctrine of law that says an administrative agency must not be arbitrary and capricious, must have some basic reason related to its functions for what it does.

I felt it was none of the business of the commissioner of parks to insist on a charge, that that was not part of his function. He was there to protect the people of the city and to protect the parks. He was not there to produce theater or tell anyone how they should do it. He could say, "We've got too little park space," or, "That's not a proper park function," but what he was saying was, "This is fine for the park, but I want you to charge money." At that point, it would be none of his business, and I thought that the court might well interfere.

We lost at the Supreme Court at special term. The judge, a nice man, decided against us on June 2, 1959, saying that it wasn't up to the court to run the parks. You're always disheartened by losing, but I didn't think it was hopeless. I thought that we ought to have a fair shot on appeal. At first, it didn't occur to Joe that we could appeal or that we had any hope. He was rather pleased and surprised when he found out.

Joseph Papp: There were days, I'm telling you, when there was no movement whatsoever, and it looked terrible. Then, after losing in lower court, it looked as though we were going to write it off. With the mayor coming out and saying what he said, where do we turn to? I didn't know about a higher court at that time, that there was such a thing as appellate court that even handled things of this kind. Those days were very dismal, we were just wallowing around. I thought it was the end of it.

JUDGE J. MCNALLY, APPELLATE DIVISION
IN THE MATTER OF SHAKESPEARE WORKSHOP,
APPELLANT AGAINST ROBERT MOSES,
AS COMMISSIONER OF PARKS OF THE CITY OF
NEW YORK, RESPONDENT
JUNE 17, 1959

In no aspect of the case do we perceive a rational basis for the respondent's insistence upon an admission charge contrary to the wishes, policy and purposes of the petitioner. Nor do we see any connection between the power and duty of the respondent to preserve the parks and their functions and the requirement of a minimum admission charge . . .

No useful park purpose is served by the requirement that petitioner make an admission charge and retain ninety percent thereof when petitioner desires no part of it. Such a requirement incident to the issuance of a park permit is clearly arbitrary, capricious and unreasonable. When, as here, it is apparent that the sole substantial ground for the denial of the permit is arbitrary, capricious and unreasonable, the determination should and must be vacated and set aside.

Colleen Dewhurst:[23] There was a moment when I picked up the *New York Times* and saw that Joe had literally beat the government. I was stunned. He had no name, no political push, nothing. We had all been saying, "Come on, you can't win that." That's why I laugh now, when someone says, "Well, of course, Joe Papp will get into it and he'll have his way." And I say, "No, that's not why he'll have his way. There was a day when there was no way he could have it." I know a lot of people who have power, but he's probably the only person I know who has real power, because he had it before he had the trimmings.

[. . .]

Samuel J. Silverman: I rather expected that if we won, there would be some kind of attempt to appeal, but the corporation counsel, Charles H. Tenney, who appeared for the city and was a close friend of Mayor Wagner's, never tried to appeal to the court of appeals.

The decision came down just before the summer recess, there may not have been time to go to the court of appeals, but they could have asked for a

23. The actress was an important part of the Festival's early years, including playing Kate in the pivotal production of *Taming of the Shrew* outdoors at the East River Amphitheater in 1956, the production that, written about enthusiastically by longtime *New York Times* critic Brooks Atkinson, marked the sudden rise in the company's fortunes. The NYSF would move to Central Park the following summer.

stay until the fall. It would not have been terribly hard for them to get one, and they didn't do that, either. And very soon after the appellate decision, it became clear that not only were they not going to oppose it anymore but they started to help on the financing and so on.

I think Wagner, for whatever reason, didn't have his heart in fighting this. He may have agreed with both our legal and our philosophical positions and felt, "What business is it of the commissioner of parks to insist on an admission fee if the park's not going to be hurt?" Secondly, he may have felt that charging fees if the people who were running it were willing to foot the bill was a rather unpopular position to be in. If we can have free Shakespeare for people, why not?

[. . .]

Bernard Gersten:[24] Moses believed that Joe was a communist, and he had no hesitation in using that material in a calumnious way. But on the other hand he was a pragmatist, a doer, a consummate politician, and I'm sure he did 180-degree turns in his life whenever it was appropriate.

I don't mean to sentimentalize or romanticize Moses, but I suspect that somebody who is that powerful, who'd had his own way as often as Moses did, must have a secret regard for those who defeat them. Probably somewhere deep down in his heart, he admired Joe.

Robert Moses:[25] Cultural people, by nature, training and predilection, are intolerant people, even arrogant people. They honestly believe their objective is very important. They're very self-assertive. Perhaps they have to be to succeed. Yes, I'm self-assertive myself. You have to be to get anything done. Papp is no more offensive than most of these people, and he's a hell of a lot more able. They all go in for assertion to a great extent, but they don't have the same problem we do—the duty to the people, the public job, the oath of office. They just have an idea, and that's different.

Joseph Papp: Even though we'd won, the court couldn't enforce its decision— they could only urge Moses to reconsider. And not only did he accept it, he just turned around and became supportive. He was allowed to impose "reason-

24. Executive producer of Lincoln Center Theater since 1985, Gersten may be as closely associated with the success of the New York Shakespeare Festival as anyone but the founder himself. He and Papp met and became best friends at the Actor's Lab in Los Angeles in 1948. Papp brought Gersten to the Festival in 1960, where he served as associate producer during the theater's boom years. He left in 1978.

25. Turan takes this Moses quote from *Enter Joseph Papp*, by Stuart W. Little, 1974.

able conditions" to compensate the city for any expenses, and though he could have set the amount impossibly high, he asked for twenty thousand dollars.

Even that was difficult. Suddenly there's twenty thousand dollars to be raised. It's already mid-June and we're losing time. I didn't know what the hell to do.

The next morning I got two phone calls. Edward Bernays, the head of a public relations firm, said, "I'll give you ten thousand dollars toward this thing."

The other call was from Mrs. Florence Anspacher, a woman I'd never heard of before. She said she'd like to meet me and an appointment was made at a tea room. I was in old clothes as usual and she turned out to be a very wealthy, elegant woman in her late sixties or seventies, silver-haired with transparent skin and a classic Jewish profile.

"I'm very curious," she said. "I've never given a penny to anything in my life, but I think there's something interesting in this, about the grass and all that. I'd like to give you some money toward the amount you have to raise."

She gave me ten thousand dollars and that was the beginning of a long friendship, culminating in the naming of the first and largest theater in the Public Theater after her husband.

[. . .]

Someone said, "What play?" And I said, "Let's do *Julius Caesar*." That was a calculated choice because it was about power. But I was still nervous. After all that fuss it could turn out to be a lousy production— the play could fall on its face.

Well, I went out there on opening night, the place was packed, every seat was taken. I said, "Ladies and gentlemen—" and I couldn't get any further than that. A roar, a *roar*. I mean, you never heard such a sound in your life. I just stood there and let it wash over me. That was the most amazing experience, to hear a couple of thousand people just yell at you. They felt it was their triumph, that the people had won. What a feeling that was.

As for Robert Moses, he always perplexed me somewhat. But I had a kind of respect for him, and later on, as I saw him slowly wither and become more withdrawn, as all his authority began to wane and he slowly became just an embittered man, I had the feeling you get when you watch a tall tree topple. It's a terrible thing to see a man of great success, who's achieved monumental work, end this way.

I only met him one time. I was going into City Hall and I saw this man, all bent over, coming out. He looked at me, I looked at him, and then he turned away. His face was already drawn in from age and disappointment, and I always feel bad about seeing that happen, about seeing somebody crumble who "once the world held in awe."

—*JP*

The San Francisco Mime Troupe

FOUNDED 1959

R. G. Davis

> For those of us who consider revolutionary culture neither a gimmick nor an extension of bourgeois careerism but rather as a process of thought leading to the dissolution of imperialism's hegemony, dialectical materialism (yeah, Marx) has to become the source of our inspiration.
>
> —*R. G. Davis*

There's a wonderful moment in the book *The San Francisco Mime Troupe: The First Ten Years*, written by its founder (and leader until he quit the company in 1970) R. G. Davis. It's May 1962. The Mime Troupe has just performed its first outdoor performance in Golden Gate Park, a commedia dell'arte piece called *The Dowry*, in a whirl of activity and excitement. One of the actors, Yvette Nachmias, who had been struggling with her character, a matchmaker lifted from Molière's *Scapin*, came off the stage and over to Davis, yelling excitedly. She'd had an epiphany about commedia. "The reason for the large movements and gestures is because they performed outside." They'd known it from the books on which they based their "exaggerated movements," but they hadn't really *known* it when performing in a beer hall or small theater. "Once outside," Davis writes, "theory and reality crashed together into a screaming joyous perception."

This crash of theory and reality seems, in retrospect, to describe so much of the rigorous exuberance that marked the early days of the Mime Troupe. Davis, a trained dancer who'd gone to Paris to study mime with the disciplined master Étienne Decroux, relocated to San Francisco in 1958. He became an assistant director to Herbert Blau and Jules Irving at the Actor's Workshop, and started mounting regular experimental mime performances, as well as shows in late-night hours—the *Eleventh Hour Mime*—under their auspices. These experiments, and a feeling that the Workshop was "a conservative, excessively institutionalized theater," led Davis to break with the group over the next couple of years and transform the R. G. Davis Mime Troupe into the San Francisco Mime Troupe.

Reading Davis's own account of the Troupe's first ten years, you follow the back-and-forth between ideas and action, as the company discovers commedia, articulates its evolving political convictions,

Source: "Guerrilla Theater," by R. G. Davis, *Tulane Drama Review*, Summer 1966; "Rethinking Guerrilla Theater: 1971," by R. G. Davis, *The San Francisco Mime Troupe: The First Ten Years*, 1975.

fights out issues of leadership and collectivity, moves from inside to outside, explores new (old, adapted) performance forms, such as the minstrel show, the puppet play, the parade, the Brechtian epic. You realize, at the moment Davis leaps into the air to begin a banned outdoor performance and comes down into the arms of a cop, how protest can be performance and performance protest.[26] Through it all, you can hear the clash of ideology and practice, content and structure.

"It would be difficult to exaggerate," one-time company member Robert Scheer writes in his introduction to Davis's book, "the staggering number of hours that went into the ideas and form of new plays. Outsiders were brought in to give talks, reading lists appeared and endless committees functioned and malfunctioned." Theory and reality—the dialectic of making theater.

Even the 1966 essay below, Davis's first formulation (originally published in *Tulane Drama Review*) of what it means to be a "guerrilla theater," which he distinguishes from (and prefers to) a revolutionary theater, was to be rethought and revised in 1967, 1968 and 1971. Forty years later, when he found out we meant to collect his early essay here, he insisted we represent at least some of his reassessments as well (hence the inclusion of "Guerrilla Theater—What Was It?" from his 1971 "Rethinking Guerrilla Theater: 1971"). He was right to insist. The early Mime Troupe was clearly a double process—of thought and practice, of politics and performance. It was (and miraculously still is, though Davis and the Troupe contentiously parted company in 1970) an exuberant, theatrical, radical example of ideas at play.

—TL

Guerrilla Theater[27]

Art is almost always harmless and beneficient; it does not seek to be anything else but an illusion. Save in the case of a few people who are, one might say, obsessed by art, it never dares to make any attacks on the realm of reality.[28]

----

26. When Yippie leader Jerry Rubin was called before the House Un-American Activities Committee in 1965, it was his friend Davis who suggested he wear an American Revolutionary War hat. For twenty-five dollars, Rubin bought an entire American Revolutionary costume. He was dragged from the committee room wearing it.

27. The title for this kind of theater was suggested by Peter Berg, author and member of the San Francisco Mime Troupe. [author's note]

28. *New Introductory Lectures on Psychoanalysis*, by Sigmund Freud, W. W. Norton Co., Inc., New York, 1933, p. 207. [author's note]

Freud defines theater in America, and Che Guevara tells us what to do about it:

> The guerrilla fighter needs full help from the people of the area . . .
> From the very beginning of the struggle he has the intention of
> destroying an unjust order and therefore an intention, more or less
> hidden, to replace the old with something new.[29]

This society, our society—America, USA—is chock full o'ennui. Distracted
by superficial values, and without a sense of humanness, we let machines
rule; it is easier to kill from a B-52 than to choke every Viet Cong. No one
feels any guilt, not even the poor fool dropping the bombs. Theater has contributed to alienation by presenting a performer who is hemmed in from
costume to head. He too is a number in a basket, a character "type," and he
trains his "instrument" to take orders.

All businessmen talk of *service*, and know deep in their hearts that
unearned profit is the motive. While Johnson talks of stepped-up peace
efforts, the bombing raids increase. While art and culture are dabbled with,
television grays the mind.

Movie and television stars, technical effects, equipment and the desire
for simple packaging are all obstacles to a concept of performer-as-creator in
theater-as-art.

The motives, aspirations and practice of U.S. theater must be readapted
in order to:

· Teach;
· Direct toward change;
· Be an example of change.

To teach, one must know something.

It is necessary to direct toward change because "the system" is debilitating, repressive and nonaesthetic.

The guerrilla company must exemplify change as a group. The group
formation—its cooperative relationships and corporate identity—must have
a morality at its core. The corporate entity ordinarily has no morality. This
must be the difference in a sea of savagery. There is to be no distinction
between public behavior and private behavior. Do in public what you do in
private, or stop doing it in private.

For those who like their art pure of social issues, I must say—FUCK
YOU! buddy, theater IS a social entity. It can dull the minds of the citizens,

---

29. *Guerrilla Warfare*, by Che Guevara, Monthly Review Press, New York, 1961, p. 43. [author's
note]

it can wipe out guilt, it can teach all to accept the Great Society and the Amaaaaarican way of life (just like the movies, Ma) or it can look to changing that society . . . and that's *political*.

Previous attempts at socially directed theater since the thirties have been ineffective—with the exception of the Living Theatre, the Actor's Workshop (in the fifties, and not since Ford), Off Broadway in the fifties, Joan Littlewood's theater, Roger Planchon[30] and the Berliner Ensemble. What makes this type of theater difficult? Content, style and external effects or repercussions.

If the content is too immediate, the art is newsworthy and, like today's newspaper, will line tomorrow's garbage pail. If the content is devious, symbolic or academically suggestive, the public will refuse to see it, because their minds have been flattened by television and dull jobs.

"To be stupid is a luxury only the commercial can afford."

Social theater is a risky business, both aesthetically and politically; assuming that the difficulties of style and content have been solved, the stage success can be closed because of "fire violations," obscenity or even parking on the grass. What do you do then? You roll with the punches, play all fields, learn the law, join the ACLU, become equipped to pack up and move quickly when you're outnumbered. Never engage the enemy head on. Choose your fighting ground; don't be forced into battle over the wrong issues. Guerrilla theater travels light and makes friends of the populace.

A radical theater group must offer more than the commercial theater; it must be equipped with people and imagination to compensate for the lack of heavy advertising and equipment. Entrenched power is intelligent and artful in its control. Thus operative paranoia is our appropriate state of being. Keep the caliber of performances high—any lack of skill will lose audiences who are ready and willing to attend, but not for charitable reasons. There are too many charities now.

The problem is to attract an audience to a type of theater it is accustomed to attending and discover forms that will carry the weight of "effective" protest or social confrontation, without turning theater over to twisted naturalistic symbolism, pop art, camp or happenings for the chic.

There is a vision in this theater, and it is not that of the lonely painter or novelist who struggles through his denial years, suffering, and finally breaking into the "big time." The "big time" usually means *Life* magazine commercial success. But in this case it is to continue—I repeat—to continue presenting moral plays and to confront hypocrisy in the society.

---

30. Littlewood was a brilliant British director and founder of the radical Theatre Union in 1936, renamed Theatre Workshop in 1945. Planchon was a preeminent French auteur in the post–World War II era and longtime director of Théâtre de la Cité, later Théâtre National Populaire.

Let me make this very clear. It is acceptable to criticize, to debate, to take issues with problems in society, as long as you are not effective—and as long as you gloss over the issues in such a manner as to leave the door open to that soft-pedal phrase: "There are two sides to every murder." It has been our experience in local dealings with the police and commissioners of parks that when our social comment is clear and direct and not confused by "art" or obfuscated by "aesthetic distance," we have had trouble—arrest, harassment and loss of income.

Ideally, the universities should be examples of socially committed theater. Yet academic theater, far from leading, has followed the pattern set by regional theater companies but is even less experimental and risky. Resident theaters made their stands on repertory, good literature and the Ford Foundation (not necessarily in that order) and little more is to be expected from this area. The possibility and responsibility rest with the free-swinging independent organizations which are least equipped economically to deal with the complex problems of experimentation. Commercial audiences never taught to think won't buy it—and who in showbiz would want to sell it? It is our obligation to gather audiences and *excite* them into being provoked and confronted, and into returning!

Note: We are talking about the USA and its theatrical milieu. I do not presume to make universal aesthetic judgments. Theater and the sense of dialogue are different in this country. Our aesthetic is tempered by what can be done now, and what the actual climate is.

Should we use epic Brecht? Or experiential Artaud?

Epic theater, culled from the expressionistic pre-Hitler Germany, is a historical entity appropriate for its time. To perform historical epic theater in a USA glutted with double-speak, cinemascope and newspapers is to rely upon Brecht for help. Yet Artaud here becomes an excuse for intense psychological drama and falls into the American jungle of instant improvisation, instant creation and instant coffee: all a bit watery.

Should we throw Artaud out to save our Brecht? Anything that aids in cutting through the delusions of the American way of life or the morass of missionary ideals that lead inexorably to murder is useful. Use both! But remember that they are European sources, and it is America we are confronting: perhaps baseball is the best inspiration.

HANDBOOK

Find a low-rent space to be used for rehearsals and performances: loft, garage, abandoned church or barn. If the director sleeps in, it's cheaper.

Start with people, not actors. Find performers who have something unique and exciting about them when they are on stage. For material use anything to fit the performers. Allow the performers to squeeze the material to their own shape. Liberate the larger personalities and spirits.

Commedia dell'arte has been useful for this approach. It is an open and colorful form, uses masks, music, gags, and is easily set up with backdrop and platform. Presented inside, bright lights will do; outside, there are no lighting problems.

For outdoor performances select an intimate grassy area in a park or place where many people congregate, and play Saturday or Sunday afternoons. Go where the people are—street corners, vacant lots or parks. Set up a portable stage, twelve by fifteen feet, made into eight sections with a backdrop hung on a pole strung along a goal post support. All equipment must be portable and carried in a *borrowed* three-quarter-ton truck. Set the stage so that the sun is in the face of the actors, not the audience. Begin the show by playing music, do exercise warm-ups, play and sing, parading around the area, attract an audience. Use bugles, drums, recorders and tambourines, working with simple folk tunes—rounds well done will do, even "Frère Jacques" will do. For commedia style, the masked characters have to move well to illustrate what they are saying and all must speak out so the audience can hear fifty feet away, over the street noises.

Make sure the ground is comfortable and dry for the audience. Keep the length of the show under an hour, moving swiftly, and adapting easily to accidents, dogs, bells, children. Improvise on mistakes, coincidental noises like police sirens during a chase scene. Use a funny script, adapted for your own purposes (Molière is excellent); cut out excess dialogue, update the language and clearly delineate the action.

A minstrel show is another possible form; it is obviously a good vehicle for civil rights problems. Use old minstrel books, rewriting and updating gags to the conditions of the present. Blackface is a mask too; the stereotyped minstrel will make the mask work. Try to have the actors play the music necessary for a show.

Amateurs can be used if you cast wisely. Rehearse in short intense periods, keep improving and learning even after the show opens. The show should close better than it began.

Other forms are available: morality plays, burlesque, rock-and-roll (there *must* be something in rock-and-roll for the theater). Use techniques from modern dance, vaudeville, the circus—all these theatrical events focus on the performer.

Ask a painter to do a backdrop or a sculptor to make a prop. For costumes, shop the secondhand stores—the Salvation Army helps the poor.

If you need program notes or new material find writers, politicos, poets to adapt material for your group.

When everything is ready to go, play the show for friends, learn from the performances, then take it to the people in the parks, halls, anyplace. Give it away—anything to build an audience without spending money on advertising.

The group must attract many different types of people. All can help and all can enjoy the cooperative nature of theater.

Pay the performers from donations received after the show, keep the books open, pay for all materials and anything else that is spent on production. Do not overpay, don't try to match prevailing wages (except in poverty areas). People will work for very little if the work is principled, exciting and fun.

The first steps are necessarily hectic and loosely ordered. Few long-range plans can be made. After an audience and a group have been established (in the second stage) one can begin to think of presenting conventional plays. I suggest you select short, small-cast, one-set plays. Beg, steal, borrow equipment, make your own, and rent only when necessary. Try not to purchase anything other than basic materials that can be used for two or three shows—when in doubt, invent!

One procedure which the Mime Troupe recently came upon is to join with special groups that need money and do benefits for them: Vietnam committees, SNCC, CORE,[31] children's nurseries. These groups bring the audience and you present the show in their place or a rented theater and split the take.

The problem of a regularly paid staff is that a constant production schedule has to be maintained to cover costs. But there are solutions: movie series, one-act plays, poetry readings, underground films for the second act. Organization becomes tremendously important in order to save money and energy.

Survival, and with it success, increases the dangers and the responsibility of the directors and the producer. Some traps can be avoided if the group changes its style once a year; during that change, the mind is cleansed and the soul expanded.

Protest at the box office is profitable if it's good. Good theater can be made meaningful if new audiences are developed, but once you are in the swing of radical theater, there is no stopping. You must go all the way or the enormity and power of the opposing forces will crush you. Never be caught in a politically aesthetic skirmish with grass in your pocket.

31. The Student Nonviolent Coordinating Committee (founded 1960) and Congress of Racial Equality (founded 1942) were two leading activist civil rights organizations.

One can learn from the commercial world how to package, sell and expedite. The art world knows how to create. Use both!

It is a slow and arduous path to follow but the people will come to your aid, because your cause is just and your means exciting and full of life. There are hundreds of people looking for something to do, something that gives reason to their lives, and these are the guerrillas.

. . .

Guerrilla Theater—What Was It?[32]

In 1965 we declared it possible to create theater and some life without elaborate buildings and loads of money. But what was the goal of doing this? In 1965, I stated that our purpose was to teach, direct toward change, be an example of change. In 1968, I added the thought: "We must take power." In 1970, I stopped and asked: "Could we do all the above?"

Worried that the call to action might lead to activism for its own sake, soaked with the moral justifications of a "guerrilla way of life," in 1968 I suggested we consider the problem of power in relation to teaching, directing toward change, and being an example of change. I had grown worried because, in the late sixties, we were moving in zippy political and consumer currents; instant revolutionaries, psychedelic visionaries, and rock millionaires impressed all of us and there was little time for reflection. The media became so ubiquitous that the difference between stage and street dissolved. Life-style acting, a slogan of the poetic crude communists, smogged all thoughts.

The Berliner Ensemble is the only example we have so far of an aggressive, dynamic teaching machine. During Brecht's lifetime, the Ensemble came dangerously close to Antonio Gramsci's idea of truth, rather than [Walter] Ulbricht's,[33] but who got the lesson here? [Eric] Bentley? [Martin] Esslin? While the Ensemble carved a place in history, we were swinging large slogans at square hegemony and calling for revolution of *consciousness.*

The general refusal to abide by commodity living habits found its specific reaction in a rejection of naturalism's bourgeois theater. Playacting in public for the TV cameras became the main theater. The mix began in earnest and so, too, the grand confusion. People forgot that for a theater group, whether it be guerrilla, agitprop or simply hysterical, *the presentation is the meat of the action*, even though the drama may be a contrived happening, not a literary story, or an adaptation from a play. The action in view is what we

32. "Rethinking Guerrilla Theater: 1971," by R. G. Davis, *The San Francisco Mime Troupe: The First Ten Years*, 1975.

33. A leading Communist Party figure and archetypal Stalinist in Eastern Germany after World War II, Ulbricht became head of state.

learn from. When we actually cross the picket line, punch the cop, throw the real firebomb, tear down the fence, sit in front of a truck, we are not doing theater. Actors, writers or directors who confuse theatrical representations with life will struggle desperately to approach reality and become speedfreak schizophrenics.

ONWARD

The path of relevant political theater is away from naturalism toward epic theater. Guerrilla theater, a reaction to bourgeois theater, produced a step in the right direction, but the slogans were not meaningful enough to take root, and consciousness did not change anything but hairstyles. We have treated our audiences to an ad-agency-like bombardment, by telling the "truth," protesting the "outrages," and showing examples of purity as if our "product" could be sold like cigarettes, cars or consumptive goods. The first step is to avoid sloganeering, easy access to information or one-liners. An audience is more than a group of consumers and we, as performers, are in need of a technique far greater than that of commodity manipulators.

We have not understood or believed the lessons of the past:

> We must come to the inevitable conclusion that that guerrilla fighter is a social reformer, that he takes up arms responding to the angry protest of the people against their oppressors.
>
> *—Che*

> There can be no revolutionary movement without revolutionary theory.
>
> *—Lenin*

> The truth is revolutionary.
>
> *—Gramsci*

What we do next should neither sustain prevailing conditions nor attempt to blow people's minds. Bourgeois consciousness is deep and complex. Radical theater must bring people to the point of demanding change, through giving them knowledge of the processes of their condition. Imperialism is a far larger tiger than the "bosses," the "Establishment," or the face of Truman/Eisenhower/Kennedy/Johnson/Nixon. Therefore, our weapons must deal with computerized exploitation, as well as rotten personal habits. To become an effective instrument of social criticism or revolutionary culture, a theater has to develop a tangible theory manifested in practice.

It must be conceived with intelligent care and great love. For those of us who consider revolutionary culture neither a gimmick nor an extension of bourgeois careerism, but rather as a process of thought leading to the dissolution of imperialism's hegemony, dialectical materialism (yeah, Marx) has to become the source of inspiration.

—*RGD*

Bread and Puppet Theater

FOUNDED 1962

Peter Schumann

> The arts are political, whether they like it or not. If they stay in their own realm, preoccupied with their proper problems, the arts support the status quo, which in itself is highly political. Or they scream and kick and participate in our century's struggle for liberation in whatever haphazard way they can, probably at the expense of some of their sensitive craftsmanship, but definitely for their own souls' sake.
>
> —*Peter Schumann*

Mostly, the founding of a theater is defined by physical space: if not a traditional theater venue then at least the suggestion of one, the stage and surround in which performances will happen. Bread and Puppet Theater exploded that definition, even as it has, for fifty years, exploded our notions of performance, protest and puppetry. Begun on the Lower East Side of New York City by sculptor/dancer Peter Schumann, and associated with the street protests during the Vietnam War, Bread and Puppet moved to rural Vermont to get away from what Schumann called "the stink" of the city, as well as to learn from and draw on the landscape, the natural world.

From the start, Schumann's vision was indelible—sculptures that dance through open spaces and thronged streets. It's a vision that draws its inspiration from history and from around the world. John Bell is a longtime member of the theater, and one of its principal documenters. He evokes the company's style and influences all at once:

Source: "Bread and Puppets," by Peter Schumann, *Theatre in Ireland*, Autumn 1985.

Our parades reflect those we've seen, studied or been part of: the massive, semi-chaotic Carnival parades of Basel, Switzerland; the intimate street buffoonery of the Catalan theater group Els Comediants; the straightforward determination of twentieth-century political street demonstrations; the boisterous music of New Orleans street bands; the turbulent serenity of Catholic processions of saints and relics; the pots-and-pans "rough music" of street parades going back to the Middle Ages; the dances of lion and dragon puppets at Chinese New Year street celebrations; the modernist parades designed by Russian revolutionary artists in the 1920s; and the homemade color of patriotic summer parades in Vermont villages and cities.[34]

In addition to staging plays and spectacles in response to Vietnam, capitalism, global militarism and nuclear armament, and the devastation of the environment, the company for more than twenty years held the Domestic Resurrection Circus at its home in Glover, Vermont. Working with hundreds of volunteers and drawing crowds as large as forty thousand, Bread and Puppet combined pageantry, circus and story—providing fresh-baked bread for all—to create what must be the closest thing in the U.S. to the Passion Play of Oberammergau, Germany. Indeed, the sense of religion in the purest sense has been part of the theater's ritualistic work from the beginning. In 1973, British director James Roose-Evans (*Experimental Theatre: From Stanislavsky to Today*) described a Bread and Puppet performance in London. "The actors look at us thoughtfully, gently, still rapt in the mysteries they have enacted. Without manifestos, without dogmatic utterances, without aggression, this company presents a truly poor theater, a holy theater." American scholar Margaret Croyden confirms this view: "The members of the Bread and Puppet Theater are like a tribe of primitive Christians, living in a world in which love, suffering and compassion are fundamental precepts, a world that denies the psychological and the intellectual, a world that finds man caught between social evils and his desire to be transcendent."

It's hard to think of another theater that has maintained, over so long a time (fifty years!), such clarity of vision, purity of means and consistency of ideals. People who have never seen Bread and Puppet live have experienced its imagery through film and news reports— masks of celebration and suffering, giant totemic puppets, stilt-

---

34. I'm quoting from Bell's piece "Louder Than Traffic: Bread and Puppet Parades," in Jan Cohen-Cruz's *radical street performance: an international anthology* (Routledge, New York, 1998). Jan, an expert on street performance and activist theater, was a colleague of mine at New York University's Tisch School of the Arts in the early nineties. This is as good a place as any to share my gratitude to her for enlarging my understanding of community-based theater, and for introducing me to a range of work I hadn't yet deeply considered.

walking Uncle Sams ghosted by dead children. Schumann and company have scrupulously avoided commercial co-option, continuing to create puppets and performances, Bread and Puppet's massive, compassionate offerings. At home in Vermont and elsewhere in the world, it has, literally, uniquely, made the world a stage.

—TL

————————

Bread and Puppets

We sometimes give you a piece of bread along with the puppet show because our bread and theater belong together. For a long time the theater arts have been separated from the stomach. Theater was entertainment. Entertainment was meant for the skin. Bread was meant for the stomach. The old rites of baking, and eating, and offering bread were forgotten. The bread decayed and became mush. We would like you to take your shoes off when you come to our puppet show or we would like to bless you with the fiddle bow. The bread shall remind you of the sacrament of eating. We want you to understand that theater is not yet an established form, not the place of commerce that you think it is, where you pay and get something. Theater is different. It is more like bread, more like a necessity. Theater is a form of religion. It is fun. It preaches sermons and it builds up a self-sufficient ritual where the actors try to raise their lives to the purity and ecstasy of the actions in which they participate. Puppet theater is the theater of all means. Puppets and masks should be played in the street. They are louder than the traffic. They don't teach problems, but they scream and dance and hit each other on the head and display life in its clearest terms. Puppet theater is an extension of sculpture. Imagine a cathedral, not as a decorated religious place, but as a theater with Christ and the saints and gargoyles being set into motion by puppeteers, talking to the worshippers, participating in the ritual of music and words. Puppet theater is of action rather than of dialogue. The action is reduced to the simplest dance-like and specialized gestures. Our ten-foot rod-puppets were invented as dancers, each puppet with a different construction for its movement. A puppet may be a hand only, or it may be a complicated body of many heads, hands, rods and fabric. Our puppeteers double as musicians, dancers, actors and technicians.

—PS

Chapter 7

The Artist's Journey:
School, Studio and Stage

The creation of such laboratories of the theater requires the
consecration of its members to the work of the theater with its
disappointments and blunders, its truths and revelations.

—*Richard Boleslavsky*

The Actors Studio

FOUNDED 1947

Lee Strasberg

Here is Lee Strasberg, in the words of Margaret Brenman-Gibson, a psychoanalyst and biographer of playwright Clifford Odets:

> Son of a garment-worker in Galicia, and now an artist, direc-
> tor, psychiatrist, ascetic, scholar, musicologist, rabbi, logician,
> Simon Legree and Messiah, the intense Strasberg was revered
> and deeply feared by the actors. To suffer his wrath, whether
> it be a masked, stoical iciness or a shrill maniacally enraged
> outburst, was each actor's nightmare; to be approved by him,
> the dream. The limitless power vested in him by these actors
> for their spiritual life or death was awesome.[1]

This is the Strasberg of the thirties, the Group Theatre years. In the fifties, at the helm of the Actors Studio, arguably the dominant laboratory for actors in American history, he establishes his thirty-year thrall over American acting for the stage and film, a reign of insight and intimidation. He has what Studio historian David Garfield calls a "jeweler's eye" for talent. Gordon Rogoff, who served as Studio administrative director and ombudsman-like critic, begs to differ: "If he is a genius at anything, it is in the fine art of inspiring insecurity." Whatever your point of view, there's no denying Strasberg's personal magnetism. Has anyone in our theater's history provoked more hyperbolic characterizations? In interviews leading up to the publication of *A Method to Their Madness: The History of the Actors Studio*, author Foster Hirsch was told that Strasberg was "Buddha, Moses, Oedipus, Rasputin, God, the Pope, Pontius Pilate, Hitler, Jim Jones, a sectarian, a cult leader, a doctor, a lawyer, a scientist, a guru, a Zen master, Job, a

SOURCE: *Strasberg at the Actors Studio: Tape Recorded Sessions*, by Lee Strasberg, recorded 1956, first published 1965.

1. *Clifford Odets: American Playwright (The Years from 1906–1940)*, by Margaret Brenman-Gibson, Atheneum, New York, 1981.

rabbi, a high priest, a saint, a fakir, a badger, a Jewish papa, the Great Sphinx, a Talmudic scholar, a Hassidic scholar and a human being."

The irony is that this man, so inextricably associated with the Studio—its paterfamilias, its despot, its all-seeing, artistically impeccable, personally warped, childish grown-up Messiah—was shunned at the moment of its founding. Some have even said that Strasberg was "the one man" who had to be kept out of the Studio "at all costs." (I've read this variously attributed.) The Studio was launched by producer Cheryl Crawford, director Elia Kazan and actor Robert Lewis, all leading lights of the defunct Group Theatre, and went about extending the Group's work in the realm of training. "Without the Group Theatre, there would have been no Actors Studio," according to Crawford.[2] Strasberg had led the Group with Crawford and Harold Clurman, and he had quit it in 1937. He struggled through the forties, financially and artistically, having failed to make his mark as a successful Broadway director despite many outings, and had gotten no further in Hollywood than as a director of screen tests. He was, as he always had been, a polarizing figure, and Kazan, the most successful stage and film director of the mid-century and the spearhead of the Studio, was willing to engage Strasberg in only the most minimal ways in the nascent lab. In 1951, though, after Kazan's starry rise and a parade of interim leaders at the Studio, the role of artistic director and guiding light fell to Strasberg.

Kazan, commemorating the Studio's twenty-fifth anniversary, reflected on the world into which it was born:

> No one can appreciate what the Studio means unless he can recall what the actor was in the Broadway theater before the Studio existed, a part of a labor pool, his craft scoffed at—you either had it or you didn't in those days, talent was a kind of magic, mysterious, inexplicable elite.
>
> The fact that a soul could be awakened to its potential was not recognized then. Or that acting could be studied as a course of training, not only voice and makeup and stage deportment, but the actual inner technique itself. [. . .]
>
> The great body of the profession, like the longshoreman on the waterfront, shaped up every morning, hoped to be lucky, made the rounds, waited for a phone call, lived on the curb, had nowhere to come in out of the rain.[3]

In a 1955 interview with Frederick Morton for *Esquire*, Strasberg makes a more relaxed analogy:

---

2. Crawford went on to say, "And without the Theatre Guild, there would have been no Group Theatre." This lineage—and the many ancestral lines adumbrated in this collection—is a powerful heritage, an indication of how our theater moves forward through a series of rebellions, on one hand, and seedings, on the other.

3. *A Player's Place: The Story of the Actors Studio*, by David Garfield, Macmillian, New York, 1980.

It's having a place where you can laugh together. In Europe, the theater has a café life, a restaurant life, a place where people can meet, play with ideas. You'd be surprised at the close relationship between creativity and *Kaffeeklatsch*. Seriously. That's why it's so important for the Studio to have its own building: to have a place not only for work, but for just getting together, for hanging around, for fooling around with concepts, all the things you can't do when you're *not* working, and have no time to do when you *are*.

Whatever the analogy, the fact remains that the Actors Studio—and specifically Strasberg's twice-weekly workshops for its members—has shaped the teachings of Stanislavsky (or at least the early parts of those teachings) into the American Method. The actors associated with Strasberg, the Studio and the Method—Marlon Brando, Al Pacino, James Dean, Marilyn Monroe, Shelley Winters, Geraldine Page, Lee Grant, Paul Newman, Joanne Woodward, Ellen Burstyn, Estelle Parsons—have, in turn, shaped the perception of what acting is and can be. Under Strasberg's regular, long-lived tutelage, mentorship, goading and criticism, the twentieth-century American actor, for better and worse, was born.

—*TL*

———

A Workshop for Professionals

OCTOBER 1956, THE BEGINNING OF THE SECOND SEASON AT
432 WEST 44TH STREET.

Strasberg: We now have a place, you see. That gives us a symbol, a feeling that it's permanent. We don't know what we'll do next year, but we know where we'll be next year. Everything is possible. And so I would like the people really to become a little bit more concerned. *(He hesitates.)* Well, I will say it. To hell with it! I hadn't planned to say this, because I don't know how I'll behave when I say it; I don't think it will bother me. But I saw Jimmy Dean in *Giant* the other night, and I must say that— *(He weeps.)* You see, that's what I was afraid of. *(A long pause.)* When I got in the cab, I cried. And it was funny because actually I was crying out of two reasons. It was pleasure and enjoyment, which is odd, but I must say I cried from that, too. And the other thing was seeing Jimmy Dean on the screen. I hadn't cried when I heard of his death; Jack Garfein called me from Hollywood the night it happened, and I didn't cry.[4]

4. James Dean, an early member of the Studio, who had become a sensational star through his performance in the films *Rebel without a Cause* and *Giant*, was killed in an automobile wreck shortly before this occasion at the Studio.

It somehow was what I expected. And I don't think I cried from that now. What I cried at was the waste, the waste. If there is anything in the theater which I respond to more than anything else—maybe I'm getting old, or maybe I'm getting sentimental—it is the waste in the theater, the talent that gets up and the work that goes into getting it up and getting it where it should be. And then when it gets there, what the hell happens with it? The senseless destruction, the senseless waste, the hopping around from one thing to the next, the waste of talent, the waste of your lives, the strange kind of behavior that not just Jimmy had, you see, but that a lot of you here have and a lot of other actors have that are going through exactly the same thing.

And actually the thing that I cried about wasn't only the waste. It was helplessness, because, while it is something which I feel deeply about, I haven't the slightest idea what the hell to do about it. It isn't temperament. I see other people going through the same kind of shenanigans in one way or another. I hear stories about one person, then another person. As soon as you grow up as actors, as soon as you reach a certain place, there it goes, the drunkenness and the rest of it, as if, now that you've really made it, the incentive goes, and something happens which to me is just terrifying. I don't know what to do. You can tell somebody, "Go to a psychiatrist," or, "Go here," or, "Go there," but in the meantime there is the waste.

The only answer possibly is that we somehow here find a way, a means, an organization, a plan which should really contribute to the theater, so that there should not only be the constant stimulus to your individual development, which I think we have provided, but also that once your individual development is established, it should then actually contribute to the theater, rather than to an accidental succession of good, bad or indifferent things. But I am very, very scared that despite how strongly I feel, or despite how stimulated you become, nothing will be done. Everybody will feel nice and warm and spiritual, but when we get out, the tasks of life will present themselves and the problems of "What play do I do next?" and "What movie do I do next?" and we will just continue to get so caught up that in a strange way we do not really live our lives.

It is true that when the Studio started it never tried to give any sense of theater. It started simply to help individuals to use their talent, and certainly it has accomplished that to a much greater extent than anyone ever dreamed. It has been a strange and marvelous experience seeing these things come to fruition as a result of simple, honest work, without any publicity, without anything. I'm not worried about this. This will continue. There are plenty of talented young people. The Studio will not dry up or dry out, but in recent years there has been this feeling of the senselessness of it. What the hell are you working for? The people come. They do exactly what you hoped and what they said they would do, and exactly at that moment it becomes arid. People get involved in big business, Hollywood, this here, that there, and you can't get anybody on the phone!

The individual cannot do anything, He starts with the desire. I know that is true, not only of the people here, but of everybody in the theater. You have this strange dream that somehow something happens in the theater. You don't know what, but that is the feeling that you come in with. But the dream has to be fulfilled by some kind of unified effort. And this need bothers me very, very much. [. . .] The only solution is the creation of some effort which could embody the activity of these people, [. . .] but which would at the same time mean that you need to develop, to progress and to live the kind of artistic life, the kind of career life that we all hope for when we see a talent really bloom and blossom. [. . .] To me that is the future of the Studio, that a unified body of people should somehow be connected with a tangible, consistent and contiguous effort. That is the dream I have always had. That is what got me into theater in the first place. That was the thing that got me involved in the Actors Studio. And now that you see the kind of fruition to which individual talent here can come, it becomes time to think a little bit more about our responsibility to that individual talent. We have had talents before in the American theater. Jed Harris is an enormous talent. Orson Welles is as talented as any individual you can think of. I could name you a long line of people whose talents I consider to be first rate. Still they have not contributed to theater in any measurable way except when they were trying to establish themselves. At that time you fight through, you go for what you want, but once you get where you want to be, somehow every-thing becomes a matter of working to have enough money so you can some-time or other do what you really want to do. The sometime never comes. Instead something else comes along and takes it out of you, takes it out in chunks of heart and soul and talent and mind and incentive and initiative and in every other way. I saw Jimmy Dean, I had the feeling about Jimmy. When Jack called me, I didn't cry. I just said, "I knew it. I knew it." What I felt was the utter waste—and also the sense of responsibility—but I didn't know what the hell to do. The talent we can do something about. We can feed it. We can work with it. We've made a place for it here. But this thing—I'm stuck. I don't know. And this is really the problem of the Studio.

The world has never given actors more than it gives them today—monetarily and socially on a worldwide basis. Actors are among the best-known people in the world. The faces, the images of actors are better known than the faces of our great statesmen or scientists. But it is true, too, that the actual conditions of work are for the actor extremely poor. The actor works, let's say, on a movie. It takes him months. He works in a disjointed way that hardly permits his imagination to be aroused. Then he loafs around because he's glad to loaf around after getting up all those months at six o'clock in the morning and finishing at six at night. He gets pretty tired. Then he does another picture somewhere else. Or, if he goes into a play, he works for a couple of weeks under the worst possible conditions, much more concerned with lines and positions than with really working on the play. Then the play comes into New York, and he has to run through it every night, the same play every night. The burden of a long run would have been an impossible task for any actor in the old days. It was the fact that they played different parts and therefore could revivify their imagination unconsciously that made it possible for great actors to develop, as great actors have developed, in the past. For twenty years they played the same part, but only a few times each year, and at the end of that period they could really mean it when they said, "Now I'm beginning to realize how the part should be played."

Sometimes the acting process is complicated by the fact that at the very time when you misuse your talent you are externally successful. Or at a time when you make an effort to use your talent in the proper way, you may be unsuccessful from an audience point of view. It's precisely at those moments that we need a place with an audience, not only observing from the viewpoint of simple enjoyment but able to perceive work in progress, work that may lead to something. Every time an actor changes from something he is used to to something he is not used to is fraught with danger and often with unsuccess. Even if the new thing is not well done, it may lead to a much more successful doing than anything done before. It is in that area that membership here is offered.

The Studio is a place where whatever problems actors have as actors can be worked on, can be solved. Among ourselves we sometimes say this is a place where you can fall flat on your face.

When we take people in, the primary thing we judge is talent, though I must honestly say that we directors have never found a way of defining exactly how that judgment is reached. Nonetheless, it is talent which entitles an individual to come into the Actors Studio. We hope that the people here are not any more deserving than others, but are deserving of our effort to encourage them to find the things within them that will constantly lead toward the further development of their talent. But too many of the members take their admission as a token of being singled out as better than other people, and, while I don't mind anybody on the outside thinking that, it is not really true. The choice is not solely on the basis of talent. Our vote derives from a sense of what we feel are greater capacities and possibilities in an individual than he now employs. Often we are wrong, but that makes us vote.

I know people who came back for a number of auditions. Finally they got in. The talent had not changed. Our opinions about the talent remained basically the same, but the last time they came around we saw signs of possibilities of progress that appealed to us even more than the talent. We saw a great effort to learn, to progress. That appealed to us because it is that with which we work. We deal with talent in flux, with things that might not be possible but for the existence of a place like this.

Neither life nor talent stands still. Standing still leads inevitably to retrogression. The actor does things that he has done before, perhaps more easily, but without the electrifying spark that usually arises in young people when they do their first productions. We then see the terrifying struggle that in America almost always begins with success, when the actor to maintain his career on a certain level begins to repeat and to imitate, if not someone else, what is even worse, to imitate himself and thus to pay a terrible price in his most important commodity, the very thing that singled him out at the beginning, his talent.

The recent years should have proved that the work done here for people who are already established holds at least equal importance with the work done for people who are completely unknown. These years should have proved the necessity of the professional or craft or technical demands that we make, not just on the actor, but on the good actor. The better the actor, the more the demands.

The work here is not for artistic purposes, for something that satisfies your soul and nothing else. I don't like the kind of separation in which professional work is regarded as practical, but the work at the Studio is done only when you want a little stimulus, when you're a little poor in spirits. "It's not really a necessary part of my career. Now that I've done the work and I've become successful, I don't have to participate anymore." I am exaggerating a little, but my feeling is that this is the attitude, conscious or unconscious, that a lot of the people here develop as they come to a certain professional standing. And that attitude is deadly.

With a lot of very good actors here the talent may well come to fruition. The person may go on in theater, and work here may then cease. But that person's hopes and ideals do not stop. I am referring to a member of the Studio who thinks of himself as a certain kind of actor and wants certain kinds of parts. People don't give him those parts. He insists that he will get them. He turns down things people think he is good for because he insists on other things. But when he decides to do something Off Broadway to show what he can do, his work is not commensurate with his hopes and intentions. That work should have been attempted here first. Problems of growth should be solved here, because by the time you come to the production it is just too late.

The things that I'm concerned with are technical problems, and these technical problems are not solved by the correct interpretation of a play. They are not solved by telling the actor, "If you knew what was happening in the play, you would immediately become a better actor." The voice doesn't become any better. The way of behavior on the stage doesn't become any better. The kind of inner concentration brought about by work equivalent to the singer's voice exercises does not become better by itself. These are all technical problems.

In my running engagement with Actor A here, when I say that I am disappointed or a little annoyed I don't mean there is anything wrong with his acting from the point of view of being a good actor, but that he has a deeper and more intense contribution to make than he has yet made in any of the parts he has done. But work has to be done on his acting instrument, which is composed of his mind, his emotions and his body. And this work has to be done separately, not just by understanding a part. He must deal with deep, firm things inside himself.

Otherwise the actor often fools himself. He understands the play, and he assumes that he is doing on the stage everything that he understands, when obviously he is not. That is the technical problem in any art: that an individual's understanding does not coincide with his capacity. The understanding reaches out but the capacity makes for what he actually does. That capacity is established by the technical training to which we have dedicated ourselves.

A violin we make. We pick the wood. We make it a certain size. We put things inside for vibration. We create the instrument for the violinist. The actor too employs an instrument; he brings to his art an instrument already created, and that is the human being himself with the habits, the thought processes, the emotional patterns that are already in him. All these things function in the work of acting without any awareness of them on the part of the actor or the other people in the production.

If the Studio were not here, Actor A would be just as good as he's always been and thereby would never be as good as he can be, as good as he should be in terms of the very thing that makes people say, "Now, there's an actor. What wonderful aliveness! What wonderful sensitivity!" But wonderful aliveness and sensitivity are subject to the laws of human nature. You get a little more tired. The talent gets older. The aliveness and sensitivity don't quite work when you want them to. He doesn't have to worry, of course. He will get parts; he will do television; there is a wide area of work. But he may not get the parts he wants. He may not get the things that he should do. He may not get the roles that people think of him for and yet hesitate. Those hesitations should never arise. They do arise now only because, without a firm, deep technique, acting becomes cannibalistic: we feed on our own goodness. The very moment of success in the American theater is the moment of defeat, of starting down.

Yet in art there is no age. Actors come into the Studio to find the thing that all people bring with them into the theater when they are young, when they still hope to accomplish their dreams. In art "older" doesn't mean years. Toscanini, when he died, was younger than most people around him, because he still thought he could accomplish with the orchestra what he heard in his mind. He never doubted that, and he always fought about it, and therefore he was younger than many of the people around him who had lost the sense that their dreams could at some time be accomplished.

Art grows more rich with age, not less. The inner craft, the inner vision, the emotions of the actor can continue to develop because they are not subject to any aging process entailed in the very life experience that enriches them. In every art, even in those arts where physical toil takes a toll and the person becomes actually unable to do it, the capacity, the will, the imagination to do it grow and increase. By the time his voice is gone, a singer sings more artistically, more brilliantly, because he sings not just with his voice. Even a pitcher in baseball, when he becomes an old canny pitcher, pitches more brilliantly than in the old days when he just threw the ball in and didn't care. We can see in Michelangelo a constant increase in skill. The paintings at the end of his life are greater in vision and greater in carrying out; though it took longer to do them, we do not perceive that in the pictures. The older the actor becomes, if he continues his progress, the more fully his imagination works, takes possession of his instrument more completely than it did before, becomes greater as he goes on. The old actors that I have seen have not been less. There's a richness in them as in old wine.

[. . .]

The "Method"

We are willing to be influenced by anything, to try anything. We have no fear of giving up anything here. Here there is nothing holy. Anything that can help us to become better, to fulfill better the actor's task, to contribute toward a more alive and dynamic theater is certainly worth trying and working on. A studio is not concerned with production, therefore it doesn't matter whether an individual piece of work in a studio is a failure or a success, because it is good or bad only in terms of your own needs, of your own development. In a studio it does not matter whether you agree or disagree.

A studio does not need agreement. It needs leadership—otherwise there is a formless kind of activity—but a studio can exist even without leadership if the individuals in it are avid enough in terms of their needs and their search for development.

Work such as we do can, of course, be done in a school. When we say that we are not a school, we do not mean that there is no schooling here. Obviously the whole nature of training is part of the schooling process. We are licensed as a school based on individual selection. It is not the kind that anyone gets into merely by applying. It is a school that selects the best in a certain area and certainly we have lived up to that.

People assume the Studio is a school because they are not aware that the results achieved here can be achieved in any way other than some stern, systematic and long process of study. I always have to explain that we are not a school in the sense that the work is systematic. Our work is only on a very small, part-time level, and the fact that the results we have achieved have been effected on this level only leads us to want to put the work on a firmer foundation.

In a school there are, so to say, no differences of opinion. The school is run by the people who are at the head of it. The teachers teach what they are told to teach. If they don't like it, they get out and are replaced by other teachers. The pupils have no freedom of opinion, judgment or action. If they wish to remain in the school, they do what they are asked to do. They subject themselves to the discipline which it is the school's province to create. A school has the responsibility of laying the technical foundations for each individual, of prescribing the work, right or wrong, and if an individual disagrees, he has the right to leave. In a school he has no other right.

Although there is no systematic procedure which is here attended to on principle—much as the people "outside" think there is—it is true that I have very definite ideas. Therefore the work in the Studio follows certain tendencies. But it is also true that people work here according to their own desires and initiative.

People who do only what we ask find the work of little value. When the actor does work that he feels like doing, that he feels is important for him, he leaves himself wide open to rather strong criticism. We try to contain that criticism so that it doesn't become too personal, but we do not try to stop it, because it is partly by means of the criticism, or analysis of people who have the same problems as ourselves, that we begin to try to achieve what we are capable of rather than settling for what is easy or easily successful. In these areas we are often rather stringent in our views and in our demands for criticism and self-criticism.

Those of you who were here before the public acclaim started to hit us know in all honesty that there never was any formal talk or discussion of principles of acting or of what we have called the "Method" or even of what we call the Stanislavsky approach. As you know, I only began to use Stanislavsky's name about 1955. I personally have always deliberately drawn back from using his name or encouraging any idea that we here are addicted to any kind of principle. In the early days of the Studio I was only one of the teachers, and therefore felt it would be unjust to the Studio to do so. I did my own work in the way that I presumed other people were doing theirs. Obviously I have always been clear in my own mind that my own work stems from a certain kind of approach. It has always been fed by those principles that derive from Stanislavsky. But I never do anything because anybody else said so, because Stanislavsky said so. I do something because I have tried it and think it works. When I have found that it works, I then give credit to the individual who found it. I never take credit for making it work. I am always very careful about saying that what I use is Stanislavsky's, because I am liable to misuse it or use it wrongly. I want to give Stanislavsky credit, but I don't want him to be discredited with anything that I might do. It is true that the basic elements are Stanislavsky's, but I hope I have gone beyond some of it and have contributed something of my own. Nevertheless, I feel very indebted to the work of my teachers and to whatever it is that I understand about Stanislavsky's work.

Only when the Studio's work began suddenly to be responded to outside was the word "method" actually first used, and it was used by people outside. Only because other people were saying, "Ah, Stanislavsky!" and I could not honestly say the work wasn't his, did I find myself having to temporize and say, "Well, the best things in it I suppose are Stanislavsky's. The other things come from me. I don't know." "*The* Method" was first used outside. Emphasis on the article "the" came from other people, who meant to imply that they were referring not to just any method, but to "the" particular method singled out by the Actors Studio. We would simply say "a method" or "Stanislavsky's ideas" or "Stanislavsky's method," because work in a studio is done very unsystematically—as some of you who come to my private classes are beginning to realize.

The important thing in the Stanislavsky method is that it is the opposite of a system. A system implies a theory with precise rules of what to do exactly at each moment. Systems of the past were exactly that. You had specific ways of doing things in different situations. In the Delsarte System, which was very widespread in America, you had pictures from which literally to copy each state of emotion or sequence of emotion. The place for the hands or any of the other manifestations of the body was prescribed. The Stanislavsky method is no system. It does not deal with the results to be attained and therefore sets no rules for what should be done. It only tries to show the actor the path to be followed, how he goes about finding what only he can find and what, even when he has found it, cannot be repeated the next time, but must be the next time found again.

No one can explain the mystery of talent. We try to take the mystery out of acting in the sense that we try to give to acting a craft. Nobody can object to that. However, we believe that our craft is not only for the externals of acting, but for the internals. We believe this is a craft in which one can train oneself.

When Stanislavsky said, "Don't imitate me. Don't do what I do," he did not imply that he had worked all his life and had written all his books so that other actors should not use what he had found. What he was trying to imply was that he had found principles and truths but that the actor has to know when and under what conditions to use them. If they are not properly used, the work is bad. Thus, his method is not in that sense even a method: it is a procedure. He called it "notes for the moment of difficulty." It is well not to worry about medicine when you are healthy. You need the doctor at the moment when you are ill. But you cannot cure illness and you cannot act by the book. No knowledge is greater than the ability to know when to use it.

—*LS*

New Dramatists

FOUNDED 1949

Michaela O'Harra

In 1949 there was one destination for a playwright and no path to it. The destination was Broadway. The path of university training programs, Off- and Off-Off-Broadway theaters, regional theater new-play programs, summer retreats and play labs had yet to be laid. The phrase "new-play development" had yet to be coined. A play reading might happen in a producer's office, but there were no staged reading series, few class offerings, few opportunities for playwrights to meet together, to see and hear work. As Paddy Chayefsky (Oscar-winning screenwriter of *Marty* and *Network*) described it in a 1961 talk, the young playwright's

SOURCE: An unpublished essay, "The Beginning of New Dramatists," by Michaela O'Harra.

actual contacts with the theater are made through fitful acquaintances. He knows several actors and one or two actors' bars, an assistant stage manager whom he can visit backstage on occasion. Now and then, he gets a letter from an agent's secretary, has lunch with a not-very-well-known producer who is considering doing his play. He has an occasional lunch with his agent, and perhaps some established person in the theater has taken an interest in him and takes him for a drink once or twice a year at the Plaza or Sardi's.

One might feel herself to be born an artist, but there was no way to learn the craft of playwriting, to give shape to the art within. In essence, America had grown some playwrights, but it hadn't created a profession.

Into this void stepped a tenacious young woman with a gripe and an idea: Michaela O'Harra, whose play *Honor Bright* had, for reasons she never understood, closed "out of town" on its way to a Broadway production that never happened. This added fuel to her fire. As she told *Theatre Arts* magazine in 1960,

The theater treats the newcomer, the possibly talented individual trying to break in, in the most scurrilous way possible. Producers are completely dependent on scripts for their professional life, yet the unknown playwright is treated the most cruelly of all. When he does manage to plant a script in some office, it is gone for literally what may be years. When he does get it back, it will most likely have pages rumpled and torn, coffee stains spread like Rorschach blots across it, enigmatic doodles blackening its covers. If there is any covering note sent with the script it will be curt and hypocritical, "Thank You," or more often, there is no comment at all. It is the most humiliating experience in the world.

O'Harra forged an unlikely partnership with one of the lions of Broadway, playwright (and actor) Howard Lindsay, co-author with Russel Crouse of *Life with Father*—which remains, to this day, the longest-running play in the history of the Great White Way—and, later, *The Sound of Music*, among many others. Their initial meeting is dramatized below, from the vantage point of fifty years later: O'Harra's plan, Lindsay's skepticism. Her plan, he reported in 1952, "was so inclusive I did not give it, as a whole, serious consideration." But like so many of our current theater's founding mothers, this young playwright would not take no for an answer. Together, the lion and the scrappy neophyte created a small, minimally funded program for playwrights, New Dramatists, that changed the game for theater writers and began to knit together a community of playwrights where there'd never been one.[5]

Originally, Lindsay lined up an empty cloakroom at the Hudson Theatre on Broadway for what was known for many years as the New Dramatists Committee. It would later move to New York's City Center, then to East 4th Street across the street from La MaMa ETC, before settling into its current digs in a former Lutheran mission church on 44th Street in Midtown Manhattan, down the street from the Actors Studio, another field-altering lab.[6]

—TL

Throughout the 1940s there was constant, theater-wide moaning about the dearth of new playwrights. Then, when those brilliant meteors, Arthur Miller and Tennessee Williams, flashed into Broadway's night sky, the lamentation simply changed to, "Why, oh why aren't there more?!"

In 1948 the Dramatists Guild hosted a meeting in which Rosamond Gilder of *Theatre Arts* magazine reported on a recent visit to government-subsidized European theaters. As the meeting was open to associate members (anyone who had four dollars per year for dues could be an associate), hundreds were present that afternoon.

When the floor was opened for questions and comments dozens were at once on their feet making impossible demands. "Force Congress to subsidize us!" "The Guild should produce!" "Make revivals illegal!" "Picket producers who won't do new plays!"

The harried chairman turned helplessly to the other council members seated behind their long table, poised to crawl under it. Then one man rose, walked decisively downstage and raised his hand. Howard Lindsay, star and co-author of *Life with Father*, at that time the longest running play in Broadway history.

How long he stood there answering questions I don't remember, but it must have been close to an hour. What did register indelibly was the man's astounding patience, compassion, how much he cared about the theater and its people.

---

5. I came to New Dramatists as artistic director in 1996 and worked with Michaela looking over my shoulder for many years until her death in 2007. I saw her tenacity firsthand and will always cherish the image of her stooped with age and ailment, walking with the assistance of ski pole–like sticks, making her way into the library of our church home and telling the staff what we were doing wrong, then beaming with excitement as she met the newest resident playwrights.

6. New Dramatists' Church building was spotted by actor/playwright June Havoc (Baby June of *Gypsy* fame), a member of both organizations.

I had a lot of ideas about what could be done for new playwrights, but the possibility that anyone with clout would be willing to listen to them had never occurred to me until that afternoon. I went home, composed a "dream scheme" incorporating the whole complex of ideas, dubbed "A Plan for Playwrights," and wrote the man a letter.

March 20, 1949
Dear Mr. Lindsay:

During some twelve years working in and about the theater, sometimes as a play reader for producers of films, other times as a drama editor or film and play reviewer, and when there was time, as a struggling new dramatist myself, I have become intimately acquainted with the problems baffling and frustrating the unknowns trying to write plays today. Some of these problems are nation- or theater-wide; they are big, economic or social and possibly insoluble. There are others, however. These too are big, to those of us still concerned with mastering our craft, but in another sense so minor that something direct and decisive could be done about them.

These latter problems are such knotty ones as most new dramatists have today—that of being unable to afford theater tickets; that of trying to write for a professional theater whose inner workings, from the beginning to the end of even a single production, too few of us have ever experienced; that of too much working alone with no adequate or stimulating exchange of craft information possible; and that of never being able to see our own early plays in any professional test action short of full Broadway production.

Let me contrast this with the days in which you and other now noted playwrights were learning your craft. There was live theater all over the country. Not only in New York; stock and road companies played everywhere. You saw plays constantly, all kinds of plays. In that thriving theater, with its voracious demand for scripts and people of widely varying degrees of skill and experience, even your early faulty plays were often produced, so you learned from these—or you could work in the profession; if not backstage or on stage, at odd jobs somewhere in management. One way or another you could watch or work with, talk to or learn from other writers and from actors, directors, designers and even stagehands. Constant, total exposure to theater was possible in the natural, ordinary course of things and from such exposure you learned to recognize—and learned to meet—the inexorable demands of this unique medium. Today, in 1949, this is practically impossible for new playwrights, however gifted, even after they have reached a clearly recognizable level of accomplishment.

I suggest, however, that much can be done even to "change the scene"—for the whole theater—by first changing it for new dramatists of proven potential. I believe it can be done by organized, theater-wide action under the comprehensively designed "Plan for Playwrights."

The above are opening paragraphs in a plea for the initiation in our theater of the Plan referred to. Can I persuade you to read the plea? I know of your passion for brevity—I must warn you the material is long, incorporating as it does not only detailed proposals on program but suggestions on finance. Nonetheless, I have addressed the whole to you as a leading citizen of the American theater community. I somehow believe you are the one man in the profession most likely to both read it all and to understand why it can achieve its purpose.

May I send it? Then, if it incites your interest, come to answer, whenever I can, the questions it will inevitably raise? Lengthy as the material is, it does not include all the ideas, and facts and figures, I have evolved and collected.

Very sincerely,
Michaela O'Harra

Lindsay was phenomenally successful as an actor, director, playwright and producer. He didn't know me from a pigeon in Bryant Park, but he responded within days.

March 25, 1949
Dear Michaela O'Harra:

Thank you for your note. Please send me a copy of your proposal, and I would be glad to see you any evening in my dressing room at the Empire Theatre at eight o'clock, except Wednesdays and Saturdays.

Sincerely,
Howard Lindsay

A Plan for Playwrights

The proposed organization's purposes:

- To encourage the writing of plays;
- To help playwrights develop their craft;
- To provide opportunities to meet with established dramatists and other theater professionals to gain from their knowledge and experience;

- To facilitate frequent attendance of plays;
- To make it possible for a playwright to observe the entire process of the production of a play.

These purposes would be achieved by:

- *Panel Discussions.* A panel of New Dramatists would each read a colleague's play and then meet with the author to discuss the script's strengths and weaknesses.
- *Rehearsed Readings.* A cast of actors would read a New Dramatist's play aloud, followed by a critique session.
- *A Workshop.* A New Dramatist's play would be rehearsed and staged before an audience
- *Craft Discussions.* Experienced playwrights, directors, producers and designers would meet with the New Dramatists membership and address craft problems.
- *Production Observers.* With a producer's concurrence, a New Dramatist would be assigned to observe all aspects of a specific production: including rehearsals; script, casting and production conferences; and the out-of-town tryout.
- *Theater Admissions.* As guests of the management, arrangements would be made for New Dramatists to see incoming Broadway plays.

Anticipating the meeting with Lindsay, I tried to frame an answer to every question I thought he might ask. Never once did I anticipate his very first: "How do you live?" This was accompanied by what I imagined was a meaningful glance at my fur coat. I was thrown completely off balance and stammered, "It's only muskrat! I bought it myself! On sale! Reading for Mike Todd! Someone in his office knew someone who worked for a furrier and got it for me wholesale, and I got him passes for Todd's shows!" Then I muttered that I had a cold-water flat, costing twenty-four dollars a month.

Lindsay was baffled by my inane babbling. Suspecting that his question was taken as too personal, he apologized and explained that by "you" he had meant "all you young playwrights." He thought my letter implied that in his salad days he could always earn a decent living in the theater. "Not so," he said, "I very often went to bed hungry. And I learned I could skip some meals if I drank lots of water."

He said he didn't know any young writers personally, so my letter and Plan had raised many questions: "Are you yourself typical of all those you think could benefit from your proposal? I know you speak for them, but are you representative? And, if so, are there enough of you to warrant all the time, energy, expertise—and money—this staggeringly ambitious Plan of yours would cost?"

It seemed he was saying that I had to prove to him, before "five minutes" was called, that I was some kind of genius or else he'd lose any interest he had in my proposals. I nearly turned tail and ran.

HL: Do you, yourself, think you are representative?
MO'H: Yes and no.

I knew many others. Some seemed like me in many respects. A few also read for Paramount; and sometimes we met for coffee at the Automat to discuss our common problems. Others I'd interviewed while reading scripts for Todd. All had at least one and usually many of my problems and experiences, but no one had all.

But I believed that, although individual needs vary in number and nature, other playwrights would benefit in one way or another by what I proposed. That belief grew from my experience during the two years my first play, *Honor Bright*, was held under option and twice produced by the Shubert Organization. It was like having to stand by, helplessly, watching some street kids push my child, still breathing, down into a trash-filled dumpster to suffocate and die. The experience was so traumatic, so confusing, I was disoriented for days. I had no one to talk to. Even my agent had no time for me. If I'd had peers to support me, I might well have recovered far more quickly and been able to make more and better use of the experience. For me it was so paralyzing in every way that I couldn't write for a very long time.

HL: What gave you the idea for what you call "Production Observances"?
MO'H: Sitting hunched down in dark balconies whenever I was able to con Shubert house managers into sneaking me in to watch directors and casts rehearsing new plays for Broadway.

Seeing how different directors work. Seeing how actors can convey with the lift of an eyebrow something the author has tried to do with several pages of dialogue. And I learned something about the cunning ways of actresses on my play's opening night in New Haven. One actress got a marvelous laugh on a line that never got a giggle in rehearsals. I rushed backstage, astonished. The actress chuckled, "Dearie, I'm an old hand at this game. If I'd milked that laugh before tonight our esteemed leading lady would have managed either to get it for herself or get it cut. Now she won't dare!"

HL: Was *Honor Bright* actually your first play?

MO'H: Unless you count the three-acter on one page my mother preserved for posterity, claiming I was nine at the time.

In it an old woman, aged at least twelve, was hell-bent on marriage to an old
man hell-bent on anything but. In Act One she promises to wash his clothes
every day; in Act Two to clean his house every day. He laughs at both ploys:
he's rich and can pay for such work! She wins in Act Three with a promise
to make his dinner every night, pie and ice cream.

HL: Anything else characteristic?

MO'H: For me there are always two sides to every question, every
conflict. Usually more.

This is no virtue. It's useful to me in structuring a play, but deplored by my
family and friends. An assistant once chided, "Some people leap to conclusions, you drawl."

HL: What moved you to start writing plays again? Do you know?

MO'H: I know.

It's the same thing that makes playwrights unsatisfied with all other forms
of writing. Despite my unhappy first experience, it let me in on the unique
power denied all other breeds of writers.

Playwrights' scripts have the same power hearts have: they make existence possible for bodies. What springs alive from the pages of a script is far
above, beyond and far greater than the sum of all its parts. The moment in
which a playwright first becomes aware of this power is awesome, dazzling.
It comes, usually, on an opening night during the first performance before
an audience of the first script she or he has had staged. It may be on or Off
Broadway, some regional or university theater; it may be a drama, comedy,
farce or high tragedy. As the houselights dim make-believe becomes reality;
the transmuting imaginations of the playwright, the actors, director, designers and the hundreds making up the audience all fuse to work a natural miracle. The author feels godlike.

Lindsay replied thoughtfully, "Everything possible should be done to
keep writers who've felt that at their typewriters writing plays. The catch-
word is 'possible.' You've been around long enough to realize that the whole
of your proposal—and I'm sorry to have to say this—is quite impossible.
Our theater is a disorganized, disparate lot of people who sometimes seem
more set upon destroying it than doing anything to help it survive. Equity

and the stagehands [union] would probably be against it. Actors are too involved in their own problems to worry about playwrights.

"I see only your Craft Discussions as something actually possible. Because I, myself, am willing and able to bring other professionals to talk with a group of new playwrights as you tell me are out there. If you collect six or eight, I'll arrange for them to see our new play [*Life with Mother*]. We have, alas, plenty of empty seats. We'll set up a Craft Discussion and maybe the lot of you can tell [co-author Russel] Crouse and me why audiences are staying home in droves."

I assembled a group and we analyzed the "craft mistakes" of our experienced elders. They took it graciously, Russel Crouse declaring ruefully that they should have had the meeting before they started production. This trial Craft Discussion persuaded Lindsay that there might actually be enough new dramatists around to warrant further experimentation. He took my Plan to the Dramatists Guild Council and they voted to support it. Moss Hart, then president, declared, "This is the best thing the Guild has done in years!"

But the Guild had no money to fund the project. So Lindsay and Crouse had a storage closet cleared out under some stairs of the Hudson, a theater they owned. Somebody found some old desks, chairs and a file cabinet. We got six thousand dollars from the Playwrights Company and five hundred dollars from the Katharine Cornell Fund. This paid for a phone and a miniscule stipend for whoever could be employed to start things up. That had to be me. Me because I had written up the Plan and then talked myself into a spot as uninhabited as Robinson Crusoe's island. Besides, who else had the requisite qualifications: a cold-water flat and a fur coat for use as an extra blanket?

—*MO*

Circle in the Square Theatre

FOUNDED 1950

Theodore Mann

Some theaters, in their nativity, launch movements. Others spur new theatrical styles or ways of working. On rare occasions a theater, newly minted, defines a place. For Circle in the Square, that place was Off Broadway. On April 24, 1952, a revival of Tennessee Williams's *Summer and Smoke* opened at the start-up theater in Greenwich Village's Sheridan Square, featuring an unknown Geraldine Page and directed by a young man from Panama, José Quintero. Suddenly, in addition to new talent and a new company, there was a new *place* for theater, an off-center center.

Off Broadway had been, after the boom of art-and-life experiments before the first World War, a place for actors and directors aspiring to better things. It was seen, in the words of Stuart W. Little, a tireless chronicler of the theater, as a collection of "mere dollhouse theaters busying themselves with amateur theatricals." With the artistic fruition of Circle in the Square, it became a better thing itself: a place to cultivate artists. A place to make serious work. A place to feed not just uptown theater but the culture at large. Stuart Little again:

> In this moment, in the larger sense, the Off-Broadway theater was born. Off Broadway is defined by the variety of its uses. It is a showcase for new actors and directors, a place where new talent can be discovered. It is a place to revive Broadway failures and restore the reputations of playwrights who may have been ill served in the regular commercial theater. It provides the means of encouraging the growth of theaters that exist in time and so engage the loyalties of talented professionals [so] that they can develop continuity of production and a consistent artistic policy.[7]

This theatrical relocation began with two revivals (four years apart), freshly animated plays by major American writers Williams and O'Neill, both of which had failed on Broadway. New life for older work, breathed into that work by young artists who would define a generation—Page, Jason Robards, George C. Scott, Colleen Dewhurst, later George Segal and Dustin Hoffman—eventually led to the birth

SOURCE: *Journeys in the Night: Creating a New American Theatre with Circle in the Square (A Memoir)*, by Theodore Mann, 2007.

7. *Off-Broadway: The Prophetic Theater*, by Stuart W. Little, Coward, McCann & Geoghegan, Inc., New York, 1972.

of new work for the theater generated by companies that would assert an alternative to the alternative, as Off Broadway spawned Off Off. But first there was Circle in the Square. First there was *Summer and Smoke* and *The Iceman Cometh.*

Circle was founded in 1950 by a group of hopefuls who had met and first worked together in a summer theater, the Loft Players, in Woodstock, New York. In addition to Quintero and Theodore Mann—who turned his back on lawyering to manage the theater with Quintero and take over as artistic director in 1962, a role he held for decades—the group included Emilie Stevens, Jason Wingreen, Aileen Cramer and Ed Mann (no relation to Theodore), all of whom became part of the original board. There are two genesis stories below: Theodore Mann's tale of how they discovered their unusual space, and Quintero's of the discovery of one of their most important talents. Together, these stories get to the heart of Circle's contribution—the definition of a different kind of space in a different kind of place and the discovery of a new breed of actor.

—TL

Giving Birth

We had the auction money[8]—which, in my naivete, I hoped we might start a theater with. I gravitated to Greenwich Village. The Cherry Lane Theatre and Provincetown Playhouse on MacDougal Street had been empty for several years. I went to see them and they both made me feel like the old woman who lived in that shoe. They had only ninety-nine seats with tiny stages. They felt cramped and wrong. After the summer experience, where we performed on a big stage, these two theaters seemed very limiting.

During the late forties, there was no activity known as "Off Broadway." There had been movements in the late thirties and early forties in which classic plays were performed but that quickly disappeared because rumor has it they were done poorly. In 1950, when I was looking, Off Broadway was like a ghost town with the wind blowing though the empty rows of seats at the Cherry Lane and the Provincetown.

My father suggested I look at an abandoned nightclub at 5 Sheridan Square across from Café Society Downtown. The New York State liquor authority had closed it down for violations. To its right was Louie's Tavern; to the left was Chemical Bank. I felt very cozy sitting between the money and the booze. Many nights in our coming stressful financial times I would

---

8. The group had auctioned off sets and costumes from their summer theater to raise money for this new venture.

think of drilling a hole to get at their vault. When I went inside the night-club, what I saw was a typical 1930s hotspot, though empty. There was a semicircular dance floor with three support pillars running up the center, surrounded by tables and chairs. The bandstand sat at the far end of the semicircle. The walls were plastered with painted murals of pseudo–South Pacific scenes—an excuse for naked ladies, naked palm trees and naked animals. The building was two four-story brownstones joined together. The parlors became the entertainment area. When I walked up the rickety wooden staircase to the floors above the nightclub I found ten rooms. Their former glory had faded—discarded G-strings, broken roulette wheels, dice tables and cots decorated with every kind of stain. The place looked like it hadn't been occupied for years. The rooms were a nice size and I thought cleaned up they would be perfect for us to live in—certainly better than the shacks. There was heat and running water. There was even one shower on the second floor. We could all bunk out here in these rooms and cook our meals in the old nightclub kitchen—with its big restaurant stove and mam-moth refrigerators still in place. The kitchen was equipped with silverware, pots and plates up the kazoo. There were even bread baskets—ahhh! Those infamous baskets—more on them later.

At that time, there'd been several stories in the *New York Times* about a theater in the round run by a Professor Hughes at a university out west in Washington. I thought this space would make a perfect three-sided theater similar to the Greek and Roman amphitheaters and also like Shakespeare's Globe Theatre. This was pretty grandiose thinking for a "tap dancer" from Brooklyn. I liked the idea of us doing plays in a new and different format. Something New York had never seen. The dance floor was sixteen feet wide by thirty feet deep. There was room for the actors to breathe. It would be so much more thrilling than those teeny "old woman in the shoe" theaters.

I was so charged up, I drove back to Woodstock in less than an hour. I told the board what I'd found. My adrenaline was pumping. I felt like a kid stumbling over hidden treasures. The board members got excited, too, and that night nobody slept. The next day we closed down the Maverick Theatre and drove to New York. By the time we got there it was dark. We went into the club holding up matches and everyone moving very slowly, taking in the space. When I found the light switch, there was José, standing center stage, beaming.

The board authorized me to lease the premises at the best possible terms. The next day I paid a visit to the real-estate agent, Jay D. Robilotto, who asked for a lot of money. Three thousand a month—ten times what we had in the bank. I explained to him that we were a new theater group and didn't have that kind of money. He finally agreed to accept one thousand dollars per month, which we also didn't have. I didn't know where we would get it but I just kept pushing forward. I told my dad about the meeting and he said, "Rent the space . . . I'll give you the one thousand dollars. Try it for a month and see how you like it." I promptly took the check to Jay D. who said, "Fine! But the landlord wants a seven-year lease with a security deposit of seven thousand dollars!"

I was stumped. The $383 which seemed so enormous in Woodstock shrunk to nothing in the Big City. My dad suggested, "Go back to Jay D. and ask him if you can put up the security by paying it off on a monthly basis, over the term of the lease." Jay D., who was a very elegant and well-dressed man in his sixties, who'd seen and known everything that happened in the Village, finally agreed to the deal.

A number of the Maverick actors came with us to the city—Ernie Martin, Frank McDonald, Claire Michaels, Miriam Green—and of course, the board, Jason Wingreen, Aileen Cramer, Ed Mann and Emilie Stevens. All of us set to cleaning the theater, the kitchen and the rooms upstairs. We took down the naked murals and piles of dirt followed. We removed the tables and arranged the chairs in rows. We removed the canvas and wood frames from the murals and stored them along with the nightclub tables for possible future productions. These tables, with their beautifully carved Victorian wrought iron bases, were eventually used six years later to help create Harry Hope's saloon in *The Iceman Cometh*.

Days later we were as clean as we needed to be to start life. We wanted to build a repertory company of twenty actors and we knew we had to audition, so now we began the process of finding more actors. We put a notice in the *Villager* and the theater trade paper *Show Business* about what we were doing. The board all sat behind three tables with notepads, trying to look very officious as actors auditioned. This went on for a week—then the board convened and decided on their selection of actors. The pay for actors and all the rest of us was to be twenty-five-dollars per week. Those who wished to could live upstairs in the rooms. Ed, José and Emilie continued to live on MacDougal Street. Aileen lived in her apartment on West 4th Street. Geno [Mann's black labrador] and I lived in one of the second-floor rooms, right behind my new office.

If you lived in one of the studios you had to take a turn serving as the weekly housemother. In addition, all of us, whether we lived there or not, shared in all the chores that needed to be done to maintain the theater. These included making costumes, building sets, sweeping and shoveling the snow on the sidewalk in front of the theater, keeping the men's and ladies' rooms clean and maintaining the coal-burning furnace in the basement. We named our new home the Sheridan Square Arena Theatre. In late October 1950 we started to rehearse *Dark of the Moon* by Howard Richardson and William

Berney, directed by José. I was busy doing business affairs so I only saw bits of rehearsals as I passed through the theater. They were going quite well. The actors were telling stories to get the Southern rural environment and language that was so important for the play. Emilie was responsible for the building of the sets and Aileen hired somebody that she wanted to do costumes. I can only remember her first name, which I think was Nastie—which she wasn't. She was a delightful person and a hard worker. Finally, after four weeks of rehearsals, we began to perform.

Dark of the Moon featured a new addition to the company: James Ray as the witch boy. Jimmy was Southern and brought a lot of wonder to the role, an authentic nature boy. The play is based on "The Ballad of Barbara Allen" and it begins with John, the witch boy, asking the Conjur Man if he can become a human. Later in the scene, John falls in love with a human, Barbara Allen. Eventually, the Conjur Woman, played by Nadine Murray, agrees to change him into a human and tells him he'll be able to stay human forever if he is able to marry Barbara Allen—and if she remains faithful to him for one year. Through John's arrival in the town and the consequences of his bargain, the play explores the hypocrisy and unconscious prejudice of the townspeople and the town's moral figurehead, Preacher Haggler, played by Jason Wingreen.

Aileen was doing public relations for us and tried but couldn't get any critics to come from either the large or small newspapers. The only newspaper that did come was the *Villager* and they gave us a nice review. But very few people came to buy tickets. We had thought that in a city of five million we would at least have five hundred per week. But we were drawing about five to ten people a performance at $1.50 per person. Most performances the cast of twenty was larger than the audience. We were in trouble.

On top of that the police department declared us illegal. The captain said, "This space is zoned as a cabaret and you can't operate here. You have the wrong license. You need a theater license." The word theater in our name drew attention to us. If we'd just called ourselves the Sheridan Square they would have thought it was another nightclub and not bothered us. I pleaded, "Can we continue to perform, if we don't charge admission?" Begrudgingly the captain agreed. So we took down the name of the theater and continued to perform.

Remember those bread baskets? After every performance, José gave a speech and asked for money and then we'd pass the baskets around. People were stingy—very little money came in. We needed it so desperately. My heart sank when I saw the pennies, nickels and dimes. But somehow we kept going. José was so nervous making that pitch each night that he'd have a drink beforehand next door at Louie's Tavern to calm himself. As far as

I know José had never touched hard liquor before and I remember the expression on his face was one of disgust with its taste.

When we started the theater, I'd also been working in my father's law office on Broad Street. His associate had been my teacher at Brooklyn Law School in contracts, Professor Block. I consulted with him on our problem with the police. He said, "Look at the New York City code for nightclubs. There is a section which defines a cabaret." When I looked at the code, it read that a cabaret is (and I'm quoting from memory): "A place of public assembly in which there is entertainment and food and/or drink served." I thought, "Wow, this is a description of what we do!" What does drink mean? The code did not define "drink," therefore it could be a grape drink or orange juice. If so, that meant that we didn't have to serve "liquor," and that "food" could be something as simple as a brownie, and "entertainment" could be a play. "That's it! We're home free!" I felt like Sherlock Holmes having discovered the missing clue. Sherlock was always very nonchalant about his accomplishments, but I was smiling big and was overjoyed that what we were doing was allowed by the city code, with some adjustments.

Brownies, etc., were provided by the wonderful bakery of Mrs. Douglas. When I'd come in to pick up the "food" she always had the look one often sees on a baker's face—contentment and fulfillment as she wiped the flour she had been baking with off of her hands onto her apron. We could in effect satisfy the wording of the New York City code. We had met these three requirements. We forged ahead to get a license to operate a nightclub. But there was still something we had to do—come up with a new name for our space. We board members, Aileen, Ed, José, Emilie, Jason and myself, sat in my office on the second floor overlooking Sheridan Square and threw alternative names around and around. We couldn't use the word theater but we needed to convey that we were a theater-in-the-round without actually saying it. This was the dilemma. Our old name, Sheridan Square Arena Theatre, had been a dead giveaway. We sat for hours struggling to find a name. Many variations were suggested but rejected. We had run out of ideas completely. We were sitting in silence, exhausted, when someone said, "How about Circle in the Basket?" (Chicken in the Basket was a popular fast food joint at the time.) Somebody jokingly said, "How about Chicken in the Square?" We were laughing and playing a word game now. Finally, after many variations someone, I think Ed, said, "How about Circle in the Square?" That was fantastic! The word "circle" would convey theater-in-the-round and square would indicate our location. Best of all, Circle in the Square is offbeat and presents a unique, memorable visual image. You have to think before you say it. This was the time that offbeat names for music groups began to appear on the scene.

We still had to tackle the whole process of transforming this nightclub into a theater. We always were a theater and now we were pretending to be a nightclub . . . we were playacting. The casts of characters in this drama were the inspectors from the New York City Municipal Building, the police department and myself. As every good theater student knows, every play has to have an obstacle and an objective. In this case, the obstacle was securing the license to operate and our objective was to become a theater by looking like a nightclub.

In order to get the cabaret license I had to obtain permits from the fire department, health department, building and housing department, etc. So I entered the dark, murky, mysterious and secretive world of municipal bureaucracy and spent many days at the Municipal Building on Chambers Street trying to find the right person to guide me and tell me what had to be done to satisfy all the departments. I felt like a Kafka character wearing a long raincoat. One of the most helpful persons in this bureaucratic night-mare was Commissioner Henry Finkelstein, who guided me through this maze step by step, like a saint helping me to circumvent disaster.

Our task was to build the make-believe nightclub. Miraculously, a wan-dering young German named Otto came by and offered to do carpentry in exchange for a place to sleep. He was stocky, with blond wavy hair and very thick eyeglasses. I wondered—could this guy hit a nail? We desper-ately needed somebody to do the work, so I readily agreed to the swap. He became our carpenter for the special tables we had to have built, as well as the elevated wooden bench bleacher section at the far ends of the theater. The wood required for the job came from abandoned shipping crates, which I found in the streets of the meat packing district near 14th Street.

These new small wooden tables were three feet in height and nailed to the floor. The face of the table was the size of today's medium pizza—just large enough to hold a soft drink and a brownie. They were spaced in between every two customers. The Fate known as "necessity" [. . .] was helping to shape our amphitheater. [. . .]

Police regulations also required all cabaret personnel to be fingerprinted and photographed (known as a mug shot), so that each employee could be issued a cabaret identification card. The cabaret world had a tendency to attract the criminal element—bootleggers, drug dealers and ladies of the evening—and the police needed these cards to help weed them out. I had some familiarity with these cards. My dad had a financial interest in several jazz clubs on 52nd Street and I had worked at these places from time to time. [. . .]

All the young actors, not yet famous, who would come to us over the next few years, had to have these cabaret cards, including Jason Robards,

George C. Scott, Colleen Dewhurst, Geraldine Page and Peter Falk. José and all the rest of us also had to trudge downtown to the main building of the police department for this glorious initiation into the world of cabaret. I kept all of those cards in my office for safe-keeping and they are still in our archives.

Forty-five years later Jason Robards and I were at a seminar on O'Neill and he showed me his *Iceman* script, which had in it the last remaining nightclub cover-charge card. When he revealed the card, he chortled with devilish glee. "Four and a half hours for a buck fifty! They got a hell of a bargain."

[. . .]

A friend of José's from the Goodman School in Chicago had been hanging around the theater. She was long and slender, fair-haired, with a beguiling manner and face. Beautiful hands, beautiful arm movements, with gawky pigeon-toed feet and a smile that could raise the moon. Our repertory company was starting to break up so we began casting some actors from outside and José decided to cast this schoolmate in *Yerma*. She played an eighty-year-old pagan crone. She entered upstage left in the second act wearing what she called "my schmatta." Around her head she wrapped a shawl, and wore a decrepit moth-eaten long woolen dress and a burlap bag slung over her left shoulder. She walked barefoot in silence—looked around at the countryside and squinted her eyes at the glaring sun. She then wiped the sweat from her forehead with the back of her hand and slid down the center pole with her butt on the floor and knee raised to her chest, and began to tell us her story. After a few minutes she took an apple out of her bag. She wiped it on her sleeve and took a bite. Anybody who ever saw her in that play can still hear that crack of her bite and remember the humor and pain she brought to that five-minute monologue, as she continuously wiped her mouth with the back of her sleeve. Her name was Geraldine Page.

Gerry had the extraordinary ability to transform her body, and as she chewed that apple, it was as if her face and the apple became one for a moment. Her sparkling eyes roved around the audience, and then she'd take another breath and continue her story. After the scene she got up and walked out and there was a hushed silence because clearly something extraordinary had just happened on the stage.

Before the performance she'd put some dark streaks of makeup on her face and hands to age herself and look dirty. She was in her late twenties but as an actress, it was her body and her voice that told us her age and her pain. In other plays that I saw Gerry in over the years, there was always this physical transformation she achieved. You'd swear she was short, tall, fat or thin, just as the character was supposed to be. Of course, she didn't change physically but this was the art of her acting. All of this came out of her unrelenting journey for the truth of the character. I once asked her about her craft and she said, "Well, I think I come to the role as an empty vase and little by little I put buds in this vase and they bloom." She was one of the rare ones that I was so fortunate to work with.

We were so excited by Gerry that we wanted to find a play for her. This would be the first time we had ever tried to find a play for a particular actor. Previously, as I said, we would select a play and then cast the company members in a leading role. But we were now looking for a play for somebody very special, who glowed on stage.

Many members had left and we were no longer a repertory company but we were in a deep quandary over which play would be best for Gerry. So, with *Yerma* still running, I and the rest of the board all went off to read plays.

—*TM*

Circle in the Square Theatre

FOUNDED 1950

José Quintero

The Iceman Cometh

We took another partner. His name was Leigh Connell, a member of that rare, almost extinct breed which deserves to be called gentlemen. He only stayed with us for a few years, when sick of heart and body, he left the Circle and the theater and went back to his native Nashville. I knew that I would never meet the likes of him again. He walked with a cane, for as a child he had suffered from polio and the bones of his right leg had set in such a way that he was unable to bend it at the knee. He played the piano, fully understanding what the composer must have wanted to express. His knowledge of literature was vast and his evaluation of the merits of a work would shame most of our literary and theatrical critics. He loved the English language so, and the language loved him in return. His letters, for we have never stopped communicating with each other all these many years, are truly great pleasures to receive. I feel great shame, answering them, but I am comforted

SOURCE: *If You Don't Dance They Beat You*, by José Quintero, 1974.

by the knowledge that my faulty grammar and my almost total ignorance of spelling will make him smile and remember me all the more.

He is a librarian now, much happier surrounded by his beloved books, and left alone to play and listen to his favorite compositions. There is a side of the theater which is ugly, greedy, hard and unmerciful. It is crowded with crooks, slave traders, dollar worshipers, ignorant of beauty and contemptuous of talent. Leigh experienced some of it and left, filled with admiration for the few who not only could survive it, but retained the magic of their art.

It was he who said to me one day, "José, you should do an O'Neill play."

"Why do you say that?"

"I have a deep feeling that you would understand him. Besides, isn't that what this theater is for?"

"What gives you that deep feeling? About me, I mean."

"I don't know, but sometimes watching you rehearse I get the feeling that you have double vision. That you can see two realities simultaneously, never in competition with each other, and that's what gives your work an inner and outward dimension."

I didn't understand what he was talking about. I still don't.

"Which play of his do you think we should do?"

"I don't know really," he said. "There are so many of them."

"Well, suggest one."

"Do you realize, José," he went on as if he hadn't heard me, his face growing pale with anger, "that not one of his plays has been performed in the last ten years? And I am talking about in his own country. The greatest playwright America has ever produced. The trouble is shamefully simple. We don't deserve him. And still we boast of having an American theater. Who built it for these ignominious fools? The man they have forgotten. The man they jeer at and call old hat. Thank God that other more civilized people recognized and cherished his genius."

"All right. All right," I said, admiring his anger. "What play of his should we do?"

"Of course, the one that we could never do is *The Iceman Cometh*. That is the one for you. Not that you couldn't do any of the others, but right now that's the one for you. Unfortunately I think it is out of the question."

"Why?" I pleaded.

"It requires an extraordinary ensemble performance from a group of people and it also requires a truly remarkable performer to play the leading role. I don't think he exists."

I asked him to lend me his copy of the play.

I read all night, stopping a couple of times to make myself a cup of tea. Not because I was tired or sleepy; in fact it was the opposite. I was so fully awake that it frightened me. The characters in the play were frightened, too, more, far more than that. They were terrified. They were being stripped of their shabby dreams and pushed out into a burning, never-ending hall of mirrors to be strangled by an army of their own reflections. It was daylight when I finished reading *The Iceman Cometh*. I got up and opened one of the windows, looking down at the street, which was already filling up with people and cars and trucks. I was lucky, I thought.

Although I was dazed and, certainly after a first reading, ignorant of the multifaceted nature of its theme, I knew that the ceiling of Harry Hope's crummy, bum-inhabited bar was that of the Sistine Chapel. O'Neill may have stretched a layer of cobwebs to hide it, or to prove his point, but there it was. If Hickey wanted to kill, with the salesmanship which is a gift of the devil, the pipe dreams of his friends, his pals, his bums—and lead them on to death, as he had done with his saintly wife Evelyn—he would have to lead God out of that crummy bar, too, and kill His pipe dream. The one that we mortals are made in the image of Him, and therefore have a bit of Him in all of us. Yes, Hickey, the cold iceman of death, would have to kill God and His pipe dream, and kill us for inventing God, our biggest pipe dream. After all, Hickey was not the son of a preacher for nothing. "Ministers' sons are sons of guns." But can any mortal whose conscience was molded out of Judeo-Christian clay by a god of his own creation, dare undertake such a task without plunging himself into insanity? And who can give him back his sanity? Go on, Hickey, look around you. Your pals, your friends, your bums are sitting in their accustomed places, by their accustomed tables at Harry Hope's bar. They can give you back your sanity, but they're corpses. They're dead. You killed them by killing their pipe dreams. They have you trapped. Their death proves you totally mad because their belief in your madness is their only way back to life. I understand what made you do it, Hickey. We're all sons of preachers and we're all sons of guns. How can we reconcile them both? How can the judge and the accused live in the sinful embrace of lovers? We all marry Virgins, whatever their second name may be: Rachel, Mary, Helen, Rosalie, Jessica or Evelyn. Virgins have their pipe dreams, too. Don't they keep on saying, as in your case, Hickey, "I know you won't do it again, Teddy." "I forgive you, Teddy." "I love you, Teddy." "I know you don't mean it, Teddy." Oh, virgins are suckers for pipe dreams.

And we love our pipe dreams about virgins. It is a sin to fuck. It is a terrible sin to fuck the Virgin, and you picked up a nail from some tart in Altoona, Hickey. You thought you were cured, but you weren't, and infected the immaculate, clean Evelyn. But being the Virgin, she did her best to make you believe she fell for your lies about how traveling salesmen get things from drinking cups and trains, and she forgave you . . .

Where did I get the nerve to think I could do this play? All I have to do is walk two blocks up, turn right, walk another block and be at the Circle in the Square, where I had to do this play. On my way I opened the script and began to read the cast of characters. My God, I thought, suddenly rooted at a corner, unable to move although the light was green, these are not bums. What O'Neill's got here are representatives, ambassadors from every major and revered institution. All of the characters at Hope's bar are not Americans and they're not all of the same race or religion or of the same political convictions. Take Harry Hope, the Irishman, for instance, "the governor," as they call him. He is, or was—for it really doesn't make much difference, as it all takes place within shabby dreams anyway—very high up in the cobweb of Tammany Hall. Ed Mosher, his Jewish brother-in-law, the traveling man, the one-time con man, the one that gets the better deal until he gets caught. Pat McGloin, part-time police lieutenant, part-time crook. Willie Oban, the American dream, tall, rich, white, Protestant, Harvard Law School alumnus. Joe Mott, black, one-time proprietor of a gambling house where all white folks always said he was white, and Christ, how much he wanted to believe them. Piet Wetjoen, one-time leader of a Boer commando—they call him "the General." And he has a captain, too, a captain of the British Infantry, very clipped, very proper, very officers' club, called Cecil Lewis. There's Jimmy Tomorrow, who wrote, as a correspondent, impassionate articles about the Boer War. He is not alone. There is another man of letters at Hope's, Hugo Kalmar, who fought with all he had to free the holy dignity of man, writing chain-breaking editorials for anarchist periodicals. There's Larry Slade, a true believer of the freedom of the human spirit, one-time Syndicalist-Anarchist. Blooming in the soil of shabby dreams are three fading, man-bruised, crepe-paper lilies: Cora, Pearl and Margie. What nationality they are, it doesn't matter. They were expelled from the Garden of Eden, and that's all that's needed. They are hookers, and hookers have an ancient, and unshakable, past. Cora is going to marry Chuck Morello, the Italian day bartender at Harry Hope's. The one that wears a chain with a tarnished medal around his neck. No wonder she never made it to the wedding. She's too loaded, in her room, on sherry flips. "She's had twenty since ten o'clock this morning," says Rocky, the make-believe realist, night bartender, "and it ain't even twelve o'clock yet." And last, but not least, there's the young Eugene O'Neill, going by the name of Don Parritt, who in desperation tries to commit suicide by slashing his wrists and spurting blood all over Harry Hope's bar. Christ, I whispered to myself, is there no end, no boundaries to this play?

If their pipe dreams are shabby, it's because they're a tiny piece of the mirage of the institutions they represented. They didn't get kicked out because they cheated or killed, but because they got caught. Getting caught is the cardinal sin. It can destroy the whole mirage. So go, run, before we all get caught. There's a lot of places to hide and they're all called Harry Hope's bar. Find it, and there you can continue to live. Sure, you'll be able to come back, and soon, very soon. Because you are, that never changes. How can it? A man's got to be in order to be. The light changed to green, but I still couldn't move. I was terrified.

Ted found out that Miss Jane Rubin was the agent that handled all of Eugene O'Neill's plays. He called her and after answering a few questions such as when, where, who and how, she told him that no O'Neill play was being released at that time. Two days later Miss Rubin called and said that Mrs. O'Neill wanted to meet me the next day. She lived at the Lowell Hotel on 65th Street between Madison Avenue and Park. I was to be there at three o'clock.

I was there on time. The Lowell is a very small, exclusive hotel. The two gentlemen behind the desk looked at me.

"I'm here to see Mrs. O'Neill."

"What's your name?"

"José Quintero."

They made me spell it.

"Does Mrs. O'Neill know you?"

"No. We're about to meet this afternoon."

"We'll have to check, young man. You are not by any chance trying to crash in, in order to meet her?"

Not being able to answer, I turned around and walked out. I walked very fast down the block, almost to the corner of Park, and leaned against one of the frail trees that looked as scrawny as I did and shamelessly cried. I wiped my tears, knowing I had to go back, which I did.

"Well, did you check and is Mrs. O'Neill expecting me or not?"

Obviously they had, because their attitude was entirely different. "We are terribly sorry, Mr. Quintero," and they pronounced my name perfectly. "She is expecting you. You must understand, we have to be very careful."

There were three ordinary-looking elevators across the lobby except that they had mirrors framed by vines of small gold leaves and little pink roses.

I ran back to the desk and asked, "Which one do I take? I forgot to ask you what floor."

"We're so sorry. Take any one to the fourth floor and it's apartment 1A."

When I arrived on the fourth floor, her door was open and she stood there to greet me.

"Mr. Quintero?"

"Yes. It was most kind of you to let me come to see you."

"Your hands seem to be unsteady and wet. Are you frightened of me?"

"Yes," I said.

"Oh, nonsense. You put your hand in mine and you come with me. I'm going to show you my collection." She took me through a hall, past the living room and down a long hallway that led to her bedroom. She said, "You sit right there," which was the edge of her large and very handsome bed, "and I will show you my collection of hats."

Of course, I didn't know at the time that she wore nothing but black. She pulled open the doors of her closets and they were filled with boxes and boxes containing her collection of hats. All black. She modeled at least twenty for me and finally she brought out a box and set it on the bed and said, "This is very special. I want to know what you think about it."

She opened the box and out of it came a black hat with a long tail of black chiffon. Without going to the mirror she put it on and draped the veil around her neck in an almost Oriental way, for it covered her forehead and her neck and fell long and thin down her back.

"How do you like this one?"

"That's the most beautiful one of them all," I said.

"This is the one I wore when I buried him." As she took off her hat she said, "You have hands like my husband's. I must say, it felt very strange when you came in and shook my hand. It felt like Gene's hand. That's why I acted a little nervous. Such thin wrists. Just like his. You don't happen to be Irish, do you?"

"No. I'm Spanish, like your name, Monterey."

"Well, that's not my real name. My name was Tossinger.[9] I am Danish and Dutch and maybe a little French. But here I am showing my hats and talking about my ancestry. Come into the living room and let me offer you something, a drink, a cup of tea or coffee perhaps. I am not such a bad hostess as you must think, but I see so very few people that my manners, without my being aware of it, are becoming a little rusty."

Her apartment was filled with pictures of herself with O'Neill or of either one alone.

"This was taken when we lived in France. And that was taken by Carl Van Vechten. He and Fania were dear friends of ours. The dark one over there was taken in that beautiful house I built for him at Marblehead. Come closer. See how angry his eyes got. I have always been afraid of that picture. I also built him," she continued as if to change the subject, "a magnificent house in California. It was before the war. It faced the sea and he would run down the hill every afternoon and go swimming. But now what will you like?"

9. O'Neill's biographers, Arthur and Barbara Gelb and Louis Schaeffer, list the spelling of Carlotta's original name as Tharsinge—Hazel Nielson Tharsinge.

"A scotch and water, if it is all right."

Her living room was mostly decorated with some very fine Chinese pieces. Her desk was piled with paper, dominated by a large, round, magnificent glass. Her bookshelves were filled with copies of O'Neill's works and books on Oriental art.

"You seem very fond of Oriental art. That is a magnificent screen over there."

"Oh, yes, I am. These are just a few pieces I managed to keep when we decided to sell the house in Marblehead and live . . . well, that's a long story. But my love for the Orient was fostered by my father. He was a botanist and all of his help was Chinese. Maybe that's why I went to the Orient with O'Neill. He was married then and I was married, too, and when we got to the Orient he went on a binge. My husband, you must understand, was a black Irishman. I was a Tory. I taught him how to dress, even what tie to wear and he called me 'the Tory.'"

"Mrs. O'Neill."

"Don't call me Mrs. O'Neill. Call me Carlotta."

"Were you ever a dancer?"

"A dancer? No, not me. You may be mistaking me for my mother."

"Was your mother?"

"Good heavens no. She was a society lady from San Francisco."

"Mrs. O'Neill . . . Carlotta . . ."

"I know," she interrupted. "You want to talk about *The Iceman Cometh*. I can see the anxiousness in your eyes. Now you remind me of the first time I saw O'Neill. I was very beautiful once. The kind of people I came from thought being an actress was a disgrace, but I went down to the Provincetown Theater to *The Hairy Ape*. When they moved it uptown and I took over the female leading role, we were rehearsing and one day O'Neill came and sat in the empty theater. Somebody pointed him out to me. You know he looked. As I said, there was a time I was worth looking at."

"You still are."

"Thank you, kind sir, but never mind what I said. *Iceman* broke his heart and mine, too, which was not any new thing. We broke each other's hearts time and time again. He thought that I broke his more times than he did mine. But he was wrong. Sometime I would like to tell you, but not now. I'm sounding morbid and you didn't come here to hear a sad tale. You came here to get the rights for the play."

"Yes," I said.

"You can have them. I trust you. I like you," she said as she stood against the sun setting through the windows, looking very beautiful with her short black hair and her flawless skin.

"I hope it turns out well this time," she said. "Not only for O'Neill, but for you also."

"Thank you."

"Will you come and see me every once in a while and tell me how it's going? I get so lonesome here. Will you come and lunch with me next Monday?"

"I would love to."

"I'll tell you more about him. Maybe it will make you understand the *Iceman* better."

First of all, the play cast itself by a chain of highly bizarre and extraordinary experiences.

David Hays had designed all of the plays we had done at the Circle after *Summer and Smoke*, and would move on to Broadway with me for *Long Day's Journey into Night*. I met David when I went to do a project at Boston University and brought him to the Circle to design *The Cradle Song*. To this day, I consider him the greatest and most resourceful designer I have worked with. His work has the deceiving simplicity of the Orient and, when called for, the frenzy of a Caribbean carnival. Throughout those years, we traveled from one reality to another as joyfully as children cross a stream by jumping from rock to rock.

I called David and asked him to read *The Iceman Cometh*. "That's going to be our new adventure," I told him.

Isabel, the most efficient and beautiful secretary I will ever have, who had become as much a part of the Circle as the rest of us, placed an ad that I was beginning to interview actors, which was to appear the following Wednesday.

Thursday morning, I went to the Circle very early. It must have been seven-thirty. I wanted to avoid, at all costs, running into a mob of actors waiting outside, although they had been summoned for ten.

The street was almost empty and so mysteriously quiet that I had the feeling I was breaking delicate glass bubbles as my feet pressed upon the pavement. In short, I was scared—petrified.

I reached the door of the Circle and, as I was to turn the key, a girl whom I had not seen, for she was hiding against the stairs, jumped and grabbed my wrist. "There is nobody inside," she whispered.

"It's much too early for anything," I answered. She pressed my wrist a little tighter.

"Open the door and let's go in. Or are you frightened?"

"Look, dear," I said. "I am not interviewing clowns for a circus, so why don't you go home, throw away that ridiculous orange-red wig, those overly long false lashes and, while you are at it, those other false things that you are wearing. Then wash your face, get into a simple dress and call for an appointment."

"You know," she said, "I'm going to tell you something."

"What's that?"

"That you are a stupid bastard and a hell of a rotten director. Here you are looking at an actress who can play the hell out of one of those hookers in that play you are casting, and you can't even see it."

"Excuse me," I said. "I have a very busy day ahead of me."

"You go right ahead, you wonderful man, but I am going to sit here until you give me that role. You think I am kidding? Just wait and see."

When I reached my office, I took my coat and tie off. After I hung them in the closet, I rolled up my sleeves, saying, "If it's going to be like this, I am ready."

When we returned to the office, Jason Wingreen was there. "I know there is nothing for me in this play, but I'm here to help in any way I can."

"Thank you, Jason," I said. "You know that this one is going to be a bitch to cast. Let's start from the beginning. Where am I going to find a sixty-year-old Irishman to play Harry Hope? I'm forgetting about Hickey for the moment."

"Jesus, José! That's a tough one. It would have to be someone who came to New York with the Irish players and stayed. Hey! That gives me an idea. Let's try to locate P. G. Kelly. He may know of someone."

"I'll try," said Isabel. "Is he in *Player's Guide?*"

"I think so."

"Jason, why don't you use Ted's office and try to find him."

"Okay."

"People are beginning to come," said Leigh, hearing the footsteps on the nearby stairs.

"Go out," I said, "and take their names and addresses and I'll begin to see them in a few minutes. Isabel, get me Jason Robards on the phone, please."

Jason and I had worked together at the Circle before. He had come to see me when I was casting a new play called *American Gothic* by Victor Wolfson. So many things, things that have changed the course of both our lives, have happened between Jason and myself, that it is difficult to remember the exact details of that first meeting. I know that we both sensed that we had known each other before, if not actually, in a trail of individual experiences that matched each other. I spent quite a long while talking to him about things unrelated to the play, which is something I usually don't do with actors. One thing that delighted me was my discovery that Jason, as good-looking as he was and is, had a clown's face. It is a personal thing with me that I believe that all great actors and actresses fundamentally have to be great clowns. Vulnerable, foolish painted faces disguising their capabilities to perform and feel every action and emotion known to man with a self-deprecating farcical gesture. And people laugh. They are great salesmen. They also own the myth of the broken heart. But can you imagine anything more horrifying than an enraged clown revenging himself for suffering a lifetime of your humiliating laughter, the circus dark with smashed spotlights, thin blades of moonlight stealing through the ceiling of the big tent? A clown, when he is not conforming to the strict and binding rules of the arena, must seek his own amusement mocking the world and its lofty institutions, insatiably drowning his self-hatred and loving the defenseless. The single daisy in a field of weeds. Jason I recognized as an actor and a clown at our first meeting. That very day I cast him in the leading role, which was good but undemanding. How deep and great a clown he was destined to prove years later as a salesman of death!

After we exchanged hellos, I told him I was casting *The Iceman Cometh*, and that I had a wonderful part for him, Jimmy Tomorrow; and asked him if he could come by the next day about five in the afternoon.

When I put the phone down, I said to Isabel, "Well, I think I have cast the first part. Write down Jason Robards as Jimmy."

By two o'clock, I had seen about thirty to forty people, but unfortunately no one seemed to be right for anything.

[. . .]

On my way out I met Ted in the hall. He said, "The casting is getting you down, isn't it? Come into my office. I want to talk to you seriously about that."

We went into his office and he closed the door.

"Now, José, you know that I have never interfered with the casting of any play you've done."

"Right. Of course you also know that I wouldn't let you."

"Have you thought about Hickey?"

"No, I haven't given that poor, guilt-ridden, insane clown a thought."

"You don't have a play if you don't have a Hickey."

"Goddamn, Ted, don't you think I know it?" I picked up an eraser from his desk, and opening and closing my hand, I kept saying, "Now you see it. Now you don't. Now you see it, now you don't. Funny, isn't it? Then why don't you laugh? I am here to make you laugh and make you have the greatest time of your life. Wait till you see what I have planned for your birthday. It's so great you'll never forget it. And I am going to do all of that because I love you, you see, for I am here to save your goddamned soul . . ."

"Well, have you finished?"

"No, I haven't even started. How can I? I don't have Hickey. We can't even look forward to his coming, for I haven't the vaguest idea where to find him."

"I think some of his madness has rubbed off on you already. You'll never find an actor that can play him, even if you go on interviewing people for a year."

"What do you suggest, then?"

"You are going to have to find a name."

"A name. What do you mean?"

"You know what I mean when I say a name. Someone who is up there already because he has proven he has got what it takes. Talent, personality . . ."

"And box office appeal," I added. "That is really what you mean. Isn't it?"

"If you want to take it that way, you just go right ahead, but you'll never get to do that play unless you follow my advice."

[. . .]

I got up and stretched, looking out the window. The sun already disappeared behind the houses in back of the Circle. It's the end of the day, I thought. And Jason hadn't come. I asked Leigh if he had seen him. Leigh told me he had, but that Jason had wanted to wait till I had seen everybody. I asked Leigh to fetch him.

Jason came in. He was wearing an old tweed coat.

"Hi there, Jason."

"Hi, José." He tried to laugh that all-embracing, warm, pulsating laugh of his, but it got choked up and disappeared some.

"Look, Jason, you have come to tell me that you don't like the part, and, hell, I can understand that. We are old friends, and there will be other plays . . ."

"No, no. That's not it at all. The part of Jimmy Tomorrow is fine, but I would like you to do me a favor. I want you to let me read for Hickey."

"But, Jason, I know you, and you know that I never . . ."

"Please, I know I don't look like the way O'Neill describes him, physically. José, since I read this play and that part especially, I have not been the same. I didn't sleep last night. I stayed in the little kitchen, and the words were not coming from the book to me, but from me," and he hit his chest with his fists. "Just listen to me, please."

"Just listen." He took the book out of one of the pockets of his tweed jacket. He opened it toward the end. Hickey's last hour-long speech.

"*I picked up a nail from some tart in Altoona. The quack I went to got all my dough and then told me I was cured and I took his words. But I wasn't and poor Evelyn . . .*" He threw the book away. "I know it by heart anyway." Then he focused those tormented eyes on me. "But she did her best to make me believe she fell for my lie about how traveling salesmen get things from drinking cups on trains. Anyway she forgave me . . ." He kept on with the speech, and I sat there watching him gouge his eyes out and tear the very flesh from his bones. His arms stretched out, begging for the crucifixion. Rivers of sweat distorting all his features. But driving his points cleanly, with the precision and clarity of the mad, of the holy, of the devil.

"Wait. I'll show you. I always carry her picture." He reached into his pocket and it came out empty.

"What's the matter, Jay? What'd you do with it? Did you lose it? Did you forget it? Come on, answer me," I demanded.

He just kept staring at me. The realization of what he had done drained all energy out of his body, leaving his mouth open, saliva running from the corners of it, taking in air without making the slightest effort to do so.

"Speak, man. Answer me. Did you leave it at home?"

"No," came a grunt from that open mouth. "I'm forgetting," he continued in the voice of a deaf person who late in life is uttering his first words. "I tore it up afterward." The beginning of a smile pulled the muscles of his face upward as he said, still staring at me, "I didn't need it anymore."

A silence followed, just as O'Neill demanded. A silence like that in the room of a dying man, where you hold your breath, waiting for him to die. "But I'm not going to die like that, José," he said. "No, I can't die like that. But what—what can I do?" he stuttered, opening his arms toward me, begging me.

"Explain. Explain why you did it, Jay. You must have had a good reason. You must have had a powerful reason."

"Christ yes, I did. I swear to God, I did." A wave of energy rushed into his being as he pounded his fist on my desk. "I—I loved Evelyn. So I began to hate her pipe dream. But all the time I saw how crazy and rotten of me that was, and it made me hate myself all the more." Little rivers of sweat scarred his face, but he made no effort to erase them. "I bet," he said, every word like a knife sinking deep into his flesh, "that you'd never believe, José, that I could have so much hate in me. How could you, you always saw me as a good-natured, happy-go-lucky slob."

"Enough!" I shouted.

He stopped, went to pick up the book where he had thrown it, put it inside his coat pocket and smiling said, "Thanks, old buddy. I guess I had to get it out." He opened and closed the door behind him. I could hear his footsteps as he walked through the hall and down the stairs. Then an enormous silence oozed out of me, invaded the room and soon the entire building. I don't know how long I sat there, warmly erased by the silence and the pale blue tinted light which slid through the windows.

Isabel and Leigh came back.

"Isabel, call Jason's house and ask for Hickey. Don't either one of you leave this room until you get him. I'm going next door," I said, picking up my copy of *The Iceman Cometh* and putting it inside one of the pockets of my jacket. "And when you join me, I swear by God Almighty, I'm going to stake you to a drink, you two gorgeous bums."

This production began the O'Neill revival, ran for two years and made Jason a star.

—*JQ*

La MaMa Experimental Theatre Club

FOUNDED 1961

Ellen Stewart

> You must see my theater. I want you to see my theater because it will be beautiful some day.
>
> —*Ellen (La Mama) Stewart*[10]

If Circle in the Square defined Off Broadway, La MaMa ETC epitomized the explosive, underground theater beyond. La MaMa stands for Off Off Broadway and more. In a string of dingy fire-traps in New York's East Village, and finally in a pair of buildings on East 4th Street, La MaMa became not only the progenitor (along with the much shorter-lived Caffe Cino) of experimental playwriting in America, but also the country's first, foremost, and longest-thriving *world* theater. And what a world it is.

"La MaMa is both an institution and a person," writes Barbara Lee Horn. In other words, to talk about the theater is to talk about the extraordinary woman who shared its name until her death early in 2011, Ellen (La Mama) Stewart. Reportedly, playwright Maria Irene Fornés once said that "Ellen Stewart is like a madwoman who held a piece of junk in her hand and said it was pure gold—and in five years

SOURCE: "How It All Began," by Ellen Stewart, from La MaMa's Thirtieth Commemorative Program, 1992.

10. Quoted in "Mother Is at Home at La MaMa," by Patricia Bosworth, *New York Times*, on March 30, 1969. Thanks to my student Jaeeun Joo at Yale School of Drama for finding this article, as well as *Ellen Stewart and La MaMa: A Bio-Bibliography*, by Barbara Lee Horn (Greenwood Press, Westport, CT/London, 1993). Much of the same material found in Horn's book is told much more energetically in David A. Crespy's *Off-Off Broadway Explosion: How Provocative Playwrights of the 1960s Ignited a New American Theater* (Back Stage Books, New York, 2003).

it was pure gold." A lot more is known about the theater, though, than about its founder and fifty-year matriarch. Stewart's personal history, a portion of which is told in her own words below (taken from a commemorative program on the theater's thirtieth anniversary) is, for the most part, an enduring mystery. "Some sources say she is Creole," says her bio-bibliographer Horn, quoting this passage from *Current Biography*:

> and the French-like cadence of her speech, as well as her birthplace, Alexandria, Louisiana, would seem to support that assertion, but according to most reports she is descended from Geechees, the slaves who settle along the Ogeechee River in Georgia.

"Other sources," Horn continues, "claim that she was born in a Cajun parish of Louisiana, that she has been married five times and has one son, Larry Hovell, who was born in 1943. Marriages take her to Chicago, Detroit, and to the middle-class suburbs of Long Island." Off-Off Broadway chroniclers Albert Poland and Bruce Mailman add that, once in those suburbs, "she went mad, suffered a breakdown, and lost her hair [. . .] and fled."[11] There are other versions, including Stewart's own, below, which has her coming from Chicago, where she at one time admitted to being born.

The theater's biography is much better known: it started with a voice coming to Stewart, a struggling fashion designer, on a trip to Morocco. The first playwrights she set out to serve were her foster brother, Fred Lights, a Yale Drama School–trained writer who'd suffered a debilitating blow in his first Broadway outing, and their dear friend Paul Foster. She set up shop in a rat-infested basement and kept getting closed down by the city—for occupancy violations, fire violations, building violations. Once police tried to arrest her for running a brothel, when the stream of white men visiting this black woman's apartment raised suspicions. Regardless of the court orders, she kept re-opening, even when she got thrown in jail for it. She moved from space to space, rallying help, standing guard on the front steps during shows to forestall any cops who might be coming to stop a performance. She remade the company, from café to club to theater, in order to slip through the loopholes in municipal regulations, and even evaded closure by direct order of the powerful Robert Moses as he tried to clean the city up for the 1964 World's Fair. She began every performance from 1963 on by ringing a bell and saying, "Welcome to La MaMa, dedicated to the playwright and all aspects of the theater."

11. This and the Fornés quote above come from *The Off Off Broadway Book*, edited by Poland and Mailman (Bobbs-Merrill Company, New York, 1972).

The playwright always came first at La MaMa, even as she expanded her family of artists to include directors—Tom O'Horgan, Andrei Serban, Meredith Monk, Marshall Mason, Elizabeth Swados— and companies like the Open Theater, Mabou Mines, Ping Chong's Fiji Theatre Company, Talking Band and many others. "Some of the plays we do have been called crashing bores," she told *Times* reporter Patricia Bosworth. "But with them the playwright learns. He learns that he can fail and his soul won't be crushed for it. In our culture playwrights can be eaten alive by the success-failure syndrome. [. . .] Before you fail, you try—and after you fail you must be encouraged to try again until something beautiful comes out. The ability to create is a dangerous and wonderful thing." The proof of that danger and wonder is in an almost endless list of more than two thousand plays by an array of America's most original writers: Foster, Fornés, Sam Shepard, Lanford Wilson, Ed Bullins, Harvey Fierstein, Rochelle Owens, Jean-Claude van Itallie, Adrienne Kennedy, Megan Terry, Leonard Melfi and more.

But just as her family circle grew larger and the plays she produced grew wilder as she moved to successively larger spaces, so the circle of her world appeared to expand infinitely, starting in 1965 when she sent a pair of La MaMa troupes out for simultaneous tours of Europe. She brought Jerzy Grotowski's Polish Laboratory Theatre to the States for the first time, sponsored and presented work from India, Korea, Indonesia, the Philippines, Nigeria, Japan, Colombia, Israel—more than seventy nations, from every continent. The circle that began with her playwright brother expanded to touch what the long-term director of the International Theatre Institute, Martha Coigney, calls "universal language, global vision." Elizabeth Swados began at La MaMa as a teenaged composer with Serban and the Great Jones Repertory Company, before going on to create and direct work of her own. She's written of Stewart:

> She prescribes countries for the doldrums and makes sure an artist can get to the desert or ancient chapel she thinks will help him or her grow. She matches composers, actors and dancers with directors, designers and choreographers from halfway across the globe. Nothing stops Ellen when she senses a fitting combination. She materializes her plane tickets the way magicians bring out white doves. "Baby—you want to go to hear the Pygmies? You're going to the Ituri Forest? Just tell me when you want to leave."
>
> —TL

_____

How It All Began

I came to New York in 1950. I came from Chicago to go to the Traphagen Fashion Institute. Colored people couldn't go to a school like that in Chicago. I was supposed to meet a friend who lived in New York. Two Chicago friends had come along with me. We waited at Grand Central "under the clock," but my friend never showed up. I had only sixty dollars. I didn't want to tell anyone in Chicago what had happened. My friends left New York, but I was too proud to go back home. I had to find a job. I got lost and went into St. Patrick's—I didn't know it was St. Patrick's then. I lit a candle and asked for a job. Thirty minutes later, I had one. I was to be a porter at Saks. Sundays, I'd get on the subway and go anywhere, exploring the city wherever I got off the train. One Sunday, I discovered Delancey Street and all those little shops with clothes and fabric. I wanted to be a dress designer and there was all this wonderful fabric! You could look at anything you liked. You could try things on. No one said anything to you. And this little man— my Papa Diamond—came out of this shop. He was wearing a little black cap on his head. He tried to sell me some fabric. I told him I had no money. He said, "Come inside. Maybe you'll see something you like better." Finally, he understood I really hadn't a cent. Also, that I didn't have anybody, no family in New York. It was love at first sight, my papa Abraham Diamond!

He adopted me on the spot. I became the artist daughter. Every Sunday, I'd come and spend the day with his family. When I left, he'd give me a piece of fabric in a package. I'd open it when I got home. I had a little sewing machine in my room. Every week, I'd make a dress or an outfit and wear it the following Sunday. He'd show me all around the street—his daughter, the designer. Now, at Saks Fifth Avenue, the colored had to wear blue smocks at work. The white didn't. So there I was, like Cinderella, under my smock. It all happened very fast. I'd come to Saks in May. With the interest in my little home-made clothes, by August I was one of the executive designers. I designed for eight years—and I never got to design school at all. In the meantime, my Papa Diamond told me that when he came to New York from Romania at age eleven, he was the first to put out a pushcart in the Delancey Street area. He said I should have a pushcart, too. And, if I pushed the pushcart for other people, it would take me where I wanted to go! Then I got very sick. I had many operations. I didn't know if I was going to live. I went to Morocco. My Papa Diamond came to me in a vision and told me to get my pushcart. So I left Morocco to return to New York. I decided my pushcart would be a little theater where my brother Fred Lights, and Paul Foster, could have their plays performed. That's exactly what I did. And that's why La MaMa is often referred to as a "pushcart."

I believe very much in the universality of man. I still use that term: man. I think communication helps what I call universalization—and the theater helps to communicate beyond one's own language. At La MaMa, we do nothing without some kind of text, but I want our La MaMa playwrights, in creating, to think about playmaking, not about playwriting. So no matter what is spoken, the audience will see something on stage that also communicates. No matter what the audience, I want them to make a connection with what's happening on the stage. That's the kind of work I'm interested in. The other kind—which is what most of American theater is about—is not of interest to me. I believe young people must have a chance to start and learn, even if the work, the production, isn't remarkable.

I want to let them have that chance. We have produced more than 1,400 plays now at La MaMa, and most of them have been American. We have not been remiss in that. I think we have a better track record than any other theater in America on that score. I also feel that music is integral to what happens in the theater, so for me the composer is also a playmaker. We've counted over five hundred original musical scores for La MaMa plays. I feel very strongly that some day we will have to do more than just say "hello" to other people. There has to be a visceral understanding among men—not just a greeting. So I try to use La MaMa as a pushcart to help push us in this direction.

—ES

The Open Theater

FOUNDED 1963

Joseph Chaikin

> Under the surface, all theaters are works-in-process, changing and growing, refining practices and clarifying vision. Vision, therefore, is determined to a great extent by time. Is the ideal version of the theater—any theater whose story is collected in this book—anticipated from the beginning, the way some manifestos suggest? Or are the guiding principles of the company worked out in action? Many of the visions anthologized here are articulated in retrospect, haloed by the glow of memory and nostalgia; does reminiscence lend idealization to the ideal?

SOURCE: *The Presence of the Actor*, by Joseph Chaikin, 1972.

493

More than any, though, the in-process nature of the Open Theater was right out in the, yes, "open," the very name of the company.
Begun as a workshop for actors in the winter of 1963, this assemblage of seventeen actors, four playwrights and a couple of dramaturgs (though they weren't called that) was brought together by
two former Living Theatre actors, Joseph Chaikin and Peter Feldman.
The actors, "not wanting to be committed to a specific approach,
refrained from self-definition and resisted formulating a unified aesthetic," as Margaret Croyden puts it. Chaikin and others devised a
series of exercises, some adapted from the games of Viola Spolin and
the techniques of Nola Chilton, with whom many of the actors had
studied. They were looking for something beyond naturalism, what
Feldman called in his personal notes "levels of reality which usually
are not expressed in situations: the elusive, irrational, fragile, mysterious or monstrous lives within our lives."

Chaikin became, and remained, the spiritual, questing, charismatic leader of the loose collective. Through his continuous questioning of the forms and purposes of their lives and work,

> he began to elaborate a theater vision that was open, radical,
> and had no Way—in an aesthetic, moral, even political sense.
> It was his credo that the deepest possibilities of the theater
> were still unknown, and a new expressiveness could be liber-
> ated upon the stage through the creative intervention of the
> performer. The fragile life of acting even could suffuse the spirit
> of the dramatic text and challenge its claim to finality. [. . .] For
> the ensemble was to celebrate, perhaps more than any mod-
> ern troupe in our time, the virtues of the work-in-progress, the
> commedia of life in the process of becoming itself.[12]

"What I wanted most from the Open Theater," Chaikin later said,
"was that it could be a place of discovery, breaking down, exploring,
a place of re-perceiving—through the theater, through images and
breathings and pulses. It was a laboratory."[13] Chaikin was most interested in pure research, "unfixing" the limits of acting and the theater. To accomplish that, he set out on a fluid journey that redefined
collaboration in the theater, as members of the ensemble worked
together, led separate research, created plays through improvisation—famously with writers Jean-Claude van Itallie, Megan Terry and
Susan Yankowitz—and taught each other.

12. William Coco, "The Open Theater [1963–1973]: Looking Back," *Performing Arts Journal*, 21,
1983.

13. Ibid.

Not surprisingly, then, the company's largest crises came when their monastic, laboratory work flowered into actual productions. The success of the work, once out in the world, brought tension to the group—the pull of independent careers, the tug of product-thinking, conflicts over the course of pursuit. The company, like the experiments it tackled, kept re-forming.

This deep process orientation came from Chaikin himself, who led the troupe as much by the example of his own openness to others, and the discipline of his inquiry, as by charisma. You can hear the questioning, the resistance to categories and easy answers, in the very tone of his language here. Theater is process, first last and always. This refusal to live in yesterday's answers was, perhaps, Chaikin's greatest gift. When the company disbanded in 1973—at a height of its public success—several other experimental companies, including the Talking Band, Medicine Show and Omaha Magic Theatre, grew out of the questions that still hung in the air.

—TL

About 1960 I went to the Living Theatre. I got a part in a play they were doing, Paul Goodman's *From the Cave*. We rehearsed it for ten weeks, because everything kept going wrong technically—with the company, with the building; there was the threat of bankruptcy, and we kept being stopped, and the production kept being delayed. When the play opened it was a disappointment, but this put me into the repertory of the Living Theatre. I played in *Many Loves* by William Carlos Williams, and eventually I got into *The Connection*, with a part for which I was ill-suited. After several months I realized I couldn't stand being in *The Connection* anymore, and I went to a different theater where I played in *Ghelderode*, a Yeats play and an e. e. cummings play—mostly poetic theater. Then that closed, and I called up the Living Theatre and said: "I have to go back to office work unless you give me work. I'll take anything." They said: "The only thing is *The Connection*. You can go back into that." So I went back into it.

We had made a European tour during my first period with the Living Theatre and then we went to Europe again, this time adding a Brecht play, *In the Jungle of Cities*. After that, back to New York and a part in *Man Is Man*. This was the beginning of a radical change for me, and the end of a certain aspiration. Until the Brecht play I had been interested in a fancy career for myself as an actor, and I thought the opportunity to play this role would give me all the chance in the world to further this career. I thought I was very happy: it was the beginning of stardom—Off Broadway was just coming to be important—and I was playing a major role in a new play, with a company that was noticed and called interesting. I had a New York agent and a personal manager as well, and a lot of projects waiting. They would say: "We've got to get good reviews, and then we have to take them in such and such a way, and a movie will show up, and a this will show up . . ." We were trying to find out exactly how to label me—was I a young character or a character juvenile or an offhand young leading actor—exactly what was I?

But in doing the role every night, saying the lines, finding my own involvement with the play, I changed little by little. Like Galy Gay in the play, it came mostly from considering the lines of the play, night after night after night. And saying them. Studying them and saying them: there is a time when he turns to the audience and says, "Who am I? If they cut off my arm and my head, would the arm recognize the head?" It was particularly the responsibility of coming out to the audience and talking directly to them— something I had never had to do before—knowing that what I said to the audience I didn't believe, and then coming to believe what I was saying. The other thing was the Becks. I had become involved with them originally simply as an actor to whom they had offered a part—not a very good part, but one that might lead to better ones. Behind this thinking was my ambition to be seen, my hope that I might really "get somewhere." But while I was with the Becks my idea of "somewhere" became very confused.

Politics was what undid it. I had resisted that aspect of their theater, because it had seemed ridiculous and unnecessary to me. The world didn't seem to me to be all that bad. I used to say to them again and again, "Are you a theater or are you a political movement? You can't be both." I was very determined to define my path, and it was their ambivalence about what they were doing that made my path appear clearer to me.

We had many conversations, and many fights. And what Judith and Julian were saying and doing, the lines of Galy Gay which I was saying every night to the audience, and the conversations I got into at that time began to have an impact on me. I started getting involved in political things, and getting involved in demonstrations, and getting arrested and going to jail. I was only there a couple of nights at a time, but it had a lasting effect on me. I began to feel that the political aspect of the Living Theatre, which had looked so ridiculous, was very necessary. And the fact that it *was* ridiculous didn't make it any less necessary.

I began thinking, shortly after that, that I would like to know more about acting than I had access to through the classes I had been going to, or through the Living Theatre. At that time the Living Theatre was not really interested in acting at all, and hardly explored the actor's own powers or the ensemble experience. The constant state of emergency at the Living Theatre prevented that. So I began working with writers and actors from Nola Chilton's class after she had gone to Israel—people who wanted to continue working together even though she was gone. When the Living Theatre went to Europe in 1963, I did not.

Our new group began meeting once a week, and then twice a week. Our first problem arose when the actors wanted to continue exactly as Nola had done when she worked with them, and I wanted us to try other things. And again there was a certain dogmatic hurdle: *this* is the way, and another way is not the way. It was a very transient situation, where people came and went. We took a long time to see if we could trust each other, and given the way we defined the question, we found we couldn't. There were a number of experiments within a classroom and workshop situation; some of them were attempts to relate and understand certain Brechtian ideas, some of them were political, some were ideas I had for a long time and wanted to develop with other people, and a great many of them were simply to take away the wall, the boundary—that limit we felt through our training. We began by doing things like tying up our hands and legs and trying to perform a task with another actor, trying to find some other way than using naturalistic mannerisms.

The internal questions were: "What direction should we take?" and "Do you think we can get along with each other?" At this point there were two schools of thought, one that felt we should be basically a communal group doing theater, and the other that felt we should be a group of theater professionals. These questions occurred again and again. And then we said, "Well, what name should we give ourselves?" And we thought of all kinds of names, including the Genesis, the Spiral, and the Open Theater. I liked the Open Theater because it was an unconfining name, it implied a susceptibility to continue to change. The name would serve to remind us of that early commitment to stay in process, and we called ourselves that. Very early in our meetings, even before we started calling ourselves the Open Theater, we were a formless group. The initial form came about as a result of the people who originally made up the group. Lee Worley, Peter Feldman and Meg Terry were there from the start. Their temperaments and talents largely shaped the first period of the Open Theater. After meeting for two or three or four months, Jean-Claude van Itallie was brought to a workshop by Gordon Rogoff. His role in the early stages, and our collaboration from that point, beginning with short scenes through *America Hurrah* and *The Serpent*, had a great deal to do with all that followed.

. . .

Julian Beck said that an actor has to be like Columbus: he has to go out and discover something, and come back and report on what he discovers. Voyages have to be taken, but there has to be a place to come back to, and this place has to be different from the established theater. It is not likely to be a business place. One has to be able to imagine and feel an alternative realm of behavior in order to play it. The spectator will feel that what is true on the stage is what most represents himself—that realm which he most identifies with as his "real life" and perhaps that one which he most inhabits. But at the same time, the realm which is played recommends a "reality" which he may adopt.

Everything we do changes us a little, even when we purport to be indifferent to what we've done. And what we witness, we also do.

[. . .]

Winter 1965

The organization of the Open Theater has changed its face already so many times that it is hard to know what is referred to as the Open Theater. The structure and emphasis are always changing: I have no idea what will happen in the future. But even if we were to melt away now, I think we would have already unfixed what previously seemed almost immovable in our work. Somehow, our minds are stirred. The movies have come such a distance in understanding their art and broadening it, while the stage remains stuck in the thirties. But everything—including impenetrable audiences—is changing, and the old work is no longer enough. If Stanislavsky were alive, would he be working in the same way, or would he be exploring? The obvious answer is the challenge of his example, which our theater rarely meets.

Only some of our work and thought are in social terms. Much of the work is abstract and nonliteral. When we begin on a new form or idea, we have no way of knowing if it will result in anything visible or lends any clarity. Often it doesn't.

—*JC*

American Conservatory Theater

FOUNDED 1965

William Ball, et al.

> Some artists are fortunate because they can create a sculpture and work alone in a studio like a painter. A theater artist cannot exist or succeed alone. There are no soloists in our business. We are all *interdependent*. We call ourselves a community art. Our success is based on the relationship of one artist to another, or one craftsman to another. A.C.T. is a *group* of two hundred people bound together in service of one idea.
>
> —*William Ball*

The American Conservatory Theater began without a home or, rather, it began in what was meant to be a three-year home—the Pittsburgh Playhouse—where it lasted only six months. In May 1965—with a manifesto/statement of purpose (below) written by wunderkind director William Ball—lighting designer Jules Fisher, actor Edward Hastings, voice teacher Kristin Linklater and producer Robert Whitehead joined Ball in signing the company's incorporation papers for nonprofit status. In July, the company began its short-lived but earth-shaking season of fourteen plays in repertory in Pittsburgh. But whether the board of the Playhouse couldn't suffer Ball's ambitions or the need to share space among three organizations (A.C.T., the Playhouse itself and the drama department of Carnegie Institute of Technology, Ball's alma mater), this was the end of A.C.T.'s residency. Ball and company went in search of a city.

He had already ruled out New York, where he'd been offered the helm of the two-year-old Repertory Theater of Lincoln Center after his *Tartuffe* made a splash there. During that play's run Lincoln Center's first leaders, Elia Kazan and Robert Whitehead, had been ousted. In a 1981 interview in the *San Francisco Chronicle*, Ball replays the scene:

> The conditions [in New York] were so awful that I nearly had a nervous breakdown. I brought a tape recorder to hear the sound cues, and the union people said I couldn't turn it on; it was going to cost me two days' salary for sixteen men. The sets were delivered without doorknobs. In the middle of the rehearsal the board of directors fired Whitehead and Kazan.

SOURCE: Manifesto written in 1965 by William Ball, et al., later published in *The Creation of an Ensemble: The First Years of the American Conservatory Theater*, by John R. Wilk, 1986.

This great effort of two years, the great hope of the Lincoln Center was dissolving, and they told me to go back to rehearsal, as though nothing had happened and you could go right on creating theater. Here I'd come all this distance to what I thought were the highest professional standards, and what did I find? A profession? No. It was madness.

So New York was out. Pittsburgh was a closed door. After some touring and flirtations with other options, including the thought of staying peripatetic, A.C.T. rang in 1967 from its new home on the San Francisco Bay. The first season lasted twenty-two weeks and offered sixteen productions in rotating rep, for a total of 296 performances. It drew 222,685 in paid admissions, taking in $799,150 at the box office. Forty-seven actors played 187 roles, not including the roles in which they were double cast or for which they understudied. Ball's goal was "to have so much, such a splashy repertory that it was an undeniable experience. We had to dazzle our audience and overwhelm them." This dazzle stands in direct contrast to A.C.T.'s predecessor in San Francisco, the Actor's Workshop, which was defiantly standoffish with regard to popular support. Julius Novick sums it up: the Workshop believed, in Herbert Blau's words, "Give an audience a chance, and it will certainly be wrong." For Ball, "To succeed a theater must have an audience!"

Integral to Ball's idea of professionalism was a lifetime of training. Hence, the birth of the theater was inseparable from the birth of a training conservatory. The models were European. The energy, pure American. As critic Martin Gottfried put it, "I doubt whether there is a single director in America so wound up in the new kind of theater, so messianic. The company and the conservatory were his dream."

Gottfried, like many others, considered Ball "the finest director in America."

He is training them to discipline flamboyance and then apply it to productions that he stages with all the devices of grand opera, ballet, mime and magical full-throated theater. Combining these primary theater colors with an unrelenting demand for such basics as voice control, diction, movement and facial expression, and pumping them up with the inspirational effect of his own genius, he blends directorial creativity with respect for a playwright's purposes.

Ball's trademark was the excessive, the overmuch. Here was American theater at its most theatrical, flamboyance at its most disciplined. Here was a troupe formed around the needs of the actor, under the firm, fiery hand of a single man.

—TL

Statement of Purpose of the American Conservatory Theater Foundation

1. Whereas, the United States is the only country in the civilized world without a national conservatory of theater art, and there is no immediate likelihood of one being created within our existing theatrical structures.

2. The commercial theater is so heavily burdened with the pressures of immediate projects, that it cannot be expected to provide development and training for theater artists.

3. Such training as exists in universities and professional schools often suffers from inadequate standards and is often limited by the highly individualistic stamp of one teacher or method.

4. There is no consistently available link for young professionals of these schools and the competitive commercial theater.

5. The creative artists in many professional theater structures often find their work limited or dominated by institutionalism, financial or pedagogic interference or the personal whim of a proprietary interest.

6. The theatrical trade unions generally refuse or are unable to use their power to initiate constructive programs toward revitalizing the theater.

7. The metropolitan theater audience consists mainly of hit-followers; the minority of thoughtful theater lovers is offered little in the way of a sustained meaningful repertoire.

8. A handful of drama critics find themselves in a position to shape the canons of theater art and the tastes of the entire nation; that their mere opinion may make or break the self-esteem, progress and longevity of an artist or company.

9. The exaggerated values of "fame and fortune" and the panicky competitiveness accompanying them have intimidated most theatrical artists to the point of paralysis; these myths have misled others in the conviction that their work has achieved an incontestable excellence, that their venerated talents are no longer in need of training and extension.

10. Every day, innovators announce new theater projects, each determined in his own way to solve the problems of today's theater; but lacking valid experience and research they are frequently unaware that their formulas for tomorrow's theater have already proven yesterday's mistakes.

THEREFORE WE RESOLVE TO FOUND:
THE AMERICAN CONSERVATORY THEATER

1. As a nonprofit tax-exempt educational institution resembling the European concept of Conservatory—adapted so that development and performances are integral and inseparable parts of the professional's creative life. Training and production shall be indigenous, the one to the other, not working as separate programs with separated personnel. All participants in the Conservatory—as in a ballet company—will always be in training.

2. To bring together the finest directors, authors, playwrights, actors and educators in the theater arts to provide comprehensive advanced training to a large professional company and to make this aggregate training available to representatives of regional theaters and educators in university and professional schools of drama.

3. To restore to the creative artist himself the right to leadership in shaping and fulfilling his own potential.

4. To determine the qualifications for membership and welcome as participants in the Conservatory any union person who demonstrates creative ability and who agrees to participate in the triple role of student, instructor and production artist. It shall not, however, demonstrate prejudice against gifted young talent merely because they are not union members.

5. To engage artists on long contracts so that within an explorative atmosphere, with reasonable security, the adventuresome artist may test his potential.

6. To structure the Conservatory Theater to insure the maximum freedom from proprietary interference, and to vest in the artistic directors of the Conservatory the authority to determine continuity and policies of the Foundation.

7. To build and rely completely upon a subscribed membership audience [by] offering a meaningful repertoire at a popular, accessible ($4.95 top) price scale.

8. To enlist the cooperation of national leaders, publishers, editors and theater critics themselves in an experiment by which television and journalistic reviewing will be limited to exclude both praise and disparagement of the repertory performances for a period of three years; in return, the Conservatory Theater will agree to limit advertising to exclude "quotes" from any source.

9. To found the American Conservatory Theater upon the observed and reported experience of all related theater proj-

ects; principles derived from research and experience collated from former theater projects with the aim to avert the misjudgments that have caused so many projects to founder; to leave provision for expansion and adjustment within the charter and bylaws; to encourage, through future programs (already drafted) the growth of playwriting, criticism, design, architecture, opera, mime and theater literature; to provide a receptacle for the focus of isolated theater projects and to aid all efforts toward unity and economy in the national theater.

DEFINITION

The American Conservatory Theater combines the concept of resident repertory theater with the classic concept of continuous training, study and practice as an integral and inseparable part of the performer's life.

The American Conservatory Theater is simultaneously an educational and performing organization. The purpose in the first three years is to provide actors, craftsmen, directors and designers with a triple-pronged program. Each participant in the program will:

1. Develop his own artistic potential through study.
2. Teach the younger professionals.
3. Perform wide repertoire.

As the project is aimed at broadening the expressive ability of the actor and director, all available techniques for acting and directing will be used as sources. An eclectic program will be explored with a wide range of theory and experiment, while performance will serve to apply and test techniques.

The training program of the Conservatory will be concurrent with the program of presentations. Training will be woven into the rehearsal pattern by stage managers specifically engaged for the purpose of preparing the daily schedule and assignments of personnel. [. . .]

Our goal is to awaken in the theater artist his maximum versatility and expressiveness.

—WB, et al.

Yale Repertory Theatre (Originally Yale School of Drama Repertory Theatre)

FOUNDED 1967

Robert Brustein

> . . . to ensure
> That what was bravely founded will endure,
> Not as an academic appanage,
> But as the White Hope of tomorrow's stage.
> We need a White Hope for the Great White Way!
>
> *—Lee Wilson Dodd,*
> *A Prologue for the Opening of*
> *the University Theatre at Yale University*[14]

When George Pierce Baker left Harvard University in 1925 to plan and chair the Yale School of Drama, taking his famous 47 Workshop in playwriting and production with him, the journalist Heywood Broun quipped, "Yale: 47; Harvard: 0." Forty-two years later, Robert Brustein brought to the famous drama school professional theater and, in the process, experienced—and catalyzed—culture shock. In 1980, Brustein would reverse Baker's journey, leaving Yale and founding the first professional theater at Harvard, American Repertory Theater.

What is the role of academia in the theater, and what is the role of theater in academia? These are the questions that both Baker and Brustein had to confront. By redirecting the teaching of theater toward the actual, practical stage, Baker transformed academic training in the early years of the American art theater. Brustein brought the professional theater into a collision with Ivy League culture, and so changed both.[15]

Source: *Making Scenes: A Personal History of the Turbulent Years at Yale, 1966–1979*, by Robert Brustein, 1981.

14. Thanks to Iris O'Brien Dodge, Sergi Torres and Jen Wineman, my students at Yale, for bringing this dedication to my attention.

15. On the subject of the interrelatedness of academia and theater: this book would not have been possible without the comprehensive contributions of editor Weldon B. Durham and contributors to the second and third volumes of his encyclopedic *American Theatre Companies*. The second covers the years 1888–1930, and the final volume, 1931–86. Both were published by the Greenwood Press, Westport, Connecticut, in 1987 and 1989, respectively. While not every theater in *An Ideal Theater* appears in Durham, many do. The remarkable detail and specificity of historical information makes his collection an invaluable reference, not to mention an example of fine and helpful scholarship.

It helps that Brustein has also been one of the theater's smartest and most argumentative critics. His teaching career at Columbia University (prior to Yale) and his long tenure as drama critic for the *New Republic*, beginning in 1959, prepared him not only for the task of making over the moribund Yale School of Drama and starting up a progressive new theater linked to it, but also for furthering his artistic agenda through his critical writings. Moreover, Brustein's drive to make his case has given us fifteen (and counting) eloquent, provocative books on the contemporary theater, including *Making Scenes: A Personal History of the Turbulent Years at Yale, 1966–1979*, from which this chapter's first excerpt is taken.

Brustein oversaw training for a generation of actors, playwrights, directors, designers, technicians, arts administrators (a category he added at Yale) and dramaturgs, the latter a profession he helped establish in the U.S. (He tried to train critics, but the attempt to integrate them into a nurturing environment for theater artists proved unworkable.) His hiring and programming sought to merge the best in theater history with the best in contemporary, experimental theater—Jonathan Miller's production of Aeschylus' *Prometheus Bound* and the Open Theater's *Viet Rock*, for example. He fought to establish and keep resident artists in his theater, tenaciously holding on to an acting company. He brought fresh avant-garde perspectives—and directors—to classical work, perhaps Yale's and, later, ART's most distinctive artistic stamp. And he combined political theater with artistic elitism, ensemble techniques with the best of Stanislavsky's teachings, and dared, even within the conservative groves of academe, to remain on the cutting edge of writing and design. More vocally than his contemporaries, he also eschewed the lures of Broadway, in favor of an alternative ideal.

If Brustein was, almost literally, the dean of American theater for many years, he has also managed to remain one of our nation's theater's unrelenting critics—taking on commercialism, political correctness, the dumbing down of culture, and the loss of standards of excellence and of the original intent of the nonprofit theater movement. By his own admission, he led his theaters with the doggedness of an Ibsen character standing alone against the corruptions of the world. Unlike Ibsen's righteous, solitary heroes, though, Brustein, by surrounding himself with a family of artists and by training four decades of students in what he calls "the repertory ideal," was rarely fighting alone.

—TL

Kingman[16] believed that a major obstacle in the way of attracting distinguished faculty to Yale was the city of New Haven, which, whatever it was in the past, had now become something of a cultural and aesthetic wasteland. In Kingman's mind, Yale had the obligation to provide some of the artistic life that the city lacked, and it was partly for this reason that he encouraged public performance in the schools of music and drama, where theory had always prevailed. He believed that Yale also had a responsibility to the nation to provide it with not just "leaders of men"—in its traditional role of developing bankers, corporation executives, lawyers, engineers, doctors and architects—but also scholars, musicians, painters, sculptors and theater artists.

Partly for these reasons, he endorsed my plan to create a new professional theater on the grounds of the university. To me, it seemed an inevitable—indeed, an essential—step. When the School of Drama was founded in 1927, following George Pierce Baker's move from Harvard, the central locus of theatrical activity, whether for art or entertainment, was Broadway, but the same theatrical conditions did not continue during the years of Baker's successors. The American theater began to develop alternatives—not only Off Broadway, which existed during the early years of the century, but Off Off Broadway and the decentralized resident theater movement. Despite these developments, however, the School of Drama continued to prepare its students as if nothing but Broadway existed, even after Broadway had ceased to be a hospitable place for the serious American drama. Moreover, the school's training procedures had become antiquated, and, as a result, students considered them useless for providing either practical opportunities or viable alternatives. It is a melancholy fact that by the fifties and sixties only a very small proportion of Drama School graduates (most of them designers) were entering the American theater profession.

Some were going into college or high school theater departments, some into business, some into advertising. The school had largely lost its reputation as a training institution or a breeding ground for talent. Acting students, for example, were accepted not through auditions but on the basis of academic records and recommendations. My plan was to transform the place from a graduate school, devoted to fulfilling requirements and granting MFA degrees, into a professional conservatory, concerned with developing artists for the American stage. The Master of Fine Arts degree would still be offered after the satisfactory completion of three years of work, but passing courses would no longer be the goal of the work; instead, the student would be encouraged to develop his or her talent. The shift was subtle, but it was important. It suggested a commitment to growth rather than to academics.

16. Kingman Brewster, president of Yale Univesity from 1963–77.

It was perfectly conceivable, for example, that a gifted acting student might complete three years at the school, playing leading roles and even entering the company afterward, without ever having completed the degree requirements. The degree would be important to the student, not to the school, and it was up to the student to obtain it. Our emphasis would be on training— and training for a well-defined purpose.

This shift to a conservatory structure raised certain problems for the university, though it never seemed to bother Kingman. Yale was a system of schools and colleges administered by deans and, as such, was bound to feel uncomfortable with a professional school that subordinated its academic function. A conservatory of this nature could survive in the university only by sufferance, and would always be particularly vulnerable at Yale, which considered undergraduates the central constituency. It also meant that undergraduates would have much less access to the school than they had in the past, when anyone who registered was allowed to join the acting classes with the drama students. The undergraduates had their own program in theater administered by the Drama School, which we were to improve as the years went on, and they had many outlets for acting and directing, including the Yale Dramat and the numerous dramatic societies in the residential colleges. But they always objected to being segregated from the graduate-professional activities of our acting and directing students. The objections were understandable but, to my mind, unanswerable. Because of its professional thrust, its selective admission process, and its collaborative nature, the School of Drama would never be able to satisfy undergraduate demands as easily, say, as the School of Art, with its system of lecture courses. As long as it guarded its own integrity and autonomy, the school would always seem a little peripheral to the rest of the university. Indeed, nothing could guarantee its survival except the support of the central administration.

This support remained firm and constant as long as Kingman remained president. Whenever I mentioned the odd nature of the school in an academic setting, he simply shrugged. He approved of my changes, and he didn't seem to care whether they fit a neat pattern within the university. He did, however, refuse one of my requests for change; I didn't want to be called a dean. The title made me uncomfortable; it smacked of academic robes and punitive behavior. How do you communicate with creative people in something called the Office of the Dean? But Yale was an institution administered by deans, and Kingman couldn't release me from the office without violating the charter of the university. I was stuck with the title and, worse, I was stuck with the psychological impact of the title on the minds of faculty and students alike. It created subtle barriers, difficult to overcome, and it affected perceptions of me in a way I couldn't change.

Nevertheless, the dean of the school had another title more appropriate to the situation—director of the theater. This was helpful, considering my plans for the formation of a professional company at Yale. In my mind, the company had become the key to the training. If the American theater had lost its way, then schools of drama were obliged, I thought, to break a new path. It was essential to create a professional model in order to inform the training, determine the aesthetic, develop a laboratory and provide a potential avenue of future employment. The analogy I proposed to Kingman was the School of Medicine in its relationship to the Yale–New Haven Hospital. Yale faculty participated in both these institutions, while students took classes in one and practiced internship in the other. Like the hospital, the professional theater could help to bridge a gap between the academic and the urban community; and like the practicing doctors, the practicing artists could provide an up-to-date source of instruction for young people in the field.

Professional instruction was crucial to the realization of the conservatory idea. Kingman had already made it possible through his earlier decision to abolish future tenure appointments at the school. This was a brilliant if controversial move; without it, I doubt if I could have proceeded at all. The school's tenure policies were unquestionably responsible for many of its problems, particularly its stodginess. Tenure was originally invented in order to protect academic freedom, not to sink creative people into an atmosphere of staleness and paralysis. To offer lifetime protected positions to instructors in a professional school was to encourage separation between theory and practice; it was to substitute security for growth. Tenure discouraged practice by rewarding academic achievement instead of artistic endeavor, and since art is a process of continual change, people who did not practice their profession were not really prepared to teach it. A professional company at Yale would provide instructors in all the areas of theater—acting, directing, design, playwriting, stage management, dramaturgy, technical production and theater administration—and while it wouldn't guarantee that all would be inspired teachers, they would certainly be lively and informed, and what they couldn't give in continuity of instruction would be provided by a permanent resident staff.

My hope, at the time, was to involve everybody at the school with the theater and everybody at the theater with the school, so that the two related structures would ultimately become interdependent, indistinguishable, one. This took years to accomplish, and ran into unexpected difficulties of a kind to be later described. But bringing in professional people had one immediate advantage: it exposed the tenured faculty to new developments in the theater. This was important because a few of them had become curiously isolated in New Haven. An elder, respected faculty member, for example, surprised me by saying he had not seen any New York productions for years, including Peter Brook's *Marat/Sade* (then considered one of the most seminal shows of the decade). He wasn't alone; most of the others hadn't seen it either. Too busy. Too many committees. Too many classes. Too far to go. A few years later I would find myself making some of the same excuses for my failure to get out of New Haven. How easy it was to lose track of the advances in your field.

The last and most important reason for forming a permanent company at Yale was to state as strongly as possible that the Yale School of Drama was now devoted to training students not for teaching careers, not for college theater, not for Broadway, not for television, not for the movies, but rather for the resident theaters that were just then beginning to burgeon in the larger cities of the country. I thought that resident theaters had much in common with universities—both were nonprofit institutions representing a real alternative to the profit-making corporate world. If one informed the mind, the other informed the imagination; both were at their best when challenging, provocative, adventurous, taking risks. Why wasn't it possible for the university to provide not only a library for learning but a living library for art—offering not only the best that had been thought and written but the best that was being invented and created? I began to envision not only professional theaters and art museums in places like Yale but also resident dance and opera companies, symphony orchestras, string quartets—an alliance of art and learning that would make the university a cultural capital. I had no idea, at the time, how easily nonprofit institutions could be drawn into the vortex of the prevailing system or how shaky were their values.

From the beginning, however, I had in mind a professional theater to be staffed primarily by people who had completed the training at the school, who shared *its* values. The idea was hardly a new one. In Europe, theater conservatories were common enough in relation to professional companies— the Old Vic School, for example, which trained young actors for the Old Vic Theatre. In the United States, too, George Balanchine and Lincoln Kirstein had developed the New York City Ballet Company out of the School of American Ballet; while such musical training grounds as the Juilliard School and the New England Conservatory continued to provide musicians for such orchestras as the New York Philharmonic and the Boston Symphony. As an idea for theater, however, the conservatory notion was a relatively new concept in America, and not as readily accepted. People tended to think that actors were discovered in a Hollywood drugstore rather than trained in performance studios. And since Broadway drew its talent from casting calls rather than from schools or workshops, the organic relationship between a conservatory and a professional theater had to be continually justified, articulated and explained.

When I outlined the idea to Curtis Canfield, former dean of the school, he assured me that the acting students would never stand for it. This surprised me, since I thought that anybody would welcome the opportunity to supplement the work done in all-student projects with contact with experienced professionals, both in the classroom and on stage. Didn't young actors partly learn from watching distinguished performances? Didn't young directors partly learn by assisting distinguished artists? What I hadn't anticipated was the American resistance to the European master-apprentice system. We had always been plagued by the belief that acting was a matter of instinct, which gifted people pulled out of the air, instead of a technique to be learned, as one learned the violin or the harp. And we were just heading into the late sixties, when all notions of "authority" would come under question and any kind of apprenticeship would be considered an unacceptable form of self-subordination.

There would have been no problem had I been able to entrust these students from the start—as I learned to do soon after—with responsible roles in the professional productions, but I had inherited two years of students whose talents were then unknown to me, who had developed under an entirely different system. The incoming actors would have the opportunity to start their training from scratch; those already at the school would have to keep some continuity with the old program lest the changes prove unsettling. For this reason I consented, against my better instincts, to approve certain projects (a student production of *Hamlet*, for example), that were clearly beyond the reach of the participants as well as to feature a traditional faculty-directed project (Dean Canfield's production of O'Neill's sea plays with an all-student cast) on the main stage. Before long, I would learn just who among the students could be entrusted with good roles with a professional company, and who among them was capable of designing, directing, managing and writing plays for a professional theater. But until I had more familiarity with the talents of the second- and third-year students, I planned to offer them a compound not only of method and practice but of apprenticeship and observation as central components of the intensified approach to training I hoped to introduce.

For these reasons I ignored Dean Canfield's warning and brought my proposal to the Drama School acting students in the spring of 1966 (some months before I officially took up my duties at Yale). As Canfield had predicted, this group received my plan without much enthusiasm, even with some traces of hostility. Some of my ideas—such as increasing the number of acting faculty from two to eleven, and the number of contact hours from eight to twenty-five per week—were appealing to the student actors. But my proposal to invite visiting companies, and eventually to form our own, caused considerable consternation. One young actor (ironically, he would join our company when he graduated) coldly rejected the idea that professionals could teach him anything, either on stage or off. "We can play the roles as well as anyone you bring in," he said, with the others nodding their approval. "That is, unless you get in someone like Morris Carnovsky." It was more than youthful arrogance. These students actually believed they were equal or superior to anyone acting on the stage. A few months later an instructor showed his class the Olivier film of *Henry V*, and, receiving no response, asked who thought he could do it better. Almost all in the class raised their hands.

At this particular meeting the best I could do was assure the acting students they would benefit from the changes. But at the same time that they were objecting to playing supporting roles in professional productions, Stella Adler was objecting to their playing any roles at all, even in the student projects. Stella had been one of my first new faculty appointments. A good friend of Norma's[17] and mine for a number of years, she had been running a studio in New York where she gained a reputation as a brilliant, inspiring teacher: she had taught Brando, De Niro and Pacino, and she had taught my wife, who later assisted her at her studio. A leading actress with the Group Theatre, Stella was one of the few who had actually worked with Stanislavsky in the Soviet Union. Her disagreements with Lee Strasberg over what she took to be his misapplication of Stanislavsky theory were a continuing source of lively debate in New York theatrical circles.

Stella had done little acting in recent years, and had stopped altogether after an ill-fated production in England of Arthur Kopit's *Oh Dad, Poor Dad*. She didn't have a lot of respect for most directors, and she didn't think much of most critics either. Stella's ambiguous attitude toward acting inevitably communicated itself to her students. It was to her the most ennobling—but also the most difficult—of the arts. As a result, some of her charges tended to consider performing an ordeal; it was said that if you could get through Stella's training, nothing would ever frighten you again. Whatever she thought about the terrors of acting, however, she certainly demonstrated, through her own example, that a great actor had to be a great human being. Ageless, magnificently beautiful, heavy-lidded and white-maned, she dressed like a French courtesan and lived in an apartment furnished like a Venetian brothel, but she had the regal dignity of an English queen. Stella Adler struck admiration, love and fear into the hearts of all who knew her—at once the most intelligent and seductive of women, witty and scholarly, generous and loving, one of the great myths of the American stage, whose boards she shunned as a result of wounds of which she never spoke.

17. Brustein's wife, Norma Brustein, an actress and teacher at Yale.

When I finally agreed to Kingman's offer in March of 1966, Stella was the obvious choice to head the acting department. She stood at the very heart of the American theater—which, in one sense, meant that her techniques were designed for realism. But she also knew and appreciated Shakespeare, and she had a deep understanding of Ibsen, Strindberg and, especially, Chekhov, all of whom she taught in a famous script breakdown course. I believed that Stella would help us navigate the extremes of artificial, English-style "rep" acting, on the one hand, and narrow Actors Studio naturalism, on the other. I wanted to develop an actor capable of playing any role ever written, from the Greeks to the most experimental postmodernists. Of all the New York acting teachers who had come from the Group Theatre, Stella was clearly the most versatile, the most demanding, the most passionate—and, I thought, the most open to a continually changing theater.

I arrived at her apartment in March, accompanied by Jeremy Geidt, whom I had just persuaded to teach acting also; later he was to become one of the key figures in our acting company. Jeremy had performed extensively with British companies, had taught at the Old Vic School, and had come to the United States as a member of the English satirical group called the Establishment. He seemed eminently qualified to train in a variety of areas, including Shakespeare, mask work, satirical improvisation and games theater—an unlikely mishmash of styles, which pleased me. Upon our arrival in Stella's luxurious Fifth Avenue living room, she eyed Jeremy suspiciously. She distrusted English actors because she found them mannered, lacking in truth. Over tea, however, Jeremy quickly disarmed our hostess: endowed with the barrel chest of a Toby jug and the delicious vocabulary of a foul-mouthed sailor, Jeremy assailed Stella's ears with his salty theater anecdotes and his obscene jokes. For a few moments she looked at him quizzically; soon after, they were fast friends.

Stella had not yet decided to commit herself to Yale. She worried about the travel, the salary, the classroom space. After an hour of discussion, I asked her point-blank if she would accept the job. "I'll do it," she said, fluttering her eyelids and pursing her lips. "I'll do it . . . *for you*." Only two things stood in the way. She insisted on teaching all her classes over a period of a day and a half per week, and she wanted to be assured that her acting students would not perform in public for the first two years of training.

Stella had a way of getting whatever she wanted, and she had already reduced the two of us to jelly; still, this last seemed to me an excessively stringent demand, and I resisted it. Jeremy and I believed that acting students learned as much from getting up in front of an audience as they did from scene work and exercises; we couldn't imagine a program in which actors were prevented from acting. I feared that the students wouldn't be able to imagine it either, and that Stella was asking for trouble. Nevertheless she remained firm. Stella was convinced that performance was earned only after strenuous training; otherwise, the actor only calcified bad habits. In this, she was following Stanislavsky, who had prohibited his students from performing for an even longer period. But I didn't think she was being sufficiently sensitive to the impatience of American students or their need to display their talents. Stella remained steadfast on the issue; so did I. Finally, we compromised. Students would be asked to refrain from public performance only during their first year of training—and they would be given the chance to act before an audience at the end of that year, in a faculty-directed project.

[...]

I was embracing the new job in earnest, finding the most enjoyment in recruiting faculty. I had no administrative experience whatever, and the unfamiliar tasks of being a dean were already changing my life, even before I officially took office on the first of July. For the first time, I began to wake up in the middle of the night, remembering something I had forgotten, and make notes on a pad beside the bed. My nocturnal restlessness brought sharp looks, and occasionally sharp jabs, from Norma, who valued her uninterrupted slumber. "Don't sleep like a great man," she said one night, quoting Stella's immortal remark to Harold Clurman, "just sleep." But sleep was never to be the same again for me. The waking hours were much too full of anxieties.

Norma herself was displaying certain anxieties about the future. Our visits to New Haven in the spring had been personally supervised by Kingman, who took great trouble to organize dinner parties with people he thought we might like to meet. Among these were John Hersey, then master of Pierson College, and his charming wife, Barbara, who quickly became two of our closest friends in New Haven. But Norma remained very worried about the formality of life in this community, where, she had heard, the center of social life was the Lawn Club, and invitations to tea or dinner were personally delivered to your door by New Haven matrons wearing white gloves and Peck & Peck suits. In New York our friends were mostly cantankerous intellectuals and artists, who often concluded an evening with a screaming quarrel. By contrast, New Haven struck us both as rather decorous. Would Yale be able to accept our outspoken, freewheeling style? And was this sedate community prepared to accommodate the kind of provocative theater we were hoping to establish?

The unspoken worry was over being Jewish in an essentially Gentile community. Brewster, patrician though he was, had no apparent difficulty with people of other racial or religious groups, but Yale itself had traditionally been a protected WASP enclave, and vestiges of anti-Semitism still remained. Stella certainly noticed a difference during her first visit to the Drama School: John Gassner was the only Jew on the entire faculty. Furthermore, the two or three homosexuals were in the closet, leading hidden lives as exemplary family men. "How can you have a theater," she asked, "without Jews and homosexuals?" And without them, how could you have a university or a cultural community? At one of those early dinner parties Norma and I felt obliged to attend in New Haven, one of the guests—a curator of old maps—fixed us with a frozen smile over dessert and said, "I hope you're not coming here expecting to find the Promised Land?" We found this a curious allusion. Neither Norma nor I had ever been oversensitive to anti-Semitic innuendo, but then neither of us had ever before lived in such a rarefied community.

—RB

American Repertory Theater

FOUNDED 1980

Robert Brustein

On March 21, 1980, the American Repertory Theater opened *A Midsummer Night's Dream*, its initial production at the Loeb Drama Center at Harvard. It was the first day of spring and it rained.

The A.R.T., to use the cheeky acronym by which our theater was quickly known, was a company of seventy actors, directors, designers, administrators and technicians that had decamped from Yale the previous year after thirteen seasons in New Haven. The move was a result of a celebrated dust-up between me and the new Yale president, the late A. Bartlett Giamatti, a commotion that ended my thirteen-year tenure as dean of the Yale School of Drama and founding artistic director of the Yale Repertory Theatre.

Whatever the unpleasant controversy attending our departure, we were now happily ensconced in new headquarters in Cambridge. Through the dedicated preparation of many good people, under the careful and tireless supervision of managing director Robert Orchard, we had accomplished what before had seemed unlikely if not impossible—the establishment of a not-for-profit resident theater with a permanent company of actors in an area

SOURCE: Brustein's unpublished memoir: *Commotions Recollected in Tranquility.*

traditionally disinclined to support subsidized theater. Over the years, many ambitious and even distinguished companies with historic names like Theatre on the Green (Group 20), the Massachusetts Repertory Company, the Cambridge Theatre Company, the Brattle Theatre Company and the Theatre Company of Boston, among others, had come and gone in the Boston area, leading the critic Carolyn Clay to quip: "Boston is to first-rate regional repertory what the Bermuda triangle is to small craft." Still, here we were, the only large professional theater in town, in the process of launching a rather sizable craft into the Bermuda triangle—not only a season of classical and new plays, but the first credit courses in drama in Harvard history.

Two months before leaving New Haven for Cambridge, my first wife, Norma, had died, leaving me and my fifteen-year-old son, Danny, adrift and bereft. But despite the difficulty of the transition to a new city, a new community and a new culture, it was not a bad time. We had the endorsement of Derek Bok, president of Harvard University, and Henry Rosovsky, dean of the faculty of Arts and Sciences. We had been welcomed with considerable enthusiasm by the press, notably the *Boston Herald* and the *Boston Globe*, which ran an editorial celebrating our arrival. The major theater critics, Elliot Norton and Kevin Kelly, were not disguising their pleasure over our presence in town. Mayor Kevin White had organized a huge party in our honor at the Parkman House. And in our very first season, before having staged a single play, we had amassed thirteen thousand subscribers whereas in New Haven, at the height of our popularity, we had barely managed to attract six thousand. The A.R.T. no doubt derived some luster from its novelty value and from all those media-soaked years at Yale. But we were also floating on the success of a tour the previous season to the Loeb Drama Center with two extremely well-received shows: Andrei Serban's playful production of *Sganarelle* (four short Molière farces) and Walt Jones's nostalgic *The 1940's Radio Hour*. As I wrote with satisfaction in my account of the Yale years, *Making Scenes*, Cambridge had received our work like parched earth soaking up rain.

Our strategy in the initial season was to lead from strength without sacrificing our experimental thrust. We also hoped the opening productions would help define our artistic identity. Alvin Epstein's staging of *A Midsummer Night's Dream*, featuring Purcell's exquisite music from *The Faerie Queene* expertly played by the Banchetto Musicale, had already proven itself twice in New Haven as a signature piece of the company. It would not only illustrate our commitment to renovating classical plays, it would also demonstrate how a literary text could be enhanced by the addition of music. So would another season offering, the Elisabeth Hauptmann–Bertolt Brecht–Kurt Weill *Happy End*, one of the musical triumphs of the years at Yale.

In addition to featuring plays from our past repertoire, the first season was designed to demonstrate our devotion to young American playwriting with the professional premiere of Mark Leib's *Terry by Terry*. And, finally, we hoped to emphasize our interest in talented young directors by providing twenty-one-year-old Peter Sellars with his professional stage debut, before he had even graduated from Harvard. Sellars was commissioned to direct and co-adapt (with our Russian-speaking business manager, Sam Guckenheimer) Gogol's *The Inspector General*.

A Midsummer Night's Dream was if anything better received in Cambridge than it had been in New Haven. Boston is a music-loving town, and the combination of Purcell's resonating arias and choruses, Shakespeare's soaring verse and Epstein's inventive direction, proved to be irresistible. The production was performed by a gifted young company of actors and designers, most of them, like Mark Linn-Baker in the role of Puck and Marianne Owen playing Hermia, recent graduates of the Yale Drama School. They were led by their former teachers, the dancer-actor Carmen de Lavallade as a sinuous Titania, and the irrepressible Jeremy Geidt as Quince. New company members John Bottoms playing Bottom and Max Wright playing Flute were also prominent in the cast. And the whole event was performed on a gorgeous wooden scoop, designed by one of our graduated designers, Anthony Straiges, backed by a huge shimmering moon. Though the staging caused a little grumbling about what was perceived by some to be deviations from established traditions, the general refrain was ecstatic—letters and calls testifying to how happy everyone was that we were there.

The press response was equally positive, the one sour note being about my own performance as Theseus. I had undertaken the role partly to save a salary, partly as a symbolic way for me to welcome our new public to the theater in the robes of the Duke. The symbolism seemed lost on the critics and so was my performance. No doubt I wasn't much good in the part, my attention that first season being deflected by matters other than rehearsals. When we reprised the production the following season at Boston's Wilbur Theatre, where WBGH videotaped it for national television, I exercised an artistic director's discretion by replacing myself with another actor.

Our second production, *Terry by Terry*, which played in rotating repertory with *Midsummer*, and which featured some of the same performers, was the first new American work we staged in Cambridge. The author, Mark Leib, a graduate both of Harvard and the Yale Drama School, provided a highly literate evening of two one-act plays about the same character, first as a child who refuses to speak (Mark Linn-Baker), then as a blocked writer caught in a raging Strindbergian relationship (Robertson Dean). Despite some walkouts during previews, the play was tolerated by our audiences, and hailed by most of the reviewers (especially the *Harvard Crimson*) as the work of a very promising new talent.

Happy End, on the other hand, was nowhere near as successful in Cambridge as it had been in New Haven. Instead of treating it as a flawed but neglected work that featured some of Kurt Weill's finest songs, virtually every reviewer felt compelled to tell us that *Happy End* was inferior to the *The Threepenny Opera*. It must be admitted that our production was less integrated than it had been in New Haven, but I believe the problem was other. Very few of our Brecht offerings, with the later exception of *The Threepenny Opera*, were destined to attract large audiences or positive reviews in the Boston area. In New Haven, we were considered a small-town Berliner Ensemble, exploring the whole Brecht-Weill canon—including the full-scale opera, *The Rise and Fall of the City of Mahagonny*, as adapted by our dramaturg Michael Feingold. Indeed, it was Feingold's success with Brecht and Weill that gained us the permission of Lotte Lenya (Weill's widow and principal performer) to do the American premiere of *Happy End* in Feingold's jaunty adaptation.

At Yale, Brecht's caustic ironies and mordant worldview, not to mention Weill's tinny syncopated rhythms, were keystones of our style. In Cambridge, on the other hand, a town as infatuated with English culture today as it was in Colonial times, the favorite playwrights were Bernard Shaw and Tom Stoppard, not Bertolt Brecht or Frank Wedekind or Georg Büchner or Heiner Müller, or any of the other Germans we would be force-feeding audiences in succeeding years.

It was, however, our final production of the season, the Sellars's version of Gogol's *The Inspector General*, that caused what might be described as a bit of a commotion. Although he always took great liberties with the classics, even as an undergraduate, Sellars was then, and has remained, a genuine favorite of the Harvard community, as well as of the *Boston Globe*. Nevertheless, at the first preview two hundred people walked out before the act break. With Max Wright playing the Mayor, Jeremy Geidt as Osip and Mark Linn-Baker as Khlestakov, we had a fine cast stimulated by a strong if eccentric directorial concept. But the professional company chafed a bit over the inexperience of this young Turk, who had hitherto worked only with undergraduates and puppets, and the reviews were mixed. Some critics chafed at the literal translation that Sellars created with Sam Guckenheimer in order to simulate Gogol's linguistic peculiarities (featuring such nuggets as: "I have outlived my own mind."). Some were turned off by what they perceived to be self-conscious and irrelevant effects, notably a huge pineapple residing on stage for no other reason than the fact that in the Russian language pineapple was a pun on one of Gogol's phrases. Elliot Norton, particularly unhappy at the sight of what he took to be a huge head of Stalin passing upstage, felt compelled to remind us that Gogol had died a hundred years before the Soviet dictator was born. By contrast, Kevin Kelly of the *Globe* was won by the show, and the undergraduate community was in ecstasy. But we were already getting a hint of the kind of controversy that would color our future work in Cambridge.

The debate was over the proper role of a professional theater in an academic community. *The Inspector General* to a greater extent, *Midsummer* to a lesser, signified to some people that we were disdainful of tradition and dedicated to corrupting the classics. The A.R.T. was functioning in a community with dozens of distinguished educational institutions, many of whose members (behaving like a Yankee Académie française) expected us to conform to certain academic rules and regulations. The majority of the professoriate was dedicated to preserving the past. We were more concerned with bringing the past into the present and thereby creating a theater of the future. It was a timeworn conflict between the ancients and the moderns (now called theorists and practitioners) that neither side would ever resolve.

Furthermore, the A.R.T. was sharing the Loeb Drama Center with the Harvard-Radcliffe Dramatic Club, a well-entrenched undergraduate theater club, which resented our coming because we had reduced the club's time on the main stage from eighteen weeks to twelve. Although the HRDC had unlimited access to the smaller experimental theater and rarely seemed comfortable on the more professional main stage, the issue was territorial. The undergraduates felt expelled from their own theater space, while our own company was unhappy about having to abandon the Loeb for six key weeks in the fall and six in the spring with a corresponding loss in precious income.

Moreover, we had just festooned the handsome, if somewhat institutional, exterior of the building with colorful banners, designed by Lou Bakanovsky, not only a Harvard architecture professor but a member of Ben Thompson's celebrated Cambridge Seven. This act of vandalism didn't arouse quite the level of outrage I had provoked at Yale when we painted the Green Room red. Indeed, the design had even been approved by Hugh Stubbins, the original architect of the Loeb. But although it was hardly an arbitrary move, it was enough to provoke the neighbors who raised the complaints you inevitably hear whenever anything changes on Brattle Street. It also annoyed John Loeb, the building's chief donor, who reminded us that the space he had helped endow was meant to be a "drama center" for undergraduates, not a theater, and therefore not a place for decoration. It was a distinction that puzzled us at the time, though it seemed compelling enough to Mr. Loeb. His son John Jr. even suggested that the family might be more inclined to help the A.R.T. if the offending banners were removed.

I countered that we were trying to attract the paying public to living architecture, not to a mausoleum. I have since come to understand that this was precisely the problem. What was actually bothering Mr. Loeb was the professionalization of his building. An extracurricular academic space dedicated to amateur production and undergraduate workshops was being turned into a full-fledged professional theater with a busy box office, fundraising appeals, subscription drives, advertising, yes, and attention-getting banners. Loeb was eventually to grow more friendly to us, even providing scholarship money (for a Harvard graduate) when we later started a training institution. But I don't think he ever fully approved of our presence on campus performing a season of plays.

Neither for that matter did many members of the university community. During its 350-year history, Harvard had steadfastly refused to approve what it called "technical" or "vocational" courses in the arts (theoretical courses in the arts, of course, were commonplace). It was, as a matter of fact, this resistance to practical theater that led professor George Pierce Baker to abandon Harvard and move to Yale. While teaching his celebrated English 47 playwriting course to a Harvard community that included Eugene O'Neill, Sidney Howard and Philip Barry, Baker had requested a space in which to stage their plays. This was rudely denied. ("We don't teach people how to butcher meat either," one of his Harvard colleagues muttered.) After a member of the Harkness family offered the university a million dollars to build a suitable space for Baker—and Harvard uncharacteristically turned down the bequest—Baker took the money to New Haven and founded the Yale University Department of Drama (later to become the Yale School of Drama).

After serving as dean of that school for thirteen years, I had completed Baker's circuit and returned his idea to Harvard. There in the early years I was to face some of the same resistance that had plagued my predecessor fifty years earlier. In kind, not in intensity. If the A.R.T. never entirely won the hearts of the Harvard faculty, the momentum behind our arrival made it relatively easy in a short period of time for us to introduce practical credit courses in theater, closely monitored by a faculty group called the Committee on Dramatics. The undergraduate courses (in acting, directing, design, dramaturgy, criticism and the like) were deemed acceptable as long as they conformed to what were called the "Bakanovsky guidelines" (named after committee member Lou Bakanovsky, the same genial professor of visual arts and environmental studies who had designed our banners). Those "guidelines" essentially called for a reading list and a component of theory and history, easy enough to supply. But while we were empowered to offer a "Program in Drama" for undergraduates, we never managed to pass a drama

major or even a drama concentration through the various Harvard committees. As for the professional school of theater that I had proposed when we
first negotiated our contract, this was peremptorily rejected on the grounds
that Harvard didn't even have an undergraduate drama major. We would
not develop our training program until five years had passed, and we had
discovered the secret codes and nomenclatures required to pull the Harvard
behemoth around by its obstinate whiskers.

We were learning about the enduring power of tradition, about how
ivy has the power to crumble stone. Harvard had been founded by some
of the same Puritans who had colonized Boston, fleeing England following
the restoration of the Stuart kings. One of Oliver Cromwell's first official
acts, during the Puritan Interregnum, was to shut down all the theaters and
make production of plays illegal. In true Cromwellian fashion, the Reverend Increase Mather, pastor at the Old North Church in Boston, had thundered that: "The Natural Effects of Stage-Plays have been very pernicious
. . . Multitudes, especially of Young Persons, have thereby been Corrupted
and Everlastingly Ruined." In Cromwell's time, the only way plays could
be performed was if they included music, and could thereby be identified
as "operas." Clearly, music was sacred for the Puritans, while theater was
profane, being associated with harlots, orange girls, erotic behavior and (as
a result of boys playing women's parts) transvestitism, an act expressly condemned in the Book of Deuteronomy. I suspect that may explain why Boston musical institutions have always been able to attract the funding and
support that are denied the Boston stage.

Most support for the arts in the area, however, came largely from private philanthropists. Even the Boston Symphony had trouble raising money
from private foundations or local corporations. There is, as a matter of fact,
not a single arts funding agency exclusive to the entire Boston area, and local
corporate philanthropy has always been relatively stingy and grudging. Boston banks and insurance companies make gifts ranging from five hundred
dollars to five thousand dollars to arts institutions with budgets ranging anywhere from five hundred thousand dollars to fifty million dollars. Boston is
home to more arts organizations per capita than any other city, including
New York, Chicago and San Francisco. But the city is also unique in its niggardly government funding and its low level of foundation support (the city
gives less than a million dollars a year to arts and culture, ranking it forty-
eighth among the nation's fifty largest cities).

That was why some national foundations had initially urged us, upon
leaving New Haven, to forget about Boston and move to Chicago. After
almost a quarter of a century in residence, the A.R.T. is still not able to
attract more than forty thousand dollars in local corporate support. The area

almost seems to pride itself on being last among cities of its size for giving to the arts, proudly pointing to the Museum of Fine Arts and the Boston Symphony Orchestra as evidence that Boston remains the "Athens of America," for all its Yankee thriftiness.

And the state of Massachusetts has not been much better, except for one glorious period in the eighties when, under the leadership of Anne Hawley, the Massachusetts Cultural Council grew in size and ambition to become second only to the New York State Council in its enterprise and funding. Alas, it wasn't long before the legislature slashed sixty-two percent from that budget, and Hawley, dispirited, left her post to become the leader of the Isabelle Stuart Gardner Museum. The office of Mayor Kevin White had a cultural department but it was woefully underfunded. And while Harvard gave a subvention to the Loeb Drama Center for supervising undergraduate theater that eventually reached $750,000, the figure was well below the four-million-dollar subsidy that Yale University gave to the Drama School and Repertory Theatre. Moreover, Derek Bok did not seem to have the financial autonomy at Harvard that Kingman Brewster enjoyed at Yale. Over the years, Harvard's FAS (Faculty of Arts and Science) subvention would rise by inflationary increments, and in time the university would prove more generous in its support of the A.R.T. But it was very clear in the early years that my chief daily task was going to be the relentless pursuit of cultivated people with large pockets.

This unreliable climate threatened to make us considerably more dependent on the box office and the media than we ever were at Yale. It was also to have a sobering effect on the scale of our civic ambitions. Soon after arriving in Cambridge, Rob Orchard and I got the idea that Boston could use a free outdoor theater, similar to Joe Papp's Shakespeare in the Park, and we believed that the A.R.T. was ideally suited to provide it. Admittedly, we had other motives in addition to civic virtue. From a fundraising perspective, we wanted to demonstrate that the A.R.T. was not just a Harvard plaything but a resource for the entire city. From an image standpoint, we wanted to be perceived as native citizens rather than as carpetbaggers from another city. And from a budgetary point of view, we wanted to reduce production costs by staging the first play of every new season under the summer auspices of the city before we brought it to Cambridge in the fall. The price tag—a modest twenty thousand dollars—would not only cover actors' salaries during the summer months but help shorten rehearsal time in the fall. I pitched the idea to Kathy Kane, the mayor's cultural commissioner, who was so enthusiastic that she quickly organized a benefit to foot the bill.

The benefit—a performance of *A Chorus Line*—drew only sixty-five people and lost two thousand dollars. Nevertheless, we were encouraged to proceed with our plans. Tremendously excited by the thought of a new cultural initiative in Boston, we started rehearsing Andrei Belgrader's production of *As You Like It* for a two-week performance in the courtyard of Government Center. We didn't have a Rosalind in our resident company so, after auditions in New York, we eventually cast a young actress from Tennessee named Cherry Jones, who seemed to have exactly the right kind of twinkle, mischief and wholesomeness for the part. She was to remain a crucial member of the A.R.T. for the next twelve years, returning thereafter on an irregular basis from her distinguished stage career to take parts with the company.

As You Like It opened in August to an audience of two thousand cheering people. Although the actors had to battle wind, dust, rain, heat, police sirens and low-flying planes, there was not an empty seat to be had throughout the summer run. It drew poor reviews both from Kelly and Norton which puzzled us. The production had been a rousing success in New Haven, with its combination of Arcadian charm and Romanian goofiness, and its ingenious use of miniaturized puppets in the forest scenes. But in Boston there was one visual effect that clearly irritated a lot of people, including the critics. In the last scene of the play, when Hymen descends to bless the various couples, the actress playing the part was wearing a headdress consisting of female breasts and male sexual organs.

Considering that Hymen was the Goddess of Marriage, it wasn't an inappropriate item of clothing. But during the summer, and later in the fall when we opened the show in Cambridge, we received a number of protests from audience members, along with a warning from the head of the Committee on Dramatics to think twice before doing Shakespeare again in this community. In an admonitory lecture that was no doubt intended as friendly advice, she also suggested that we hold a debate about the true function of what she called "academic theater."

As for our plan to bring outdoor Shakespeare to Boston every summer, this too foundered on the rocks of finances. We waited for the twenty-thousand-dollar check promised from the mayor's office. And waited. And called. And waited. Finally, a check arrived, ten months later, for eighteen thousand dollars, accompanied by an explanation that the city was passing on to the A.R.T. the two-thousand-dollar loss from the benefit it had organized to raise money for us in the first place. As a needy not-for-profit theater we were in no position to add the city's shortfall to our growing deficits, so we had to abandon what could have been a really exciting civic venture.

It was a little worrisome that instead of the community subsidizing us, the city fathers were expecting us to subsidize the community. Another troublesome omen was a summer story in the magazine section of the *Boston*

Globe which, while generally enthusiastic about our first season, predicted looming problems if we continued to flout the tastes of Boston audiences. Furthermore, our fundraising efforts were not bearing much fruit, and we were projecting troublesome deficits between two hundred thousand dollars and four hundred thousand dollars at the end of the second season. ("Anything over one hundred thousand dollars will jeopardize the whole enterprise," we were warned by Dean Rosovsky.) Instead of declining, our subscription base actually managed to rise a little that year—to fourteen thousand members. But there were growing signs, as Carolyn Clay announced in the alternative newspaper, the *Boston Phoenix*, that "the honeymoon was over."

The debate on "academic theater" requested by our committee chairman took place in November. Director Alvin Epstein and professor of English Harry Levin represented the A.R.T. while Stanley Cavell, an eminent professor of philosophy with an interest in film, and Robert Chapman, my predecessor as director of the Loeb Drama Center, represented Harvard. Moderating the debate was our new dramaturg Michael Kustow. Kustow, former associate director of the Royal Shakespeare Company during Peter Hall's regime and more recently director of special projects at the National Theatre, was ideal for the moderator's role because he was a gracious, intelligent and well-informed Englishman. But we were all taken aback by the ferocity of the objections to our work. Chapman launched a defense of amateur production in which he called undergraduate theater infinitely more exciting than professional performance, while Cavell expressed his cheerful disdain not only for Belgrader's *As You Like It* but also for Alvin's *A Midsummer Night's Dream*. Both productions could have been improved, he affirmed, had the Harvard faculty been consulted during the process. "Use us," he urged with a good-natured smile. "Use us!" Levin contributed his memories of how the Loeb had evolved, how no one had wanted a theater on Brattle Street, and how the whole idea had foundered until someone invented the rubric "Drama Center." I was learning how important the right nomenclature was in this neighborhood. I was thinking of William Davenant who had managed to fool the Puritans by putting on plays and calling them "operas."

While certainly spirited, the debate was for the most part friendly. It may even have helped to lance some festering boils. After almost thirty years as a professor of English, I should have known that nothing upsets us academics more than not being able to express our opinions, and we were obviously playing to a highly opinionated and literate audience that had strong feelings about what they saw. When we did a classic, some subscribers would even come to the theater with a copy of the play, thumbing through it like a musical score, marking any deviations from the original text. I don't think more than a handful of Harvard faculty shared Harold Bloom's conviction that Shakespeare should be read in the study, not seen or heard on the stage. (Bloom, my Yale colleague and friend, had written, in *Shakespeare: The Invention of the Human*, that the worst productions he could remember of *A Midsummer Night's Dream* were those of Peter Brook and Alvin Epstein, which he called "a Yale hilarity.") But a great majority strongly resented any departure from the play they held in their hands or in their heads. Noel Lord Annan, an English critic recently invited to Harvard, admonished us miscreants, to the vocal approval of the English department, to: "Respect the verse, honor the text." The debate had been a good way of letting off academic steam. Only later would I learn how to provide relief more regularly for the tensions between an intelligent, conservative audience and a progressive, impudent theater.

—RB

Coda:

Theater, Theater Everywhere

The Florida Wheel

Hallie Flanagan

We played Okahumpka[1] and they came in by oxcart
They came in with lanterns to see *Twelfth Night*.
An old man barefoot, helping children from an oxcart,
Said, "They may be pretty young to understand it
But I want they should all be able to say
They've seen Shakespeare—
I did once, when I was a kid."
We played Live Oak, Madison, Monticello
We played Lake City and Tallahassee
We played Marianna and Callahan
We played DeFuniak Springs.

We played Palatka, county seat of Putnam County
A citrus center, northern end of the citrus belt.
We played *Everyman*. The actors like *Everyman*:
"A different kind of acting and a different kind of play
But we like it."
The audience liked it, too.

Wauchula was the place where we played musical comedy
And no one laughed.
The director went out and said "What's the matter?"

SOURCE: "The Florida Wheel," by Hallie Flanagan, was originally written for *Federal Theatre Magazine*, and later published in Flanagan's *Arena: The Story of the Federal Theatre* in 1940. It was presented on NBC national hook-up in special broadcast for Federal Theatre from Hollywood, on June 26, 1939, in a program which included Lionel Barrymore, Edward Arnold, James Cagney, Dick Powell, Joan Blondell, Walter Abel, Edward G. Robinson, Al Jolson, Bette Davis, Henry Fonda, Gale Sondergaard, Ralph Bellamy and Gloria Dickson.

1. Trading textual accuracy for geographical, I've corrected the spelling of several Florida towns Flanagan seems to have gotten wrong.

"Don't you like it? Why don't you laugh? Why don't you clap?"
An old lady said,
"We'd like to laugh but we're afraid to interrupt the living actors
It don't seem polite.
We'd like to clap but we don't know when.
We don't at the pictures."

We played Sanford, the Celery City
A big shipping center on the St. John's River
The biggest celery center in the USA.
We played there in November
When we came back in March
The kids in the street called the actors by their play names
"Hello, Malvolio! Hello, Olivia! Hello, Sir Toby Belch!"

In St. Augustine we played *The Nativity*
On Christmas Eve
In St. Augustine, Fountain of Eternal Youth
People laughed
But when the church doors opened
There lay the Child
Everyone was silent
You could hear a star fall.

West out of Jacksonville lies rural Florida
"They won't want you there, they're only crackers"
But we wanted to play the turpentine camps.

We played Eustis, Clermont, Tavares
We played Mount Dora and Howey-in-the-Hills
We played Yalaha
And once in Umatilla at a Crippled Children's Home
The leading actor, one from the big time, said,
"God, why haven't we been doing this
All
Our
Lives?"
[. . .]

New theaters
American theaters
Theaters in the making
Theaters from the past
Of the present
Pointing to the future

—HF

Source Notes

Chapter 1

The Hull-House Dramatic Association (Later, Hull-House Players)
Twenty Years at Hull-House, by Jane Addams, 1910, copyright © 1961 by Henry Steele Commager. Used by permission of Signet, an imprint of Penguin Group (USA) Inc., New York.

The Carolina Playmakers
"Drama in the South," an address delivered by Frederick H. Koch at the Playmakers Theatre in Chapel Hill, North Carolina, on April 5, 1940, for the Southern Regional Theatre Festival, commemorating the founding of the Carolina Playmakers. Published in *Pioneering a People's Theater*, edited with a foreword by Archibald Henderson, copyright © 1945 by the Carolina Playmakers. Used by permission of the University of North Carolina Press, Chapel Hill, NC, www.uncpress.unc.edu.

Barter Theatre
The excerpt is from an unpublished memoir by Robert Porterfield. Used by permission of Barter Theatre.

The Federal Theatre Project
Arena: The Story of the Federal Theatre, copyright © 1940 by Hallie Flanagan. Duell Sloan Pearce Publishers, New York.

The Wisconsin Idea Theater
Grassroots Theater: A Search for Regional Arts in America, by Robert E. Gard, 1955. Copyright © 1999, with a foreword by David H. Stevens and an introduction by Maryo Gard Ewell, by the Board of Regents of the University of Wisconsin System. Reprinted by permission of the University of Wisconsin Press, Madison, WI.

Roadside Theater
The excerpt is copyright © 2008 by Dudley Cocke. Originally published on the Roadside Theater website: www.roadside.org. Used by permission of the author.

Cornerstone Theater Company
The excerpt is from Cornerstone Theater Company Newsletter: October 1987, Act Two, Scene 1, copyright © 1987 by Cornerstone Theater Company, Bill Rauch and Alison Carey, co-founders, et al. Used by permission of Cornerstone Theater Company.

Chapter 2

The Yiddish Art Theatre
"Can New York Support a Better-Quality Yiddish Theatre?" by Maurice Schwartz, 1918. Published in *Der Tag*, 2 March 1918: 3. Translated for this publication by Joshua Waletzky. Used by permission of the translator.

KRIGWA Players
The excerpt is copyright © 1926 by W. E. B. Du Bois. Originally published in the July 1926 issue of *The Crisis*. Courtesy of Crisis Publishing Co., Inc., the publisher of the magazine of the National Association for the Advancement of Colored People.

The Negro Theatre Project, Federal Theatre Project
(aka, Negro Theatre Unit, Harlem Theatre Project)
Run-Through: A Memoir, copyright © 1972 by John Houseman. Simon & Schuster, New York. Reprinted by permission of Russell & Volkening as agents for the author.

The Free Southern Theater
From a series of letters by Doris Derby, Gilbert Moses and John O'Neal. Later published in *The Free Southern Theater*, by The Free Southern Theater, 1969. Bobbs–Merrill Company, New York. Used by permission of the authors.

El Teatro Campesino
"The Flat Bed Truck Years 1965–1970," copyright © 1966 by Luis Miguel Valdez. Originally published in the July 1966 issue of *Ramparts* magazine. Used by permission of the author.

The Negro Ensemble Company
"For Whites Only?" copyright © 1966 by Douglas Turner Ward. Originally published in the *New York Times*, on August 14, 1966.

The National Theatre of the Deaf
"The Premiere" is from *Lessons in Laugher: The Autobiography of a Deaf Actor*, by Bernard Bragg, as signed to Eugene Bergman, copyright © 1989 by Gallaudet University Press. Reprinted by permission of the author and Gallaudet University Press, Washington, D.C.

Chapter 3

The Chicago Little Theatre
Too Late to Lament: An Autobiography, copyright © 1956 by Maurice Browne. Indiana University Press, Bloomington, IL.

The Neighborhood Playhouse
The Neighborhood Playhouse: Leaves from a Theatre Scrapbook, copyright © 1959 by Alice Lewisohn Crowley. Theatre Arts Books, New York. Used by permission of the Neighborhood Playhouse.

The Washington Square Players
The Magic Curtain: A Story of a Life in Two Fields, copyright © 1951 by Lawrence Langner. Dutton & Company, New York. Reprinted by Kessinger Publishing LLC, Whitefish, MT, 2007. Used by permission of The Estate of Lawrence Langner.

The Provincetown Players
The Road to the Temple: A Biography of George Cram Cook, copyright © 1927 by Susan Glaspell. Frederick A. Stokes Company, New York. New edition printed in 2005, edited and with a new introduction and bibliography by Linda Ben-Zvi. McFarland & Company, Inc., Jefferson, NC, www.mcfarlandpub.com. Used by permission of McFarland & Company, Inc.

The Theatre Guild
The Theatre Guild: The First Ten Years, copyright © 1929 by Lawrence Langner. Later published by Brentanos, New York, in a version edited by Walter Prichard Eaton. Used by permission of The Estate of Lawrence Langner.

Oregon Shakespeare Festival
As I Remember, Adam: An Autobiography of a Festival, copyright © 1975 by Angus Bowmer. Oregon Shakespeare Festival, Ashland, OR. Used by permission of Oregon Shakespeare Festival.

Chapter 4

The Group Theatre
The Fervent Years, written by Harold Clurman in 1945, copyright © 1957 by Harold Clurman. Used by permission of Alfred A. Knopf, a division of Random House, Inc., New York. Any third party use of this material, outside of this publication, is prohibited. Interested parties must apply directly to Random House, Inc. for permission.

The Mercury Theatre
Run-Through: A Memoir, copyright © 1972 by John Houseman. Simon & Schuster, New York. Reprinted by permission of Russell & Volkening as agents for the author.

The Second City
Days and Nights at the Second City: A Memoir, with Notes on Staging Review Theatre, copyright © 2002 by Bernard Sahlins. Ivan R. Dee, Chicago. Used by permission of Rowman & Littlefield Publishing Group, Inc., New York.

The Ridiculous Theatrical Company
Unpublished essays, circa 1980s, by Charles Ludlam. Later published in *Ridiculous Theatre: Scourge of Human Folly: The Essays and Opinions of Charles Ludlam*, by Charles Ludlam, compiled and edited by Steven Samuels, copyright © 1992 by The Estate of Charles Ludlam. Theatre Communications Group, New York.

The Performance Group
Environmental Theater, copyright © 1973 by Richard Schechner. Hawthorn Books, New York. Used by permission of Applause Theatre & Cinema Books, LLC, an imprint of Hal Leonard Corporation, Milwaukee, WI.

Steppenwolf Theatre Company
"No Money, Just Each Other and the Theatre," copyright © 1998 by Gary Sinise. Originally published in *North Shore*, August 1998. Used by permission of Makeitbetter.net.

Chapter 5

The Civic Repertory Theatre
With a Quiet Heart: An Autobiography, copyright © 1953 by Eva Le Gallienne. Viking Press, New York. Used by permission of The Estate of Eva Le Gallienne.

Theatre '47
Theatre-in-the-Round, copyright © 1951 by Margo Jones. Rinehart & Company, New York. Used by permission of The Estate of Margo Jones.

Alley Theatre
"Alley Theatre: First Legitimate Playhouse on Main Street, Houston, Texas (we hope)," copyright © 1947–48 by Nina Vance. From Nina Vance/Alley Theatre Papers; Special Collections and Archives, University of Houston Libraries, University of Houston, Texas. Used by special arrangement of the Special Collections and Archives, University of Houston.

Arena Stage
"Theatres or Institutions?" copyright © 1969–70 by Zelda Fichandler. Originally published in *Theatre 3*, International Theatre Institute (ITI) of the U.S., New York. Used by permission of the author.

Minnesota Theater Company (Guthrie Theater)
A New Theatre, copyright © 1964 by Tyrone Guthrie. McGraw-Hill, New York. Used by permission of McGraw-Hill.

Ford Foundation Program in Humanities and the Arts
"The Arts and Philanthropy," by W. McNeil Lowry, was delivered at Brandeis University, under the auspices of the Poses Institute of Fine Arts, on December 10, 1962. Copyright © 1963 by the Poses Institute of Fine Arts, Brandeis University, Waltham, MA.

The Repertory Theater of Lincoln Center
"Diary of a Madman, or How to Build a Classical Theater on Five Dollars a Day," copyright © 1972 by Jules Irving. Originally published in the *New York Times*, on July 16, 1972. Used by permission of The Estate of Jules Irving.

The Mark Taper Forum
"Reflections on Beginnings," copyright © 1968 by Gordon Davidson. Originally published in *Theatre 1*, 1967–68, volume 1, International Theatre Institute (ITI) of the U.S., New York. Used by permission of the author.

The Theatre of the Living Arts

The excerpt is an untitled essay, copyright © 1967 by André Gregory. Originally published in the *Tulane Drama Review*, Summer 1967, volume 1, number 4. Used by permission of the author.

Chapter 6

The Living Theatre

The diaries of Judith Malina, 1951; later compiled and published in *The Diaries of Judith Malina: 1947–1957*, copyright © 1984 by Judith Malina. Grove Press, New York. Used by permission of the author.

The Living Theatre

The meditations of Julian Beck, 1961–63; later compiled and published in *The Life of the Theatre*, copyright © 1972 by Julian Beck. City Lights, San Francisco. Later published by Limelight Editions, Applause Theatre & Cinema Books, LLC, an imprint of Hal Leonard Corporation, Milwaukee, WI, 2004.

The Actor's Workshop

The Impossible Theatre: A Manifesto, copyright © 1964 by Herbert Blau. Macmillan, New York. Used by permission of the author.

The New York Shakespeare Festival

"The Price of This Ticket Is Responsibility," by Joseph Papp, was originally published in the *New York Herald Tribune*, on March 16, 1958. The letter to Robert Moses, by Joseph Papp, was originally published in the *New York Times*, on May 4, 1959. "Sponsor of Free Shakespeare Says It Would Help More Than Hinder," by Joseph Papp, was originally published in the *New York Times*, on July 24, 1960. All used by permission of The Estate of Joseph Papp. *Free for All: Joe Papp, The Public, and the Greatest Theater Story Ever Told*, by Kenneth Turan and Joseph Papp, with the assistance of Gail Merrifield Papp, copyright © 2009 by The Estate of Joseph Papp and the New York Shakespeare Festival. Used by permission of Doubleday, a division of Random House, Inc., New York.

The San Francisco Mime Troupe

"Guerrilla Theater," copyright © 1966 by R. G. Davis. Originally published in the *Tulane Drama Review*, Summer 1966, volume 10, number 4. "Rethinking Guerrilla Theater: 1971," copyright © 1975 by R. G. Davis, *The San Francisco Mime Troupe: The First Ten Years*, Ramparts Press, Palo Alto, CA. Both used by permission of the author.

Bread and Puppet Theater

"Bread and Puppets," copyright © 1985 by Peter Schumann. Originally published in *Theatre Ireland*, Autumn 1985, number 11. Used by permission of the author.

Chapter 7

The Actors Studio

Strasberg at the Actors Studio: Tape-Recorded Sessions, by Lee Strasberg, recorded in 1956. Published in *Strasberg at the Actors Studio: Tape-Recorded Sessions*, copyright © 1965 by Lee Strasberg and Robert H. Hethmon, edited by Robert H. Hethmon. Viking Press, New York. Reprinted by Theatre Communications Group, New York, 1991.

New Dramatists

"The Beginning of New Dramatists" is an unpublished essay by Michaela O'Harra. Used by permission of New Dramatists, Inc.

Circle in the Square Theatre

Journeys in the Night: Creating a New American Theatre with Circle in the Square (A Memoir), copyright © 2007 by Theodore Mann. Used by permission of Limelight Editions, Applause Theatre & Cinema Books, LLC, an imprint of Hal Leonard Corporation, Milwaukee, WI.

Circle in the Square Theatre

If You Don't Dance They Beat You, copyright © 1974 by José Quintero. Little Brown & Company, New York. Used by permission of The Estate of José Quintero.

La MaMa Experimental Theatre Club

"How It All Began," by Ellen Stewart, was originally published in La MaMa's Thirtieth Anniversary Commemorative Program, on April 24, 1992. Used by permission of La MaMa E.T.C.

The Open Theater

The Presence of the Actor, copyright © 1972 by Joseph Chaikin. Atheneum, New York. Reprinted by Theatre Communications Group, New York, 1991.

American Conservatory Theater

Manifesto written in 1965 by William Ball, et al. Later published in *The Creation of an Ensemble: The First Years of the American Conservatory Theater*,

Yale Repertory Theatre (Originally Yale School of Drama Repertory Theatre)

American Repertory Theater

Coda

The Florida Wheel

Index